CHILD AND ADOLESCENT THERAPY

Child and Adolescent Therapy

Cognitive-Behavioral Procedures

SECOND EDITION

Edited by
PHILIP C. KENDALL

The Guilford Press
New York   London

© 2000 Philip C. Kendall and The Guilford Press
Published by The Guilford Press
A Division of Guilford Publications, Inc.
72 Spring Street, New York, NY 10012
www.guilford.com

Printed in the United States of America

This book is printed on acid-free paper.

Last digit is print number: 9 8 7 6 5 4 3 2 1

Library of Congress Cataloging-in-Publication Data is available
from the Publisher.

ISBN 1-57230-556-8

*To my spouse, Sue, for her support, enthusiasm,
and intellectual curiosity.*
—PCK

About the Editor

Philip C. Kendall, PhD, ABPP, is the Laura H. Carnell Professor of Psychology, Head of the Division of Clinical Psychology, and Director of the Child and Adolescent Anxiety Disorders Clinic at Temple University. An internationally recognized expert on clinical child psychology and clinical psychological research, Dr. Kendall has published widely on many topics but is perhaps best noted for his development and evaluation of cognitive-behavioral treatments for anxiety in youth. Author or coauthor of over 300 research publications and books, Dr. Kendall has twice been a Fellow at the Center for Advanced Study in the Behavioral Sciences, Stanford, California, and is a Fellow of the American Association for the Advancement of Science (AAAS) and of the American Psychological Association (APA). He served on the Child and Adolescent Mental Disorders Task Force for the National Academy of Sciences, Institute of Medicine, the William T. Grant Foundation Consortium for "School-Based Promotion of Social Competence," and the Examination Committee of the American Association of State and Provincial Psychology Boards (overseeing the national licensure examination), and has been a Consultant to the World Health Organization and a Distinguished Visiting Professor to the United States Air Force.

Dr. Kendall has served several professional organizations and publications, including, as Editor, the *Journal of Consulting and Clinical Psychology* and *Cognitive Therapy and Research*. He is the President-Elect of Division 53 (Clinical Child Psychology) of the APA and previously served as the President of the Association for Advancement of Behavior Therapy, as a member of the Board of Directors of the Council of University Directors of Clinical Training Programs, as a Diplomate Examiner for the American Board of Professional Psychology, and as a member of the Scientific Program Committee for the World Congress on Cognitive and Behavioral Therapy.

Dr. Kendall has been the recipient of several NIMH research grants for the study of the nature and treatment of youth. Among his awards are the Outstanding Alumnus Award from the Phi Kappa Phi Honor Society of Old Dominion University, the Psychology Department's Outstanding Alumnus Award from Virginia Commonwealth University, the State of Pennsylvania Distinguished Contribution to the Science and Profession of Psychology Award, and the "Great Teacher Award" from Temple University.

Contributors

Michelle D. Bronik, MS, Department of Educational Psychology, University of Texas, Austin, Texas

Muniya Choudhury, MA, Division of Clinical Psychology, Department of Psychology, and Child and Adolescent Anxiety Disorders Clinic, Temple University, Philadelphia, Pennsylvania

Brian C. Chu, MA, Division of Clinical Psychology, Department of Psychology, and Child and Adolescent Anxiety Disorders Clinic, Temple University, Philadelphia, Pennsylvania

Craig Colder, PhD, Department of Psychology, State University of New York at Buffalo, Buffalo, New York

A. J. Finch, Jr., PhD, ABPP, Department of Psychology, The Citadel, Charleston, South Carolina

David P. FitzGerald, PhD, Department of Psychiatry and Behavioral Sciences, Duke University Medical Center, Durham, North Carolina

Stephen P. Hinshaw, PhD, Department of Psychology, University of California, Berkeley, California

Julia A. Hoke, MS, Department of Educational Psychology, University of Texas, Austin, Texas

Grayson N. Holmbeck, PhD, Department of Psychology, Loyola University Chicago, Chicago, Illinois

Philip C. Kendall, PhD, ABPP, Division of Clinical Psychology, Department of Psychology, and Child and Adolescent Anxiety Disorders Clinic, Temple University, Philadelphia, Pennsylvania

Laura Kenealy, MS, Department of Psychology, Loyola University Chicago, Chicago, Illinois

Neville J. King, PhD, Faculty of Education, Monash University, Clayton, Victoria, Australia

Annette M. La Greca, PhD, Department of Psychology, University of Miami, Coral Gables, Florida

John E. Lochman, PhD, Department of Psychology, University of Alabama, Tuscaloosa, Alabama, and Division of Medical Psychology, Duke University Medical Center, Durham, North Carolina

W. Michael Nelson III, PhD, ABPP, Department of Psychology, Xavier University, Cincinnati, Ohio

Thomas H. Ollendick, PhD, Child Study Center and Department of Psychology, Virginia Polytechnic Institute and State University, Blacksburg, Virginia

Sandra S. Pimentel, MA, Division of Clinical Psychology, Department of Psychology, and Child and Adolescent Anxiety Disorders Clinic, Temple University, Philadelphia, Pennsylvania

Janay Boswell Sander, MS, Department of Educational Psychology, University of Texas, Austin, Texas

Wendy Shapera, MS, Department of Psychology, Loyola University Chicago, Chicago, Illinois

Anthony Spirito, PhD, Department of Psychiatry and Human Behavior, Brown University School of Medicine, Rhode Island Hospital, Providence, Rhode Island

Kevin D. Stark, PhD, Department of Educational Psychology, University of Texas, Austin, Texas

Anne Updegrove, PhD, Illinois Masonic Medical Center, The Wellington Center, Chicago, Illinois

James W. Varni, PhD, Department of Psychiatry, University of California, San Diego, School of Medicine, Center for Child Health Outcomes, Children's Hospital and Health Center, San Diego, California

Venette Westhoven, MS, Department of Psychology, Loyola University Chicago, Chicago, Illinois

Janet M. Whidby, PhD, Department of Psychiatry and Behavioral Sciences, Duke University Medical Center, Durham, North Carolina

Mary G. Yancy, MS, Department of Educational Psychology, University of Texas, Austin, Texas

Preface

The previous decade of the science and practice of mental health services for children and adolescents witnessed noteworthy developments and advances. If you work with children and adolescents you are probably already aware of at least some of these changes and examples of progress. After completing this volume, you will be on top of the field.

"Youth" is emerging as a fundamental focus for the field of mental health. For example, at the National Institute of Mental Health, where programs of research are evaluated for potential funding, there is renewed interest in investigations involving youth—so much so that there is the new requirement that investigators/applicants include or justify why they are not including children and adolescents in their proposed research. Although this may at first promote the rash effort by a few to try to apply adult treatments to children without proper attention to developmental factors, the mere placing of an emphasis on children and adolescents by such a prestigious institution will no doubt have a favorable impact on the research of the forthcoming decades.

"Adolescents" and "families" are both hot topics. The increased focus on adolescents is the result of a combination of forces. Social issues have been highlighted through crises in the schools, including egregious instances of extreme violence, and by concerns relating to adolescent sexual activity and health. At the same time, there have been advances in developmental theories and their application. Families have long been seen as important in the psychological treatment of youth, but early applications of family therapy were not empirically based; some researchers have suggested that the development of family therapy may have been delayed for this reason. In contrast, many of the contemporary family and parent training therapies that are receiving attention are emerging from an empirical background and receiving empirical evaluations. "Family" treatment has moved into the family of empirically evaluated interventions for children and adolescents.

The 1990s drew increased attention to those psychological treatments that had been subjected to empirical examination: What treatments had been tested and which had been found to produce beneficial gains? Several therapies emerged as having received empirical support, and it is these treatments that are likely to be the nucleus of the next decade. Doctoral, intern, and residency training programs are making decisions with regard to the types of therapy they wish to teach to their trainees, funding and health management agencies are considering which treatments to fund and/or reimburse, and the educated consumer is increasingly seeking out those services that have been supported by science. The good news is that this book includes detailed descriptions of some of the very programs, often manual-based, that have been identified as empirically supported.

Not a cookie-cutter operation, a manual-based therapy is not conducted exactly the same way for everyone. The designation "manual-based" indicates that the goals and strategies for the treatment sessions are prepared in advance and can be monitored along with progress. But the written word can be lifeless, and one needs to breathe energy into the manuals. It is hoped that the sections referred to as "sitting in on therapy" will provide the reader with an opportunity to see how the strategies and components of treatments described in a manual are actually put into practice. It is worth noting that several second editions of the treatment manuals are referred to in this second edition of *Child and Adolescent Therapy*.

The treatments described in this book have benefited from the research literature describing the nature of the disorder being treated as well as from the literature on the efficacy and effectiveness of the various programs. Similarly, the treatments have benefited from the clinical cases seen and/or supervised by the authors of the programs. I have learned a great deal from the research reports of the Child and Adolescent Anxiety Disorders Clinic at Temple University, but I have also learned from my clinical cases and their individual needs and situations.

The opening chapter provides a description and discussion of the guiding theory for work with children and adolescents. Consideration is given to the need to consider problem solving, cognitive information processing, emotions, and interpersonal relations, while at the same time staying performance-based. The chapter also addresses a conceptualization of the therapist as a coach, a temporal model for the development of coping, the role of normal development in youth, and the nature of rational therapist expectations for change. The chapters that follow represent major contributions by leading clinicians/researchers. Each chapter summarizes the background research, the assessment procedures, and the treatment process. Along with the description of the in-session treatment procedures is a review of the empirical evaluations of the intervention. There are chapters dealing with aggression, attention-deficit/hyperactivity disorder, anger, depression, and anxiety; also addressed are special populations and topics such as pediatrics and health, and adolescents. My intent from the outset has been to direct the work toward the practitioner and the researcher. Not surprisingly, therefore, whereas most chapters provide hands-on descriptions for the practitioner, the closing chapter considers the current status of numerous treatments in terms of their empirical support.

I wish to thank each of the contributors for their participation in the present volume. Without them, the book would lack the diversity of applications and the needed breadth of perspective; with them, the book is an impressive representation of the field at the start of the 21st century. I also wish to thank Ms. Linda Custer for her conscientiousness and quality assistance in the preparation of the manuscript. To my graduate students and colleagues, to the many children who have been part of the research and clinical programs described in this book, and to the universities, medical schools, school systems, and other settings that have cooperated over the years, I offer a collective thank you. Last, for her support and understanding, I thank my spouse, Sue, and for their opening my eyes to new ways to see things, I thank my children, Reed and Mark.

PHILIP C. KENDALL
Temple University

Contents

III. INTERNALIZING DISORDERS

PART I

GUIDING THEORY

CHAPTER 1

Guiding Theory for Therapy with Children and Adolescents

Philip C. Kendall

It is difficult, and unwanted, for a therapist to be atheoretical when designing, implementing, or evaluating treatment programs. Although it is true that no one theory accounts for or explains all human emotion, thought, and action, theory nevertheless provides proper guidance for all clinical endeavors.

Descriptions of any one of the various psychological therapies are related, in large measure, to some form of a guiding theory. For some therapies, the theory is an extrapolation from clinical experiences; for others, the applied theory is an adaptation of a complementary theory from a more basic area of psychology, and in still others, the theory is built upon and extended from empirical research observation.

For clinical work, the most direct and useful theories are those that propose to explain the processes of change. Given our special attention to children and adolescents, we can benefit greatly from consideration of theories that deal with psychological change in youth and that address aspects of human development. What may be alarming, especially to those well versed in either theories of behavior change or those of development, is that there is precious little connection in applied work between these two arenas. In this chapter, along with consideration of other related themes, I outline a cognitive-behavioral theory in which behavioral events, associated anticipatory expectations and postevent attributions, and ongoing cogni-

3

tive information processing and emotional states combine to influence behavior change. Relatedly, the theory adapts to the different challenges facing different levels of development. The theory is problem-solving oriented, deals directly with cognitive information processing, incorporates emotional and social/interpersonal domains, employs structured and manual-based procedures, and emphasizes performance-based interventions. A closer look at each of these features is informative.

Why adopt a problem-solving orientation? It is truthful to state that, without exception, humans routinely experience problems that require solutions. Quite simply, problems occur! The ability to recognize a problem and address it (problem solving) is an essential ingredient to adequate adjustment in childhood, as well as across the life span. Different developmental challenges face youth as they move through childhood and adolescence, and these youth differ in their ability to recognize a problem and to generate and consider possible solutions. Importantly, their ability to generate alternative solutions and competently evaluate each option will form an important basis for the quality of their psychological health. The problem-solving orientation is seen in many of the empirically supported psychological treatments (see Lonigan, Elbert, & Johnson, 1998) for disorders of youth (Kazdin & Weisz, 1998; Ollendick & King, 1998).

Why emphasize cognitive information processing? Problems occur, without provocation or effort. Solutions to problems, in contrast, do not materialize from thin air, nor are they handed to someone carte blanche. And, in instances when solutions appear to jump out, they are not always the optimal solutions. Rather, successful solutions often emerge from an individual's active use of thinking—or, as we call it, involvement with cognitive strategies. These strategies are not transmitted from parents through genetic codes, but they are acquired through experience, through observation, and through interaction with others. For our purposes, the use of cognitive strategies can be maximized through planned intervention. Styles of information processing have profound effects on how one makes sense of the world and one's experiences in it, and dysfunctional information processing requires attention and modification (e.g., Ingram, Miranda, & Segal, 1998). Correcting faulty information processing and/or teaching strategies to overcome a deficiency in information processing (Kendall, 1993) are both valuable steps in treatment of the psychological disorders of youth.

Why be concerned with emotions? Our emotional states, both positive (Diener & Lucas, 1999) and negative, influence our cognitive and behavioral abilities. Learning about the nature and regulation of our emotions can provide a solid building block for advancing well-being. It simply is not enough to know how to think through problems; extreme states of emotional arousal can interfere with efforts to think reasonably! Effective cognitive problem solving requires an understanding of the experience and modification of emotions (Southam-Gerow & Kendall, 2000).

Why focus on social and interpersonal domains? Mental health professionals are interested in effective adaptation and adjustment (coping) in social situations. Stated differently, the important psychological problems in need of solutions are not *im*personal problems (e.g., how to distribute weight when loading a trailer) but are *inter*personal (social) ones (e.g., how to adjust to changing physiology and family roles). It is worth noting that developmental theory has underscored the importance of social relationships (peers [see Hartup, 1984] and family) to psychologically healthy adjustment, and it is this social domain that takes on special importance in clinical interventions. It is the social domain—both peers and family members—in which the individual interacts reciprocally.

Why follow a manual-based or structured approach to treatment? Like theory, structure provides an organization for the treatment: an understanding of the problem and the nature of its experience for the youth, as well as an arranged set of progressive experiences that will optimize beneficial gains for the youth. A manual-based approach helps shape explicit goals, offers a suggested pace, and provides sequenced steps for movement toward the goals: manuals are *not* inflexible or rigid blueprints. Likewise, workbooks for the child–client to use in learning new skills allow for structured practice. For example, the *Stop and Think Workbook* (Kendall, 1992a) provides training materials for use of cognitive strategies to control impulsivity, whereas the *Coping Cat Workbook* (Kendall, 1992b) teaches skills for managing unwanted anxious arousal. Organization and structure guide treatment; they are not inflexible boundaries.

Why stress performance-based interventions? Some interventions, often targeting adults, may be geared toward helping the client gain insight or understanding. Other interventions, such as those focused on youth, intend to teach skills and/or remediate skills deficits in thinking, emotions, or action, and it is through performance-based procedures that such goals are best reached. Practice of new skills, with encouragement and feedback, leads to further use and refinement of those skills. Proper contingencies are implemented to shape involvement, to firm up intrinsic interest, or to promote motivation in otherwise disinterested participants. For youth, it simply is not enough to talk about what may be needed; practice is a part of the optimal intervention.

This collected work of several therapists holds together in terms of these dimensions. As will become more evident throughout the book, the guiding cognitive-behavioral theory has more than one facet and is appropriate in multiple applications. The theory places greatest emphasis on helping youth to advance their cognitive information processing in social contexts by using structured, behaviorally oriented practice, while concurrently paying attention to the participant youth's emotional state and involvement in the tasks of the treatment. As central as a guiding theory is to the provision of interventions, it is nevertheless crucial that the intervention be examined and evaluated for effectiveness. A guiding theory is necessary but not sufficient. Empirical support for an intervention is a priceless key to the choice of one intervention over another.

TOWARD A WORKING DEFINITION

There are numerous forms of psychosocial intervention designed to facilitate child and adolescent adjustment and remediate their psychological distress. At times, it is easy to wonder and speculate about the similarities and differences that actually exist among the different treatment philosophies (for an interesting and informed look into four different child therapies, see Fishman, 1995). Until a series of empirical studies of the specific therapies are undertaken, we can only speculate about the distinct and overlapping features of different therapies from their written descriptions. In an effort to provide a working definition applicable to the cognitive-behavioral approaches, consider them as a rational amalgam: a purposeful attempt to preserve the demonstrated positive effects of behavioral therapy within a less doctrinaire context and to incorporate the cognitive activities of the client into the efforts to produce therapeutic change (Kendall & Hollon, 1979). Accordingly, cognitive-behavioral treatments use enactive performance-based procedures and structured sessions (e.g., manuals, workbooks) as well as cognitive intervention strategies designed to produce changes in thinking, feeling, and behavior.

The cognitive-behavioral analyses of child and adolescent disorders and adjustment problems, as well as related analyses of treatment-produced gains, include considerations of the child's internal and external environment and represent an integrationist perspective (e.g., Meichenbaum, 1977). The model places greatest emphasis on the learning process and the influence of the contingencies and models in the environment, while underscoring the centrality of the individual's mediating/information-processing style in the development and remediation of psychological distress. The hyphenated term "cognitive-behavioral" is not intended as a direct insult to the role of emotions or the impact of the social context. Rather, it is a hybrid representing an integration of cognitive, behavioral, emotion-focused, and social strategies for change. Abandoning an adherence to a singularly behavioral model, the cognitive-behavioral model includes the relationships of cognition and behavior to the emotional state and functioning of the organism in the larger social context.

Affect has been assigned to both primary and ancillary roles in childhood psychopathology. Emotions were given a primary role by Bernard and Joyce (1984); child psychopathology was said to be caused by emotional problems.

In other writings (e.g., Santostefano & Reider, 1984), cognition and emotion were considered "one and the same" (p. 56) and thereby given a comparable etiological contribution. I argue that while cognition and emotion are interrelated, the variance in the etiology of some disorders may be best accounted for by cognitive assessments and analyses, whereas some other disorders may be best understood by a more direct appraisal of emotions. Still other disorders are best viewed as largely behavioral. Anxious children behave in frightened ways (avoiding situations), for example, and they not only misperceive threat and danger in an otherwise routine environment, but also fail to recognize and understand the modifiability of their own emotions (Southam-Gerow & Kendall, 2000). It is not that any one domain is always primary or uniformly accounts for the most variance. Rather, cognition, emotion, and action vary in their potency across the different types of psychological difficulties and disorders.

Because behavioral patterns in the external world and cognitive interpretations in the internal world pertain to social/interpersonal contexts (peers and family), the cognitive-behavioral perspective must consider the importance of the social context. Social/interpersonal factors play a crucial role in the design of and outcomes from therapy. For children and adolescents, the centrality of the social context must be underscored. Indeed, a satisfactory relationship with peers is a crucial component of a child's successful adjustment, and an understanding of peer and social relationships is required for a meaningful assessment of a child's needs and for the accomplishment of an effective intervention. Similarly, the role of the family can not be contested, for this social microcosm sets many of the rules and roles for later social interaction.

Acknowledgments of peer and family contributions to child and adolescent psychopathology, however, far outweigh the research database that is currently available, and the need for further inquiry in these areas cannot be overemphasized. This statement is especially true with regard to treatment: parents are regularly involved in many of the programs designed for their children in spite of the fact that there is a limited empirical database on the optimal nature of their involvement. Yes, do involve parents, but how best to do so? For example, parents can serve as consultants when they provide input into the determination of the nature of the problem. When parents are seen as contributing to or maintaining some aspect of the child's problem, the parents may become co-clients in the treatment itself. Parents may also be involved as collaborators in their child's treatment when they assist in the implementation of program requirements. Cognitive-behavioral interventions assess, consider, and incorporate social/interpersonal matters into their programs. Involvement of parents and changing the family system should be used in conjunction with the nature of the treatment and the needs of the child. Future research in this arena will further inform the ideal involvements of parents.

THERAPIST AS COACH: THE POSTURE OF THE THERAPIST

For the past 20 years, I have struggled when searching for the words to try to describe the mental attitude that is recommended for therapeutic work with youth. Using the term "posture" to refer to one's mental attitude, although not exact or ideal, can help to describe the cognitive-behavioral therapist working with children and adolescents. The word "coach," too, carries useful connotations. I choose to describe three characteristics of the therapist's posture using the terms "consultant," "diagnostician," and "educator," all within the umbrella of a supportive yet exacting coach who can bring the best out of someone with opportunities and feedback. After 20 years of using the term in a certain way, I am now very comfortable with the therapist as "coach."

By referring to the therapist as a consultant, I am referring to the therapist as a person who does not have all the answers, but one who has some ideas worthy of trying out and some ways to examine whether the ideas have value for the individual client. Telling a child and/or adolescent exactly what to do is *not* the idea; giving the client an opportunity to try something and helping him or her to make sense of the experience is the idea. The therapist as consultant strives to develop skills in the client that include thinking on his or her own and moving toward independent, mature problem solving. The consultant (therapist) is a problem-solving model working with the client. When the client asks, "Well, what am I supposed to do?", the therapist might reply, "Let's see, what do you want to accomplish here?", and then, "What are our options?" or "What's another way we could look at this problem?" The exchange is geared toward facilitating the process of problem solving, but without forcing a specific solution. The youngster and therapist interact in a collaborative problem-solving manner.

"Diagnostician" is a term that might suggest the process of labeling within a diagnostic system (e.g., DSM-IV, ICD-10), but although this process is not criticized, it is not the thrust of the meaning of the term when used here to describe the therapist's mental posture. The mental attitude associated with "diagnostician" is one of being confident to go beyond the verbal report and/or behavior of the client and his or her significant others. A diagnostician is one who integrates data and, judging against a background of knowledge of psychopathology, normal development, and psychologically healthy environments, makes meaningful decisions. This aspect of the term "diagnostician" is that which I underscore. Consider the following example: Suppose that you win a brand new Jaguar automobile. You are driving it around for 2 days and you notice a "clug-clug" sound in the front end when you make a right-hand turn. There is no noise when you go straight or when you turn left. The noise has you perplexed, so you contact a mechanic and tell him that the front tie-rod ends need repair. You leave the car for repair and pick it up at the end of the day. Your tie-rod ends have been replaced. Would you be satisfied?

My answer is a definite "no." Why should I be satisfied when the mechanic relied on me as the diagnostician? What do I know about tie-rod ends? I just won the car, I am not a mechanic, and I should not be diagnosing the problem. The auto mechanic is the expert who should be making the determinations. He should ask for a description of the problem and look under the hood! The mechanic should not fix what I say is wrong, because I am not the Jaguar expert. He can use my descriptions of the problem and consider my ideas as helpful information, but he should nevertheless make his own determination. Similarly, we (mental health professionals/educators) cannot let others tell us what is wrong and what needs to be fixed when we are working with children and adolescents with psychological problems. That a parent says an adolescent has an anxiety disorder is not, alone, sufficient reason to undertake an anxiety treatment program. That a parent or teacher says that a child is hyperactive is not sufficient reason to initiate a medication regimen and/or cognitive-behavioral therapy. The fact that a parent or teacher suspects or suggests hyperactivity in a child is a valuable piece of information, but there are several rival hypotheses that must be considered. For example, the child's behavior may be within normal limits but appears as troubled when judged against inappropriate parental (teacher) expectations about child behavior. When the parent expects too much "adult-like behavior" from a child, the essential problem does not lie within the child. There is also the possibility of alternative disorders: Hyperactivity may be the term used by the referring parent, but aggressive noncompliance may be a better description in terms of mental health professionals' communications and targeting the treatment. Also, the child's identified problem may be a reflection of a dysfunctional family interaction pattern, with the parenting styles needing the greatest attention, not the child per se. In a nutshell, the cognitive-behavioral therapist serves as a diagnostician by taking into account the various sources of information and, judging against a background of knowledge, determines the nature of the problem and the optimal strategy for its treatment.

The therapeutic posture of a cognitive-behavioral therapist entails being an educator. The use of "educator" here is intended to communicate that I am talking about interventions for learning behavior control, cognitive skills, and emotional development, and about optimal ways to communicate to help someone to learn. A good educator stimulates the students to think for themselves. An active and involved coach is a good educator. Let us consider the following sports story. You are off to a weeklong golf camp for adults. You arrive and learn that for your $2,600 fee, you will lie on the couch and tell your instructor how you feel about golf, about the clubs, about hitting the ball, and about your early experiences with golf. How would you respond? Your answer might be, "Excuse me, but I'd like to im-

prove my golf game. My short irons are weak, and my driving is terrible."
The instructor might then reply, "What is it about driving that you don't
like? Does it make you feel uneasy to be the driving force?" "No—no," you
reply. "My drive is weak—I think my backswing is too quick." "Aha," he
mumbles, "backswing. Is there any meaning to that? Are you nervous
about your back, or backside perhaps?" An interpretive approach is not
seen as optimally instructive toward an improved game of golf. Some observation and comment about what needs to be changed (diagnostician) is
needed, but the week will prove more successful following opportunities
for practice with feedback.

In contrast to the scenario just described, what would a good educator
(coach) do? He or she would first get you out on the links and watch you
play, not taking your self-report as perfect truth, but instead observing how
you hit the ball and determining for him- or herself (diagnostician) if your
backswing is too quick. The observations would take place on different occasions, using different clubs, and approaching long and short holes. Then,
there would be some feedback about strengths and weaknesses, and some
discussion of alternatives and options (consultant). For example, the educator might inform you that your drives are inconsistent because your waist is
shifting when it should not—and it may be that you need to practice with a
pole in the ground at your side to get feedback about when your waist is
moving. Videotaping might be used, along with modeling by the expert,
and group lessons could be integrated as well, before you play the course
and keep score. Importantly, a good educator/coach does not make all players play the game the same way. A good coach observes how each student is
playing and helps to maximize strengths while reducing hindrances. If a
player uses a cross-finger grip for driving but a noncrossed grip for putting,
there is no reason to force the player always to cross fingers—if the putting
is effective, there is no need to force conformity. Individualized attention
means that individuals can and should do things a bit differently.

A good educator/coach also pays attention to what the learner is saying to him- or herself, as this internal dialogue can be interfering with performance. Walking up to address the ball and thinking, "I can't hit this low
iron—the ball's going to go into the rough" is not a preferred internal dialogue. An effective therapist, just like an effective teacher or coach, is involved in the cognitive and behavioral process. More on this later in this
chapter.

The posture, or mental attitude, of the cognitive-behavioral therapist
working with children and adolescents is one that has a collaborative quality (therapist as consultant), integrates and decodes social information
(therapist as diagnostician), and teaches through experiences with involvement (therapist as educator). A quality coach has many of these characteristics, and it is not difficult to suggest that the child therapist view him- or
herself somewhat as a mental health coach. A high-quality intervention, be

it provided by a psychologist, psychiatrist, school counselor, special educator, classroom teacher, or parent, is one that alters how the client makes sense of experiences and the way the client will behave, think, and feel in the future. Such coaching and correction in thought and action place the client on track toward improved adjustment.

CONSIDERING COGNITION

Many psychologists, teachers, and mental health professionals have viewed cognition as inaccessible. True, cognition refers to a complex system, but the system can be subdivided for added access and increased understanding. For instance, it has been suggested (Ingram & Kendall, 1986, 1987; Kendall & Ingram, 1987, 1989) that cognitive content (events), processes, products, and structures can be distinguished, the idea being that cognition is not a singular or unitary concept.

Cognitive structures can be defined as memory, and the manner in which information is internally represented in memory. Cognitive content refers to the information that is actually represented: the contents of the cognitive structures. Cognitive processes are the procedures by which the cognitive system operates: how we go about perceiving and interpreting experiences. Cognitive products (e.g., attributions) are the resulting cognition that emerges from the interaction of information, cognitive structures, content, and processes. Psychopathology may be related to problems in any or all of these areas, and effective therapy includes consideration of each of these factors for each individual client. Although these concepts are complex, a simple, though not everyday, example can help to illustrate their meaningful interrelationships.

Consider the experience of stepping in something a dog left on the lawn. Have you ever had such an experience? If this were to happen to you now, what would you say to yourself? The typical first reaction ("Oh, sh_____") is a self-statement that reflects dismay. This self-statement may be made by most of the people having just made such a misstep, but these same people then proceed to *process* the experience quite differently, and it is important to understand how these individuals process the same experience differently. For example, some people might process the event by beginning to think about the potential for social embarrassment ("Did anyone see me?"), some might become self-denigrating ("I can't even walk"), while others might be inattentive to the processing of environmental cues and may simply keep walking! The manner of processing the event contributes meaningfully to the behavioral and emotional consequences for the individual.

After the unwanted experience (i.e., stepping in it) and a processing of the event, conclusions are reached regarding the causes of the misstep—

cognitive products, such as causal attributions, which may vary across individuals. Some may attribute the misstep to their inability to do anything right: Such a global internal and stable attribution often characterizes depression (Abramson, Seligman, & Teasdale, 1979; Stark et al., Chapter 5, this volume). An angry individual, in contrast, might see the experience as the result of someone else's provocation ("Whose dog left this here—I bet the guy knew someone would step in it!"); attributing the mess to someone else's intentional provocation is linked to aggressive retaliatory behavior (see Lochman et al., Chapter 2, and Nelson & Finch, Chapter 4, this volume). Cognitive content, processes, and products are involved in each individual's making sense of environmental events.

Cognitive structures, or templates, are an accumulation of experiences in memory and serve to filter or screen new experiences. The anxious child, for instance, brings a history to new events: the memory of the past. Also referred to as a cognitive schema, this structure for anxious children/adolescents is threat—threat of loss, criticism, or harm (see Kendall et al., Chapter 6, this volume). An individual who brings an anxiety-prone structure to the misstep experience noted earlier would see the threat of embarrassment and the risk of germs, and process the experience accordingly. Anxious cognitive processing of the misstep experience might include self-talk such as, "What if somebody notices the bad smell; they'll think I'm dirty" or "What if germs get into my shoes and then to my socks, and my feet? Should I throw these shoes away?" Anxiety, as seen in this example of cognitive processing of an event, is laced with perceptions of threat and social evaluation.

Cognitive structures can serve to trigger automatic cognitive content and information processing about behavioral events; that is, after several real or imagined experiences, the person can come to have a characteristic way of making sense of events. Attributions (cognitive products) about the event and its outcomes reflect the influence of the preexisting structure. Therapeutically, cognitive-behavioral interventions seek to provide experiences that attend to cognitive content, process, and product (paying attention to the child's self-talk, processing style, and attributional preferences), so that the child/adolescent can be helped to build a cognitive structure that will have a positive influence on future experiences.

What is a healthy way to think about and deal with having just made such a misstep? It would certainly be detrimental if one were to think, "It's good luck to step in s_____," because that might lead one to seek out and intentionally step in it more frequently. Good luck is not likely to accrue and this would not be healthy thinking. To say "Good thing I had my shoes on" might be reasonable, as it reflects the absence of self-punitiveness and has an accepting quality. Likewise, "Good thing it was a small dog" reflects self-talk that is not overly harsh. The person might then process the experience by thinking that cleaning is necessary, some time will be needed to do an adequate job, and that, next, time, one might be more careful and look where one is walking. With regard to an attribution, a person might conclude: "I made a mistake—maybe rushing too much" or "I haven't stepped in it for over a year. Maybe I can go for over 2 years before the next misstep." Such an attribution reflects acceptance of a minor error and hints that increasing the time between mistakes (not never doing it again) is a reasonable goal.

Cognitive-behavioral interventions provide an arena to challenge the youth's existing structures. Knowing that we all, figuratively, step in it at times, what is needed is a structure for coping with these unwanted events when they occur. In-session role-playing experiences are ideal opportunities for learning, and with the focus on cognitive activities during the experience, they bolster the impression made on the client's current and future information processing.

Recall that a goal of treatment is to alter the cognitive structure of the child/adolescent such that he or she will think, feel, and behave differently in the future. Might I be so bold as to now suggest that I have already altered your cognitive structure for the rest of your life! Indeed, I am confident that I have done so. When you next step in a dog mess, you will think of me (this chapter). You will step in it and have a self-statement that reminds you of this passage. Even if I would like for you not to think of me, I probably cannot stop it. I cannot chemically or surgically remove the memory and I cannot, effectively, ask you not to think of me. The present experience has altered your cognitive structure in such a way that you will think differently the next time you step in it. So, too, the therapeutic activities in many interventions, when accompanied by careful attention to the child's thinking, result in a major alteration on the child's view of future events and experiences.

Not all dysfunctional cognition is the same. Understanding the nature of the cognitive dysfunction has very important implications for the optimal design of treatment. One central issue for children and adolescents concerns cognitive processing and the differentiation between *cognitive deficiency* in processing and *cognitive distortion* in processing. Processing deficiencies refer to an absence of thinking (lacking careful information processing where it would be beneficial), whereas distortions refer to dysfunctional thinking processes. I have elsewhere (Kendall, 1981) made this distinction to highlight the differences between the forerunners of cognitive-behavioral therapy with adults who focused on modifying distorted thinking (e.g., Beck, 1976; Ellis, 1971) and early cognitive-behavioral training with children that dealt mostly with teaching to remediate deficiencies in thinking (e.g., self-instructions; Kendall, 1977; Meichenbaum & Goodman, 1971). This processing distinction can be furthered when other childhood and adolescent disorders are considered. Anxiety and depression, for example, are typically linked to misconstruals or misperceptions of the

Artist: Peter J. Mikulka, PhD

social/interpersonal environment. There is active information processing, but it is distorted (illogical, irrational, crooked). In a series of studies of depressed children, for example, depressed youngsters viewed themselves as less capable than did nondepressed children when, in fact, teachers (the source of objective outsiders' judgment) saw the depressed and non-depressed groups of children as nondistinct on the very dimensions that the depressed youth saw themselves as lacking (Kendall, Stark, & Adam, 1990). In the teachers' eyes, the depressed children were not less competent across social, academic, and athletic dimensions. It was the depressed children who evidenced distortion through their misperception (underestimation) of their competencies.

Hyperactive and impulsive children, in contrast to anxious and/or depressed youngsters, are often found to act without thinking and perform poorly due to the lack of forethought and an absence of planning. Here, cognitive deficiencies are implicated. These children are not engaging in careful information processing and their performance suffers as a result. Consider the case of a small group of youngsters playing soccer. Twelve players are on the soccer field; some are kicking at the ball, others are looking around and talking, while others are standing still. A nonparticipating child sits on the sidelines and, when asked why he is not playing, replies, "I can't play. I'm not good at soccer." In reality, the child can stand, talk, kick at a ball, and so on, and could easily participate at a modest skills level.

The child's comment reflects mistaken perceptions of demands in the situation and suggest that he thinks he could not play as well as the others—that they are good players, but he is not. This is a distorted perception, and such thinking is tied to feelings of inadequacy, isolation, and withdrawal. Contrast this overly self-critical and isolating style of the withdrawn and depressive child to the impulsive child who, when seeing the soccer game, runs directly onto the soccer field and starts after the ball. He is kicking and running but does not yet know what team he is on, who is on his team with him, or which goal he is going to use. His difficulties emerge more from failing to stop and think (cognitive deficiency) than from active but distorted processing of information.

The terms "deficiency" and "distortion" have been used in the extant literature to describe features of cognitive dysfunction (Kendall, 1993, 2000). In the many instances where the terms have been employed, their use has been, even if unwittingly, consistent with my distinction. For instance, Prior (1984; often citing Hermalin & O'Connor, 1970) described the considerable evidence concerning "the nature of the cognitive deficits in autism" (p. 8) (e.g., suggested inability to use meaning to aid recall). The dominant role assigned to distortions (errors) by rational–emotive theory is evident in DiGiuseppe and Bernard's (1983) comment that "emotional disturbance develops because of one of two types of cognitive errors: empirical distortions of reality that occur   (inferences) and exaggerated and distorted appraisals of inferences" (p. 48). In contrast, Spivack and Shure (1982) contend that deficits in interpersonal cognitive problem-solving skills carry etiological clout, and Meichenbaum (1977) and Kendall (1977) have described impulsivity as a disorder resulting from mediational deficits.

To further illustrate the differences between distortions and deficiencies, consider the role of cognition in overcontrolled and undercontrolled childhood disorders. Anorexia, most often observed in adolescent females, is related to setting perfectionistic goals and demands, carrying an inaccurate view of the self (e.g., self-perception of body), and being "too good" behaviorally. These features of an overcontrolled problem reflect cognitive distortions. Anxiety and depression are also considered internalizing problems and they, too, evidence cognitive distortions that are dysfunctional—misperceptions of demands in the environment, misperceptions of threat and danger, attributional errors (e.g., depression: Hammen & Zupan, 1984; Prieto, Cole, & Tageson, 1992; anxiety: Daleiden, Vasey, & Williams, 1996; Kaslow, Stark, Printz, Livingston, & Tsai, 1992). In contrast, impulsive acting-out and aggressive behavior, often more characteristic of young boys, is in part related to a lack of self-control, a failure to employ verbal mediational skills, and a lack of social perspective taking. The undercontrolled problem child seems to evidence a deficiency in activating and following careful and planful cognitive processing. In aggression (Kendall & MacDonald, 1993), there is evidence of both cognitive deficiency and cognitive distortion (Kendall, Ronan, & Epps, 1990). There are data to suggest that aggressive youth have deficiencies in interpersonal problem solving (Deluty, 1981) and data to document that they also show distortions in their processing of information (e.g., Lochman & Dodge, 1998; Edens, Cavell, & Hughes, 1999; see also Lochman et al., Chapter 2, and Nelson & Finch, Chapter 4, this volume). Limited ability to generate alternative, nonaggressive solutions to interpersonal problems is an example of their deficiencies, while misattribution of the intentionality of others' behavior (Dodge, 1985) demonstrates a tendency for distorted processing. My argument is that (1) undercontrol versus overcontrol (or externalizing vs. internalizing; see Achenbach, 1966) is an important behavioral differentiation; (2) distortions versus deficiencies is an important cognitive differentiation; and (3) there are meaningful relationships between the two (Kendall & MacDonald, 1993). Internalized problems are linked more to maladaptive, distorted processing, whereas externalizing problems reflect, in part, deficiencies in processing. Moreover, recognition of this distinction and use of interventions that direct themselves appropriately to the needed arena have benefits for participating youth.

DEVELOPING COPING OVER TIME: A TEMPORAL MODEL

Both empirical research and clinical theory continue to document and stress the role of cognitive concepts such as expectations, attributions, self-statements, beliefs, distortions and deficiencies, and schemata in the development of both adaptive and maladaptive behavior patterns. Interestingly, these same concepts play important roles in the process of behavioral change. However, the interrelationships of these and other cognitive factors themselves have yet to be fully clarified. How are the functional effects of self-statements similar to or different from those of attributions? How does an individual's maladaptive cognitive structure relate to his or her level of irrational beliefs? Do inconsistent or anxious self-statements reduce interpersonal cognitive processing and problem solving? Quite simply, we know only a modest amount about the organization and interrelations of the cognitive concepts receiving theoretical and research attention.

A model with some potential utility is one built on development and organized along a temporal dimension. The developmental model must take into account and be able to reflect the role of cognition associated with behavior across time (e.g., the cognition that occurs before, during, and after events). Because events do not occur in a vacuum (they are typically social), and because behavior is determined by multiple causes, the model must allow for the feedback that results from multiple, sequential behavioral events. Again, this involves development over time; that is, a person's cognitive processing before an event varies, depending on the outcomes of previous events. Thus, the model must allow for fluctuations in pre-event cognition associated with the different outcomes (e.g., successful, unsuccessful) of prior events. Moreover, because repetitions of cognitive-event sequences will eventually result in some consistency in cognitive processing, the model must highlight the eventual development of more regularized cognitive processing (e.g., cognitive structures, cognitive styles).

Figure 1.1 offers an illustration of the proposed model. The figure depicts the flow of cognition across multiple behavioral events that vary in their emotional intensity. The starting point is a hypothetical initial behavioral event (BE), and the model moves from the initial BE point at the left in Figure 1.1 to the cognitive consistency that results (at the right of the figure). Attributions are the cognitive concepts often studied at the culmination of a behavioral event:

How do children disambiguate the causes of their behavior once it has already taken place? Stated differently, of all the possible explanations for behavior that can be proposed, how do youth explain their own and others' behavior to themselves? Attributions are temporally short-lived in that their occurrence is at the termination of an event. Nevertheless, their effects can be long-lasting. One could assess an attribution long after an event, although numerous factors (e.g., recall from memory) may interfere with accurate recall. Typically, attributions are preferably assessed immediately after the behavioral event has taken place.

Repetition of behavioral events (multiple BEs in Figure 1.1) and repetition of the related cognitive processing will result in some degree of consistency in both behavior and cognition. The figure illustrates that cognitive consistency (i.e., a cognitive structure, beliefs, an attributional style) results

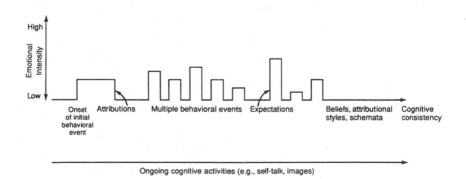

FIGURE 1.1. A temporal model of the flow of cognition across behavioral events of different emotional intensity. Self-statements and images occur at any point and can be studied at various points in the temporal flow. Problem-solving processes also occur at various points, especially where conflicts arise.

after multiple events. These cognitive variables (consistencies over time) are more stable than a single attribution. More stable cognitive style variables may be more predictive in a general sense but are less predictive in specific situations than the actual cognition at the time of the specific behavioral event. Upon the accumulation of a history of behavioral events and event outcomes, the child or adolescent entertains more precise anticipatory cognition (i.e., expectancies). Expectancies have been described, for example, as outcome expectancies and self-efficacy expectancies (Bandura, 1977). Other anticipatory cognition includes intentions, plans, and commitments. These latter variables may be more stable and consistent over time than situationally specific expectancies. A generalized expectancy (e.g., locus of control), by its very general, transsituational nature, can also be seen as an attributional style. For instance, the generalized expectancy of an external locus of control could be present both before (expectancy) and after (attribution) an event. Before the event, the person's externality leads to an anticipation of having a minimal effect: "Why bother to speak up? No one listens to me." After the event, when a decision has been reached without the individual's input, the event is attributed to powerful others: "See, the big mouths always get their way."

In addition to the cognition factors mentioned thus far, other cognitive variables have been demonstrated to be important in a cognitive-behavioral analysis—variables such as imagery, self-statements, and cognitive problem-solving skills. These factors occur at all points along the temporal flow depicted in Figure 1.1, and assessments of these factors (e.g., self-talk) can prove valuable in understanding and treating children and adolescents.

Emotional forces are crucial in the design and conduct of interventions, and in the eventual permanence of effective intervention outcomes. The intensity of emotion is represented vertically in Figure 1.1. The higher the bar, the higher the emotionality: A high bar indicates a behavioral event that is more emotionally intense. Emotional intensity contributes because the more intense the experience, the greater the impact on the development of a cognitive structure (schema). Accordingly, minor events, in terms of emotional involvement, may have a limited influence of attributions, future expectations, and behavior, whereas an emotionally significant event has greater impact on the development of a cognitive structure and on future thinking and action. One strives to design and implement therapy as an emotionally positive and involving experience, leading to coping and adaptive cognitive processing. As will be discussed in more detail later in this chapter and in other chapters throughout this book, therapy can help to reduce the client's support for dysfunctional thinking/schema, and it can help to construct a new schema through which the client can identify and solve problems—movement toward coping.

With specific reference to therapy for children and adolescents, an effective program is one that intentionally plans and capitalizes on creating behavioral experiences with intense positive emotional involvement, while paying attention to the anticipatory and after-the-fact cognitive activities of the participants. The therapist guides both the youngster's attributions about prior behavior and his or her expectations for future behavior. Thus, the youngster can acquire a cognitive structure for future events (a coping template) that includes the adaptive skills and accurate cognition associated with adaptive functioning.

ASPIRATIONS

To what end does the cognitive-behavioral therapist aspire? What goals are set before us as worthy of conscientious effort? To answer these questions, we will consider (1) the trajectory of normal development, (2) rational therapist expectations about behavior change, and (3) theoretical models that detail the nature of our goals.

Normal Developmental Trajectory

From birth, the human organism is set on a course of development that, in general, moves toward the acquisition of coping skills, self-direction, autonomy, and happiness in life; that is, when developmental trajectories are not deflected, an organism moves toward a satisfying self-determined role. Assuming such a trajectory, what place do cognitive-behavioral interventions serve?

Interventions for children and adolescents can be therapeutic, preventive, or enhancement focused. Ameliorative interventions (therapy) are designed to help youth overcome problems that already exist, whereas prevention attempts to forestall problems before they emerge. Enhancements are aimed at the improvement of the quality of life for individuals not currently in distress or necessarily at risk for maladaptation. The clear majority of cognitive-behavioral interventions are therapeutic, with a substantial number being currently or potentially preventive, and fewer still serving to enhance an adequate adjustment. It is considered advantageous to work to serve currently suffering individuals as well to prevent future suffering by intervening to help build self-determined persons.

Children and adolescents, as clients, require that the therapist give special consideration to treatment goals. To what extent does the therapist want to help the client make a better adjustment to the present life situation? To what extent does the therapist want to help the client to alter his or her life situation? When family members, school personnel, and other adult authorities are involved, the matter becomes even more complicated. Adjusting to a life situation that is psychologically unhealthy may not be advised, yet one cannot always alter a life situation as dramatically as might be construed when thinking of optimal adjustment for the client. The resolution offered by the cognitive-behavioral approach is one that focuses on individual problem solving. The client is given skills that can be used to make self-determinations—skills that are in natural agreement with the developmental move toward autonomy. Problem-solving skills allow for individual choices, unique to the client, that are optimal for the individual at the time. A child or adolescent client is supported through the thinking processes, encouraged to consider alternative solutions, rewarded and encouraged for effort, and helped to practice the skills needed for future challenges to adjustment. In this manner, the child or adolescent is guided through the process of becoming an active participant in a problem-solving process that, while it does not dictate which answers to choose, does allow for choice and self-determination. Helping to identify options, think through options in a careful manner, and guide the testing and evaluation of options is a goal of cognitive-behavioral therapy.

To return to the notion of a natural developmental trajectory, psychologically healthy adjustment, as it unfolds in nature, builds on resolutions to prior challenges. Managing frustration contributes to competence. When one is on a fault-free course of adjustment, interventions may appear to be unnecessary. However, when challenges do not present themselves, or when prior challenges have not been met successfully, new skills are needed and, to the extent possible, the acquisition of those general skills that can be applied to a multitude of new challenges are most promising. By demonstrating, teaching, and honing problem-solving skills, the cognitive-behavioral therapist's efforts coincide with changes to adjustment. The goal is a better-prepared individual—prepared for the inevitable difficulties of life with a set of skills that can facilitate problem resolution.

Rational Therapist Expectations

The best hitter in major league baseball hits approximately .340, professional bowlers do not bowl 300 routinely, and not every play in football leads to a touchdown. Perhaps even more striking, Michael Jordan—consensually the best basketball player ever—has a lifetime shooting percentage of approximately 49%. Yet we, as mental health professionals, often carry expectations that we (and our therapies by implication) are expected to help almost all of our clients. To expect such a success rate is irrational, maladaptive, and likely to be associated with other distressing problems.

Rational therapist expectations include the belief that interventions will be helpful in the movement toward successful adjustment and that individuals who acquire the skills communicated in therapy will at some time experience the benefit of those skills. What is irrational is to expect that any child, with any problem, can be "fixed" using psychotherapy, cognitive-behavioral or otherwise. The notion that therapy provides a "cure" is a troublesome and misleading belief (see Kendall, 1989).

Children and adolescents do not, automatically, evidence benefit from psychological forms of therapy. And, even in cases where some success is obvious, the chance of relapse remains ever present. If relapse does occur, was the therapy ineffective? Should therapy be expected to prevent all relapses as a part of the "cure" of psychopathology? A reasonable and rational expectation for therapists to hold is that psychotherapy does not cure maladaptation. Therapy does provide help, but the help is more in the form of a strategy for the *management* of psychopathology. The anxiety-disordered adolescent, for example, will not receive a treatment that will totally remove all perceptions of situations as anxiety provoking or totally eliminate self-evaluative concerns, but the treated youth will be able to employ newly acquired strategies in the management of anxious arousal when it does occur. The angry–aggressive and deficient child may not erase all impulses for immediate action, but he or she will have available skills that can be implemented when more cautious, thoughtful action is needed. To expect cures is irrational; to expect to impart the wisdom that, through experience, will facilitate adjustment is sage.

Dealing with relapse, or relapse temptations, is part of life. Even our most successful clients will be challenged by the many opportunities for decisions that are less than optimal. Our goal is not to "have all go well forever," but to improve upon the trajectory that was evident before treatment began. To alter a nonadaptive trajectory is to produce therapeutic gains, and such an expectation is rational.

Social anxiety and depressive symptomatology are common emotional difficulties. Many therapists working with children and adolescents deal with problems of detrimental anxiety and unwanted depression. Youth with these emotional problems have, as part of their distress, a maladaptive way of processing their world that requires intervention. As is true with adult clients suffering from these same disorders, cognitive-behavioral interventions strive to rectify the distorted information processing that is linked to the emotional distress. Unfortunately, the popular press has overpromoted an idea that has been labeled the "power of positive thinking." Do we want our clients to become big-time positive thinkers? Is such a goal a rational and desired outcome of treatment? As it turns out, theory suggests, and research evidence supports, the notion that it is *not* so much the power of positive thinking that is related to emotional adjustment or improvement in treatment as it is the reduction in negative thinking. I have elsewhere referred to this as "the power of nonnegative thinking" (Kendall, 1984). As we achieve reductions in overly negative and harsh cognitive processing, we reduce negative thinking and we reduce associated psychological distress (Treadwell & Kendall, 1996).

Would you want to be someone who always thinks positively? Individuals who think or talk to themselves in only positive terms are not psychologically healthy. Rather, we all experience life events that have negative features and a rational individual accepts these inevitabilities. One would not want to be thinking only positive thoughts when in a difficult situation. For example, imagine that you are on an intercontinental airplane trip. During excessive air turbulence, you find yourself sitting next to someone who sees everything positively. The turbulence causes the door to open and the person next to you says, "Ah, fresh air." Not exactly a rational response. There are times when a negative thought or two is quite reasonable. Purely positive information processing is, when judged against reality, somewhat distorted. If purely positive thinking is not the goal, and adjustment is related to a reduction in negative thinking, what then should therapists hold as a rational expectation for the outcome of interventions? Should treatments be designed to reduce the negative, self-critical styles of thinking of the anxious and depressed youth?

An answer lies in the ratio of positive to negative thinking. The ratio of positive to negative thinking that has been found to be associated with adjustment is .62:.38 (see Kendall, Howard, & Hays, 1989; Schwartz & Garamoni, 1989). These findings are reported for older adolescents, but the concept holds true for younger persons as well. Generally speaking, this 2:1 ratio suggests that positive thinking occupies two-thirds of the thinking, whereas negative thinking occupies one-third of the thinking in individuals who are not maladjusted (see also Treadwell & Kendall, 1996). Depressed cases, identified psychometrically and clinically, show a 1:1 ratio: the 50–50 split reflecting an equal frequency of positive and negative thinking—an internal dialogue that evidences conflict between the positive and the negative.

How does this affect the expectations held by therapists? I suggest that knowing an optimal ratio of positive to negative thinking is 2:1 serves as a guide for the therapist. Overly optimistic thinking is not necessarily healthy, and shifting too much toward a 1:1 ratio is unhealthy as well. It is healthy to acknowledge certain unwanted situations, accept a negative thought or two, and then proceed to counter the negative aspects with some positive thinking. Positive thinking helps overrule negative thinking, but negative thinking should not be totally eliminated.

Although we all have our share of exceptional successes, is it the case that children and adolescents typically strive to (1) display their newly acquired skills and (2) thank the therapist for the help? Sometimes, as the many fortunate therapists can attest, children and/or their parents do offer a warm and genuine "thanks." However, it is also quite possible (even likely) that children and adolescents learn from their therapeutic interactions but, for a variety of reasons, do not want to let us know. They sometimes act as if they were right all along and did not need nor benefit from therapy. It is irrational for therapists to expect that all clients will, at posttreatment, demonstrate that they have benefited from our interventions.

It is possible that there will be beneficial effects, but that these effects will not be readily evident immediately at the end of treatment. I refer to this, admittedly optimistically, as "sleeper effects." Beneficial learning took place, but the evidence of the learning does not appear until a later point in development, or until a different situation emerges. For example, completion of a therapy that provides an opportunity for learning social problem-solving skills might not produce immediate use of these skills. It may be that after the passage of time, the percolation of the ideas at various times, and the successful use of parts of the problem-solving process, the child/adolescent client comes to employ and recognize the benefits of a problem-solving approach. It has been my experience, for instance, that interpersonal skills learned by a child during early childhood take a temporary backseat to the social pressure of peers. After further developmental changes, the skills acquired earlier can emerge without conflict and better serve the individual's current adjustment.

Continuing an optimistic line of thought, it is also possible for "spillover" effects to occur. Spillover effects refer to the beneficial gains associated with a child's treatment that may be evident in the parents, siblings, or other nontarget participants in the treatment. For example, a child participates in and successfully completes a cognitive-behavioral treatment for an anxiety disorder (see Kendall et al., Chapter 6, this volume). At the end of treatment he or she is less avoidant and more participatory in the activities of his or her peers. As a result, the child is spending less emotionally draining time with the parents and is less demanding and troublesome to them. The tension between the parents, which had been in part linked to the child's anxious distress, diminishes in conjunction with the child's overcoming the unwanted anxiety. The effects of the treatment spill over onto other nontarget arenas. In this example, although such effects may occur, it is likely that they will be more likely and more pronounced with increased involvement of the child's parents.

Conceptualization of Change

Children and adolescents with behavioral and emotional difficulties have associated maladaptive qualities in cognitive information processing. For the depressed adolescent who is misattributing negative outcomes to internal–global–stable features, as well as for the impulsive/hyperactive child who is active in behavior but deficient in planful forethought, modifications of the cognitive processing are in order. Theoretically speaking, how might we conceptualize the needed changes? How best to describe the nature of the cognitive changes that are a part of the goals of treatment?

Some cognitive distortions, as noted in earlier discussion, require modification. New experiences, with guided processing of the experiences, will help to straighten out crooked thinking. What is being suggested is that the existing cognitive structure is not erased, but that new skills and means of construing the world are built, and these new constructions come to serve as new templates for making sense of future experiences. Therapy does not provide a surgical removal of unwanted cognitive structures, but it offers to help to build new schemata with new strategies that can be employed in place of the earlier dysfunctional ones.

Therapy offers exposure to multiple behavioral events with concurrent cognitive processing, such that new cognitive structures can be built over time (recall the discussion tied to Figure 1.1). Positive emotional tones can increase the potency of the experience and add to its impact on the youth's developing new views. As these new perceptions are incorporated into the child's more overarching view of the world and his or her place in it, future experiences are construed differently (less maladaptively). Using newly acquired skills and constructed schemata, the individual moves forward to face and confront new challenges in ways that manage former maladaptive tendencies.

CLOSING

It is worth noting that children and adolescents do not call or refer themselves for services from a mental health professional. Quite the contrary, individuals other than the child or adolescent, such as parents, teachers, or guardians, are often the initiators of psychological interventions. In contrast, adults, who themselves are in personal suffering, seek their own mental health services—they are suffering and they seek help for themselves. The fact that children are sent for treatment, whereas adults often seek it, is an important distinction that has clinical implications. Children and adolescents must, on their own, come to see the potential benefits of therapy. Accordingly, efforts to create a pleasant affective environment and a motivation for further participation are essential.

One of the main challenges facing the developing organism is the movement toward autonomy and independence. Central to this movement is the family, specifically, the parents, and their supportive or constraining styles. Child and adolescent clients are not fully capable, as yet, to be entirely independent, and family, school, and other contextual influences must be considered. Indeed, although the thrust of the present theory is on individual change, multiple influences have been considered and incorporated.

In the present analysis, little discussion has been assigned to factors such as trust, respect, and relationship as part of the therapeutic process. It is not because these matters are unimportant, but rather because they are *essential* to all forms of therapeutic interventions; they need not be given special reconsideration here. Suffice it to say, factors that contribute to a strong relationship are to be encouraged, as are behavioral patterns that clearly communicate mutual respect and trust. The cognitive-behavioral theory outlined herein is one that complements and contributes to basic clinical wisdom about positive adult–child interactions and building an open and trusting relationship. Similarly, this chapter has not discussed the issues facing empirically supported treatments. Nevertheless, treatments that have empirical support are clearly preferred over those that have no such evidence, as the content provided by the contributing authors to this book attest.

ACKNOWLEDGMENTS

I express gratitude to the many graduate students and faculty of the clinical psychology doctoral training program, Temple University, for their helpful input.

REFERENCES

Abramson, L. Y., Seligman, M. E. P., & Teasdale, J. D. (1978). Learned helplessness in humans: Critique and reformulation. *Journal of Abnormal Psychology, 87,* 49–74.

Achenbach, T. M. (1966). The classification of children's psychiatric symptoms: A factor analytic study. *Psychological Monographs, 80*(Whole No. 615).

Bandura, A. (1977). Self-efficacy: Toward a unifying theory of behavior change. *Psychological Review, 84,* 191–215.

Beck, A. T. (1976). *Cognitive therapy and the emotional disorders.* New York: International Universities Press.

Bernard, M. E., & Joyce, M. R. (1984). *Rational emotive therapy with children and adolescents: Theory, treatment strategies, preventive motives.* New York: Wiley.

Daleiden, E. L., Vasey, M. W., & Williams, L. L (1996). Assessing children's state of mind: A multitrait, multimethod study. *Psychological Assessment, 8,* 125–134.

Deluty, R. H. (1981). Alternative-thinking ability of aggressive, assertive and submissive children. *Cognitive Therapy and Research, 5,* 309–312.

Diener, E., & Lucas, R. (1999). Personality and subjective well-being. In D. Kahneman, E. Diener, & N. Schwarz (Eds.), *Well-being: The foundations of hedonic psychology* (pp. 213–239). New York: Russell Sage Foundation.

DiGiuseppe, R., & Bernard, M. E. (1983). Principles of assessment and methods of treatment with children: Special consideration. In A. Ellis & M. E. Bernard (Eds.), *Rational–emotive approaches to the problems of childhood* (pp. 45–88). New York: Plenum Press.

Dodge, K. (1985). Attributional bias in aggressive children. In P. C. Kendall (Ed.), *Advances in cognitive-behavioral research and therapy* (Vol. 4, pp. 75–111). New York: Academic Press.

Edens, J., Cavell, T., & Hughes, J. (1999). The self-systems of aggressive children: A cluster-analytic investigation. *Journal of Child Psychology and Psychiatry, 40,* 441–453.

Ellis, A. (1971). *Growth through reason.* Hollywood, CA: Wilshire Books.

Fishman, K. D. (1995). *Behind the one-way mirror: Psychotherapy with children.* New York: Bantam Books.

Hammen, C., & Zupan, B. (1984). Self-schemas, depression, and the processing of personal information in children. *Journal of Experimental Child Psychology, 37,* 598–608.

Hartup, W. W. (1984). Peer relations. In P. Mussen (Ed.), *Handbook of child psychology.* New York: Wiley.

Hermalin, B., & O'Connor, W. (1970). *Psychological experiments with autistic children.* Oxford, UK: Pergamon Press.

Ingram, R. E., & Kendall, P. C. (1986). Cognitive clinical psychology: Implications of an information processing perspective. In R. E. Ingram (Ed.), *Information processing approaches to clinical psychology* (pp. 3–21). New York: Academic Press.

Ingram, R. E., & Kendall, P. C. (1987). The cognitive side of anxiety. *Cognitive Therapy and Research, 11,* 523–537.

Ingram, R. E., Miranda, J., & Segal, Z. V. (1998). *Cognitive vulnerability to depression.* New York: Guilford Press.

Kaslow, N., Stark, K., Printz, B., Livingston, R., & Tsai, S. (1992). Cognitive Triad Inventory for Children: Development and relation to depression and anxiety. *Journal of Clinical Child Psychology, 21,* 339–347.

Kazdin, A. E., & Weisz, J. R. (1998). Identifying and developing empirically supported child and adolescent treatments. *Journal of Consulting and Clinical Psychology, 66,* 19–36.

Kendall, P. C. (1977). On the efficacious use of verbal self-instructional procedures with children. *Cognitive Therapy and Research, 1,* 331–341.

Kendall, P. C. (1981). Assessment and cognitive-behavioral interventions: Purposes, proposals and problems. In P. C. Kendall & S. D. Hollon (Eds.), *Assessment strategies for cognitive-behavioral interventions* (pp. 1–12). New York: Academic Press.

Kendall, P. C. (1984). Behavioral assessment and methodology. In G. T. Wilson, C. M. Franks, K. D. Brownell, & P. C. Kendall, *Annual review of behavior therapy: Theory and practice* (Vol. 9, pp. 39–94). New York: Guilford Press.

Kendall, P. C. (1989). The generalization and maintenance of behavior change: Comments, considerations, and the "no-cure" criticism. *Behavior Therapy, 20,* 357–364.

Kendall, P. C. (1992a). *Stop and think workbook* (2nd ed.). Ardmore, PA: Workbook Publishing.

Kendall, P. C. (1992b). *Coping cat workbook.* Ardmore, PA: Workbook Publishing.

Kendall, P. C. (1993). Cognitive-behavioral therapies with youth: Guiding theory, current status, and emerging developments. *Journal of Consulting and Clinical Psychology, 61,* 235–247.

Kendall, P. C. (2000). *Childhood disorders.* London: Psychology Press.

Kendall, P. C., & Braswell, L. (1993). *Cognitive-behavioral therapy for impulsive children* (2nd ed.). New York: Guilford Press.

Kendall, P. C., & Hollon, S. D. (1979). Cognitive-behavioral interventions: Overview and current status. In P. C. Kendall & S. D. Hollon (Eds.), *Cognitive behavioral interventions: Theory, research and procedures* (pp. 1–13). New York: Academic Press.

Kendall, P. C., Howard, B. L., & Hays, R. C. (1989). Self-referent speech and psychopathology: The balance of positive and negative thinking. *Cognitive Therapy and Research, 13,* 583–598.

Kendall, P. C., & Ingram, R. E. (1987). The future for cognitive assessment of anxiety: Let's get specific. In L. Michelson & M. Ascher (Eds.), *Anxiety and stress disorders: Cognitive-behavioral assessment and treatment* (pp. 89–104). New York: Guilford Press.

Kendall, P. C., & Ingram, R. E. (1989). Cognitive-behavioral perspectives: Theory and research on depression and anxiety. In P. C. Kendall & D. Watson (Eds.), *Anxiety and depression: Distinctive and overlapping features* (pp. 27–54). New York: Academic Press.

Kendall, P. C., & MacDonald, J. P. (1993). Cognition in the psychopathology of youth, and implications for treatment. In K. S. Dobson & P. C. Kendall (Eds.), *Psychopathology and cognition* (pp. 387–430). San Diego: Academic Press.

Kendall, P. C., Ronan, K., & Epps, J. (1990). Aggression in children/adolescents: Cognitive-behavioral treatment perspectives. In D. Pepler & K. Rubin (Eds.), *Development and treatment of childhood aggression* (pp. 341–360). Hillsdale, NJ: Erlbaum.

Kendall, P. C., Stark, K., & Adam, T. (1990). Cognitive deficit or cognitive distortion in childhood depression. *Journal of Abnormal Child Psychology, 18,* 267–283.

Lochman, J., & Dodge, K. (1998). Distorted perceptions in dyadic interactions of aggressive and nonaggressive boys: Effects of prior expectations, context, and boy's age. *Development and Psychopathology, 10,* 495–512.

Lonigan, C., Elbert, J., & Johnson, S. B. (1998). Empirically supported psychosocial interventions for children: An overview. *Journal of Clinical Child Psychology, 27,* 138–145.

Meichenbaum, D. (1977). *Cognitive-behavior modification: An integrative approach.* New York: Plenum Press.

Meichenbaum, D., & Goodman, J. (1971). Training impulsive children to talk to themselves: A means of developing self-control. *Journal of Abnormal Psychology, 77,* 115–126.

Ollendick, T., & King, N. (1998). Empirically supported treatments for children with phobic and anxiety disorders. *Journal of Clinical Child Psychology, 27,* 156–167.

Prieto, S., Cole, D., & Tageson, C. (1992). Depressive self-schemas in clinic and nonclinic children. *Cognitive Therapy and Research, 16,* 521–534.

Prior, M. (1984). Developing concepts of childhood autism: The influence of experimental cognitive research. *Journal of Consulting and Clinical Psychology, 52,* 4–16.

Santostefano, S., & Reider, C. (1984). Cognitive controls and aggression in children: The concept of cognitive-affective balance. *Journal of Consulting and Clinical Psychology, 52,* 46–56.

Schwartz, R. M., & Garamoni, G. L. (1989). Cognitive balance and psychopathology: Evaluation of an information processing model of positive and negative states of mind. *Clinical Psychology Review, 9,* 271–294.

Southam-Gerow, M., & Kendall, P. C. (2000). Emotion understanding in youth referred for treatment of anxiety disorders. *Journal of Clinical Child Psychology, 29.*

Spivack, G., & Shure, M. B. (1982). The cognition of social adjustments: Interpersonal cognitive problem-solving thinking. In B. B. Lahey & A. E. Kazdin (Eds.), *Advances in clinical child psychology* (Vol. 5, pp. 323–372). New York: Plenum Press.

Treadwell, K. R. H., & Kendall, P. C. (1996). Self-talk in anxiety-disordered youth: States-of-mind, content specificity, and treatment outcome. *Journal of Consulting and Clinical Psychology, 64,* 941–950.

PART II

EXTERNALIZING DISORDERS

CHAPTER 2

Cognitive-Behavioral Assessment and Treatment with Aggressive Children

John E. Lochman, Janet M. Whidby,
and David P. FitzGerald

Aggression is a set of primarily interpersonal actions that consist of verbal or physical behaviors that are destructive or injurious to others or to objects (Bandura, 1973; Lochman, 1984). Although almost all children display some aggressive behavior, it is only when aggression is exceptionally severe, frequent, and/or chronic that it becomes indicative of psychopathology.

Children with high levels of aggressive behavior are most often diagnosed as having conduct disorders or oppositional defiant disorders, but aggressive behavior can be comorbid with other diagnostic categories as well. Children with subclinical conditions or a variety of other primary diagnoses (e.g., attention-deficit/hyperactivity disorder, dysthymia, posttraumatic stress disorder) may have periodic or chronic bursts of aggressive behavior as well. A common characteristic of all seriously aggressive children is that they have intense negative effects on the people who interact with them. Peers are victimized, teachers are disrupted from their teaching activities, and parents are frustrated with being unable to control these children's coercive and provocative behaviors. Because of these intense, flagrant effects on others, aggressive children are referred for mental health services at higher rates than are children with most other forms of psychopathology (Lochman & Lenhart, 1995).

31

Longitudinal research has indicated that aggressive behavior is quite stable during childhood and adolescence, and that aggression is more consistent over time than most other behavioral patterns (Gesten, Langer, Eisenberg, Simcha-Fagan, & McCarthy, 1976; Huesmann, Eron, Lefkowitz, & Walder, 1984; Lochman & the Conduct Problems Prevention Research Group, 1995; Olweus, 1979). Children who display a wide range of different kinds of aggressive, antisocial behavior, and who are highly antisocial in multiple settings (e.g., home, school, community) are at greatest risk for continued disorder (Loeber & Dishion, 1983; Loeber & Schmaling, 1985). These children display a progressive accumulation, or "stacking," of a variety of problem behaviors as they develop further along the trajectory to conduct disorder (Lochman & the Conduct Problems Prevention Research Group, 1995; Loeber, 1990), and they are at risk for a wide range of negative outcomes, including adolescent drug and alcohol use, cigarette smoking, school truancy and dropout, early teenage parenthood, delinquency, and violence (Coie, Lochman, Terry, & Hyman, 1992; Kellam, Ensminger, & Simon,1980; Kupersmidt & Coie, 1990; Lochman & Wayland, 1994; Lynskey & Fergusson, 1995; Miller-Johnson et al., 1999; Swaim, Oetting, Edwards, & Beauvais, 1989; Tremblay et al., 1992; Wills & Filer, 1996; Windle, 1990).

Problem youth typically do not differ from their peers on just one dimension, such as aggressiveness, but instead vary on multiple behavioral dimensions related to poor self-control, leading to the high correlation among delinquency, substance use, and depression (Wills & Filer, 1996). These self-control difficulties may be the result of deficits in children's executive cognitive functioning, which controls self-regulation of goal-directed behavior (Giancola, Martin, Tarter, Pelham, & Moss, 1996; Seguin, Pihl, Harden, Tremblay, & Boulerice, 1995). As individuals accumulate increasing numbers of risky problem behaviors, their odds for violent behavior increase (Lochman, in press). By age 14, risk taking, drug selling, gang membership, early initiation of violence, and peer delinquency all combine to become the strongest predictors of later violence (Herrenkohl et al., 1998). Thus, it is clinically important to anticipate co-occurring negative outcomes and comorbidity of risk factors. For example, aggressive children who are also socially rejected by their peers have twice the risk rate for middle school adjustment problems of children who are only aggressive (Coie et al., 1992), adolescents with conduct disorder who are also depressed have an earlier onset of alcohol use than do adolescents with conduct disorder only (Miller-Johnson, Lochman, Coie, Terry, & Hyman, 1998), and aggressive children who also have attention-deficit/hyperactivity disorder (ADHD) have more violent offending and greater substance use than do children who are only aggressive (Thompson, Riggs, Mikulich, & Crowley, 1996). Because aggression is a broad risk factor, it has become an important focus for intervention.

In this chapter, we present a social-cognitive model for aggression, and discuss the cognitive-behavioral assessment techniques and intervention strategies associated with this model. An anger coping program is described. We review only cognitive-behavioral therapy results and procedures with aggressive children and do not cover adolescence or impulsive, hyperactive behaviors. Hinshaw (Chapter 3, this volume) addresses attention-deficit/hyperactivity disorder, which frequently accompanies childhood aggression.

CONCEPTUAL FRAMEWORK FOR COGNITIVE-BEHAVIORAL THERAPY: IDENTIFYING MEDIATIONAL PROCESSES

Cognitive-behavioral therapy (CBT) focuses upon the perceptions and thoughts of aggressive children as they encounter perceived threats and frustrations. The techniques and goals of CBT are directed at children's deficiencies and distortions in their cognitive processing of events, and at their regulation of emotions, especially anger. Anger is the mood that people have most difficulty controlling (Goleman, 1995), and intense, uncontrolled anger arousal can be a central component of aggression and externalizing behavior problems (Lochman, Dunn, & Wagner, 1997; Zillmann, 1994). Anger corresponds to the "fight" response in the fight–flight arousal mechanism; this innate action tendency involves an attack on the agent perceived to be blameworthy (Lazarus, 1993). Refinements in CBT techniques have arisen largely because of new research and models of these deficiencies in children's self-regulation and processing of social conflicts, and parent and community contextual factors that influence these dysfunctional cognitive-affective processes. Before examining CBT with aggressive children, we first review two of the major areas of conceptual roots for CBT and then examine the social-cognitive model used as a foundation for our Anger Coping Program.

Historical Roots of Cognitive-Behavioral Therapy

A number of factors have influenced the sharp increase in interest and development of CBT procedures with children over the last two decades (Hughes, 1988; Kendall & Braswell, 1985; Meyers & Craighead, 1984). The two factors that have important implications for this chapter are social learning theories and research on self-regulation.

Social Learning Theories

The social learning theories (SLTs) developed by both Rotter and Bandura represent early precursors of current CBT approaches with children. In

Rotter's SLT (Rotter, Chance, & Phares, 1972), the potential, or likelihood, of a specific behavior being emitted by an individual was the result of situationally specific reinforcement values and of expectancies that the reinforcement could be attained with the specific behavior. While external consequences were assumed to be important determinants of an individual's behavior, the behavior was seen as the direct product of the individual's cognitive evaluations of the value of the available reinforcements and the success that was expected in attaining the reinforcement. If the value of a reinforcement was high (e.g., a portable stereo) but the expectation for attaining the reinforcement with a socially approved behavior was low (e.g., getting a job and saving for the stereo), then the individual would logically use other behaviors for which he or she had higher expectations for successful reinforcement acquisition (e.g., breaking into an apartment to steal a stereo). Each decision about a behavior would be influenced by expectations for an array of positive and negative consequences. Rotter's SLT emphasized the situational specificity of these cognitive processes, but it recognized that cross-situational cognition also developed in the form of generalized expectancies (e.g., locus of control) and reinforcement values (needs or goals).

Bandura's (1977) SLT added an emphasis on other cognitive factors, such as an individual's expectations about competently enacting a given behavior (efficacy expectations), self-reinforcement, and the tendency to attend selectively to certain observed models (Hughes, 1988). The concept of modeling in Bandura's theory has had a major influence on CBT with children. Modeling influences the initial acquisition of behaviors, as we learn behaviors by observing others engaging in them, as well as the performance of already acquired behaviors. Certain characteristics of models, such as their prestige and the consequences that result from their performed behavior, have been to influence individuals' attention to the model, to encode of the model's behavior, and, ultimately, to display the model's effectiveness (Bandura, 1977). The constructs evident in these SLTs foreshadow many of our current concepts in CBT.

Research on Self-Regulation

Another primary empirical influence on CBT has been the investigation of self-regulation. The two strands of developmental research that played a key role in Meichenbaum's early application of CBT to children (Meichenbaum & Goodman, 1971) was the research of Luria and Vygotsky, and Mischel's work on delay of gratification. According to Vygotsky (1978), the child's internalization of control on tasks is a gradual, stepwise process, in which the caregiver first controls and guides the child's activity; then, the adult and child begin to share in the initiation of problem solving, although the adult still guides when the child fails; finally, the caregiver supportively permits the child to exercise control (Brown, 1987). Mischel's research has exemplified the importance of cognitive mechanisms such as attention and strategy production in the developmental change in the ability to delay gratification (Kopp, 1987), which is a central aspect of self-regulation. Similarly, research on executive cognitive functioning (ECF) has found that it involves the self-regulation of goal-directed behavior and encompasses higher-order cognitive abilities such as attentional control, cognitive flexibility, planning, and self-monitoring (Giancola, Zeichner, Yarnell, & Dickson, 1996). Boys with ECF deficits have been found to have higher rates of reactive aggression several years later (Giancola, Moss, et al., 1996), apparently because these weaknesses in their higher-order cognitive abilities lead to failures in self-regulation.

In Vygotsky's theory, internal psychological processes have a social basis. Thoughts mirror interpersonal transactions that are observed and experienced, and the transactions become internal communication when they have been transformed through experience into an intrapersonal process (Brown, 1987). This emphasis on the socialization provided by caregivers in the formation of these cognitive processes is consistent with the assumption in attachment theory that children's "working models," which provide them with their basic expectations about their interpersonal environment, are derived from their relationships with caregivers (Bretherton, 1995; Lochman & Dodge, 1998; Shaw & Bell, 1993).

Implications of These Historical Roots

The theoretical and empirical work on SLTs and on self-regulation has had a clear, but often indirect, impact on all forms of CBT with children (Hughes, 1988; Kendall & Braswell, 1985). Perhaps more importantly, these conceptual roots also can guide our thinking about the future evolution of CBT with children. Five implications for CBT that arise from this brief review include (1) examination of additional and, ideally, theoretically interrelated cognitive processes such as outcome expectations and reinforcement values; (2) exploration of cognitive processes that are situational; (3) emphasis on developmental changes in cognition in CBT; (4) integration of understanding of basic cognitive processes such as attention, retrieval, and organization of information in memory into social information-processing models and into CBT, and (5) consideration of the importance of early caregivers on the evolution of children's cognitive controls, schemas, and self-regulation. The latter point is an essential one, since collateral intervention with parents and teachers has become an important area of emphasis in the literature on CBT with children. We return to these implications as we propose a social information-processing model for aggressive children, and again after we examine current CBT approaches with these children.

Social-Cognitive Model of Anger and Aggression

The Anger Coping Program we use with aggressive children is based on an evolving, empirically-based social-cognitive model (Lochman et al., 1997; Lochman, Fitzgerald, & Whidby, 1999; Lochman & Lenhart, 1993; Lochman, Nelson, & Sims, 1981) of how anger develops in children and results in aggressive responses. In these types of information-processing models, Kendall (1985; Kendall & MacDonald, 1993; see also Chapter 1, this volume) differentiated between cognitive deficiencies, which involve an insufficient amount of cognitive activity, and cognitive distortions, which involve misperceptions. Both types of responses can be seen in aggressive children's social-cognitive dysfunctions.

The model presented here originally derived in large part from Novaco's (1978) conceptualization of anger arousal in adults and has been substantially affected by Dodge's (1986; Crick & Dodge, 1994) social information-processing model. In our social-cognitive model, the child encounters a potentially anger-arousing stimulus event, but the emotional and physiological reaction is due to the child's perception and appraisal of the event rather than the event itself. These perceptions and appraisals can be accurate or inaccurate, and are derived from prior expectations that filter the event and from the child's selective attention to specific aspects, or cues, in the stimulus event. If the child has interpreted the event to be threatening, provocative, or frustrating, he or she may then experience physiological arousal and also become engaged in another set of cognitive activities directed at deciding upon an appropriate behavioral response to the event. The internal arousal has a reciprocal interaction with the child's appraisal processes, because he or she has to interpret and label the emotional connotations of the arousal, and the increased arousal narrows the child's attention to certain types of cues associated with possible threat. These three sets of internal activities—(1) perception and appraisal, (2) arousal, and (3) social problem solving—contribute to the child's behavioral response and to the resulting consequences the child elicits from peers and adults and experiences internally as self-consequences. These consequent reactions from others can then become stimulus events that feed back into the model, becoming recurrent, connected behavioral units.

We review the social-cognitive deficiencies and distortions that have been found in research with aggressive children and propose how other cognitive, physiological, and familial factors could affect these social-cognitive products. The social-cognitive processes we have described account for sequential activation of situational, moment-to-moment processes, but they do not specify the structural relationship between more basic cognitive activities and social cognitions. Social information-processing models have only recently begun to indicate how enduring, cross-situational cognitive schemas affect immediate, momentary processing (Lochman, White, & Wayland, 1991; Crick & Dodge, 1994; Lochman & Lenhart, 1995; Lochman & Dodge, 1998). Similarly, the effects of psychophysiological processes and family influences on children's social information-processing have only become an active area of investigation in the last decade.

In this chapter, we use an adaption of the Cognitive Taxonomic System (Ingram & Kendall, 1986; Kendall & Ingram, 1989) to organize the relevant sets of cognitive activities into three clusters, which are then integrated into our model. Schematic propositions are the stored information in cognitive structures in memory. Cognitive operations are various procedures that process stored and incoming information (e.g., attention, encoding, retrieval) and, in our case, can be separated from the content of social-cognitive products. Social-cognitive products are the results of interaction among stored schematic proportions, cognitive operations, and incoming sensory data about stimulus events, and include social-cognitive appraisals, social problem solving, and cognitive-emotional linkage. Finally, the roles of key social influences, especially parents and peers, are noted.

Social-Cognitive Products

Social-Cognitive Appraisals

These social-cognitive products consist of the first two stages in Crick and Dodge's (1994) reformulated social information-processing model: cue utilization and attributions about others' intentions. Aggressive children have been found to perceive and encode cues in the environment around them in a different manner than do nonaggressive children. Social-cognitive researchers have had children listen to series of audiotaped and videotaped segments in which child actors describe and portray hostile, benevolent, and neutral situations. After listening to, or viewing, the segments, the children were asked to remember as many cues as they could. In comparison with nonaggressive children, aggressive children and adolescents have been found to recall fewer relevant cues (even after controlling for intelligence levels) (Lochman & Dodge, 1994) and to remember more of the last statements they hear, indicating that they have a developmental lag in their cue utilization (Milich & Dodge, 1984).

Another developmental lag has been evident in aggressive boys' tendencies to decide to attend to few cues while attempting to interpret the meaning of other's behavior (Dodge & Newman, 1981). When given an opportunity to listen to as many taped statements about a child's intentions as they wished, nonaggressive boys listened to 40% more cues before making a decision than did aggressive boys. In addition, aggressive children have been found to encode and retrieve significantly more cues that convey hostile connotations than do nonaggressive children (Dodge, Pettit, McClaskey, & Brown, 1986; Gouze, 1987; Lochman, 1989; Milich & Dodge, 1984). McKinnon, Lamb, Belsky, and Baum (1990) have suggested that these cue encoding biases can be the result of aggressive children's earlier social interactions with their parents, because children who experience primarily negative or aggressive interactions with their parents are more likely to attend to cues of hostility and aggression in others.

These findings indicate that aggressive children are hypervigilant in scanning their social environment, attending to more immediate ones, especially hostile cues, than do nonaggressive children. Aggressive children do not appear to use sustained search strategies in examining the environment and thus do not planfully consider more complex inferences about others' behavior.

In the milliseconds after cues are perceived, aggressive children form inferences about others' intentions, and these efforts to decipher the meaning of others' behavior have been found to be significantly influenced by their higher rate of detection of hostile cues and their prior expectations that others will be hostile toward them (Dodge & Frame, 1982). As a result, aggressive boys have been found to be 50% more likely than nonaggressive boys to infer that antagonists in hypothetical provocations act with hostile rather than neutral or benign intent (Dodge, 1980). This attributional bias about others' intentions has been replicated in a series of studies with both aggressive boys and girls, using experimental stimuli consisting of written or videotaped hypothetical vignettes and live observation of another child knocking down a block building that the aggressive child made (Dodge et al., 1986; Guerra & Slaby, 1989; Milich & Dodge, 1984; Nasby, Hayden, & DePaulo, 1980; Sancilio, Plumert, & Hartup, 1989; Steinberg & Dodge, 1983; Waas, 1988). This hostile attributional bias has been found to be equally evident in both preadolescent and adolescent severely aggressive boys (Lochman & Dodge, 1994), again suggesting that these appraisal difficulties become well established during early socialization experiences in the home, neighborhood, and peer group.

In actual competitive dyadic discussions with nonaggressive peers, aggressive boys not only tend to overperceive the peer's aggressiveness, but they also substantially underestimate their own aggressiveness (Lochman, 1987; Lochman & Dodge, 1998). These distorted perceptions by aggressive children during live interactions have been found to occur on both competitive and cooperative tasks, and are due to aggressive boys' prior expectations (Lochman & Dodge, 1998). Due to their distorted perceptions of the peer and of themselves, aggressive boys implicitly attribute responsibility for the conflict to the peer. This pattern of distorted perceptions and interpretation of others in early stages of a conflict sequence can contribute to the boys' subsequently feeling quite justified in responding in an intensely aggressive manner.

Social Problem Solving

While cognitive distortions are evident in aggressive children's appraisal processes, cognitive deficiencies are more evident in their social problem-solving difficulties. In this chapter, social problem solving refers to the last four of Crick and Dodge's (1994) stages, and includes goal selection, generation of alternative solutions, consideration of consequences of solutions, and behavioral implementation of solutions (Allen, Chinsky, Larcen, Lochman, & Selinger, 1976). Generation of solutions and consideration of consequences are social-cognitive products in our model. Mixed findings exist as to whether aggressive children in general actually generate fewer solutions than nonaggressive children (Deluty, 1981; Dodge et al., 1986; Kendall & Fischler, 1984; Lochman & Lampron, 1986; Richard & Dodge, 1982; Rubin, Bream, & Rose-Krasnor, 1991), but evidence does indicate that boys with the very highest level of aggressive behavior, in comparison with moderately aggressive boys, have a marked paucity in the range of problem solutions they consider (Lochman & Dodge, 1994; Lochman, Lampron, Burch, & Curry, 1985). In contrast to these qualified findings about the quantitative aspect of the social problem-solving process, aggressive children have displayed consistent and characteristic deficiencies in the content or quality of the solution they generate.

Using measures with hypothetical open-middle and open-ended vignettes, aggressive children have been found to generate fewer verbal assertion and compromise solutions than do nonaggressive children (Asarnow & Callan, 1985; Deluty, 1981; Joffe, Dobson, Fine, Marriage, & Haley, 1990; Lochman & Dodge, 1994; Lochman & Lampron, 1986), along with more direct action solutions (Lochman & Dodge, 1994; Lochman & Lampron, 1986), more help-seeking or adult intervention solutions (Asher & Renshaw, 1981; Lochman, Lampron, & Rabiner, 1989; Rabiner, Lenhart, & Lochman, 1990), and more physically aggressive solutions (Richard & Dodge, 1982; Slaby & Guerra, 1988; Waas, 1988; Waas & French, 1989). Aggressive children have been found to consider more aggressive responses in their second or third solution to a problem, indicating they have more aggressive, ineffective backup solutions to social problems (Evans & Short, 1991; Richard & Dodge, 1982). When subtypes of aggressive children have been examined, boys with more severe conduct disorder diagnoses produce more aggressive/antisocial solutions in vignettes about conflicts with parents and teachers, and fewer verbal/nonaggressive solutions in peer conflicts, in comparison to boys with oppositional defiant disorder (Dunn, Lochman, & Colder, 1997). The findings about verbal assertion are particularly important, since nonaggressive children, by verbally labeling what they want in a simple, direct manner, are better able to indicate their intentions to those around them. Aggressive children's nonverbal direct actions, in contrast, can easily lead their peers to assume that their intentions may have been hostile, and can lead to progressive escalations of aggression.

At the next stage of problem solving, children evaluate the solutions they have generated and decide which solution would produce the best outcome for them. Aggressive children evaluate aggressive behavior as less negative (Deluty, 1983) and more positive (Crick & Ladd, 1990) than do nonaggressive children. Aggressive children believe that aggressive behavior will lead to tangible rewards and have a positive outcome (Hart, Ladd, & Burleson, 1990; Perry, Perry, & Rasmussen, 1986), will reduce others' aversive behavior (Lochman & Dodge, 1994; Perry et al., 1986), and will result in a positive image and not create suffering in others (Slaby & Guerra, 1988). Recent research has found that these beliefs about the acceptability of aggressive behavior lead to deviant processing of social cues, which in turn then mediates or leads to children's aggressive behavior (Zelli, Dodge, Lochman, Laird, & the Conduct Problems Prevention Research Group, 1999), underscoring the importance of recognizing that these information-processing steps have bidirectional and recursive effects, rather than strictly linear effects on each other.

In the attempt to enact behaviorally the solutions they have selected, aggressive children have been found to be less adept at enacting positive or prosocial behaviors (Dodge et al., 1986). Thus, aggressive children's beliefs that they will be less successful enacting prosocial behaviors than aggressive behaviors (Erdley & Asher, 1993) may reflect reality and emphasize the need for social skills training embedded within the cognitive-behavioral intervention for these children.

Appraisal of Internal Arousal and Emotional Reactions

The manner in which aggressive children perceive, or label, the arousal they begin to experience during conflicts constrains the kinds of behavioral responses they consider using. Aggressive children have distortions in this affect-labeling process, as they are more apt to label affect-arousing situations as producing anger rather than other emotions, such as sadness (Garrison & Stolberg, 1983). It is likely that certain responses children deem appropriate for sadness-evoking situations would not be considered appropriate for anger-evoking situations, thus serving to narrow the range of solutions that aggressive children would consider. In addition, there appear to be important developmental changes that occur in the affect-labeling patterns of aggressive children. As aggressive boys pass into early adolescence, they become even more likely to minimize their endorsement of negative affective states during stressful situations and social conflicts, especially avoiding affective expression of feelings related to vulnerability (e.g., sadness, fear). Instead, aggressive adolescent boys strive to act unconcerned or even to have positive, "happy" emotional reactions to threatening events (Lochman & Dodge, 1994).

The relationship between aggression and affective factors such as empathy has also received attention. This body of research explores the hypothesis that empathic responding inhibits one's tendency to engage in aggressive or antisocial interpersonal acts. In Feshbach and Feshbach's (1982) three-component model, empathy consists of (1) the capacity to discriminate another's emotional state (affect identification); (2) the ability to assume the perspective and role of another (cognitive perspective taking); and (3) the ability to respond emotionally (affective responsivity). This model thus suggests that empathy is a complex intrapsychic and interpersonal phenomenon that involves several cognitive and affective skills.

In two extensive reviews of the literature on the relationship between empathy and antisocial and prosocial behaviors (Eisenberg & Miller, 1987; Miller & Eisenberg, 1988), the authors concluded that empathy is positively correlated to prosocial behaviors and negatively correlated with antisocial behaviors. Empathy is defined by these authors as a form of "emotional matching" in which a vicarious emotional response is consistent with, or identical to, another's emotional state. The relationship between empathy and pro- and antisocial behavior appears to be influenced by such factors as age, the method of assessing behavior, and the means of assessing empathy (Eisenberg & Miller, 1987; Miller & Eisenberg, 1988). In studies that use questionnaire methods to assess empathy, these authors concluded that there is stronger evidence for the relationship between empathy and pro- and antisocial behaviors among school-age children and adolescents than preschool children. Questionnaires provide "trait" or dispositional measures of empathy that typically assess one's general understanding of others' emotions, weaknesses, and degree of emotional responsiveness across a range of situations. Evidence for the relationship between empathy and behavior is weakest or nonexistent when empathy is measured by asking children to indicate their emotional responses to hypothetical vignettes presented as brief pictures or stories. Picture story methods provide "state" measures of empathy that assess children's immediate response to stimuli designed to elicit emotional reactions. As Eisenberg and Miller note, inconsistent results may be due to different methods of assessing empathy for different-age children, or to actual developmental differences in children's capacity for empathic responding. The moderating effect of age on the relationship between behavior and empathic responsivity is unknown. For instance, Slaby and Guerra (1988) noted that some of the beliefs of antisocial aggressive youths would interfere with their ability to develop appropriate empathy skills. Cohen and Strayer (1996) found empathy to be lower among youth with conduct disorder than comparison youth and related inversely to antisocial and aggressive attitudes for all youth tested.

*Individual Differences among Aggressive Children's
Social-Cognitive Processes*

When assessing individual children, as we soon discuss, it is important to
identify the specific patterns of appraisal and the problem-solving difficulties of each aggressive child. As noted earlier, children with conduct disorder have a wider range of social problem-solving deficits than do children
with oppositional defiant disorder (Dunn et al., 1997) and, in a similar
way, more severely aggressive, violent boys have poorer social problem-
solving skills than do moderately aggressive boys (Lochman & Dodge,
1994). A similar pattern exists for children who are both aggressive and
rejected by their peer group in comparison to aggressive children who are
relatively accepted by their peer group (French, 1988; Lochman, Coie,
Underwood, & Terry, 1993; Rabiner et al., 1990). A particularly useful distinction has been made between reactive and proactive aggressive children
(Crick & Dodge, 1996; Dodge & Coie, 1987; Dodge, Lochman, Harnish,
Bates, & Pettit, 1997), with direct implications for information-processing
patterns. Reactive aggressive children, who display intense anger and
arousal as they impulsively respond with aggression to perceived provocations, have a broad range of social-cognitive problems, including encoding
and attributional distortions as well as social problem-solving deficits. Reactive aggressive children are also more likely to be victimized by their
peers (Schwartz et al., 1998), to have comorbid affective distress, and to
come from families that use harsh discipline (Dodge et al., 1997). Reactive
aggressive children have been found to have more deficits in executive cognitive functioning and to be more at risk for substance abuse (Giancola,
Moss, et al., 1996). Proactive aggressive children, in contrast, engage in aggressive behavior in a more planful, less emotionally aroused way and have
higher levels of psychopathy (Cornell et al., 1996); their primary social-
cognitive difficulty is their strong belief that aggressive strategies will work
for them (Dodge et al., 1997).

Cognitive Operations

The operations used to manipulate information that individuals encounter
externally and internally include attention, retrieval processes from short
and long-term memory, and concept formation and problem-solving processing. External information is evident in cues from the environment
around the individual, and internal information is present in physiological
cues and in images, thoughts, or beliefs accessed from memory. Attention
can be conceived as an operation that assists other cognitive operations
such as encoding and retrieval (Cohen & Schleser, 1984); thus, the efficiency and quality of the attentional operations can have major effects on
the quality of other cognitive operations and products.

There is suggestive evidence that links deficiencies in sustaining and focusing attention to aggression in children. Mirsky (1989) administered a variety of attentional measures, including the Continuous Performance Task (CPT), to adolescents involved in a 10-year follow-up of a population sample. Aggressive adolescents had difficulty concentrating and sustaining attention on the CPT in comparison to other adolescents. These attentional deficits produced impairments in encoding information, so that individuals did not perceive relevant bits of information (omission errors), and they perceived information that was not present (commission errors, or intrusions). Similar impairments on attention tasks have been found with aggressive children (Agrawal & Kaushal, 1988), and with children with ADHD who are comorbid for conduct disorder or oppositional disorder (Werry, Elkind, & Reeves, 1987). Children with ADHD have a basic problem with self-control (Gold, 1998; Barkley, 1997), and ADHD is the most common comorbid diagnosis in children with conduct disorder. These children who are comorbid for ADHD and conduct disorder are most likely to display these attentional difficulties and to display behavioral activation rather than behavioral inhibition (Matthys, van Goozen, de Vries, Cohen-Kettenis, & van Engeland, 1998); they also have more wide-ranging and intense problems, including earlier age of onset of severe conduct problems, more violent offending, and earlier and greater substance use (August, Realmuto, MacDonald, Nugent, & Crosby, 1996; Frick, 1998; Thompson et al., 1996).

These attentional impairments may also be related to a distinct pattern of deficiencies in retrieval from short-term memory for aggressive children. Lochman (1989) examined group differences in basic recall and attention (using Santostefano & Roder's [1984] Leveling–Sharpening House Test) and a parallel social-cognitive measure of utilization of social cues (audiotape recall measure; Milich & Dodge, 1984). In comparison with non-aggressive boys, the aggressive boys had higher rates of intrusive commission errors on the recall tasks. Since a similar pattern was evident for both social and nonsocial stimuli, the cue perception deficits appeared to be partly due to operational defects.

In addition to deficient retrieval from short-term memory, which has an impact on distortion in appraisal processes, aggressive children have characteristic styles of retrieving known strategies from long-term memory, which contribute to social problem-solving deficiencies. Lochman, Lampron, and Rabiner (1989) found that children responding to the Problem-Solving Measures for Conflict (PSM-C) in the usual open-middle format, which simulates automatic retrieval processes, had different patterns of responses than children responding to the PSM-C with a multiple-choice format. The multiple-choice format simulated more deliberate, comparative retrieval processes, similar to a process of carefully sifting through stored solutions in "memory bins." In the open-middle condition, aggressive elementary school boys produced significantly more direct action solutions and tended to produce fewer verbal assertion solutions than nonaggressive children, replicating the Lochman and Lampron (1986) results. In the multiple-choice condition, both aggressive and nonaggressive boys had higher rates of verbal assertion solutions and lower rates of direct action solutions than occurred in the open-middle condition; however, aggressive boys still had lower rates of verbal assertion and higher rates of help-seeking solutions than did nonaggressive boys. Thus, aggressive boys' solutions to social problems seemed to be affected by salience effects during retrieval from long-term memory, as well as by learned patterns stored in memory. In a subsequent study, Rabiner et al. (1990) replicated these findings while using a more direct paradigm in which automatic retrieval processes were forced by requiring children to provide responses immediately, while deliberate processing was facilitated by having children wait 20 seconds after hearing the problem vignette before responding.

Schematic Propositions

In Ingram and Kendall's (1986) cognitive taxonomic system, cognitive propositions, defined as the content of cognitive structures, are essentially personal information or general knowledge stored in memory (e.g., belief, expectations). Cognitive structure is the architecture of functional psychological mechanisms such as short-term memory, long-term memory, cognitive networks, and memory nodes. Propositions and structure are classified as categories of schemas, but only the schematic propositions are relevant for our discussion here. Schematic propositions, which are also similar to the "cognitive structures" identified by Meichenbaum (1985) and others, are ideas and thoughts stored in memory that have a direct influence on how new pieces of information, or cognitive products, are processed moment by moment. Schemas are regarded as conservative, because preexisting beliefs are accepted over new ones, and they are self-centered, because they draw on personal beliefs over information or experiences from other sources (Fiske & Taylor, 1984). With stronger schemas, children's perceptions become more filtered and potentially more distorted (Lochman & Dodge, 1998), and schemas can operate quickly outside of conscious awareness (Erdley, 1990) in a manner similar to the automatic preemptive information processing evident in aggressive children's social problem solving (Lochman, Lampron, & Rabiner, 1989; Rabiner et al., 1990). Recent conceptualizations of social information-processing models have suggested that children's schemas, acquired through prior socialization, may have powerful effects on how children appraise the meaning of interpersonal behavior and how they decide to respond to perceived social problems (e.g., Crick & Dodge, 1994; Lochman & Dodge, 1998; Lochman & Lenhart, 1995). Classes of schematic proposition, which have been found to be related to children's aggressive behavior, and which, therefore, may influence social-cognitive products, are goal values, generalized outcome expectations, beliefs, and perceived competence and self-worth.

In a study of the direct effect of adolescents' social goals on their solutions to social problems, Lochman, Wayland, and White (1993) used an SLT framework (Rotter, et al., 1972) to examine boys' ratings of (1) the value of four social goals in a conflict situation (avoidance, dominance, revenge, affiliation), (2) the solution they would use to accomplish each goal, and (3) their level of expectation that they could attain the goals with their selected responses. Aggressive boys had significantly higher value ratings for the dominance and revenge goals and lower ratings for an affiliation goal in comparison to nonaggressive boys. This dominance-oriented pattern of social goals was found to be associated with adolescents' delinquency and substance-use rates. Although aggressive and nonaggressive boys endorsed similar patterns of behavioral solutions to attain each of the goals, aggressive boys had substantially different solutions they would use to gain their main goal than non-aggressive boys. This suggests the direct effect of goals (schematic proposition) on problem solutions (cognitive products). Due to overvaluing dominance and revenge goals, aggressive boys had more aggressive and verbal assertion solutions and fewer bargaining solutions than did nonaggressive boys. These results also are consistent with Brion-Meisel and Selman's (1984) view that developmental changes take place in children's interpersonal negotiation tactics. While simple verbal assertion strategies are competent and adaptive means of resolving social conflicts in the preadolescent years, by midadolescence, complex mutual bargaining and cooperation strategies appear to be more normative for nonaggressive boys.

In a conceptually related study of goals, Rabiner and Gordon (1992) found that aggressive-rejected children were less able to integrate self-oriented and other-oriented concerns than average and popular boys. In another study documenting aggressive children's self-oriented goals for dominance, Boldizar, Perry, and Perry (1989) used the Rotter et al. (1972) social learning framework to examine outcome values. In their goal-oriented outcome values, aggressive children were found to place more value on achieving control of the victim and less value on suffering by the victim, retaliation from the victim, peer rejection, or negative self-evaluation. These sets of findings about goals and outcome values are also consistent with moral reasoning research in which children consider the consequences of their hypothetical actions. Aggressive children and adolescents have a lower level of moral reasoning (Edelman & Goldstein, 1981; Jurkovic & Prentice, 1988; Nucci & Herman, 1982), generally at a preconventional level; that is, they primarily attempt to avoid punishment by authority figures and do not act cooperatively to bolster the positive consequences for themselves and others.

In addition to the stored schematic representation of their goal and outcome values, aggressive children have certain patterns of expectations of achieving their outcomes/goals. Aggressive children have been found to be more confident that aggressive behavior will produce tangible rewards and reduce aversive treatment from others in comparison with nonaggressive children (Lochman & Dodge, 1994; Perry et al., 1986). In Slaby and Guerra's (1988) study of beliefs, antisocial aggressive youth similarly believed that aggressive behavior would increase self-esteem, would avoid a negative image, would not cause victims to suffer, and that it was a legitimate response. This set of beliefs could certainly inhibit the formation of cognitive products involving accurate empathy.

In addition to the goals and expectations identified already, it is likely that other generalized expectations (e.g., locus of control) and other types of schematic propositions such as self-esteem would have effects on social-cognitive products. Lochman and Lampron (1986) have found that aggressive children have lower levels of self-worth than nonaggressive boys, and their self-esteem and perceptions of competence have been found to be responsive to CBT (e.g., Lochman, Burch, Curry, & Lampron, 1984). Self-esteem weaknesses appear to be most pronounced in certain types of aggressive children and are most clearly detected at certain developmental periods. Lochman and Lampron (1985) found that high-aggressive preadolescent boys who also had low levels of social status with their peers had the most pronounced impairment in self-esteem. Since this same category of boys has been noted subsequently to have higher levels of depressive and anxiety symptoms (Lochman, Wayland, & Cohen, 1990), it appears that children's conceptions of their worth and esteem have strong associations with affective states, as well as serving as cognitive schemas. Although aggressive preadolescent boys have expressed lower self-esteem and more dysphoric affect than nonaggressive boys, by early adolescence, aggressive boys report very high levels of self-esteem and little dysphoria (Lochman & Dodge, 1994). This developmental shift as they enter adolescence is likely due to aggressive boys avoidance of being perceived as vulnerable. Researchers are only beginning to understand the complex network of associations among stored cognitive representations, physiological arousal, and affective states.

Noncognitive Influences

Psychophysiology and Arousal

In speculation about parameters that influence social-cognitive products and aggression, the role of children's arousal state has been noted (Dodge, 1985; Lochman, 1984). It has been hypothesized that children's initial appraisals of an event can produce immediate increases in arousal, possibly due to a classically conditioned reaction in which a stimulus has become capable of automatically eliciting an aroused psychophysiological state in an individual. In comparison to nonaggressive peers, boys with oppositional defiant disorder have been found to have low-level heart rates during baseline, nonstress periods, but then to have sharp increases in heart rate during provocation and frustration (van Goozen, Matthys, Cohen-Kettenis, Gispen-de Wied, et al., 1998). In the latter study, boys with high levels of both externalizing behavior problems and anxiety had the sharpest increases in cortisol following provocation, indicating that they experienced much more stress in these situations than did aggressive boys without anxiety. Once aroused, preemptive cognitive processing becomes likely, as the individual responds quickly and automatically. In this way, it is anticipated that arousal would produce marked influences on social-cognitive products, as well as being influenced by social-cognitive appraisals.

Aggressive children's cognitive processing is noticeably affected by arousal. Dodge and Somberg (1987) found that threat-induced arousal affected children's attributions. After overhearing an audiotaped confederate threatening to fight them, aggressive boys made more hostile attributions of others' intentions in hypothetical vignettes and tended to be less accurate in detecting cues that indicated the provocation may have been accidental. Craven, Lochman, and Wells (1997) examined the relationship between attributional processes and physiological arousal. As in the van Goozen, Matthys, Cohen-Kettenis, Gispen-de Wied, et al. (1998) study, highly aggressive boys had the lowest resting heart rate but the sharpest increase in heart rate following an experimental threat. In this study, boys were told that an unknown peer was waiting in another room to work with them on a task. They were then told that the peer was agitated and threatening to initiate a conflict. As boys' heart rates increased during the study, they began to display more hostile attributional biases on vignette measures, indicating that their increasing cognitive distortions were accompanied by increases in physiological arousal.

While these studies support the assumption that aggressive children's preemptive cognitive operations can further impair their social-cognitive product, they have not examined the direct effect of biological arousal on cognition. Arousal has been conceptualized as an end product of the activational properties of the neuroendocrine and sympathetic nervous system (Brain, 1984; Raine, Venables, & Williams, 1990). In this regard, aggressive adolescents have been found to have higher levels of serum and salivary testosterone than nonaggressive adolescents (Christiansen & Knussmann, 1987; Dabbs, Jurkovic, & Frady, 1988; Olweus, Mattesson, Schalling, & Low, 1980), although other studies have not found this effect (van Goozen, Matthys, Cohen-Kettenis, Thijssen, & Van Engeland, 1998). Testosterone levels have been found to fluctuate in response to provocations, and testosterone affects brain areas such as the hypothalamus, associated with the production of aggressive behavior. Olweus (1984) has suggested that testosterone may have a direct effect on frustration tolerance, which in turn influences adolescents' aggressive behavior. Research has suggested that other androgens, involving high levels of DHEAS (dehydroepiandrosterone sulphate) and androstenedione (van Goozen, Matthys, Cohen-Kettenis, Thijssen, et al., 1998), and measures of serotonergic function (low levels of 5-HIAA and HVA) (Halperin et al., 1997; van Goozen, Matthys, Cohen-Kettenis, Westenberg, & van Engeland, in press) may be more substantially related to children's levels of attentional problems, aggression, and delinquency, and to the history of aggressive behavior in these children's parents. Comparative research with animals has supported the link between low serotonergic functioning and high levels of hyperactivity and impulsivity (Gainetdinov et al., 1999). Continued research on the integrated assessment of biological, psychophysiological, and social-cognitive processes will be critical in the years ahead.

Parental, Peer, and Teacher Influences

We assume that parents and other adult caregivers, and, subsequently, children's peers have a formative influence on children's schematic propositions and social-cognitive products. Research on families of aggressive children indicate that parents and siblings display high levels of aversive behavior, as well as other maladaptive parental processes, such as vague "beta" commands, inaccurate monitoring of children's behavior, low cohesion, and rigid or chaotic control efforts (Bry, Catalano, Kumpfer, Lochman, & Szapocznik, 1999; Forehand & Long, 1988; Patterson, 1986; Rodick, Henggeler, & Hanson, 1986). Lochman and Dodge (1990) found that, in comparison with nonaggressive boys' parents, parents of aggressive boys report that they and other adult caregivers provide high levels of verbally and physically aggressive behavior to the target children, and also high levels of verbally aggressive behavior in adults' relationships in the household. Children who have been exposed to more marital conflict have been found to be hypervigilant to hostile words on a laboratory task, making more false-positive and fewer false-negative memory errors, indicating that marital conflict leads to schemas about interpersonal conflict that then impact children's information processing (O'Brien & Chin, 1998). These results imply that children's social-cognitive products may be affected through modeling of their parents' ways of perceiving and responding to conflicts with spouses and children, and through parents' socialization of their children's schemas and working models (Lochman & Dodge, 1998; Shaw & Bell, 1993).

A more direct test of the transmission of social-cognitive products from parents to children involves assessing the attributional processes of parents. Following findings of attributional biases in child-abusing parents (e.g., Larrance & Twentyman, 1983), Dix and Lochman (1990) found that in contrast to a nonaggressive group, mothers of aggressive boys attributed the cause of children's misdeeds more to a negative disposition within the children rather than to the external circumstances. Thus, aggressive children's attributional biases appear to mirror the attributional biases of their parents. Similarly, children's problem-solving skills have been found to be associated with parents' problem solving about how to handle child-rearing problems (Sayed, Lochman, & Wells, in press). Thus, parents' behavior and cognitions are closely linked to their children's social-cognitive processes and behavior, and intervention should be directed at both aggressive children and their parents.

Similar investigations can begin to examine the relationship between the social-cognitive products of additional significant others in children's lives (peers, teachers, other relatives) and aggressive children's appraisal and problem-solving processes. It is clear that children's peer relationships are linked to their aggressive behavior. Children who are both aggressive and rejected by their peer group are at risk for more negative outcomes in adolescence than are children who are aggressive but accepted by their peer group (Coie et al., 1992). Children who gravitate to deviant peer groups by early adolescence (sometimes because of prior rejection from their peer group at large) receive frequent models, reinforcement and peer pressure to engage in increasingly antisocial behavior, and they then increase their rates of school truancy, delinquency, and substance use (Dishion, Patterson, & Griesler, 1994; Wills, McNamara, Vacarro, & Hirkey, 1996).

Summary

Table 2.1 summarizes the cognitive distortions and deficiencies that we have reviewed in this section.

ASSESSMENT OF AGGRESSION IN CHILDREN

Conducting a thorough assessment of the factors related to a child's aggressive tendencies is an extremely important part of designing a comprehensive treatment plan. In this section, a rationale is provided for evaluating children on a number of behavioral and social-cognitive variables. Implications for assessment from empirical research are noted, followed by a proposed model for an in-depth evaluation procedure.

We have used a battery of all these types of assessment tools in clinical research with our school-based Anger Coping and Coping Power Pro-

TABLE 2.1. Cognitive Characteristics of Aggressive Children

Social-cognitive products

Social-cognitive appraisals
  Overly sensitive to hostile cues
  Bias in attributing hostile intentions to others
  Underestimate own aggressiveness

Social problem solving
  Limited repertoire of solutions for the most aggressive youth
  For preadolescent aggressive children: few verbal assertion solutions and excess
    direct action solutions
  For aggressive adolescents: few cooperative solutions
  Aggressive backup solutions

Appraisal of internal arousal
  Overlabeling of affective arousal as anger
  Associated with increased hostile attributional biases
  Low levels of empathy

Cognitive operations

Difficulty in sustaining attention
Retrieval of salient, less competent solutions when automatically retrieving solutions
  from long-term memory

Schematic propositions

Higher value on social goals of dominance and revenge rather than affiliation
Less value placed on outcomes such as victim suffering, victim retaliation, or peer
  rejection
Expectation that aggressive behavior will produce tangible rewards and reduce
  aversive reactions
Bias in expecting that others will be excessively aggressive in upcoming interactions
Low self-esteem in the preadolescent period

grams. In our clinic-based Conduct Disorders Program, we have used selected subsets of the measures and have often informally assessed for
aspects of the social-cognitive deficiencies and distortions during comprehensive structured and unstructured interviews. We anticipated that the
breadth of the assessment battery would be affected by practical factors.

Behavior Presentation of the Child

It is important to look at aggression within the context of all other observable behavior problems, interaction styles, and environmental factors. Often, these patterns of behavioral problems vary with respect to the environmental context (e.g., location, home vs. school; person involved, peer vs.
teacher). Therefore, it is important to obtain information from as many
sources as possible.

Behavioral Rating Scales

Probably the best way to easily obtain a "reading" of the breadth and severity of the problem is through the use of the behavioral checklist (McMahon & Forehand, 1988). A checklist allows assessment of a broad range of behaviors, including low-frequency behaviors (e.g., aggression, stealing); it requires little time to administer and incorporates the perceptions of significant others (e.g., parents, teachers) in the child's life.

Probably the most commonly used and best validated behavioral rating scale is the Child Behavior Checklist (CBCL; Achenbach & Edelbrock, 1983; Achenbach, 1991). Several features make this measure particularly useful: extensive normative data, access to perceptions from multiple informants (parents teachers, and children); provision of both broadband (e.g., externalizing-internalizing) and narrowband (e.g., aggression) syndromes, and evaluation of prosocial behavior (a relatively rare quality among child behavior checklists). Other useful rating scales include the Revised Behavior Problem Checklist (RBPC; Quay & Peterson, 1983), the Eyberg Child Behavior Inventory (ECBI; Eyberg, 1980), and the Missouri Child Behavior Checklist (Sines et al., 1969).

Interviews

Interviews with aggressive children, their parents, and teachers can be extremely helpful in identifying situational variables related to the occurrence of aggressive behavior. Several structured interview formats (e.g., for parents, Forehand & McMahon, 1981; teachers, McMahon & Forehand, 1988; and children, Patterson & Bank, 1986) may be used to access information from a specific informant. Perhaps more helpful are interview formats with parallel forms for parent and child, allowing for comparison of different perceptions and convergence of reported problem areas. For these purposes, interviews such as the Child Assessment Schedule (CAS; Hodges, 1987) and the Diagnostic Interview Schedule for Children (DISC; Costello, Edelbrock, Dulcan, & Kalas, 1984) may be most useful, as they allow for important distinctions regarding the setting and objects of aggression (e.g., toward peers and siblings, cruelty to animals). The CAS, DISC, and other similar diagnostic interviews provide information about both externalizing (e.g., overactivity) and internalizing (e.g., depression, anxiety) symptoms, the presence of which may provide critical information in developing a comprehensive understanding of the context in which the aggressive behavior occurs. The interview of antisocial behavior (Kazdin & Esveld-Dawson, 1986) may be particularly useful in determining patterns of covert–overt symptomatology. We have found that with children who have fairly serious problems with aggression, the use of a less-structured clinical interview may also be helpful, especially in uncovering a child's attributions and reasoning about a particular incident. For instance, some children and young adolescents attribute their poor reasoning in aggressive interactions to the use of drugs or association with a particular set of peers. Their descriptions of relatively extreme acts of violence (e.g., muggings) may provide researchers important clinical "hunches" about their capacity for empathy, their assessment of their own self-control, and their sense of remorse.

Behavioral Observations

Behavioral observations may yield some of the most useful information about aggressive children (McMahon & Estes, 1997; McMahon & Forehand, 1988). The aforementioned measures may be subject to children's perceptual biases or motivation to deny specific behavior problems. Comparing data obtained from direct observation, checklists, and interviews is most likely to reveal treatment targets (e.g., school-based intervention with peers, parent–child interaction).

The assessment procedure should include as many opportunities to observe behavior as possible. Conducting screenings in a group format with potential group members has the advantage of allowing clinicians to observe peer interactions as well as to obtain a preview of important group composition and cohesion issues. Parent–child interactions also should be observed during the assessment period. The seating behavior that occurs prior to conducting a parent–child interview often informs clinicians about family structure, especially if the child verbally or behaviorally dictates where the parent should sit. Other important behaviors to observe during a parent–child interview include interrupting, withdrawal, and the affective valence of the interaction. Hostile interactions devoid of affective warmth or humor require increased treatment attention to the parent–child relationship. Finally, individual child assessments grant clinicians a sampling of the child's social and verbal skills as well as the opportunity to establish a personal rapport that will assist the upcoming group's success.

Peer Ratings

Not surprisingly, many aggressive children have problematical peer relations. They are judged as being less socially competent by parents (e.g., Achenbach & Edelbrock, 1983) and teachers (e.g., Dodge & Frame, 1982), and lower in social acceptance by peers (e.g., Coie, Dodge, & Coppotelli, 1982). Use of peer evaluations may be particularly helpful in identifying a subgroup of aggressive socially rejected children who exhibit a combination of risk factors (e.g., attentional and learning problems, low self-esteem, peer-rejected status) that point to possible situational facts related to their experience of frustration and aggressive outbursts

(Dodge, Coie, & Brakke, 1982; Lahey, Green, & Forehand, 1980; Lochman, Coie, et al., 1993; Lochman & Lampron, 1985). Lochman and Lampron (1985) found that another group of highly aggressive, more socially accepted children reported higher general and school-related self-esteem, even in comparison to socially accepted boys who were less aggressive. Since these children enjoy greater social acceptance and self-esteem, they may be less motivated to cooperate with treatment efforts to reduce their aggressive behavior.

Evaluation of Social-Cognitive–Affective Characteristics

As presented in the social-cognitive model of aggression, the current literature on aggressive children clearly indicates that particular characteristics of their social-cognitive style differ in a meaningful way from nonaggressive children. Based upon empirical findings, measures are proposed for use in a "battery" of assessment techniques for clinical evaluation. It is important to caution that while meaningful group differences exists on these measures, the psychometric properties are yet to be determined. Therefore, the following procedures are offered for consideration as a means by which to collect relevant clinical information along with other measures (e.g., IQ and achievement tests, behavioral checklist) using well-established psychometric properties.

Most experienced researchers and clinicians readily agree that highly aggressive children seem to perceive the social world very differently than nonaggressive children (see Table 2.1). The goal of a social-cognitive assessment battery is to refine a clinician's understanding of a particular aggressive child's social information processing, using the general framework presented in Table 2.1.

Social-Cognitive Products

To answer the question of what a child attends to and encodes when presented with information in a social situation, Dodge (1980) and his colleagues (Dodge & Frame, 1982; Dodge & Newman, 1981; Dodge et al., 1986; Milich & Dodge, 1984) have developed a number of interesting measures to test a series of related hypotheses about aggressive children's skills for encoding different types of social cues. Dodge and Frame (1982) have presented videotaped "hypothetical situations" to children, in which a child experiences hostile, benign, or neutral outcomes in a peer interaction. Children's responses to this measure can be used to evaluate their (1) ability to recall cues freely from the interaction, (2) recognition of events that actually occurred, (3) "mistaken" accounts of the event (commission errors, intrusions), and (4) attributions and expectations about a hypothetical peer's intentions as to future behavior. Generally, aggressive children tend to attend to and remember hostile cues selectively in interaction with peers, particularly when they are asked to imagine being a participant in the interaction.

A second general question about aggressive children's way of thinking is, What kinds of ideas do they have about how to interact and "solve" social situation? How does this aforementioned style of information processing influence their strategies (or lack thereof) in social problem solving? In evaluating the actual content of social problem-solving solutions, a number of factors need to be considered: (1) the type of social task (e.g., peer group entry, initiating friendships, resolving conflict situations); (2) the persons involved in the hypothetical situation (peers, teachers, parents); (3) the apparent intentions (hostile, benevolent, ambiguous).

Lochman and Lampron (1986) evaluated aggressive children's social problem-solving strategies in two types of situational variables while holding constant a third variable—the type of social task. The PSM-C presents hypothetical stories involving only interpersonal conflict and systematically varies the type of antagonist (peer, teacher, parent) and his or her expressed intent (hostile or ambiguous frustration of the protagonist's wishes). On this measure, aggressive boys, compared to nonaggressive boys, had lower rates of "verbal assertion" solutions for conflicts with peers and those involving a hostile antagonist (of any type; peer, parent, or teacher). They had higher rates of direct action solutions for conflicts with teachers and hostile antagonists, and a higher rate of physically aggressive solutions in peer conflicts.

The following examples illustrate deficits in appraisal and problem-solving strategies exhibited by two aggressive boys. These boys' responses to the same stimuli from the PSM-C (Lochman & Lampron, 1986; Dunn et al., 1997) and Milich and Dodge's Recall Test are provided.

M. is a 15-year-old, highly aggressive and sociopathic youth referred for evaluation and treatment following adjudication for property offenses and assault charges. J., a 12-year-old male referred for treatment to address chronic oppositional behavior in school, is particularly prone to respond in a passive–aggressive manner in response to adult authority, and to have trouble labeling emotions. Both boys responded to the following story from the PSM-C:

> Some of Ed's friends borrowed his soccer ball during lunch period but did not return it. When Ed came out of school at the end of the day, the other boys had already starting playing with it again. Ed was supposed to go right home after school, and he wanted to have his soccer ball back. The story ends with Ed walking home with his soccer ball. What happens in between Ed not having his soccer ball, and later, when he walked home with it?

M.'s immediate response represents an attempt to seek help from an authority:

> "They wouldn't let Ed have the ball, right? So Ed went to the principal and told him the situation. He went back to the kids and told them to give Ed the soccer ball back, and if they messed with Ed, they would be expelled from school. Because Ed is the kind of person who doesn't like violence or to fight—he has values and stuff."

M.'s initial backup solutions:

> "He could have gone up there, say, for instance if he had a knife or something. He could have cut one of them up."

M.'s final solution:

> "He could have come over to the school with his mother. His mother could have got the ball back."

Thus, after paying lip service to prosocial thinking, M. generated an extremely antisocial response and then resorted to immature help seeking.

J.'s initial response represents a direct action solution:

> "Ed went up and act like he was fixing to play with the soccer ball, but took the ball and walked away with it."

J.'s backup solution:

> "He could have just took the soccer ball without playing with them."

> "He could have went home and next morning seen them playing and gone up to them and taken it without asking."

> "Next morning if it's in the locker he could have went in the locker and took it out."

J. is clearly fixated on direction action solutions, which characterize each of the four problem-solving strategies he provided. Together, these boys demonstrate aggressive boys' tendency to rely on physically aggressive or direction action solutions and to be deficient in their use of verbal assertion.

M.'s and J.'s responses to a series of five hostile, benevolent, and neutral audiotaped statements on one segment of Milich and Dodge's (1984)

Recall Test (this segment contains two positive, five hostile, and two neutral statements) were as follows:

> M.: "He stole somebody's money. He hit this boy so hard that his nose started bleeding. He hates this boy named Kenny so much that he wishes his arms would fall off."

> J.: "There was this boy who made him so mad that he punched him in the nose. There was this other boy who was crippled. The boy helped him get his lunch. One day, he told this boy to beat up this other boy."

Both boys exhibited a tendency to overrecall hostile cues and to include hostile commission errors or intrusions, as they remembered some items in hostile terms rather than in their original positive or neutral form.

Clearly, aggressive children not only perceive social situations in a different light, but they tend to generate solutions to problematic situations that are maladaptive. This pattern leads to the question of "Why?" Are there particular beliefs or expectations or goals that aggressive children hold that relate to, or perhaps lead them to, their unskilled handling of social situation? In addition to assessing the answers to these questions during interview, several experimental measures can also be useful. The Outcome-Expectation Questionnaire and Self-Efficacy Questionnaire (Perry et al., 1986), measures of beliefs and expectations (Slaby & Guerra, 1988), and a measure of social goals (Lochman, Wayland, & White, 1993) have all been used to distinguish aggressive children and adolescents from less aggressive peers. Assessments of such schematic propositions permit a more detailed and coherent understanding of aggressive children's maladaptive behavior and approaches for intervention with them.

Schematic Propositions

A measure of a child's relative evaluation of social goals such as dominance, revenge, avoidance, and affiliation assists clinicians in determining how consistent a child's social behavior is with his or her stated goals. A measure adapted from Lochman, Wayland, and White (1993) allows clinicians to view a child's relative ranking of these social goals. These rankings can then be placed in context with the child's other social-cognitive characteristics. For example, some aggressive children, with poor ability to manage their arousal, may endorse prosocial goals and adequate problem-solving strategies but may be unable to exercise behavior consistent with these goals because of their self-control deficits. The knowledge gained from such an assessment profile has clear treatment indications.

Appraisal of Internal Arousal

Aggressive children often have difficulty differentiating their own negative affect, tending to overlabel negative affective arousal (fear, sadness) as anger. An aggressive child's unstructured self-report of his or her negative affect can provide some insight into the child's feeling identification skills. Of course, these feeling identification skills are a prerequisite for understanding the emotions of others. Social perspective taking and empathy are tapped by Bryant's (1982) Empathy Index for Children and Adolescents. Assessing children's empathic tendencies can also establish how receptive they might be to change in general, and to cognitive-behavioral techniques in particular.

Other Domains of Functioning in the Aggressive Child

A thorough assessment of familial/parental functioning is necessary, so that a complete picture of the behavioral contingencies and influences can be outlined. McMahon and Forehand's (1988) chapter on assessment of conduct disorders is an excellent resource. Parental and marital adjustment need to be thoroughly investigated to determine what types of social problem-solving styles are being modeled and to evaluate the degree to which parents are able to be receptive to intervention efforts. Commonly used instruments for which there is adequate psychometric validation include the following. (1) for parental depression, the Beck Depression Inventory (BDI, Beck, Rush, Shaw, & Emery, 1979), the Depression Adjective Checklist (DACL; Lubin, 1967); (2) for parental stress, the Parenting Stress Index (PSI; Abidin, 1983; (3) for marital adjustment, Locke's Marital Adjustment Test (MAT; Locke & Wallace, 1959) and the Dyadic Adjustment Scale (DAS; Spanier, 1976). Measures that can yield an assessment of the child's exposure to marital hostility and experience of direct or indirect use of force include the O'Leary–Porter Scale (Porter & O'Leary, 1980) and the Conflict Tactics Scale (CTS; Straus, 1979). The Child Perceptions of Marital Discord Scale (CPMD; Emery & O'Leary, 1982) has been found to be a useful index of child distress and a correlate of parental report of aggression (Wayland, Schoenwald, & Lochman, 1989).

In addition to assessment of familial and parental functioning, it is well know that children with aggressive behavior disorders often have other cognitive–academic deficits (for a brief overview, see McMahon & Forehand, 1988). A thorough evaluation of intellectual and academic strengths and weaknesses should be conducted. An accurate assessment of the type of obstacles and frustrations experienced in the learning environment (e.g., specific learning disabilities, especially reading) may shed some light on the reasons why children may be perceived as defensive, defiant, or argumentative by teachers and peers. Also, in order to streamline the assessment of verbal and nonverbal cognitive skills, a cognitive screening instrument, such as the Kaufman Brief Intelligence Test (K-BIT; Kaufman & Kaufman, 1990), provides essential information about basic cognitive strengths and weaknesses and a child's readiness for cognitive-behavioral techniques.

Measures of the aggressive child's subjective experience are also important and have implications for response to treatment (e.g., Lochman et al., 1985). The Coopersmith Self-Esteem Inventory (CSI; Coopersmith, 1967) and the Self-Perception Profile for Children (Harter, 1985) yield self-ratings of competence in a number of areas (e.g., home vs. school, cognitive vs. social). Given the high likelihood that the aggressive child has difficulties in multiple areas (e.g., academic achievement, peer relations), it is important to be aware of areas of functioning about which a child may feel particularly sensitive as well as those for which he or she has a sense of pride and accomplishment. The Piers–Harris Children's Self-Concept Scale (Piers & Harris, 1964) is useful because it provides a gross measure of several affective factors. These factors usually contribute and/or maintain aggressive behavior, such as a child's evaluation of his or her popularity and competency skills. This scale also seems to provide greater insight into depressive symptoms/tendencies in some populations.

Parent Assessment

As indicated earlier, every attempt should be made to include the parent and/or parent surrogate in the assessment process. Along with the previously discussed formal behavioral rating scales completed by parents, less formal behavioral scales are useful. In our clinical work, we devised a CD/ODD Symptom Severity (Disruptive Behavior) Checklist, based on the specific diagnostic criteria for conduct disorder and oppositional defiant disorder in DSM-IV (American Psychiatric Association, 1994).

Another extremely important essential ingredient is the assessment of parental willingness to be involved in the treatment process. To expedite this process, the parents' screening/assessment group is conducted simultaneously with the child's assessment process. This format allows group leaders to discuss a parent's role in the intervention and at the same time gauge a parent's interest, as well as availability, in participating in a weekly parenting group.

COGNITIVE-BEHAVIORAL THERAPY WITH AGGRESSIVE CHILDREN

CBT addresses the deficient and distorted social-cognitive processes in aggressive children, including distortions in their perceptions of others' and their own behavior, biases in their attribution of hostile intentions to others, and overreliance on nonverbal direct action solutions and underreliance on verbal assertion and verbal negotiation solutions. CBT programs can include training in self-instruction, social problem solving, perspective taking, affect labeling, or relaxation, and most programs include a combination of several of these techniques. All of these programs have a common focus on children's social cognitions during frustrating or provocative situations.

Anger Coping Program

To provide a sample of the kinds of cognitive-behavioral techniques that can be used with aggressive children, we describe our Anger Coping Program, which is a somewhat briefer version of a more recent Coping Power Program (Lochman & Wells, 1996). The Coping Power Program is currently being evaluated in two grant-funded studies, and the additional components of this program are briefly described in a subsequent section. We address the major content and process issues that constitute the foci of CBT interventions (see Lochman et al., 1999, for a session-by-session description of the Anger Coping Program). The school-based Anger Coping Program has been developed and refined over a period of 20 years and consists of eighteen 45- to 60-minute sessions. Sessions are highly structured, with specific goals, objectives, and structured exercises outlined for each session. This model was designed for use with elementary-school-age children and has been used primarily with 4th- and 5th-grade boys. Thus, groups are typically homogeneous with respect to age, gender, and presenting problem/psychiatric symptomatology (aggressive and disruptive behavior). Although our model has more often been implemented in schools, it can easily be adapted for use in clinic settings.

We believe there are several advantages to the use of group therapy as the modal form of treatment. Peer and group reinforcement are frequently more effective with children than reinforcement provided in a dyadic context, or by adults (Rose & Edelson, 1987). This may be especially true for children with disruptive behavior disorders, who, research suggests, are relatively resistant to social reinforcement. Additionally, the group context provides *in vivo* opportunities for interpersonal learning and development of social skills.

The Anger Coping Program addresses both cognitive and affective processes, and is designed to remediate skills deficits in conflictual situations involving affective arousal. Specific goals are to increase children's awareness of internal cognitive, affective, and physiological phenomena related to anger arousal; enhance self-reflection and self-management skills; facilitate alternative, consequential, and means–end thinking in approaching social problems; and increase children's behavioral repertoires when faced with social conflict. To do so, sessions are organized around teaching specific social-cognitive skills. The major components of the program, which consist of self-management/monitoring skills, perspective-taking skills, and social problem-solving skills, are presented in this section, along with process variables such as the behavioral management system, goal setting, and interpersonal group process.

Pragmatic and Logistical Issues

Although group therapy has the previously discussed advantages, individual therapy that addresses the components discussed below may be indicated in several instances. First, individual therapy may be indicated to assist a child in preparing to enter a group. This possibility is likely if a child is unable to participate in groups either because of disruptive behavior (e.g., ADHD) or perhaps a comorbid anxiety disorder. Second, a child may benefit from individual therapy as a "step down" from a successful group experience that requires continued practice and skills acquisition.

School-based delivery of services often depends upon the level of support from school administrators and personnel, and usually serves children who have a wider range of aggression relative to clinic-referred children. Clinic-based groups often contain children who are experiencing frequent, intense, and problematic levels of aggression, although some children in school-based groups are just as behaviorally disturbed. As such, the clinic groups are typically smaller (4–5 members) than school-based groups, which may contain larger numbers of children (5–7 members).

A large room with an adequate number of chairs and a place to hang posterboard is necessary, regardless of service site. A chalkboard or "wipe-erase" marker board is helpful but not necessary, as writing can be done on posterboard. The comorbidity of disruptive behaviors (e.g., ODD and ADHD) creates the need to plan the physical environment. It is best to have as few visual, tactile, and auditory distractions as possible, within the recognized limitation that group rooms often have multiple users/uses. The group rules portion of the first session also should include the "coming/going to group rules" to encourage expected and appropriate behavior during this transition.

Self-Management Skills

First, children are taught to become more competent observers of internal states related to affective arousal. As is true of other skills taught, this process occurs throughout the entire course of treatment. Through modeling, observation, structured exercises, and group discussion, children are taught to identify physiological and affective cues of anger arousal. For example, they are asked to define the concept of anger in terms of its affective and behavioral concomitants (e.g., "Anger is the feeling you have when you think you cannot get something you want, or do something you want to do, or when you feel provoked") (Lochman, Lampron, Gemmer, & Harris, 1987, p. 347). Children are asked to identify environmental cues and precipitants by generating examples of anger-arousing stimuli (e.g., situations both at home and at school that make them angry with peers and authority figures). Next, physiological aspects of anger arousal are addressed. A videotaped instruction is used to introduce the topic, showing a boy displaying several overt symptoms of anger arousal. The signal function of these cues is emphasized, and group brainstorming/discussion is used to identify a variety of physiological cues of anger (blood rushing to one's face, quickening pulse, increased muscle tension, affective flooding). Children are asked to identify the specific ways in which they and others experience anger arousal (facial and gestural expression, tone of voice, body posture, thoughts, statements, action). This implicitly communicates to them that people differ in their internal experience of, and behavioral response to, anger and is intended to help children become better observers of a wide range of cues regarding their own and others' anger. Children may be encouraged to differentiate their affective experience of anger on the dimension of intensity (e.g., to generate situations that make them angry "on a scale of 1 to 10"; to label affective states of different intensity, such as "simmering," "steaming," "boiling"). The phenomenological experience of anger can thus be conceptualized as occurring on a continuum, and children can be taught to identify affective and physiological symptoms at lower and more manageable levels of affective arousal, and to link affective states of different intensity to specific environmental events or cues. One such method of helping children concretize their understanding of these issues is the use of role plays. Children can be asked to provide "Academy Award portrayals" of anger arousal and anger coping, including nonverbal and verbal cues.

In addition to self-monitoring strategies designed to increase awareness of environmental triggers, and affective and physiological states related to anger, cognitive self-control strategies are also taught. Instruction in this area attempts to address deficiencies in verbal mediation strategies that help to regulate behavior. Children are helped to appreciate the impact of cognition on subsequent affective arousal and behavior, and are instructed on the role of internal dialogue in enhancing or decreasing the experience of anger arousal. This concept is taught through the construct of "self-talk." Through repeated instruction, children are helped to identify anger-enhancing and anger-reducing cognitions, and to understand the impact of private speech on emotions and behavior. A series of verbal taunting games is particularly useful in concretizing this concept. In this application, children receive insults or taunts from other group members and discuss their thoughts and feelings in response to this structured provocation. Stimuli are presented in a hierarchical format, progressing from relatively distanced stimuli (e.g., taunting of puppets) to increasingly more threatening stimuli (direct taunting of group members). Instruction on self-talk is combined with exercised designed to increase awareness of individual perceptual processes. For example, group members may be asked to identify the kinds of assumptions they are most likely to make in situations of social conflict, and the kinds of anger-reducing statements that are most likely to facilitate adaptive coping. In this way, children are encouraged to develop a repertoire of coping statements that will work specifically for them. Other self-control techniques are discussed and rehearsed as well, including visualization, distraction, and relaxation. Through discussion of self-monitoring techniques, children are implicitly taught that the triggers for anger arousal vary from individual to individual, and from event to event. The awareness of these triggers is then used to prompt children to employ their self-management skills.

Sitting in on Therapy

The following interactions occurred in the context of a self-control exercise that is part of the Anger Coping Group Treatment Model (see Lochman et al., 1999). The exercise has group members taunt a target child under controlled circumstances to develop the child's ability to respond adaptively to provocation. The child is physically separated by a "safety circle" outlined on the floor and typically begins this "hot-seat" exercise with "coaching" support from a group coleader, who stands with the child in the circle, in this case, Coleader 1. A "safe environment" for the child can also be achieved by having the group members sit around a table.

COLEADER 1: Okay, B., before we begin this first time, is there anything that is "off-limits"?

B.: No.

COLEADER 1: You're sure?

B.: Yeah.

COLEADER 2: Okay, for this first time, each person will spend one minute in the "hot seat."

MEMBERS: Ye ah.

COLEADER 1: Are you ready, B.?

B: Yeah.

COLEADER 1: Okay, then, Go!

MEMBER 1: Look at that hat on his head, all dirty and stuff!

MEMBER 2: Yeah, look at his hat! (*laughing*)

MEMBER 3: Do you ever wash that thing?

B: Yeah, I wash it! Look at your hat! You . . .

COLEADER 1: (*interrupting*) Remember, B., we're practicing our self-control strategies.

B.: Okay. Okay.

COLEADER 2: Okay, guys, keep going.

MEMBER 2: Your mama make that hat for you? (*Other members laugh and point.*)

COLEADER 1: B., I can see that you're making a fist and your teeth are clenched.

B: (*He unclenches his fist as he begins to take several deep breaths.*) Okay. That's right (*to himself*), "They don't even know my mama. They're just trying to get me mad. There's nothing wrong with my hat."

MEMBER 4: B.'s mama made that dirty, funky hat! (*Members laugh.*)

COLEADER 1: Keep your cool, B.

MEMBER 3: He needs the hat to cover up his ugly face!

B: (*to himself*) I'm gonna stay calm. They just want me to fight and I'm not going to.

This activity demonstrates the need for leaders to shape and to support children's skill acquisition. Group members are reminded that these are *skills*, that they require practice to become effective, and that there will be times when they do not perform them competently. This type of anticipatory guidance validates the children's frustration with learning a difficult and new skill.

One activity in this section includes verbal taunting during a domino-building task. One group member builds a tower for 30 seconds, using one hand, while the others taunt him. Each member receives a turn building a tower, and the highest tower wins. The discussion after the task centers on how hard it is to concentrate on the domino building, how group members keep their concentration focused, if they started to feel antsy, if the anger hurts their concentration, if the players use self-talk to help them do well, and how anger management is critical for winning.

In summary, through hierarchical exposure to stimuli of increasing threat, behavioral rehearsal, and group discussion, children are encouraged to develop and practice using cognitive and affective self-reflection/self-monitoring strategies for situations involving interpersonal conflict. Children are provided opportunities to write "scripts" that include the set of skills and coping strategies they have been developing, and practice these skills through the use of videotapes.

Social Perspective-Taking Skills

Research suggests that children with externalizing disorders exhibit egocentric and distorted perceptions of social situations (Chandler, 1973; Dodge, 1980; Lochman, 1987). As noted earlier, these social cognitive deficiencies involve difficulty integrating self- and other-oriented concerns (Lochman & Lenhart, 1995), overattribution of hostile intent on the part of others (Dodge, 1980) and deficient perspective-taking skills (Kendall, Zupan, & Braswell, 1981). Such maladaptive interpersonal processing places aggressive children at high-risk for dysfunctional social relationships (e.g., a child who quickly assumes hostile intent on the part of others may respond to social conflict based on an inaccurately perceived threat; a child who has difficulty adopting others' perspective may quickly disregard others' views or needs, and respond entirely from his or her own vantage point). A series of perspective-taking exercises is presented to address these issues, employing a variety of techniques (structured exercises, role plays, modeling, and group discussion). Perspective-taking instruction attempts to improve children's ability to infer accurately other's thoughts and intentions (cognitive perspective taking), and to enhance their understanding of others' feelings and internal emotional states (affective perspective taking). Children are asked to differentiate individual cognitive and affective processes by identifying similarities and differences between people, by delineating alternative interpretations of social cues, and by generating inferences of what others may be thinking or feeling. For example, a prototypical exercise presents children with an ambiguous picture, asks them to generate, independently, "stories" about the picture, and engages them in a discussion about differences in their perceptions of the same stimulus. Another perspective-taking and empathy-induction option is the use of videotaped clips of poignant emotional scenes from popular movies. Perspective-taking instruction is routinely provided when children present examples of conflict with peers, teachers, and family members, and is used to address interpersonal conflict as it arises in the group. Thus, this component of the intervention continues throughout the course of the group.

Social Problem-Solving Skills

Aggressive children exhibit deficiencies in their ability to resolve interpersonal problems successfully. The Anger Coping Program addresses the deficient problem-solving strategies exhibited by aggressive boys by helping them to identify conflictual situations as problematical, and by encouraging them to increase their repertoire for responding to these situations. A sequential, stepwise model of handling social conflict is presented, including the following three components: problem identification; generation of multiresponse alternatives; and evaluation and prediction of consequences for their actions. A variety of techniques are used to help children learn and implement this model, including modeling, instruction in divergent and consequential thinking, practice generating and elaborating solutions, and behavioral rehearsal. The latter is accomplished through role playing and the use of videotaping, in which children develop scripts for handling conflictual situations and enact them on videotape. Children are encouraged to incorporate into these scripts the personalized menu of anger-coping strategies (self-talk, conflict resolution strategies) they have developed over the course of the group. A critical aspect of this instruction involves helping children to identify a potentially problematical situation early on, before it escalates to a point where they are unable to respond adaptively. Children's use of direct action solutions is discouraged, while their use of verbal expression, discussion, and negotiation solutions is reinforced. Attention is also placed on identifying how solutions are affected by social goals, how solutions can be competently enacted, and how there is a need to have backup solutions when initial solutions fail or when obstacles arise in the implementation of a solution. In summary, the social problem-solving component provides children with a model for responding to social conflicts and encourages qualitative and quantitative improvements in their range of coping solutions.

In addition to structured exercises, children also use social problem-solving with the real-life problems they bring into the group. In a recent group session, Bob began talking about an incident that had led to a 5-day suspension from school the prior week. Rather than continue with the scheduled group activity, the bulk of the session was spent in group problem solving about this situation. Bob described how the incident began when he and another boy disagreed over who could sit on a cushion in the library. After a brief exchange of insults, the two boys were quiet for the remainder of the library period. However, as the class left the library, Bob got in the other boy's face and reinitiated the verbal assaults in a more provocative way. When the boy responded with verbal insults, Bob knocked him down and kept hitting him, until the assistant principal pulled Bob away. The group discussion included a focus on perspective taking with regard to the other boy's intentions, which did not initially appear to be as purposefully malevolent as Bob had perceived, and with regard to the assistant principal's intentions. In a spirited discussion, the group noted that the assistant principal may have been either mean or trying to protect the combatants when he grabbed Bob and swung him around (most group members eventually decided he was trying to be protective). After several ways of handling the initial "cushion" problem were suggested to Bob, he asked each of the group members how they would have handled it. When the group member with the most streetwise demeanor suggested a nonconfrontational solution, Bob tentatively decided to try that strategy in the next conflict. Notable aspects of this discussion included how assaultive incidents often escalate from trivial initial problems, how Bob had great difficulty letting his anger dissipate after the initial provocation, how Bob's anger disrupted his ordinarily adequate social cognitions through preemptive processing, and how the group members were instrumental in providing training in social perspective taking and social problem solving.

Process Variables in the Anger Coping Program

Three process variables are of central therapeutic importance in the anger coping model: a behavior management system, in which the social microcosm of the group is used to encourage prosocial behavior and to facilitate group cohesiveness; goal-setting activities, which provide a structured vehicle to encourage generalization of treatment effects; and use of the interpersonal "here-and-now" of the group to encourage development of the context of the group.

Behavior Management System. The primary mechanism for encouraging a "positive peer culture" is early development of group rules and specification of a behavior management system. Children are involved in the process of instituting rules, which allows them to assume psychological ownership of group norms and sensitizes them to aspects of behavior that would interfere with group process. Their participation in developing this shared social contract facilitates group cohesion and helps to minimize the power struggle that can evolve between adults and children with conduct-disorder. Contingency management techniques such as response cost or reward systems (Sulzer & Mayer, 1972) are essential to enable group leaders to shape, maintain, and reinforce desired behavior (participation, prosocial behavior). It is helpful to display group rules at each session and to provide children with frequent feedback about their behavior (e.g., review number of points earned at the end of each session or periodically during the session). By seeing their peers received corrective feedback on a regular basis, group members can come to feel less concern about "saving face" when they are also corrected. As children accumulate points to be exchanged for individual and group rewards, they are provided opportunities to delay immediate gratification, often a problem area for children with disruptive behavior disorders. Additionally, group contingencies provide a useful vehicle for further developing group cohesion. With respect to successful implementation of the behavior management system, it is useful to provide children with corrective feedback early on and to provide such feedback in a neutral, matter-of-fact manner. This early "detoxification" of corrective feedback helps to defuse aggressive children's tendencies to overpersonalize adult feedback and respond with oppositional or challenging behavior.

Goal Setting. Each week, children are encouraged to target a problematic behavior, to set a goal regarding behavior change, and to monitor their ability to meet their goal. Weekly goal sheets are used to help children concretize this process. Goals are selected with input from group leaders, teachers, and parents, and individualized treatment goals are developed for each child based on the particular social-cognitive deficits or distortions exhibited by that child. Children are helped to set realistic expectations regarding change in problematical behaviors, and teachers may be contacted to provide external monitoring of children's progress. Goal setting thus provides a structured vehicle to enhance generalization of treatment effects, encourage children to assume responsibility for changing problematical aspects of their behavior, and facilitate the development of self-monitoring skills. Goal-setting and monitoring can be enhanced when combined with a parent group that includes behavioral management skills training. Such a group allows parents to increase their ability to set and monitor behavioral limits effectively.

In addition to goals set for individual behavior in domains outside the group (school, home), setting "in-group" goals that children and their peers monitor also increases self-monitoring skills. At the end of group, children assess their success, and this can be integrated with the feedback from other group members' observations. Using such in-group goals also has the advantage of establishing the "positive peer culture" needed for group cohesion. In-group goals can also be used for the group as a whole. For example, having a group goal of all members avoiding "strikes" in conjunction with a group incentive may improve the group members' ability to monitor themselves and their peers for appropriate and prosocial behavior. "In-group" goals are particularly useful for adolescents, as well as for children whose parents cannot consistently monitor "out-of-group" goals.

Interpersonal Group Process. The spontaneous interaction that occurs among group members throughout the course of treatment provides an excellent opportunity to assess children's interpersonal styles and deficits, and to identify peer relationship difficulties. Through modeling, coaching, and shaping of their behavior, children can be helped to develop listening skills, interact in a prosocial manner, increase their ability to respond in a verbally assertive manner; and better understand the perspective of their peers. The inevitable tensions that arise among group members, and children's negative reactions to corrective feedback from leaders, provide *in vivo* opportunities to work with children on issues of anger control. Thus, in addition to the "cold" processing that occurs in structured exercises and role plays, "hot" processing provides an excellent opportunity to guide children in the use of newly acquired skills, that is, to label anger arousal as it occurs, and to practice the use of anger management techniques. In summary, through the social microcosm of "here-and-now" group process, there is much opportunity for interpersonal learning through modeling, processing of interpersonal conflict, *in vivo* social skills instruction, and opportunities to practice more adaptive means of interacting with peers.

Coping Power: An Extension of the Anger Coping Program

The Coping Power Program (Lochman, in press; Lochman & Wells, 1996) is a lengthier, multicomponent version of the Anger Coping Program, designed to enhance outcome effects and to provide for better maintenance of gains over time. The Coping Power Program (CP) has added additional sessions to the basic anger coping framework to create a CP Child Component (for a total of 33 group sessions), addressing additional substantive areas such as emotional awareness, relaxation training, social skills enhancement, positive social and personal goals, and dealing with peer pressure. Other elements of the CP Child Component include regular individual sessions (about once every 3–4 weeks) to increase generalization of the program to the children's actual social situations, and periodic consultation with teachers, especially for children who have made some progress in groups but who still have recurrent behavioral problems at school. The Coping Power program also has a CP Parent Component, which is designed to be integrated with the CP Child Component and to cover the same 15- to 18-month period of time. The 16 parent group sessions address parents' use of social reinforcement and positive attention, their establishment of clear house rules, their behavioral expectations and monitoring procedures, their use of appropriate discipline strategies, their family communication, their positive connection to school, and their stress management. The CP Parent Component also includes periodic home visits to promote generalization of skills.

Overview of Cognitive-Behavioral Therapy Outcome

In this section, we summarize the results of outcome research using CBT with aggressive children and of studies examining child and treatment characteristics that are predictive of treatment outcomes. These studies have begun to establish that CBT with aggressive children is an empirically supported therapy (Kendall, 1998). More detailed reviews of CBT outcome research with aggressive children and adolescents are available elsewhere (Kazdin, 1987, 1995; Lochman, 1990; Lochman & Wells, 1996; McMahon & Wells, 1989; Southam-Gerow & Kendall, 1997).

Outcome Effects

Early, simple pre- and posttreatment studies indicated that children's aggressive and disruptive behavior changed following CBT. After studies indicated that CBT could help children behave less impulsively in impersonal problem-solving tasks (e.g., Meichenbaum & Goodman, 1971), Goodwin and Mahoney (1975) developed a similar procedure to modify children's covert self-statements during a verbal taunting game. The 3 treated boys had marked increases in coping responses and improved levels of non-disruptive classroom behavior. Robin, Schneider, and Dolnick (1976) trained 11 emotionally disturbed children in the turtle technique, which involved imagery training and social problem solving, and resulted in reductions in aggressive classroom behavior. Lochman et al. (1981) developed the initial form of the Anger Coping Program for 12 second- and third-grade aggressive children. The children improved in teachers' daily ratings of on-task behavior and ratings of aggressive behavior.

Based on promising findings from pre- and posttreatment studies, more controlled research was begun. These studies can be grouped into those that had negative, mixed, or generally positive treatment effects. Three studies have not found changes in aggressive behavior following CBT, although two of these did produce improvements in the cognitive processes that were hypothesized to mediate the behavior (Camp, Blom, Herbert, & van Doornick, 1977; Coats, 1979; Dubow, Huesmann, & Eron, 1987). In comparison to a control condition, Camp et al. (1977) found that aggressive second-grade boys had become less cognitively impulsive, less inattentive, and that they generated more problem solutions after their involvement in the 6-week Think Aloud Program. However, teacher-rated aggression did not improve. Similarly, Coats (1979) found that boys treated in a 2-week intervention demonstrated better delay of gratification and less verbal aggression, but they made no gains relative to an attention control group in off-task classroom behavior or in teacher-rated aggression. Dubow et al. (1987) found that not only did the 5-week cognitive training not produce a relative reduction in teacher-rated aggressive behavior, but also these treated children were actually rated as more aggressive than an attention–play condition at 6-month follow-up.

Four studies with mixed findings have found improvements on some, but not all, behavioral measures. Forman's (1980) cognitive restructuring treatment produced reductions in inappropriate classroom behavior, although a response–cost procedure was more effective in reducing teachers' ratings of aggressive behavior and classroom disturbance. In a CBT intervention with day-camp children, Kettlewell and Kausch (1983) found that treated children had less self-reported anger, fewer time-out restrictions, and improvements in coping self-statements and generation of problem solutions. However, relative to a control condition, these children did not have improvements in counselor or peer-rated aggression. Using brief affective imagery training, Garrison and Stolberg (1983) found that aggressive children became more capable of accurately identifying which situations evoke compound anger, and teacher-observed aggression tended to decrease, but the changes were modest. Finally, in a recent broad-based intervention for black, lower-class, socially rejected children, Lochman, Coie, et al. (1993) used a combination of CBT and social skills training with three annual cohorts. While the first two cohorts of treated children displayed little improvement in comparison to a control condition, the third cohort evidenced more positive results. Treated aggressive-rejected children had significantly higher peer ratings for social preference and prosocial behavior by posttreatment, and they tended to have reductions in teachers' ratings of aggression. This year-long, school-based intervention was progressively revised over the 3 cohort years, with the last and most successful intervention year emphasizing more contingency contracting and reframing of who wins in interpersonal conflicts.

Stronger treatment effects have been documented in several programmatic research efforts (Southam-Gerow & Kendall, 1997). Kendall, Ronan, and Epps (1991) adapted their CBT program for use with impulsive children to treat day-hospitalized CD children. Comparing 20 sessions of CBT with a "current conditions treatment" in a crossover design, CBT-treated children had improvements in teachers' ratings of their self-control and prosocial behavior and in their perceived social competence. However, reductions in cognitive impulsivity were not noted, and the treatment gains that were present at posttreatment did not persist to a 6-month follow-up. In the second programmatic research effort (Kazdin, 1995), Kazdin, Esveldt-Dawson, French, and Unis (1987b) used a 20-session problem-solving skills training (PSST) program with psychiatric inpatient children and did find follow-up effects. Relative to two control conditions, PSST produced significant reductions in parents' and teachers' ratings of aggressive behavior at posttesting and at 1-year follow-up. These results were replicated in several studies that combined PSST with parent behavioral management training (Kazdin, Siegel, & Bass, 1992; Kazdin, Esveldt-Dawson, French, & Unis, 1987a), and in another study using PSST with antisocial children treated in outpatient and inpatient settings (Kazdin, Bass, Siegel, & Thomas, 1989). Treated children in the latter study improved behaviorally in both home and school settings, indicating the generalization of intervention effects. In addition, the combined child-and-parent intervention program (Kazdin et al., 1992) was found to produce the greatest and most long-lasting improvements in children's behavior compared to either intervention alone. These findings argue for the importance of providing cognitive-behavioral intervention to both aggressive children and their parents (Southam-Gerow & Kendall, 1997).

Several recent studies from other research groups have documented that these combined effects of child-and-parent cognitive-behavioral interventions can also be apparent with children in the 4- to 7-year age range (Webster-Stratton & Hammon, 1997), producing positive effects on both children's problem-solving and parent–child relations, and on longer-term outcomes such as delinquency and school adjustment at age 12, over 4 years after intervention (Tremblay, Pagani-Kurtz, Masse, Vitaro, & Pihl, 1995). Universal preventive interventions directed at entire child populations in communities rather than high-risk groups have also been found to produce significant positive effects on adolescent antisocial behavior and substance use (Hawkins et al., 1992; Kellam & Rebok, 1992). Combining universal interventions directed at classroom teachers, along with comprehensive, long-lasting interventions targeted at high-risk children and their families, has been shown in initial analyses to produce significant improvements even in the highest risk first-graders, suggesting the potential utility of this type of intensive, multicomponent intervention with the "early starting" (Moffitt, 1993) conduct problem children who have the poorest prognosis and the greatest likelihood of negative adolescent outcomes (Conduct Problems Prevention Research Group, 1999). This program, known as Fast Track, has produced clear improvements in children's social relations, social cognitions, reading achievement, and behavior, and in parents' warmth and discipline at the end of the first-grade year, and it is designed to be delivered to these very high risk children through their 10th-grade year to prevent serious delinquency, substance use, and conduct disorder.

A programmatic series of controlled studies has also examined the Anger Coping Program described in this chapter. In comparison with a minimal treatment and untreated control condition, Lochman et al. (1984) found that treated aggressive elementary schoolboys had reductions in independently observed disruptive–aggressive off-task classroom behavior, reduction in parents' ratings of aggression, and improvements in self-esteem. Other ratings by teachers and peers did not indicate improvement. The posttreatment behavioral improvements in this study have been replicated in subsequent studies (e.g., Lochman & Curry, 1986; Lochman, Lampron, Gemmer, Harris, & Wyckoff, 1989), and gains in classroom on-task behavior have been found in a 7-month follow-up (Lochman & Lampron, 1988). While some maintenance of treatment effects was evident in a 3-year follow-up, at age 15, these results were mixed (Lochman, 1992). In comparison to an untreated condition of aggressive boys, Anger Coping Program boys maintained their gains in self-esteem, displayed better problem-solving skills, and had significantly lower levels of substance use. On these measures, the treated boys were in the same range as nonaggressive boys at follow-up, and the results indicated important prevention effects on adolescent substance use. However, continued reduction in off-task behavior and in parents' ratings of aggression were only evident for Anger

Coping Program boys who had received a six-session booster treatment for themselves and their parents during the next school year. Without the booster treatment, the reductions in aggressive behavior were not maintained.

Building on these findings, the multicomponent Coping Power intervention, which used the Anger Coping Program as a foundation, has been developed and is being evaluated in two randomized, controlled intervention trials (Lochman, in press; Lochman & Wells, 1996). Initial outcome analyses of this Coping Power Program have found improvements in boys' social competence, social information processing, and aggressive behavior, and in parents' parenting practices and marital relationship, for children and families who received Coping Power in comparison to an untreated aggressive control group. These findings were found to be maintained at a 1-year follow-up, and the highest risk boys receiving Coping Power were also found to have lower substance-use rates at the 1-year follow-up.

Clinical and Treatment Characteristics as Predictors of Outcomes

While efforts to find which aspects of CBT are most effective with which types of aggressive children are still in the rudimentary stages, some initial findings have emerged. Kendall et al. (1991) have found that CBT for children with conduct disorder has been most effective in reducing conduct problems with children who had initially lower perceived levels of hostility and a more internalized attributional style. Lochman et al. (1985) found that boys in the Anger Coping Program who had greatest reductions in aggressive behavior relative to the control condition were initially the poorest social problem solvers. In addition, better outcomes tended to occur for boys with more initial somatization and anxiety behaviors, and lower social acceptance from peers, suggesting that these boys may have been more motivated for treatment because of a desire to alleviate distress and decrease peer rejection. Interestingly, those boys in the untreated condition who improved the most spontaneously had better problem-solving skills and higher self-esteem. The differential correlates of improvement for the treated and untreated conditions suggest that the Anger Coping Program was most successful with those boys who were the poorest problem solvers and most in need of intervention.

In studies of treatment characteristics that might augment the effects of the Anger Coping Program, Lochman et al. (1984) found that inclusion of a behavioral goal-setting component tended to lead to lower aggression and disruptiveness. In this component, boys set weekly goals for themselves in their group meetings; these goals were monitored daily by teachers, and there was contingent reinforcement for successful goal attainment. Similar evidence for the effectiveness of homework assignments in CBT has been obtained by Kazdin et al. (1989). In addition, more widespread improvements in classroom behavior have been noted when the Anger Coping Program was offered in an 18-session format instead of the original 12 sessions (Lochman, 1985). We have not found that inclusion of limited forms of structured teacher consultation (Lochman, Lampron, Gemmer, et al., 1989) or additional self-instruction training on nonsocial, academic tasks (Lochman & Curry, 1986) augments the basic Anger Coping program's effects, although we are currently examining whether teacher and parent training groups, offered as an universal intervention, can enhance the effects of the Coping Power Program for targeted, high-risk children.

Implications for Cognitive-Behavioral Therapy Outcome Research

As Kazdin (1987, 1995) has noted, these research results present a generally positive and promising view of the effects of CBT with aggressive children. However, because of the mixed posttreatment and follow-up findings, further program development and outcome research is clearly needed. Future outcome research should address the following issues (see also Lochman 1990): (1) follow-up assessments in designs that include control conditions and direct behavioral observation measures; (2) further exploration of child and treatment characteristics that predict outcome; and (3) more intensive CBT programs for childhood aggression, since research in treatment of chronic behavioral problems should focus on creating clinically meaningful improvement (Kazdin, 1987). More intensive CBT programs might include behavior modification components in school settings, longer treatment periods with follow-up boosters, and behavioral parent training, since all of these treatment components and characteristics have had documented effects on childhood aggression.

Issues and Recommendations

Ethnic and Community Context

There are several ethnic and community factors that may delimit the transferability and the consistent use of the anger coping strategies for aggressive boys and adolescents, especially among African-American, low-income individuals. First, parents indirectly and/or directly may promote the use of physically aggressive problem-solving strategies by their greater dependence on corporal punishment, as well as actively teaching their children to retaliate when confronted with physically or verbally aggressive situations. These covert and overt messages may cause a child or adolescent to underutilize some of their new problem-solving skills and alternatives to aggression. It is important to keep in mind that many of these messages have developed as the result of many urban parents' ongoing struggle to protect their boys on the one hand, while trying to inculcate responsibility on the other. Of course, much of this struggle is primarily a result of living in an impoverished neighborhood, along with the long-term effects of racism and discrimination. Another factor that may also serve to delimit the effectiveness of treatment is conflicting messages about the use of aggression among parents and other authority figures, such as school personnel. Equally important is the fact that there are survival mechanisms within the low-income community that are antithetical to those espoused by the Anger Coping Program; that is, peers who are assaultive or physically threatening—which a child or adolescent might encounter in their community—may require the use of physically aggressive strategies. Finally, if children or adolescents have had a traumatizing event occur in their community involving themselves, a peer, or family member—which renders these alternative strategies as counterintuitive—then this will significantly limit the long-term use of these alternative problem-solving skills.

One technique that might serve to offset some of these limitations is to investigate further the relationship between the duality of roles and the use of a phenomenon called "code switching" (Johnson & Farrell, 1997; Fellows Milburn, 1996). This technique serves as a mechanism specifically to train children or adolescents to have a different code of behavior depending on the context in which they finds themselves. This is really quite similar to the duality of roles premise, which has been promulgated throughout the years since slavery as a survival mechanism for African-Americans. A focus on code-switching could provide greater insight about how to maximize mastery as well as apply these critical social skills.

Adaptation of Cognitive-Behavioral Therapy to Early Elementary-School-Age Children

The behavioral and social-cognitive characteristics of younger children require group leaders to modify the structure and content of group sessions. Five- to 7-year-olds are active and less skilled in important group behavior such as turn taking, sitting in one's seat, and making relevant comments. Children in this age group also are egocentric with regard to perspective-taking skills and typically do not demonstrate a sequential problem-solving style. Information on how to alter group sessions to accommodate these behavioral and social cognitive differences can be found in Lochman et al. (1999).

Adaptation of Cognitive-Behavioral Therapy to Middle-to-Late Adolescents

The emotional–behavioral–cognitive development of middle-to-late adolescents require group leaders to modify the structure and content of group sessions. The role of peer pressure is an important factor as well. Based on work with adolescents in several settings, a general outline of the various structural and content changes can be found in Lochman et al. (1999).

Future Directions for Cognitive-Behavioral Therapy

When we wrote this chapter (Lochman, White, & Wayland, 1991) for the previous edition of this book, we identified the three most compelling emerging themes for CBT assessment and intervention to be (1) the inclusion of cognitive-behavioral parent assessment and therapy, (2) the intensification and broadening of CBT programs, and (3) an increasing focus on universal (primary) prevention and on indicated and selected (secondary) prevention. Clear signs exist that the evolution of CBT with aggressive children has moved in these directions. They remain an important focus for continued intervention development.

The most striking deficiency in many CBT programs and research with aggressive children has been the neglect of children's caregivers, especially parents. Intervening with these caregivers can be critical in strengthening treatment effects and in maintaining generalization of effects over time. The best-documented, effective treatment for childhood aggression is behavioral parent therapy (Kazdin, 1987, 1995; Lochman, 1990; Lochman, 1999; Long, Forehand, Wierson, & Morgan, 1994; McMahon & Wells, 1989; Wells, 1995). Behavioral parent training can focus on altering the deficient parenting skills and parental aggressiveness that are so often evident in families of aggressive children, thereby reinforcing the behavioral changes children begin to make in CBT. Behavioral training for teachers could similarly be useful. Perhaps more critically, parent treatment can, over time, promote changes in parents' appraisal distortions and social problem-solving deficiencies. As parents change these pathological thinking patterns, which are shared by their children, children can begin responding to the parents' and teachers' modeling of more adaptive and competent cognitive processes.

A CBT program can be broadened by including an emphasis on cognitive schemas and operations, and cognitive appraisal and coping with arousal, as well as social-cognitive products. By focusing on children's social goals, expectations of achieving goals, and labeling and coping with affective states and concomitant arousal, we can impact key processes that are critical in successful use of self-instruction or social problem solving. To intensify CBT programs, intervention periods can be lengthened to reinforce the changes that are made in social-cognition and behavior. Lengthier treatment also permits the development of closer therapeutic relationships, and it is in the context of these relationships in individual or group therapy that children can begin to examine, trust, and try out others' perceptions of interpersonal events. These perceptual changes are slow in coming, since they involve revisions in internalized styles of attending to and interpreting events. In contrast, social problem-solving skills can be altered more rapidly through role playing and discussion. The intensification of treatment can involve use of booster treatment periods, and of more intensely "bunched" treatment, as in day-camp or day-treatment settings.

CBT can be easily and effectively adapted for universal, selected, and indicated prevention programs (Conduct Problems Prevention Research Group, 1992; Lochman & Wells, 1996). To facilitate development of these programs, risk markers (e.g., temperament, parenting skills; Colder, Lochman, & Wells, 1996) for childhood aggression will have to be identified during the preschool and early elementary school period. With a preventive orientation, CBT-based services can be provided in settings that give a broad access to children (e.g., school, pediatric clinics, day care, community athletic facilities), as we have successfully done in the Fast Track, Anger Coping and Coping Power Programs. Through early identification, and by not having to rely on caregivers' compliance with referrals to clinics, CBT can be provided for children and their caregivers at a time when children's self regulation processes are being internalized.

REFERENCES

Abidin, R. R. (1983). *Parenting Stress Index—Manual*. Charlotteville, VA: Pediatric Psychology Press.

Achenbach, T. M. (1991). *Manual for the Child Behavior Checklist/ 4–18 and 1991 Profile*. Burlington: University of Vermont, Department of Psychiatry.

Achenbach, T. M., & Edelbrock, C. S. (1983). *Manual for the Child Behavior Checklist and Revised Child Behavior Profile*. Burlington: University of Vermont, Department of Psychiatry.

Agrawal, R., & Kaushal, K. (1988). Attention and short-term memory in normal children, aggressive children, and nonaggression children with attention deficit disorder. *Journal of General Psychology, 114*, 335–343.

Allen, G. J., Chinsky, J. M., Larcen, S. W., Lochman, J. E., & Selinger, H. V. (1976). *Community psychology and the schools: A behaviorally oriented multilevel preventative approach*. Hillsdale, NJ: Erlbaum.

American Psychiatric Association. (1994). *Diagnostic and statistical manual of mental disorders* (4th ed.). Washington, DC: Author.

Asarnow, J. R., & Callan, J. E. (1985). Boys with peer adjustment problems: Social cognitive processes. *Journal of Consulting and Clinical Psychology, 53*, 80–87.

Asher, S. R., & Renshaw, P. D. (1981). Children without friends: Social knowledge and social skill training. In S. R. Asher & J. M. Gottman (Eds.), *The development of children's friendships* (pp. 273–296). New York: Cambridge University Press.

Bandura, A. (1973) *Aggression: A social learning analysis*. Englewood Cliffs, NJ: Prentice-Hall.

Bandura, A. (1977). *Social learning theory*. Englewood Cliffs, NJ: Prentice-Hall.

Barkley, R. A. (1997). *ADHD and the nature of self-control*. New York: Guilford Press.

Beck, A. T., Rush, A. J., Shaw, B. F., & Emery, G. (1979). *Cognitive therapy of depression*. New York: Guilford Press.

Boldizar, J. P., Perry, D. G., & Perry, L. C. (1989). Outcome values and aggression. *Child Development, 60*, 571–579.

Brain, P. F. (1984). Biological explanations of human aggression and the resulting therapies offered by such approaches: An initial evaluation. In R. J. Blanchard & D. C. Blanchard (Eds.), *Advances in the study of aggression* (pp. 64–102). Orlando, FL: Academic Press.

Bretherton, I. (1995). Attachment theory and developmental psychopathology. In D. Cicchetti & S. L. Toth (Eds.), *Rochester Symposium on Developmental Psychopathology: Emotion, cognition, and representation*. Rochester, NY: University of Rochester Press.

Brion-Meisel, S., & Selman, R. L. (1984). Early adolescent development of new interpersonal strategies: Understanding the intervention. *School Psychology Review, 13*, 278–291.

Brown, A. (1987). Metacognition, executive control, self-regulation and other more mysterious mechanisms. In F. E. Weinert & R. H. Kluve (Eds.), *Metacognition, motivation and understanding* (pp. 65–116). Hillsdale, NJ: Erlbaum.

Bry, B. H., Catalano, R. F., Kumpfer, K. L., Lochman, J. E., & Szapocznik, J. (1999). Scientific findings from family prevention intervention research. In R. Ashery (Ed.), *Family-based prevention interventions* (pp. 103–129). Rockville, MD: National Institute of Drug Abuse.

Bryant, B. K. (1982). An index of empathy for children and adolescents. *Child Development, 53*, 413–425.

Camp, B. W., Blom, G. F., Herbert, F., & van Doornick, W. J. (1977). "Think Aloud": A program for developing self-control in young aggressive boys. *Journal of Abnormal Child Psychology, 5*, 157–169.

Cartledge, G., & Fellows Milburn, J. (1996). A model for teaching social skills. In G. Cartledge (Ed.), *Cultural diversity and social skills instruction: Understanding ethnic and gender differences* (pp. 45–85). Champaign, IL: Research Press.

Chandler, M. J. (1973). Egocentrism and antisocial behavior: The assessment and training of social perspective-taking skills. *Developmental Psychology, 9*, 326–332.

Christiansen, K., & Knussmann, R. (1987). Androgen levels and components of aggressive behavior in men. *Hormones and Behavior, 21*, 170–180.

Coats, K. I. (1979). Cognitive self instructional training approach for reducing disruptive behavior of young children. *Psychology Reports, 44*, 127–132.

Cohen, D., & Strayer, J. (1996). Empathy in conduct-disordered and comparison youth. *Developmental Psychology, 32*, 988–998.

Cohen, R., & Schleser, R. (1984). Cognitive development and clinical implications. In A. W. Meyers & W. E. Craighead (Eds.), *Cognitive behavior therapy with children* (pp. 45–68). New York: Plenum Press.

Coie, J. E., Dodge, K. A., & Coppotelli, H. (1982). Dimensions and types of status: A cross-age perspective. *Developmental Psychology, 18*, 557–570.

Coie, J. D., Lochman, J. E., Terry, R., & Hyman, C. (1992). Predicting early adolescent disorder from childhood aggression and peer rejection. *Journal of Consulting and Clinical Psychology, 60*, 783–792.

Colder, C. R., Lochman, J. E., & Wells, K. C. (1997). The moderating effects of children's fear and activity level on relations between parenting practices and childhood symptomatology. *Journal of Abnormal Child Psychology, 25*, 251–263.

Conduct Problems Prevention Research Group. (1992). A developmental and clinical model for the prevention of conduct disorder: The Fast Track Program. *Development and Psychopathology, 4*, 509–527.

Conduct Problems Prevention Research Group. (1999). Initial impact of the Fast Track prevention trial for conduct problems: I. The high-risk sample. *Journal of Consulting and Clinical Psychology, 67*, 631–647.

Coopersmith, S. (1967). *Antecedents of self-esteem*. San Francisco: Freeman.

Cornell, D. G., Warren, J., Hawk, G., Stafford, E., Oram, G., & Pine, D. (1996). Psychopathy in instrumental and reactive violent offenders. *Journal of Consulting and Clinical Psychology, 64*, 783–790.

Costello, A. J., Edelbrock, C. S., Dulcan, M. K., & Kalas, R. (1984). *Testing of the NIMH Diag-*

nostic Interview Schedule for Children (DISC) in a clinical population (Contract No. DB-81–0027, final report to the Center for Epidemiological Studies, National Institute for Mental Health). Pittsburgh: University of Pittsburgh.

Craven, S., Lochman, J. E., & Wells, K. C. (1997). *Examination of the physiological, emotional and cognitive processes in boys' responses to peer provocations at three levels of aggression.* Unpublished manuscript, Duke University, Durham, NC.

Crick, N. R., & Dodge, K. A. (1994). A review and reformulation of social information-processing mechanisms in children's social adjustment. *Psychological Bulletin, 115,* 74–101.

Crick, N. R., & Dodge, K. A. (1996). Social information-processing mechanisms in reactive and proactive aggression. *Child Development, 67,* 993–1002.

Crick, N. R., & Ladd, G. W. (1990). Children's perceptions of the outcomes of aggressive strategies: Do the ends justify the means? *Developmental Psychology, 26,* 612–620.

Dabbs, J. M., Jr., Jurkovic, G. L., & Frady, R. L. (1988). *Saliva testosterone and cortisol among young male prison inmates.* Unpublished manuscript, Georgia State University, Atlanta, GA.

Deluty, R. H. (1981). Alternative-thinking ability of aggressive, assertive, and submissive children. *Cognitive Therapy and Research, 5,* 309–312.

Deluty, R. H. (1983). Children's evaluation of aggressive, assertive and submissive responses. *Journal of Consulting and Clinical Psychology, 51,* 124–129.

Dishion, T. J., Patterson, G. R., & Griesler, P. C. (1994). Peer adaptations in the development of antisocial behavior: A confluence model. In L. R. Huesmann (Ed.), *Aggressive behavior: Current perspectives* (pp. 61–95). New York: Plenum Press.

Dix, T., & Lochman, J. E. (1990). Social cognition and negative reactions to children: A comparison of mothers of aggressive and nonaggressive boys. *Journal of Social and Clinical Psychology, 9,* 418–438.

Dodge, K. A. (1980). Social cognition and children's aggressive behavior. *Child Development, 51,* 162–170.

Dodge, K. A. (1985). Attributional bias in aggressive children. In P. C. Kendall (Ed.), *Advances in cognitive-behavioral research and therapy* (Vol. 4, pp. 75–110). New York: Academic Press.

Dodge, K. A. (1986). A social information-processing model of social competence in children. In M. Perlmutter (Ed.), *The Minnesota Symposia on Child Psychology: Vol. 18. Cognitive perspectives on children's social and behavioral development* (pp. 77–125). Hillsdale, NJ: Erlbaum.

Dodge, K. A., & Coie, J. D. (1987). Social information processing factors in reactive and proactive aggression in children's peer groups. *Journal of Personality and Social Psychology, 53,* 1146–1158.

Dodge, K. A., Coie, J. D., & Brakke, N. P. (1982). Behavior patterns of socially rejected and neglected preadolescents: The roles of social approach and aggression. *Journal of Abnormal Child Psychology, 10,* 389–410.

Dodge, K. A., & Frame, C. L. (1982). Social cognitive biases and deficits in aggressive boys. *Child Development, 53,* 620–635.

Dodge, K. A., Lochman, J. E., Harnish, J. D., Bates, J. E., & Pettit, G. S. (1997). Reactive and proactive aggression in school children and psychiatrically impaired chronically assaultive youth. *Journal of Abnormal Psychology, 106,* 37–51.

Dodge, K. A., & Newman, J. P. (1981). Biased decision-making processes in aggressive boys. *Journal of Abnormal Psychology, 90,* 375–379.

Dodge, K. A. Pettit, G. S., McClaskey, C. L., & Brown, M. M. (1986). Social competence in children. *Monographs of the Society for Research in Child Development, 51*(2, Serial No. 213).

Dodge, K. A., & Somberg, D. R. (1987). Hostile attributional biases among aggressive boys are exacerbated under conditions of threat to the self. *Child Development, 58,* 213–224.

Dubow, E. F., Huesmann, L. R., & Eron, L. D. (1987). Mitigating aggression promoting prosocial behavior in aggressive elementary schoolboys. *Behaviour Research and Therapy, 25,* 527–531.

Dunn, S. E., Lochman, J. E., & Colder, C. R. (1997). Social problem-solving skills in boys with conduct and oppositional defiant disorders. *Aggressive Behavior, 23,* 457–469.

Edelman, E. M., & Goldstein, A. P. (1981). Moral education. In A. P. Goldstein, E. G. Carr, W. S. Davidson, III, & P. Mohr (Eds.), *In response to aggression: Methods of control and prosocial alternatives* (pp. 235–315). New York: Pergamon Press.

Eisenberg, N., & Miller, P. A. (1987). The relation of empathy to prosocial and related behaviors. *Psychological Bulletin, 101,* 91–119.

Emery, R., & O'Leary, D. (1982). Children's perceptions of marital discord and behavior of boys and girls. *Journal of Abnormal Child Psychology, 10,* 11–24.

Erdley, C. A. (1990). *An analysis of children's attributions and goals in social situations: Implications of children's friendship outcomes.* Unpublished manuscript, University of Illinois, Champaign, IL.

Erdley, C. A., & Asher, S. R. (1993, March). *To aggress or not: Social-cognitive mediators of children's responses to ambiguous provocation.* Paper presented at the biennial meeting of the Society for Research in Child Development, New Orleans, LA.

Evans, S. W., & Short, E. J. (1991). A qualitative and serial analysis of social problem-solving in aggressive boys. *Journal of Abnormal Child Psychology, 19,* 331–340.

Eyberg, S. M. (1980). Eyberg Child Behavior Inventory. *Journal of Clinical Child Psychology, 9,* 29–40.

Feshbach, N. D., & Feshbach, S. (1982). Empathy training and the relation of aggression: Potentialities and limitations. *Academic Psychology Bulletin, 4,* 399–413.

Fiske, S. T., & Taylor, S. W. (1984). *Social cognition.* Reading, MA: Addison-Wesley.

Forehand, R., & Long, N. (1988). Outpatient treatment of the acting out child: Procedures, long term follow-up data, and clinical problems. *Advances in Behaviour Research and Therapy, 10,* 129–177.

Forehand, R. L., & McMahon, R. J. (1981). *Helping the noncompliant child: A clinician's guide to parent training.* New York: Guilford Press.

Forman, S. G. (1980). A comparison of cognitive training and response cost procedures in modifying aggressive behavior of elementary school children. *Behavior Therapy, 11,* 94–100.

French, D. C. (1988). Heterogeneity of peer-rejected boys: Aggressive and nonaggressive subtypes. *Child Development, 59,* 976–985.

Frick, P. J. (1998). *Conduct disorders and severe antisocial behavior.* New York: Plenum Press.

Gainetdinov, R. R., Wetsel, W. C., Jones, S. R., Levin, E. D., Jaber, M., & Caron, M. G. (1999). Role of serotonin in the paradoxical calming effect of psychostimulants on hyperactivity. *Science, 283,* 397–401.

Garrison, S. R., & Stolberg, A. L. (1983). Modification of anger in children by affect imagery training. *Journal of Abnormal Child Psychology, 11,* 115–130.

Gesten, J. C., Langer, T. S., Eisenberg, J. G., Simcha-Fagan, D., & McCarthy, E. D. (1976). Stability and change in types of behavioral disturbance of children and adolescents. *Journal of Abnormal Child Psychology, 4,* 111–127.

Giancola, P. R., Martin, C. S., Tarter, R. E., Pelham, W. E., & Moss, H. B. (1996). Executive cognitive functioning and aggressive behavior in preadolescent boys at high risk for substance abuse/dependence. *Journal of Studies on Alcohol, 57,* 352–359.

Giancola, P. R., Moss, H. B., Martin, C. S., Krisci, L., & Tarter, R. E. (1996). Executive cognitive functioning predicts reactive aggression in boys at high risk for substance abuse: A prospective study. *Alcoholism: Clinical and Experimental Research, 20,* 740–744.

Giancola, P. R., Zeichner, A., Yarnell, J. E., & Dickson, K. E. (1996). Relation between executive cognitive functioning and the adverse consequences of alcohol use in social drinkers. *Alcoholism: Clinical and Experimental Research, 20,* 1094–1098.

Gold, P. W. (1998). Lack of attention from loss of time. *Science, 281,* 1149–1150.

Goleman, D. (1995). *Emotional intelligence.* New York: Bantam Books.

Goodwin, S. F., & Mahoney, J. J. (1975). Modification of aggression through modeling: An experimental probe. *Journal of Behavior Therapy and Experimental Psychiatry, 6,* 200–202.

Gouze, K. R. (1987). Attention and social problem solving as correlates of aggression in preschool males. *Journal of Abnormal Child Psychology, 15,* 181–197.

Guerra, N. G., & Slaby, R. G. (1989). Evaluative factors in social problem solving by aggressive boys. *Journal of Abnormal Child Psychology, 17,* 277–289.

Halperin, J. M., Newcorn, J. H., Kopstein, I., McKay, K. E., Schwartz, S. T., Siever, L. J., & Sharma, V. (1999). Serotonin, aggression, and parental psychopathology in children with attention-deficit disorder. *Journal of the American Academy of Child and Adolescent Psychiatry, 36,* 1391–1399.

Hart, C. H., Ladd, G. W., & Burleson, B. R. (1990). Children's expectations of the outcomes of social strategies: Relations with sociometric status and maternal disciplinary style. *Child Development, 61,* 127–137.

Harter, S. (1985). *The Self-Perception Profile for Children: Revision of the Perceived Competence Scale for Children* (manual). University of Denver, Denver, CO.

Hawkins, J. D., Catalano, R. F., Morrison, D. M., O'Donnell, J., Abbott, R. D., & Day, L. E. (1992). The Seattle Social Development Project: Effects of the first four years on protective factors and problem behavior. In J. McCord & R. E. Tremblay (Eds.), *Preventing antisocial behavior: Interventions from birth through adolescence* (pp. 139–161). New York: Guilford Press.

Herrenkohl, I. T., Maguin, E., Hill, K. G., Hawkins, J. D., Abbott, R. D., & Catalano, R. F. (1998). *Developmental predictors of violence in late adolescence.* Unpublished manuscript, University of Washington, Seattle, WA.

Hodges, V. K. (1987). Assessing children with a clinical research interview: The Child Assessment Schedule. In R. J. Prinz (Ed.), *Advances in behavioral assessment of children and families* (pp. 65–81). Greenwich, CT: JAI Press.

Huesmann, L. R., Eron, L. D., Lefkowitz, M. M., & Walder, L. O. (1984). Stability of aggression over time and generations. *Developmental Psychology, 20,* 1120–1134.

Hughes, J. N. (1988). *Cognitive behavior therapy with children in schools.* New York: Pergamon Press.

Ingram, R. E., & Kendall, P. C. (1986). Cognitive clinical psychology: Implications of an informational processing perspective. In R. E. Ingram (Ed.), *Information processing approaches to clinical psychology* (pp. 3–21). New York: Academic Press.

Joffe, R. D., Dobson, K. S., Fine, S., Marriage, K., & Haley, G. (1990). Social problem-solving in depressed, conduct disordered and normal adolescents. *Journal of Abnormal Child Psychology, 18,* 565–575.

Johnson, J. H., Jr., & Farrell, W. C., Jr. (1997). *The Durham Scholars Program: An evaluation research proposal.* Chapel Hill: University of North Carolina Department of Geography, Sociology, and the Kenan-Flagler Business School.

Jurkovic, G., & Prentice, N. M. (1977). Relation of moral and cognitive development to dimensions of juvenile delinquency. *Journal of Abnormal Psychology, 86,* 414–420.

Kaufman, A., & Kaufman, N. (1990). *Kaufman Brief Intelligence Test (K-BIT) Manual.* Circle Pines, MN: American Guidance Service.

Kazdin, A. E. (1987). Treatment of antisocial behavior in children: Current status and future directions. *Psychological Bulletin, 102,* 187–203.

Kazdin, A. E. (1995). *Conduct disorders in childhood and adolescence* (2nd ed.). Thousand Oaks, CA: Sage.

Kazdin, A. E., Bass, D., Siegel, T., & Thomas, C. (1989). Cognitive-behavioral therapy and relationship therapy in the treatment of children referred for antisocial behavior. *Journal of Consulting and Clinical Psychology, 57,* 522–535.

Kazdin, A. E., & Esveldt-Dawson, K. (1986). The Interview for Antisocial Behavior: Psychometric characteristics and concurrent validity with child psychiatric inpatients. *Journal of Psychopathology and Behavioral Assessment, 8,* 289–303.

Kazdin, A. E., Esveldt-Dawson, K., French, N. H., & Unis, A. S. (1987a). Effects of parent management training and problem-solving skills training combined in the treatment of antisocial child behavior. *Journal of the American Academy of Child and Adolescent Psychiatry, 26,* 416–424.

Kazdin, A. E., Esveldt-Dawson, K., French, N. H., & Unis, A. S. (1987b). Problem-solving skills training and relationship therapy in the treatment of antisocial child behavior. *Journal of Consulting and Clinical Psychology, 55,* 76–85.

Kazdin, A. E., Siegel, T. C., & Bass, D. (1992). Cognitive problem-solving skills training and parent management training in the treatment of antisocial behavior in children. *Journal of Consulting and Clinical Psychology, 60,* 733–747.

Kellam, S. G., Ensminger, M. E., & Simon, M. B. (1980). Mental health in first grade and teenage drug, alcohol and cigarette use. *Drug and Alcohol Dependence, 5,* 273–304.

Kellam, S. G., & Rebok, G. W. (1992). Building developmental and etiological theory through epidemiologically based preventive intervention trials. In J. McCord & R. E. Tremblay (Eds.), *Preventing antisocial behavior: Interventions from birth through adolescence* (pp. 139–161). New York: Guilford Press.

Kendall, P. C. (1985). Toward a cognitive-behavioral model of child psychopathology and a critique of related interventions. *Journal of Abnormal Child Psychology, 13,* 357–372.

Kendall, P. C. (1998). Empirically-supported psychological therapies. *Journal of Consulting and Clinical Psychology, 66,* 3–6.

Kendall, P. C., & Braswell, L. (1985). *Cognitive-behavioral therapy for impulsive children.* New York: Guilford Press.

Kendall, P. C., & Fischler, G. L. (1984). Behavioral and adjustment correlates of problem-solving:Validation analyses of interpersonal cognitive problem-solving measures. *Child Development, 55,* 879–892.

Kendall, P. C., & Ingram, R. E. (1989). Cognitive behavioral perspective: Theory and research. In P. C. Kendall & D. Watson (Eds.), *Anxiety and depression: Distinctive and overlapping features.* New York: Academic Press.

Kendall, P. C., & MacDonald, J. P. (1993). Cognition in the psychopathology of youth and implications for treatment. In K. S. Dobson & P. C. Kendall (Eds.), *Psychopathology and cognition* (pp. 387–427). San Diego: Academic Press.

Kendall, P. C., Ronan, K. R., & Epps, J. (1991). Aggression in children–adolescents: Cognitive-behavioral treatment perspectives. In D. Pepler & K. Rubin (Eds.), *Development and treatment of childhood aggression* (pp. 341–360). Toronto: Erlbaum.

Kendall, P. C., Zupan, B. A., & Braswell, L. (1981). Self-control in children: Further analyses of the Self Control Rating Scale. *Behavior Therapy, 12,* 667–681.

Kettlewell, P. W., & Kausch, D. F. (1983). The generalization of the effects of a cognitive-behavioral treatment program for aggressive children. *Journal of Abnormal Child Psychology, 11,* 101–114.

Kopp, C. B. (1987). The growth of self-regulation: Caregivers and children. In N. Eisenberg (Ed.), *Contemporary topics in developmental psychology* (pp. 34–56). New York: Wiley.

Kupersmidt, J. B., & Coie, J. D. (1990). Preadolescent peer status and aggression as predictors of externalizing problems in adolescence. *Child Development, 61,* 1350–1362.

Lahey, B. B., Green, K. E., & Forehand, R. (1980). On the independence of ratings of hyperactivity, conduct problems, and attention deficits in children: A multiple regression analysis. *Journal of Consulting and Clinical Psychology, 48,* 566–574.

Larrance, D. T., & Twentyman, C. T. (1983). Maternal attributions and child abuse. *Journal of Abnormal Psychology, 92,* 449–457.

Lazarus, R. S. (1993). From psychological stress to the emotions: A history of changing outlooks. *Annual Review of Psychology, 44,* 1–21.

Lochman, J. E. (1984). Psychological characteristics and assessment of aggressive adolescents. In C. R. Keith (Ed.), *The aggressive adolescent: Clinical perspectives* (pp. 17–62). New York: Free Press.

Lochman, J. E. (1985). Effects of different treatment lengths in cognitive behavioral interventions with aggressive boys. *Child Psychiatry and Human Development, 16,* 45–56.

Lochman, J. E. (1987). Self and peer perceptions and attributional biases of aggressive and nonaggressive boys in dyadic interactions. *Journal of Consulting and Clinical Psychology, 55,* 404–410.

Lochman, J. E. (1989, February). *Hardware versus software: Land of deficiency in social-cognitive processes of aggressive boys.* Paper presented at the first annual meeting of the Society for Research in Child and Adolescent Psychopathology, Miami, FL.

Lochman, J. E. (1990). Modification of childhood aggression. In M. Hersen, R. Eisler, & P. M. Miller (Eds.), *Progress in behavior modification* (Vol. 25, pp. 48–86). Newbury Park, CA: Sage.

Lochman, J. E. (1992). Cognitive-behavioral intervention with aggressive boys: Three-year follow-up and preventive effects. *Journal of Consulting and Clinical Psychology, 60,* 426–432.

Lochman, J. E. (1999). *Parent and family skills training in indicated prevention.* Unpublished manuscript, University of Alabama, Tuscaloosa, AL.

Lochman, J. E. (in press). Preventive intervention with precursors to substance abuse. In W. J. Bukoski & Z. Sloboda (Eds.), *Handbook of drug abuse theory, science, and practice.* New York: Plenum Press.

Lochman, J. E., Burch, P. R., Curry, J. F., & Lampron, L. B. (1984). Treatment and generalization effects of cognitive-behavioral and goal-setting interventions with aggressive boys. *Journal of Consulting and Clinical Psychology, 52,* 915–916.

Lochman, J. E., Coie, J. D., Underwood, M., & Terry, R. (1993). Effectiveness of a social relations intervention program for aggressive and nonaggressive rejected children. *Journal of Consulting and Clinical Psychology, 61,* 1053–1058.

Lochman, J. E., & the Conduct Problems Prevention Research Group. (1995). Screening of child behavior problems for prevention programs at school entry. *Journal of Consulting and Clinical Psychology, 63,* 549–559.

Lochman, J. E., & Curry, J. F. (1986). Effects of social problem-solving training and self-instruction training with aggressive boys. *Journal of Clinical Child Psychology, 15,* 159–164.

Lochman, J. E., Dunn, S. E., & Wagner, E. E. (1997). Anger. In G. Bear, K. Minke, & A. Thomas (Eds.), *Children's Needs II* (pp. 149–160). Washington, DC: National Association of School Psychology.

Lochman, J. E., & Dodge, K. A. (1990, January). *Dysfunctional family and social-cognitive process with aggressive boys.* Paper presented at the annual meeting of the Society for Research in Child and Adolescent Psychopathology, Costa Mesa, CA.

Lochman, J. E., & Dodge, K. A. (1994). Social-cognitive processes of severely violent, moderately aggressive and nonaggressive boys. *Journal of Consulting and Clinical Psychology, 62,* 366–374.

Lochman, J. E., & Dodge, K. A. (1998). Distorted perceptions in dyadic interactions of aggressive and nonaggressive boys: Effects of prior expectations, context, and boys' age. *Development and Psychopathology, 10,* 495–512.

Lochman, J. E., FitzGerald, D. P., & Whidby, J. M. (1999). Anger management with aggressive children. In C. Schaefer (Ed.), *Short-term psychotherapy groups for children* (pp. 301–349). Northvale, NJ: Aronson.

Lochman, J. E., & Lampron, L. B. (1985). The usefulness of peer ratings of aggression and social acceptance in the identification of behavioral and subjective difficulties in aggressive boys. *Journal of Applied Developmental Psychology, 6,* 187–198.

Lochman, J. E., & Lampron, L. B. (1986). Situational social problem-solving skills and self-esteem of aggressive and nonaggressive boys. *Journal of Abnormal Child Psychology, 14,* 605–617.

Lochman, J. E., & Lampron, L. B. (1988). Cognitive behavioral interventions for aggressive boys: Seven months follow-up effects. *Journal of Child and Adolescent Psychotherapy, 5,* 15–23.

Lochman, J. E., Lampron, L. B., Burch, P. R., & Curry, J. F. (1985). Client characteristics associated with behavior change for treated and untreated boys. *Journal of Abnormal Child Psychology, 13,* 527–538.

Lochman, J. E., Lampron, L. B., Gemmer, T. V., & Harris, R. (1987). In P. A. Keller & S. R. Heyman (Eds.), *Innovations in clinical practice: A source book* (Vol. 6, pp. 339–356). Sarasota, FL: Professional Resource Exchange.

Lochman, J. E., Lampron, L. B., Gemmer, T. C., Harris, R., & Wyckoff, G. M. (1989). Teacher consultation and cognitive-behavioral interventions with aggressive boys. *Psychology in the Schools, 26,* 179–188.

Lochman, J. E., Lampron, L. B., & Rabiner, D. L. (1989). Format and salience effects in the social problem-solving of aggressive and nonaggressive boys. *Journal of Clinical Child Psychology, 18,* 230–236.

Lochman, J. E., & Lenhart, L. A. (1993). Anger coping intervention for aggressive children: Conceptual models and outcome effects. *Clinical Psychology Review, 13,* 785–805.

Lochman, J. E., & Lenhart, L. A. (1995). Cognitive behavioral therapy of aggressive children: Effects of schemas. In H. P. J. G. van Bilsen, P. C. Kendall, & J. H. Slavenburg (Eds.), *Cognitive behavioral approaches for children and adolescents: Challenges for the next century* (pp. 145–166). New York: Plenum Press.

Lochman, J. E., Nelson, N. W., III, & Sims, J. P. (1981). A cognitive behavioral program for use with aggressive children. *Journal of Clinical Child Psychology, 13,* 527–538.

Lochman, J. E., & Wayland, K. K. (1994). Aggression, social acceptance and race as predictors of negative adolescent outcomes. *Journal of the American Academy of Child and Adolescent Psychiatry, 33,* 1026–1035.

Lochman, J. E., Wayland, K. K., & Cohen, C. (1990, August). *Prediction of adolescent behavioral problems for subtypes of aggressive boys.* Paper presented at the American Psychological Association Annual Convention, Boston, MA.

Lochman, J. E., Wayland, K. K., & White, K. J. (1993). Social goals: Relationship to adolescent adjustment and to social problem-solving. *Journal of Abnormal Child Psychology, 21,* 135–151.

Lochman, J. E., & Wells, K. C. (1996). A social-cognitive intervention with aggressive children: Prevention effects and contextual implementation issues. In R. D. Peters & R. J. McMahon (Eds.), *Preventing childhood disorders, substance use, and delinquency* (pp. 111–143). Thousand Oaks, CA: Sage.

Lochman, J. E., White, K. J., & Wayland, K. K. (1991). Cognitive behavioral assessment and treatment with aggressive children. In P. C. Kendall (Ed.), *Child and adolescent therapy: Cognitive-behavioral procedures* (pp. 25–35). New York: Guilford Press.

Locke, H. J., & Wallace, K. M. (1959). Short marital adjustment and prediction tests: Their reliability and validity. *Marriage and Family Living, 21,* 251–255.

Loeber, R. (1990). Development and risk factors of juvenile antisocial behavior and delinquency. *Clinical Psychology Review, 10,* 1–41.

Loeber, R., & Dishion, T. J. (1983). Early predictors of male delinquency: A review. *Psychological Bulletin, 94,* 68–99.

Loeber, R., & Schmaling, K. B. (1985). Empirical evidence for overt and covert patterns of antisocial conduct problems: A meta-analysis. *Journal of Abnormal Child Psychology, 13,* 337–352.

Long, P., Forehand, R., Wierson, M., & Morgan, A. (1994). Does parent training with young noncompliant children have long-term effects? *Behaviour Research and Therapy, 32,* 101–107.

Lubin, B. (1967). *Manual for the Depression Adjective Check List.* San Diego: Educational and Industrial Testing Service.

Lynskey, M. T., & Fergusson, D. M. (1995). Childhood conduct problems, attention deficit behaviors, and adolescent alcohol, tobacco, and illicit drug use. *Journal of Abnormal Child Psychology, 23,* 281–302.

Matthys, W., van Goozen, S. H. M., de Vries, H., Cohen-Kettenis, P. T., & van Engeland, H. (1998). The dominance of behavioural activation over behavioural inhibition in conduct disordered boys with or without Attention Deficit Hyperactivity Disorder. *Journal of Child Psychology and Psychiatry, 39,* 643–651.

McKinnon, C. E., Lamb, M. E., Belsky, J., & Baum, C. (1990). An affective-cognitive model for mother–child aggression. *Development and Psychopathology, 2,* 1–13.

McMahon, R. J., & Estes, A. M. (1997). Conduct problems. In E. J. Mash & L. G. Terdal (Eds.), *Assessment of childhood disorders* (3rd ed., pp. 130–193). New York: Guilford Press.

McMahon, R. J., & Forehand, R. (1988). Conduct disorder. In E. J. Mash & L. G. Terdal (Eds.), *Behavioral assessment of childhood disorders* (2nd ed., pp. 105–153). New York: Guilford Press.

McMahon, R. J., & Wells, K. C. (1989). Conduct disorders. In E. J. Mash & R. A. Barkley (Eds.), *Treatment of childhood disorders* (pp. 73–134). New York: Guilford Press.

Meichenbaum, D. (1985). *Stress inoculation training.* New York: Pergamon Press.

Meichenbaum, D. H., & Goodman, J. (1971). Training impulsive children to talk to themselves: A means of developing self control. *Journal of Abnormal Psychology, 77,* 115–126.

Meyers, A. W., & Craighead, W. E. (1984). Cognitive behavior therapy with children: A historical, conceptual, and organizational overview. In A W. Meyers & W. E. Craighead (Eds.), *Cognitive behavior therapy with children* (pp. 1–18). New York: Plenum Press.

Milich, R., & Dodge, K. A. (1984). Social information processing in child psychiatric populations. *Journal of Abnormal Child Psychology, 12,* 471–490.

Miller, P. A., & Eisenberg, N. (1988). The relation of empathy to aggressive and externalizing/antisocial behavior. *Psychological Bulletin, 103,* 324–344.

Miller-Johnson, S., Lochman, J. E., Coie, J. D., Terry, R., & Hyman, C. (1998). Comorbidity of conduct and depressive problems at sixth grade: Substance use outcomes across adolescence. *Journal of Abnormal Child Psychology, 26,* 221–232.

Miller-Johnson, S., Winn, D. M., Coie, J., Maumary-Gremaud, A., Hyman, C., Terry, R., & Lochman, J. E. (1999). Motherhood during the teen years: A developmental perspective on risk factors for childbearing. *Development and Psychopathology, 11,* 85–100.

Mirsky, A. F. (August, 1989). *The neuropsychology of attention: Developmental neuropsychiatric implications.* Paper presented at the 97th Annual Convention of the American Psychological Association, New Orleans, LA.

Moffit, T. E. (1993). Adolescence-limited and life-course persistent antisocial behavior: A developmental taxonomy. *Psychological Review, 100,* 674–701.

Nasby, W., Hayden, B., & DePaulo, B. M. (1980). Attributional bias among aggressive boys to interpret unambiguous social stimuli as displays of hostility. *Journal of Abnormal Psychology, 11,* 257–272.

Novaco, R. W. (1978). Anger and coping with stress: Cognitive-behavioral intervention. In J. P. Foreyet & D. P. Rathjen (Eds.), *Cognitive behavioral therapy: Research and application* (pp. 135–173). New York: Plenum Press.

Nucci, L. P., & Herman, S. (1982). Behavior disordered children's conception of moral, conventional, and personal issues. *Journal of Abnormal Child Psychology, 10,* 411–426.

O'Brien, M., & Chin, C. (1998). The relationship between children's reported exposure to interparental conflict and memory biases in the recognition of aggressive and constructive conflict words. *Social Psychology Bulletin, 24,* 647–657.

Olweus, D. (1979). Stability of aggressive behavior patterns in males: A review. *Psychological Bulletin, 86,* 852–875.

Olweus, D., Mattesson, A., Schalling, D., & Low, H. (1980). Testosterone, aggression, physical and personality dimensions in normal adolescent males. *Psychosomatic Medicine, 42,* 253–269.

Patterson, G. R. (1986). Performance models for antisocial boys. *American Psychologist, 41,* 432–444.

Patterson, G. R., & Bank, L. (1986). Bootstrapping your way in the nomological thicket. *Behavioral Assessment, 8*, 49–73.

Perry, D. G., Perry, L. C., & Rasmussen, P. (1986). Cognitive social learning medicators of aggression. *Child Development, 57*, 700–711.

Piers, E. V., & Harris, D. B. (1964). Age and other correlates of self-concept in children. *Journal of Educational Psychology, 55*, 91–95.

Porter, B., & O'Leary, K. D. (1980). Marital discord and child behavior problems. *Journal of Abnormal Child Psychology, 8*, 287–295.

Quay, H. C., & Peterson, D. R. (1983). *Interim manual for the Revised Behavior Problem Checklist*. Unpublished manuscript, University of Miami, Miami, FL.

Rabiner, D. L., & Gordon, L. V. (1992). The coordination of conflicting goals: Differences between rejected and nonrejected boys. *Child Development, 63*, 1344–1350.

Rabiner, D., Lenhart, L., & Lochman, J. E. (1990). Automatic versus reflective social problem-solving in popular, average, and rejected children. *Developmental Psychology, 26*, 1010–1016.

Raine, A., Venables, P. H., & Williams, M. (1990). Relationships between central and aotonomic measures of arousal at age 15 years and criminality at age 24 years. *Archives of General Psychiatry, 47*, 1003–1007.

Richard, B. A., & Dodge, K. A. (1982). Social maladjustment and problem-solving in school-aged children. *Journal of Consulting and Clinical Psychology, 50*, 226–233.

Robin, A. L., Schneider, M., & Dolnick, M. (1976). The turtle technique: an extended case study of self-control in the classroom. *Psychology in the Schools, 73*, 449–453.

Robins, L. N. (1978). Sturdy childhood predictors of adult antisocial behavior: Replications from longitudinal studies. *Psychological Medicine, 8*, 611–622.

Rodick, J. D., Henggeler, S. W., & Hanson, C. L. (1986). An evaluation of family adaptability and cohesion evaluation scales and the circumplex model. *Journal of Abnormal Child Psychology, 14*, 77–87.

Rose, S. D., & Edleson, J. L. (1987). *Working with children and adolescents in groups*. San Francisco/London: Jossey-Bass.

Rotter, J. B., Chance, J. E., & Phares, E. J. (1972). *Applications of a social learning theory of personality*. New York: Holt, Rhinehart & Winston.

Rubin, K. H., Bream, L. A., & Rose-Krasnor, L. (1991). Social problem solving and aggression in childhood. In D. J. Pepler & K. H. Rubin (Eds.), *The development and treatment of childhood aggression* (pp. 219–248). Hillsdale, NJ: Erlbaum.

Sancilio, M., Plumert, J. M., & Hartup, W. W. (1989). Friendship and aggressiveness as determinants of conflict outcomes in middle childhood. *Developmental Psychology, 25*, 812–819.

Santosterfano, S., & Roder, C. (1984). Cognitive controls and aggression in children: The concept of cognitive-affective balance. *Journal of Consulting and Clinical Psychology, 52*, 46–56.

Sayed, J. C., Lochman, J. E., & Wells, K. C. (in press). Children's social problem-solving strategies: Relationships to parental child-rearing practices. *Merrill–Palmer Quarterly*.

Schwartz, D., Dodge, K. A., Coie, J. D., Hubbard, J. A., Cillessen, A. H., Lemerise, E. A., & Bateman, H. (1998). Social-cognitive and behavioral correlates of aggression and victimization in boys' play groups. *Journal of Abnormal Child Psychology, 26*, 431–440.

Seguin, J. R., Pihl, R. O., Harden, P. W., Tremblay, R. E., & Boulerice, B. (1995). Cognitive and neuropsychological characteristics of physically aggressive boys. *Journal of Abnormal Psychology, 104*, 614–624.

Shaw, D. S., & Bell, R. Q. (1993). Developmental theories of parental contributions to antisocial behavior. *Journal of Abnormal Child Psychology, 21*, 493–518.

Sines, J. O., Pauler, J. D., Sines, L. K., & Owen, D. R. (1969). Identification of clinically relevant dimensions of children's behavior. *Journal of Consulting and Clinical Psychology, 33*, 728–734.

Slaby, R. G., & Guerra, N. G. (1988). Cognitive mediators of aggression in adolescent offenders: 1. Assessment. *Developmental Psychology, 24*(4), 580–588.

Southam-Gerow, M. A., & Kendall, P. C. (1997). Parent-focused and cognitive-behavioral treatments of antisocial youth. In D. M. Stoff, J. Breiling & J. D. Maser (Eds.), *Handbook of antisocial behavior* (pp. 384–394). New York: Wiley.

Spanier, G. B. (1976). Measuring dyadic adjustment: New scales for assessing the quality of marriage and similar dyads. *Journal of Marriage and the Family, 38,* 15–28.

Steinberg, M. D., & Dodge, K. A. (1983). Attributional bias in aggressive adolescent boys and girls. *Journal of Social and Clinical Psychology, 1,* 312–321.

Straus, M. A. (1979). Measuring intrafamily conflict and violence: The Conflict Tactics (CT) Scales. *Journal of Marriages and the Family, 41,* 79–88.

Sulzer, B., & Mayer, G. R. (1972). *Behavior modification procedures for school personnel.* Hinsdale, IL: Dryden.

Swaim, R. C., Oetting, E. R., Edwards, R. W., & Beauvais, F. (1989). Links from emotional distress to adolescent drug use: A path model. *Journal of Consulting and Clinical Psychology, 57,* 227–231.

Thompson, L. L., Riggs, P. D., Mikulich, S. E., & Crowley, T. J. (1996). Contributions of ADHD symptoms to substance problems and delinquency in conduct-disordered adolescents. *Journal of Abnormal Child Psychology, 24,* 325–348.

Tremblay, R. E., Masse, B., Perron, D., LeBlanc, M., Schwartzman, A. E., & Ledingham, J. E. (1992). Early disruptive behavior, poor school environment, delinquent behavior, and delinquent personality: Longitudinal analyses. *Journal of Consulting and Clinical Psychology, 60,* 64–72.

Tremblay, R. E., Pagani-Kurtz, L., Masse, L. C., Vitaro, F., & Pihl, R. O. (1995). A bi-modal preventive intervention for disruptive kindergarten boys: Its impact through mid-adolescence. *Journal of Consulting and Clinical Psychology, 63,* 560–568.

van Goozen, S. H. M., Matthys, W., Cohen-Kettenis, P. T., Gispen-de Wied, C., Wiegant, V. M., & van Engeland, H. (1998). Salivary cortisol and cardiovascular activity during stress in oppositional-defiant disorder boys and normal controls. *Biological Psychiatry, 43,* 531–539.

van Goozen, S. H. M., Matthys, W., Cohen-Kettenis, P. T., Thijssen, J. H. H., & van Engeland, H. (1998). Adrenal androgens and aggression in conduct disordered prepubertal boys and normal controls. *Biological Psychiatry, 43,* 156–158.

van Goozen, S. H. M., Matthys, W., Cohen-Kettenis, P. T., Westenberg, H., & van Engeland, H. (in press). Plasma monoamine metabolites and aggression: Two studies of normal and oppositional defiant disorder children. *European Neuropsychopharmacology.*

Vygotsky, L. S. (1978). *Mind in society: The development of higher psychological processes* (M. Cole, V. John-Steiner, S. Scribner, & E. Souberman, Eds. and Trans.). Cambridge, MA: Harvard University Press.

Waas, G. A. (1988). Social attributional biases of peer-rejected and aggressive children. *Child Development, 59,* 969–975.

Waas, G. A., & French, D. C. (1989). Children's social problem solving: Comparison of the open middle interview and children's assertive behavior scale. *Behavioral Assessment, 11,* 219–230.

Wayland, K. K., Schoenwald, S. K., & Lochman, J. E. (1989, August). *Marital adjustment, family conflict and children's perceptions of marital discord.* Paper presented at the American Psychological Association Annual Convention, New Orleans, LA.

Webster-Stratton, C., & Hammon, M. (1997). Treating children with early-onset conduct problems: A comparison of child and parent training interventions. *Journal of Consulting and Clinical Psychology, 65,* 93–109.

Wells, K. C. (1995). Parent and family management training. In L. Craighead, W. E. Craighead, A. Kazdin, & M. Mahoney (Eds.), *Cognitive-behavioral interventions* (pp. 213–236). New York: Pergamon Press.

Werry, J. S., Elkind, G. S., & Reeves, J. C. (1987). Attention deficit, conduct, oppositional, and anxiety disorders in children: III. Laboratory differences. *Journal of Abnormal Child Psychology, 15,* 409–428.

Wills, T. A., & Filer, M. (1996). Stress-coping model of adolescent substance use. In T. H. Ollendick & R. J. Prinz (Eds.), *Advances in clinical child psychology* (Vol. 18, pp. 91–132). New York: Plenum Press.

Wills, T. A., McNamara, G., Vaccaro, D., & Hirkey, A. E. (1996). Escalated substance use: A longitudinal grouping analysis from early to middle adolescence. *Journal of Abnormal Child Psychology, 105,* 166–180.

Windle, M. (1990). A longitudinal study of antisocial behavior in early adolescence as predictors of late adolescent substance use: Gender and ethnic group differences. *Journal of Abnormal Psychology, 99,* 86–91.

Zelli, A., Dodge, K. A., Lochman, J. E., Laird, R. D., & the Conduct Problems Prevention Research Group. (1999). The distinction between beliefs legitimizing aggression and deviant processing of social cues: Testing measurement validity and the hypothesis that biased processing mediates the effects of beliefs on aggression. *Journal of Personality and Social Psychology, 77,* 150–166.

Zillmann, D. (1994). Cognition–excitation interdependencies in the escalation of anger and angry aggression. In M. Potegal & J. F. Knutson (Eds.), *Biological and social processes in dyads and groups* (pp. 45–71). Hillsdale, NJ: Erlbaum.

CHAPTER 3

Attention-Deficit/
Hyperactivity Disorder
The Search for Viable Treatments

Stephen P. Hinshaw

Of necessity, this chapter takes a somewhat different approach from its counterparts in this volume. The chief reason is that, unlike the other disorders, conditions, and problems represented in the companion chapters, many children with attention-deficit/hyperactivity disorder (ADHD) have proven quite refractory to the types of treatment procedures that are typically categorized as cognitive-behavioral. Indeed, in the last 15 years, mounting negative evidence regarding the potential benefits of cognitive-behavioral treatment for children with ADHD has rendered the field nearly moribund. Furthermore, even when one considers approaches that are more strictly behavioral than cognitive in focus, for which better evidence regarding ADHD-related efficacy exists, seminal investigations completed in the 1990s indicate the superiority of pharmacological treatments with respect to important outcome domains (MTA Cooperative Group, 1999a; Pelham, Carlson, Sams, Vallano, & Dixon, 1993). Thus, a viable question arises as to the viability of psychosocial treatment procedures, particularly those utilizing a cognitive/mediational approach, for youth with ADHD.

What is the true state of affairs? For one thing, cognitively based interventions, which may be successful with subclinical cases or school-identified "impulsive" children, may simply not be powerful enough for clinical samples of children with ADHD. Yet, despite the relatively stronger effects of medication, psychosocial treatments grounded in behavioral contingencies can indeed make a positive impact on ADHD-related symptomatology (Hinshaw, Klein, & Abikoff, 1998). In these pages, I contend that cognitive additions to behaviorally based interventions may be clinically beneficial, particularly for extending their benefits over time and across settings, but I also state clearly that the field must be cognizant of current evidence regarding the clear limitations of strictly cognitive procedures for individuals with clinical levels of ADHD.

Thus, how to organize this chapter? Do I provide a detailed description of cognitively based treatment procedures, which, in the present case, have proven to improve the functioning of the population of interest? Or do I take a "review chapter" approach, considering critically the nonsupportive empirical investigations and the potential reasons for the lack of significant benefit of such treatments for this diagnostic category? My solution is to attempt both. In the spirit of promoting empirically supported treatments (Kazdin & Weisz, 1998; Kendall, 1998; Ollendick & King, Chapter 9, this volume), I emphasize strategies that clearly blend "behavioral," contingency-based programs with "cognitive," mediational strategies. I also feature treatments that can influence the crucially important domains of social functioning and peer relations, which are major sources of impairment for children with ADHD (Hinshaw, 1999; Whalen & Henker, 1992). Furthermore, by devoting attention to the mechanisms that may underlie ADHD related symptomatology and impairment, I raise the issue of just what types of psychosocial treatments will need to be developed in the future, both as supplements to medication-based interventions and as procedures that may be able to stand on their own.

As in the first edition of this chapter (Hinshaw & Erhardt, 1991), I must point out two key facts. First, traditional, contingency-based, "behavioral" treatments clearly contain a number of cognitive elements (e.g., the child is involved in the selection of reinforcers; reward schedules are thinned as the child takes on more responsibility for self-management; effective behavior management programs emphasize the child's need for planning and problem solving). Thus, the distinction between behavioral and cognitive elements is necessarily indistinct. Second, if they are to be at all effective for children with clinical levels of ADHD, cognitive procedures must explicitly include contingency management and other empirically supported behavioral strategies. The road to intrinsic motivation for most children and adolescents with ADHD begins with skills building and behavior management, extrinsically rewarded, before internal, cognitive changes will appear. In short, given the pressing need to develop, investigate, and disseminate any effective psychosocial treatments for the multiple problems related to ADHD, I prefer not to debate what is "behavioral" and what is "cognitive" in these pages, but rather to focus on an integrated conception of cognitive-behavioral interventions as inclusive of affect, motivation, family and school contexts, as well as modification of cognitions per se (Braswell & Bloomquist, 1991; Kendall & MacDonald, 1993).

FUNDAMENTALS OF ADHD

I begin with an overview of ADHD, emphasizing (1) important subtypes of this condition; (2) comorbidity—the extensive overlap of ADHD with other behavioral, emotional, and learning disorders; (3) the substantial impairment in key functional domains that ADHD engenders; (4) important assessment principles regarding the accurate evaluation of this diagnostic category; (5) recent information on etiology, including genetic liability, early biological risk factors, and relational influences; and (6) current theoretical advances regarding ADHD's underlying processes and mechanisms. Historical conceptions of this disorder are described in Hinshaw and Erhardt (1991) and Schachar (1986); more detailed coverage of ADHD-related issues appears in recent references (e.g., Barkley, 1998; Hinshaw, 1999; Tannock, 1998). My objective herein is to give appreciation of the complex psychobiological, familial, school-related, and social transactions in which ADHD yields such clear impairment, and in which treatment efforts must be directly made, as well as the types of underlying deficits pertinent to this disorder, which may serve as foci for more conceptually derived interventions in the future.

Description and Subtypes

The diagnostic criteria for ADHD mandate developmentally extreme symptoms in the domains of inattention/disorganization or hyperactivity/impulsivity that are of early onset (before the age of 7 years), long-standing (at least 6 months' duration), pervasive (displayed in multiple situations), and impairing (see American Psychiatric Association, 1994). Because difficulties with allocating sustained attention to academic tasks, inhibiting behavior in the face of temptation for immediate gain, and refraining from excess motor behavior are nearly ubiquitous in early to middle childhood, particularly in structured educational settings, critics have contended that ADHD has been overdiagnosed in the 1990s (e.g., Diller, 1998). Yet substantial evidence supports the validity of ADHD on the basis of such important features as diagnostic reliability, coherence of the syndrome, cross-cultural manifestations, and evidence for clear impairment that emanates from the symptom picture when an appropriate diagnosis is made (Barkley, 1998; Hinshaw, 1999; Lahey & Willcutt, in press).

Subtypes of ADHD that are listed in the fourth edition of the *Diagnostic and Statistical Manual of Mental Disorders* (DSM-IV; American Psychiatric Association, 1994) pertain to the types of symptoms that are displayed[1]; that is, children with extreme levels of inattention (but not hyperactivity/impulsivity) are categorized as the predominantly inattentive type; those with high degrees of hyperactivity/impulsivity (but not inattention) are placed in the predominantly hyperactive/impulsive type; and those with impairing symptoms in both domains comprise the combined type. Importantly, despite their different presentations, all ADHD subtypes have been shown to be valid (Lahey et al., 1994). Whereas epidemiological studies suggest that, in community samples, the inattentive type is the most prevalent (e.g., Lahey & Willcutt, in press), the combined type is the most likely to be referred for clinical services. Thus, clinicians who treat ADHD must contend most often with multiple problems of sustaining attention, managing impulse control, and regulating excessive motor activity, in addition to the crucial impairments and comorbidities that pertain to this multifaceted symptom presentation (the following sections).

Once believed to be a transient disorder limited to childhood, ADHD has clearly been shown to persist through adolescence in a majority of cases, and through young adulthood in a plurality (Johnston, in press; Klein & Mannuzza, 1991). Viable intervention during a child's early years may therefore prevent a lifetime of accumulating difficulties. The overall prevalence of ADHD appears to be approximately 3–5% of the school-age population (American Psychiatric Association, 1994), with boys more likely than girls to meet diagnostic criteria, particularly for the hyperactive/impulsive and combined types. Girls with ADHD are, in fact, an understudied population; treatment research with female samples is rare but extremely needed.

A basic description of symptom patterns of inattention, impulsivity, and hyperactivity does not begin to do justice to the extent and kinds of problems that children and adolescents with ADHD experience in everyday interactions with parents, teachers, friends, and the world at large. Such youth often have marked difficulties managing and coping with many requirements of society, with resultant decrements in self-esteem and self-perceptions (Slomkowski, Klein, & Mannuzza, 1995; Treuting & Hinshaw, 2000). The intensity of reactions, the lack of emotion regulation, the poor judgment, the "out of sync" quality of social interactions, the clear problems with keeping organized, and the long-term risk for substance abuse and delinquency—all combine to document the devastating impact of ADHD on children, families, and schools.

Comorbidity

It is a relative rarity to witness a case of ADHD that is unaccompanied by one or more additional disorders (Bird, Gould, & Staghezza-Jaramillo, 1994). In other words, comorbidity is the rule rather than the exception with respect to ADHD (Hinshaw, Lahey, & Hart, 1993; Jensen, Martin, &

Cantwell, 1997). First, in approximately half of the cases of ADHD, there is clear association with significant levels of aggressive-spectrum symptomatology, which, in psychiatric terminology, may qualify for diagnoses of oppositional defiant disorder (ODD) or conduct disorder (CD) (see Hinshaw, 1987; Jensen et al., 1997). Children with combinations of ADHD and such disruptive disorders are at marked risk for a host of severe difficulties, including virulent family histories of both ADHD and antisocial-spectrum problems, deficits in verbal skills, grave levels of peer rejection, and a long-term course marked by substantial risk for continuing antisocial behavior patterns (see Hinshaw, 1999). When referred for treatment, youth with this pattern of comorbidity present a blend of intraindividual and family-related difficulties that is difficult to alter.

Second, it may come as somewhat of a surprise to learn that ADHD also displays rather strong overlap with so-called "internalizing" disorders, those marked by a predominance of anxious, withdrawn, and even depressive features (Biederman, Newcorn, & Sprich, 1991; Treuting & Hinshaw, 1999). In fact, up to one-third of youth with ADHD show such patterns of comorbidity (Jensen et al., 1997; MTA Cooperative Group, 1999b).[2] Although less is known about such overlap than about the ADHD–aggression linkage, evidence is accumulating that youth with ADHD plus significant anxiety disorders may show different patterns of treatment response than do ADHD youngsters without such comorbidity (MTA Cooperative Group, 1999b), a topic to which I return in discussing moderators of treatment outcome.

Third, about one in five or six children with ADHD also displays a marked learning disability, defined as a large disparity between academic performance (usually in reading) and IQ. When ADHD is combined with such learning disabilities, the typical stimulant medication treatments that are employed facilitate some aspects of achievement but do not appear to alter the underlying processing deficits—for example, phonemic awareness and phonologic processing related to reading—that compromise learning. Thus, psychosocial interventions that directly target academic problems are a priority, particularly for this subgroup.

In short, the strong degree of overlap between ADHD and other, significant psychiatric syndromes signals both the considerable distance the field must travel to understand the mechanisms responsible for such association and the clear clinical challenges presented by children and adolescents with these multiple-symptom pictures.

Impairment

When clinically significant levels of ADHD are present, the syndrome is associated with clear impairment in precisely those domains of functioning that are essential for competence in development (Hinshaw, in press). Such impairment is evident even (1) when impairment criteria are eliminated from the diagnostic algorithm, thereby preventing the potential for circular reasoning, and (2) comorbid disorders are controlled for, signifying the specific linkage of impairment to ADHD rather than to associated conditions (e.g., Lahey et al., 1994).

First of all, even in cases without comorbid learning disabilities, ADHD is strongly related to poor school-related and academic performance, as evidenced by both lowered achievement test scores and such other indicators as retention, expulsion, special education placement, and dropping out (Barkley, 1998; Hinshaw, in press). School-based intervention is therefore essential for contending with ADHD.

Second, family-related impairment has been clearly documented, as evidenced by high rates of discordant parent–child interactions, substantial parenting stress and distress, and higher-than-expected levels of marital dissatisfaction and divorce among families with an ADHD child (Barkley, 1998). Although relational disturbances have been causally linked to the development of ADHD symptoms in one investigation of high-risk, inner-city families (Carlson, Jacobvitz, & Sroufe, 1995), for the most part, it appears that the aforementioned indicators of distress result from (rather than cause) ADHD. In reality, transactional, reciprocal patterns of causation are most likely. Regardless of the direction of the causal arrow, meaningful interventions for ADHD must directly target home life and family interaction patterns.

Third, perhaps the most devastating impairment relates to the strong tendency for children with ADHD to experience substantial levels of rejection from their peers (Pelham & Bender, 1982; Hinshaw & Melnick, 1995). Indeed, ADHD youngsters may be disliked to a greater extent than nearly all other diagnostic groupings; they come to be rejected by age-mates after quite brief periods of interaction, measurable in minutes or hours (Erhardt & Hinshaw, 1994; Bickett & Milich, 1990), and negative regard from peers is quite stable once it has formed. Because peer rejection has been repeatedly linked with poor long-term outcomes such as school dropout, delinquency, and mental health problems in adulthood (Parker & Asher, 1987), it is no wonder that ADHD is documented to be a persistent disorder with long-term consequences for compromised development. Peer rejection is nearly universal for children with comorbid ADHD and aggression, but even when aggressive behavior is not present, ADHD children are still more quite likely to encounter significant peer disapprobation (Hinshaw & Melnick, 1995). It is noteworthy that the inattentive type of ADHD is more clearly associated with peer neglect than with active peer rejection, which characterizes the hyperactive/impulsive and combined types (Lahey et al., 1994, 1998). As with school- and home-related impairments, the problems with social interactions and peer relations of children with ADHD are a crucially salient target for intervention strategies.

Fourth, another domain of notable impairment for children with ADHD relates to their penchant for accidental injuries, including those that can be quite severe—falling and breaking bones, being hit by cars; swallowing poisons accidentally (see Hinshaw, in press). By late adolescence, high rates of driving-related impairments and accidents pertain to ADHD samples (Barkley, 1998). Many of these types of accidents relate directly to the problems with impulse control that plague those ADHD children in the hyperactive/impulsive and combined types. Thus, another challenge for designers of treatments is contending with and preventing the damaging effects of accidental injury, which (in the case of head injuries) may serve to exacerbate ADHD-related symptomatology. Finally, ADHD is associated with marked impairments in such crucial life skills as motoric competence, performance of self-care skills, and overall independence (Stein, Szumowski, Blondis, & Roizen, 1995). That is, despite normal-range IQ scores, many children and adolescents with ADHD have failed to attain the kinds of adaptive functioning necessary for successful performance in society. Although this domain is not often considered in the development of treatment strategies for ADHD, it would be wise to do so.

Overall, clear ADHD-related impairments in crucial domains relevant to healthy development (1) serve to validate the status of ADHD as a "real" clinical disorder with devastating consequences, (2) emphasize the need for development of viable preventive and clinical intervention strategies, and (3) highlight the need for policy initiatives related to societal accommodations related to ADHD.

Assessment and Evaluation

Space permits only a brief outline of assessment-related principles for the accurate evaluation of ADHD; for detailed coverage, see Barkley (1998), as well as Hinshaw and Nigg (1999). First and foremost, ADHD cannot be accurately evaluated in a brief, 5- to 10-minute examination of the child and discussion with parents (as may be all too common in some pediatric practices). There are a host of reasons why children show high levels of inattention or overactivity at school or home—including neurological disorders, reactions to traumatic stressors (including abuse), or dysfunction in the family system, to name just three—and the process of differential diagnosis cannot be performed casually or quickly. Indeed, one essential aspect of a viable assessment is a thorough history of the child and family, in order to place ADHD-related symptomatology in historical and situational context, and to rule out a host of alternate conceptualizations.

Second, even the most sensitive clinicians cannot typically discern ADHD-related symptomatology on the basis of the child's behavior in the clinic. Indeed, children with ADHD are often quite responsive to novelty; during an office visit, a child with markedly disorganized and disruptive behavior patterns at school or home can often "hold it together" quite well. Thus, false-negative appraisals may result. Information from parents and teachers, who see the child as he or she typically performs in daily life functions, is essential for assessment and diagnosis. Well-normed rating scales, which allow parent and teacher perspectives on typical functioning, are therefore quite helpful in the evaluation process (Hinshaw & Nigg, 1999).

A third point is that because of the multiplicity of problems displayed by most children with ADHD, as well as the high rates of comorbidity that pertain to ADHD, narrowly constructed "ADHD checklists" are not as helpful in the diagnostic workup as are broader scales that afford information about internalizing and acting-out behavior patterns as well as inattention/hyperactivity per se (Hinshaw & Nigg, 1999). Narrower, ADHD-specific scales can be utilized at the next stage, in order to probe subtypes of ADHD and yield finer-grained examination of specific symptom patterns, but only after the broader range of psychopathology has been ascertained. Individual testing is typically necessary to discern achievement patterns and, potentially, neuropsychological correlates, but it does not establish the behavioral basis for diagnosis.

Fourth, although it may be essential to include the child's own perspectives during the evaluation process, and although children themselves may be optimal informants with respect to both internalizing symptomatology and noteworthy antisocial behaviors, youth are rather dramatic underreporters of ADHD-related symptomatology. Thus, in establishing a diagnosis of ADHD, the child's self-report should be deemphasized in favor of information from parents and teachers. Yet the child's own information is often crucial regarding internalizing disorders and thought disturbance.

Fifth, whereas neurological and medical evaluations may be necessary in the process of differential diagnosis, positive findings in these domains are not at all required for a diagnosis of ADHD. Furthermore, whereas laboratory tasks measuring attentional functioning are yielding important empirical findings related to underlying mechanisms, they are not, at present, sufficiently sensitive or specific to be of much use in the evaluation of individual children to rule in or rule out ADHD. In short, despite active investigation into fundamental cognitive, attentional, and information-processing mechanisms pertinent to the underpinnings of ADHD (to be discussed), the diagnosis remains a behavioral one.

Finally, evaluation of ADHD does not stop with the initial workup, nor should it be limited to ADHD symptoms per se. Ongoing assessment throughout treatment, incorporating information about associated internalizing and externalizing problems, family interaction patterns, self-perceptions, school performance, and peer relations, is necessary to monitor the success (or lack thereof) of the chosen intervention strategies (Hinshaw, March, et al., 1997). Repeated evaluation throughout and beyond treatment need not be as time-consuming as the initial workup; brief symptom checklists and ongoing appraisals of functioning can be performed economically with proper planning.

Risk Factors and Etiology

Perhaps the most important message to convey regarding the broad topic of causal factors related to ADHD is that there is no single etiological sequence or pathway leading to this disorder. In other words, what the field conceptualizes as the syndrome of ADHD is actually quite heterogeneous, both symptomatically and etiologically (Hinshaw, 1994). A key hope for future research is that ADHD's multiple developmental pathways can be better elucidated.

1. In the past decade, a series of twin studies have yielded evidence for startlingly high estimates of the heritability of ADHD, in the neighborhood of .7–.8 (see review in Tannock, 1998). Although these estimates may be inflated, in some cases, because of the use of maternal estimates of ADHD symptomatology (which may invoke contrast effects in the appraisal of dizygotic, or fraternal, twins), the evidence clearly supports the fact that ADHD is as heritable as schizophrenia or depression, even approaching figures associated with bipolar disorder. An important corollary here is that such strong heritability estimates pertain to dimensions of ADHD symptomatology and not to a diagnostic category per se; what tends to be inherited is a vulnerability to the spectrum of ADHD-related behaviors rather than a "disorder" (Levy, Hay, McStephen, Wood, & Waldman, 1997). Also, I must point out that heritability refers to the proportion of individual differences in a trait that is attributable to genetic, rather than environmental, influences; it does not speak to the joint roles of genes and environment in shaping a given person's symptom picture, nor to the strong roles that environments can play in altering phenotypic expression of highly heritable traits (e.g., Rutter et al., 1990; Hinshaw & Park, 1999).

Quite recently, several candidate genes have been linked to the expression of ADHD—most notably, the dopamine transporter gene and the gene responsible for creating the fourth known neural receptor for dopamine (the DR4R gene; for a review, see Tannock, 1998). It is quite conceivable that in the next decade, these or other "susceptibility" genes will be established as providing known liability for a subset of cases of ADHD.

An important clinical implication from the strongly heritable nature of ADHD is that biological relatives of children and adolescents with ADHD are themselves quite likely to display subclinical or clinical manifestations of the disorder. Treatment of ADHD, which of necessity involves active family cooperation and collaboration, is therefore a continuing challenge when family disorganization, denial, and/or lack of follow-through are part of the genetic legacy of the disorder.

2. Other biological (but nongenetic) risk factors have been found to

contribute substantially to ADHD. One salient example is low birth weight (defined as birth at under 2,500 grams, or approximately 5.5 pounds), which has been demonstrated in rigorous investigations to predict subsequent ADHD with specificity (e.g., Breslau et al., 1996; Whitaker et al., 1997). In fact, a host of prenatal and perinatal risk factors, including birth complications and maternal ingestion of tobacco, alcohol, and other psychoactive substances, predispose to later ADHD-related symptomatology (Tannock, 1998). At a policy level, the lack of our society's emphasis on adequate prenatal care appears to be a major culprit in the genesis of this major form of child psychopathology.

3. Because of recent emphasis on these biological contributions to ADHD, some commentators have contended that parenting and early socialization are not relevant to ADHD-related behavioral manifestations and impairment. Such positions betray a misunderstanding of the nature of heritability and an unfortunate tendency toward biological reductionism. First, the early temperamental proclivities that are "inherited" must necessarily interact with the early rearing environment to produce clinical-level manifestations. Thus, temperament–parenting "fit" (Chess & Thomas, 1984) is an understudied yet crucial variable in the genesis of ADHD. Second, investigations conducted at my own summer research programs for children with ADHD show clearly that parenting attitudes and practices are related to impairments (and strengths) in boys and girls with this disorder. For example, Anderson, Hinshaw, and Simmel (1994) demonstrated that the degree of maternal negativity and hostility directed toward a son with ADHD—even controlling for the negativity and noncompliance directed by the boy toward his mother—predicted levels of covert antisocial behavior (stealing) and general noncompliance exhibited at our naturalistic summer setting. In addition, Hinshaw, Zupan, Simmel, Nigg, and Melnick (1997) found that the strongest predictor of positive sociometric status among boys with ADHD was the degree to which their mothers displayed authoritative (warm, limit setting, encouraging autonomy) parenting beliefs. Indeed, such a maternal parenting style outperformed the boys' own behavioral interactions with one another in predicting such social competence; it also served as a protective factor against peer rejection in the ADHD sample. In short, despite the strongly biological underpinnings of ADHD, family socialization is critical in shaping the types of aggressive and antisocial comorbidity—and even the peer-related competencies—that are crucial for the long-term outcomes of youth with this disorder.

Underlying Mechanisms

The search for the "fundamental deficit" of ADHD has a long and tortuous history. Because of the multiple etiological pathways to ADHD described earlier, it appears that there is no "theory of everything" related to this condition. The search for the nature of basic ADHD-related deficits continues.

In terms of neuroanatomical localization of ADHD, nearly every region of the brain, from the brain stem to the prefrontal lobes, has been invoked as fundamentally involved in ADHD-related symptomatology. Frontal and frontal–striatal circuits have received the most consistent support in recent years (Barkley, 1998; Tannock, 1998), with implications for "executive" deficits in planful behavior and in the regulation of motor output. More explicitly psychological theories have also been proffered, but some that were once ascendant (e.g., a fundamental deficit in sustained attention) are highly debated (Barkley, 1997b). Is ADHD a problem of oversensitivity to reward? Of poorly regulated arousal? Of fundamental problems in motivation? Of dysregulation of emotional control? Of verbal mediation? Each of these positions has been advanced (Hinshaw, 1994), but none has received unequivocal support. Complicating matters further, models that emphasize overactivity and behavioral impulsivity cannot readily contend with the inattentive type of ADHD, which features hypoactivity, a sluggish tempo, and even an apparently different type of attentional deficit from that found in more hyperactive/impulsive variants.

Barkley's (1997a, 1997b) unifying theory of ADHD has captured considerable interest in the latter part of the 1990s. Noting its qualitatively distinct nature, Barkley omits the inattentive type and posits that the fundamental deficit in combined and hyperactive/impulsive types of ADHD—and a highly heritable one—is found in the individual's difficulties with basic inhibitory processes, such as those related to the need to suspend a previously rewarded or prepotent response, or to control "interference." Barkley contends that this fundamental deficit in inhibitory control spurs cascading problems in four distinct executive functions, subserved by the frontal lobes; these problems, in turn, portend poorly planned and poorly integrated motor responses. Despite its preliminary nature (Hinshaw, 1998), Barkley's theory admirably leads to testable hypotheses and has already generated considerable research.

To the extent that it is accurate, this model implies that the core deficit of ADHD occurs at a basic neuropsychological level of inhibitory processing, which is temporally prior to (and, indeed, sets the stage for) such verbal processes as self-directed speech (Berk & Potts, 1991). One implication is that interventions attempting to teach self-regulation through verbal self-control may be occurring too late and too far downstream for clinical success. Indeed, as noted at the outset, treatments emphasizing verbal mediation have proven notoriously unsuccessful with clinical samples of youth with ADHD.

Summary

ADHD is a disorder involving long-standing, developmentally extreme, and pervasive difficulties in attentional deployment, impulse control, and regulation of excessive motor behavior. Its subtypes are focused around the "poles" of inattentive/disorganized versus hyperactive/impulsive domains. Often occurring with comorbid conditions—most notably, antisocial-spectrum disorders, internalizing syndromes, and/or learning deficits—ADHD yields clear, even devastating impairment in key domains (school functioning, home life, peer relations, accidental injuries, adaptive behavior) that are highly related to long-term success. The symptom composite is strongly heritable; yet other biological risks (prenatal insult, low birth weight) exist, and the "fit" of temperamental style with parenting practices is critical for expression of impairments and competencies. Among a host of competing explanations, fundamental problems in inhibitory control appear central for the combined and hyperactive/impulsive types; but the field has not yet conclusively demonstrated knowledge of such underlying processes. Perhaps the clearest message is that, left untreated, ADHD portends a lifelong pattern of compromised functioning, mandating the development and promotion of effective treatment procedures.

BEHAVIORAL AND COGNITIVE-BEHAVIORAL TREATMENTS: RATIONALE AND FINDINGS

Conceptual Underpinnings of Behavioral and Cognitive Interventions

Paraphrasing from the previous section, children with ADHD lack behavioral compliance and control; they fail to display intrinsic motivation for task completion; they do not display rule-governed behavior; and they respond erratically under typical home and classroom conditions of delayed and inconsistent reward (Barkley, 1998; Hinshaw, 1994). On these grounds, ADHD would appear to be tailor-made for intervention programs that feature regular and consistent reinforcers. Such reinforcement could pave the way toward skills building and behavior management, with the gradual development of intrinsic motivation in task performance.

A long-standing issue with respect to contingency-based programs for such children is the extent to which gains will generalize across situations or maintain over time, once such structured extrinsic reinforcement is absent. Several decades ago, a key rationale for adding cognitive components to behavioral contingencies was to foster explicitly just such "extensions" of treatment gains, by teaching the child to manage his or her own behavior through problem-solving, verbal mediation, and error-coping strategies. Indeed, the 1970s witnessed a surge of interest in the application of cognitive-behavioral treatment procedures to children and adolescents with this disorder. Innovators such as Meichenbaum (1977) contended that the regulatory deficits of what was then termed "hyperactivity" were extremely well-matched for the types of self-instructional, problem-solving interventions that were being developed (for empirical evidence, see Bugental, Whalen, & Henker, 1977).

From a somewhat different perspective, Kendall and MacDonald (1993) differentiate two fundamental classes of cognitive disturbance in child psychopathology. First, cognitive *distortions* pertain to certain child disorders—for example, anxiety and depression, with their often-displayed overgeneralization and catastrophizing; aggression and conduct disturbance, with their characteristic "hostile attributional bias" in the face of ambiguous social situations. A host of cognitive therapeutic strategies have been developed to modify and redirect such cognitive distortions. Second, cognitive *deficiencies* apply to other conditions, most saliently ADHD, which is characterized by deficient problem solving and verbal mediation, as well as a general cognitive immaturity (Barkley, 1997a, 1998).[3] In contrast to altering distorted cognitions, it may be a far more difficult task to remediate deficient thinking patterns and strategies. Furthermore, as discussed earlier, it is conceivable that the core deficit of ADHD occurs "preverbally," so that approaches based on verbal mediation do not directly tackle the underlying mechanism. I return to this issue in the final section of the chapter.

Relevant Outcome Research

To frame the illustrations of treatment procedures that are a major focus of the chapter, I first give a brief overview of empirical evidence regarding behavioral and cognitive-behavioral interventions as applied to ADHD. Despite some promising initial findings regarding cognitively based interventions in early research (see reviews of Hinshaw & Erhardt, 1991; Kendall & MacDonald, 1993), when cognitive-behavioral procedures were then applied in experimental trials with clinical samples of youth with ADHD (e.g., Abikoff & Gittelman, 1985; Abikoff et al., 1988), treatment gains were found to be almost nonexistent (see Abikoff, 1991; Hinshaw & Erhardt, 1991). Whereas children with subclinical levels of attentional deficits or impulsivity can benefit from intervention focused on verbal mediation (Braswell & Bloomquist, 1991), and whereas children with aggressive behavior have also been found to show improvement with cognitive-behavioral treatments targeted to problem-solving skills (see Lochman et al., Chapter 2, this volume), youngsters with diagnostic levels of ADHD appear to be quite refractory to these kinds of treatment.

Exceptions to the general trend can be found in the short-term trials conducted earlier in my own career, in which (1) cognitive-behavioral training for anger control was shown to be superior to cognitive training in empathy (Hinshaw, Henker, & Whalen 1984a), and (2) the addition of a cognitive, self-evaluation procedure enhanced the effects of behavioral reinforcement for promoting improved social behavior in playground settings

(Hinshaw, Henker, & Whalen, 1984b). Note that in these trials, which measured only acute effects of the interventions, the effective treatments were truly cognitive-behavioral in nature. Only when cognitive-mediational procedures for anger management and self-evaluation were paired with traditional, behavioral contingency management did significant gains emerge. No evidence was found for clinically sufficient benefits of self-instructional training or mediational strategies alone. Thus, an initial lesson for practitioners contemplating clinical work with children or adolescents with ADHD—and one that I emphasize throughout—is that any cognitive aspects of intervention must clearly be linked with behavioral reinforcement strategies.

To place this discussion in a larger context of behavioral intervention strategies for children and adolescents with hyperactive and "externalizing" behavioral difficulties, I utilize and extend a tripartite framework for describing behavioral interventions (see Hinshaw et al., 1998; Pelham & Hinshaw, 1992).

1. *Direct contingency management.* The most "basic" level of behavioral intervention involves the direct application of positive and negative contingencies in carefully engineered environments, usually special education or residential settings. With such procedures, strong effects of reward programs and response–cost contingencies on behavioral and academic targets have been repeatedly demonstrated, usually through single-case experimental designs (see review in Pelham & Hinshaw, 1992). It is important to note that the programmatic research of O'Leary, Pfiffner, and colleagues has shown that prudent negative consequences, including time-out and response–cost, are particularly effective for children with ADHD, so long as rewarding contingencies are also used. A major issue, however, is the transportability and generalizability of such highly individualized, direct contingency management programs to home, school, and peer settings.

2. *Clinical behavior therapy.* The most common application of behavioral procedures to children with disruptive and attentional problems involves this category of interventions, in which parents and teachers receive consultation from a behavioral expert in such tactics as measuring behavior, targeting problems for intervention, devising a reinforcement menu and token reward program, utilizing consistent (and nonphysical) punishment procedures, and coordinating programs between home and school. Thus, the "clientele" for such behavior therapy consultation consist of key adults in the child's environment, who receive training in the implementation of home- and school-based behavioral programs. Such interventions have led to significant gains for children with ADHD (Hinshaw et al., 1998). As expected, however, improvements are not as large as those from direct contingency management per se, and benefits typically fall short of normalization or full clinical significance. Furthermore, the outcome measures that show

improvement usually constitute ratings from the same parents and teachers who conduct the intervention, potentially involving a positive "halo" from satisfaction with the treatment rather than from objectively observed social or academic improvements.

3. *Cognitive-behavioral interventions.* Here, the intervention is typically conducted directly with the child, either individually or in small-group formats. Common procedures include training in (1) self-instructions, designed to enhance verbal mediation and self-control by fading from adult-directed instruction to child "overt" speech, to child self-directed speech that is "covert"; (2) problem solving, with the aim of providing a scheme for better planning of social and academic behavior; (3) self-reinforcement, so that there is less dependence on adult sources of reward; and (4) error coping, in order that the child redirect him- or herself from mistakes or problematic situations. Application of these procedures to analogue tasks, actual academic work, and interpersonal situations is performed according to systematic curricula. As noted earlier, despite the success of these kinds of cognitive, mediational strategies with subclinical populations of "impulsive" children, or with children at risk for aggression, applications to youth with ADHD have not yielded significant improvement in any measured domains. Although one might consider ADHD to be an ideally suited group for such applications, the empirical data dictate otherwise.

To these three prototypes of behavioral intervention, I add an additional modality:

4. *Social skills training.* This type of treatment is typically performed in small groups, where clinicians utilize discussions of relevant concepts (e.g., cooperation, validation), repeated behavioral rehearsal, and direct reward of socially skilled behaviors to promote better interpersonal interactions (for an early prototype, see Oden & Asher, 1977). Because the clinical focus is on direct work with children or adolescents rather than application of contingencies in school settings or consultation with adults, such a social skills intervention is quite similar to cognitive-behavioral treatment in terms of format. The key distinction, however, is that social skills training typically deemphasizes verbal self-instructions or training in self-reinforcement and focuses on rehearsal and direct rewards to the group members for better approximations of socially competent behavior. Clearly, however, some cognitive components are utilized (see Pfiffner & McBurnett, 2000). Although early manifestations of social skills training produced mixed results with children with ADHD and other kinds of disruptive children, more recent and systematic applications have produced robust benefits (Pfiffner & McBurnett, 1997). Excerpts from this curriculum appear later in the chapter.

Both direct contingency management and clinical behavior therapy procedures appear to be attempts to shape the environment of the individual with ADHD, by providing clear rewards and punishments, by altering parent and teacher expectations, and by making appropriate accommodations in task demands. Cognitive-mediational and social skills treatments, on the other hand, prioritize changing the inner workings of the child, through the teaching of self-instructional speech, problem-solving strategies, self-evaluation and self-reinforcement skills, and explicit instruction in peer-related competencies. In terms of viable clinical practice, however, this differentiation between "outer" environmental strategies versus "inner" cognitive/psychological treatments is more apparent than real (see, e.g., Kendall & MacDonald, 1993). The goal of any environmental modification for youth with ADHD is subsequently to encourage better behavior, academic performance, and social competence in more naturalistic settings—through thinning of reward schedules, fading of prompts and cues, and even the addition of cognitive self-evaluation, self-reinforcement, and error-coping strategies to promote generalization and maintenance. Similarly, any cognitive procedures that are expected to be useful for this population cannot be taught in a vacuum; direct rewarding of the use of self-control treatments, extensive behavioral rehearsal, and altering home and school environments to encourage self-regulation must supplement the direct work with the individual. In fact, the social skills curriculum of Pfiffner and McBurnett (1997) expressly incorporated supplemental parent training, designed to promote the gains from the child therapy groups. Given the daunting nature of the task at hand—to develop viable intervention procedures for this extremely impairing condition, any partisanship about what is "behavioral" versus what is "cognitive" is bound to be counterproductive. Investigators and practitioners of cognitive-behavioral procedures must be cognizant of multiple facets of a child's functioning, including affective, behavioral, cognitive, familial, and school-related facets (Kendall & MacDonald, 1993).

Comparison and Combination with Stimulant Medication

A crucial issue in evaluating treatment outcome research for youth with ADHD pertains to the high levels of efficacy that have been shown for pharmacological treatment for this population (Klein & Wender, 1995; Greenhill & Osman, 1999). Indeed, the use of stimulant medications is sufficiently prevalent and effective (at least in the short run) that no discussion of psychosocial treatment procedures for ADHD can be complete without considering the medication as a standard of comparison.

Stimulant medications produce, in over 80% of carefully diagnosed youth with ADHD, clear benefit with respect to core symptomatology, associated impairments in home and school domains, and the reciprocal interactions of parents, teachers, and, to some extent, peers (Hinshaw & McHale, 1991; MTA Cooperative Group, 1999a; Swanson, McBurnett, Christian, & Wigal, 1995). Individual differences in medication response are vast, however. Furthermore, the role of medications with respect to actual academic progress is less clear. Critically, pharmacological benefits last only as long as the medication is in the child's system (Gillberg, Melander, van Knorring, & Janols, 1997). In this latter respect, stimulant treatment of ADHD is quite similar to typical behavioral intervention, which also tends not to persist beyond the life of the contingencies that are put in place. Indeed, a major impetus for the development and promotion of cognitive-behavioral treatments for ADHD 25 years ago was the hope that such mediational procedures—"portable coping strategies," in the terminology of Meichenbaum (1977)—could promote generalization and maintenance of contingency-based gains for this population. A continuing challenge for the entire field is the discovery of any interventions that can produce lasting benefits for the core symptoms and often-devastating impairments that pertain to ADHD.

In addition, medications may induce side effects, most of which are manageable but, in some cases, can be prohibitive. Furthermore, medication alone is rarely sufficient to normalize a child's or adolescent's functioning across relevant functional domains, and in some cases, the benefits of initially successful medication treatment can dissipate over time. Thus, limitations of pharmacological intervention mandate that psychosocial/behavioral treatments continue to be developed and investigated (for a more complete discussion, see Hinshaw & Erhardt, 1991).

Well-conducted, head-to-head comparisons of behavioral versus pharmacological procedures during the current decade have yielded provocative results. First, even powerful direct-contingency management procedures have been found to produce smaller effect sizes regarding important behavioral outcomes than stimulant medication (Pelham et al., 1993). Thus, even the strongest behavioral treatments may not fare as well as medications in terms of magnitude of effect. Second, in the Multimodal Treatment Study of Children with ADHD (MTA)—a long-term (14-month) comparison of systematic medication management versus an intensive combination of clinical behavior therapy (over 35 parent-training sessions paired with regular teacher consultation) plus direct contingency management (8-week summer treatment program as well as a paraprofessional aide in the child's classroom setting)—the medication procedures proved superior with regard to ADHD symptomatology, associated disruptive behaviors, and indicators of social skills (MTA Cooperative Group, 1999a). Note that such findings apply to averaged outcomes across participants; whether certain subgroups of children with ADHD exhibited preferential treatment response to psychosocial as opposed to medication treatments remains a key unanswered question (see the section later on moderators of outcome).

Another important question concerns the incremental benefit of combining effective behavioral or psychosocial treatments with medication-based interventions. Initial research, reviewed in Pelham and Murphy (1986), consistently revealed that combined treatment regimens yielded greater levels of improvement than single-modality interventions, even if the differences were not always statistically significant. Larger-scale clinical trials have produced mixed evidence: Hechtman and Abikoff (1995) found no significant increment from adding systematic behavioral and other psychosocial treatments to individually titrated medication, whereas the MTA Cooperative Group (1999a, 1999b) showed that the ancillary outcomes of internalizing comorbidity, family relations, and some indicators of social skills responded optimally to combination treatment, which outperformed medication alone. Additional analyses suggest strongly that, even for core ADHD-related symptomatology, combined treatment procedures were significantly more likely to produce large benefits; that is, excellent clinical response was highest with combined treatment.

Hence, a continuing question for the field is whether combination treatments may be better able to arrest the pernicious trajectory traveled by many children with ADHD. Relatedly, given the limitations of both behavioral and pharmacological treatments for producing lasting benefits, there is still an open question as to whether the right kinds of cognitive extensions of contingency management may help to extend benefits so that they are "internalized" by the child. Finally, for the minority of children with ADHD who either show prohibitive side effects to medication or whose families are not comfortable with a pharmacological approach, psychosocial treatments must be able to stand on their own.

Summary

In this section, I have provided an overview of key trends from three decades of behavioral (and pharmacological) intervention research for children with ADHD. With respect to behavioral interventions, direct contingency management can yield large effects for youth with this disorder, but usually in highly specialized settings and only so long as the contingencies are in effect. Clinical behavior therapy consultation with parents and teachers also yields significant (albeit short-lived) improvement, but gains are typically smaller (falling short of clinical significance) and are usually restricted to outcomes comprising ratings from the parents and teachers who are the recipients of the intervention (Hinshaw et al., 1998). Crucially, cognitive treatments designed to enhance mediation and problem solving have failed to yield positive effects for children and adolescents with clinical levels of ADHD. On the other hand, combining cognitive procedures with specific contingencies and extensive behavioral rehearsal (Hinshaw et al., 1984a, 1984b) may still be promising. Furthermore, social skills training, a broad category of intervention that overlaps to some extent with cognitive-behavioral strategies, has recently shown promise when rehearsal, specific contingencies, and coordination with parent-training efforts are combined with cognitive strategies designed to promote social competence (Pfiffner & McBurnett, 1997). As for pharmacological intervention, stimulant medication treatment provides a standard against which psychosocial treatments are typically compared in terms of the prevalence of stimulant treatment and the evidence for strong effects. These effects are typically superior to those of behavioral intervention but last only as long as pills are ingested; and evidence exists that combining behavioral with pharmacological approaches may yield optimal benefits in several key domains of functioning. In short, the types of cognitive-mediational approaches that have been found effective for other child populations are clinically insufficient for children with ADHD, mandating that I extend my illustrative review to procedures that explicitly combine cognitive strategies with direct contingency management, behavioral rehearsal, and training for generalization to nontherapy settings and maintenance over time.

RELEVANT PROCEDURES

Before describing exemplars of treatment procedures, I first note that an essential aspect of intervening with the population under consideration is coordination and collaboration; that is, given (1) the multiple problems and impairments displayed by children and adolescents with ADHD across diverse settings (home, school, peer groups, leisure activities) and (2) the need, in many instances, for treatments to span educational, family-related, social, and behavioral goals, consistency in service delivery and coordination of efforts is paramount. If services are fragmented, and if educators, medical personnel, psychologists, and paraprofessionals do not coordinate efforts, it is virtually a guarantee that intervention effects will be limited and spotty. The disorganization manifested by most individuals with ADHD must be countered by intensive organization and coordination among those attempting to forge more consistent environments and more productive performance.

Intervention for Social Skills

The social skills training (SST) curriculum of Pfiffner and McBurnett (1997, 2000) provides for just such coordination in that it includes as one condition in their randomized clinical trial supplemental parent groups, the purpose of which is to teach parents to support the transfer or generalization of social skills to their children's home and play environments. For the child-focused SST program, I excerpt from the manualized examples of the behavioral and cognitive-behavioral procedures (Pfiffner & McBurnett, 2000).

In this training program, participants (boys and girls with ADHD, with group size ranging from 6 to 9) receive a total of eight 90-minute weekly groups. The goals—to improve relationships with both peers and adults—are addressed through (1) remediating skills knowledge deficits, (2) remediating skills performance deficits, (3) fostering the child's recognition of verbal and nonverbal social cues, (4) teaching adaptive responding to new problem situations that arise, and (5) promoting generalization. For an overview, I quote from the manual (Pfiffner & McBurnett, 2000):

> The group includes a highly structured, high-density contingency management program. This reward system serves not only to increase the motivation of the children to participate but creates a more playful, "game-like" atmosphere for them. Specific skills are selected each day from the current skill module being taught. The session always begins with a clear introduction of the "skill of the week." These skills are presented didactically and through modeling (using enthusiasm and humor!). They are then taught to students using prompting, shaping, and rehearsal during "skill games" and role plays. Children are actively involved in generating examples, participating in the role plays, and evaluating when, where, and why to use the skill. To promote generalization, counselors prompt or suggest role plays for three different situations: 1) with peers, 2) in the classroom, and 3) at home with siblings or parents. . . . Feedback, both during training and activities, includes attempts to help children self-monitor and self-evaluate their social behavior (e.g., "Did you show 'accepting' when you were called 'out' in the game? Did you use your 'ignoring' skill to deal with that problem?"). If a child has not grasped a key concept (as revealed through lack of participation or inability to succeed at a task), the concept is reviewed verbally and practiced.

Note that the SST explicitly includes a high-density reward program in addition to cognitive elements, exemplifying the prior discussion's emphasis of integrated cognitive-behavioral intervention for children with ADHD, based on a clear contingency management system.

Following a review of the children's usage of the previous week's skill at home and school, the instructional format begins, during each session, with brief didactic instruction regarding the new "skill of the week" (e.g., good sportsmanship, accepting consequences, ignoring provocation, problem solving). The counselors then model the skill, using both pretend (e.g., through the use of puppets) and "live" modeling. Extensive role playing next takes place in the context of school, peer, and home applications of the skill; children evaluate their own and one another's skill performance.

Then, during a 30-minute indoor or outdoor "free play" game, the skills are practiced in more realistic contexts, with prompting and feedback from the counselors throughout. Tangible reinforcers (called "good sports bucks") with backup rewards (e.g., pizza party) are used during each of these group practice sessions to motivate utilization of the social skill. In addition, points can be earned throughout the session for following rules, attending, and listening; these are traded for child-selected activities at the end of the training session. Response–cost is part of the system, in that points can be lost for such behaviors as interrupting, name-calling, cursing, aggressing, and destroying property. In-room time-outs are also in place for aggressive or disruptive behavior.

I now give specific, manualized examples from Session 2 of the SST curriculum, which focuses on "Accepting" as the skill of the week.

Introduce the Accepting Module

Announce (with a finger drum roll) that the skill of the week is Accepting. Counselors will hide a piece of paper with the word "Accepting" written on it somewhere in the room. Tell the children that they are going to pretend to be detectives. First, they are assigned the mission to find the piece of paper. . . . Once it is found, they have the mission of figuring out how to show good acceptance by watching the counselors. One counselor will role play being a teacher, and the other, a student.

Role Play Description: The student is on the playground playing dodgeball, her favorite game, and really wants to win. She ends up getting hit by the ball and must sit out of the game until the next round. She shows the right way to accept (going to the end of the line, "good sport" face and body, etc.). The teacher praises the behavior.

Ask the children what clues they detected that showed good accepting. Encourage them to come up with the following by asking what the counselor looked like, what she did, and what she said. Write the children's ideas on poster board or chalkboard.

- staying calm
- following rules
- following directions right away
- good sport face
- verbalizing compliance (e.g., "OK, I'll do that")
- continuing to get along with others

Announce that "good sport bucks" will be given each time the children show good accepting.

Now, the counselors will role play the wrong way to accept (leaving the game, clenching fists, calling names, etc.). The teacher will give consequences for the non-accepting behavior (benching the student for the rest of recess). As always, the role play should be animated and entertaining. . . .

Role Plays

Children will volunteer to participate, and each child gets a chance. The children who are not participating will vote on how well the actors showed accepting skills in the role play by thumbs up vote.

Role Play Example: Peter's favorite game is basketball. A group of kids were playing on the court at recess. Peter really wanted to play and they needed another kid. Peter also had some homework he needed to finish. He chose to do his homework and then play. He finished really quickly and ran over to join the game. When he got there they had already found another kid to play and they had enough. . . .

Later, during the Free Play module, children play small-group board games or outdoor sports, with the opportunity to earn "good sport bucks" for appropriately demonstrating and utilizing the skill of the week. These "bucks" can be traded for credits toward a pizza party. Also, a Good Sport Thermometer is used as a visual aide for goal setting and self-evaluation. At the bottom level (1), the rating is that all of the kids showed poor acceptance; at the top (5), all showed good acceptance (furthermore, if everyone showed "super" acceptance, they "break" the thermometer). The children predict the group's performance before the game and review ratings afterwards. Counselors prompt and encourage throughout the game, with a careful review afterwards.

Finally, in the treatment condition termed SST-PG (parent-mediated generalization), parents meet in groups simultaneously with the child SST groups. They receive similar instruction as do the children; they also observe some of the SST sessions from behind a one-way mirror. In the main, parents learn how to prompt and reinforce their children's budding use of the social-cognitive skills at home. Finally, they establish a daily report card with their child's teacher, who rates the target behavior of "getting along with peers" on a daily basis. Parents provide the backup reward of "good sports bucks" at home for the child's earning of high teacher ratings on this criterion. Some evidence for the incremental ability of this additional parent intervention to promote generalization and maintenance of socially skilled behavior was found (Pfiffner & McBurnett, 1997). Certainly, it demonstrates the broader principles of extending cognitive-behavioral intervention to the natural environment espoused by Braswell and Bloomquist (1991) and Kendall and Macdonald (1993).

Self-Evaluation Procedures

As in the last edition of this volume (Hinshaw & Erhardt, 1991), I supply information about a procedure that aims to provide explicit training in self-monitoring and self-evaluation, two essential skills for academic, behavioral, and social competence that appear to be quite deficient in most children with ADHD (e.g., Douglas, 1983; Hinshaw, 1992). Indeed, deficient "checking" of task performance and a resultant array of academic errors, behavioral chaos, and social rejection are hallmarks of ADHD. Children with this disorder appear to pay poor attention not only to adults who give them directions and commands but also to their own behavioral performance. Thus, explicit training in the ability to self-monitor and self-evaluate one's performance in the context of initial goals appears critical. At least, in the short run, procedures that encourage, rehearse, and reward such accurate self-monitoring and self-evaluation aid in the social behavior of children with ADHD (Hinshaw et al., 1984b).

The procedure in question has been utilized most often in small-group therapy formats, but it can also be applied in individual training sessions. The overall goal of the "Match Game" procedure is to encourage a more self-reflective approach to any academic, behavioral, or social enterprise. It can only be used when behavioral contingencies and token rewards for appropriate behavior are established and in place, thereby exemplifying the type of integrated cognitive-behavioral intervention that is most likely to prove successful for youth with ADHD. In fact, the goal of self-evaluation training is to extend the benefits of reward programs for children with ADHD by encouraging them to "take over" the monitoring of progress usually left up to the supervising adults. Hence, self-evaluation exercises such as the Match Game do not stand on their own but, rather, should be paired with a social skills, problem-solving curriculum to encourage the child's generalization and maintenance of skills learned.

During a given session, the leaders begin by introducing a salient skill or concept to be learned and practiced. For example, *Cooperation* may be the day's focus (or, in other sessions, *Paying Attention*, or *Helping Others*). This behavioral skill is defined by the group leaders and discussed by the group; key definitional features are written down for public display to facilitate recognition and recall (see the earlier section on SST for extended discussion of this type of work with children). Next, role plays (of both good and poor examples of the criterion behavior) are performed, first by the leaders and then by the group members. The children must thus have a clear understanding of the target behavior and a clear sense of how to perform that behavior before they can begin to practice self-evaluation. During the next portion of the session, the group members are periodically rewarded for their display of the criterion behavior while performing academic work or playing a social game. For purposes of the Match Game, rewards are in the form of points, with 5 signaling excellent behavior and 1, no semblance of the criterion. (Points are, of course, redeemable for subsequent backup reinforcers.) The leaders occasionally remind the children to be thinking of how well they are performing with respect to the criterion— in the example that follows, cooperating.

Soon, the leaders announce that it is time to play the Match Game.

Stopping the activity and revealing sheets displayed in Figure 3.1, they explain that each participant will try to guess or match which point on the rating scale has been earned. The pair of leaders then models a Match Game session: Pretending to be a child, one leader voices her thought processes regarding how well her behavior matched the criterion: "In that work period, I kept following the rules of the game, I shared my materials. . . . Yeah, I was really cooperating. But, oh yeah, I did grab the ball a couple of times, and I got upset when I thought Billy did a better job than I did of playing. Overall, though, I think that I did a pretty good job of cooperating—I'll give myself a 4."

The other adult, modeling the trainer, then might say the following: "Well, Betty, you did start out with good cooperation—I noticed that your hands were to yourself and that you really took turns well. You did share the ball, too. But you did get quite upset when the other team won a round, and when you grabbed the ball away, Billy could have been hurt. So I believe that you earned a 3—okay for cooperating, with some excellent work but also some examples of poor cooperation, too." Essential here is the behavioral specificity of the leader's "report," which is designed to model and motivate specific recall on the part of the children. Note that during this modeled Match Game, it works best for the trainer role playing the child to slightly overestimate her score, in anticipation of the overly generous interpretations of many children with ADHD.

At the conclusion of this role-played Match Game, each child then individually completes a rating form, while the leaders privately discuss the ratings they will award. The key part of the training now occurs, as the children, in sequence, discuss their self-ratings—and, crucially, their reasons for the ratings they make—and the leaders, in turn, discuss *their* ratings of the child, noting precise examples of good and poor performance. (Videotaping of sessions, with children watching their behavior patterns, can also be effective if used judiciously.) The child receives, as token reinforcement, the number of points awarded by the trainer. Yet the point total is doubled (alternatively, 3 bonus points can be awarded) in the event of accurate self-evaluation—in other words, when there is a "match." Initially, the bonus can occur for self-ratings that are within a point of the adult rating. Over time, only accurate matches (or ratings that either match perfectly or are one point below the adult rating) would receive the bonus.

During its initial phases, the Match Game can be played several times within a training session, with emphasis again placed on eliciting the child's reasons for his or her particular self-rating and on the leaders' rewarding the accuracy of the self-evaluation. Gradually, the time span for self-evaluation can be lengthened. In addition, note that the wise (if devious) child with ADHD may soon learn that intentional misbehavior (earning a 1 or 2 rating from the adult) can easily be matched—"I completely messed up so I'll give myself a 1"—thus earning a bonus. Across sessions, then, the criterion

The Match Game

name: _____

date: _____

working on:

_____

I THINK THAT YOU'LL SAY THAT I WAS...

1	**2**	**3**	**4**	**5**
NOT AT ALL GOOD	A LITTLE GOOD	OK	PRETTY GOOD	GREAT

____   ____   ____   ____   ____

FIGURE 3.1. "Match Game" form used for self-evaluation training.

should be tightened so that only adult ratings of at least 3 (or even 4) will receive a bonus with accurate self-evaluation. The behavioral target can shift over sessions in accordance with the curriculum, so that social and behavioral goals, as well as attentional and academic objectives, can be "matched."

The ultimate goal is for the child to require less and less adult reinforcement, as self-evaluation becomes an end unto itself. Of course, periodic "checks" by the adult are necessary—even normally functioning children receive adult feedback, grades, honors, and the like. Clinically, extending the Match Game from the clinic setting to home and school environments, where parents and teachers providing the adult criterion ratings, should be employed to generalize the benefits of self-evaluation on improved academic and social behavior. Thus, while the child is learning the Match Game, the parent training and school-consultation components of an integrated and integrative cognitive-behavioral program should include rationale, explanation, and instruction in its use.

Anger Management

Anger is a component of certain forms of aggressive behavior (see Lochman et al., Chapter 2, and Nelson & Finch, Chapter 4, this volume). Because children with ADHD—particularly those with comorbid disruptive behavior disorders—tend to emotionally overreact (Melnick & Hinshaw, in press) and distort interpretations of interpersonal provocations (Milich & Dodge, 1984), they are prone to display retaliatory, reactive aggression, which places them at high risk for interpersonal rejection. Thus, instruction in and rehearsal of anger management skills are often indicated. My presentation here is brief; see Nelson and Finch (Chapter 4, this volume) and Lochman et al. (Chapter 2, this volume) for additional therapeutic strategies.

In the curriculum outlined here, as in the previous two sections, procedures that are both behavioral (i.e., repeated rehearsal of the anger-control strategies; explicit reward for successive approximations) and cognitive (i.e., reframing of the interpersonal stimulus, self-monitoring of the attempted plan) are salient. Indeed, as found in Hinshaw et al. (1984a), rehearsal-based, cognitive-behavioral intervention for anger control clearly surpassed a treatment emphasizing solely cognitive elements of emotion recognition and empathy enhancement. Basing psychosocial intervention on a strong behavioral foundation for children with ADHD cannot be overemphasized.

Utilizing elements from Novaco (1979) regarding adult anger management, the curriculum again utilizes peers—in a group training format—to facilitate improved self-control. Because the training procedures (and the behavioral provocations that are used to generate outcome assessment data) involve the active use of group provocation to provide a realistic environment for the practice of anger control, I highlight at the outset that this is not a curriculum that should be attempted "cold." In fact, several initial sessions are mandatory, as is group leadership that balances clinical sensitivity with a commitment to enhanced self-regulation on the part of the participants.

The unit is initiated when leaders ask that the children disclose those names and phrases used by peers that really "get under their skin," writing these down and explaining that the group will make use of such words to help practice self-control in later sessions. Such open disclosure could lead to embarrassment or even ridicule unless there is a clear atmosphere of trust in the group, and unless the children know that the leaders will not let any use of the names get out of hand. Again, even this initial step must be based on the establishment of solid group process before it is attempted.

As the actual training begins, leaders raise the topic of name-calling and teasing, probing how much of a problem the youngsters perceive this issue to be and asking for suggestions as to how best to cope with this problem. As always, the children's initial plans are carefully written down; after discussion, good versus not so good ideas are discussed and sorted through. Next, the pair of leaders engages in a spontaneous (but preplanned) mock argument, with the "victim" initially responding in a verbally retaliatory fashion. The goal is to surprise the children and promote discussion of "what happened" and "what else could the leader who was teased have done better?" Leaders typically need to walk the group through the steps of this provocation afterwards, in order to draw out the sequence of events (and ensuring that the group realizes it was a role play). The "argument" can then be repeated, this time incorporating the children's suggestions for greater self-control on the part of the victim.

Anger may develop quite rapidly in individuals with emotional dysregulation, including many children with ADHD. Thus, another phase of training involves prompting the participants to reflect on "how they know" when they are becoming upset or angry. For older, verbally skilled children, knowledge of incipient feeling states may be relatively accessible ("I can feel my blood start to boil"). Yet for younger children or those with little access to internal processes, this exercise is indeed a difficult one.

The active cognitive-behavioral training procedures are then put into place. Each child first generates (with ample adult support) several specific procedures that he or she will use to "pair up" with the developing feelings of anger—feelings, sensations, and cues that can now be better monitored. Following group discussion and individual consultation, the child selects a specific alternative to anger, rehearsing it while the group provides ever-increasing levels of verbal provocation and teasing (using the names initially generated and placed onto each child's list). For children in the early elementary grades, chosen strategies may be quite behavioral in nature (e.g., sitting on one's hands, covering one's ears), whereas children closer to adolescence may be able to utilize more sophisticated cognitive mediational strategies to supplement specific behavioral actions. The repeated practice of the selected strategy under conditions of provocation—with feedback from both the leaders and the group, and incorporation of adjustments based on such feedback—appears to be the essential ingredient for the learning of anger control.

Again, clinical issues are salient here. If the provocation exercises are rote and "staged," there will not be sufficient affect to motivate any need to employ the newly learned strategies (and the entire procedure will fall flat). If, alternatively, the leaders fail to enforce rules of "No touching" and "Stop the teasing on our cue," the procedures could be markedly counterproductive.

Modifications of these anger-control procedures have been incorporated in the intensive Summer Treatment Program curriculum of Pelham and Hoza (1996) and Pfiffner and McBurnett (1997). While not clinically sufficient alone, this cognitive-behavioral procedure may be an important component in helping to address a fundamental interpersonal problem for many youth with ADHD. Note that evidence from Hinshaw, Buhrmester, and Heller (1989) suggests that combining active anger management with relatively high-dosage levels of stimulant medication can lead to optimal self-regulation.

MEDIATORS AND MODERATORS OF TREATMENT OUTCOME

Kazdin and Weisz (1998) highlight that identification of those factors that predict and shape treatment response are of the utmost importance in child therapy research. Moderators are defined as preexisting characteristics that influence treatment response, such as family characteristics, social class, comorbidity, or the child's developmental level. Mediators are those variables occurring during treatment—such as attendance, "dosage" received, relationship with therapist, and the like—that act to explain the process of effective treatment (see Kraemer, Stice, Kazdin, Offord, & Kupfer, 1999). Because of the paucity of controlled clinical trials, however, and the rather small samples that have been investigated, the field has not accumulated much knowledge of such influences on treatment response in children with ADHD. As a result, there is substantial need to identify background variables and therapeutic processes that are linked to outcome.

With respect to cognitively oriented treatments, the child's age or developmental level must certainly be considered as a key moderator of intervention response; that is, children in the preschool- or early elementary-school-age range may lack the cognitive sophistication and abstract thinking abilities to demonstrate self-reflective strategies in the service of self-control. Therapeutic strategies for youngsters of this age should probably be quite concrete (e.g., Hinshaw et al., 1984a). Yet, as highlighted in this chapter, even older children with ADHD show a poor response to exclusively cognitive interventions, perhaps validating the contention that ADHD encompasses an overall developmental immaturity (see, e.g., Barkley, 1997a). In other words, one potential explanation for the relative lack of efficacy of cognitive strategies with ADHD (in distinction to the success rates with other diagnostic categories) is that youth with this disorder continue to function, verbally and emotionally at a level younger than their chronological years.

The comorbidity of ADHD with additional behavioral, emotional, and learning disorders is another prime candidate as a moderator variable. Past research has been largely inconclusive in this regard, primarily because of the lack of statistical power in earlier investigations.[4] A study with a sufficient sample size for moderator analyses is the previously noted MTA, a long-term (14 months of treatment), large-scale ($N = 579$), multisite, randomized clinical trial for 7- to 10-year-old children with carefully diagnosed ADHD (combined type). To reiterate, eligible families were assigned randomly to (1) medication management, (2) intensive behavioral treatment, (3) combined treatment (both of the above treatments), or (4) community care (assessment and referral to community practitioners). The behavioral treatment condition was quite intensive in the MTA, comprising 27 group parent-training sessions plus eight individual sessions, school consultation from the same therapist who conducted the parent intervention; a paraprofessional aide in the child's classroom for 3 months, helping the teacher's implementation of the consultation; and an intensive 8-week summer treatment program. Note that this package blends clinical behavior therapy for parents and teachers, intensive contingency management during the summer treatment program, a classroom aide, plus cognitive features embedded in the summer program and the higher "levels" of the school consultation. As indicated earlier, for the assessment domains of ADHD symptoms, associated oppositional/aggressive behaviors, and parent and peer indicators of social skills, the combined treatment was equivalent to medication management, with both yielding stronger outcomes than behavior therapy or community referral (which did not differ). Yet for other outcome domains (associated internalizing features, parent–child relations, teacher-appraised social skills), the combination treatment outperformed the other conditions.

In terms of moderators of outcome, comorbid oppositional defiant disorder or conduct disorder did not appreciably alter the main findings. Yet comorbidity with an anxiety disorder—characterizing approximately one-third of the sample who demonstrated overanxious disorder, separation anxiety disorder, multiple phobias, and so on—was important clinically. Specifically, ADHD/anxious participants who received behavior therapy performed equivalently to ADHD/anxious children in the medication and combination treatment conditions. On the other hand, the ADHD participants without significant anxiety showed the same pattern of outcome as was found in the overall analyses, where (for core ADHD symptoms) medication and combination interventions were superior to behavior therapy (MTA Cooperative Group, 1999b). In other words, for the outcome variables of parent-reported ADHD symptomatology and internalizing features, comorbid anxiety disorder status predicted an enhancement of the effectiveness of behavior therapy procedures (note that anxious vs. nonanxious participants performed comparably with medication; the moderator effect was specific to the behavioral intervention). Mechanisms responsible for this effect are not readily apparent: The ADHD/anxious group was not more severe symptomatically than the nonanxious subgroup at baseline, and it is unknown whether families in this condition were somehow more motivated for treatment. This moderator finding does, however, suggest that clinicians carefully appraise comorbidity in children with ADHD and consider that highly anxious youth with ADHD may fare relatively better with an exclusively behavioral/psychosocial approach.

The MTA Study selected only children with the combined type of ADHD. All too little is known about the potentially differential treatment responses of children with the inattentive type, with its predominance of learning problems, peer neglect, and anxiety-related symptoms. Furthermore, in terms of such potential mediators as treatment fidelity, treatment intensity, or client–therapist relationship variables, almost nothing is known. A clear priority for subsequent research in the field is identification of those subgroups that respond optimally to behavioral (or pharmacological) treatments and those intervention-related processes that predict particularly strong benefit.

CURRENT STATUS AND FUTURE DIRECTIONS

The main themes from this chapter can be summarized as follows.

1. ADHD is an impairing and often chronic disorder, characterized by inhibitory dysregulation and resulting from substantial genetic and prenatal risk operating transactionally with family and school environments. Its impact on multiple life domains mandates intensive intervention in childhood.
2. Self-instructionally based cognitive interventions are not sufficiently powerful to influence the symptomatology or course of ADHD; their use is not empirically supported.
3. More traditional behavioral treatments form the basis of effective psychosocial intervention for this condition, despite their relatively

short-term benefits and their relatively weaker effects than those of medication.

4. Cognitive enhancements of such contingency-based interventions in the realms of social skills training, intervention for self-evaluation, and promotion of anger management may be valuable for enhancing social competence and promoting maintenance of treatment gains.

5. No treatments to date, either pharmacological or psychosocial in nature, are typically sufficient for the multiple problems, impairments, and long-term course related to ADHD; prevention and alteration of the trajectory of ADHD remain elusive goals.

In the limited space available, I elaborate on these conclusions and speculate about the directions that future treatment research will need to take for youth with ADHD.

How Well Do Behavioral Approaches—with or without Cognitive Enhancement—Meet the Needs of Children with ADHD?

As discussed earlier, the features of behavioral interventions, including a graduated approach to teaching, consistent positive reinforcement, and clear negative consequences for misbehavior, all appear well-suited to the disorganized style and stimulus-bound nature of children and adolescents with ADHD. It is not clear, however, that direct contingency management or clinical behavior therapy programs truly remediate any underlying deficit. Rather, they attempt to rework environmental contingencies in the hopes of promoting skills learning and reducing problem behavior. Perhaps this is as much as can be expected at present, but greater hopes for lasting change would certainly seem to derive from treatment of core mechanisms of ADHD-related psychopathology. I also point out that (1) behavioral programs take considerable effort to mount and maintain, and (2) there is no automatic transfer of gains once the contingent reinforcers are tapered.

In this light, the claims of early cognitive-behavioral theorists and practitioners regarding ADHD continue to be conceptually appealing. For example, treatments intended to foster intrinsic motivation and self-regulation would be preferable to operant behavioral approaches, with their focus on extrinsic reinforcement and environmental shaping (Douglas, Parry, Marton, & Garson, 1976; Meichenbaum, 1977; Henker, Whalen, & Hinshaw, 1980; Whalen, Henker, & Hinshaw, 1985). In addition, from this perspective, verbal self-instructions would facilitate the development of internal speech (often lacking, delayed, or nonproductive in children with ADHD; see Berk & Potts, 1991); problem solving strategies would foster a more reflective cognitive style; self-reinforcement would bring control of contingencies "inside" the child; and error-coping procedures would constitute a built-in self-correction mechanism.

Yet the empirical data do not support the apparently valid conceptual rationale of those who advocate cognitive interventions. What is the nature of this "disconnect"? For one thing, the multiple cognitive, motivational, behavioral, and emotional problems that characterize clinical-range youth with ADHD may simply prevent the conceptually appealing cognitive principles and strategies from ever getting learned (Hinshaw & Erhardt, 1991). For another, the frequent comorbidity of ADHD with clinically significant aggression means that one is often attempting to intervene with youngsters at severe risk for achievement deficits, highly disorganized familial functioning (and "loaded" family histories of disorder), neuropsychological difficulties, and extreme peer rejection (Hinshaw, 1999). Such severe psychopathology is quite resistant to the field's most intensive treatment efforts. Also, as highlighted earlier, the underlying deficit in ADHD may be closely linked with fundamental problems in inhibitory control that occur "preverbally," prior to the potentially ameliorative effects of verbal self-regulation. Finally, as described earlier, cognitive therapies may be better situated to alter *distortions* in belief systems than to replace or supplement *deficiencies* in cognitive strategies (see Kendall & MacDonald, 1993).

For all of these reasons (and more), cognitive approaches have met with an extremely difficult target with respect to children with diagnosable ADHD. Truly integrated cognitive-behavioral treatments, based on contingency management, have yielded documentable benefits. Yet, as just indicated, these treatments may be best considered as rehabilitative rather than truly curative, at least as currently administered.

How Can Underlying Problems of Inhibitory Control Be Addressed?

Assuming that at least part of the underlying deficit of ADHD is linked to inhibitory control mechanisms (Barkley, 1997a, 1997b), how can clinicians influence such primary difficulties? Will sophisticated computer games of the future be able to help a child entrain more reflective, inhibited responding? Will it be possible, in other words, for repeated trials of successful inhibition of prepotent responses to "reset" the inhibitory control mechanisms? Importantly, if such proves to be the case, will gains be imprinted in neural architecture, automatically transferring to the child's home behavior and school performance? If so, that would signal a huge advance over current behavioral, cognitive, or pharmacological treatments, none of which generalize to periods beyond the active intervention. Regarding medication, will more specific, targeted pharmacological treatments be able to narrow in on receptor subtypes that mediate inhibitory control? The answers to all such questions are, at present, unknown.

More basically, can consistent application of more traditional reinforcement programs, which aim to reinforce planful, nonimpulsive actions
and developing skills, serve (over time) to rewire key brain regions and neural tracts toward the end of facilitating inhibitory control? If so, then perhaps there is a more fundamentally curative role for behavioral contingency
management, particularly if it is employed with utter consistency and early
in development. Indeed, perhaps the field's efforts have been occurring too
late developmentally. In the case of autism, for example, extremely early
and intensive behavioral intervention may be beneficial in altering the
course of disorder, at least in relatively mild cases (see McEachin, Smith, &
Lovaas, 1993). It is conceivable that with early identification, a similar type
of "immersion" could benefit preschool-age youngsters with ADHD, although the exact nature of the educational, behavior management, and psychological inputs necessary to effect lasting change is still unknown. Intervention with an organism and brain that are still relatively "plastic" would
clearly be preferable to performing rehabilitation with a child or adolescent
who has undergone many years of failure and negative self-esteem. I must
note, however, that the accurate identification of which overactive, impulsive preschoolers truly have ADHD (as opposed to transitory behavior patterns) is far from an exact science at this point. Genetic testing may be able
to offer some prediction of risk in the not-too-distant future, but in absence
of major locus genes, this prediction will be likely to suffer from uncer-
tainty.

At another level, even though Barkley's neuropsychological model of
ADHD posits that basic inhibitory deficits occur prior to such executive
functions as verbal mediation, implying that cognitive self-instructional
training targets a process that follows from (rather than precedes) inhibitory control, it is not always the case that successful interventions must occur at levels of "primary" psychopathology. For example, in adult depression, few would argue that depressive cognitions and interpersonal
consequences of depression temporally precede affective symptoms. On the
contrary, depressed mood and somatic features antecede the onset of depressive cognitions and interpersonal alienation and rejection. Nonetheless,
cognitive therapy and interpersonal therapy have clearly been found to benefit major depression (Craighead, Craighead, & Ilardi, 1998). In other
words, successful treatments need not be linked explicitly to etiological factors.

Consider the parallels between ADHD and such severe and often
intractible disorders as schizophrenia and bipolar disorder, for which exclusively psychological/behavioral treatments have proven largely insufficient.
In each of these highly heritable conditions, complex psychobiological
causal pathways have been traced, but the core underlying mechanism(s)
remain obscure. Regarding schizophrenia, social skills interventions have
effected clear improvements in community functioning, and family treat-

ments enhance the benefits of antipsychotic medications (Koplewicz & Liberman, 1998). For bipolar disorder, the clearly beneficial nature of adjunctive individual and group therapies designed to enhance self-awareness and medication adherence cannot be overlooked (Craighead, Miklowitz, Vajk, & Frank, 1998). Thus, there may well be a place for psychosocial therapies in such chronic, heritable disorders. For ADHD, the significant benefits of contingency-based behavioral interventions (though less robust, overall, than those of medication)—and the potential for additive effects over and above exclusively pharmacological treatments—are thus precedented by parallels from severe, biologically based adult disorders.

Where Should Intervention Research Be Headed?

I close with a brief discussion of several additional points that bear consideration for the field's development of subsequent treatment efforts.

1. Intervention efforts directed specifically toward functional impairments have much to recommend them. In particular, organizational skills, social competence, and academic remediation are three key target domains for youth with ADHD. Even if a given treatment fails to address the "underlying" psychopathology of ADHD, successful remediation of impairments in such crucial domains may greatly facilitate the adaptive functioning and long-term course of youth with ADHD. No better example can be found than that of social skills treatments for schizophrenia (see the preceding section). Indeed, in the clinical examples section of this chapter, two of the three exemplars pertained to enhancing social competence (social skills training, anger management).

Along this line, it is tempting to ponder somewhat different targets from the field's traditional treatments. Because Hinshaw, Zupan, et al. (1997) found that authoritative parenting served as both a potentiating factor for ADHD boys' peer acceptance and a buffer against peer rejection, it is conceivable that parenting interventions should attempt to promote, more specifically, the warmth, limit setting, and promotion of independence that characterize this child-rearing style. Many behavioral interventions for parents target similar skills and attitudes, but usually by means of quite directive coaching in rewards and punishments. A more expanded set of goals might yield greater benefit. Along this line, given the parental psychopathology that often appears in conjunction with ADHD, it may be important, if not essential, to deal with maternal depression, paternal substance use, or extreme marital conflict prior to or independently of a focus on the child's ADHD-related problems.

In addition, given the major problems in independent, adaptive functioning in youth with ADHD (Hinshaw, in press; Stein et al., 1995), intervention directed toward enhancing independence may be of great benefit.

Furthermore, as youth with ADHD approach adolescence, more concentrated work on organizational skills appears to be a major target.

2. Almost no research efforts have been directed toward the treatment of children and adolescents with the inattentive type of ADHD. Whereas such youth do not demonstrate the kinds of disruptive, impulsive behaviors that frequently get their counterparts with the hyperactive/ impulsive and combined types of ADHD in conflicts with authority and with the peer group, they clearly show impairment in social, academic, and personal domains (Lahey et al., 1994, 1998), and their high rates of comorbidity with internalizing features are troubling. Stimulant medications appear to be effective for this subgroup, but often at relatively low dosage levels, with the potential for troublesome side effects if doses are pushed too high. Psychosocial intervention trials with this subtype are indicated.

3. Much more needs to be learned about combining psychosocial treatment strategies with medications for ADHD. Although some recent trials suggested almost no incremental benefit of behavioral treatments over and above stimulant medications alone (Hechtman & Abikoff, 1995), the MTA Study revealed additive effects for combined treatment in the realms of teacher-reported social skills, internalizing comorbidity, and parent–child relationships (MTA Cooperative Group, 1999a). Furthermore, combined treatments were more likely than solely pharmacological efforts to yield large, clinically "excellent" gains. Yet the field still does not know about many related issues, such as the following: What is the optimal temporal patterning of combining these treatment modalities? Should the interventions be started simultaneously? Should behavioral approaches be tried first, with medications added only if needed? Alternatively, are medications the treatment of choice, with adjunctive behavioral treatments to be utilized after pharmacological control of symptoms? Furthermore, do the potential benefits of combination treatments appear over longer time periods than the acute effects of either intervention modality alone? That is, perhaps combination treatments are particularly likely to alter the course of ADHD, an effect that would not become apparent in short-term trials. As well, optimal medication treatment may be sufficiently powerful with respect to core symptomatology that further improvements from behavioral approaches are difficult to discern; yet incremental gains may be far more apparent in domains of functional impairment (academic achievement, social relationships) that are not measured as easily or readily in most clinical trials.

4. As I have highlighted throughout this chapter, cognitive-behavioral approaches must clearly incorporate (a) explicit reward programs and behavioral contingencies, as well as (b) parent and teacher involvement, if optimal benefits are desired. Altering thinking patterns or teaching problem solving in the absence of either clear contingencies or explicit programming

for generalization and maintenance is not likely to show any kind of success for youth with ADHD.

5. Kazdin (1987) has highlighted that externalizing disorders of childhood (e.g., aggression, ADHD) are best conceptualized as chronic, rather than acute, conditions. Our treatment efforts to date, however, as well as current patterns of mental health funding, tend to view these problems as deserving of short-term intervention models. Changing models of treatment, public perception, and health care financing are certain to be key issues regarding intervention approaches for ADHD in the years ahead. Certainly, the evidence presented herein suggests strongly that concentrated, intensive efforts during childhood will pay later dividends in terms of preventing the often-devastating consequences of ADHD to individuals, families, and society.

NOTES

1. For the category of conduct disorder, on the other hand, subtypes are formed on the basis of age of onset rather than symptom presentation (American Psychiatric Association, 1994).
2. ADHD subtypes show asymmetrical patterns of comorbidity: There is a strong likelihood that children with the combined type of ADHD will display association with aggression and antisocial behavior, whereas youngsters with the predominantly inattentive type will show overlap with internalizing features (Paternite, Loney, & Roberts, 1996). Nonetheless, in clinical samples of children with the combined type of ADHD, comorbidity with anxiety disorders may still comprise up to one-third of cases (MTA Cooperative Group, 1999b).
3. Note that aggressive conduct disorder features both cognitive distortion (hostile bias in attributing negative social contact) and cognitive deficiencies (Kendall & MacDonald, 1993).
4. In pharmacological research with ADHD, there is some evidence that children with comorbid anxiety disorders show a less pronounced response to stimulant medications than do nonanxious children with ADHD (DuPaul, Barkley, & McMurray, 1994; Pliszka, 1989).

REFERENCES

Abikoff, H. (1991). Cognitive training in ADHD children: Less to it than meets the eye. *Journal of Learning Disabilities, 24,* 205–209.

Abikoff, H., Ganeles, D., Reiter, G., Blum, C., Foley, C., & Klein, R. G. (1988). Cognitive training in academically deficient ADHD boys receiving stimulant medication. *Journal of Abnormal Child Psychology, 16,* 411–432.

Abikoff, H., & Gittelman, R. (1985). Hyperactive children treated with stimulants: Is cognitive therapy a useful adjunct? *Archives of General Psychiatry, 42,* 953–961.

American Psychiatric Association. (1994). *Diagnostic and statistical manual of mental disorders* (4th ed.). Washington, DC: Author.

Anderson, C. A., Hinshaw, S. P., & Simmel, C. (1994). Mother–child interactions in ADHD and comparison boys: Relationships to overt and covert externalizing behavior. *Journal of Abnormal Child Psychology, 22,* 247–265.

Barkley, R. A. (1997a). *ADHD and the nature of self-control.* New York: Guilford Press.

Barkley, R. A. (1997b). Behavioral inhibition, sustained attention, and executive functions: Constructing a unifying theory of ADHD. *Psychological Bulletin, 121,* 65–94.

Barkley, R. A. (1998). *Attention-deficit/hyperactivity disorder: A handbook for diagnosis and treatment* (2nd ed.). New York: Guilford Press.

Berk, L. E., & Potts, M. (1991). Development and functional significance of private speech among attention-deficit hyperactivity disordered and normal boys. *Journal of Abnormal Child Psychology, 19,* 357–377.

Bickett, L., & Milich, R. (1990). First impressions formed of boys with attention deficit disorder. *Journal of Learning Disabilities, 23,* 253–259.

Biederman, J., Newcorn, J., & Sprich, S. (1991). Comorbidity of attention deficit hyperactivity disorder with conduct, depressive, anxiety, and other disorders. *American Journal of Psychiatry, 52,* 464–470.

Bird, H., Gould, M. S., & Staghezza-Jaramillo, B. M. (1994). The comorbidity of ADHD in a community sample of children aged 6 through 16 years. *Journal of Child and Family Studies, 3,* 365–378.

Braswell, L., & Bloomquist, M. L. (1991). *Cognitive-behavioral therapy with ADHD children: Child, family, and school interventions.* New York: Guilford Press.

Breslau, N., Brown, G. G., DelDotto, J. E., Kumar, S., Ezhuthachan, S., Andreski, P., & Hufnagle, K. G. (1996). Psychiatric sequalae of low birth weight at 6 years of age. *Journal of Abnormal Child Psychology, 24,* 385–400.

Bugental, D. B., Whalen, C. K., & Henker, B. (1977). Causal attributions of hyperactive children and motivational assumptions of two behavior change approaches: Evidence for an interactionist position. *Child Development, 48,* 874–884.

Carlson, E. A., Jacobvitz, D., & Sroufe, L. A. (1995). A developmental investigation of inattentiveness and hyperactivity. *Child Development, 66,* 37–54.

Chess, S., & Thomas, A. (1984). *Origins and evolution of behavior disorders.* New York: Brunner/Mazel.

Craighead, W. E., Craighead, L. W., & Ilardi, S. S. (1998). Psychosocial treatments for major depressive disorder. In P. E. Nathan & J. M. Gorman (Eds.), *A guide to treatments that work* (pp. 226–239). New York: Oxford University Press.

Craighead, W. E., Miklowitz, D. J., Vajk, F., & Frank, E. (1998). Psychosocial treatments for bipolar disorder. In P. E. Nathan & J. M. Gorman (Eds.), *A guide to treatments that work* (pp. 240–248). New York: Oxford University Press.

Diller, L. H. (1998). *Running on Ritalin.* New York: Bantam Books.

Douglas, V. I. (1983). Attention and cognitive problems. In M. Rutter (Ed.), *Developmental neuropsychiatry* (pp. 280–329). New York: Guilford Press.

Douglas, V. I., Parry, P., Marton, P., & Garson, C. (1976). Assessment of a cognitive training program for hyperactive children. *Journal of Abnormal Child Psychology, 4,* 389–410.

DuPaul, G. J., Barkley, R. A., & McMurray, M. B. (1994). Response of children with ADHD to methylphenidate: Interaction with internalizing symptoms. *Journal of the American Academy of Child and Adolescent Psychiatry, 33,* 894–903.

Erhardt, D., & Hinshaw, S. P. (1994). Initial sociometric impressions of ADHD and comparison boys: Predictions from social behaviors and from nonbehavioral variables. *Journal of Consulting and Clinical Psychology, 62,* 833–842.

Gillberg, C., Melander, H., van Knorring, A.-L., & Janols, L.-0. (1997). Long-term stimulant treatment of children with attention deficit hyperactivity disorder symptoms: A randomized, double-blind, placebo-controlled trial. *Archives of General Psychiatry, 54,* 857–864.

Greenhill, L. L., & Osman, B. O. (1999). *Ritalin: Theory and patient management* (2nd ed.). Larchmont, NY: Mary Ann Liebert.

Hechtman, L. T., & Abikoff, H. (1995, October). *Multimodal treatment plus stimulants vs. stimulant treatment in ADHD children: Results from a 2-year comparative treatment study.* Paper presented at the annual meeting of the American Academy of Child and Adolescent Psychiatry, New Orleans, LA.

Henker, B., Whalen, C. K., & Hinshaw, S. P. (1980). The attributional contexts of cognitive intervention strategies. *Exceptional Education Quarterly, 1,* 17-30.

Hinshaw, S. P. (1987). On the distinction between attentional deficits/hyperactivity and conduct problems/aggression in child psychopathology. *Psychological Bulletin, 101,* 443–463.

Hinshaw, S. P. (1992). Intervention for social skill and social competence. *Child and Adolescent Psychiatric Clinics of North America, 1,* 539–552.

Hinshaw, S. P. (1994). *Attention deficits and hyperactivity in children.* Thousand Oaks, CA: Sage.

Hinshaw, S. P. (1998). Review of R. A. Barkley's *ADHD and the nature of self-control. Journal of Developmental and Behavioral Pediatrics, 19,* 209–211.

Hinshaw, S. P. (1999). Psychosocial intervention for childhood ADHD: Etiologic and developmental themes, comorbidity, and integration with pharmacotherapy. In D. Cicchetti & S. L. Toth (Eds.), *Rochester Symposium on Developmental Psychopathology: Vol. 9: Developmental approaches to prevention and intervention* (pp. 221–270). Rochester, NY: University of Rochester Press.

Hinshaw, S. P. (in press). Is ADHD an impairing condition in childhood and adolescence? In P. S. Jensen & J. R. Cooper (Eds.), *Diagnosis and treatment of attention-deficit hyperactivity disorder: An evidence-based approach.* Washington, DC: American Psychiatric Press.

Hinshaw, S. P., Buhrmester, D., & Heller, T. (1989). Anger control in response to verbal provocation: Effects of methylphenidate for boys with ADHD. *Journal of Abnormal Child Psychology, 17,* 393–407.

Hinshaw, S. P., & Erhardt, D. (1991). Attention-deficit/hyperactivity disorder. In P. C. Kendall (Ed.), *Child and adolescent therapy: Cognitive-behavioral procedures* (pp. 98–128). New York: Guilford Press.

Hinshaw, S. P., Henker, B., & Whalen, C. K. (1984a). Cognitive-behavioral and pharmacologic interventions for hyperactive boys: Comparative and combined effects. *Journal of Consulting and Clinical Psychology, 52,* 739–749.

Hinshaw, S. P., Henker, B., & Whalen, C. K. (1984b). Self-control in hyperactive boys in anger-inducing situations: Effects of cognitive-behavioral training and of methylphenidate. *Journal of Abnormal Child Psychology, 12,* 55–77.

Hinshaw, S. P., Klein, R. G., & Abikoff, H. (1998). Childhood attention-deficit hyperactivity disorder: Nonpharmacologic and combination approaches. In P. E. Nathan & J. M. Gorman (Eds.), *A guide to treatments that work* (pp. 27–41). New York: Oxford University Press.

Hinshaw, S. P., Lahey, B. B., & Hart, E. L. (1993). Issues of taxonomy and comorbidity in the development of conduct disorder. *Development and Psychopathology, 5,* 31–49.

Hinshaw, S. P., March, J. S., Abikoff, H., Arnold, L. E., Cantwell, D. P., Conners, C. K., Elliott, G. R., Halperin, J., Greenhill, L. L., Hechtman, L. T., Hoza, B., Jensen, P. S., Newcorn, J. H., McBurnett, K., Pelham, W. E., Richters, J. E., Severe, J. B., Schiller, E., Swanson, J. M., Vereen, D., & Wells, K. C. (1997). Comprehensive assessment of childhood attention-deficit hyperactivity disorder in the context of a multisite, multimodal clinical trial. *Journal of Attention Disorders, 1,* 217–234.

Hinshaw, S. P., & McHale, J. P. (1991). Stimulant medication and the social interactions of hyperactive children: Effects and implications. In D. G. Gilbert & J. J. Connolly (Eds.), *Personality, social skills, and psychopathology: An individual differences approach* (pp. 229–253). New York: Plenum Press.

Hinshaw, S. P., & Melnick, S. (1995). Peer relationships in children with attention-deficit hyperactivity disorder with and without comorbid aggression. *Development and Psychopathology, 7,* 627–647.

Hinshaw, S. P., & Nigg, J. T. (1999). Behavior rating scales in the assessment of disruptive behavior problems in childhood. In D. Shaffer, C. P. Lucas, & J. Richters (Eds.), *Diagnostic assessment in child and adolescent psychopathology* (pp. 91–126). New York: Guilford Press.

Hinshaw, S. P., & Park, T. (1999). Research issues and problems: Toward a more definitive science of disruptive behavior disorders. In H. C. Quay & A. E. Hogan (Eds.), *Handbook of disruptive behavior disorders* (pp. 593–620). New York: Plenum Press.

Hinshaw, S. P., Zupan, B. A., Simmel, C., Nigg, J. T., & Melnick, S. M. (1997). Peer status in boys with and without attention-deficit hyperactivity disorder: Predictions from overt and covert antisocial behavior, social isolation, and authoritative parenting beliefs. *Child Development, 64,* 880–896.

Jensen, P. S., Martin, D., & Cantwell, D. P. (1997). Comorbidity in ADHD: Implications for research, practice, and DSM-V. *Journal of the American Academy of Child and Adolescent Psychiatry, 36,* 1065–1079.

Johnston, C. (in press). The impact of attention-deficit hyperactivity disorder on social and vocational functioning in adults. In P. S. Jenson & J. R. Cooper (Eds.), *Diagnosis and treatment of attention-deficit/hyperactivity disorder: An evidence-based approach.* Washington, DC: American Psychiatric Press.

Kazdin, A. E. (1987). Treatment of antisocial behavior in children: Current status and future directions. *Psychological Bulletin, 102,* 187–203.

Kazdin, A. E., & Weisz, J. R. (1998). Identifying and developing empirically supported child and adolescent treatments. *Journal of Consulting and Clinical Psychology, 66,* 19–36.

Kendall, P. C. (1998). Empirically supported psychological therapies. *Journal of Consulting and Clinical Psychology, 66,* 3–6.

Kendall, P. C., & MacDonald, J. P. (1993). Cognition in the psychopathology of youth and implications for treatment. In K. S. Dobson & P. C. Kendall (Eds.), *Psychopathology and cognition* (pp. 387–427). San Diego: Academic Press.

Klein, R. G., & Mannuzza, S. (1991). Long-term outcome of hyperactive children: A review. *Journal of the American Academy of Child and Adolescent Psychiatry, 30,* 383–387.

Klein, R., & Wender, P. (1995). The role of methylphenidate in psychiatry. *Archives of General Psychiatry, 52,* 429–433.

Koplewicz, A., & Liberman, R. P. (1998). Psychosocial treatments for schizophrenia. In P. E. Nathan & J. M. Gorman (Eds.), *A guide to treatments that work* (pp. 190–211). New York: Oxford University Press.

Kraemer, H. C., Stice, E., Kazdin, A. E., Offord, D., & Kupfer, D. (1999). *How do risk factors work? Mediators, moderators, independent, overlapping, and proxy-risk factors.* Unpublished manuscript, Stanford University Department of Psychiatry, Stanford, CA.

Lahey, B. B., Applegate, B., McBurnett, K., Biederman, J., Greenhill, L., Hynd, G., Barkley, R. A., Newcorn, J., Jensen, P., Richters, J., Garfinkel, B., Kerdyk, L., Frick, P. J., Ollendick, T., Perez, D., Hart, E. L., Waldman, I., & Shaffer, D. (1994). DSM-IV Field Trials for attention deficit hyperactivity disorder in children and adolescents. *American Journal of Psychiatry, 151,* 1673–1685.

Lahey, B. B., Pelham, W. E., Stein, M. A., Loney, J., Trapani, C., Nugent, K., Kipp, H., Schmidt, E., Lee, S., Cale, M., Gold, E., Hartung, C. M., Willcutt, E., & Baumann, B. (1998). Validity of DSM-IV attention-deficit/hyperactivity disorder for younger children. *Journal of the American Academy of Child and Adolescent Psychiatry, 37,* 695–702.

Lahey, B. B., & Willcutt, E. (in press). Validity of the diagnosis and dimensions of attention-deficit hyperactivity disorder. In P. S. Jenson & J. R. Cooper (Eds.), *Diagnosis and treatment of attention-deficit/hyperactivity disorder: An evidence-based approach.* Washington, DC: American Psychiatric Press.

Levy, F., Hay, D. A., McStephen, M., Wood, C., & Waldman, I. (1997). Attention-deficit hyperactivity disorder: A category or a continuum? Genetic analysis of a large-scale twin study. *Journal of the American Academy of Child and Adolescent Psychiatry, 36,* 737–744.

McEachin, J. J., Smith, T., & Lovaas, O. I. (1993). Long-term outcome of children with autism who received early intensive behavior therapy. *American Journal of Mental Retardation, 97*, 359–372.

Meichenbaum, D. H. (1977). *Cognitive-behavior modification: An integrative approach*. New York: Plenum Press.

Melnick, S. M., & Hinshaw, S. P. (in press). Child emotion regulation and parenting in boys with ADHD and nondiagnosed boys: Predictions to social behaviors and peer competence. *Journal of Abnormal Child Psychology*.

Milich, R., & Dodge, K. A. (1984). Social information processing in child psychiatry populations. *Journal of Abnormal Child Psychology, 12*, 471–489.

MTA Cooperative Group. (1999a). Fourteen-month randomized clinical trial of treatment strategies for attention-deficit hyperactivity disorder. *Archives of General Psychiatry, 56*, 1073–1086.

MTA Cooperative Group. (1999b). Effects of comorbid anxiety, poverty, session attendance, and community medication on treatment outcome in children with attention-deficit/hyperactivity disorder. *Archives of General Psychiatry, 56*, 1088–1096.

Novaco, R. W. (1979). The cognitive regulation of anger and stress. In P. C. Kendall & S. D. Hollon (Eds.), *Cognitive-behavioral interventions: Theory, research, and procedures* (pp. 241–283). New York: Academic Press.

Oden, S., & Asher, S. R. (1977). Coaching children in social skills for friendship making. *Child Development, 48*, 495–506.

Parker, J. G., & Asher, S. R. (1987). Peer relations and later personal adjustment: Are low-accepted children at risk? *Psychological Bulletin, 102*, 357–389.

Paternite, C. E., Loney, J., & Roberts, M. A. (1996). A preliminary validation of subtypes of DSM-IV attention-deficit/hyperactivity disorder. *Journal of Attention Disorders, 1*, 70–86.

Pelham, W. E., & Bender, M. E. (1982). Peer relationships in hyperactive children: Description and treatment. In K. Gadow & I. Bialer (Eds.), *Advances in learning and behavioral disabilities* (Vol. 1, pp. 365–436). Greenwich, CT: JAI Press.

Pelham, W. E., Carlson, C. L., Sams, S. E., Vallano, G., & Dixon, M. J. (1993). Separate and combined effects of methylphenidate and behavior modification on boys with attention-deficit hyperactivity disorder in the classroom. *Journal of Consulting and Clinical Psychology, 61*, 506–515.

Pelham, W. E., & Hinshaw, S. P. (1992). Behavioral intervention for attention-deficit hyperactivity disorder. In S. M. Turner, K. S. Calhoun, & H. E. Adams (Eds.), *Handbook of clinical behavior therapy* (2nd ed., pp. 259–283). New York: Wiley.

Pelham, W. E., & Hoza, B. (1996). Intensive treatment: A summer treatment program for children with ADHD. In E. D. Hibbs & P. S. Jensen (Eds.), *Psychosocial treatments for child and adolescent disorders: Empirically based strategies for clinical practice* (pp. 311–340). Washington, DC: American Psychological Association.

Pelham, W. E., & Murphy, H. A. (1986). Behavioral and pharmacological treatment of hyperactivity and attention-deficit disorders. In M. Hersen & S. E. Breuning (Eds.), *Pharmacological and behavioral treatment: An integrative approach* (pp. 108–147). New York: Wiley.

Pfiffner, L., & McBurnett, K. (1997). Social skills training with parent generalization: Treatment effects for children with attention deficit disorder. *Journal of Consulting and Clinical Psychology, 65*, 749–757.

Pfiffner, L., & McBurnett, K. (2000). *Social skills training manual*. Unpublished manuscript, University of Chicago, Department of Psychiatry, Chicago, IL.

Pliszka, S. R. (1989). Effect of anxiety on cognition, behavior, and stimulant response in ADHD. *Journal of the American Academy of Child and Adolescent Psychiatry, 28*, 882–887.

Rutter, M., Bolton, P., Harrington, R., LeCouteur, A., Macdonald, H., & Simonoff, E. (1990). Genetic factors in child psychiatric disorders: I. A review of research strategies. *Journal of Child Psychology and Psychiatry, 31*, 3–37.

Schachar, R. (1986). Hyperkinetic syndrome: Historical development of the concept. In E. A. Taylor (Ed.), *The overactive child* (pp. 19–40). London: MacKeith.

Slomkowski, C., Klein, R. G., & Mannuzza, S. (1995). Is self-esteem an important outcome in hyperactive children? *Journal of Abnormal Child Psychology, 23,* 303–315.

Stein, M. A., Szumowski, E., Blondis, T. A., & Roizen, N. J. (1995). Adaptive skills dysfunction in ADD and ADHD children. *Journal of Child Psychology and Psychiatry, 36,* 663–670.

Swanson, J. M., McBurnett, K., Christian, D. L., & Wigal, T. (1995). Stimulant medications and the treatment of children with ADHD. In T. H. Ollendick & R. J. Prinz (Eds.), *Advances in clinical child psychology* (Vol. 17, pp. 265–322). New York: Plenum Press.

Tannock, R. (1998). Attention deficit hyperactivity disorder: Advances in cognitive, neurobiological, and genetic research. *Journal of Child Psychology and Psychiatry, 39,* 65–99.

Treuting, J., & Hinshaw, S. P. (in press). Depression and self-esteem in boys with attention-deficit/hyperactivity disorder: Relationships with comorbid aggression and explanatory attributional mechanisms. *Journal of Abnormal Child Psychology.*

Whalen, C. K., & Henker, B. (1992). The social profile of attention-deficit hyperactivity disorder: Five fundamental facets. *Child and Adolescent Psychiatric Clinics of North America, 1,* 395–410.

Whalen, C. K., Henker, B., & Hinshaw, S. P. (1985). Cognitive-behavioral therapies for hyperactive children: Premises, problems, and prospects. *Journal of Abnormal Child Psychology, 13,* 289–308.

Whitaker, A. H., Van Rossem, R., Feldman, J. F., Schonfeld, I. S., Pinto-Martin, J. A., Torre, C., Shaffer, D., & Paneth, N. (1997). Psychiatric outcomes in low-birth-weight children at age 6 years: Relation to neonatal cranial ultrasound abnormalities. *Archives of General Psychiatry, 54,* 847–856.

CHAPTER 4

Managing Anger in Youth

A Cognitive-Behavioral Intervention Approach

W. Michael Nelson III and A. J. Finch, Jr.

Anger, aggression, and violence in children and adolescents have become increasingly recognized as having an adverse effect upon individuals, others, and society at large. The upsurge in rates of violent crime among youth (Fingerhut & Kleinman, 1990) is consistent with the increasing number of children and adolescent who exhibit aggressive, assaultive, and violent behavior (Richters, 1993). Graphic acts of violence with children and adolescents as perpetrators are becoming increasingly common in newspaper, magazine, and television headlines, to the point that, unfortunately, they can be considered even commonplace in the 1990s. Most recently, the tragedy at Columbine High School in Littleton, Colorado, where 12 students and one teacher were killed by two adolescents, who then committed suicide, has been labeled an "American Tragedy." For children and adolescents themselves, early aggression seems to foreshadow problems in adulthood (Kazdin, 1987), with such aggression predicting later violence, including frequent fighting by late adolescence, partner assault, and conviction for violent offenses by the early thirties (Farrington, 1991, 1994; Stattin & Magnusson, 1989).

Among nations, the United States ranks first in its rates of interpersonal violence (American Psychological Association, 1993). Although there was a 61% increase in arrests for violent offenses between 1988 and 1994, the juvenile arrest rate for homicide increased a staggering 90% between

1987 and 1991, and it has remained fairly constant since this time (Snyder & Sickmund, 1995). Disruptive, aggressive, and delinquent child and adolescent behavior accounts for almost 25% of all special services in school and almost half of all juvenile referrals to community mental health agencies (e.g., Gilbert, 1957; Lorion, Cowen, & Caldwell, 1974; Stewart, deBlois, Meardon, & Cummings, 1980; Stouthamer-Loeber, Loeber, & Thomas, 1992). Highly aggressive children have also been shown to be at high risk for adult crime, alcoholism, drug abuse, unemployment, divorce, and mental illness (e.g., Farrington, 1995; Horne & Sayger, 1990; McCord & McCord, 1960; Robins, 1966).

Aggressive and violent behavior not only have severe consequences for the perpetrator but also for others, including siblings, parents, teachers, peers, and strangers, who are targets of such behavior aimed at causing serious harm. The disruptive influence of having a highly aggressive individual in the family in terms of the effects on siblings and parents is well documented (e.g., Kazdin, 1995). Those youth with a history of severe aggressive and antisocial behavior are generally more likely to continue such acts as they grow up, oftentimes leaving many victims of murder, rape, robbery, spousal and child abuse, arson, and drunk driving (Farrington, Loeber, & VanKamman, 1990; Kazdin, 1995).

The impact of aggression and violence in terms of its effect on communities and societies is penetrating. Climates of fear, intimidation, and depravation in many communities results from the threat or reality of violence (Richters & Martinez, 1993). The highest rates of referral from mental health services among youth involve aggressive, acting-out, and disruptive behavior patterns. The monetary costs of treatment make aggressive acting out one of the most costly mental health problems in the United States today (Lipsey, 1992; Robins, 1981).

Although there appears to be stability of aggression over time, this does not mean that such behavior in children and adolescents is immutable. In fact, there is some evidence that physical altercations and aggressive acting out generally decrease from childhood to adulthood (e.g., Loeber & Stouthamer-Loeber, 1998). There appear to be three developmental types of highly aggressive, violent individuals: (1) a life-course type, (2) a limited-duration type, and (3) a late-onset type (Moffitt, 1993; Moffitt, Caspi, Dickson, Silva, & Stanton, 1996; Loeber & Stouthamer-Loeber, 1998). The life-course type accounts for the largest proportion of highly aggressive persons emerging in later life. Some exhibit extreme aggression and antisocial behavior in childhood, while for others, this pattern of behavior does not emerge until adolescence. The limited-duration type of individual outgrows aggression in either elementary school or late adolescence. Finally, violent behavior in the late-onset type emerges only during adulthood and may be a function of overcontrol that diminishes as inhibitions against anger abate.

Overall, it does appear that aggressive behavior is susceptible to change with systematic interventions (e.g., Southam-Gerow & Kendall, 1997; Tate, Reppucci, & Mulvey, 1995; Wasserman & Miller, 1998). Thus, the notion that early-onset and stable forms of aggression during childhood and adolescence develop into stable personality traits is not entirely accurate. There is evidence and subsequent hope that when exposed to effective interventions, at-risk youth can not only learn to deal with problems in other ways than aggression and violence but also lead productive lives. Thus, the clinical picture is not all doom and gloom.

A variety of intervention strategies have been evaluated for more seriously acting-out children with conduct disorder, such as psychotherapeutic and medication interventions, and home, school, and community-based programs, as well as hospital and residential treatment (for reviews, see Brandt & Zlotnick, 1988; Dumas, 1989; Eyberg, Boggs, & Algina, 1995; Kazdin, 1987; Miller, 1994; Pepler & Rubin, 1991; Stoff, Breiling, & Maser, 1997; U. S. Congress, 1991). In fact, Kazdin (1993) described several criteria in evaluating the promise of intervention programs, including: (1) a theoretical conceptualization of the disorder that guides treatment, (2) a conceptualization supported by research, (3) outcome research supporting the treatment's efficacy, and (4) outcome related to processes identified in the conceptualization of the disorder. Currently, there are no treatments that adequately meet all of these criteria, although two interventions seem more promising for children who severely act out—the family-focused therapies derived from social learning theory and the child-focused cognitive-behavioral interventions (Kazdin, 1987; Miller & Prinz, 1990; Southam Gerow & Kendall, 1997). This chapter focuses primarily on the cognitive-behavioral interventions.

THEORIES, CONCEPTS, CENTRAL FEATURES, AND CATEGORIZATION OF ANGER AND AGGRESSION

A variety of terms used to describe acting-out behavior in children and adolescents result in confusion and lack of precision. Our difficulties in understanding acting out in youth comes not only as a function of the entanglement of terms used to describe such behavior but also from the differing conceptional models that are employed in understanding such emotion and behavior. The value of any psychological theory is measured, at least in part, by its usefulness in improving assessment and therapeutic intervention procedures. Interest in several traditional theories of aggression has diminished, particularly as deficiencies in their conceptional and derived therapeutic techniques have become apparent. Among these are theories that view aggressive behavior, like virtually all other social behavior, as being under instinctual control (instinctual theory: McDougall, 1931); that view aggression as an expression of a death instinct (psychoanalytic theory:

Freud, 1920); that consider aggressive behavior to consist of clearly organized response patterns released in each species by specific external or
"sign" stimuli (ethological theory: Lorenz, 1966); and that view aggression
as a frustration-produced drive (frustration–aggression hypotheses: Dollard, Doob, Miller, Mower, & Sears, 1939). It is the social learning
(Bandura, 1986) and cognitive-behavioral theories (Novaco, 1978, 1979)
that have emerged and been sustained as the most widely held theories of
aggressive behavior in children and adolescents (Nelson, Hart, & Finch,
1993). Social learning theory holds that aggressive behaviors are learned either through direct experience or observation. The cognitive-behavioral
model expands this position and views *anger* as an intense emotional response to frustration or provocation, characterized by heightened automatic arousal, changes in central nervous system activity, and cognitive labeling of the physiological arousal as anger. Thus, aggression is viewed as
only one of the potential overt expressions of the subjective experience of
anger.

As previously indicated, it is important to clarify the terms used to describe acting-out behavior in children and adolescents. *Anger* is the internal
experience of a private, subjective event (i.e., emotion) that has cognitive
(e.g., thoughts, self-statements, private speech, images, attributions) and
physiological components. *Aggression* involves behavioral acts that inflict
bodily or mental harm on others (Loeber & Hay, 1997). Aggression causes
less serious harm than *violence*, where the aggressive acts cause serious
harm (e.g., aggravated assault, rape, robbery, homicide; Loeber &
Stouthamer-Loeber, 1998). There are two primary classification approaches in describing aggressive acting out in youth: (1) the empirically investigated, multivariate statistical approaches that distinguish among dimensions of externalized (typified by impulsive, overactive, aggressive,
antisocial actions) and internalized (characterized by dysphoric, withdrawn, anxious, somaticizing features) conflict (Achenbach, 1991; Quay,
1986); and (2) the more clinically derived DSM-IV (American Psychiatric
Association, 1994). The diagnostic categories of "conduct disorder" (CD)
and "oppositional defiant disorder" (ODD) are the two primary classification categories for youth in DSM-IV, while antisocial personality disorder is
reserved for adults. Despite the wide acceptance of these classification systems, they do not necessarily provide better understanding of the problem
for the practicing clinician. There are more clinically useful ways of categorizing the levels of aggressive behavior of children and adolescents. Practicing clinicians, in obtaining assessment information from the children/ad-
olescents, their parents, teachers, and significant others, can categorize the
anger and aggression exhibited by children in terms of levels of anger and
aggression.

Distinctions among various levels of anger and aggression are an important first step not only in clinical assessment, but also in setting the stage for cognitive-behavioral interventions. Such clinically useful diagnostic distinctions, as opposed to the clinically derived DSM-IV and empirically derived (e.g., Achenbach Child Behavior Checklist) classification systems, not only assist the therapist in planning appropriate interventions but also help the family of the youngster accurately assess the severity and dangerousness of the aggressive behavior. This distinction is particularly important in dealing with clients whose primary problems are anger and aggression, in that their behavior frequently elicits strong emotional responses not only in family members and significant individuals around them, but also in the therapist. Such emotional reactions may result in the immediate assumption that the youngster is "bad" or more seriously dangerous than is actually the case.

In general, therapists tend to err in the direction of assuming greater danger than is warranted (Buchanan, 1997; Limandri & Sheridan, 1995; Monahan & Walker, 1990). As such, a therapist's assessment in evaluating a problem may be skewed because of the level of fear a parent or teacher may have in attempting to manage the youngster who seems out of control. Therefore, it is important to distinguish among anger, threats of violence against others, and actually carrying those threats out. In such a diagnostic process, parents and significant others need to be sensitized to and recognize the differences among anger, verbal aggression, and different levels of physical aggression, in the sense that such behaviors range from being obnoxious and inflammatory to seriously harmful or violent. By differentiating anger and aggression in a more clinically-useful fashion, a clearer and more realistic picture of the seriousness of the problem can be ascertained. The relevant dimensions of anger, aggression, and violence in the clinically useful classification system (adapted from Price, 1996) are depicted in Table 4.1 and explained below.

Level 1: The Impatient/Annoying/Irritating Child

Youngsters at Level 1 whine, complain, and become enraged whenever they are told "no," do not get their way, or are challenged. They raise their voices, hold their breath, and their faces become red. Such anger is "controlled" and they may even turn such anger against themselves and say, "I hate myself; I'm always doing the wrong thing; I'm stupid, etc."

Level 2: The Stubborn/Dramatic Child

Children and adolescents at Level 2 stubbornly refuse to follow directions or comply with requests. They become enraged and exhibit verbal aggression in the sense of swearing, calling others names, hurling insults, and so

TABLE 4.1. Relevant Dimensions in a Clinically Useful Classification System

	Anger	Verbal aggression directed at self	Verbal aggression directed at others	Physical aggression against inanimate objects	Physical aggression against others	Violence
Level 1	•	•				
Level 2	•	•	•			
Level 3	•	•	•	Minimal damage •		
Level 4	•	•	•	Severe damage •		
Level 5	•	•	•	•	Unintentional harm	
						Intentional harm
Level 6	•	•	•	•	•	•

on. Such verbally assaultive behavior may be interpreted by parents as indicating that their child is on the verge of violence. Children's dramatic behavior often is sufficient (in terms of intensity and/or frequency) to convince adults that their children are "out of control" when, in fact, they are angry and expressing this feeling only verbally. A 15-year-old who takes a few steps toward his mother and calls her a "bitch" demonstrates Level 2 behavior.

Level 3: The Threatening Child and the Beginning of Damage

At Level 3, children become increasingly angry (in terms of frequency and/or intensity) and the range of their verbal aggression includes threats to injure or kill parents, siblings, peers, and/or animals. It should be noted that at Level 3, youngsters have never really injured any human being or living thing. They are still primarily engaged in verbal aggression and threats, although they may have caused minimal damage to nonvaluable inanimate objects. A 10-year-old kicks his chair and it puts a good-size dent in the plaster wall, but the fact that he avoids throwing knives, glasses, or objects at the television demonstrates that he is still cognizant of how serious more severe forms of aggression against inanimate objects might be. Thus, he is clearly thinking about how far he is going, even though parents (or therapist) may interpret this behavior as clearly "out of control."

Level 4: The "Taking It Up a Notch" Child

Children at Level 4 are purposely and intentionally venting their anger against inanimate objects by seriously damaging or destroying things. They become so enraged that they exhibit aggressive behavior such as punching a hole in the wall, throwing an object through a window, or breaking increasingly valuable objects. Youngsters may actually threaten to hit a family member with an object or weapon such as a baseball bat, hammer, or knife. However, the most important distinction to make at this level is the fact that there is no actual physical contact or harming of another. These teenagers, when they become enraged, may threaten others but keep a distance between the person they view as the antagonist and themselves. They usually retreat or storm out of the room, however, when approached. Most parents believe that their child is very dangerous at this time and can become quite intimidated by him or her. Nevertheless, these youngsters are exhibiting some cognitive and behavioral control in the sense that their verbal aggression against others and their physical aggression against inanimate objects is not escalating into actual physical violence against others.

Level 5: The Assaultive Child

At Level 5, the child has moved well beyond expressions of verbal anger and physical aggression exhibited against inanimate objects to physical aggression involving acts that inflict bodily harm on others. Thus, actual physical aggression often accompanies verbal threats. At this level, however, the aggression does not involve violence or serious bodily injury. Such behavior includes pushing, shoving, shouldering, hitting, and throwing objects at others that would not result in serious harm (e.g., tennis ball, pencil, plastic cup, stuffed animal). Actual physical injuries at this level are minor, and such injuries tend to be more incidental than directly intentional. For example, a 12-year-old boy might throw a tennis ball across the room and accidentally hit his sister. Even though she may have fallen down and bruised her arm, this injury is basically unintentional insomuch as he did not anticipate the outcome. Although it may be difficult, it is important to assess whether the adolescent has actually made a choice to injure someone physically or whether the injury was an unintentional outcome of an angry/aggressive outburst. At this point, the parents are usually very frightened and legitimately fearful that their child might truly lose control and physically harm someone in a violent fashion.

Level 6: The Violent Child

Adolescents or children at Level 6 exhibit violent behavior that causes serious harm and is dangerous to others. They deliberately throw dangerous objects at others or attack others with their fists, with the intention to injure them. Weapons may be more deliberately used, such as when a 15-year-old girl deliberately struck her 9-year-old brother with a tree limb because he would not give her a ball. The important dimension in Level 6 is actually violent behavior, where physical harm is intended and occurs. At this stage, parents feel intimidated, hopeless, and even abused. They may seem "shell-shocked" or "burned out" because of the humiliation and abusiveness they have suffered over the years. They may even feel resigned to the violence that has escalated from verbal expressions of anger to aggression against inanimate objects, to aggression unintentionally resulting in minor bodily harm, to actual violence toward others. Parents often view their situation as being so terrible that they no longer have any control over the situation whatsoever, and feel lost, abandoned, and hopeless. Price (1996) refers to these parents as being "emotionally and physically abused" by their children.

THE COGNITIVE-BEHAVIORAL TREATMENT
OF ANGER AND AGGRESSION IN YOUTH

Cognitive-behavioral treatment draws upon the rich traditions of behavior modification, rational–emotive, and cognitive therapy, and integrates knowledge about social cognition (Dodge, 1991). As such, cognitive-behavioral treatment interventions do not involve a single therapeutic technique, but rather consist of multiple intervention components: (1) problem-solving and social skills education, (2) coping models, (3) role playing, (4) *in vivo* experiences and assignments, (5) affective education, (6) homework assignments, and (7) operant conditioning, most typically response–cost (Kendall & Braswell, 1993). In addition, therapeutic interventions include a variety of self-control strategies that not only teach the child to inhibit aggressive behavior through the use of cognitive processing (in other words, to put thought between the environmental stimulus or "trigger" and the overt aggressive response) but also teach alternative skills to inhibit acting in an aggressive fashion. The cognitive-behavioral approach is unified by the principles of learning theory and information processing, and therefore is not simply a loose technical eclecticism.

   To date, there have been only two attempts to meta-analyze studies of anger management (Beck & Fernandez, 1998; Tafrate, 1995). However, Tafrate's survey was confined to adult samples. On the other hand, Beck and Fernandez's study involved not only adults and children, but also incorporated unpublished studies. Their final sample consisted of 50 nomothetic studies that included 1,640 participants and provided at least one anger-related measure of change. They included only cognitive-behavioral interventions for anger, which typically involved multiple intervention techniques. Their results indicated that cognitive-behavioral interventions were suggestive of moderate treatment gains in that the average treatment participant improved more than 76% of the control participants. Twenty-five of the 35 studies (two articles reported results of two different studies) used in their meta-analytic calculations had different samples of children and/or adolescents. These 25 studies were examined as to the number of participants, sex, age, intervention techniques, outcome measures, and results.[1] There were multiple cognitive-behavioral interventions employed in these studies (e.g., self-monitoring, self-instruction, problem solving, relaxation, assertion training, goal setting, perspective taking). In addition, samples included youth ranging in age from 8 to 21 years. Seventeen samples involved males only, and eight involved males and females. Outcome measures also varied but, typically, self-reported anger was utilized as the dependent variable for these younger populations. When self-reported anger was not feasible, behavioral ratings of aggression and/or ratings by significant others were often employed as dependent variables.

THE COGNITIVE-BEHAVIORAL MODEL OF ANGER

Guided by the cognitive-behavioral model of anger (see Figure 4.1), cognitive-behavioral therapy includes a set of general therapeutic interventions that are individually tailored to fit the child's specific circumstances in terms of dealing with external environmental stimuli and/or internal stimuli and the specific aggressive responses to these stimuli. Any model of anger needs to be not only comprehensive enough to guide the clinician in effectively utilizing therapy interventions but also simple enough for the child or adolescent to understand (at least with the assistance of the therapist) the nature of his or her anger and subsequent aggressive behavior. Thus, the cognitive-behavioral model provides the framework not only for the therapist to understand the child but also for the child to understand his or her problems that have necessitated therapy.

The cognitive-behavioral model is based on the rationale that children's emotions and subsequent actions are regulated by the way they perceive, processes, and/or mediate environmental events. The problem or environmental events themselves do not directly determine how persons feel or what they actually do in any given circumstance. Anger is a subjective reaction to day-to-day problems or "triggers." The experience of the emotion of anger is an integration of cognitive processing of physiological events (cognitive arousal theory of emotion; Mandler, 1984; Schachter, 1964; Schachter & Singer, 1962). It is assumed that aggressive youngsters lack the necessary psychological resources for coping with problems and are, therefore, prone to react in an aggressive fashion when encountering a provoking situation. Thus, the cognitive-behavioral model is a skills-deficit

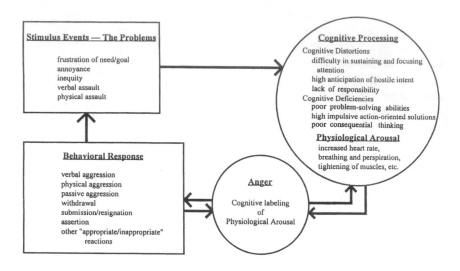

FIGURE 4.1. Cognitive-behavioral model of anger and aggression.

model. In order to cope with problems or stressors, the child needs to develop the necessary skills to effectively manage the subjective state of anger, which then results in more adaptive behavioral reaction. Specific cognitive-behavioral intervention techniques involve both direct action procedures (e.g., assertion training, relaxation techniques) and/or cognitive interventions (e.g., self-talk, problem solving, humor). In the former procedures, the focus is on teaching the child alternative ways of responding to problems or stress. In the latter cognitive techniques, the focus is on changing the child's cognitions concerning anger-provoking situations or the processing of such situations. In both cases, the desired outcome is a more adaptive change in subsequent behavior.

THE THERAPEUTIC RELATIONSHIP AND THE STRESS INOCULATION PARADIGM FOR AGGRESSIVE YOUTH

It is essential that clinicians have not only a conceptual model of anger and aggression to understand such emotions and behavior but also a model in which a variety of intervention techniques can be conceptualized and integrated into an effective therapeutic intervention treatment plan (Finch, Nelson, & Ott, 1993; Meichenbaum, 1977; Novaco, 1979). The stress inoculation model provides such a framework and can be seen in Table 4.2.

However, before discussing specific stress inoculation strategies, it is

TABLE 4.2. Four Phases in the Stress Inoculation Training Model

1. Assessment
2. Educational Phase (cognitive preparation)
3. Skills Acquisition Phase (rehearsal)
4. Application Training (practice, practice, and more practice . . .)

important to consider the type of therapeutic relationship that a cognitive-behavioral therapist attempts to establish with aggressive youth. Such clients provide a variety of different challenges in therapy because of their dysfunctional beliefs, self-statements, and ways of interacting with others. Aggressive youngsters may believe that no one understands them, especially because they frequently believe that it is others who provoke them into aggressive responses. They may believe that "Others will get me if I don't get them first" or "If I don't push other people, I will get pushed around." Not only do angry youngsters frequently not want to come to therapy but also when forced to do so by parents or others in authority, they often view the therapist in the same negative light in which they perceive adults outside of therapy. Thus, therapists "have their work cut out for them" in trying to establish a positive therapeutic relationship with aggressive children and adolescents.

Cognitive-behavioral interventions are best grounded in a "collaborative empiricism" (Beck, Rush, Shaw, & Emery, 1979; see also Kendall, Chapter 1, this volume). In other words, a collaborative relationship is established with the child so that the "therapist–client team" works against the common opponent, anger/aggression. It is essential to form such a collaborative relationship with acting-out youngsters, who frequently view adults or authority figures as "the enemy." Such relationships are forged by aligning with children to assist the therapist in developing better skills to avoid suffering aversive consequences after behaving in a maladaptive, aggressive fashion. Most acting-out children are acutely aware of the fact that it is they who "end up in hot water" or "get the short end of the stick" in many situations, even though they frequently minimize or deny their own responsibility in the aggressive cycle or chain of events. Thus, they view themselves as victims in most situations. Attempts to convince them otherwise, especially in initial contacts, frequently lead to a rift in the therapist–client relationship. Consequently, it is recommended that therapists "side-step" such a power struggle and form an alliance with the youngster against what can be conceptualized as "the enemy"—unbridled anger and subsequent maladaptive aggression or violence. It is during the early phases of treatment that the groundwork is established in the therapeutic relationship.

Although it is better to continue multimethod assessment over the course of treatment in order to ascertain any therapeutic gains, this may not always be feasible for practicing clinicians who frequently rely more on self- or parent-report devices. For experimental studies in assessing anger management interventions, it is important to assess during at least two time periods, once initially for selection for treatment/therapy, and once immediately before intervention is to begin. In this way, the actual status of the client immediately preceding treatment can be ascertained, as well as the issue of stability of self-report measures (Kendall & Flannery-Schroeder, 1995; Kendall, Hollon, Beck, Hammen, & Ingram, 1987).

For the practicing clinician, it is also important to note that there are likely gender-related differences in forms of overt aggression. Girls tend to be nominated more by their peers as relationally aggressive, while boys are described more frequently as overtly aggressive (e.g., Cairns, Cairns, Neckerman, Ferguson, & Gariepy, 1989; Crick & Grotpeter, 1995; Lagerspetz, Bjorkqvist, & Peltonen, 1988). Overt aggression involves both direct verbal and physical aggression that can be harmful to others, whereas relational aggression tends to be more harmful to others indirectly, causing damage to peer relationships by way of manipulation and control (Crick, Casas, & Mosher, 1997). This is an important factor to remember when developing anger hierarchies during the initial assessment and treatment.

The first stage of treatment, the Assessment Phase, involves a thorough multimodal process to identify the external environmental stimuli and/or internal "triggers." Assessment techniques not only help the clinician understand the interconnections between cognition, emotion, and behavior but also can be utilized to develop the collaborative alliance between therapist and child. The second stage, the Educational Phase, involves teaching children about the nature of their feelings of anger and how subsequent aggressive behavior can be self-defeating and "get them into trouble." Thus, the Educational Phase sets the stage for the youngster to become more aware of how the anger experience (involving cognitions and physiological events) can lead to maladaptive acting out. This increased awareness involves a self-observation or self-monitoring of autonomic and physiological processes, so that the child can better understand the two components of anger (feelings and cognitions) and how these can be utilized in the third stage, the Skills Acquisition Phase, to better manage anger and subsequent aggression. Thus, these self-observations are utilized to increase the child's awareness of not only the environmental "triggers" for anger and aggressive acting out but also to help him or her recognize the maladaptive cognitive–physiological–behavioral chain. Finally, in the Application Training Phase, children are exposed in a hierarchical fashion to progressively more problematic situations in order to practice their newly learned anger management skills.

We have developed a treatment workbook, *Keeping Your Cool* (Nelson & Finch, 1996), that integrates five of the most often utilized cognitive-behavioral intervention techniques for use with acting-out children into a structured, yet flexible, intervention regimen. Such a prevention program can be utilized as a primary or secondary intervention strategy. In fact, The *Summary Report of the American Psychological Association Commission on Violence and Youth* (American Psychological Association, 1993) indicated that "primary prevention programs that promote social and cognitive skills seem to have the greatest impact on attitudes about violent behavior among children and youth" (p. 56) and "secondary prevention programs that focus on improving individual affective, cognitive, and behavioral skills . . . offer promise of interrupting the path toward violence for high-risk or predeliquent youth" (p. 56). The *Keeping Your Cool* workbook has integrated a number of these empirically supported procedures into a psychoeducational workbook format—verbal self-instructions, relaxation training, problem solving, assertion training, and humor. These particular procedures were selected because of their individually demonstrated usefulness and their theoretical consistency within the cognitive-behavioral model of anger management. The use of verbal self-instructions as a treatment approach grew out of the theories of Vygotsky (1962, 1934/1987) and Luria (1959, 1961). These two Soviet psychologists suggested that verbal commands need to be internalized in order for a child to gain voluntary control over overt behavior. A potential model for this development of control was presented by Luria and later utilized by Meichenbaum and Goodman (1971) in modifying an impulsive cognitive style in normal children. Subsequently Finch, Wilkinson, Nelson, and Montgomery (1975) and Kendall and Finch (1976, 1978) applied these procedures with children referred for emotional problems, and Rath (1992) has demonstrated their effectiveness with disadvantaged children. Kendall and Braswell (1993) have summarized the research in this area, identifying a number of factors influencing the effectiveness of self-instructional training.

Relaxation training usually follows a set of procedures first introduced by Jacobsen (1938). Various muscle groups are isolated and the feeling of relaxation is enhanced by comparison with tension. These procedures have been modified for children by Koeppen (1974). Relaxation training has been found to be useful in children not only for the reduction of anxiety (Eisen & Silverman, 1993), depression (Dujovne, Barnard, & Rapoff, 1995; Reynolds & Coats, 1986), and anger (Deffenbacher, Lynch, Oetting, & Kemper, 1996), but also for the increase of positive psychological attitudes (Benson, Kornhaber, Kornhaber, & LeChanu, 1994). In addition, there is some suggestion that relaxation training may be more effective with physical symptoms than cognitive ones (Eisen & Silverman, 1993). We have found this finding to be consistent with our clinical work with angry children. Most of the children and adolescents who have anger management problems tense their muscles as their anger increases. This increase in tension seems to be a signal that is often interpreted by the individual as a preparation for some aggressive act. Through relaxation training, the individual is taught to reinterpret these signals as a call to engage in relaxation.

The third treatment strategy in the *Keeping Your Cool* workbook is problem solving. Problem-solving skills have been identified as deficient in a variety of disorders. For example, training in problem solving has been employed in the treatment of depression (Clarke, Lewinsohn, & Hops, 1990), marital problems (Jacobson, 1984), and anger (Lochman & Curry, 1986). Clinically, aggressive children and adolescents appear markedly deficient in solving their interpersonal problems. Their first response to a wide range of problem situations is anger, and they seem to lack other skills in seeking alternative solutions. A variety of studies have found problem-solving training to be helpful with these youngsters (Barrett, 1998; Dangel, Deschner, & Rasp, 1989; Eargle, Guerra, & Tolan, 1994; Spivack, Platt, & Shure, 1976).

Assertiveness training has been a widely used and popular intervention, as indicated by the publication of the seventh edition of Alberti and Emmons's self-help book, *Your Perfect Right* (1995). Within the anger management area, the rationale for the use of assertiveness training is that individuals have difficulty standing up for themselves and/or making their needs known to others in an appropriately assertive manner. As a result of these skills deficits, they respond in an aggressive or angry manner. With children and adolescents, assertiveness training has been found to be effective in improving self-concept (Waksman, 1981), raising self-esteem in minority females (Stewart & Lewis, 1986), increasing appropriate interaction with teachers (Pentz, 1980), and decreasing self-reported aggressiveness (Dong, Hallberg, & Hassard, 1979).

Humor, by design, is comical or amusing and therefore elicits an incompatible emotional response with anger. Its use in psychotherapy (Buckman, 1994; Chapman & Chapman-Santana, 1995; Fry & Salameh, 1993) and assessment (Bernet, 1993; Dana, 1994) has been widely discussed. Specific guidelines for its use with children and adolescents have been published (Ventis & Ventis, 1988). Despite all the discussion about the use of humor, there is a dearth of research on the effectiveness of its use. It has been our clinical impression that humor not only can be an effective tool in the reduction of tension and anger with children and adolescents but also can serve to improve the collaborative therapeutic relationship between the therapist and the client.

Although the use of psychotherapy training manuals has been debated (e.g., Addis, 1997; Strupp & Anderson, 1997), we hope that the manual and workbook provide clinicians with concrete descriptions and procedures of intervention techniques, as well as a theoretical framework to guide or augment treatment. The workbook format is not meant to be a mechanical set of rules but rather is a way of structuring interventions for therapists wanting to use a cognitive-behavioral approach. In addition, such workbooks may become increasingly useful for clients, as increasing pressure from third-party reimbursers and policymakers frequently caps the number of therapy sessions available to clients. Workbooks can expand the therapeutic armaments of the clinician by providing a way to offer more structured interventions outside of the typical therapy hour.

Thus, the *Keeping Your Cool* workbook offers a sequential, stepwise program to teach cognitive-behaviorally based anger management skills to acting-out youth. The five specific intervention strategies or "plays" presented in the workbook help children identify potentially problematic situations early on, process the environmental cues, of which they become more accurately aware, and provide a variety of anger management skills they can draw upon in dealing with day-to-day problem or anger-provoking situations. These basic strategies in the workbook are also augmented by other cognitive-behavioral techniques found to have some empirical support in the cognitive-behavioral literature—goal setting, self-monitoring, perspective taking, and changing irrational beliefs.

Phase I: Assessment

The assessment of anger in children is both a multidimensional process and one that is likely to be shaped by the nature of the anger management problems presented. However, certain core components should be considered. The initial decision concerns with whom the therapist should meet for the initial interview. Some therapists would suggest that parents should be seen initially, to determine the nature of the problem; others suggest meeting with the child alone initially, and still others suggest meeting with the entire family during this initial session. We recommend that the entire family be seen during the initial session if at all possible. The reason for this approach is to directly observe the interactions among family members and to avoid the perception by the child that anything secretive is being planned. Children with anger management problems generally have a history of conflict with authority figures and are quick to believe that they are in trouble again. Having their parents meet with another authority figure, without personally hearing what is said, has the potential to result in a negative perception by the child. Many of these children have fears about what will be said, and their misconceptions are generally worse than what is actually conveyed.

Another advantage of meeting with the entire family at once is to observe the interactions of the family members. Considerable information about interactions, respect, and lines of communication can be learned quickly by observing interactions firsthand. Estimations of how best to deal with issues of compliance and sabotage can be assessed quickly. In addition, the clinician can obtain some indication of how angry the parents are with the child, and with each other, about the problem. Such information can be very useful once treatment begins.

After the initial session with the entire family, the next session can be divided between meeting with the parents alone and/or with the child. During these meetings, more detailed information is obtained about specific behaviors, including a description of general and specific incidences of problems in dealing with anger. Care should be taken to ensure that the child is not made to feel defensive. By the time the child meets with the therapist, he or she has been lectured, scolded, punished by many adults, and often feels guilty and defensive. Often, the natural response is to withdraw and remain silent. Minimization is to be expected, and the therapist is likely to need a "warm up" period with the child in which other issues are discussed rather than the specific problems that brought the child to the office. An alliance with the child against a specific problem or "common enemy" (anger) needs to be established, but this alliance may have to be developed slowly and indirectly.

Interviewing children can take a variety of different directions. Children with anger management problems frequently answer even open-ended questions with one- or two-word answers, or simple shrugs. Given that many of the factors that the cognitive-behavioral therapist wants to explore are private (e.g., negative self-statements), the therapist must be patient and supportive of the child. Frequently, children will minimize or present themselves in the "best light." We have found that confrontation, rather than helping, only increases the child's defensiveness. A more indirect approach may be necessary. The following case material with 11-year-old Josh illustrates this point.

Inside the Therapist's Office

THERAPIST: Tell me about the last time you were angry with your sister.

JOSH: I was running late getting ready for school . . .

THERAPIST: Tell me a little more about your "running late." What happened?

JOSH: She called me a "slug."

THERAPIST: When she called you a slug, what did you do?

JOSH: I told her that it made me mad when she called me a slug, and she said she was sorry.

[Comments: The therapist knew that Josh actually threw his books at his sister and a physical fight followed, in which Josh was so angry/aggressive that his mother had to seek assistance in controlling him. However, the therapist also believed that Josh was attempting to place himself in the best light. The therapist believed that, if confronted, Josh would simply react in a more defensive manner. The therapist responded with a "side step."]

THERAPIST: I wonder if you would tell me about another time your sister made you mad and you did not handle it so well. Tell me about a time you kind of lost it with her.

[*Comments*: Here, the therapist is giving Josh permission to share freely an incident that is selected because he did not handle his anger very well. By definition, there is no need for Josh to present himself in the best light.]

As a number of interview techniques for use with children with anger management problems have previously been presented (Finch, Nelson, & Moss, 1993), only a brief discussion is included here. In many cases, we have found it very useful to have the child "run a movie" of an incident. Children are familiar with VCR terms such as "pausing," "reversing," and "rerunning" from their home videos and seem to have little difficulty engaging in this activity. The therapist simply asks the child to close his or her eyes and visualize the event. Next, the child is asked to "play" the scene and provide the therapist with a verbal description of what is being played. The therapist can help the child focus attention by asking specific questions about internal dialogue, visual images, physiological sensations, and other potentially important details. While the child is providing this description, the therapist needs to "record" the scene (take detailed notes) for later "play back" and "editing" during future sessions.

Younger children (below about 10 years of age) frequently have difficulty with "running a movie." Their attention typically drifts and they appear to need a more concrete approach. With this age group we have attempted a variety of other approaches. One of the most useful has been "action figure drawings." In this task, the child is asked to describe the scene and the therapist makes a stick figure drawing of the described scene. The therapist can ask questions to help "make the drawing," while actually obtaining information about the desired feelings, thoughts, and physical sensations. Internal dialogue can be noted with bubbles (as utilized in cartoons), while external speech is noted by a continuous line. Children tend to enjoy this task and it can help to develop a sense of collaboration that becomes highly useful later in therapy.

Other procedures for assessing anger with children include self-report measures. Because anger is an internal feeling and not an external behavior, self-report measures provide the most direct means of assessing it. As has been pointed out by Quay and La Greca (1986), internal self-statements and emotions are difficult for parents and teachers to identify accurately. There are serious questions that have to be realized when self-report measures are being used. As Finch and Politano (1994) have pointed out, self-report measures assume that the child is willing and able to report his or her internal feelings. This fact makes the development of a trusting and collaborative relationship even more important in the assessment of anger.

One of the most useful measures that we have found in the self-report of anger is the Children's Inventory of Anger (ChIA; Nelson & Finch, in press). The ChIA consists of 48 items that require children to rate how the items apply to them on a 4-point scale ranging from "I don't care. That situation doesn't even bother me. I don't know why that would make anyone mad (angry)" to "I can't stand that! I'm furious! I feel like really hurting or killing that person or destroying that thing!" The items are written on a fourth-grade reading level and involve a variety of situations that might occur at home, at school, in peer interactions, and in other potentially anger-provoking situations. A number of other self-report measures have also been found to be useful. The Children's Action Tendency Scale (CATS) is a self-report inventory developed to evaluate levels of assertiveness in children (Deluty, 1979). One of the various potential responses to conflict situations is anger or aggression. The CATS has been found to be useful in a variety of situations and has acceptable levels of reliability.

Information about the child's anger management can be obtained from parents and teachers as well as other individuals who may have the opportunity to observe the problem. These individuals can provide important information for the therapist about the child's behavior, precipitating evens, and the subsequent outcomes. This information often proves highly useful in individually tailoring a treatment program for the particular child. In addition, children are not always the best reporters of their own behavior. Sometimes they are unaware of their own behaviors, while at other times, they deny/minimize their role in the situation.

As was discussed by Finch, Nelson, and Moss (1993), the therapist should focus the interview with significant others on obtaining information on the following:

1. The informant's view of the child's complaint, symptoms, and stressors.
2. The informant's view of the child's current environment (home, school, peers).
3. The informant's view of the child's development and history.
4. The informant's expectations about the child's future.

More general measures of behavior can be obtained from behavioral checklists. Popular rating scales frequently employed include the Behavioral Assessment System for Children (BASC; Reynolds & Kamphaus, 1992) and the Child Behavior Checklist (Achenbach & Edelbrock, 1983). Both of these scales provide different forms to be completed by parents, teachers, and older children. These different perspectives can be very useful in evaluating the effectiveness of treatment as well as planning it.

Another useful anger scale is the Children's Hostility Inventory (Kazdin, Rodgers, Colbus, & Siegel, 1987). This scale consists of 38 items related to hostility and aggression that can be completed by parents. It is clinically useful to ask the children themselves to respond to these items and then to compare their responses to those of their parents. Frequently, the clinician can gain some understanding of the differences in perspective between parents and their children. However, there are not data available on the psychometric properties of this scale when completed by children.

On a more informal basis, we have found it useful to use behavioral role playing of anger-provoking situations. In these role-playing situations, anger-provoking interactions are staged and the child is asked to respond to them. After a few minutes of "warmup," most children are able to become comfortable with these situations and fall into the same behaviors that have led to their being referred. We have been surprised at the number of times children have become angry in these artificial situations. It is important to establish the "ground rules" before these role-playing situations are initiated in order to have clearly defined limits and signals to "stop the action." Parents, siblings, and peers can be used successfully when clearly defined escape plans are established. The amount of information that can be obtained by using such "staged" interactions is very impressive.

Phase II: Educational Phase

Although an extension of the Assessment Phase rather than a discrete shift in therapy, the Educational Phase has four main purposes: (1) to continue forming a collaborative alliance with the child to work against the common "enemy," anger; (2) to help the child further understand the nature of his or her anger and subsequent aggressive behavior; (3) to quickly recognize the cognitive–affective–behavioral links early in the anger-arousing response chain; and (4) to continue to identify and recognize the specific environmental stimuli or problems that "trigger" the anger–aggression response pattern. First, the strategy of joining with the child to form a "team" works better with aggressive youngsters because it helps avoid the aversive consequences that typically follow maladaptive aggressive acting out; the goal of collaborative empiricism is facilitated. Second, in a collaborative attempt to teach the child the two components of anger (cognitions and physiological processes) that precede aggressive behavior, the child is given the clear message that he or she can control and better manage his or her own thoughts/images and feelings, and is not a helpless victim solely at the mercy of anger-engendering stressors. The workbooks provide specific psychoeducational tasks to augment the therapist's skillful, persuasive efforts aimed not only at teaching the child about his or her own experience of anger but also at setting the stage for how the intervention strategies in the skills acquisition phase can be utilized to short circuit the maladaptive cognitive–affective–behavioral reaction.

The understanding of anger and aggression is integrated into the cognitive-behavioral framework of personality and presented as the "ABCs of personality." In other words, an individual's personality and the experience of anger is determined by how one thinks (A), feels (B), and acts (C). This ABC paradigm is derived from the rational–emotive model (Ellis, 1971, 1973; Ellis & Grieger, 1977) A, the activating experience, refers to the external event, problem, or "trigger" to which the child is exposed. B, the belief, refers to the chain of thoughts, images or specific self-verbalizations that result in internal feelings and subsequent actions (behaviors) the adolescent goes through in response to A. Thus, B symbolizes the cognitive processes that occur within the adolescent in response to external events. Such processes include the child's appraisal of the situation, anticipated reactions of others, and self-statements in response to activating events. Finally, C, the consequences, refers to the environmental reactions that result from others reacting to the behavior of the adolescent.

Inside the Therapist's Office

The following is a brief interaction between the therapist and Freddie, a 14-year-old young man referred for his anger management problems.

THERAPIST: I understand that you and your mom had a big fight Saturday.

FREDDIE: Yeah, she wouldn't leave me alone (*very angry tone*).

THERAPIST: Tell me a little more about it.

FREDDIE: She told me I was grounded (*angry tone*).

[*Comments*: This is a fairly typical exchange with an adolescent. The therapist finds him- or herself in the middle of an interaction. It seems likely that Freddie's mother grounding him is an event that happened as part of a more complex interaction and was not the start of it.]

THERAPIST: Let's start over. What time did you get up Saturday morning?

[*Comments*: This is a closed-ended question that the therapist hopes will help Freddie begin discussing the interaction at the beginning and at a less emotionally charged part of the interaction.]

FREDDIE: On Saturday I don't have to get up until mom gets home from exercise. That is usually around 10 (*matter-of-fact tone*).

THERAPIST: Does she call you or do you just get up when she gets home?

FREDDIE: She comes in and calls me. I get dressed while she is cooking breakfast.

THERAPIST: So she cooks breakfast on Saturday?

FREDDIE: Yeah, during the week we usually eat cereal or toast, but on Saturday Mom cooks a big breakfast and she and I eat together.

THERAPIST: During the week, I guess things are pretty rushed, with you getting ready for school and your mom getting ready for work. But on Saturday, it sounds like that is a little more relaxed.

FREDDIE: (*Nods.*)

THERAPIST: So you had breakfast together. Then what happened?

FREDDIE: She told me to start cleaning up my room. I was supposed to clean it on Friday afternoon but Will came over.

THERAPIST: So you didn't clean it up on Friday.

FREDDIE: No, we played on the computer and then watched a movie.

THERAPIST: So here is the room still waiting to be cleaned. What happened then?

FREDDIE: I went upstairs and started cleaning; it was a big mess with all my stuff everywhere. I'm not the neat type. (*Smiles.*)

THERAPIST: (*Laughs.*) It seems to come easily to some folks. Then what happens?

FREDDIE: I was cleaning when Trip called and asked if I wanted to go to the beach in the afternoon. Mom said I could, if I got my room cleaned.

THERAPIST: Umhum.

FREDDIE: Mom left to take my grandmother to the grocery store. She doesn't drive.

THERAPIST: I guess she depends on your mom a lot.

FREDDIE: Yea. Mom has to take her lots of places.

THERAPIST: What happens with the room?

FREDDIE: Will calls and we talk for a while. Then I just didn't want to clean it anymore. I watched television for a while and then Mom came back home.

THERAPIST: About how long was she gone?

FREDDIE: An hour and a half.

THERAPIST: Then what happened?

FREDDIE: She comes in and starts telling me I had better get busy if I'm going to the beach with Trip and his parents.

THERAPIST: She wanted you to start back cleaning your room.

FREDDIE: Yeah, she said I hadn't done anything since she left, and I had to get it done before I could go to the beach.

THERAPIST: What did you say?

FREDDIE: I told her I could clean it up when I got back, and she said I had to have it cleaned before I could go to the beach.

THERAPIST: How were you feeling?

FREDDIE: I was getting a little mad—that's bullshit! That is what you do with babies, not 14-year-olds! . . . Yeah and then I couldn't find my bathing suit.

THERAPIST: Another delay.

FREDDIE: So I start back cleaning and then Trip calls and says they are ready to go to the beach.

THERAPIST: And your room was still a mess.

FREDDIE: Pretty much. I start to leave and Mom says I can't go.

THERAPIST: Umhum.

FREDDIE: I told her that was bullshit, and she said not to talk to her that way.

THERAPIST: I started to leave and she told me to stop, that I was not going. I went back to my room and slammed the door.

THERAPIST: Is that when you threw the Coke?

FREDDIE: Yea. I was drinking a Coke and just threw it.

THERAPIST: Sounds like you were pretty angry then.

FREDDIE: Damn straight. What was Trip going to think?—"Freddie's mother won't let him go." Such bullshit.

THERAPIST: Is this when you got grounded?

FREDDIE: Yeah, for a whole week.

THERAPIST: And then you trashed your room?

FREDDIE: Yeah, I dumped everything out.

From a cognitive-behavioral model, the above interaction is replete with a series of escalating interactions that can be conceptualized as a string of ABCs. This scenario depicts a fairly typical situation with a single parent who is dealing with a variety of demands and stressors. There is a 14-year-old who is self-focused (not atypical) and believes that *all* things should go his way. In addition, he is engaging in all-or-none thinking in which he is either a "baby" or grown. A series of interactions lead to an escalating series of emotional/behavioral reactions.

In this interaction, we can assume that the mom is already being pushed by Freddie, who has not done what he has said he would do—clean his room on Friday. Freddie finds himself faced with a boring task that he really does not want to do. In the ABC conceptualization, first there is the loss of the trip to the beach—a very desirable activity. This is an activating (A) event for Freddie. He is disappointed and believes he is being treated like a "baby" (a previously mentioned concern). In addition, he thinks that things *must* go his way and is fearful of being teased by his friends and "losing face" with them. This could be unfortunate, but it is a major disaster to Freddie's way of thinking. This type of belief (B) leads to angry feelings and a subsequent aggressive outburst that is very frightening to his mother. She grounds him (C) for his inappropriate behavior.

Later in the session, the therapist explores with Freddie his irrational belief system and attempts to help him understand how his self-talk and dysfunctional beliefs served to escalate his anger and resulted in an even more undesirable outcome.

Phase III: Skills Acquisition

The third phase within the training stress inoculation model is designed to provide the child with specific techniques, both cognitive and behavioral, to use during the coping process. During this phase, self-management strategies are targeted at the cognitive, affective, and behavioral levels, as anger-reducing self-talk, relaxation techniques, problem-solving skills, assertion training, and humor are introduced and taught. By having the "stage set" during the educational phase, children are further presented with the notion that what they ultimately do in any situation (behavior) is basically a function of how they feel (feelings), which, in turn, is more a function of how they think about a situation and what they say to themselves (e.g., explicit self-talk and thoughts). Thus, aggression is not triggered merely by environmental events but rather by the way in which these events are perceived and processed. Children with anger-control problems have been found to exhibit egocentric and distorted perceptions of social situations (Chandler, 1973; Dodge, Price, Bachorowski, & Newman, 1990; Lochman & Dodge, 1998). In general, aggressive children typically selectively attend to and remember hostile cues in their interactions with others (Dodge et al., 1990). Children with anger-control problems exhibit tendencies to over-recall hostile cues and may even remember situations in hostile terms, even if they were originally positive or neutral (Milich & Dodge, 1984). Perspective taking is a key cognitive element in adolescents' understanding of relationships (e.g., Chandler & Boyes, 1982). Aggressive children and adolescents overattribute hostility on the part of others (e.g., Dodge, 1985; Lochman, Meyer, Rabiner, & White, 1991) in that they quickly assume hostile intent on the part of others and subsequently are more likely to respond in an aggressive fashion based on inaccurately perceived threats. This distorted "viewpoint" of aggressive youth understandably makes them particularly prone to impulsively react aggressively in a wide range of problem situations. One's ability to take the perspective of others and make inferences about their thoughts and attentions is called cognitive perspective taking. One's understanding of the feelings and internal emotions of others is called affective perspective-taking. Both are clearly influenced by developmental factors (e.g., Kimball, Nelson, & Politano, 1993). Such maladaptive interpersonal processing exacerbates the difficulties aggressive children have in interpersonal situations. Thus, aggressive youngsters quickly seem to assume that others will behave in a hostile fashion toward them and are more likely to respond in an aggressive fashion based on inaccurately perceived threats. The "Perspective Check" exercises in the workbook provide therapists with opportunities to deal with such distorted perspective-taking and to help youngsters infer more accurately others' thoughts and intentions (cognitive perspective taking) and subsequently to enhance their understanding of others' feelings and emotional states (affective perspective taking). Workbook tasks assist adolescents in accurately identifying similarities and differences among individuals by considering alternative interpretations of social cues and considering alternative inferences about what others may be thinking or feeling. For example, using the "Perspective Check" cartoon (see Figure 4.2), the child is asked, "How does the boy on the ground feel watching the boy fall off the mountain?" or "How does Joe in the Fracture Clinic feel?" and "How do their perspectives differ?"

The basic educational purpose in these tasks is to help adolescents better understand the idea that individuals (including themselves) frequently misinterpret the intent, thoughts, and/or feelings of others. This idea may also be presented by having the therapist ask how the class bully or someone with a "chip on their shoulder" might respond to someone asking, "Where'd you get that?" (in a gruff voice) and how his or her response would be different from that of someone else, who did not have a "chip on their shoulder." In this way, adolescents learn to evaluate more accurately the intent of others by considering additional alternatives to hostile intent. Again, they are empowered in the sense that it is clarified how their hostile perceptions and appraisals in interpersonal situations, and their subsequent interpretation of others as threatening, can be altered, and they can engage in other cognitive or behavioral activities directed at developing more effective behavioral responses to problems.

The use of anger-reducing self-verbalization and humor are employed in a systematic fashion that involves overt cognitive modeling, overt external guidance; overt self-guidance, faded overt modeling; faded overt self-guidance; covert guidance modeling, and covert self-guidance. The basic strategy is to have individuals engage in anger reducing self-talk or to think of something funny to "short-circuit" the cognitive-affective behavioral aggression chain.

Interventions at the cognitive level involve four of the five anger-management skills in the stress inoculation model—self-talk, problem solving,

FIGURE 4.2. "It's all in how you look at it" cartoon exercise.

assertion training, and humor. The following are brief descriptions of how these intervention techniques are presented in the *Keeping Your Cool* workbook. For each anger-management skill, the technique is outlined in a "Playbook" that is employed in sessions and for homework. In this way, the skill to be learned is taught in a step-by-step, simplified fashion. Thus, we hope the reader can better understand how these "Plays" are run for individual children and adolescents. Play 1 (Self-Talk) fundamentally involves teaching the child to engage in anger-reducing self-talk rather than his or her well-learned anger-increasing self-talk in response to problem situations (see Figure 4.3). We hope that such a change in private speech results in different feelings, behaviors, and consequences in response to problems that the aggressive youngster frequently encounters.

A similar playbook is employed for Play 5 (Humor) (see Figure 4.4). Again, the basic strategy is to insert different cognitive processes between the anger-provoking situation and subsequent behavior.

Problem-solving and assertion training are more complex skills that involve systematic training. Play 3 (Problem Solving) basically teaches children the problem-solving process. The Problem-Solving Playbook is depicted in Figure 4.5. As can be seen, the problem-solving sequence involves the following steps:

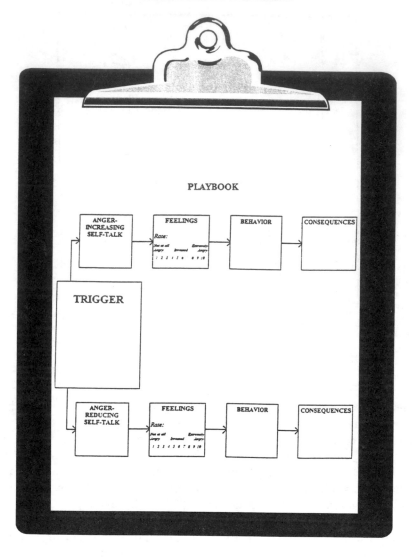

FIGURE 4.3. The Self-Talk Playbook.

1. *Stop*: What's the problem?
2. *Think*: What can I do? Brainstorm the solutions.
3. *Evaluate*: What's the best solution?
4. *Act*: Try it out.
5. *React*: Did it work?

Play 4 (Assertion Training) is a more complex set of skills that is beyond the scope of this chapter to review. Nevertheless, the basic strategy is

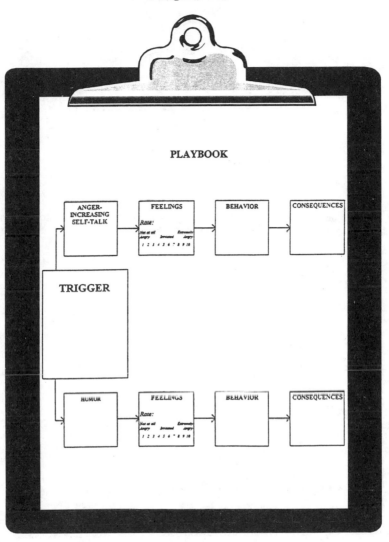

FIGURE 4.4. The Humor Playbook.

to teach aggressive adolescents alternative responses to situations that typically evoke anger and aggression. The basic format of assertion training involves assisting youth (1) to distinguish among aggressive, passive–aggressive, and assertive responses; (2) to identify their personal rights in various situations; (3) to identify and change irrational thoughts supporting nonassertive behavior; and (4) to practice assertive responses to various anger arousing situations. The first step involves sharpening the children's ability to recognize the various ways of responding to different problems

PLAYBOOK

1. <u>STOP</u>: What's the problem?

Who: _____ What: _____ When: _____

Where: _____ Why: _____

2. <u>THINK</u>: What can I do? Brainstorm solutions.

Think of as many solutions as you can. Don't worry about whether it's a good or bad solution because this will make it harder for you. Just "brainstorm!"

SOLUTION

1) _____
2) _____
3) _____
4) _____
5) _____

3. <u>EVALUATE</u>: What's the best solution?

For each SOLUTION in #2, write down what you think would happen, OUTCOME, if you did it. RATE each solution as + (good) or - (bad). Then pick the best.

SOLUTION	OUTCOME	RATING + OR -
1) _____	_____	___
2) _____	_____	___
3) _____	_____	___
4) _____	_____	___
5) _____	_____	___

Pick the best solution and circle it.

4. <u>ACT</u>: Try it out. Run the play.

5. <u>REACT</u>: Did it work? If it did, great! If it didn't, either try it again or "go back to the drawing board" by picking another solution from Step #3.

FIGURE 4.5. The Problem-Solving Playbook.

and to help identify their "Personal Rights" (see Figure 4.6). The Assertion Playbook is depicted in Figure 4.7.

Play 2 (Relaxation) involves teaching youngsters deep-breathing and relaxation techniques to use as an anger-reducing coping skill. The intervention takes place at the affective level and not the cognitive level, as do self-talk, humor, problem solving, and assertion training. Again, it is beyond the scope of this chapter to detail the specifics of relaxation training,

---

YOUR BILL OF RIGHTS

1. You have the right to experience and express your feelings.

2. You have the right to voice your opinion about things.

3. You have the right to be treated with respect.

4. You have the right to say "no" to others and not feel guilty.

5. You have the right to take time to slow down and think.

6. You have the right to change your mind.

7. You have the right to be different or "your own person."

8. You have the right to ask for things you want.

9. You have the right to make mistakes.

10. You have the right to feel good about yourself.

Can you think of any others?

11. _____

12. _____

13. _____

FIGURE 4.6. Your Bill of Rights.

although children are encouraged to rate their ability to relax by using the Relax-O-Meter (see Figure 4.8).

Overall, the goal is to help the child recognize the cognitive–physiological elements of anger, to decide whether or not expression of anger is appropriate, and then either to communicate feelings (anger) in a nonhostile, more adaptive manner, or to engage in some form of problem-solving action that might include direct expressing of feelings.

Inside the Therapist's Office

In the following transcript, the therapist works with a boy to help him see the potential benefits of learning how to manage his anger. Although many youngsters we see with anger-management problems do not admit they have a problem, they do recognize that they are not obtaining what they want in life. They are the ones who frequently find themselves in trouble and losing various privileges. In the following exchange, the therapist attempts to form a "partnership" with the 12-year-old youngster, Noel, in managing his anger and thus preventing the experience of negative consequences.

THERAPIST: We've been talking about anger and the various problems that people have with anger management. Do you have any ideas about your anger and how you can better manage it, so you won't keep getting into trouble?

NOEL: Yeah, I got the idea, but I wouldn't have no problem if my mom would just get off my case. She just needs to get a life and stop trying to live mine.

THERAPIST: That may or may not be true. Anyway, you feel like she keeps after you a little too close, and you want a little more room to be your own person. And that's reasonable.

NOEL: Damn right. I just need for her to keep off my case.

THERAPIST: What I think we should do is to try and increase the amount of time you are off restrictions. What do you think?

NOEL: I spend most of my life on restrictions and it isn't fair.

THERAPIST: Okay. From what you and your mom have said, it seems that you and your mom have more fights when you are on restrictions.

NOEL: We are locked up together and Dad is at sea [he is in the Navy] and we fight like cats and dogs and I keep getting more restrictions—hell, I can only sit on the couch and watch the grass in the yard grow.

[*Comments*: Noel, his 17-year-old sister, and his parents lived in Navy base housing. When his father is at sea, his mom and Noel have a very difficult time. When Noel is on restriction, he and his mom have more difficulty and disagree extensively. Noel's sister has a part-time job and is usually not around. The sequence of events usually consists of Noel breaking a rule and being placed on restriction. Once he is on restriction, Noel and his mom's disagreements escalate and Noel explodes with anger. His angry outburst leads to additional restrictions and increases the amount of time he spends with his mom. Thus, a cycle of anger evoking events is set in motion.]

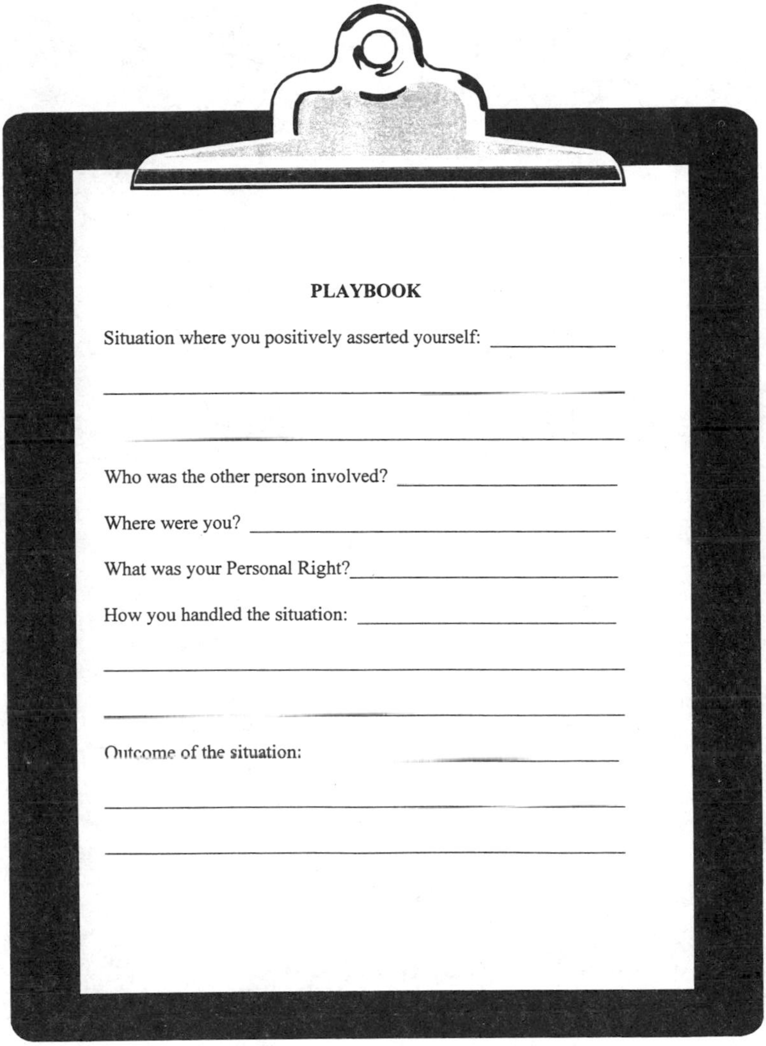

PLAYBOOK

Situation where you positively asserted yourself: _____

_____

_____

Who was the other person involved? _____

Where were you? _____

What was your Personal Right?_____

How you handled the situation: _____

_____

_____

Outcome of the situation: _____

_____

_____

FIGURE 4.7. The Assertion Playbook.

THERAPIST: I bet you'd like to reduce the number of times you are placed on restriction and to decrease the length of time you end up serving on restriction.

NOEL: Make Mom get a life!

THERAPIST: That's an idea, but I don't think that is something you and I are going to make happen.

NOEL: Got that right.

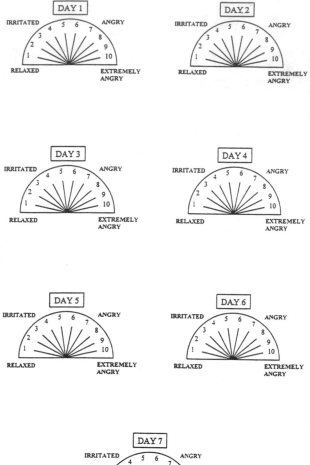

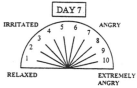

FIGURE 4.8. The Relax-o-Meter.

THERAPIST: But, you and I can work together in getting you more "time off for good behavior." We can work on ways to help you prevent restriction and to get off it sooner when you do get on it.

NOEL: I've really got to have more freedom.

THERAPIST: Okay, we have a goal. And, it seems that you agree that it would be good if I could help you get on restrictions less and get off them more quickly?

NOEL: Yes—you bet your sweet ass, it would be.

THERAPIST: Good! Now let's look at what anger is and see where we can break the chain of events that leads to your getting into trouble.

The therapist has formed an agreement with Noel to help him gain a desirable and mutually agreed-upon goal—being on restriction less and being released from restriction sooner. This goal is likely to meet both Noel's needs (more freedom) and to decrease the angry outbursts that resulted in the referral for psychological treatment. Most of Noel's restrictions are related to angry/aggressive outbursts, and once his restriction is imposed, he has his "sentence" increased because of such angry outbursts. Noel sees the "problem" as being his mom's fault but now is willing to work to develop skills that will decrease his restrictions.

Phase IV: Application Training

After the youngster has become proficient in the skills taught during Phase III, the therapist provides the opportunity to test these skills in controlled situations. Thus, the emphasis is on practicing the newly-learned anger management skills. The workbook allows the gradual build-up to the more difficult interactions in an anger hierarchy. It is designed to ensure that the child understands and has learned the anger-management strategies before having to apply them in emotionally arousing anger situations, thus optimizing successful outcomes. This is accomplished by having the therapist and child engage in structured role-play scenarios in therapy sessions to "test" the newly learned skills. This practice is done in both imaginal and direct-action role-play scenarios, employing a hierarchy of anger situations that the child is likely to encounter in real life. Once the child is proficient, the therapist can use "barbs" (Kaufmann & Wagner, 1972). A "barb" is a provocative statement that is applied in situations other than in the training/therapy situation. The rationale and procedure are explained to the child, whom the therapist then warns, "I'm going to barb you" (e.g., "Don't look at me like that! You're grounded tomorrow!"). Parents, teachers, staff members, and other significant individuals deliver the barbs and record the child's responses for review and discussion in following therapy sessions. Overall, homework assignments are very familiar to children and play a pivotal role in cognitive-behavioral interventions. It is the main mechanism to foster generalization of treatment effects into the real world by providing a structure in which the child practices anger-management skills. The implication also is that children (as well as parents) are taught that improvement in their situation is a product of their own efforts rather than those of the therapist.

INTEGRATION OF INDIVIDUAL AND FAMILY INTERVENTIONS: FUTURE DIRECTIONS

There is an increasing awareness of the benefits of involving parents in the treatment of children and adolescents. Such involvement has ranged from an exclusive focus on parent training treatments (e.g., Patterson, 1982, 1986) to parents' indirect supporting roles in cognitive interventions (e.g., Kendall & MacDonald, 1993). Within the child-focused cognitive-behavioral treatments, it is likely that broadening these to include parent training could facilitate treatment efficacy. Although several treatment programs have combined some type of parent training with individual cognitive-behavioral approaches (e.g., Horne & Sayger, 1990; Kazdin, Esveldt-Dawson, French, & Unis, 1987; Kazdin, Siegel, & Bass, 1992; Webster-Stratton & Hammond, 1997), more research on the implications of active involvement of parents in these more individually tailored treatment programs is needed. For example, Kazdin et al. (1992) found problem-solving training combined with parent management training to be superior for children and adolescents (ages 7 to 23 years) referred for severe antisocial/aggressive behavior. In addition, Brestan and Eyberg (1998) reviewed 82 controlled studies involving psychosocial interventions for child and adolescent conduct problems and found videotape modeling parent-training programs and those based on Patterson and Gullion's (1968) manual, *Living with Children*, to be effective. Recent reviews (Chamberlain & Rosicky, 1995; Estrada & Pinsof, 1995) found that family interventions consistently improved child and parent functioning in their analyses of the scientific evidence for the effectiveness of family-based approaches in the treatment of aggressive children with conduct disorders. Thus, the involvement of parents in treatment programs seems like a good idea, as the family plays a critical role in a child's development. Nevertheless, there can be difficulties with parental participation in a child's treatment. Involving more than one person in a treatment program can make it more complex for the therapist to manage. Furthermore, therapists using parent-based child interventions for youth with conduct disorders have found that it is often difficult to persuade parents to participate (e.g., Hawkins, von Cleve, & Catalano, 1991) and attrition rates are high (Forehand, Middlebrook, Rogers, & Steffe, 1983). In addition, parents of highly aggressive children can be as difficult to work with as the children themselves, because parents of acting-out children have shown a higher frequency of deviant behavior, exhibit less mature moral judgment, and have been found to be more rejecting, to use harsh power-assertive punishment, to model aggressive criminal behavior, and to be erratically permissive and inconsistent in enforcing rules (e.g., Hetherington & Martin, 1986). Also they are simply "worn out" in dealing with their children, and although they may love them, they may not like them at the beginning of therapy. Despite these difficulties, the potential benefits for involving parents are notable insofar as treatment gains need not only to be generalized to the home, school, and elsewhere, but also to be maintained over time. Because the parents, in large part, contribute to the environment in which a child develops over time, they can contribute to the generalization and treatment gains over time and prevent relapse. Although it is beyond the scope of this chapter, Kazdin and Kendall (1998) outlined a blueprint for progress in treatment research that recommends expanded assessment, addressing a broad range of treatment questions, evaluating "clinical significance," replicating findings, and exploring how to make use of research findings for practicing clinicians.

Key issues still remain as to what type of interventions are most effective for specific children, how best to integrate the various parent-training components with individual interventions, and how to determine the conditions under which therapeutic interventions are maximally effective (e.g., school/community-based programs). In this endeavor, any intervention components need to be fundamentally based on social learning, cognitive-behavioral, and behavioral principles. Parents of acting-out youngsters need to be taught to observe the child carefully and to identify clearly positive and maladaptive behaviors. Most parent training focuses on how to reinforce children's attempts at better managing their anger and to deal effectively with incidents when their children do not manage their anger. Consistency, negotiation, and behavioral contracting are all elements of parent training that have been employed for years, and for which manuals for parents and therapist are available (e.g., McMahon, Forehand, & Guest, 1981; Patterson & Forgatch, 1987; Patterson & Gullion, 1971; Patterson, Reid, Jones, & Conger, 1975). These and other techniques, especially from strategic family therapists, also offer the potential to augment individual child/adolescent treatment interventions (e.g., Price, 1996; Sells, 1998). Remember that cognitive-behavioral treatments are also "behavioral" in nature, in the sense that the use of clear, effective consequences for severe acting out should be integrated with the more "cognitive" approaches. For example, in employing the *Keeping Your Cool* workbook, Nelson has had some success teaching the anger-management skills to angry/aggressive parents who have problems with managing their own anger, with the caveat that they are then to teach their acting-out child these self-control techniques. In this way, both the adult (typically the father) and child are treated, and the parent is "hooked" into treatment himself by having to help his child. Such a task alters the father–son relationship and places the father more in the role of an educator than disciplinarian. Not only does this therapeutic intervention provide the father with needed anger-management skills, but it also aims at shifting and ultimately improving the father–son relationship. Coupled with such an approach is also the "behavioral" side, where parents are coached in developing consequences that are effective in stopping extreme aggressive acting out without being abusive.

Considerable progress toward refining theoretical models, making meaningful differential diagnoses, and formulating adequate treatments for aggressive behavior has been made. Nevertheless, much more remains to be done. It is likely that neither parent training nor cognitive-behavioral approaches alone will suffice to treat all the problems of highly aggressive children and adolescents. Being equipped with the best possible therapeutic approaches and the continued empirical evaluation of these interventions will hopefully lead us to become even better able to assist children and adolescents in developing into adults who are healthy, productive members of society.

NOTE

1. A copy of a summary table of the child/adolescent studies cited in the Beck and Fernandez (1998) study is available from W. Michael Nelson III, Elet Hall, Xavier University, Cincinnati, OH 45207-6511.

REFERENCES

Achenbach, T. M. (1991). *Manual for the Child Behavior Checklist/4-18 and 1991 profile.* Burlington: University of Vermont, Department of Psychiatry.

Achenbach, T., & Edelbrock, C. (1983). *Manual for the Child Behavior Checklist and Revised Behavior Profile.* Burlington: University of Vermont, Department of Psychiatry.

Addis, M. E. (1997). Evaluating the treatment manual as a means of disseminating empirically validated psychotherapies. *Clinical Psychology: Science and Practice, 4,* 1–11.

Alberti, R., & Emmons, M. (1995). *Your perfect right.* San Luis Obispo, CA: Impact.

American Psychiatric Association. (1994). *Diagnostic and statistical manual of mental disorders* (4th ed.). Washington, DC: Author.

American Psychological Association. (1993). *Summary report of the American Psychological Association Commission on violence and youth: Vol. 1. Violence and youth: Psychology's response.* Washington, DC: Author.

Bandura, A. (1986). *Social functions of thought and action: A social cognitive theory.* Englewood Cliffs, NJ: Prentice-Hall.

Barrett, P. (1998). Evaluation of cognitive-behavioral group treatments for childhood anxiety disorders. *Journal of Clinical Child Psychology, 27,* 459–468.

Beck, R., & Fernandez, E. (1998). Cognitive behavioral therapy in the treatment of anger: A meta-analysis. *Cognitive Therapy and Research, 22,* 63–74.

Beck, A. T., Rush, A. J., Shaw, B. F., & Emery, G. (1979). *Cognitive therapy of depression.* New York: Guilford Press.

Benson, H., Kornhaber, A., Kornhaber, C., & LeChanu, M. (1994). Increases in positive psychological characteristics with a new relaxation–response curriculum in high school students. *Journal of Research and Development in Education, 27,* 226–231.

Bernet, W. (1993). Humor in evaluating and treating children and adolescents. *Journal of Psychotherapy Practice and Research, 2,* 307–317.

Brandt, E. E., & Zlotnick, S. J. (1988). *The psychology and treatment of the youthful offender.* Springfield, IL: Thomas.

Brestan, E. V., & Eyberg, S. M. (1998). Effective psychological treatments of conduct-disordered children and adolescents: 29 years, 82 studies, 5,272 kids. *Journal of Clinical Child Psychology, 27,* 180–189.

Buchanan, A. (1997). The investigation of acting on delusions as a tool for risk assessment in the mentally disordered. *British Journal of Psychiatry, 170*(Suppl. 32), 12–14.

Buckman, E. (Ed.). (1994). *The handbook of humor: Clinical applications in psychotherapy.* Malabar, FL: Krieger.

Cairns, R. B., Cairns, B. D., Neckerman, H. J., Ferguson, L. L., & Gariepy, J. L. (1998). Growth and aggression 1: Childhood to early adolescence. *Developmental Psychology, 25,* 320–330.

Chamberlain, P., & Rosicky, J. G. (1995). The effectiveness of family therapy in the treatment of adolescents with conduct disorders and delinquency. *Journal of Marital and Family Therapy, 21,* 441–459.

Chandler, M. (1973). Egocentrism and antisocial behavior: An assessment and training of social perspective-taking skills. *Developmental Psychology, 9,* 326–332.

Chandler, M., & Boyes, M. (1982). Social-cognitive development. In B. Wolman (Ed.), *Handbook of developmental psychology* (pp. 387–402). New York: Wiley.

Chapman, A., & Chapman-Santana, M. (1995). The use of humor in psychotherapy. *Arquivos de Neuro-Psiquiatria, 53,* 153–156.

Clarke, G., Lewinsohn, P., & Hops, H. (1990). *Adolescent coping with depression course.* Eugene, OR: Castalia.

Crick, N. R., Casas, J. F., & Mosher, M. (1997). Relational and overt aggression in preschool. *Developmental Psychology, 33,* 579–588.

Crick, N. R., & Grotpeter, J. K. (1995). Relational aggression, gender, and social-psychological adjustment. *Child Development, 66,* 710–722.

Dana, R. (1994). Humor as a diagnostic tool in child and adolescent groups. In E. Buckman (Ed.), *The handbook of humor: Clinical applications in psychotherapy* (pp. 41–51). Malabar, FL: Krieger.

Dangel, R., Deschner, J., & Rasp, R. (1989). Anger control training for adolescents in residential treatment. *Behavior Modification, 13,* 447–458.

Deffenbacher, J., Lynch, R., Oetting, E., & Kemper, C. (1996). Anger reduction in early adolescents. *Journal of Counseling Psychology, 43,* 149–157.

Deluty, R. H. (1979). Children's Action Tendency Scale: A self-report measure of aggressiveness, assertiveness, and submissiveness in children. *Journal of Consulting and Clinical Psychology, 47,* 1061–1071.

Dodge, K. A. (1991). The structure and function of reactive and protective aggression. In D. J. Pepper & K. H. Rudin (Eds.), *The development and treatment of childhood aggression* (pp. 210–218). Hillsdale, NJ: Erlbaum.

Dodge, K. A. (1985). Attributional bias in aggressive children. In P. C. Kendall (Ed.), *Advances in cognitive-behavioral research and therapy* (pp. 73–110). New York: Academic Press.

Dodge, K. A., Price, J. M., Bachorowski, J., & Newman, J. P. (1990). Hostile attributional biases in severely aggressive adolescents. *Journal of Abnormal Psychology, 99,* 385–392.

Dollard, J., Doob, L. W., Miller, N. E., Mowrer, O. H., & Sears, R. R. (1939). *Frustration and aggression.* New Haven, CT: Yale University Press.

Dong, Y., Hallberg, E., & Hassard, H. (1979). Effects of assertion training on aggressive behavior of adolescents. *Journal of Counseling Psychology, 26,* 459–461.

Dujovne, V., Barnard, M., & Rapoff, M. (1995). Pharmacological and cognitive behavioral approaches in the treatment of childhood depression: A review and critique. *Clinical Psychology Review, 15,* 589–611.

Dumas, J. E. (1989). Treating antisocial behavior in children: Child and family approaches. *Clinical Psychology Review, 9,* 197–222.

Eargle, A., Guerra, N., & Tolan, P. (1994). *Journal of Child and Adolescent Group Therapy, 4*, 229–242.

Eisen, A., & Silverman, W. (1993). Should I relax or change my thoughts? A preliminary examination of cognitive therapy, relaxation training, and their combination with overanxious children. *Journal of Cognitive Psychotherapy, 7*, 265–279.

Ellis, A. (1971). *Growth through reason: Verbatim cases in rational–emotive therapy*. California: Science & Behavior Books.

Ellis, A. (1973). *Humanistic psychotherapy: The rational–emotive approach*. New York: McGraw-Hill.

Ellis, A., & Grieger, R. (1977). *Handbook of rational–emotive therapy*. New York: Springer.

Estrada, A. U., & Pinsof, W. M. (1995). The effectiveness of family therapies for selected behavioral disorders of childhood. *Journal of Marital and Family Therapy, 21*, 403–440.

Eyberg, S. M., Boggs, J. R., & Algina, J. (1995). New developments in psychosocial, pharmacological, and combined treatments of conduct disorders in aggressive children. *Psychopharmacology Bulletin, 31*, 83–91.

Farrington, D. P. (1991). Childhood aggression and adult violence: Early precursors and life outcomes. In D. J. Pepler & K. H. Rubin (Eds.), *The development and treatment of childhood aggression* (pp. 5–29). Hillsdale, NJ: Erlbaum.

Farrington, D. P. (1994). Childhood, adolescent, and adult features of violent males. In L. R. Huesmann (Ed.), *Aggressive behavior: Current perspectives* (pp. 215–240). New York: Plenum Press.

Farrington, D. P. (1995). The development of offending and antisocial behavior from childhood: Key findings from the Cambridge Study in Delinquent Development. *Journal of Child Psychology and Psychiatry, 36*, 929–964.

Farrington, D. P., Loeber, R., & Van Kamman, W. B. (1990). Long-term clinical outcomes of hyperactivity–impulsivity–attention deficit and conduct problems in childhood. In L. N. Robins & M. Rutter (Eds.), *Straight and devious pathways from childhood to adulthood* (pp. 62–81). Cambridge, UK: Cambridge University Press.

Finch, A. J., Jr., Nelson, W. M., III., & Moss, J. H. (1993). Childhood aggression: Cognitive-behavioral therapy strategies and interventions. In A. J. Finch, Jr., W. M. Nelson, III, & E. S. Ott (Eds.), *Cognitive-behavioral procedures with children and adolescents: A practical guide* (pp. 148–205). Boston: Allyn & Bacon.

Finch, A. J., Jr., Nelson, W. M., III, & Ott, E. S. (1993). *Cognitive-behavioral procedures with children and adolescents: A practical guide*. Boston: Allyn & Bacon.

Finch, A. J., Jr., & Politano, P. M. (1994). Projective techniques. In T. H. Ollendick, N. J. King, & W. Yule (Eds.), *International handbook of phobic and anxiety disorders in children and adolescents* (pp. 381–393). New York: Plenum Press.

Finch, A., Wilkinson, M., Nelson, W. M., III, & Montgomery, L. (1975). Modification of an impulsive cognitive tempo in emotionally disturbed boys. *Journal of Abnormal Child Psychology, 3*, 47–51.

Fingerhut, L. A., & Kleinman, J. C. (1990). International and interstate comparisons of homicide among young males. *Journal of the American Medical Association, 263*, 3292–3295.

Forehand, R., Middlebrook, J., Rogers, T., & Steffe, M. (1983). Dropping out of parent training. *Behaviour Research and Therapy, 21*, 663–668.

Freud, S. A. (1920). *A general introduction to psycho-analysis*. New York: Boni & Liveright.

Fry, W., & Salameh, W. (Eds.). (1993). *Advances in humor and psychotherapy*. Sarasota, FL: Professional Resources Press.

Gilbert, G. M. (1957). A survey of "referral problems" in metropolitan child guidance centers. *Journal of Clinical Psychology, 13*, 37–42.

Hawkins, J. D., von Cleve, E., & Catalaro, R. F. (1991). Reducing early childhood aggression: Results of a primary prevention program. *Journal of the American Academy of Child and Adolescent Psychiatry, 30*, 208–217.

Hetherington, E. M., & Martin, B. (1986). Family interaction. In H. C. Quay & J. S. Werry

(Eds.), *Psychopathological disorders of childhood* (2nd ed., pp. 332–390). New York: Wiley.

Horne, A. M., & Sayger, T. V. (1990). *Treating conduct and oppositional defiant disorders in children*. Elmsford, NY: Pergamon Press.

Jacobsen, R. (1938). *Progressive relaxation*. Chicago: University of Chicago Press.

Jacobson, H. (1984). A component analysis of behavioral martial therapy: The relative effectiveness of behavior exchange and problem solving training. *Journal of Consulting and Clinical Psychology, 52,* 295–305.

Kaufmann, L., & Wagner, B. (1972). Barb: A systematic treatment technology for temper control disorders. *Behavior Therapy, 3,* 84–90.

Kazdin, A. E. (1987). Treatment of antisocial behavior in children: Current status and future directions. *Psychological Bulletin, 102,* 187–203.

Kazdin, A. E. (1993). Treatment of conduct disorder: Progress and directions in psychotherapy research. *Development and Psychopathology, 5,* 277–310.

Kazdin, A. E. (1995). *Conduct disorder in childhood and adolescence* (2nd ed.). Thousand Oaks, CA: Sage.

Kazdin, A. E., Esveldt-Dawson, K., French, N. H., & Unis, A. S. (1987). Effects of parent management training and problem-solving skills training combined in the treatment of antisocial child behavior. *Journal of the American Academy of Child and Adolescent Psychiatry, 26,* 416–424.

Kazdin, A. E., & Kendall, P. C. (1998). Current progress and future plans for developing effective treatments: Comments and perspectives. *Journal of Clinical Child Psychology, 27,* 217–226.

Kazdin, A. E., Rodgers, A., Colbus, D., & Siegel, T. (1987). Children's Hostility Inventory: Measurement of aggression and hostility in psychiatric inpatient children. *Journal of Clinical Child Psychology, 16,* 320–328.

Kazdin, A. E., Siegel, T. C., & Bass, D. (1992). Cognitive problem-solving skills training and parent management training in the treatment of antisocial behavior in children. *Journal of Consulting and Clinical Psychology, 60,* 733–747.

Kendall, P. C., & Braswell, L. (1993). *Cognitive-behavioral therapy for impulsive children*. New York: Guilford Press.

Kendall, P. C., & Finch, A. J., Jr. (1976). A cognitive-behavioral treatment for impulsive control: A case study. *Journal of Consulting and Clinical Psychology, 44,* 852–857.

Kendall, P. C., & Finch, A. J., Jr. (1978). A cognitive-behavioral treatment for impulsivity: A group comparison study. *Journal of Consulting and Clinical Psychology, 46,* 110–118.

Kendall, P. C., & Flannery-Schroeder, E. C. (1995). Rigor, but not rigor mortis, in depression research. *Journal of Personality and Social Psychology, 69,* 892–894.

Kendall, P. C., Hollon, S. D., Beck, A. T., Hammen, C. H., & Ingram, R. E. (1987). Issues and recommendations regarding use of the Beck Depression Inventory. *Cognitive Therapy and Research, 11,* 289–299.

Kendall, P. C., & MacDonald, J. P. (1993). Cognition in the psychopathology of youth and complications for treatment. In K. S. Dobson & P. C. Kendall (Eds.), *Psychopathology and cognition* (pp. 387–432). San Diego: Academic Press.

Kimball, W., Nelson, W. M., III, & Politano, P. M. (1993). The role of developmental variables in cognitive-behavioral interventions with children. In A. J. Finch, W. M. Nelson, III, & E. S. Ott (Eds.), *Cognitive-behavioral procedures with children and adolescents: A practical guide* (pp. 25–66). Boston: Allyn & Bacon.

Koeppen, A. (1974, October). Relaxation training for children. *Elementary School Guidance and Counseling*, pp. 14–21.

Lagerspetz, K. M. J., Bjorkqvist, K., & Peltonen, T. (1988). Is indirect aggression more typical of females? Gender differences in 11–12 year children. *Aggressive Behavior, 14,* 403–414.

Limandri, B., & Sheridan, D. (1995). Prediction of intentional interpersonal violence. An introduction. In J. C. Campbell (Ed.), *Assessing dangerousness: Violence by sexual offenders, batterers, and child abusers* (pp. 1–19). Thousand Oaks, CA: Sage.

Lipsey, M. W. (1992, October–November). *The effects of treatment on juvenile delinquent: Results from meta-analysis*. Paper presented at the NIMH Meeting for Potential Applicants for Research to Prevent Youth Violence, Bethesda, MD.

Lochman, J., & Curry, J. (1986). Effects of social problem-solving training and self-instruction training with aggressive boys. *Journal of Clinical Child Psychology, 15*, 159–164.

Lochman, J. E., & Dodge, K. A. (1998). Distorted perceptions in dyadic interactions of aggressive and nonaggressive boys: Effects of prior expectations, context, and boys' age. *Development and Psychopathology, 10*, 495–512.

Lochman, J. E., Meyer, B., Rabiner, D., & White, K. (1991). Parameters influencing social problem solving of aggressive children. In R. Prinz (Ed.), *Advances in behavioral assessment of children and families* (Vol. 5, pp. 31–63). Greenwich, CT: JAI Press.

Loeber, R., & Hay, D. F. (1997). Key issues in the development of aggression and violence from childhood to early adulthood. *Annual Review of Psychology, 48*, 371–410.

Loeber, R., & Stouthamer-Loeber, M. (1998). Development of juvenile aggression and violence: Some common misconceptions and controversies. *American Psychologist, 53*, 242–259.

Lorenz, K. (1966). *On aggression*. New York: Harcourt Brace Jovanovich.

Lorion, R. P., Cowen, E. L., & Caldwell, R. A. (1974). Problem types of children referred to a school-based mental health program: Identification and outcome. *Journal of Consulting and Clinical Psychology, 42*, 491–496.

Luria, A. (1959). The directive function of speech in development and dissolution. *Word, 15*, 341–352.

Luria, A. (1961). *The role of speech in the regulation of normal and abnormal behaviors*. New York: Liveright.

Mandler, G. (1984). *Mind and body: Psychology of emotion and stress*. New York: Norton.

McCord, W., & McCord, J. (1960). *Origins of alcoholism*. Stanford, CA: Stanford University Press.

McDougall, W. (1931). *An introduction to social psychology*. London: Methuen.

McMahon, R. J., Forehand, R., & Guest, D. L. (1981). Effects of knowledge of social learning principles on enhancing treatment outcome and generalization in a parent training program. *Journal of Consulting and Clinical Psychology, 49*, 526–532.

Meichenbaum, D. (1977). *Cognitive-behavior modification: An integrative approach*. New York: Plenum Press.

Meichenbaum, D., & Goodman, J. (1971). Training impulsive children to talk to themselves: A means of developing self-control. *Journal of Abnormal Psychology, 77*, 115–126.

Milich, R., & Dodge, K. A. (1984). Social information processing in child psychiatric populations. *Journal of Abnormal Child Psychology, 12*, 471–490.

Miller, L. S. (1994). Preventive interventions for conduct disorders: A review. *Child and Adolescent Psychiatric Clinics of North America, 3*, 405–420.

Miller, G. E., & Prinz, R. J. (1990). Enhancement of social learning family intervention for childhood conduct disorder. *Psychological Bulletin, 108*, 291–307.

Moffitt, T. E. (1993). Adolescence-limited and life-course-persistent antisocial behavior: A developmental taxonomy. *Psychology Review, 100*, 674–701.

Moffitt, T. E., Caspi, A., Dickson, N., Silva, P., & Stanton, W. (1996). Childhood-onset versus adolescent-onset antisocial conduct problems in males: Natural history from ages 3 to 18 years. *Development and Psychopathology, 8*, 399–424.

Monahan, J., & Walker, L. (Eds.). (1990). *Social science in law: Cases and materials* (2nd ed.). Westbury, NJ: Foundation Press.

Nelson, W. M., III, & Finch, A. J., Jr. (1996). *Keeping your cool: The anger management workbook* (Parts 1 and 2). Ardmore, PA: Workbook Publishing.

Nelson, W. M., III, & Finch, A. J., Jr. (in press). *Children's Inventory of Anger (ChIA) manual*. Los Angeles: Western Psychological Services.

Nelson, W. M., III, Hart, K. J., & Finch, A. J., Jr. (1993). Anger in children: A cognitive behavioral view of the assessment–therapy connection. *Journal of Rational–Emotive and Cognitive-Behavior Therapy, 11,* 135–150.

Novaco, R. W. (1978). Anger and coping with stress. In J. P. Foreyt & D. P. Rathjen (Eds.), *Cognitive behavior therapy: Research and application* (pp. 241–286). New York: Plenum Press.

Novaco, R. W. (1979). The cognitive regulation of anger and stress. In P. C. Kendall & S. D. Hollan (Eds.), *Cognitive-behavioral interventions: Theory, research, and procedures.* New York: Academic Press.

Patterson, G. R. (1982). *Coercive family process.* Eugene, OR: Castalia.

Patterson, G. R. (1986). Performance models for antisocial boys. *American Psychologist, 41,* 432–444.

Patterson, G. R., & Forgatch, M. (1987). *Parents and adolescents living together: Part 1. The basics.* Eugene, OR: Castalia Press.

Patterson, G. R., & Gullion, M. E. (1971). *Living with children: New methods for parents and teachers.* Champaign, IL: Research Press.

Patterson, G. R., Reid, J. B., Jones, R. R., & Conger, R. W. (1975). *A social learning approach to family intervention* (Vol. 1). Eugene, OR: Castalia Press.

Pentz, M. (1980). Assertion training and trainer effects on unassertive and aggressive adolescents. *Journal of Counseling Psychology, 27,* 76–83.

Pepler, D. J., & Rubin, K. H. (Eds.). (1991). *The development and treatment of childhood aggression.* Hillsdale, NJ: Erlbaum.

Price, J. A. (1996). *Power and compassion: Working with difficult adolescents and abused parents.* New York: Guilford Press.

Quay, H. C. (1986). Conduct disorders. In H. C. Quay & J. S. Werry (Eds.), *Psychopathological disorders of childhood* (3rd ed., pp. 35–72). New York: Wiley.

Quay, H. C., & La Greca, A. M. (1986). Disorders of anxiety, withdrawal, and dysphoria. In H. C. Quay & J. S. Werry (Eds.), *Psychopathological disorders of children* (3rd ed., pp. 73–110). New York: Wiley.

Rath, S. (1992). Cognitive-behaviour intervention with disadvantaged tribal school children: An empirical study. *Indian Journal of Clinical Psychology, 19,* 4–9.

Reynolds, W., & Coats, K. (1986). A comparison of cognitive-behavioral therapy and relaxation training for the treatment of depression. *Journal of Consulting and Clinical Psychology, 54,* 653–660.

Reynolds, C., & Kamphaus, R. (1992). *Behavior Assessment System for Children: Manual.* Circle Pines, MN: American Guidance Services.

Richters, J. E. (1993). Community violence and children's development: Toward a research agenda for the 1990's. *Psychiatry, 56,* 3–6.

Richters, J. E., & Martinez, P. E. (1993). Violent communities, family choices, and children's chances: An algorithm for improving the odds. *Development and Psychopathology, 5,* 609–627.

Robins, L. N. (1966). *Deviant children grown up: A sociological and psychiatric study of sociopathic personality.* Baltimore: Williams & Wilkins.

Robins, L. N. (1981). Epidemiological approaches to natural history research: Antisocial disorders in children. *Journal of the American Academy of Child Psychiatry, 20,* 566–580.

Schachter, S. (1964). The interaction of cognitive and physiological determents of emotional state. In L. Berkowitz (Ed.), *Advances in experimental social psychology* (pp. 49–80). New York: Academic Press.

Schachter, S., & Singer, J. (1962). Cognitive, social and physiological determinants of emotional state. *Psychological Review, 69,* 379–399.

Sells, S. P. (1998). *Treating the tough adolescent: A family-based, step-by-step guide.* New York: Guilford Press.

Snyder, H. N., & Sickmund, M. (1995). *Juvenile offenders and victims: A national report* (Document No. NCJ-153569). Washington, DC: U.S. Department of Justice, Office of Juvenile Justice and Delinquency Prevention.

Southam-Gerow, M. A., & Kendall, P. C. (1997). Parent-focused and cognitive-behavioral treatments of antisocial youth. In D. M. Stoff, J. Breiling, & J. D. Moser (Eds.), *Handbook of antisocial behavior* (pp. 384–394). New York: Wiley.

Spivack, G., Platt, J., & Shure, M. (1976). *The problem-solving approach to adjustment.* San Francisco: Jossey-Bass.

Stattin, H., & Magnusson, D. (1989). The role of early aggressive behavior in the frequency, seriousness, and types of later crime. *Journal of Consulting and Clinical Psychology, 57,* 710–718.

Stewart, C., & Lewis, W. (1986). Effects of assertiveness training on the self-esteem of black high school students. *Journal of Counseling and Development, 64,* 638–641.

Stewart, M. A., deBlois, S., Meardon, J., & Cummings, C. (1980). Aggressive conduct disorder of children: The clinical picture. *Journal of Nervous and Mental Disease, 168,* 604–615.

Stoff, D. M., Breiling, J., & Maser, J. D. (Eds.). (1997). *Handbook of antisocial behavior.* New York: Wiley.

Stouthamer-Loeber, M., Loeber, R., & Thomas, C. (1992). Caretakers seeking help for boys with disruptive and delinquent behavior. *Comprehensive Mental Health Care, 2,* 159–178.

Strupp, H. H., & Anderson, T. (1997). On the limitations of therapy manuals. *Clinical Psychology: Science and Practice, 4,* 76–82.

Tafrate, R. C. (1995). Evaluation of treatment strategies for adult anger disorders. In H. Kassinove (Ed.), *Anger disorders: Definition, diagnoses, and treatment* (pp. 109–130). Washington, DC: Taylor & Francis.

Tate, D. C., Reppucci, N. D., & Mulvey, E. P. (1995). Violent juvenile delinquents: Treatment effectiveness and implications for future action. *American Psychologist, 50,* 777–781.

United States Congress, Office of Technology Assessment. (1991). *Adolescent health* (OTA-H-468). Washington, DC: U. S. Government Printing Office.

Ventis, W., & Ventis, D. (1988). Guidelines for using humor in therapy with children and young adolescents. *Journal of Children in Contemporary Society, 20,* 179–197.

Vygotsky, L. (1962). *Thought and language.* New York: Wiley.

Vygotsky, L. (1987). Thinking and speech. In *The collected works of L. S. Vygotsky: Vol. 1. Problems of general psychology* (N. Minick, Trans.). New York: Plenum Press. (Original work published 1934)

Waksman, S. (1981). A controlled evaluation of assertion training with adolescents. *Adolescence, 19,* 277–282.

Wasserman, G. A., & Miller, L. S. (1998). The prevention of serious and violent juvenile offending. In R. Loeber & D. P. Farrington (Eds.), *Serious and violent juvenile offenders: Risk factors and successful interventions* (pp. 197–247). Thousand Oaks, CA: Sage.

PART III

INTERNALIZING DISORDERS

CHAPTER 5

Treatment of Depression in Childhood and Adolescence
Cognitive-Behavioral Procedures for the Individual and Family

Kevin D. Stark, Janay Boswell Sander, Mary G. Yancy,
Michelle D. Bronik, and Julia A. Hoke

To effectively treat youth, it is important to have a thorough empirical understanding of the disorder within the age group of interest. In this chapter, relevant research is discussed. Additional relevant research regarding cognitive, interpersonal, and family disturbances are discussed by Stark, Laurent, Livingston, Boswell, and Swearer (1999). The development of emotion regulation skills is a growing area of research that was not covered in our chapter in the previous edition of this volume (Stark, Rouse, & Livingston, 1991), so this topic is discussed here. A biological and a potential psychosocial pathway to the development of depressive disorders are described, and an integrated model of childhood depression is proposed.

On a more practical level, we have attempted to describe the link between assessment and a cognitive-behavioral treatment for depressed youth. This discussion is followed by a section on the treatment of depressed youth. The assessment tools and treatment program described are appropriate for youngsters from 9 to 14 years old who are suffering from a unipolar depressive disorder. First, basic research on the prevalence, natural course, and predictors of the duration of a depressive episode are discussed.

PREVALENCE OF DEPRESSION

More youths are experiencing depressive disorders, and the age of onset is earlier than in the past. In general, prevalence rates progressively increase with age until late childhood and early adolescence, when the rate rapidly increases and continues to increase through late adolescence, when it reaches adult levels. Until early adolescence, the prevalence rates for males and females are equal. During early adolescence, the number of girls begins to exceed the number of boys experiencing a depressive disorder. The reasons for this gender difference are unknown, but this represents an area in need of research, as it has implications for prevention and intervention efforts.

Depressive disorders among preschoolers from the general population are relatively rare and associated with extreme abuse or neglect (Kashani & Carlson, 1987; Kashani & Ray, 1983). The prevalence rates of major depression and dysthymic disorder for school-age children range from 0.4% to 1.85% and 0.6% to 2.5%, respectively (Anderson, Williams, McGee, & Silva, 1987; Costello et al., 1988; Kashani et al., 1983; Kashani, Orvaschel, Rosenberg, & Reid, 1989). Existing research indicates that prevalence rates for adolescents are higher than those reported for children. Results from a large high school population indicated that the prevalence rate for unipolar depression was 2.9% (Lewinsohn, Hops, Roberts, Seeley, & Andrews, 1993), which is very similar to the 3% reported by Rohde, Lewinsohn, and Seeley (1991), but significantly lower than the 8% reported by Kashani et al. (1990). In investigations where rates of major depression and dysthymic disorder have been reported separately, the rates have ranged from 0.4% to 4.7% and 1.1% to 3.3% (Kashani et al., 1990; McGee et al., 1990; McGee & Williams, 1988). It is difficult to draw conclusions about the prevalence of depressive disorders among youth because of the limited number of studies and various methods employed, and because some investigators report rates of both major depression and dysthymic disorder, while others only report rates of major depression. The omission of information on dysthymic disorder is problematic, because research indicates that it may be more insidious than major depression relative to its long-term impact on the psychosocial adjustment of youth, and it appears to be more resistant to treatment (Kovacs, Feinberg, Crouse-Novak, Paulauskas, & Finkelstein, 1984). A substantial percentage of youth also report low levels of chronic dysphoria and low self-esteem (Stark et al., 1991), which may represent a developmental precursor to a depressive disorder.

Higher prevalence rates are found among youth from a variety of special populations. Children with learning difficulties appear to be at risk, as youngsters enrolled in special education classes (20–50%) (Mattison, Humphrey, Kales, Hernit, & Finkenbinder, 1986) and in an educational diagnostic clinic suffer from higher rates of depression (49%) (Weinberg, Rutman, Sullivan, Penich, & Dietz, 1973). As would be expected, the prevalence rates are high for youths who are receiving mental health services (e.g., Brady & Kendall, 1992). The prevalence rate in the literature of depression among elementary-school-age children from psychiatric clinics ranges from 2.1% (Christ, Adler, Isacoff, & Gershansky, 1981) to 61% (Weinberg et al., 1973). Studies of inpatient children have reported a range from 26% (Asarnow & Bates, 1988) to 58% (Carlson & Cantwell, 1980) or 59% (Kashani, Venzke, & Millar, 1981; Petti, 1978). Hodges and Siegel (1985) noted that prevalence rates for adolescent psychiatric patients have ranged from 13% to 60%, while Petersen et al. (1993) reported that depression rates averaged 42% across studies of clinic samples. Children with a variety of medical problems including headaches (40%) (Ling, Oftedal, & Weinberg, 1970), orthopaedic problems (23%) (Kashani et al., 1981), cancer (17%) (Kashani & Hakami, 1982), and general medical problems (Kashani et al., 1981) experience high rates of depression.

NATURAL COURSE OF DEPRESSION

Longitudinal research indicates that major depression and dysthymia follow different natural courses. The average duration of an episode of major depressive disorder is reported to be between 32 and 36 weeks (Kovacs et al., 1984; McCauley et al., 1993; Strober, Lampert, Schmidt, & Morrell, 1993). The rate of recovery tends to be slow, with the greatest improvement starting between the 24th and 36th week (Strober, Lampert, Schmidt, & Morrell, 1993). Within 6 months of the onset of an episode of major depressive disorder, the episode has remitted for 40% of the children. At 1 year, 80% of the children are no longer experiencing a depressive episode (McCauley et al., 1993). The natural course of dysthymic disorder is more protracted, with the average episode length being 3 years (Kovacs et al., 1984). A chronic course is reported for a significant percentage of depressed children (McCauley et al., 1993; McGee & Williams, 1988; Strober et al., 1993), although it is not clear whether these figures vary between major depression and dysthymic disorder.

Longitudinal research addresses another important characteristic of depressive disorders: They are recurrent. Over a 3-year period, 54% of a sample of depressed youth experienced another depressive disorder (McCauley et al., 1993), and over a 5-year period, 72% of a sample of depressed youth experienced another episode of depression (Kovacs et al., 1984). Thus, it appears that depressed youth are at risk for experiencing additional depressive episodes.

PREDICTORS OF DURATION OF AN EPISODE

A few variables have been identified that appear to predict the duration of a depressive episode. Age of onset may be a predictor, but results of this research have been contradictory (Kovacs et al., 1984; Harrington, Fudge, Rutter, Pickles, & Hill, 1990; McGee & Williams, 1988). Severity is a predictor of the duration of an episode, with more severe episodes having a more protracted course (McCauley et al., 1993). Family dysfunction is associated with a more protracted course (McCauley et al., 1993). Finally, gender has been associated with the overall severity and course of a depressive disorder, with females experiencing more severe and protracted episodes. Some youngsters who are depressed will later develop bipolar disorder (Kovacs et al., 1984). It appears that an episode of psychotic depression (Strober et al., 1993) or comorbid attention-deficit/hyperactivity disorder (ADHD) may be a risk factor for the later occurrence of bipolar disorder (Carlson & Kashani, 1988).

PSYCHOSOCIAL ASPECTS OF DEPRESSIVE DISORDERS: DISTURBANCES IN AFFECT REGULATION

Depressive symptoms and disorders have been conceptualized as a failure to regulate negative affect (Cole & Kaslow, 1988). Understanding the normative progression of emotion regulation across development informs the creation of developmentally sensitive treatments. Four trends characterize the typical development of affect regulation: (1) progression from other-regulation to self-regulation (Cole & Kaslow, 1988; Dunn & Brown, 1991; Rossman, 1992; Thompson, 1991); (2) expansion of children's emotion regulation repertoire with age (e.g., Kopp, 1989; for contradictory results, see Masters, 1991); (3) a shift from more behavioral strategies to cognitive strategies (Altshuler & Ruble, 1989); and (4) an increased emphasis on situational characteristics.

Development of Emotion Regulation

Infancy

Caregivers accomplish most infant emotion regulation by acting to alleviate distress or to maintain optimal levels of arousal during interaction (Thompson, 1991). When arousal levels are kept relatively low, infants are able to modify their own mood using reflex behaviors, such as eye closing and nonnutritive sucking, or learned behaviors, such as self-distraction (Kopp, 1989). Subsequent social and motor development during later infancy equip infants with a wider array of techniques (facial expressions, verbalizations) for engaging caregivers to alleviate distress, and for self-soothing (rubbing themselves, grasping a toy).

Quality of attachment has been hypothesized to be associated with affect regulation (Cole & Kaslow, 1988) and provides one model for understanding continuities in emotion regulation over the course of development. Cicchetti, Ganiban, and Barnett (1991) suggest that an infant's working model of attachment, which includes expectations about a caregiver's responsiveness, influences emotion regulation. For example, securely attached infants, whose working model includes the idea that caregivers will keep aversive affect within manageable limits, express negative affect directly and expect to be soothed and reassured.

Early Childhood

In early childhood, language becomes a major tool for emotion regulation. Language is used by caregivers to facilitate children's emotion regulation (Thompson, 1991), by young children in their efforts at self-regulation (Cole & Kaslow, 1988; Kopp, 1989), and, most often, to enlist the aid of the caregiver in meeting their emotional needs (Dunn & Brown, 1991). The development of language also signals a growth in representational skills and subsequent social-cognitive understanding of emotion, including an understanding of the origins of emotions, consequences of emotion expression, and techniques for emotion regulation (Masters, 1991; Thompson, 1991). Understanding the possible antecedents for an emotion guides the young child's attempts to control that emotion; understanding the consequences of expressing emotions may motivate the child's efforts to self-regulate.

Early childhood also marks the emergence of more active and planful forms of emotion regulation, and it is at this point that the responsibility for affect regulation begins to shift from parent to child (Cicchetti et al., 1991). Preschoolers develop a limited repertoire of self-regulatory strategies, based on their emergent understanding of emotion, including regulating sensory intake, seeking nurturance, using reassuring self-talk, escaping the situation, and changing their goals for an interaction (Thompson, 1991). Although, toddlers and preschoolers are laying the foundation for competent self-regulation of emotions, most of their affect regulation, is still accomplished by parents and other adults.

Middle Childhood

The emotion-regulation abilities of school-age children are characterized by an increasing reliance on self-regulation, although the influence of parents remains strong (Kliewer, Fearnow, & Miller, 1996). The increase in emotion regulation strategies seen during middle childhood may be the result of the greater number of cognitive strategies reported by older children (Altshuler & Ruble, 1989). Cognitive strategies reported by school-age children include thinking happy thoughts, redirecting attention, focusing on the benefits of regulation, reframing the situation, changing attributions of causality, and recalling earlier emotional experiences (Thompson, 1991).

Rossman's (1992) study of emotion-regulation strategies found that younger children report more behavioral distraction, such as playing or watching television, whereas older children report using cognitive distraction, such as thinking about something else.

During middle childhood, children become more adept at choosing emotion regulation strategies based on characteristics of the emotion-provoking situation. Before middle childhood, children's strategies tend to be aimed directly at changing some aspect of the situation (i.e., primary control or problem-focused). With increasing age, children report using more secondary control strategies aimed at maximizing their goodness of fit with an uncontrollable situation (Band & Weisz, 1988). Research by Kliewer (1991) suggests that the majority of stressors reported by young children (e.g., death of a pet) are perceived as uncontrollable; thus, the emergence of secondary control strategies is important for the development of overall emotion-regulation competence. This finding is consistent with other research, which reveals that older children pay more attention to context than do younger children when choosing emotion-regulation strategies (Saarni, 1989).

Emotion regulation in middle childhood is also characterized by a growing reliance on peers (Thompson, 1991). Peers serve as a resource for managing negative affect and may convey expectations about appropriate emotion expression and inflict punishment if expectations are violated (Kopp, 1989). For example, elementary-school-age children may exclude from play peers who display intense sadness or anger.

Adolescence

In accordance with the view of identity formation as the major task of adolescence, emotion regulation during this period is characterized by the solidification of a theory of personal emotion (Thompson, 1991). This theory, or schema, has its roots in early childhood, when children first realize that their emotional experiences may differ from those of others. The theory of personal emotion becomes more integrative and consistent during adolescence and guides efforts to regulate mood. Adolescents have developed self-schemas that represent their coping with negative emotions (e.g., "I don't let my emotions show" or "I can't handle my feelings; they are too powerful").

Emotion Regulation and Depression

Research has consistently linked depression with emotion dysregulation, although it is unclear whether emotion regulation deficits precede the onset of depression (Shaw, Keenan, Vendra, Delliguadri, & Giovannelli, 1997) or grow out of depressive symptoms (Garber, Braafladt, & Weiss, 1995).

Casey (1996) concludes that it is most likely a combination of the two that best explains the relationship between depression and emotion regulation. Support for this relationship is reviewed below.

A mood disturbance is the defining characteristic of depressive disorders. Depressed children have difficulty altering negative affect once they are experiencing it, as they tend to generate more passive, less effective methods to regulate mood and hold lower expectations for the efficacy of strategies generated by others (Garber & Robinson, 1997). Consequently, Garber et al. (1995) suggested that children with depression use emotion-regulation strategies less often because they do not expect them to work. Moreover, observational ratings of depressed children have revealed less competent regulation of sad affect (Breen & Weinberger, 1995).

Depressed children are also more likely to report using strategies that may exacerbate distress (Garber, Braafladt, & Zeman, 1991). Specifically, depressed girls tended to avoid direct problem solving in interpersonal situations, and depressed boys tended to act in aggressive ways that exacerbate interpersonal conflict. Depressed children also reported significantly less use of pleasant activities relative to nondepressed children (Garber et al., 1991). Moreover, the interpersonal disturbances observed in depressed children (e.g., Rudolph, Hammen, & Burge, 1995) may prevent them from effectively seeking support as a means of regulating affect.

It is possible that risk factors, such as maternal depression, may act through their influence on the development of emotional regulation. The children of depressed mothers tend to exhibit maladaptive affect regulation (Cicchetti et al., 1991; Garber et al., 1991). Accordingly, mothers who are depressed show deficits in the very skills needed to foster adaptive affect regulation skills in their children. Depressed mothers tend to exhibit more negative affect (Cohn, Campbell, Matias, & Hopkins, 1990), less sensitive responding (Campbell, Cohn, & Meyers, 1995), and more difficulty balancing behavioral control and autonomy granting (Kochanska, Kuczynski, Radke-Yarrow, & Welsh, 1987). Depressed mothers also react to negative affect in their children with more criticism and less encouragement of problem solving, which may hinder children's attempts to develop effective affect-regulation strategies (Garber et al., 1991).

ETIOLOGY OF DEPRESSIVE DISORDERS DURING CHILDHOOD

It is likely that there are multiple etiological pathways to the development of depressive disorders during childhood. Thus, although there may be a limited number of paths, they are going to differ between children. The predominant etiological models are stress–diathesis models, in which stress is hypothesized to interact with a vulnerability within the child (the etiological pathway) to produce a depressive disorder. The stressors may take any of several forms (chronic strains, daily hassles, major life events) and may be chronic or have an acute onset. The diathesis (which represents the pathway) also varies across theories and probably across youngsters, and includes deficits in the production of neurotransmitters (Schildkraut, 1965), depressogenic schemas (Beck, 1967), an insidious attributional style and hopelessness (Abramson, Metalksy, & Alloy, 1989), social skills disturbances (Lewinsohn, 1975), or a lack of perceived competence (Cole & Turner, 1993), to note just some of the variables that have received empirical attention and support. It is our belief that a combination of biological, cognitive, behavioral, and familial/environmental variables reciprocally interact with each other and with stress to produce and maintain a depressive disorder (Stark et al., 1991). The following section describes biological models of the etiology of depressive disorders.

Biological Aspects of Depression

There is substantial evidence that biological and genetic factors are associated with depressive disorders (Koplewics, Klass, & Kafantaris, 1993; Thase & Howland, 1995). Most biological theories of depression assume dysfunction of one or more neurochemical systems in the brain (Thase & Howland, 1995). The "classic" biogenic amine theory suggests that depression is caused by depletion of monoamines at critical synapses in the brain (Schildkraut, 1965). The monoamine system includes the neurotransmitters norepinephrine, serotonin, and dopamine. In individuals with depression, the levels of these neurotransmitters are hypothesized to be below a critical level. The biogenic amine theory, in its original form, was too simplistic. Subsequent modifications of this model have emphasized long-term changes in receptor function. For each neurotransmitter, many different receptor sites exist. Hence, depression may stem from a disruption in these specialized receptor sites, rather than from a general neurotransmitter deficit within the monoamine system (Kolb & Whishaw, 1996). Additionally, there is an increasing appreciation of the synergistic action of multiple neurotransmitter systems (Feldman, Meyer, & Quenzer, 1997).

Newer generation antidepressants serve to further refine our understanding of the neurobiology of depression, as they target specific neurotransmitters. Selective serotonin reuptake inhibitors (SSRIs) such as fluoxetine (Prozac), paroxetine (Paxil), fluvoxamine (Luvox), and sertraline (Zoloft), although structurally different from each other, all specifically affect the serotonin system, leading to the conclusion that depression involves abnormal serotonergic functioning (Kolb & Whishaw, 1996). Two newer antidepressants, venlafaxine (Effexor) and nefazodone (Serzone), affect the neurotransmitters serotonin and norepinephrine. Both serotonin and norepinephrine are found in the limbic system, which controls such functions as eating, sleeping, and emotion, which often involve definitive disturbances associated with depression. Serotonin and norepinephrine also modulate the secretion of hormones by the hypothalamic–adrenal system (Kolb & Whishaw, 1996). Within the hypothalamic–adrenal system, the adrenal glands at times oversecrete hydrocortisone, or cortisol, which has been associated with stress. When stressed, hypothalamic neurons, regulated by norepinephrine neurons in the locus coeruleus, secrete corticotropin-releasing hormone, which stimulates the production of adrenocorticotropin (ACTH) by the pituitary. ACTH then stimulates the adrenal glands to produce cortisol. In individuals with depression, the stress reaction of the body may be abnormal. Many antidepressant medications affect norepinephrine receptors, thus possibly influencing the stress system as well. Both stress-related hormones and neurotransmitters influence many aspects of cerebral functioning (Kolb & Whishaw, 1996).

Hormonal and neuroendocrine systems may be involved in depression. Hormonal changes during puberty, especially estrogen levels in girls, may be linked with depression. Girls appear to release more growth hormone (GH) than boys (Burke & Puig-Antich, 1990). Age and puberty may interact in the control of GH release, which was found to be greater during sleep of prepubertal children with depression but not nondepressed prepubertal children or adolescents (Burke & Puig-Antich, 1990). The hypothalamic–thyroid system may contribute to depression as well. Some patients with clinical depression have exhibited mild hypo-thyroidism, with thyroid replacement therapy decreasing depressive symptoms (Shelton, Hollon, Purdon, & Loosen, 1991). Fewer thyroid symptoms have been noted, however, in prepubertal children (Burke & Puig-Antich, 1990), suggesting possible age mediation.

It is important to note that our current knowledge about the neurochemistry of depression is based primarily on adult studies and that few studies have specifically examined the neurochemistry of child and adolescent depression. Little is known about relative rates of development in different neurotransmitter systems, and these systems may function differently at different stages of development (Emslie, Weinberg, Kennard, & Kowatch, 1994; Speier, Sherak, Hirsch, & Cantwell, 1995). Furthermore, extant research has failed to consider simultaneously the reciprocal relationship between biological and psychosocial variables when evaluating the relationship between biological variables and depression. It has been assumed that the biological variables always precede or supersede psychosocial disturbances, but this is unlikely to be true for all cases of depression.

Cognitive–Interpersonal Pathway

An emerging paradigm among cognitive theorists is to integrate cognitive and interpersonal theories as a means of describing a potential pathway for the development of depressive disorders (Baldwin, 1992; Rudolph, Hammen, & Burge, 1997; Shirk, 1998; Stark, Schmidt, & Joiner, 1996). These theorists have typically integrated either Beck's cognitive theory (e.g., Beck, 1967) or Abramson's (e.g., Abramson et al., 1989) learned hopelessness theory of depression (e.g., Abramson, 1999; Flynn & Garber, 1999; Stark, Schmidt, Joiner, & Boswell, 1999) with interpersonal theories. Our own work has concentrated on an integration of Beck's cognitive theory of depression with attachment theory (Stark et al., 1999). Beck's cognitive theory provides an empirically supported explanation of the cognitive disturbances that are evident among depressed youth as well as some hypotheses about how these disturbances develop, and attachment theory provides a description of a process through which the cognitive disturbances may develop in the very young child within the family context and then influence future development.

Briefly, from the cognitive perspective, depressive disorders are characterized by a disturbance in cognition that is activated by specific vulnerabilities to stressful events (Hammen & Goodman-Brown, 1990). Once activated, the disturbance in cognition produces a negative distortion in perceptions about the self, the world, and the future (the cognitive triad; Beck, 1967). Driving the cognitive disturbance are dysfunctional core schemas that are hierarchically linked to other less central but related schemas. Schemas are hypothesized to serve as filters that guide what is attended to, how it is perceived, and what meaning is derived from stimuli. Schemas combine with environmental events to produce the individual's conscious thoughts. The most central or core schema is the self-schema. The self-schema is comprised of the individual's most central rules for life. It is presumed to facilitate encoding, storage, and retrieval of self-relevant information. Support for the existence of a self-schema that may facilitate the processing of self-relevant information in children is evident (Prieto, Cole, & Tageson, 1992). The self-schema of depressed individuals is unrealistically negative and characterized by a sense of loss or unlovability and may account for such symptoms as selective attention to, and personalization of, salient events (Beck, Rush, Shaw, & Emery, 1979).

Whereas Beck (1967) hypothesizes that a negative self-schema guides the information processing of depressed individuals, and empirical support for this contention is evident for depressed adults, support for this contention with depressed youth has not been forthcoming. Rather, research to date, with children has indicated that nondepressed youths possess a positive self-schema, which is lacking in depressed youngsters (Hammen & Zupan, 1984; Jaenicke et al., 1987; Zupan, Hammen, & Jaenicke, 1987). However, in one study, Zupan and colleagues (1987) found evidence of a stronger negative self-schema among the depressed youngsters. It is possible that the lack of a positive self-schema is a developmental precursor to a negative self-schema. The absence of an adaptive self-schema would lead to an imbalance in information processing, in which fewer instances of positive self-relevant information are processed and internalized into the overall sense of self. The lack of a positive self-schema, or the existence of a pervasively negative self-schema, is hypothesized to lead to a negative bias in information processing that serves to confirm the depressed individual's less positive or negative sense of self, world, and future. Emerging research suggests that children's schemas evolve through a developmental process that eventually leads to a structuralized sense of self.

Cole and Turner's (1993) research indicates that the schematic functioning of depressed youth is not as structuralized as that of depressed adults. A child's self-schema affects his or her perceptions of experiences and is simultaneously shaped by these experiences. Thus, if the youngster's life experiences are chronically stressful or in other ways unhealthy, they will be integrated into and shape the sense of self, which will become structuralized over time through repeated learning experiences. Once structuralized, the self-schema guides information processing and the youngster tends to attend selectively to information that confirms the sense of self and ignores schema-inconsistent information. However, if the youngster's environment changes, or if the youngster is exposed to other corrective experiences, the overall development of the self-schema may change as these alternative experiences become internalized through repeated learning experiences and form an adaptive self-schema or a less potent negative self-schema.

Although research supports many of the tenets of the cognitive model of depression in children, the key question is: How does the self-schema develop? Beck et al. (1979), as well as other cognitive theorists (e.g., Freeman, 1986; Young & Lindemann, 1992), hypothesize that depressive schemas are formed through early learning experiences, especially those within the family. Young (1991) hypothesizes that maladaptive schemas could be the result of inadequate parenting or ongoing aversive experiences within the family milieu, such as repeated criticism or rejection. Mahoney (1980) hypothesizes that schemas are hierarchically organized according to the time at which they develop, with those developing earliest influencing the subsequent development of other schemas. The first schema to develop is the self-schema, and as the first, it influences the development of other schemas. Attachment theory offers some direction for understanding how the family may contribute to the earliest development of schematic functioning.

Attachment is defined as a set of behaviors that characterize the style of interaction between the child and his or her caretakers, particularly during stressful situations. Attachment behaviors are hypothesized to reflect the youngster's internal working model. The internal working model (Bowlby, 1980) is a cognitive representation of the self, of others in the relational world (especially the primary caretaker), and of the relationship between the child and the primary caregiver (Berman & Sperling, 1994). As such, these cognitive representations that comprise the internal working model are analogous to the cognitive theorists' concept of core schema. Thus, from the cognitive perspective, the internal working model consists of the self-schema, a schema that represents an amalgam of significant others, and a schema about the relationship between the child and his or her primary caretaker. In fact, interpersonal theorists have used the schema concept within their definitions of the internal working model. For example, Bretherton (1990) describes the internal working model as an interconnected hierarchy of schema of self, world, and others, which feed interactively and reciprocally into one another. Bretherton's description of the internal working model is similar to Mahoney's (1980) description of the organization of an individual's information-processing system. The internal working model, like the core schema, is hypothesized to provide the framework for expectations that guide interactions with others in new and existing relationships. To borrow from cognitive-behavioral theory, more specifically, Bandura's (1978) concept of reciprocal determinism, the child's interpersonal behavior leads to reactions of others that then impact the child and his or her perceptions of the interaction, as well as expectations for future relationships. In addition, the outcome of the interaction provides the child with information about the self. For example, if a new friendship is formed, the child could interpret the result to mean "I am likable", "People enjoy being with me", "I am good at making friends." Oftentimes, the child's interactions with others confirms his or her expectations and the underlying schema. In a similar fashion, the cognitive representations of relationships appear to guide information processing that is related to the youngster's view of self (Rudolph et al., 1995). For example, children who display negative maternal schemas report expectations of aversive and undesirable outcomes within their family, and their self-descriptions are associated with cognitive representations of parents and peers. These results indicate that children may maintain cognitive representations of relationships, including self and others, that influence information encoding and retrieval, and expectations of future experiences.

Both cognitive theory and attachment theory are concerned with the child's developing sense of self. On the one hand, Beck postulated that the sense of self is formed within an interpersonal context, yet the self-schema is the central variable in information processing. From both cognitive and interpersonal perspectives, the self-schema is shaped by interpersonal experiences. From the cognitive perspective, the schema is shaped by experiences within an interpersonal context at the same time that it filters and constructs perceptions about these experiences. While attachment theory is concerned with the developing sense of self, greater emphasis is placed on the schemas that represent relationships and significant others. These schemas interact with the self-schema but are hypothesized to influence the development of self. Thus, these interpersonal variables are hypothesized to be prepotent and impact the developing sense of self. Cognitive theorists would agree that the self-schema is connected to a schema of others, but that the self-schema is prepotent and more influential in the sense that it develops first and influences the development of the schema about other people.

Like the cognitive theorists, interpersonal theorists have suggested mechanisms through which the child's internal working model is developed. It has been hypothesized that consistency in interactions in the caregiving environment leads to internalization of the attachment relationship (Colin, 1996). Bretherton (1990) hypothesized that the internal working model is internalized through communications between the child and caregiver. While interpersonal theorists hypothesize that the internal working model is internalized through interactions with significant others, the actual process that leads to internalization is not stated. This is a point where cognitive theory may be integrated, as cognitive theorists hypothesize that the internalization process results from repeated learning experiences. For example, if a mother's interactions with her child are repeatedly characterized by loving, caring, warm interactions, the child learns that he or she is lovable. Perhaps Colin (1996) is referring to learning as the process when she notes that *consistency* in the interactions leads to internalization.

The coherence and organization of the relationship between the child and the primary caregiver, and within the family in general, determine whether an attachment is secure or insecure. Main (1996) outlined the broad research in attachment in the last two decades. Infant attachment has been empirically defined according to four broad classifications, including one secure classification and three insecure classifications. Classifications are made based on interactions between the primary caregiver and the infant in a laboratory setting. Kobak, Sudler, and Gamble (1991) suggest that an insecure and anxious attachment, which is often linked to a psychologically unavailable or rejecting caregiver, fosters an internal working model of self as unlovable, particularly if the developing youth is unable to distinguish between negative parenting behaviors and negative self. In other words, the child may interpret the mother's rejection or unavailability as evidence that he or she is unworthy of attention, bad, or unlovable. As noted earlier, Beck hypothesizes that an unlovable self-schema is at the core of depression. Priel and Shamai (1995) hypothesize that an insecure–ambivalent attachment style, characterized by the youngster's hypervigilance to the caregiver and high dependence on others, is related to expectations that the primary caregiver as well as significant others will not support the youngster in stressful situations. Based on the earlier discussion of the acquisition of emotion-regulation skills, this attachment style would prevent the child from learning how to regulate his or her own emotions. Thus, attachment theorists hypothesize that the nature of the attachment style determines the child's schemas of relationship with the primary caregiver, others, and the self, and that these schemas interact and influence each other.

Research is beginning to explore the relationship between attachment styles and depression. Cowan, Cohn, Cowan, and Pearson (1996) investigated parental attachment styles in relation to externalizing and internalizing disorders and adjustment in preschool and kindergarten children. Their results indicated that parents' attachment styles predicted children's adjustment in kindergarten in terms of internalizing and externalizing disorders. Kobak et al. (1991) reported an association between depressive symptoms and preoccupied attachment strategies among adolescents in the general population. In the only study using a clinical population, Rosenstein and Horowitz (1996) reported that adolescents' and mothers' attachment styles were highly related. In addition, adolescents with a mood disorder were more likely to be classified as insecure–preoccupied. Although several studies have linked insecure attachment to depression, it should be noted that attachment behaviors are internalized through repeated learning experiences and become schemas. The schemas guide information processing, which is hypothesized to lead to the development of a depressive disorder. In addition, attachment behaviors impact the development of the child's emotion-regulation skills and expectations for social support. Thus, an insecure attachment style does not cause depression. It may be better characterized as a risk factor for the development of a depressive style of thinking, a deficit in emotion-regulation skills, and a failure to use social support that stems from the expectation that others are not going to help eliminate stress or be soothing—all of which increase the risk for depression. In contrast, secure attachment may act as a protective factor that leads to the development of an adaptive style of processing information and healthy emotion regulation and coping skills. From our perspective, insecure attachment is the context in which a negative sense of self, world, and future begins to develop. Thus, it represents a cognitive interpersonal pathway to the development of depression.

Cognitive and interpersonal theorists suggest that schemas are formed through early childhood experiences within the family, yet no research has directly tested this hypothesis with very young children. However, in research with youngsters in middle childhood, Stark, Schmidt, and Joiner (1996) reported that a youngster's sense of self, world, and future could represent the internalization of messages, verbal and nonverbal, that he or she receives from interactions with parents. We believe that children are active information processors who derive meaning from day-to-day interactions, and that the self-schema, as the most basic core schema, develops first through learning experiences within the family. Each interaction with the world represents a learning experience that provides the developing child with information about the self. As the self-schema develops, it becomes more structuralized and guides information processing in a fashion that confirms the developing sense of self. Furthermore, the child begins to construct an environment that confirms this sense of self through his or her perceptions and actions. Thus, from the cognitive perspective, the diathesis for a depressive disorder would be a negative sense of self, or as research with children indicates, the lack of a positive sense of self, which is formed through early interactions with caregivers and maintained by interactions within the family and with peers, as well as through other day-to-day experiences.

The cognitive-interpersonal pathway concept has implications for a debate that is evident in the depression literature about the veracity of the depressed individual's information processing. Alloy and Abramson (1979) have hypothesized that the negatively toned information processing of depressed individuals is a reflection of their reality rather than a distortion in information processing. In contrast, Beck has argued that the information processing of depressed adults is characterized by a distortion that leads to the negative bias in their information processing. In other words, from Abramson and Alloy's perspective, the depressed individual's negative cognitions are an accurate reflection of the negative experiences they are having, whereas from Beck's perspective, the depressed individual sees things in an unrealistically negative (distorted) manner. In the case of depressed youth, both perspectives may be true. The schemas of depressed youth are hypothesized to be realistic in the sense that they represent the internalization of unhealthy or unpleasant experiences. Thus, during the developmental period, the information processing of depressed youth is realistic, as the negative life experiences are becoming internalized. Once these experiences are structuralized, depressed youth continue to use these schemas to guide their information processing and to derive meaning from their experiences. These schemas operate in situations outside of the original context in which they developed and now cause a distortion in information processing. For example, a child may have a realistic schema: "Everyone that I get close to is going to hurt me." Consequently, when this child becomes an adolescent, he or she believes that other's actions are designed to be hurtful or will lead to emotional pain even when the other person is not doing anything that is intended to be hurtful. Thus, later in life, the youngster will experience difficulties with intimacy as the schema is applied to new relationships and the youngster misinterprets others' actions as intentionally hurtful.

AN INTEGRATED MODEL OF DEPRESSIVE DISORDERS DURING CHILDHOOD

Based on research, it is believed that depression is associated with disturbances in cognitive, interpersonal, familial and biochemical functioning, as well as deficits in critical emotion-regulation skills (for a review, see Stark et al., 1999). Furthermore, a reciprocal relationship exists among these disturbances, and they reciprocally interact with a deficit in emotion regulation. Thus, a disturbance in one area would affect, and be affected by, each of the other domains. For example, a biochemical disturbance would affect mood, vegetative functioning, and information processing, and leave the youngster more vulnerable to the effects of stress. The disturbance in mood and information processing would feed back to, and impact, the biochemical disturbance and affect the youngster's behavior, which in turn impacts relationships with others. The behaviors and reactions of significant others may be misperceived due to distortions in information processing that lead to a confirmation of, or the activation of, dysfunctional schemas. Once activated, these dysfunctional schemata guide information processing. Depending on the age and learning history of the youngster, the schemas may be more or less structuralized and thus open to, and shaped by, new experiences.

The following example may clarify some of the major tenets of the model. A child may have a genetic predisposition toward depression that stems from having a depressed parent. This predisposition would place the child at risk for developing a neurochemical diathesis. The depressed parent would be a chronic stressor. Depressed mothers, for example, tend to perceive more misbehavior in their children than actually exists, which increases the number of punitive interchanges and creates a negative affective tone at home (Forehand et al., 1988). Moreover, depressed mothers have difficulty engaging their children in the types of interactions necessary for teaching affect regulation skills. The attachment behaviors would likely be characterized by an insecure style and the internal working model would be one of contradictions. The schema about relationships would characterize relationships as fraught with pain and unreturned love.

Children are active constructors of their environments, both in terms of their actions and perceptions. They try to make sense of, or derive meaning from, interactions with the environment and especially from interactions with significant others. The message that a youngster might surmise from repeated punitive interactions with the depressed mother would be "I'm bad." In addition, the lack of emotional availability of the depressed parent, along with the negative interactions, would lead to the self-perception, "I'm unlovable." If these messages are communicated often enough and accompanied by other learning experiences that communicate the same message, this self-view becomes internalized and structuralized as a core schema that guides information processing. The other schemas that comprise the internal working model would become structuralized in a similar fashion and guide interpersonal behavior. The youngster would be unlikely to get close to others, as he or she would expect to be hurt and rejected. Thus, the youngster's behavior would reinforce his or her internal working model and prevent schema-inconsistent learning experiences. During times of stress, the youngster would not seek social support due to a history of not getting it. Thus, the youngster would not have access to the interpersonal warmth and sense of security that come from social support during stressful times. The extent to which children feel supported, safe, and secure predicts the use of adaptive mood regulation strategies by children (Kliewer & Lewis, 1995). Thus, the youngster would fail to learn essential mood regulation skills. In addition, the child would not have access to the consoling conversations that often produce a reframing of what is happening and how it is likely to impact one's life. Schemas serve as filters that eliminate schema-inconsistent information and process schema-consistent information that further strengthens the developing sense of self and the rest of the internal working model. Furthermore, this negative style of thinking and other depressive symptoms, as well as the youngster's "standoffish" behavior, may be aversive to peers, which could lead to further isolation, alienation, or rejection. Thus, within this example, biological (genetic predisposition), cognitive (self-schema, internal working model), behavioral (distant, aversive interpersonal behavior), and interpersonal/family (depressed parent, negative messages) disturbances reciprocally interact with each other and a deficit in mood regulation skills to produce and maintain a depressive disorder.

It has been hypothesized (e.g., Beck et al., 1979) and research (Stark, Schmidt, & Joiner, 1996) is emerging that supports the notion that the core schemas are formed through early learning experiences and communications within the family. We refer to this as the cognitive interpersonal pathway. In the case of the depressed youngster, schemas that make the youngster vulnerable to stress may develop as a result of interactions that are characteristic of an insecure attachment, negative evaluative statements directed at the child from parents, a history of abuse, and interactions that communicate rejection (Puig-Antich et al., 1985), and parental overreliance on punitive procedures (Poznanski & Zrull, 1970). It is important to note that the child, through genetic predispositions and temperament factors, plays a role in constructing this environment. Furthermore, the youngster's behaviors impact the environment in a fashion that supports the developing schema.

It is within the family milieu that the child develops crucial attachment behaviors, interpersonal skills, and the expectations that guide interpersonal relationships. In the case of the depressive family milieu, the child learns a more impulsive and angry style of interacting, and rejection or a lack of support is expected (Stark, Humphrey, Crook, & Lewis, 1990). As the child develops, he or she begins to interact with others, and these interactions are guided by the youngster's internal working model. These interactions are both shaped by, and shape, existing social skills, affect regulation skills, as well as the youngster's schema about social situations (internal working model). The depressed youngster behaves in an impulsive and angry style that leads to rejection. This rejection in turn leads to the development of a sense of self that is comprised of a poorly developed positive self-schema and a more active negative self-schema (Prieto et al., 1992), a negative world schema (Kaslow, Stark, Printz, Livingston, & Tsai, 1992), and negative schema about interpersonal relationships, as well as the self within these relationships. In addition, rejection may lead to withdrawal (Kazdin, Esveld-Dawson, Sherick, & Colbus, 1985), which insulates the youngster from corrective learning experiences. As the youngster matures and faces new stressors, he or she does not have the parental (Stark et al., 1990) or peer social support (e.g., Blechman, McEnroe, Carella, & Audette, 1986) necessary to help buffer their impact. The impact is further heightened through negative distortions in information processing (Kendall, Stark, & Adam, 1990) and a deficit in mood regulation skills. Affect interacts with the previously mentioned variables in a reciprocal fashion. The youngster may experience dysphoria due to the perception of social or familial rejection, the conflictual and punitive atmosphere within the family milieu (Forehand et al., 1988), or from biochemical imbalances. Similarly, the mood disturbance impacts the youngster's information processing and behavior, and he or she lacks the skills necessary for moderating or changing the dysphoria.

Once developed, schemas can be either active or latent. It is possible that they become active through a variety of means. A traumatic or stressful event that is related to the content of the schema may occur and trigger its activation. Once activated, schemas guide information processing, which leads to depressed affect and the accompanying depressive symptoms. With time, disturbances in cognition reciprocally impact brain chemistry perhaps through a stress-like reaction.

What might be the link between stress, cognition, and biochemical functioning? As noted earlier, stress impacts a child's neurochemical functioning. Stressful events have both a direct impact on biological functioning and an indirect effect through the individual's perceptions of stress and the potential harm he or she may experience. The depression-prone individual, due to errors in information processing that are a reflection of early learning experiences, may believe that he or she does not possess the skills or abilities to cope effectively with stress. In addition, these individuals are more likely to perceive a wider variety of events as potentially harmful, which leads to greater stress. Social support is a buffer for the effects of stress, but due to the youngster's internal working model, he or she is less likely to seek social support or to receive it. Stress appears to impact the hypothalamic–adrenal system, causing the adrenal glands to oversecrete hydrocortisone or cortisol. When stressed, hypothalamic neurons, regulated by norepinephrine in the locus coeruleus, secrete corticotropin-releasing hormone, which stimulates the production of ACTH by the pituitary.

ACTH then stimulates the adrenal glands to produce cortisol. Stress-related hormones and neurotransmitters influence many aspects of cerebral functioning (Kolb & Whishaw, 1996). This may lead to a disruption in the neurotransmitter system, as well as produce many of the symptoms of depression.

ASSESSMENT

Tools for assessing the presence and severity of depressive disorders in children have been discussed in numerous journal articles (e.g., Kazdin, 1987; Kendall, Cantwell, & Kazdin, 1989), and chapters (e.g., Reynolds, 1984). Since these discussions remain timely and complete, descriptions of all of the available measures and their psychometric properties are not repeated here. Rather, the focus is on the application of a few selected measures and the way they are used to inform intervention.

Measures of symptom severity, including self-report questionnaires such as the Children's Depression Inventory (Kovacs, 1981), interviews such as the Schedule for Affective Disorders and Schizophrenia for School-Age Children (K-SADS; Orvaschel & Puig-Antich, 1987), and parent report measures such as the Child Behavior Checklist (Achenbach & Edelbrock, 1983) serve as a means of assessing the presence and severity of depressive symptoms. Following best-practices guidelines, we assess for the presence and severity of a depressive disorder using a semistructured interview, the K-SADS, with the child and his or her caregivers. The K-SADS has been used for many years and continues to be revised and updated (Orvaschel & Puig-Antich, 1987). There are two versions of the K-SADS: Present Episode and Epidemiological. Both interviews cover the major psychological disorders of childhood, including depression. Thus, they enable the interviewer to assess for the presence and severity of comorbid conditions. While the K-SADS requires extensive training and is designed for use in research, its format is flexible enough that it can be adapted by the skilled interviewer for clinical practice.

The Present Episode format is used to assess the presence and severity of symptoms at two potentially different points in the disorder. The youngster is queried about the presence and experience of each symptom when it was most severe during the present episode, and how it was experienced over the past week. Since the interview is oriented to the present episode and depression is episodic, we have altered the administration procedure to gather more information about the history of the disorder. Two time lines that have a mood rating along the vertical axis and meaningful anchors (day school started, Thanksgiving, Christmas, birthday, etc.) along the horizontal axis are used. One time line is for the past year and the other is for the lifetime. If a child indicates the presence of a depressive disorder, then the interviewer instructs the child in how to graphically depict the way that the disorder has varied in severity during the previous year. Similarly, the youngster is asked whether he or she had ever experienced depression in the past, and if an affirmative answer is given, the child is asked to use the time line to illustrate the onset and course of previous episodes.

The K-SADS provides the interviewer with sample questions and anchors for severity ratings for symptoms of each disorder. The anchors reflect a range of phenomenological experience from nonexistent to most severe. The interviewer is free to rephrase, reword, or use different questions from the samples to assess the desired information. For example, the questions for assessing dysphoria appear in Figure 5.1, and the anchors for rating severity appear in Figure 5.2. As is true for all of the symptom anchors, severity of dysphoria is determined through combining information about the frequency and duration of dysphoric mood with the degree of psychic pain experienced. Assessment of the severity of the phenomenological experience of the symptom, and not just its frequency and duration, is one of the strengths of this interview. The interview assesses additional characteristics of each symptom. With respect to dysphoria, the quality of the sadness is assessed, since clinically depressed youths report that their experience of sadness is distinct from the sadness they feel when an unpleasant event occurs. Dysphoric mood can vary in the degree to which it is both associated with and reactive to environmental events. A more severe experience is evident when the youngster's mood disturbance is not associated with environmental events and attempts to cheer the child up have no impact.

Both the child and primary caregiver are interviewed regarding the child's symptoms. The child is considered the best source of information re-

---

How have you been feeling?
Would you say you are a happy child or a sad child?
Mostly happy or mostly sad, unhappy, empty, like crying. Is this a good feeling or a bad feeling?
Have you had any other bad feelings?
Do you have a bad feeling all the time that you can't get rid of? Have you cried or been tearful?
Do you feel (_____) all the time, some of the time?
Does it come and go?
How often?
Every day?
How long does it last?
All day?
How bad is the feeling?
Can you stand it?

FIGURE 5.1. Sample questions for the K-SADS for assessing dysphoria. From Orvaschel and Puig-Antich (1987).

0. No information.
1. Not at all or less than once a week.
2. Slight: Occasionally has dyphoric mood at least once a week for more than 1 hour.
3. Mild: Often experiences dysphoric mood at least three times a week for more than 3 hours each.
4. Moderate: Most days feels "depressed" (including weekends) or over 50% of awake time.
5. Severe: Most of the time feels depressed and it is almost painful. Feels wretched.
6. Extreme: Most of the time feels extreme depression, which "I can't stand."
7. Very extreme: Constant unrelieved, extremely painful feelings of depression.

FIGURE 5.2. Anchors for rating severity of the child's experience of dysphoria.

garding the experience of depressive symptoms. Since depression is a covertly experienced disorder, only the youngster is aware of the subjective symptoms. Because younger children are not accurate reporters of time-related information, such as when the episode first began, parents are considered the better source of information. However, the parents' own mental health is considered when interpreting ratings of the child's depressive symptoms.

In addition to the interview, we recommend use of a self-report measure as a means of further quantifying the subjective severity of depressive symptoms. Although the interview provides the clinician with the opportunity to establish rapport and to inquire about each symptom, the self-report questionnaire, due to the difference in assessment format, often results in additional information. The youngsters' responses to the Children's Depression Inventory (CDI) items are compared to their responses to the same symptom ratings on the interview, and differences are discussed.

Assessment–Treatment Link

Results of the interview and self-report questionnaire provide a measure of the severity of the episode. Research suggests that more severe disorders will have a more protracted course (McCauley et al., 1993). The therapist may use this information to plan for a more intense intervention and a more protracted course of treatment. The intensity may be increased through scheduling more frequent meetings and coordinating other adjunctive interventions, such as pharmacological treatments and family therapy. In addition, admission to a psychiatric hospital may be considered and recommended. The diagnostic interview also guides treatment through the identification of comorbid conditions.

Information about symptoms from the interview guides treatment as procedures are chosen to intervene with each symptom. Of great concern to the clinician is determining whether the youngster is suicidal. If the youngster is at risk for suicidal behavior, steps are immediately taken to ensure the youngster's safety and to provide hope and relief from the overwhelming stress. The sources of stress are identified and the youngster is guided in the implementation of coping skills for managing these stressors. As an example of how symptom presence guides intervention, the type of mood disturbance determines the intervention strategies that will be employed. Dysphoria is approached with affective education, scheduling pleasant activity, and an emphasis on restructuring maladaptive schemas. Parent consultation is directed toward the identification and alteration of parental behaviors and beliefs that contribute to the development of depressive schemas and dysphoria. Excessive anger and irritability are approached with affective education designed to help the child to identify the cognitive, physical, and behavioral manifestations of anger; this heightened sensitivity is used to help the youngster identify the early signs that he or she is angry. Anger triggers from within the environment are identified, and the youngster is taught a variety of anger-management techniques. Consultation is designed to eliminate parental behaviors that contribute to an escalation of conflict, and parents are taught behavior management procedures for decreasing the frequency and intensity of angry outbursts. Anhedonia is treated with affective education, designed to help the child to recognize the presence of positive emotions, and scheduling of pleasant activity to increase the child's activity level and the experience of pleasant emotions. There is the greater likelihood of a referral to a child psychiatrist for a trial of an antidepressant. Additional examples of symptom-specific interventions are noted in Table 5.1.

A measure of symptom severity can be used as a means of assessing the effectiveness of treatment. This can be accomplished by the child completing the CDI at the beginning of every other meeting. Since children find it frustrating to repeatedly complete this questionnaire, and since it takes 10–15 minutes to complete, we have used a symptom checklist that can be completed in a brief amount of time (Stark, 1990), thus minimizing frustration and loss of treatment time.

A variety of additional measures are used to assess cognitive, interpersonal, and family variables that are relevant to the treatment of depressed youth. A few paper-and-pencil measures have been developed for assessing cognitive variables. The Automatic Thoughts Questionnaire for Children (ATQ-C; Stark, Humphrey, Livingston, Laurent, & Christopher, 1993), a version of the ATQ (e.g., Hollon & Kendall, 1980), consists of 30 depressive self-statements. The child rates the frequency of occurrence of each thought. Sample items from the ATQ-C appear in Figure 5.3. The youngster's ratings can be reviewed and used to guide cognitive interventions. For example, if the youngster indicates that he or she always has the thought, "I wish I were a better person", then the therapist would ask the child to elaborate on what this thought means. A depressed adolescent stated that

TABLE 5.1. Examples of Intervention Procedures for Depressive Symptoms

Symptom	Intervention
Insomnia	Education regarding sleep hygiene and healthy sleep behaviors, instruction and self-monitoring of adaptive sleep behaviors, progressive muscle relaxation, relaxing imagery
Hopelessness	Problem-solving training, cognitive restructuring
Poor self-esteem	Opportunities to experience success at difficult tasks, self-monitor positive qualities, and cognitive restructuring
Feeling unloved	Parent training, self-monitoring of parental behavior, cognitive restructuring
Difficulty concentrating	Self-instructional training
Excessive fatigue	Activity scheduling, including regular exercise
Excessive guilt	Attribution retraining
Appetite disturbance	Nutritional counseling
Social withdrawal	Cognitive restructuring, activity scheduling

she was a bad person because she had gone out with other boys while she was supposed to be "going with" one boy in particular. She felt that this made her unworthy of anyone's trust or affection. This belief was countered by reviewing the "evidence" of her history of being considerate of others and currently treating others with respect. In addition, she was provided with some education about the developmental appropriateness of her dating behavior.

Another useful questionnaire is the Cognitive Triad Inventory for Children, which assesses the youngster's sense of self, world, and future (CTI-C; Kaslow et al., 1992). The CTI-C consists of 36 items that are equally distributed across the three scales. Sample items appear in Figure 5.4. The youngster's scores on the three scales and on the items guide treatment. For example, if the child reports a negative sense of self, the therapist looks at the specific items that the youngster endorsed to try to further define the child's sense of self. If the youngster's negative sense of self is realistic, problem solving is used to develop plans for self-improvement. It appears that providing the youngster with opportunities to work toward and achieve meaningful self-improvement is one of the most effective means of improving the sense of self. If the youngster's sense of self reflects a distortion in self-evaluative information processing, then cognitive restructuring procedures are used to help the youngster obtain a more realistic and positive sense of self.

The My Standards Questionnaire—Revised (Figure 5.5; Stark, 1990) is a measure of youngsters' personal standards, perceptions of parents' standards, and self-evaluations in 10 areas of importance to youth. In ad-

1. I feel like I'm up against the   Not at all   Sometimes   Fairly often   All the time
   world.
2. I'm no good.   Not at all   Sometimes   Fairly often   All the time
3. Why can't I ever succeed.   Not at all   Sometimes   Fairly often   All the time
4. No one understands me.   Not at all   Sometimes   Fairly often   All the time
5. I've let people down.   Not at all   Sometimes   Fairly often   All the time
6. I don't think I can go on.   Not at all   Sometimes   Fairly often   All the time
7. I wish I were a better person.   Not at all   Sometimes   Fairly often   All the time
8. I'm so weak.   Not at all   Sometimes   Fairly often   All the time
9. My life's not going the way I   Not at all   Sometimes   Fairly often   All the time
   want it to.
10. I'm so disappointed in myself.   Not at all   Sometimes   Fairly often   All the time
11. Nothing feels good anymore.   Not at all   Sometimes   Fairly often   All the time
12. I can't stand this anymore.   Not at all   Sometimes   Fairly often   All the time
13. I can't get started.   Not at all   Sometimes   Fairly often   All the time
14. What's wrong with me.   Not at all   Sometimes   Fairly often   All the time
15. I wish I were somewhere else.   Not at all   Sometimes   Fairly often   All the time
16. I can't get things together.   Not at all   Sometimes   Fairly often   All the time
17. I hate myself.   Not at all   Sometimes   Fairly often   All the time
18. I'm worthless.   Not at all   Sometimes   Fairly often   All the time
19. I wish I could just disappear.   Not at all   Sometimes   Fairly often   All the time
20. What's the matter with me?   Not at all   Sometimes   Fairly often   All the time

FIGURE 5.3. Sample items from the Automatic Thoughts Questionnaire for Children (Stark, Humphrey, Laurent, Livingston, & Christopher, 1993).

1. I do well at many different things.   Yes   Maybe   No
2. Schoolwork is no fun.   Yes   Maybe   No
3. Most people are friendly and helpful.   Yes   Maybe   No
4. Nothing is likely to work out for me.   Yes   Maybe   No
5. I am a failure.   Yes   Maybe   No
6. I like to think about the good things that will happen for me in   Yes   Maybe   No
   the future.
7. I do my schoolwork okay.   Yes   Maybe   No
8. The people I know help me when I need it.   Yes   Maybe   No
9. I think that things will be going very well for me a few years   Yes   Maybe   No
   from now.
10. I have messed up almost all the best friendships I have   Yes   Maybe   No
    ever had.
11. Lots of fun things will happen for me in the future.   Yes   Maybe   No
12. The things I do every day are fun.   Yes   Maybe   No

FIGURE 5.4. Sample items from the Cognitive Triad Inventory for Children (Kaslow, Stark, Printz, Livingston, & Tsai, 1992).

dition, the youngsters are instructed to rank-order the 10 areas according to their personal importance. A child's standards are compared to his or her self-evaluations to identify discrepancies in standards and performance. Discrepancies in areas of personal import to the child become targets of intervention. If the failure to perform or achieve standards is something that is changeable and under youngsters' personal control, children can be helped to develop plans for self-improvement. If youngsters are performing or achieving up to a reasonable standard but fail to perceive this due to a negative distortion in information processing, then cognitive restructuring procedures are used to alter these unrealistically negative self-evaluations.

Since the self-schema directs information processing, it should be reflected in a youngster's responses to a projective measure that requires him or her to construct the meaning of the stimulus. In a recent investigation (Swearer, Stark, & Sommer, 1999), the thematic apperception test (TAT) responses of youngsters with a conduct disorder, or comorbid depression and conduct disorder, were coded for self-schema. The self-schemas of youth with comorbid depression and conduct disorder were characterized by defectiveness, social undesirability, and failure to achieve, whereas the self-schemas of youth with conduct disorder only were characterized by entitlement and insufficient self-control. Although a story construction method introduces inference, as it is assumed that the youngster's projection onto the characters in the story is a reflection of his or her own thinking, it is possible to code self-schemas reliably, and the differences found were consistent with theoretical predictions. The youngster's self-schema as expressed in responses to the TAT can be used as a guide to interview the youngster to evaluate the hypothesis that the projective responses reflect his or her self-schema. If the interview verifies the hypothesis, and the youngster indicates that he or she is worthless, unlovable, or defective, then cognitive restructuring procedures are used.

The therapist continually observes the children's behavior within the therapeutic relationship and uses his or her own observations and reactions to the children as a means of assessing their interpersonal skills. In addition, the Matson Evaluations of Social Skills in Youths (Matson, Rotatori, & Helsel, 1983), a 62-item self-report questionnaire, assesses youngsters' perceptions of their social skills across five dimensions, including appropriate social skills, inappropriate assertiveness, impulsive recalcitrant, jealousy/withdrawal, and overconfidence. When a disturbance in interpersonal skills or functioning is identified, then the therapist determines whether it is due to a maladaptive schema, such as "If I get close to someone they will hurt me," or due to a skills deficit, such as a failure to engage in age-appropriate behaviors. Depressed youngsters have negative expectancies and maladaptive thoughts during interpersonal exchanges that inhibit social in-

1. How popular do you have to be to feel really good about (absolutely satisfied with) yourself?

0	1	2	3	4	5	6	7	8	9	10
I don't care if anyone likes me.					Average					The most popular person in school

2. How good do your grades have to be to feel really good about (absolutely satisfied with) yourself?

0	1	2	3	4	5	6	7	8	9	10
0% I can fail everything.	30%	40%	50%	60%	70% Average All C's	75%	80%	85%	90%	100% All A's

3. How good looking do you have to be to feel really good about (absolutely satisfied with yourself?

0	1	2	3	4	5	6	7	8	9	10
Ugly					Average					Like a model

1. How popular do your parents think you ought to be?

0	1	2	3	4	5	6	7	8	9	10
Least popular person in school					Average					Most popular person in school

2. What grades do your parents think you ought to make?

0	1	2	3	4	5	6	7	8	9	10
I fail everything.					Average All C's					All A's

3. How good-looking do your parents think you ought to be?

0	1	2	3	4	5	6	7	8	9	10
Not at all					Average					Like a model

1. How popular or unpopular are you?

0	1	2	3	4	5	6	7	8	9	10
No one likes me.					Average					The most popular person

2. How good are your grades?

0	1	2	3	4	5	6	7	8	9	10
I fail everything.					Average grades					All A's

3. How good looking are you?

0	1	2	3	4	5	6	7	8	9	10
Ugly					Average					I look like a model

FIGURE 5.5. Sample items from the first three scales of the My Standards Questionnaire—Revised (Stark, 1990).

teractions as well as the implementation of appropriate social behaviors. If a cognitive disturbance is causing a performance deficit, then cognitive restructuring procedures, especially behavioral homework assignments, are used to build new, more adaptive schemas and automatic thoughts. When a maladaptive pattern of behavior is recognized, the therapist shares his or her observations and helps the youngster identify thoughts surrounding it. Subsequently, they develop a plan for preventing the maladaptive behavior from reoccurring and replace it with a more adaptive behavior that serves the same function (assuming that the function is a healthy one). Oftentimes this information is used to develop social skills building exercises that are taught and rehearsed in individual therapy and then practiced as therapeutic homework. In a properly running group, the depressed child experiences safety, acceptance, support, and positive feedback that leads to some restructuring of negative beliefs about social situations and about the self in a social context.

Guiding the assessment of family functioning is the belief that the family represents the context in which the child develops essential cognitive and interpersonal skills. The therapist observes and assesses the family with the goal of identifying interaction patterns that could produce and maintain maladaptive schemas, beliefs, information-processing errors, and maladaptive interpersonal behaviors. Perhaps the most effective method for accomplishing this is to join the family and observe their interactions in times of stress. In addition, we have developed a few measures that are designed to aid in the assessment of interaction patterns that could contribute to the development of a depressive style of thinking. To assess characteristics of the family milieu that are associated with depressive disorders, we have developed a children's version of the Self-Report Measure of Family Functioning (Stark et al., 1990). Sample items appear in Figure 5.6. This measure has undergone extensive revision and currently consists of 65 items and 13 scales that reliably assess important characteristics of the family environment, including cohesion, expression, conflict, nontransient conflict, disengagement, enmeshment, organization, democratic family style, authoritarian family style, laissez-faire family style, sociability, active recreational orientation, and intellectual/cultural orientation. Another measure that has proven very useful in differentiating depressed youths from those with other disorders (Schmidt, Stark, & Carlson, 1999) is the Family Messages Measure (Stark, Schmidt, & Joiner, 1996). This 36 item self-report questionnaire assesses messages about the self, world, and future that the child perceives receiving from each parent. Separate versions have been constructed for mother's and father's messages. Sample items from the self, world and future scales appear in Figure 5.7. Results of the questionnaires serve as hypotheses that are tested during observation of family interactions. Once identified, the behaviors and cognitions that lead to the maladaptive interaction can be explored and modified.

1. Family members really help and support one another.

Never true   A little true   Sometimes true   Pretty much true   Very true

2. Family members feel free to say what is on their minds.

Never true   A little true   Sometimes true   Pretty much true   Very true

3. We fight in our family.

Never true   A little true   Sometimes true   Pretty much true   Very true

4. We go to lectures, plays, or concerts.

Never true   A little true   Sometimes true   Pretty much true   Very true

5. We go to movies, sporting events, camping, etc.

Never true   A little true   Sometimes true   Pretty much true   Very true

6. Family members attend church, synagogue, or Sunday school.

Never true   A little true   Sometimes true   Pretty much true   Very true

7. Family members miss appointments.

Never truc   A little true   Sometimes true   Pretty much true   Very true

8. Our family gets together with friends.

Never true   A little true   Sometimes true   Pretty much true   Very true

9. Our family believes that whatever happens is because we make it happen.

Never true   A little true   Sometimes true   Pretty much true   Very true

10. Each family member does as they wish without concern about the other members.

Never true   A Little true   Sometimes true   Pretty much true   Very true

FIGURE 5.6. Sample items from the Self-Report Measure of Family Functioning—Child Form (Stark, Humphrey, Crook, & Lewis, 1990).

TREATMENT PROGRAM

Overview

Based on the previously reviewed research and the integrated model of childhood depression, the child is one of a number of participants in the intervention. Significant others from within the child's primary environments also are targets through parent training, family therapy, and consultation. Intervention with the parents, family, and school is necessary to (1) support the individual work being completed with the child; (2) encourage the development of new adaptive schemas and rules for processing information; (3) encourage the use of coping skills in the extratherapy environment; and (4) change environmental events that contribute to the development and maintenance of the cognitive, interpersonal, and familial disturbances that underlie the depressive symptoms.

1. My father tells me that I'm good at different things.   Never   Sometimes   Always

2. My father says that schoolwork is just something that must get done.   Never   Sometimes   Always

3. My father believes that most people are friendly and helpful.   Never   Sometimes   Always

4. Nothing I do seems to satisfy my father.   Never   Sometimes   Always

5. My father tells me that I'm a failure.   Never   Sometimes   Always

6. When I talk with my father about the future, it looks bright.   Never   Sometimes   Always

7. I hear my father say that I do well at school.   Never   Sometimes   Always

8. My father tells me that he will help me whenever I need it.   Never   Sometimes   Always

9. My father tells me that I will do well in the future.   Never   Sometimes   Always

10. My father wonders how anyone could be friends with me.   Never   Sometimes   Always

11. My father tells me that being grown up is no fun.   Never   Sometimes   Always

12. My father tells me that I can have an enjoyable future.   Never   Sometimes   Always

FIGURE 5.7. Sample items from the Family Messages Measure—Father Version (Stark, Kendall, et al., 1996).

A therapist's manual that describes the intervention in a session-by-session format (Stark & Kendall, 1996) and an accompanying children's workbook (Stark, Kendall, et al., 1996) have been developed. The manual describes the intervention in detail. The description of the intervention that follows is organized by type of disturbance to emphasize the parallelism among the empirically established disturbances, the assessment tools used to assess the presence and nature of the disturbances, and the intervention strategies developed for each disturbance. In other words, for each disturbance, there is a parallel assessment and intervention strategy. Modifications are made to address environmental disturbances such as parental psychopathology, a history of abuse, substance abuse, marital discord, neglect, and abandonment. The prototypical order of implementing the various treatment components is outlined in Table 5.2.

Child

Affective Disturbance

Emphasis during the initial treatment sessions is on developing the therapeutic relationship, helping youngsters gain a better understanding of their
emotional experiences, and teaching them the link between thoughts, feelings, and behaviors. Moreover, recognition of emotions and an understanding of the relationship between thoughts, feelings, and behaviors is the cor-
nerstone on which other mood-regulation and coping skills are built.

TABLE 5.2. Session-by-Session Outline of the Action Treatment Program

Session 1

Introductions
Establish appropriate expectations

Session 2

Affective education
    Identify and label emotions
Establish a within-group incentive system
Self-monitoring pleasant emotions

Session 3

Affective education
    Identify emotions, link emotions to thoughts and behavior
Introduction to active coping orientation
Self-monitoring pleasant emotions

Session 4

Affective education
    Internal and external cues of emotions, coping with unpleasant
    emotions, link emotions to thoughts and behavior
Extend coping orientation
Pleasant events scheduling
Self-monitoring pleasant emotions

Session 5

Affective education
    Internal and external cues of emotions, coping with unpleasant
    emotions, link emotions to thoughts and behavior
Introduction to problem solving
Self-monitoring pleasant emotions

Session 6

Affective education
    Internal and external cues of emotions, coping with unpleasant
    emotions, link emotions to thoughts and behavior
Pleasant events scheduling and self-monitoring pleasant emotions
Problem-solving game

TABLE 5.2. (*continued*)

Session 7

Affective education
  Internal and external cues of emotions, coping with unpleasant
  emotions, link emotions to thoughts and behavior
Pleasant events scheduling
Problem-solving game

Session 8

Affective education
  Internal and external cues of emotions, coping with unpleasant
  emotions, link emotions to thoughts and behavior
Application of problem solving to mood disturbance

Session 9

Application of problem solving to mood disturbance
Missing solution activity

Session 10

Introduction to relaxation
Exercise and mood

Session 11

Problem solving applied to interpersonal problems
Pleasant events scheduling
Relaxation as a coping strategy

Session 12

Problem solving applied to interpersonal situations
Focus on self-evaluation of solution implementation
Relaxation as a coping strategy

Session 13

Spontaneous use of problem solving
Relaxation and problem solving

Session 14

Introduction to cognitive restructuring
Identification of depressogenic thoughts

Session 15

Practice catching negative thoughts
Cognitive restructuring

Session 16

Improve understanding of cognitive restructuring
Practice catching negative thoughts
What's the evidence?
What to do when a negative thought is true

Session 17

Alternative interpretation

(*continued on next page*)

TABLE 5.2. (*continued*)

Session 18

Alternative interpretation
Identifying negative expectations
Introduce What if?

Session 19

What if?

Session 20

Review of cognitive restructuring procedures
Introduction to assertiveness training
Generate and rehearse coping statements

Session 21

Positive assertiveness
Generation of coping statements

Session 22

Assertiveness training
Generation of coping statements

Session 23

Identify personal standards
Introduction to self-evaluation training
Identification of areas in need of personal improvement

Session 24

Establish goals and subgoals for self-improvement

Sessions 25–28

Self-evaluation training/Working toward self-improvement

Sessions 29 and 30

Termination issues
Programming for generalization

Note. From Stark and Kendall (1996).

Affective educational activities are used to accomplish these as well as additional therapeutic objectives.

Depressed youths are experiencing either dysphoria, anger, anhedonia, or a mix of mood disturbances. While some of the intervention strategies specifically target the mood disturbance, all of the treatment components have as their goal an improvement in mood. Thus, it is assumed that the mood disturbance will be progressively modified as youngsters begin to cope with the various symptoms of depression and perceive themselves, life in general, and the future in a more positive and realistic fashion.

Based on a coping skills model, the goal is to teach youngsters to use their mood as a cue to engage in various coping activities. The first step to this process involves establishing a vocabulary for describing affective experiences and an empathic understanding of what children are experiencing. Depressed youth typically do not have an adequate set of labels for the range of their affective experiences (everything is referred to as "bad" or "sad"), or they mislabel them. For example, many children describe irritability as "bad," which may mean something completely different to another person. Thus, they have a difficult time communicating how they are feeling, and they find this frustrating or they misinterpret it to mean that no one understands them.

CHILD: No one understands me.

THERAPIST: You are right, I don't understand how you are feeling now. But this discussion and the sharing of your thoughts and feelings is helping me to understand. I understand better than before. It takes time and talking to each other to gain that understanding. It can be frustrating. It leaves you thinking that I don't and won't understand you, so I can't help you.

While discussing how the child has been feeling, the therapist also inquires about what the child may have been thinking and what was happening, thus trying to establish the link between thinking, environmental experiences, and feelings.

THERAPIST: You mentioned that you felt really sad when your mom used that tone of voice. So, what she said was buried by the way it was said?

CHILD: Yes!

THERAPIST: What were you thinking when you heard that tone—what does that tone mean to you?

CHILD: She is angry with me.

THERAPIST: If she is angry with you, what does that mean to you?

CHILD: That she doesn't want anything to do with me. That I am just a pain.

THERAPIST: So, when you hear that tone, you think that Mom doesn't want anything to do with you—that she doesn't love you?

The therapist chooses questions that will help identify patterns in events that are associated with a downturn in mood and then tries to identify the thoughts and meanings associated with those events. In addition, the goal is to help the child become aware of the cues that he or she is experiencing certain emotions and to cue into thoughts and actions associated with them.

When working with groups of depressed youth or with a youngster who is especially defensive, a series of games (Stark, 1990; Stark & Kendall, 1996) can be used to help the youngster(s) learn the names of various emotions. In addition, the activities improve youngsters' ability to recognize when they are experiencing particular emotions and to identify them in others. The relationship between emotions, thoughts, and behavior is illustrated through these activities. Moreover, strategies for coping with unpleasant emotions and the thoughts that accompany them are identified. The games have been described in detail elsewhere (e.g., Stark, 1990).

One of the primary tools for altering mood is activity scheduling, which is the purposeful scheduling of enjoyable and goal-directed activities in the child's day. Enactment of these activities helps the youngster obtain reinforcement and combat the withdrawal, passivity, and sedentary lifestyle associated with an episode of depression. They also provide the child with distraction from preoccupation with negative thinking and lead to cognitive restructuring as the child sees that life can be enjoyable. A child can readily recognize the relationship between "doing fun things and feeling good." This relationship can be established by discussing the youngster's week. When a typically enjoyable activity is mentioned during the meeting, the therapist can inquire as to how the child was feeling while engaged in that activity.

THERAPIST: You mentioned that you played street hockey with your friends from the neighborhood after school. How did you feel while playing hockey?

CHILD: Good.

THERAPIST: Hmm, what did we just learn about what to do to help yourself feel good?

CHILD: Play street hockey?

THERAPIST: Yes. What other fun things do you do that help you to feel good?

After exhausting the list, then the therapist might inquire: "Why do you think that playing street hockey, etc., helps you to feel good?"

CHILD: Because I'm with my friends.

THERAPIST: Okay, so being with other people helps you to feel good. What does that suggest?

CHILD: That I should do things with friends?

THERAPIST: Yes, most kids have more fun when they are with their friends than when they are alone. Why else do you think it helps you to feel good?

CHILD: Because I am doing something I like to do.

THERAPIST: That is true. Why else do you think it helps you to feel good?

CHILD: Because I'm not thinking about my problems.

THERAPIST: Right. Doing fun things gives you a chance to get away from thinking about all of the stuff that is going on. Playing is a distraction. Another thing we just learned is that when your head is full of negative thoughts about all of the things that are going on, you feel sad and when you aren't thinking about those things, you feel better. So, what seems to be causing your sadness?

Thus, the link between thoughts, actions and feelings can be established. If the child is upset about events that he or she might be able to change, then problem solving would be used to develop a plan for changing those experiences.

The therapist, child, and parents work together to identify activities that the child enjoys, and then they schedule the time and day that the child will be able to do the activities. Children are instructed to self-monitor their engagement in pleasant activities and to rate their overall mood for the day within a diary. We have created a workbook and diary form that facilitates this self-monitoring (see Figure 5.8). As sessions progress, youngsters complete a contract in which they agree to try progressively to increase their activity level. Over time, the mood ratings and frequency of pleasant activities can be graphed to provide "evidence" that a relationship exists between engagement in pleasant activities and mood. In addition, as discussed elsewhere (Stark, 1990), the graph can be used to identify activities that have an especially powerful effect on mood.

It is important to include in the schedule some mastery activities (activities that have an instrumental value). Completion of such tasks provides youngsters with a sense of accomplishment or mastery. For example, completion of a major school project, more homework assignments, a household project, or a hobby kit might lead to a sense of mastery. In addition, completion of such activities may eliminate a source of stress. The child and therapist work to combat pessimism and inertia through breaking the mastery activity down into manageable steps, creating a schedule to complete each step, and developing coping statements that can be used when the youngster begins to stall or get stuck in negative thinking.

Procedures for helping depressed children manage their irritability, anger, and anhedonia have been described elsewhere (e.g., Stark, 1990). It is very difficult for children to follow through and use anger management strategies. It usually is necessary for parents to encourage the child to cope by coaching, modeling the use of these strategies, and by establishing an incentive program. In some instances, it also is possible for parents to cue the child that he or she is becoming angry. Telling an angry person

M	T	W	TH	F	S	S	Things I like to do
0	0	0	0	0	0	0	Lowest ever
55	5	5	5	5	5	OK	
10	10	10	10	10	10	10	On top of the world

FIGURE 5.8. Pleasant Events Diary.

that he or she is angry can often escalate the problem. One child stated that she thought her parents were making fun of her whenever they told her that she was starting to get angry, and this belief would inflame her anger. Consequently, a great deal of preplanning and rehearsal are necessary. A neutral cuing system, typically involving some agreed-upon non-inflamatory phrase, something that is humorous, or a hand signal (time-out), can be used to help the youngster without exacerbating the problem.

Problem-Solving Set

As youngsters acquire a better understanding of their emotions, accurately identify them, and recognize their relationship to behavior and thinking, we begin to teach them to adopt a problem-solving set toward life. They are taught that unpleasant affect, problems, and disappointments represent problems to be solved. For example, feeling angry is a cue that a problem exists and that the youngster needs to develop a plan for eliminating the stressor and/or managing the feelings. Problem solving also counters rigidity and hopelessness as the youngsters see that there may be some options of which they were previously unaware. Children also gain a sense of self-efficacy as they experience success and mastery over the environment.

The problem-solving procedure is a modification of the one described by Kendall (e.g., Kendall & Braswell, 1993). We add a "Psych-Up" step to the procedure between problem identification and solution generation. Children learn the problem-solving steps through education, modeling, coaching, rehearsal, and feedback. Board games are used as a fun and engaging medium for teaching the steps. They provide the youngsters with almost immediate feedback through a game-related consequence (e.g., your checker gets jumped) for not following the steps. In addition, the children readily see the advantages to following the steps. As they begin to understand and correctly apply each of the six steps, the therapist teaches the youngsters to apply the process to problems in daily life.

THERAPIST: What did your mom say when you asked if your friend could spend the night?

CHILD: She said Yes.

THERAPIST: Now what do you think she will say the next time you ask her?

CHILD: She'll probably let me.

THERAPIST: Yes, probably! Let's pretend that you really do want a friend to spend the night this Friday and she says "No." What would you think?

CHILD: See, she never lets me do anything.

THERAPIST: So, you would get stuck in the negative thinking again. But if you thought to yourself: Okay, last time she said "Yes." This time she said "No." Maybe there is a reason so I'll ask her if there is another day when he can spend the night, like maybe on Saturday or next weekend instead. Then what might happen? And if you just believed your negative thought of "She never lets me do anything" and didn't ask her this other way, would your friend be able to sleep over?

When teaching depressed youth problem solving, the therapist and child are faced with the child's negative thinking. To depressed children, a problem means that there is something wrong with them, or it represents an impending loss. "If I were smarter, or nicer, or thinner, and so on, then I wouldn't have these problems." In addition, they feel overwhelmed by problems, as if they cannot solve them, and that even if they did solve an existing problem, it would simply be replaced by another one. To help combat this pessimism, the children are taught to use "Psych-Up" statements. This pessimism has to be combated over time through concrete evidence from their life experiences that demonstrates that they can overcome problems.

The third step is generation of alternative solutions. Children are taught to brainstorm as many possible solutions as they can without evaluating them. This is difficult for depressed youngsters since they typically come up with more reasons why a plan will not work than why it will work. Even when they cannot identify specific reasons for it not working, they base their prediction on how they are feeling (emotional reasoning). When beginning to learn to generate solutions, children often are limited in the range and number of possibilities that they can generate. Consequently, they have to be taught additional possibilities. It is important to teach depressed children not to evaluate the alternatives while they are trying to generate them, since they have a tendency to believe that nothing will work. Thus, youngsters may once again short-circuit the process and think that they cannot solve the problem. As treatment progresses and the problems they work on are drawn from real-life situations, emphasis is placed on developing solutions that are reasonable and realistic for the context of the adolescent's world, not just socially acceptable within an adult's world.

The fourth step involves predicting the likely outcomes for each possible solution. As youngsters progress into real-life problems, the therapist often has to help them recognize potential positive outcomes as well as limitations and self-defeating consequences of other possibilities. Once again, it is necessary at this step to combat pessimism. The fifth step involves reviewing possible solutions, choosing the best one, and enacting the plan. The final step is evaluating progress toward solving the problem and the outcome of the chosen solution. If the outcome is a desirable one, the child self-reinforces. If the outcome is undesirable, the youngster reconsiders possible solutions, chooses an appropriate "Psych-Up" and alternative solution, and enacts it. Once again, coping statements for unsuccessful plans have to be included in the treatment.

Interpersonal Behavior

The relationship that develops between the child and therapist has therapeutic value. The youngster learns how to trust someone and how to deal in a healthy fashion with intimacy. In addition, through the acceptance provided by the therapist, the youngster learns that he or she is likable and worthy. As social disturbances become evident during the natural exchanges between the child and therapist, the therapist addresses them directly through feedback and by teaching the youngster more adaptive behavior. The cognitive disturbances that underlie the maladaptive behavior are countered with more adaptive self-statements.

Maladaptive Cognitions

Children are taught various strategies for identifying and altering their maladaptive cognitions. With one exception, these treatment components typically appear late in therapy due to the fact that they require the youngster to become more self-focused, which would exacerbate depressive symptoms early in treatment. In fact, the one exception, altering faulty information processing, is included early in treatment because it is designed to redirect the youngsters' attention from negative thoughts and feelings to more pleasant emotions and positive thoughts appear to produce an elevation in mood and energy. In addition, our goal is to provide youngsters with a base of potential coping skills that they can use to moderate the severity of symptoms prior to directing them to tune into and try to counter or change maladaptive cognitions. It also appears that the improvement in mood and symptoms that results from other intervention components provides youngsters with some personal distance from their maladaptive thoughts and beliefs, which seems to open them up for change.

Altering Faulty Information Processing. Depressed children tend to pay attention to the negative things that are occurring in their lives to the exclusion of the positive. This disturbance may stem from a variety of errors in information processing. To counter this, children are taught to self monitor positive events and pleasant emotions. This serves as a method for directing children's attention to more positive things, thus breaking the cycle of negative attention. It helps children see that there are positive things going on in their lives. Youngsters may be taught to observe behaviors, thoughts, feelings, or physical reactions and make a judgment about their occurrence or nonoccurrence. In addition, they may be instructed to monitor what is happening when they have a specific thought or emotion.

The first step in teaching children to self-monitor is to define collaboratively the phenomena to be observed and identify examples and non-examples of them. It is useful to begin the training with a behavior that is likely to occur during the session, which gives the therapist an opportunity to help children tune into the occurrence of the behavior, to check for accuracy of self-monitoring, to model the procedure if necessary, and to reward the children for successful and accurate self-monitoring.

> "Today I would like you to tell me whenever you do something well during our meeting. For example, you might notice that you remembered to bring up things for us to discuss, you might be good at telling me about what you are thinking, or maybe you learned some useful things today."

After identifying and defining the target for self-monitoring, which is pleasant activities and emotions early in treatment, the children and therapist devise a method for recording its occurrence or nonoccurrence, and determine when and how often to record. It is important to devise a system that allows youngsters to record the occurrence of the target immediately after it occurs. We have created (Stark, Kendall, et al., 1996) and used emotion diaries. At first, each page in the diary has a series of cartoon characters expressing different pleasant emotions. The youngsters circle the ones they experience each day. As treatment progresses, more and more emotions are added and a check sheet is used.

Altering Automatic Thoughts. The consciousness of depressed children is dominated by negative automatic thoughts. Especially prevalent are negative self-evaluative thoughts. As these thoughts are identified, the cognitive restructuring procedures discussed later, with cognitive modeling and self-instructional training, can be used to alter them directly. Automatic thoughts are targeted by the therapist throughout treatment, and youngsters learn how to identify and modify them on their own later in treatment.

The first step for using either procedure is to help children recognize and be aware of the tendency to think negatively. This is accomplished through education, thinking aloud while playing games that require self-verbalizations (e.g., puzzles), and helping children catch negative thoughts as they occur during games and other activities. It is especially important to watch for signs that a child's mood has changed within the session and then to ask the child to state what he or she is thinking. After catching a negative thought, the youngster is taught to replace it. One method to accomplish this is therapist modeling of more adaptive thoughts.

Cognitive modeling involves the therapist verbalizing his or her thoughts, or verbalizing more adaptive thoughts that the children might use to replace existing thoughts or ones that they might have the next time a particular situation arises. In addition to using cognitive modeling when specific thoughts are being targeted, the therapist thinks aloud whenever he or she confronts a problem or some other situation that enables him or her to model adaptive thoughts for the child. This is done throughout treatment as a means of planting seeds of more adaptive thinking.

When depressed children are having an especially difficult time replacing thoughts, self-instructional training (Meichenbaum, 1977) is used to help them internalize any set of self-statements that guide their thinking and/or behavior. In our work with depressed children, we have used Kendall's (e.g., 1977) adaptation of Meichenbaum's procedure. Any content of thoughts can be taught. It is especially useful with children who are experiencing a deficit in their verbal-mediational skills, such as those who simply explode and exert no control over their emotions.

Changing Dysfunctional Schemas. One of the ultimate goals of treatment is changing dysfunctional schemas. The program includes a number of the cognitive restructuring procedures developed by Beck and colleagues (1979), including (1) What's the evidence?, (2) What's another way to look at it?, (3) What if?, and (4) behavioral experiments. Children are taught to be "thought detectives" who identify maladaptive thoughts and (1) evaluate the evidence for the thought, (2) consider alternative interpretations, and/or (3) think about what really would happen if the undesirable event occurred. These procedures are used throughout treatment by the therapist, although the goal is for the children to learn how to restructure their negative thoughts independently. This is accomplished through therapist modeling, and the techniques are taught to the youngsters through activities (see Table 5.3).

Behavioral Experiments. Perhaps the most efficient way to change children's thinking is to strategically alter behaviors that serve as the base of evidence for their thoughts. Altering behavior, and the resultant change in outcomes, provides children with immediate, direct, and concrete contradictory evidence for an existing maladaptive schema, or supportive evidence for a new, more adaptive schema. This process of assigning personal experiments requires creativity, as the therapist must first be able to identify a maladaptive thought or schema, bring it to the child's recognition, work with the child to establish the necessary evidence to support or refute the thought or schema, and then devise a behavioral assignment that directly tests the validity of it.

THERAPIST: You said that you don't believe that your dad loves you or even likes you. Let's test that belief out by doing an experiment. What would be evidence that your father loves you?

CHILD: He would spend time with me, kiss me, hug me.

THERAPIST: How about other things that he does that tell you he loves you? How about, he asks you about school and other things that you do. He helps you with schoolwork. He might ask you to join him when he does things. He might play games or watch TV with you. (*Child nods in agreement.*) I am going to write down these things on a list and then I want you to take the list home and check off which ones occur each day on this sheet of paper. Up here, the M stands for Monday, T for Tuesday, etc. Just check which ones you notice each day. What do you think is the best time for you to do this?

CHILD: Right before going to bed.

THERAPIST: Okay, who could help remind you to do this since you are likely to be sleepy?

CHILD: Mom.

THERAPIST: Great, I'll ask her to do this and explain to her what we are doing.

TABLE 5.3. Cognitive Interventions by Session

Session	Skills training
1	Establish a sense of hope.
2	Assist participants in seeing link between thinking and emotions as examples arise.
3	Identify thoughts that are associated with emotions. Note themes in participants' thinking. Note distortions in participants' thinking.
4	Identify thoughts that are associated with emotions. Note themes in participants' thinking. Note distortions in participants' thinking. Highlight impact of negative thinking. Self-monitor positive thoughts—as the C in ACTION.
5	Reconstruct thoughts and images associated with emotions that occurred between sessions—group members help. Identify thoughts that are associated with emotions—activity. Generate negative thoughts associated with problem solving and positive coping counters for them. Note negative schemas and processing errors. Self-monitor positive thoughts.
6	Reconstruct thoughts associated with emotions that occurred between sessions. Identify thoughts that are associated with emotions. Observe for pessimism and negative self-evaluations. Identify negative thoughts during a game and develop coping counters.
7	Identify thoughts that interfere with using coping strategies, getting psyched to cope, and problem solving. Generation of coping counters for negative thoughts associated with problem solving. Group and individual identify thoughts that accompany emotions. Develop self-statements for getting psyched up for problem solving. Begin building a positive sense of self—silhouette and emotion location activity.
8	Identify thoughts that interfere with participants' trying to cope. Identify negative thoughts associated with unpleasant emotions. Build a positive sense of self—illustration activity.
9	Identify and counter thoughts that interfere with coping. Generate positive thoughts to encourage problem solving. Build a positive sense of self—cut-out activity. Identify favorite coping counters, coping bubbles on the silhouettes.
10	Identify and counter pessimistic thoughts. Present rationale for cognitive restructuring. Tune into negative thoughts—puzzle activity. Continue to build a positive sense of self—crossing out common negative thoughts. Generate thoughts that interfere with coping and development of counters—activity. Identify negative thoughts that occur during the meeting.

TABLE 5.3. (*continued*)

Session	Skills training
11	Identification of negative self-evaluations and coping counters for them. Tie cognitive restructuring to the C, O, N of ACTION. Introduce notion of thought detective. Apply What's the evidence? to past problems. Continue to build a positive sense of self—similarity to friends activity. Self-monitor personal positive qualities.
12	Present clues for identification of negative thoughts. Apply What's the evidence? to hypothetical problems. Extend thought detective analogy. Improve ability to catch negative thoughts. Continue to build a positive sense of self-reframing activity.
13	Use change of mood as a cue to tune into negative thoughts. Introduce alternative interpretation. Continue to build a positive sense of self—funny stories. Introduce self-evaluation—identification of personal standards.
14	Apply alternative interpretation activity. Continue to build positive sense of self-identity, areas for self-improvement. Establish goals and subgoals and begin working toward self-improvement.
15	Introduce What if? Practice using What if? Continue to work toward self-improvement. Use cognitive restructuring to cope with negative thoughts that impede progress toward self-improvement.
16–18	Continue to work toward self-improvement. Use cognitive restructuring to counter negative thoughts that may impede progress toward self-improvement.

Furthermore, steps have to be taken to ensure that the experiment is actually carried out as planned. In some instances, role playing ahead of time, using imagery to walk through the assignment, or writing a contract may be used to promote compliance. After the experiment has been completed, the therapist works with the child to process the results. This is an important step, since depressed youth may distort the results.

Negative Self-Evaluations

The last portion of treatment is focused on changing the depressed youngsters' negative self-evaluations. This occurs last because all of the other self-management skills, coping skills, and cognitive restructuring procedures are brought to bear on the process of working toward and recognizing self-improvement and changing the negative sense of self. Depressed children evaluate their performances, possessions, and personal qualities more negatively than nondepressed youth, and their self-evaluations tend to be negatively distorted (Kendall et al., 1990). In other words, they tend to be unrealistically and unreasonably negative in their self-evaluations. Children can be taught to evaluate themselves more reasonably and positively when it is realistic to do so. During this process, they learn to recognize their positive attributes, outcomes, and possessions. The first step of the procedure is to identify the existence and nature of the disturbance. As noted earlier, this is accomplished through completion of the My Standards Questionnaire—Revised (Stark, 1990). When children evaluate their performance as inadequate because they have set perfectionistic standards, cognitive restructuring is used to help them accept more reasonable standards. When children set realistic standards, but evaluate themselves negatively, cognitive restructuring and self-monitoring are used. The cognitive restructuring procedures "What's the evidence?" and cognitive modeling may be used. Self-monitoring of supportive evidence is used as a means to solidify the new self-evaluations. Over the course of treatment, the therapist and children review the evidence that supports the new self-evaluation. A series of activities have been developed that help youngsters build a positive sense of self (Stark & Kendall, 1996).

In some instances, children's negative self-evaluations are accurate, and they can benefit from change. In such instances, the goal of self-evaluation training is to help youngsters to translate personal standards into realistic goals, and then develop and carry out plans for attaining their goals. Following the translation process, children prioritize the areas where they are working toward self-improvement. Initially, a plan is formulated for producing improvement in an area where success is probable. The long-term goal is broken down into subgoals, and problem solving is used to develop plans that will lead to subgoal and, eventually, goal attainment. Prior to enacting plans, children try to identify possible impediments to carrying out the plans. Once again, problem solving is used to develop contingency plans for overcoming the impediments. Once the plans, including contingency plans, have been developed, children self-monitor their progress toward change. Alterations in plans are made along the way.

Parents

Parents and teachers are seen as a central link between children's acquisition of skills during therapy sessions and their application to the natural environment. The school consultation component has been described elsewhere (Stark et al., 1999). Parents begin the training component at the same time as the child begins therapy. The parent training program is designed to foster a more positive family environment through teaching parents how to (1) use positive behavior management techniques, (2) reduce conflict, (3) increase their child's role in the family decision-making process, and (4) improve their child's self-esteem.

One of the central components of the parent training program is teaching parents to use primarily positive behavior management procedures. To accomplish this objective, procedures have been borrowed from Barkley (1997). Initially, parents are taught to recognize and attend to positive affect and behavior through a series of role-play activities. When they can clearly recognize positive behavior as it occurs, appropriately comment on it, and understand the notion of extinguishing undesirable behavior through nonattention, parents are assigned the task of spending 15–20 minutes each day playing with their child. They are instructed to make it an enjoyable activity in which they strive to pay particular attention to their child's positive actions. These positive behaviors are socially reinforced and recorded in a diary by parents throughout the week.

During the next few meetings, parents are taught how to use reinforcement techniques and about the impact reinforcement has on their child's mood and self-esteem. Once again, role-play activities are used to facilitate acquisition of these skills. Parents collaboratively work with the therapist to identify targets for change and develop plans to use reinforcement procedures to produce change.

In addition to reinforcement techniques, parents are taught the value of praise. Specifically, praise helps children feel good, boosts self-esteem, and can increase the occurrence of desirable behaviors. Thus, parents are instructed to praise their child a minimum of four to six times per day. Moreover, they are taught to be concrete, genuine, and specific when giving praise. They also are cautioned against using hyperbole and left-handed compliments with their child. During this time, as parents are increasing the use of praise, they are also asked to note how often they criticize their depressed child. The goal of this activity is eventually to reduce the number of criticisms by one each day, until they are eliminated.

In addition to being taught how to avoid getting caught in a coercive cycle, parents are taught to give clear and effective directives, and to use the time-out procedure and natural consequences. Following the training, parents are given an additional homework assignment to monitor their effectiveness in implementing the new disciplinary procedures and to record any problematic situations for consideration at the next meeting.

Observations of some families with depressed children have revealed an especially hostile and angry environment in which parents frequently express their anger in a destructive manner. Such personal verbal attacks shatter children's self-esteem. Although this tendency to lash out is reduced as a result of the skills taught previously, additional steps are taken to teach the parents to control their own anger. In particular, parents receive instruction in the identification of the triggers of their anger and underlying thoughts. They are taught to use their anger as a cue to leave the situation, cool off, and then take action. They use adaptive coping statements and relaxation techniques to combat their angry outbursts. The parents are then asked to apply these skills and to gauge their impact on the family as additional homework.

Some of the difficulties in the relationship between depressed youths and parents stem from parents' inability to listen empathically. Through education, parents can learn how to express empathy, using a 4-step model. The first step, active listening, includes avoiding interruptions during the child's communication and providing nonverbal cues that convey undivided attention. Second, parents are taught reflection techniques that serve the dual purpose of forcing them to listen to their child and ensure that he or she has been heard correctly. Since some parents tend to editorialize during reflection, avoidance of such remarks is stressed during role plays. The third step in the model consists of helping parents to gain an understanding of their child's feelings. The culmination of the training model involves assisting parents in the use of their new skills when interacting with their child. Again, homework is assigned to encourage skills acquisition.

Previously cited research indicates that families of depressed children often fail to engage in recreational activities. Thus, it is important to teach these families to have fun. Parents are asked to identify various low- or no-cost activities in which the family can participate. Problem solving is then used to facilitate the scheduling of such activities during the week. In addition to engaging in pleasant activities, parents are instructed to self-monitor the impact of these events on the family.

MODERATORS OF TREATMENT OUTCOME

Depressed youth are likely to experience future depressive episodes. To produce long-term maintenance effects, a treatment program must teach the youngsters skills for managing future stress and depressive symptoms. This represents a daunting task. First the child must possess the self-awareness to recognize independently and identify sources of stress and the signs that he or she is slipping into another depressive episode. Thus, an effective intervention helps youngsters develop an attitude that enables them to realistically evaluate their life experiences and tune into their affective experiences. Adopting a problem-solving philosophy toward life enables them to confront stress directly, and affective education exercises provide them with an awareness of their emotions and the associated thoughts, behaviors, and physical reactions. It takes extraordinary maturity to use the signs of stress and symptoms of depression as cues to engage coping skills. In addition, the youngsters have to remember how to apply the skills effectively. Furthermore, they have to remain motivated to try to manage stress and their symptoms in the face of the depression and the discouragement of experiencing another depressive episode. A powerful history of effective coping has to be present to build the belief that they can overcome stress and depressive symptoms. To facilitate the youngsters' awareness of their success experiences, it is helpful to provide them with concrete products that represent their success experiences. For example, a coping skills diary that includes their mood ratings, along with the coping strategies they used to overcome their dysphoria and stressful events, may be completed by the youngsters and they can be instructed in how to use the diary in the future. In some instances it may be possible to teach parents to recognize the early signs of an emerging depressive disorder in their child. The parents would then encourage the child to try to use coping skills. Special care must be taken in the cases where the depressed youngster has a depressed parent. The depressed parent's own experiences may be coloring his or her perceptions of the child's emotional experiences. The maintenance of treatment effects also may be dependent on characteristics of the primary environments within which the child functions. If the child lives within an unhealthy family environment, and research suggests that this will be the case for some depressed youths, failure to change this environment permanently may lead to a failure to produce lasting improvements in the child.

In many cases, years may pass between depressive episodes and youngsters will experience dramatic developmental changes. In addition, the youngster's life circumstances may have changed. Given these changes, it may be unreasonable to expect that most youngsters will be able to generalize what they have learned about managing their depressive symptoms to their new life circumstances. To systematically program for maintenance through regular follow-up meetings with the youngsters and their families appears to be critical. During these meetings, the youngsters and their parents can be helped to apply coping skills to new circumstances.

Since research has shown that depressed children have deficits in generating and evaluating affect regulation strategies, it is important to assess the child's affect regulation strategies and to use the results to guide the treatment plan. If a child reports developmentally immature, maladaptive, or irrelevant strategies for altering mood, then affective education strategies designed to help the youngster acquire mood regulation skills is warranted. Furthermore, the assessment and skills training should be placed within the appropriate developmental context, so that the child is not being asked to acquire emotion regulation skills for which he or she does not possess the prerequisite cognitive abilities. During certain developmental periods, children regulate emotions interdependently; thus, parents need to be involved in the intervention and may need to be taught how to respond to their child's emotional upset. If a child demonstrates adequate knowledge of affect regulation strategies, then obstacles that prevent implementation should be examined.

In general, it may be useful to instruct parents in the use of effective emotion-regulation strategies, so that they can model processes for their children. Changes in family functioning also may be desirable, as research suggests that the extent to which children feel supported, safe, and secure, predicts the use of adaptive mood regulation strategies (Kliewer & Lewis,

1995). Making changes in the overall family environment, would, then, encourage children's use of adaptive affect regulation strategies.

Overall, there is support for an association between disturbances in cognitive functioning and depressive disorders during childhood. Furthermore, the disturbances appear to be parallel to those reported in the adult literature, suggesting that cognitive therapy might be useful for depressed children. However, to intervene effectively, it is necessary to identify and understand developmental differences in cognitive processing between children and adults. To address this concern, a multitude of issues remains to be answered about the cognitive functioning of depressed children (for a review, see Garber, 1992). A consensus indicates that children's cognitive processes are adequately developed for experiencing depressive disorders by age 8. However, it is not known whether the cognitive processing assumes different forms at different ages. Some investigators find the same two broad categories of cognitions, expectations and attributions, in youths and adults (Gotlib, Lewinshohn, Seeley, Rohde, & Redner, 1993), while others have not found this (Garber, Weiss, & Shanley, 1993). In a similar vein, it is not known whether new issues arise at different points during development. For example, Garber et al. (1993) reported an increase in egocentrism with age, which could be a vulnerability factor. These youngsters are at increased risk for personalizing negative events. Likewise, they are likely to personalize undefined events. This suggests that an objective of treatment would be to help them become less self-focused. If additional developmental risk factors exist and can be identified, they may guide the nature and direction of intervention. Another developmental consideration is the degree to which the stress–diathesis models of depression are appropriate for children. Unlike adults, disturbances in cognitive processes may serve a mediational rather than moderational role in depressive disorders in children (Cole & Turner, 1993). Stressful events and negative competency feedback affect cognition, which then affects depressive symptoms. Cole and Turner (1993) suggest that this mediational relationship may be due to the cognitive disturbances not having been in existence long enough to have become structuralized. If this is true, does it mean that these disturbances in children are more amenable to change, or does it mean that intervention at this critical developmental period should be directed toward the environmental disturbances that provide the learning experiences for the dysfunctional cognitions? If the latter is the case, when the environmental disturbance is altered in a healthy way, will changes in cognition naturally follow? At least, these findings point to the importance of evaluating the primary contexts within which the child lives and devising interventions for these environmental stressors. Thus, unlike cognitive therapy with adults, the individual is not the primary and sole source of intervention. Rather, interventions directed toward the environment and significant others in the environment are equally important.

Stressful events impact cognition and have a direct relationship to depression. It appears that stressful events, perhaps daily hassles more than major life events (Dixon & Ahrens, 1992), have a direct impact on children and lead to emotional distress. With prolonged exposure, a depressive disorder eventually develops. These findings suggest that recurrent negative events lead to the perception that the world is a distressing place, life is full of pain, and it will always be this way. These results suggest that it is critical to intervene in the children's environment to eliminate or reduce the sources of stress. However, it is not clear whether the most effective way to do this is actually to alter the environment or to enhance children's coping skills for dealing with the distressing events, or both. If the hassles are of an interpersonal nature, then the intervention may be directed at children's social skills or interpersonal environment.

A self-schema appears to guide the information processing of children. Relative to nondepressed youth, the self-schema of depressed youth is less positive (e.g., Hammen & Zupan, 1984). Furthermore, this less positive self-schema affects the acquisition of new positive and negative information through selective attention, encoding, and retrieval of information (Prieto et al., 1992). These results suggest that a goal of treatment is enhancement of the youngster's sense of self. A common strategy for altering this disturbance is to have children self-monitor positive events (Stark, Reynolds, & Kaslow, 1987). However, this may not have the desired effect, and it may be especially difficult to accomplish, since the existing self-schema will be guiding information processing in a fashion that prevents the acquisition of schema-inconsistent information. Thus, positive information is likely to be overlooked. It may be necessary to train significant others within the child's environment to help with self-monitoring and with processing the outcome on a daily basis. Depressed youth have a tendency to distort self-evaluative information negatively (Kendall et al., 1990), which further inhibits the individual's chances to acquire positive self-relevant information. Once again, it may be necessary for school personnel and parents to become involved in the treatment process. While research indicates that depressed youth distort information processing, the specific errors have yet to be identified. Thus, the specific nature of the intervention is not yet clear. It is very likely that each youngster will possess a unique pattern of information-processing errors and require a unique set of intervention strategies. Once again, no research has been directed toward the elucidation of the most effective strategies for altering information-processing errors in children.

Research and theory suggest that cognitive disturbances may develop as a result of negative messages the youngster receives from his or her parents (Stark, Schmidt, & Joiner, 1996), stressful events, and negative competency feedback (Cole & Turner, 1993). Further research is needed to identify the mechanism for this. This once again highlights the importance of intervening with the child's family and school. Both environments could be the source of negative messages, stressful events, and negative competency feedback.

Although children might have cognitive disturbances that are similar to those of adults, and they may have the cognitive ability to reflect on these disturbances, do they have the same metacognitive ability as adults to be able to accurately identify, reflect upon, evaluate, and counter maladaptive cognitions? What is the best way to do this? Is it best done through traditional cognitive therapy procedures such as "What's the evidence?" and "Alternative interpretation," or are behavioral experiments the preferred mode for producing meaningful change? Does the mix of cognitive, behavioral, and environmental interventions change with developmental level?

Results from the literature regarding the formation and maintenance of maladaptive schemas should be applied to the treatment of children with depressive disorders. Multifaceted interventions that include family therapy, parent training, as well as treatment of the child appear to be necessary. The family intervention should include the identification of verbal and behavioral interactions that convey maladaptive, schema-consistent messages to the depressed child. The therapeutic question becomes, what are parents and/or other family members' communicating to the child verbally and/or through their interactions that would lead to the development and maintenance of the child's negative view of self, world, and future, and other maladaptive schemas. Once the maladaptive interactions are identified, the therapist works with the family to change them. From a cognitive-behavioral perspective, it may involve cognitive restructuring procedures to change the beliefs that underlie participants' behavior and teach family members new ways of interacting through education, modeling, rehearsal, coaching, and feedback. Parents may be taught how to communicate positive and realistic messages to their children about the children themselves, the world, and the future.

Based on research into the families of depressed youths, it is important to determine whether conflict exists within the family (Forehand et al., 1988); if so, its source should be identified and plans for reducing it should be developed. These plans may include marital counseling or individual therapy for one of the parents or another family member. Since a reduced rate of family involvement in recreational activities has been reported (Stark et al., 1990), it may prove useful to ask parents to identify various low- and no-cost activities in which the family can participate. Problem solving may then be used to facilitate scheduling such activities during the week. But this should be done cautiously, since it could create more opportunities for family conflict. Reduction in conflict and engagement in more pleasant activities could enhance the family's sense of cohesion. Research also suggests that it is important to promote inclusion of children in some of the important decisions being made by the family (Stark et al., 1990). However, a balance needs to be struck between encouraging children to participate in decisions and maintaining a sense of the parents as the executive pair in charge).

Research into the biological aspects of depression suggest that any of a number of neurochemical or neuroanatomical disturbances may lead to, or contribute to, the development of a depressive disorder. Reviews of the efficacy of tricyclic medications for depressed youth indicate that such interventions are moderately effective for depressed children, when blood levels are closely monitored, but ineffective for adolescents. Research is beginning to support the efficacy of SSRIs for depressive disorders in adolescents. The effectiveness of SSRIs for depressed children has not been examined, but it is presumed that they are effective with depressed children, since they are effective with depressed adolescents and adults.

Since many depressed youth will be experiencing at least one additional psychological disorder, therapists face a complex clinical challenge. Accurate diagnosis, treatment planning, and treatment implementation are made more difficult by the presence of multiple disorders. Nonetheless, it is important to determine the extent to which each disorder is contributing to the presenting problems and the level of distress experienced by the youngster, his or her family, and, in some cases, the community. For example, a depressed adolescent who is experiencing a comorbid conduct disorder, along with ADHD, will likely present very differently from a depressed youth who also is experiencing an anxiety disorder or obsessive–compulsive disorder. Where does the therapist begin? Is the initial point of intervention the acting out behavior or the depressive disorder? Perhaps the acting out stems from the impulsivity that is a part of the ADHD, in which case, psychiatric intervention along with parent training may be the most efficacious place to start. Experience teaches that it is difficult to treat the depressive disorder when the youngster and family are in conflict over weekly crises due to the youngster's acting out or other complicating externalizing behaviors (e.g., substance abuse, socially unacceptable sexual behavior, enactment of criminal behavior with the concomitant involvement of the judicial system). Once these other behaviors are under control, the parents are more supportive of the treatment program that is directed at alleviating depressive symptoms. For example, imagine the reaction of parents when their adolescent with conduct disorder requests to go out with friends and says, "Just trying to manage my mood, Mom." Unfortunately, no empirically based guidelines have been delineated for determining which disorder to treat first. In some instances, if there is a mistake in determining which disorder is primary or prominent and should therefore be the initial focus of intervention, then treatment may not be as effective.

The impact of comorbid conditions on the efficacy of psychosocial treatments for depressive disorders in youth has not been empirically evaluated. Existing research suggests that the comorbid conditions represent more severe disorders; thus, it is likely that more potent interventions, in terms of intensity, breadth, or duration, may be required to produce successful results. Intensity can be manipulated through frequency of meetings, structuring meetings to maintain focus and progress, and creating highly engaging, relevant treatment sessions. Breadth can be increased through designing interventions that simultaneously or sequentially impact multiple symptoms. In addition, significant others such as parents or other family members, as well as teachers, may be systematically and strategically engaged in treatment. With more complex cases in which a comprehensive treatment plan is used, and/or significant others are involved in treatment, a more protracted course may be necessary.

Clinical experience suggests that a very different treatment plan is needed to address the comorbid conditions. For example, when treating a youth who is experiencing an attention-deficit/hyperactivity disorder and a comorbid depressive disorder, we rely very heavily on parent training to manage behavior at the same time that individual work with the child is addressing depressive symptoms. In contrast, a treatment plan that emphasizes both the treatment of depressive symptoms and graded exposure and response prevention would be used with a youngster who is experiencing a depressive disorder along with obsessive–compulsive disorder.

Given the high level of co-occurrence of depression and anxiety, treatment is of particular interest. The research that examines the similarities and differences between depressive and anxiety disorders indicates that both disorders are characterized by negative affect, while depressive disorders also are characterized by low levels of positive affect, suggesting that an effective intervention for a depressive disorder would simultaneously reduce negative affect and increase positive affect. Perhaps this explains the efficacy of interventions that utilize the scheduling of pleasant events as one of the primary treatment components (Stark et al., 1987). Research on the cognitive aspects of depressive and anxiety disorders suggests that an effective intervention would target the depressed youth's negative sense of self, loss, and hopelessness. On the other hand, cognitive intervention with a youngster with anxiety disorder would focus on his or her view of aspects of the environment as threatening.

TREATMENT OUTCOME RESEARCH

Multicomponent cognitive-behavioral interventions, similar to the one noted earlier in this chapter, have demonstrated efficacy with nonclinically depressed children (Butler, Miezitis, Freeman, & Cole, 1980; Fine, Forth, Gilbert, & Haley, 1991; Stark et al., 1987; Stark, 1990) and adolescents (Kahn, Kehle, Jenson, & Clark, 1990; Reynolds & Coates, 1986), as well as clinical populations of depressed youths (Brent et al., 1997; Wood, Harrington, & Moore, 1996). The treatment programs have produced significant reductions in depressive symptoms and significant improvements in rate of remission. These results have typically been achieved while working with the child only. Thus far, inclusion of a parent training component has not appeared to produce improvements in efficacy (Lewinsohn, Clarke, Hops, & Andrews, 1990), and family therapy alone was not found to be as effective as cognitive-behavioral therapy with just the child (Brent et al., 1997). Thus, while the inclusion of these two components in the treatment program appears theoretically enticing and supported by clinical practice, research has yet to demonstrate that it is necessary or contributes anything more to the treatment than working with the child only.

The actual intervention procedures employed across studies have varied, and there have not been any dismantling studies that would help to identify the necessary and sufficient components to produce change. The typical intervention includes some form of problem-solving training, cognitive restructuring, and activity scheduling, and more adaptive self-control skills (self-monitoring, self-evaluation) are taught through completion of other treatment-related activities. Social skills training has been included as a component in some intervention programs and as a separate treatment procedure in others (Fine et al., 1991). However, the efficacy of social skills training alone is questionable. Fine and colleagues (Fine et al., 1991) reported that a therapeutic support group was more effective than social skills training at reducing depressive symptoms immediately following treatment.

Typically, the intervention programs have consisted of a limited number of sessions, typically 10 to 12, completed over a 5- to 12-week period of time. Somewhat surprisingly, this has appeared to be an adequate time frame for treatment. It is surprising in the sense that it is assumed that the youngsters are learning and applying a variety of complex skills to regulate their moods, behavior, and cognitions. Thus, they are expected to learn each skill within, typically, 3–4 meetings. Meta-analyses of problem-solving training alone indicate that it typically takes 39 one-hour sessions of training for the youngsters to be able to benefit from it. These results would seem to draw into question the assumption that the youngsters are learning and applying the skills and that this is producing the improvements.

As noted earlier in this chapter, for a treatment to be effective, it has to produce both short- and long-term effects. A trend within the outcome literature is that the youngsters continue to improve following treatment. This appears to be true for short-term as well as relatively long-term follow-up periods. The underlying mechanism for this phenomenon is not apparent. However, it is assumed that it stems from the youngsters' continuing to use, and perhaps improvement in their ability to use, the skills that they are being taught during treatment.

SUMMARY

It is evident from longitudinal research that depressed children are likely to experience another depressive disorder in the future. Thus, while depressive episodes naturally remit, treatment may speed up the recovery process or reduce the length of an episode. Given the recurrent nature of the disorder, an effective treatment must have a prophylactic effect. Research is identifying variables that appear to impact the duration of a depressive episode, including severity of the disorder, stability of the family, and gender. When treating a depressed female who is experiencing a severe episode of depression, it may be necessary to increase the intensity of the intervention or plan for a more protracted treatment. Based on epidemiological research, the occurrence of depressive disorders appears to increase with age, with a significant jump at puberty. When depressive disorders occur during the preschool and early school years they often are associated with family chaos, abuse, and neglect (Kashani et al., 1983).

The typical development of affect regulation is characterized by a shift from other-regulation to self-regulation. A number of changes occur over the course of normal development that appear to be related to overall expansion in children's affect regulation repertoire. Central among these changes is an increase in the number of cognitive strategies that can be used to control affect. Greater cognitive development also appears to enable youngsters to pay greater attention to the context of the upsetting event, which enables them to devise and utilize situation-specific methods for managing affect. In addition, this may enable the youngsters to compartmentalize the upsetting situation, thus reducing the perceived loss or threat. Furthermore, as a youngster's understanding of emotion increases, he or she can use more sophisticated strategies to regulate mood.

Parents foster competent emotion regulation by providing their children with opportunities to acquire and practice affect regulation strategies, by modeling and coaching effective emotion regulation, and by creating a family environment conducive to overall socioemotional competence. Research suggests a possible etiological pathway in which family factors associated with depression act through their influence on the development of children's affect regulation.

The cognitive model and attachment theory may complement each other, and this integration argues for greater attention to both the depressed youngster's cognitive functioning *and* the interpersonal context within which it is developed and maintained. Furthermore, it suggests that early intervention and prevention efforts may be directed at disturbances within the environments within which the youngsters' develop their schemas and other cognitive processes. Moreover, intervention solely in the cognitive domain overlooks the interpersonal context that may directly lead to the development of depression and maintain it. Similarly, interventions exclusively directed at changing the interpersonal context may meet resistance, as they would be at odds with the individual's core schema. A more complete and lasting intervention would be one that addresses the child's internal working model, other schema-relevant interactions, and learning experiences that may be contributing to the development of dysfunctional cognitive processes. This would place the interpersonal intervention within the context of the child's belief system and vice versa.

Assessment and treatment are intimately linked in the treatment of depressed youth. Results of assessment guide the choice of treatment procedures and serve as a means of assessing the effectiveness of the intervention. A variety of psychometrically sound measures are available for assessing the severity of depression. A number of additional measures of relevant cognitive, interpersonal, and family variables that inform treatment have been developed, but they have been primarily used for research purposes. Nevertheless, they hold promise for clinical use.

Cognitive-behavioral interventions have proven to be effective at reducing the severity of depression, producing a remission of the depressive episode, and speeding up recovery. Cognitive-behavioral treatments have been effective with nonclinically as well as clinically depressed children and adolescents, and the improvements have been maintained over extended periods of time. In fact, there is evidence that the youngsters continue to improve following treatment. To date, the intervention packages that have been employed have been more circumscribed than the treatment program described in this chapter. While clinical practice suggests that the more comprehensive treatment program that was described may be more effective and necessary for some youths, there is no empirical support for this contention. Are cognitive-behavioral interventions the most effective psychosocial interventions? It is not possible to determine this, since there have not been relevant comparison studies. Are cognitive-behavioral interventions as effective as the SSRIs in the treatment of depressive disorders in children? Is the combination of cognitive-behavioral therapy and medication superior to either treatment strategy alone? Once again the answers are unknown, but they are being addressed by research at this time. Nevertheless, it is clear that many depressed youth benefit from participation in cognitive-behavioral therapy.

REFERENCES

Abramson, L. Y. (1999). *Developmental maltreatment and cognitive vulnerability to depression.* Paper presented at the spring meeting of the Society for Research in Child Development, Albuquerque, NM.

Abramson, L. Y., Metalsky, G. I., & Alloy, L. B. (1989). Hopelessness depression: A theory-based subtype of depression. *Psychological Review, 96,* 358–372.

Achenbach, T. M., & Edelbrock, C. S. (1983). *Manual for the Child Behavior Checklist.* Burlington: University of Vermont.

Alloy, L. B., & Abramson, L. Y. (1979). Judgement of contingency in depressed an nondepressed students: Sadder but wiser? *Journal of Experimental Psychology: General, 108*, 441–485.

Altshuler, J. L., & Ruble, D. N. (1989). Developmental changes in children's awareness of strategies for coping with uncontrollable stress. *Child Development, 60*, 1337–1349.

Anderson, J. C., Williams, S., McGee, R., & Silva, P. A. (1987). DSM-III disorders in pre-adolescent children. *Archives of General Psychiatry, 44*, 69–76.

Asarnow, J. R., & Bates, S. (1988). Depression in child psychiatric inpatients: Cognitive and attributional patterns. *Journal of Abnormal Child Psychology, 16*, 601–615.

Baldwin, M. W. (1992). Relational schemas and the processing of social information. *Psychological Bulletin, 112*, 461–484.

Band, E. B., & Weisz, J. R. (1988). How to feel better when it feels bad: Children's perspectives on coping with everyday stress. *Developmental Psychology, 24*, 247–253.

Bandura, A. (1978). The self system in reciprocal determinism. *American Psychologist, 33*, 344–358.

Barkley, R. A. (1997). *Defiant children: A clinician's manual for assessment and parent training.* New York: Guilford Press.

Beck, A. T. (1967). *Depression: Clinical, experimental, and theoretical aspects.* New York: Harper & Row.

Beck, A. T., Rush, A. J., Shaw, B. F., & Emery, G. (1979). *Cognitive therapy of depression.* New York: Guilford Press.

Berman, W. H., & Sperling, M. B. (1994). The structure and function of adult attachment. In M. B. Sperling & W. H. Berman (Eds.), *Attachment in adults* (pp. 1–30). New York: Guilford Press.

Blechman, E. A., McEnroe, M. J., Carella, E. T., & Audette, D. P. (1986). Childhood competence and depression. *Journal of Abnormal Psychology, 95*, 223–227.

Bowlby, J. (1980). *Attachment and loss: Vol. III. Loss, sadness, and depression.* New York: Basic Books.

Brady, E. U., & Kendall, P. C. (1992). Comorbidity of anxiety and depression in children and adolescents. *Psychological Bulletin, 111*, 244–255.

Breen, M. P., & Weinberger, D. A. (1995). Regulation of depressive affect and interpersonal behavior among children requiring residential or day treatment. *Development and Psychopathology, 7*, 529–541.

Brent, D. A., Holder, D., Kolko, D., Birmaher, B., Baugher, M., Roth, C., Iyengar, S., & Johnson, B. A. (1997). A clinical psychotherapy trial for adolescent depression comparing cognitive, family, and supportive therapy. *Archives of General Psychiatry, 54*, 877–885.

Bretherton, I. (1990). Communication patterns, internal working models, and the intergenerational transmission of attachment relationship. *Infant Mental Health Journal, 11*, 237–252.

Burke, P., & Puig-Antich, J. (1990). Psychobiology of childhood depression. In M. Lewis & S. M. Miller (Eds.), *Handbook of developmental psychopathology* (pp. 327–339). New York: Plenum Press.

Butler, L., Miezitis, S., Friedman, R., & Cole, E. (1980). The effect of two school-based intervention programs on depressive symptoms in preadolescents. *American Educational Research Journal, 17*, 111–119.

Campbell, S. B., Cohn, J. F., & Meyers, T. (1995). Depression in first-time mothers: Mother–infant interaction and depression chronicity. *Developmental Psychology, 31*, 349–357.

Carlson, G. A., & Cantwell, D. P. (1980). Unmasking masked depression in children and adolescents. *American Journal of Psychiatry, 137*, 445–449.

Carlson, G. A., & Kashani, J. H. (1988). Manic symptoms in a nonreferred adolescent population. *Journal of Affective Disorders, 15*, 219–226.

Casey, R. J. (1996). Emotional competence in children with externalizing and internalizing disorders. In M. Lewis & M. W. Sullivan (Eds.), *Emotional development in atypical children* (pp. 161–183). Mahwah, NJ: Erlbaum.

Christ, A. E., Adler, A. G., Isacoff, M., & Gershansky, I. S. (1981). Depression: Symptoms versus diagnosis in 412 hospitalized children and adolescents (1957–1977). *American Journal of Psychotherapy, 35,* 400–412.

Cicchetti, D., Ganiban, J., & Barnett, D. (1991). Contributions from the study of high-risk populations to understanding the development of emotion regulation. In J. Garber & K. Dodge (Eds.), *The development of emotion regulation and dysregulation* (pp. 15–48). New York: Cambridge University Press.

Cohn, J. F., Campbell, S. B., Matias, R., & Hopkins, J. (1990). Face-to-face interactions of postpartum depressed and nondepressed mother–infant pairs at 2 months. *Developmental Psychology, 26*(1), 15–23.

Cole, D., & Turner, J., Jr. (1993). Models of cognitive mediation and moderation in child depression. *Journal of Abnormal Psychology, 102,* 271–281.

Cole, P. M., & Kaslow, N. J. (1988). Interactional and cognitive strategies for affect regulation: Developmental perspective on childhood depression. In L. B. Alloy (Ed.), *Cognitive processes in depression* (pp. 310–343). New York: Guilford Press.

Colin, V. L. (1996). *Human attachment.* Philadelphia: Temple University Press.

Costello, E. J., Costello, A. J., Edelbrock, C., Burns, B. J., Dulcan, M. K., Brent, D., & Janiszweski, S. (1988). Psychiatric disorders in pediatric primary care. *Archives of General Psychiatry, 45,* 1107–1116.

Cowan, P. A., Cohn, D. A., Cowan, C. P., & Pearson, J. L. (1996). Parents' attachment histories and children's externalizing and internalizing behaviors: Exploring family systems models of linkage. *Journal of Consulting and Clinical Psychology, 64,* 53–63.

Dixon, J. F., & Ahrens, A. H. (1992). Stress and attributional style as predictors of self-reported depression in children. *Cognitive Therapy and Research, 16,* 623–634.

Dunn, J., & Brown, J. (1991). Relationships, talk about feelings, and the development of affect regulation in early childhood. In J. Garber & K. Dodge (Eds.), *The development of emotion regulation and dysregulation* (pp. 89–108). New York: Cambridge University Press.

Emslie, G. J., Weinberg, W. A., Kennard, B. D., & Kowatch, R. A. (1994). Neurobiological aspects of depression in children and adolescents. In W. R. Reynolds & H. F. Johnston (Eds.), *Handbook of depression in children and adolescents* (pp. 143–168). New York: Plenum Press.

Feldman, R. S., Meyer, J. S., & Quenzer, L. F. (1997). *Principles of neuropsychopharmacology.* Sunderland, MA: Sinauer.

Fine, S., Forth, A., Gilbert, M., & Haley, G. (1991). Group therapy for adolescent depressive disorder: A comparison of social skills and therapeutic support. *Journal of the American Academy of Child and Adolescent Psychiatry, 30,* 79–85.

Flynn, C., & Garber, J. (1999). *Predictors of depressive cognitions in young adolescents.* Paper presented at the spring meeting of the Society for Research in Child Development, Albuquerque, NM.

Forehand, R., Brody, G., Slotkin, J., Fauber, R., McCombs, A., & Long, N. (1988). Young adolescent and maternal depression: Assessment, interrelations, and predictors. *Journal of Consulting and Clinical Psychology, 56,* 422–426.

Freeman, A. (1986). Understanding personal, cultural, and family schema in psychotherapy. In A. Freeman, N. Epstein, & K. M. Simon (Eds.), *Depression in the family* (pp. 79–100). New York: Haworth Press.

Garber, J. (1992). Cognitive models of depression: A developmental perspective. *Psychological Inquiry, 3,* 235–240.

Garber, J., Braafladt, N., & Weiss, B. (1995). Affect regulation in depressed and nondepressed children and young adolescents. *Development and Psychopathology, 7,* 93–115.

Garber, J., Braafladt, N., & Zeman, J. (1991). The regulation of sad affect: An information-processing perspective. In J. Garber & K. Dodge (Eds.), *The development of emotion regulation and dysregulation* (pp. 208–237). New York: Cambridge University Press.

Garber, J., & Robinson, N. S. (1997). Cognitive vulnerability in children at risk for depression. *Cognition and Emotion, 11,* 619–635.

Garber, J., Weiss, B., & Shanley, N. (1993). Cognitions, depressive symptoms, and development in adolescents. *Journal of Abnormal Psychology, 102,* 47–57.

Gotlib, I. H., Lewinsohn, P. M., Seeley, J. R., Rohde, P., & Redner, J. E. (1993). Negative cognitions and attributional style in depressed adolescents: An examination of stability and specificity. *Journal of Abnormal Psychology, 102,* 607–615.

Hammen, C., & Goodman-Brown, T. (1990). Self-schemas and vulnerability to specific life stress in children at risk for depression. *Cognitive Therapy and Research, 14,* 215–227.

Hammen, C., & Zupan, B. A. (1984). Self-schemas, depression, and the processing of personal information in children. *Journal of Experimental Child Psychology, 37,* 598–608.

Harrington, R., Fudge, H., Rutter, M., Pickles, A., & Hill, J. (1990). Adult outcome of childhood and adolescent depression I. Psychiatric status. *Archives of General Psychiatry, 47,* 465–473.

Hodges, K. K., & Siegel, L. J. (1985). Depression in young children and adolescents. In E. E. Beckman & W. R. Leber (Eds.), *Handbook of depression: Treatment, assessment, and research* (pp. 21–55). Homewood, IL: Dorsey Press.

Hollon, S. D., & Kendall, P. C. (1980). Cognitive self-statements in depression: Development of an automatic thoughts questionnaire. *Cognitive Therapy and Research, 4,* 383–395.

Jaenicke, C., Hammen, C., Zupan, B., Hiroto, D., Gordon, D., Adrian, C., & Burge, D. (1987). Cognitive vulnerability in children at risk for depression. *Journal of Abnormal Child Psychology, 15,* 559–572.

Kahn, J. S., Kehle, T. J., Jenson, W. R., & Clark, E. (1990). Comparison of cognitive-behavioral, relaxation, and self-modeling interventions for depression among middle-school students. *School Psychology Review, 19,* 196–211.

Kashani, J. H., & Carlson, G. A. (1987). Seriously depressed preschoolers. *American Journal of Psychiatry, 144,* 348–350.

Kashani, J. H., Carlson, G. A., Beck, N. C., Hoeper, E. W., Corcoran, C. M., McAllister, J. A., Fallahi, C., Rosenberg, T. K., & Reid, J. C. (1990). Depression, depressive symptoms, and depressed mood among a community sample of adolescents. *American Journal of Psychiatry, 144,* 931–934.

Kashani, J. H., & Hakami, N. (1982). Depression in children and adolescents with malignancy. *Canadian Journal of Psychiatry, 27,* 474–477.

Kashani, J. H., McGee, R. O., Clarkson, S. E., Anderson, J. C., Walton, L. A., Williams, S., Silva, P. A., Robins, A. J., Cytryn, L., & McKnew, D. H. (1983). Depression in a sample of 9-year-old children. *Archives of General Psychiatry, 140,* 1217–1223.

Kashani, J. H., Orvaschel, H., Rosenberg, T. K., & Reid, J. C. (1989). Psychopathology in a community sample of children and adolescents: A developmental perspective. *Journal of the American Academy of Child and Adolescent Psychiatry, 28,* 701–706.

Kashani, J. H., & Ray, J. S. (1983). Depressive related symptoms among preschool-age children. *Child Psychiatry and Human Development, 13,* 233–238.

Kashani, J. H., Venzke, R., & Millar, E. A. (1981). Depression in children admitted to hospital for orthopaedic procedures. *British Journal of Psychiatry, 138,* 21–25.

Kaslow, N. J., Stark, K. D., Printz, B., Livingston, R., & Tsai, L. (1992). Cognitive Triad Inventory for Children: Development and relation to depression and anxiety. *Journal of Clinical Child Psychology, 21,* 339–347.

Kazdin, A. E. (1987). Assessment of childhood depression: Current issues and strategies. *Behavioral Assessment, 9,* 291–319.

Kazdin, A. E., Esveldt-Dawson, K., Sherick, R. B., & Colbus, D. (1985). Assessment of overt behavior and childhood depression among psychiatrically disturbed children. *Journal of Consulting and Clinical Psychology, 53,* 201–210.

Kendall, P. C. (1977). On the efficacious use of verbal self-instructional procedures with children. *Cognitive Therapy and Research, 1,* 331–341.

Kendall, P. C., & Braswell, L. (1993). *Cognitive-behavioral therapy for impulsive children* (2nd ed.). New York: Guilford Press.

Kendall, P. C., Cantwell, D. A., & Kazdin, A. E. (1989). Depression in children and adolescents: Assessment issues and recommendations. *Cognitive Therapy and Research, 13,* 109–146.

Kendall, P. C., Stark, K. D., & Adam, T. (1990). Cognitive deficit of cognitive distortion in childhood depression? *Journal of Abnormal Child Psychology, 18,* 267–283.

Kliewer, W. (1991). Coping in middle childhood: Relations to competence, Type A behavior, monitoring, blunting, and locus of control. *Developmental Psychopathology, 27,* 689–697.

Kliewer, W., Fearnow, M. D., & Miller, P. A. (1996). Coping socialization in middle childhood: Tests of maternal and paternal influence. *Child Development, 67,* 2339–2357.

Kliewer, W., & Lewis, H. (1995). Family influences on coping processes in children and adolescents with sickle-cell disease. *Journal of Pediatric Psychology, 20,* 511–525.

Kobak, R., Sudler, N., & Gamble, W. (1991). Attachment and depressive symptoms during adolescence: A developmental pathways analysis. *Development and Psychopathology, 3,* 461–474.

Kochanska, G., Kuczynski, L., Radke-Yarrow, M., & Welsh, J. D. (1987). Resolutions of control episodes between well and affectively ill mothers and their young children. *Journal of Abnormal Child Psychology, 15,* 441–456.

Kolb, B., & Whishaw, I. Q. (1996). *Fundamentals of human neuropsychology.* New York: Freeman.

Koplewics, H. S., Klass, E., & Kafantaris, V. (1993). The psychopharmacology of childhood and adolescent depression. In H. S. Koplewics & E. Klass (Eds.), *Depression in children and adolescents* (pp. 235–253). Switzerland: Harwood Academic.

Kopp, C. B. (1989). Regulation of distress and negative emotions: A developmental view. *Developmental Psychology, 25,* 343–354.

Kovacs, M. (1981). Rating scales to assess depression in school aged children. *Acta Paedopsychiatrica, 46,* 305–315.

Kovacs, M., Feinberg, T. L., Crouse-Novak, M. A., Paulauskas, S. L., & Finkelstein, R. (1984). Depressive disorders in childhood: I. A longitudinal prospective study of characteristics and recovery. *Archives of General Psychiatry, 41,* 229–237.

Lewinsohn, P. M. (1975). The behavioral study and treatment of depression. In M. Hersen, R. M. Eisler, & P. M. Miller (Eds.), *Progress in behavior modification* (Vol. 1, pp. 16–64). New York: Academic Press.

Lewinsohn, P. M., Clarke, G., Hops, H., & Andrews, J. (1990). Cognitive-behavioral treatment for depressed adolescents. *Behavior Therapy, 21,* 385–401.

Lewinsohn, P. M., Hops, H., Roberts, R. E., Seeley, J. R., & Andrews, J. A. (1993). Adolescent psychopathology: I. Prevalence and incidence of depression and other DSM-III-R disorders in high school students. *Journal of Abnormal Psychology, 102,* 133–144.

Ling, W., Oftedal, G., & Weinberg, W. (1970). Depressive illness in childhood presenting as severe headache. *American Journal of Diseases of Childhood, 120,* 122–124.

Mahoney, M. J. (1980). Psychotherapy and the structure of personal revolutions. In M. J. Mahoney (Ed.), *Psychotherapy process: Current issues and future directions* (pp. 157–180). New York: Plenum Press.

Main, M. (1996). Introduction to the special section on attachment and psychopathology: 2. Overview of the field of attachment. *Journal of Consulting and Clinical Psychology, 64,* 237–243.

Masters, J. C. (1991). Strategies and mechanisms for the personal and social control of emotions. In J. Garber & K. Dodge (Eds.), *The development of emotion regulation and dysregulation* (pp. 182–207). New York: Cambridge University Press.

Matson, J. L., Rotatori, A. F., & Helsel, W. J. (1983). Development of a rating scale to measure social skills in children: The Matson Evaluation of Social Skills with Youngsters (MESSY). *Behavioral Research and Therapy, 41,* 335–340.

Mattison, R. E., Humphrey, J., Kales, S., Hernit, R., & Finkenbinder, R. (1986) Psychiatric background of diagnosis of children evaluated for special class placement. *Journal of Child Psychiatry, 46,* 1142–1147.

McCauley, E., Myers, K., Mitchell, J., Calderon, R., Schloredt, K., & Treder, R. (1993). Depression in young people: Initial presentation and clinical course. *Journal of the American Academy of Child and Adolescent Psychiatry, 32,* 714–722.

McGee, R., Feehan, M., Williams, S., Partridge, F., Silva, P. A., & Kelly, J. (1990). DSM-III disorders in a large sample of adolescents. *Journal of the American Academy of Child and Adolescent Psychiatry, 29,* 611–619.

McGee, R., & Williams, S. (1988). A longitudinal study of depression in nine year old children. *Journal of the American Academy of Child and Adolescent Psychiatry, 27,* 12–20.

Meichenbaum, D. (1977). *Cognitive behavior modification.* New York: Plenum Press.

Orvaschel, H., & Puig-Antich, J. H. (1987). *Schedule for Affective Disorders and Schizophrenia for School-Age Children* (Epidemiologic version, 4th ed.). Pittsburgh: Western Psychiatric Institute and Clinic.

Petersen, A. C., Compas, B. E., Brooks-Gunn, J., Stemmler, M., Ey, S., & Grant, K. E. (1993). Depression in adolescence. *American Psychologist, 48,* 155–168.

Petti, T. A. (1978). Depression in hospitalized child psychiatry patients: Approaches to measuring depression. *Journal of the American Academy of Child Psychiatry, 12,* 49–59.

Poznanski, E. O., & Zrull, J. P. (1970). Childhood depression: Clinical characteristics of overtly depressed children. *Archives of General Psychiatry, 23,* 8–15.

Priel, B., & Shamai, D. (1995). Attachment style and perceived social support: Effects on affect regulation. *Personality and Individual Differences, 19,* 235–241.

Prieto, S. L., Cole, D. A., & Tageson, C. W. (1992). Depressive self-schemas in clinic and nonclinic children. *Cognitive Therapy and Research, 16,* 521–534.

Puig-Antich, J., Lukens, E., Davies, M., Goetz, D., Brennan-Quattrock, J., & Todak, G. (1985). Psychosocial functioning in prepubertal major depressive disorders: I. Interpersonal relationships during the depressive episode. *Archives of General Psychiatry, 42,* 500–507.

Reynolds, W. M. (1984). Depression in children and adolescents: Phenomenology, evaluation, and treatment. *School Psychology Review, 13,* 171–182.

Reynolds, W. M., & Coates, K. I. (1986). A comparison of cognitive-behavioral therapy and relaxation training for the treatment of depression. *Journal of Consulting and Clinical Psychology, 54,* 654–660.

Rohde, P., Lewinsohn, P. M., & Seeley, J. R. (1991). Comorbidity of unipolar depression: II. Comorbidity with other mental disorders in adolescents and adults. *Journal of Abnormal Psychology, 100,* 214–222.

Rosenstein, D. S., & Horowitz, H. A. (1996). Adolescent attachment and psychopathology. *Journal of Consulting and Clinical Psychology, 64,* 244–253.

Rossman, B. B. R. (1992). School-age children's perceptions of coping with distress: Strategies for emotion regulation and the moderation of adjustment. *Journal of Child Psychology and Psychiatry, 33,* 1373–1397.

Rudolph, K. D., Hammen, C., & Burge, D. (1995). Cognitive representations of self, family, and peers in school-age children: Links with social competence and sociometric status. *Child Development, 66,* 1385–1402.

Rudolph, K. D., Hammen, C., & Burge, D. (1997). A cognitive–interpersonal approach to depressive symptoms in preadolescent children. *Journal of Abnormal Psychology, 25,* 33–45.

Saarni, C. (1989). Children's understanding of strategic control of emotional expression in social transactions. In C. Saarni & P. L. Harris (Eds.), *Children's understanding of emotion* (pp. 181–208). New York: Cambridge University Press.

Schildkraut, J. (1965). The catecholamine hypothesis of affective disorders: A review of supporting evidence. *American Journal of Psychiatry, 122,* 508–522.

Shaw, D. S., Keenan, K., Vondra, J. I., Delliquadri, E., & Giovannelli, J. (1997). Antecedents of preschool children's internalizing problems: A longitudinal study of low-income families.

Journal of the American Academy of Child and Adolescent Psychiatry, 36(12), 1760–1767.

Shelton, R. C., Hollon, S. D., Purdon, S. E., & Loosen, P. T. (1991). Biological and psychological aspects of depression. *Behavior Therapy, 22,* 201–228.

Shirk, S. R. (1998). Interpersonal schemata in child psychotherapy: A cognitive–interpersonal perspective. *Journal of Clinical Child Psychology, 27,* 4–16.

Speier, P. L., Sherak, D. L., Hirsch, S., & Cantwell, D. P. (1995). Depression in children and adolescents. In E. E. Beckham & W. R. Leber (Eds.), *Handbook of depression* (2nd cd., pp. 467–493). New York: Guilford Press.

Stark, K. D. (1990). *Childhood depression: School-based intervention.* New York: Guilford Press.

Stark, K. D., Humphrey, L. L., Crook, K., & Lewis, K. (1990). Perceived family environments of depressed and anxious children: Child's and maternal figure's perspectives. *Journal of Abnormal Child Psychology, 18*(5), 527–547.

Stark, K. D., Humphrey, L. L., Laurent, J. L., Livingston, R., & Christopher, J. C. (1993). Cognitive, behavioral, and family factors in the differentiation of depressive and anxiety disorders during childhood. *Journal of Consulting and Clinical Psychology, 61,* 878–886.

Stark, K. D., & Kendall, P. C. (1996). *Treating depressed children: Therapist manual for "Action."* Ardmore, PA: Workbook Publishing.

Stark, K. D., Kendall, P. C., McCarthy, M., Stafford, M., Barron, R., & Thomeer, M. (1996). *ACTION: A workbook for overcoming depression.* Ardmore, PA: Workbook Publishing.

Stark, K. D., Laurent, J., Livingston, R., Boswell, J., & Swearer, S. (1999). Implications of research for the treatment of depressive disorders during childhood. *Applied and Preventive Psychology: Current Scientific Perspectives, 8,* 79–102.

Stark, K. D., Reynolds, W. M., & Kaslow, N. J. (1987). A comparison of the relative efficacy of self-control therapy and a behavioral problem-solving therapy for depression in children. *Journal of Abnormal Child Psychology, 15,* 91–113.

Stark, K. D., Rouse, L. W., & Livingston, R. (1991). Treatment of depression during childhood and adolescence: Cognitive and behavioral procedures for the individual and family. In P. C. Kendall (Ed.), *Child and adolescent therapy: Cognitive-behavioral procedures* (pp. 165–206). New York: Guilford Press.

Stark, K. D., Schmidt, K., & Joiner, T. E. (1996). Depressive cognitive triad: Relationship to severity of depressive symptoms in children, parents' cognitive triad, and perceived parental messages about the child him or herself, the world, and the future. *Journal of Abnormal Child Psychology, 24,* 615–625.

Stark, K. D., Schmidt, K., Joiner, T. E., & Boswell, J. (1999). *Family messages: A possible pathway to the development of the depressive cognitive triad.* Paper presented at the spring meeting of the Society for Research in Child Development, Albuquerque, NM.

Strober, M., Lampert, C., Schmidt, S., & Morrell, W. (1993). The course of major depressive disorder in adolescents: I. Recovery and risk of manic switching in a follow-up of psychotic and nonpsychotic subtypes. *Journal of the American Academy of Child and Adolescent Psychiatry, 32,* 34–42.

Swearer, S., Stark, K., & Sommer, D. (1999). *The comorbidity conundrum: Cognitive, behavioral, and family factors that differentiate two groups of adolescents.* Manuscript submitted for publication.

Thase, M. E., & Howland, R. H. (1995). Biological processes in depression: An updated review and integration. In E. E. Beckham & W. R. Leber (Eds.), *Handbook of depression* (2nd ed., pp. 213–279). New York: Guilford Press.

Thompson, R. A. (1991). Emotional regulation and emotional development. *Educational Psychology Review, 3,* 269–307.

Weinberg, W. A., Rutman, J., Sullivan, L., Penick, E. C., & Dietz, S. G. (1973). Depression in children referred to an educational diagnostic center: Diagnosis and treatment. *Journal of Pediatrics, 83,* 1065–1072.

Wood, A., Harrington, R., & Moore, A. (1996). Controlled trial of a brief cognitive-behavioral intervention in adolescent patients with depressive disorders. *Journal of Child Psychology and Psychiatry and Allied Disciplines, 37,* 737–746.

Young, J. (1991). *Cognitive therapy for personality disorders: A schema-focused approach.* Sarasota, FL: Professional Resource Exchange.

Young, J. E., & Lindemann, M. D. (1992). An integrative schema-focused model for personality disorders. *Journal of Cognitive Psychotherapy: An International Quarterly, 6,* 11–23.

Zupan, B. A., Hammen, C., & Jaenicke, C. (1987). The effects of current mood and prior depressive history on self-schematic processing in children. *Journal of Experimental Child Psychology, 43,* 149–158.

CHAPTER 6

Treating Anxiety Disorders in Youth

Philip C. Kendall, Brian C. Chu, Sandra S. Pimentel,
and Muniya Choudhury

I didn't want to go to school. My body felt cold. . . . I was
tired, sad, and irritable. . . . I was thinking what if the other
kids make fun of me. Will they laugh at me? Oh what if they
laugh at me? I felt that way a lot.
                              —12-year-old boy suffering from anxiety

Mild fear and anxiety are expected experiences, consistent with normal development, but they become a concern, and potentially in need of treatment, when the fear or anxiety is disproportionate to the actual threat, and daily functioning becomes impaired. The young boy quoted here is not describing an experience of transitory anxiety that accompanies routine developmental challenges; his fear is persistent and impinges negatively on his ability to enjoy a typical childhood. Confronted with leaving the house in the morning, the boy experienced such intense physical symptoms (i.e., tired, sad, irritable) and persistent worries (e.g., "Will the other kids laugh at me?") that he refused to go to school. If such a situation were to persist, he would miss out on critical experiences. Deprived of exposure to same-age peers and school- based education, the child may be prevented from acquiring skills important for later interpersonal, professional, and emotional development.

The present chapter provides an overview of issues important to the assessment and treatment of anxiety in youth. First, the general characteristics of anxiety disorders are described, including the somatic, behavioral, and cognitive elements of anxiety in youth. Then, assessment issues are discussed, with special attention to normal developmental trajectories of anxiety and the role of families in anxiety. Recognizing the potential impact of family stress, pathology, and individual members' interpersonal/parenting styles, we explore the role of the family in the development and maintenance of a child's anxious experience. Finally, a descriptive review of the common principles and strategies of cognitive-behavioral therapy is presented and recent efficacy research evaluating these procedures is provided. One model of therapy for anxious youth is outlined in detail and illustrated by real-life session vignettes of cases seen at the Child and Adolescent Anxiety Disorders Clinic (CAADC) at Temple University. Again, it is acknowledged that families can have an impact on the course and success of treatment. A model for incorporating parents into treatment as active and collaborative participants is proposed.

THE NATURE OF ANXIETY IN YOUTH

The past decade has seen an increased commitment in research to the understanding of anxiety disorders in youth. Reviews have positioned anxiety disorders as the most common class of psychiatric disorders affecting children and adolescents (see Albano, Chorpita, & Barlow, 1996; Bernstein & Borchardt, 1991) and have provided evidence that anxiety may be persistent over time, leading to significant impairment in adulthood if left untreated (see Ollendick & King, 1994). It has been estimated that between 10% and 20% of youngsters suffer from anxiety and anxiety-related symptoms at any one time (Kashani & Orvaschel, 1988; Orvaschel & Weissman, 1986; Werry, 1986; see also Anderson, 1994).

Although there are several disorders listed within the *Diagnostic and Statistical Manual of Mental Disorders, Fourth Edition* (DSM-IV) that may be largely or primarily associated with anxiety, our focus is on three subtypes of childhood anxiety disorder that are identified in the DSM-IV (American Psychiatric Association, 1994): separation anxiety disorder (SAD), social phobia (SP), and generalized anxiety disorder (GAD).[1] SAD is the only disorder of the three that is diagnosed exclusively in children, whereas GAD and SP can be diagnosed in adult populations. This reflects a change from the revised third edition of the DSM (DSM-III-R; American Psychiatric Association, 1987) in which overanxious disorder (OAD) and avoidant disorder could also be applied. In the current nosology of DSM-IV, overanxious disorder and avoidant disorder have been subsumed under GAD and SP, respectively. The changes in the DSM-IV were intended to consolidate emotional disorders that span over childhood into adulthood.

However, given the newness of the categories, changes in diagnostic criteria may be expected as data are gathered and reported. Initial research comparing OAD and GAD, for example, suggests that changes in the diagnostic system have not affected characteristics of cases (Kendall & Warman, 1996); that is, children who met criteria for an OAD diagnosis demonstrated symptoms that qualified them for a diagnosis of GAD as well. Similar research is needed to evaluate changes in the other anxiety disorder diagnoses.

SAD involves anxiety to the point of panic upon separation from, or, for older children, in anticipation of separation from, an attachment figure. Concerns include impending danger and preoccupation with death, which result in curtailed activity away from home. Extreme shyness and withdrawal from new situations or from people characterize SP. GAD is typified by pervasive, uncontrollable worries that can occur in an array of domains, including concern about performance, family or social relations, physical health, or ruminations about future or past behavior.

Features of Anxiety

One of the well-accepted statements about anxiety is that it is a multidimensional construct that consists of somatic, cognitive, and emotional elements. In general, children who seek treatment may present with difficulties in making friends, attending activities or school, being apart from parents or loved ones, or overwhelmed with unrealistic worries and concerns. Children with anxiety disorders are often hypervigilant to criticism in evaluative situations, school situations concerning performance, peer evaluation, or avoid participation in extracurricular activities due to fear of social evaluation or excessive worries.

The most prominent motoric response to anxiety includes behavioral avoidance, but other responses may include shaky voice, rigid posture, crying, nail biting, and thumb sucking (Barrios & Hartmann, 1988). Physiologically, individuals may report an increase in autonomic nervous system activity, perspiration, diffuse abdominal pain ("butterflies in the stomach"), flushed face, gastrointestinal distress, and trembling (see also Barrios & Hartmann, 1988). However, the research with psychophysiological instruments (e.g., Beidel, 1988; 1989) suggests that, at present, psychophysiological assessments have limited clinical utility.

The cognitive distress experienced by anxious children generally includes rumination or excessive worry. Their worry may focus on the presence–absence or well-being of an attachment figure, as is seen in SAD. Fears that they or their parent may be hurt, or that their parents may leave and never return, are common among children with separation fears. Children with SP worry about social or performance situations in which they might be humiliated or embarrassed. The anxious distress may include circumscribed social situations (e.g., speaking, eating in public) or more generalized social situations, but it must include anxiety that is present in peer settings. GAD, as its name implies, is characterized by a more generalized or diffuse sense of worry about a number of issues, including fear of evaluation, self-consciousness, and rumination about past or future behavior. In each of these disorders, such worry, despite its target, is persistent, excessive, and often difficult for the child to control. Diagnostically, symptom duration is an important consideration. Whereas children experiencing the symptoms of separation (SAD) may receive a formal diagnosis after at least 4 weeks of such distress, both SP and GAD diagnoses require at least 6 months of symptom expression and impairment (American Psychiatric Association, 1994).

The study of the anxious child's emotional understanding and expression is becoming a more central focus of theorizing and research—particularly as our ability to assess and conceptualize emotional understanding and expression improves. In one study that compared anxious and normal children, it was found that anxious children did not differ from normal children in terms of their understanding of emotional cues and multiple emotions. However, and this seems quite important, anxious and normal children were significantly different in their understanding of how to (1) hide and (2) change their emotions (Southam-Gerow & Kendall, 2000). Insofar as the acts of hiding and changing emotions revolve around the ability to regulate emotions, it appears that anxious children may be limited in their capacity to understand the regulation or modification of their emotions. Therapeutically, it follows that anxious children may benefit from interventions that include efforts to improve their knowledge and ability to regulate their emotions.

It is characteristic of these disorders that the severe anxiety impairs a child's functioning to varying degrees, across a variety of situations. Studies indicate that anxiety negatively affects academic work and school performance (e.g., Dweck & Wortman, 1982), and social adjustment (e.g., Strauss, Lease, Kazdin, Dulcan, & Last, 1989). High socially anxious children, for example, have been found to report lower perceptions of social acceptance and global self-worth, and more negative peer interactions (Ginsburg, La Greca, & Silverman, 1998). Furthermore, these same authors found that children with higher levels of generalized social avoidance and distress appeared to have more pervasive deficits in their social functioning.

Experiencing a childhood that is hampered by distressing anxious arousal has long-term implications (Kendall, 1992a). Adults diagnosed with anxiety disorders have described suffering from anxious symptomatology (e.g., separation anxiety, generalized anxiety) when they were younger (Last, Hersen, Kazdin, Francis, & Grubb, 1987; Last, Phillips, & Statfeld, 1987; Pollack, et al., 1996). Moreover, comparing older and younger children with the same diagnoses has revealed that older children experience and report significantly higher levels of anxiety and depression, indicating that symptom levels may worsen over time (Strauss, Lease, Last, & Francis, 1988). Given this long-standing relationship, Gittelman (1986) described the need to address anxious problems in children as paramount.

Anxiety is not a circumscribed disorder. Children with these disorders can experience multiple additional stressors that can have an impact in a number of different areas. Children with anxiety may have an increased chance of experiencing other psychological difficulties, severe problems in other areas of their lives, or symptoms that complicate and exacerbate their anxious symptomatology. Recent reviews (Brady & Kendall, 1992; Kendall & Brady, 1995; Kendall, Kortlander, Chansky, & Brady, 1992) have revealed that comorbidity rates for children with anxiety appear to be high, with 12% of anxious children being comorbid with depression, 15% with oppositional defiant disorder, and 17% with attention-deficit/hyperactivity disorder (ADHD) (Kendall & Brady, 1995). Very commonly, in as many as 50–75% of cases, for example, the concurrent disorder experienced by the child is another anxiety disorder (e.g., Last, Strauss, & Francis, 1987). Also of interest here are findings indicating that children with comorbid diagnoses report and present with greater psychopathology and dysfunction than children with a single diagnosis (Bernstein, 1991; Strauss, Last, Hersen, & Kazdin, 1988). The existence of comorbid diagnoses requires that treatment strategies for anxious children be applied somewhat flexibly, based on such factors as the developmental level of the child and his or her presenting constellation of symptoms (see Kendall et al., 1992).

Normative Development

Normative data provide a useful starting point for understanding the content and nature of childhood anxieties and fears, as well as for evaluating the severity of the targeted anxieties and fears (see Kendall, Marrs-Garcia, Nath, & Sheldrick, 1999). As children grow and begin to experience the world around them, the content of their anxieties and fears tends to reflect changes in their perceptions of reality (Campbell, 1986). Children's fears begin with a content that is more global, imaginary, uncontrollable, and powerful, and over time become more specific, differentiated, and realistic (Bauer, 1976). Thus, for example, fears of the diffuse "boogie man" that lurks in the dark evolve into more distinct and realistic fears that include peer acceptance and school performance (Bauer, 1976). These fears may in fact be a way for children to deal with the challenges that confront them (Campbell, 1986; Morris & Kratochwill, 1983). The content of childhood fears has often been designated and described in terms of a five-factor structure based on the Fear Survey Schedule for Children—Revised (FSSC-R; Ollendick, 1983; Ollendick, Matson, & Helsel, 1985), including (1) fear of failure and criticism, (2) fear of the unknown, (3) fear of injury and small animals, (4) fear of danger and death, and (5) medical fears. Although age and gender differences exist, the factors themselves appear to be robust across age, gender, and even nationality (Ollendick, King, & Frary, 1989). However, a recent cross-cultural examination (Fonseca, Yule, & Erol, 1994) was unable to replicate the 5-factor model in non-English-speaking countries, reminding us to be cautious about generalizations across cultures.

Importantly, research examining the fears of children of different ethnicities reveals that there are more similarities than differences across these ethnicities (see Ginsburg & Silverman, 1996; Neal & Turner, 1991; Treadwell, Flannery-Schroeder, & Kendall, 1994). In their broader cross-cultural review, Fonseca et al. (1994) concluded that the most common fears endorsed by children are remarkably similar across countries and cultures; however, when examining supplemental lists to the FSSC-R, a variety of fears were also endorsed by children in different countries. Thus, although similarities may prevail, potential differences should not be forgotten.

As children grow older, the number of fears they experience generally decreases (Bauer, 1976; Draper & James, 1985), and this trend has been supported cross-culturally (see Fonseca et al., 1994). Also consistently supported are sex differences in the number of childhood fears, with maternal and self-report accounts indicating that girls exhibit more fears than boys (Bauer, 1976; Lapouse & Monk, 1959; Ollendick et al., 1985). Again, sex differences have emerged strongly in different cultures (Fonseca et al., 1994). However, as some of these authors have cautioned, it is important to consider that social desirability and sex-role stereotypes and expectations may affect not only reportability but also referability. This concern is reflected in the research, which suggests that girls are more likely to be referred for clinical attention than boys (e.g., Weisz & Weiss, 1991). In regard to clinical referral for anxiety disorders, an approximately equal number of boys and girls, ages 9–13, have been referred to the CAADC.

A Cognitive Distinction

An important distinction to be made when treating youth is between *cognitive distortions* and *cognitive deficiencies* (Kendall, 1985, 1991, 2000). Whereas deficiencies refer to an absence of thinking, distortions include thinking that is dysfunctional or biased. With deficiencies, there is a lack of forethought in situations that require some advanced consideration; with distortions, the cognitive dysfunction occurs not in the lack of information processing but in the presence of maladaptive thinking.

Making such a distinction is helpful therapeutically in that it allows clinicians to target the specific nature of the dysfunction; that is, addressing cognitive deficiencies would require eliminating impulsive acting without thinking and working toward more thoughtful and meaningful problem solving. Alternately, cognitive distortions must first be identified, recognized as problematic, and subsequently corrected. The negative self-talk, the preoccupation with the evaluations of others, and the misperceptions of threat or danger that often plague children with anxiety, for example, seem to result from a thinking process that is primarily distorted and ultimately dysfunctional. It is precisely this style of maladaptive and self-defeating thinking that becomes a treatment target for anxious children.

How do anxious children think about themselves and their world? It appears that their thoughts are often laced with negative cognition, including fear of being scared or hurt, self- critical thoughts, and thoughts of danger and threat (see Barrios & Hartmann, 1988; Daleiden & Vasey, 1997; Prins, 1986; Treadwell & Kendall, 1996; Zatz & Chassin, 1985). More specifically, the frequency of children's negative self-statements, as opposed to positive ones, are predictive of their psychological dysfunction. Following treatment, higher functioning and less anxious children engaged in fewer negative self-statements (Treadwell & Kendall, 1996; see also Kendall, 1985). Thus, armed not with positive thinking but with the "power of nonnegative thinking" (Kendall, 1984), formerly anxious children are able to maintain greater freedom from anxious symptomatology. For anxious children, it is not so much a matter of supplying positive thinking but of helping them to identify and counter their negative thinking.

Family Matters

The potential contributing role of the family in youth with anxiety disorders is receiving increased clinical and empirical attention (Fauber & Long, 1991; Sanders, 1996). The results of the "top-down" and "bottom-up" studies, which provide evidence that children with anxiety disorders are more likely to have parents with anxious symptomatology, and that parents with anxiety disorders are more likely to have children with anxious symptomatology (e.g., Last, Hersen, et al., 1987; Last, Phillips, & Statfeld, 1987; see also Ginsburg, Silverman, & Kurtines, 1995), certainly seem to implicate the role of the family in youth with anxiety disorders. Not surprisingly, it has also been found that children may imitate the fears and anxieties of their parents (Dadds, Heard, & Rapee, 1991; King, Hamilton, & Ollendick, 1988).

At the heart of much of the research investigating family variables in childhood anxiety is the notion of "control" or "perceived control" (see Chorpita, Brown, & Barlow, 1998; Ginsburg et al., 1995). In essence, such control refers to the extent to which children believe that their behavior can influence events and outcomes. Adults with anxiety and depressive disorders have described having family environments that were more likely to have limited experience with control over various events, with parental overprotection and discouragement of autonomy being related to subsequent anxiety and depression (Parker, 1983). Indeed, research indicates that the parents of youth with anxiety disorders are less granting of psychological autonomy than are parents of nonreferred children (Siqueland, Kendall, & Steinberg, 1996). Furthermore, children diagnosed with anxiety and depression are more likely to describe their families as less supportive, cohesive, and democratic in decision-making and more conflictual than other children (Stark, Humphrey, Crook, & Lewis, 1990). In examining maternal expectations and attributions of a child's ability to cope in a stressful situation, Kortlander, Kendall, and Panichelli-Mindel (1997) reported that mothers of anxious children expected their children to be more distressed and less able to perform in a given situation than mothers of nondisordered children. Similarly, mothers of high-anxious girls, as opposed to mothers of low-anxious girls, were more likely to intervene in their daughter's problem solving of a task and less likely to wait for the child to solve the task (Krohne & Hock, 1991). In a cross-cultural examination of childhood fears and anxiety by Dong, Yang, and Ollendick (1994), it was predicted that Chinese child-rearing practices and educational beliefs, which tended to be more restrictive and overprotective, should predict higher levels of anxious and depressive symptomatology in more Western contexts. The authors found support for these predictions, particularly for 11- to 13-year-old children. Considering all of these findings, each of these family factors may contribute to a child's anxious behavior. Eventually, parents must cede control, and the notion of autonomy granting is an important consideration given that families of anxious children may be overprotective. Thus, fostering independence requires treatment consideration.

Children experiencing a diminished sense of control may be more vulnerable to the experience of anxiety. Evidence suggests that this notion of perceived control mediates the relationship between a controlling family environment and the severity of negative affect (Chorpita, et al., 1998). In other words, family environments that afford limited opportunities for personal control are associated with anxiety and negative affect in children.

Several therapy models have attempted to target issues of parental control and the child's need for autonomy in treatment. One model, "transfer of control" (Ginsburg et al., 1995), sets up a system wherein the therapist transfers coping skills to the child, with the parents serving as a mediator. The therapist teaches skills to the parents and child, and then serves as a coach for the parents as they help guide their child through distressing situations. Barriers to the transfer of control, according to these authors, include parental anxious symptomatology and deficient family relations. Including the cognitive-behavioral framework, treatment strategies include contingency management, self-control management, and exposure (as seen in Kendall, 1994), as well a dyadic intervention approach that focuses on barriers in the transfer of control and targets parental anxious symptomatology as well as the problematic family relationships. For a more detailed description of this approach, see Ginsburg et al. (1995) and Silverman and Kurtines (1996).

Current research suggests that the messages, often unintentional, that parents send to their children can affect their experiences of fear and assumptions of negative consequences. What kinds of feedback are children receiving from their families that are associated with this negative affect or anxious symptomatology? The cognitive biases found in children and adolescents with anxiety disorders may be associated with a family environment that emphasizes the perception of threat and the avoidance of this threat. In one study, Barrett, Rapee, Dadds, and Ryan (1996) reported that anxious children interpreted ambiguous situations in a more threatening manner than did nonclinical children. Differing from both the nonclinical and aggressive children in their selected responses to these situations, anxious children were more likely to respond in an avoidant manner. The parents of anxious children also had significantly higher rates of threat interpretation and higher rates of predicting their children would select an avoidant response. Further reinforcing the role of the family in possibly contributing to anxious behavior, it was found that after anxious children had the opportunity to engage in a family discussion about how to act in a given situation, their avoidant responses significantly increased, whereas oppositional children's aggressive responses increased and the nonclinical children's responses became less avoidant and aggressive. This phenomenon, called the "family enhancement of avoidant and aggressive response," has clear implications for the types of preferred interventions to be implemented with families of anxious youth.

Anxiety disorders in youth are multifaceted and multidetermined. How do we come to understand the experience of a child who, for example, worries excessively about the potential rejection of his or her peers, is physically sickened by it, wants to avoid school because of it, or feels all of these things at once? How do we translate a child's worries, words of fear, and feelings of dread into a clinically meaningful account? Continuing from our developmental perspective, we now turn to the topic of assessment as a critical starting point in the treatment of childhood anxiety.

ASSESSMENT

All children are expected to experience some mild separation anxiety or specific fear(s) at different times during their childhood—it seems to happen to almost all children as they mature. Consequently, it may be difficult for an untrained appraiser to distinguish developmentally appropriate fears or anxieties from anxiety episodes that would qualify as a psychological disorder.

There is currently no single universally accepted approach to the complete assessment of all childhood anxiety disorders. Some of the assessment strategies employed with children have been derived from work with adults: Instruments designed specifically to assess anxiety in children and adolescents are needed because there are several unique features to evaluating this population. For instance, the assessment process must address the extensive developmental changes occurring during this life stage. Cognitive, socioemotional, and biological changes mean that a child of 8 or 9 is likely to be very different from a child of 12 or 13. Corresponding changes in children's expressive and comprehension abilities will also influence the suitability of particular assessment strategies, and the normative data against which behaviors will be judged developmentally appropriate must be considered (Barrios & Hartmann, 1988; Bierman, 1984; Edelbrock, Costello, Duncan, Kalas, & Conover, 1985). Consequently, multimethod assessment is essential, with information from multiple settings (school and home) and from multiple perspectives (parent, child, and teacher) (Achenbach, McConaughy, & Howell, 1987; Kendall, Pellegrini, & Urbain, 1981). As will be described, the preferred assessment methods include structured diagnostic interviewing, child self-report, behavioral observations, parent and teacher ratings, and family assessment. Although we mention psychophysiological recording, this method of assessment is not currently recommended for clinical use.

Thus far, we have described anxiety disorders in youth in a manner that is consistent with the DSM formulation: a categorical system in which a child either does or does not qualify for a diagnosis. However, it is important to recognize that the assessment of anxiety does not have to adopt a categorical system. Although there is little question about the existence of internalizing problems in childhood and adolescence, there is considerable controversy about the DSM system of classification of childhood disorders, with some mental health professionals arguing instead that the childhood disorders are best described along multiple continua (Achenbach & Edelbrock, 1978; Quay, 1977). Although a thorough review of this debate is beyond the scope of this chapter, it is noteworthy that some researchers argue that the significant overlap of symptoms among the childhood disorders raises questions regarding the discriminative validity and clinical utility of the disorders classified in the categorical system of DSM. Also, the categorical system requires that the patient display a minimum number of required symptoms in order to meet criteria for a diagnosis; a system requiring such a "threshold" for diagnosis may compromise the treatment of subclinical patients (Albano, Chorpita, & Barlow, 1996).

An alternative to a categorical system is an empirically derived dimensional system of classification, such as that developed by Achenbach and colleagues (Achenbach, 1991, 1993; Achenbach & Edelbrock, 1983). From a multivariate standpoint, Achenbach and colleagues (Achenbach, 1991; Achenbach & McConaughy, 1992) developed the Child Behavior Checklist (CBCL) and identified four specific narrowband syndromes in clinic-referred children and adolescents of various ages who present with internalizing problems: anxious–depressed, schizoid, somatic complaints, and withdrawn (this does not include the externalizing problems that can also be assessed by the CBCL). It has also been suggested that these narrowband internalizing disorders can be determined reliably (Ollendick & King, 1994).

Research in this area has contributed to the delineations represented in the fourth edition of DSM. DSM-IV is based on the prototypical approach to classification, which combines features of both the categorical and dimensional approach by identifying essential symptoms of a disorder, while allowing for nonessential variations of symptoms to occur (Barlow, 1992). Nevertheless, although considerable improvement has been made over previous DSM versions, problems remain and the classification of psychopathology in children and adolescents and some aspects of the DSM remain controversial (Albano et al., 1996).

Multiple sources of information are needed when assessing childhood anxiety. Drawing from Lang's tripartite model, fear and anxiety can have cognitive, behavioral, and psychological components (Lang, 1968), and should be assessed across all three response channels. Clinical interviews, self-report, parent and teacher ratings, behavioral observations, and family assessment are strategies that can be employed to elicit expressions of anxiety across response channels. The practice parameters for the assessment and treatment of anxiety disorders (American Academy of Child and Adolescent Psychiatry, 1993) noted important areas to emphasize in the assessment of anxiety disorders in children and adolescents. Specifically, the onset, development, and context of anxiety symptoms, as well as information regarding the child's developmental, medical, school, and social history, and family psychiatric history should be obtained (Bernstein, Borchart, & Perwein, 1996).

Instruments used to assess anxiety in children and adolescents should (1) provide reliable and valid measurement of symptoms across multiple domains (i.e., cognitive, behavioral, and psychological channels); (2) discriminate between disorders (selection/classification); (3) evaluate severity; (4) reconcile multiple observations (e.g., parent and child ratings) and (5) enable the evaluation of therapeutic change (Kendall & Flannery-Schroeder, 1998; Stallings & March, 1995). Though no instrument is currently available that meets all of these requirements, several acceptable assessment tools are available. In this section, we provide an overview of the instruments currently available for measuring anxiety in children and adolescents.

Clinical Interviews

The interview remains one of the most common methods for assessing childhood disorders in general, and anxiety specifically. Numerous interview schedules designed to be administered to both children and parents have been developed and empirically tested. They range from a highly structured format to an unstructured one and have the advantage of gleaning information about the child's developmental history from both child and parental perspectives.

Whereas an unstructured clinical interview may be acceptable in some clinical settings, the absence of standardization makes this problematic for subsequent research. The semistructured interview format has been developed to provide structure while also providing opportunities for elaboration as judged appropriate by an examiner, and it serves to increase the reliability of diagnostic assignment.

The Anxiety Disorders Interview Schedule for Children (ADIS- C/P; Silverman & Albano, 1997) is a semistructured interview developed specifically to determine DSM-IV anxiety diagnoses (assessing symptomatology, course, etiology, and severity) in youth (Silverman, 1991). The ADIS-C relies on DSM criteria for anxiety and related disorders and utilizes an interviewer–observer format, allowing the clinician to draw information both from the interview and from clinical observation. The parent interview extracts information on the child's history, while the child interview addresses symptomatology in greater detail. Final, or composite, diagnoses are based on the level of severity endorsed in each interview and the agreement in identification of pathology between parent and child interviews. Among its strengths are favorable psychometric properties (March & Albano, 1998) and clear and clinically sensitive sections for diagnosing the separate anxiety disorders in youth. Additional portions of this interview have been developed to permits diagnosis of other disorders (e.g., to assess comorbid conditions).

Another commonly used semistructured interview is the Schedule for Affective Disorders and Schizophrenia in School-Age Children (K-SADS; Puig-Antich & Chambers, 1978), which requires experienced clinicians to determine diagnoses using information generated by the interview and all other available sources and material. The Diagnostic Interview for Children and Adolescents (DICA; Herjanic & Reich, 1982) and the National Institute of Mental Health (NIMH) Diagnostic Interview Schedule for Children version 2.3 (DISC 2.3; Shaffer et al., 1996) are other highly structured interviews designed to be administered by a lay interviewer and to establish diagnoses strictly according to an established classification system.

Although these interviews are designed to elicit general diagnoses in children, not all have been found to be empirically reliable and valid for diagnosing anxiety. For general diagnoses, concordance between parent and child report during the clinical interview ranges from moderate to good, but concordance for the diagnosis of anxiety disorders is much lower (Chambers et al., 1985; Edelbrock, Costello, Duncan, Conover, & Kalas, 1986; Edelbrock et al., 1985; Hodges, McKnew, Birbach, & Roebuck, 1987). Questions concerning factual, unambiguous, and concrete information produce the highest agreement between parent and child report (Herjanic, Herjanic, Brown, & Wheatt, 1975; Herjanic & Reich, 1982); questions concerning subjective information and internalizing symptoms related to depression and anxiety produce the lowest (Herjanic et al., 1975; Herjanic & Reich, 1982; Verhulst, Althaus, & Berden, 1987). Developmental differences also have been shown to affect the reliability of parent and child reports on the clinical interview. As children age, the reliability of their reports tends to increase; conversely, the reliability of parent reports tends to decrease (Edelbrock et al., 1985).

Self-Reports

The most widely used method for assessing childhood anxiety is the self-report inventory. Because of the subjective nature of anxiety symptoms, it is extremely important to include measures that assess symptoms through the child or adolescent's viewpoint (Bernstein, Borchardt, & Perwein, 1996). Numerous inventories exist. The three instruments most frequently used to assess anxiety and fear in children and adolescents are the Revised Children's Manifest Anxiety Scale (RCMAS; Reynolds & Richmond, 1978), the Fear Survey Schedule for Children—Revised (FSSC-R; Ollendick, 1983), and the State–Trait Anxiety Inventory for Children (STAIC; Spielberger, 1973). Newer inventories, (e.g., Multidimensional Anxiety Scale for Children [MASC], Coping Questionnaire for Children [CQ-C]) are described as well, as they are likely to receive increased use and evaluation.

The RCMAS, a widely used instrument for assessing anxiety in young persons (Stallings & March, 1995), is a 37-item scale that assesses anxiety in children and adolescents ages 6–19. The scale also includes a "lie" scale to detect invalid responses. The developers of the scale describe three RCMAS factors: physiological manifestations of anxiety, worry and oversensitivity, and fear/concentration (Reynolds & Richmond, 1979), and report high retest reliability (Reynolds & Paget, 1983; Reynolds, 1981).

The STAIC is composed of two 20-item inventories: the state scale, which is designed to assess present state and situationally linked anxiety, and the trait scale, which is designed to assess stable anxiety across situations. Normative data based on a national sample of children between ages 8 and 12 years are available for the STAIC (Spielberger, 1973). Findings regarding the reliability of the scale and the validity of the state–trait distinction are mixed, however. Moreover, the information or data provided by the STAIC does not correspond with DSM anxiety categories. For these reasons, the STAIC may be best used primarily as a general screening in-strument (see Barrios & Hartmann, 1988).

The FSSC-R is the revised version of the Fear Survey Schedule for Children, developed by Scherer and Nakamura (1968). As mentioned ear-lier, five factors have been found to be measured with this instrument, in-cluding fear of failure, fear of death, fear of injury and small animals, medi-cal fears, and fear of the unknown. This 5-factor structure makes the scale useful in identifying specific sources of fear, severity of fearfulness, and treatment effects. Ollendick and colleagues (1985) provided normative data for the FSSC-R for children ages 7–18, and report high internal consistency and moderate retest reliability over a 3 month interval (Ollendick, 1983).

The Social Phobia and Anxiety Inventory for Children (SPAI-C; Beidel, Turner, & Morris, 1995) is also a reliable and commonly used self-report measure to assess anxiety in children and adolescents. The SPAI-C, a 26-item self-report that taps anxiety-arousing situations, physical and cognitive symptoms, and avoidance behavior, has demonstrated high internal consis-tency and high 2-week retest reliability (Biedel et al., 1995). It has also dis-criminated between children with social phobia and either normal children or children with externalizing problems (Beidel, Fink, & Turner, 1996).

The Multidimensional Anxiety Scale for Children (MASC; March, Parker, Sullivan, Stallings, & Conners, 1997) was developed to address the issue of a multidimensional conceptualization of anxiety. The scale covers the major domains of self-reported anxiety in children and adolescents. It is a 39-item self-report inventory containing four major factors: physical symptoms (e.g., tension), social anxiety (e.g., rejection), harm avoidance (e.g., perfectionism), and separation anxiety. This factor structure has been shown to hold for boys and girls, and for younger and older youth, and re-test reliability has been shown to be excellent over 3 weeks and 3 months (March & Albano, 1998).

A relatively unexplored, though promising, area of self-report in child-hood anxiety is that of cognitive assessment. Cognitive contents, schemas, processes, and products have been implicated in the maintenance and etiol-ogy of anxiety (e.g., Ingram & Kendall, 1987; Kendall & Ingram, 1986, 1987, 1989) but have received little empirical attention with children (Kendall & Ronan, 1990). Although the cognitive assessment of children with anxiety disorders is a promising area, relatively few scales exist. Ronan, Kendall, and Rowe (1994) developed the Negative Affectivity Self-Statement Questionnaire (NASSQ) to assess the cognitive content of anx-ious/dysphoric children. A subscale for assessing anxious self-talk was eval-uated, with results indicating favorable reliability and the ability to differ-entiate among both psychometrically defined and clinic cases of anxious and nonanxious children between 8 and 15 years old. The NASSQ consists of self-statements that participants endorse on a 1–5 scale representing the frequency that the thought occurred to them during the past week. Scale development, reliability, and validity support has been reported in Ronan et al. (1994) and Treadwell and Kendall (1996; see also Ronan & Kendall, 1997).

The Coping Questionnaire—Child Version (CQ-C; Kendall, 1994; Kendall et al., 1997) is another important instrument for cognitive assessment. This measure assesses the child's ability to cope with anxious distress in challenging situations. Analyses indicate adequate internal consistency, strong retest reliability, and document its usefulness as a measure of improvement (Kendall & Marrs-Garcia, 1999).

Self-report measures have the advantage of being economical in both time and expense, but are limited in several ways. They do not adequately address the situational specificity of childhood anxiety disorders, and some may not capture the fears and anxieties specific to the child (Kendall & Ronan, 1990). This limitation is potentially serious, since, without such information, treatment cannot be individualized nor can it address a child's unique behavioral dysfunction. The present inability of self-report inventories to account for developmental difficulties is another disadvantage. Few inventories have adequate normative data for different developmental stages, and many inventories are not modified for variations in children's comprehension abilities. For example, it is unclear whether the differences among *Never worried*, *Rarely worried*, and *Often worried* represent the same meaning for children at different stages of cognitive development or whether children at lower stages of development are capable of making such distinctions.

Self-reports may also fail to reflect the child's internal state. The inaccuracy may result from the child's desire to respond in a nondistressed or socially desirable manner. Youth with anxiety disorders approach problems with a hypersensitive concern about self-presentation and evaluation by others (Kendall & Ingram, 1989). Their preference for a favorable self-presentation may influence their performance on tasks such as self-report assessments (Kendall & Flannery-Schroeder, 1998).

Behavioral Observations

The behavioral assessment of childhood anxiety includes many structured and unstructured observational techniques. Throughout the assessment process, especially during the clinical interview, diagnosticians observe the child and note any behavior that may be suggestive of anxiety, such as fidgeting, fingernail biting, avoiding eye contact, and speaking softly. Parent and teacher rating scales, discussed below, are based on unstructured observations of the child's behavior in naturalistic settings. Unstructured observations are important but can be limited by observer bias and, especially in the case of parent and teacher ratings, typically lack appropriate observer training.

More structured observation strategies are employed in behavioral avoidance tasks (BATs), with direct observation by trained raters in naturalistic settings such as the schoolroom or playground. As an example, consider a BAT for assessing distressing anxiety associated with eating food in public. The situation could be arranged so that there would be food available, there would be trays for selecting foods, and there would be several options for places to eat the food—places that are solitary, with one person, or with many others. In a BAT, the participant would enter the situation and trained observers would record the degree of approach to the distressing situation. In this case, how far along the continuum of "not eating" to "eating among people" did the participant move? Although the structured behavioral assessment methods are advantageous because trained raters assess a child's behavior against operationalized behavior, they are limited by the absence of standardized procedures. This problem hinders the comparability across studies of data obtained with these techniques. Furthermore, neither unstructured nor structured behavioral observations are sufficient assessment techniques by themselves. As it turns out, although the total of several behavioral observation codes is correlated with the presence of anxiety, no single coded behavioral frequency appears to be pathognomic to childhood anxiety. As noted earlier, there appears to be symptom overlap among the internalizing disorders (see also Kendall & Watson, 1989) and there is between-subjects variability in the behavioral expression of anxious symptomatology.

Parent and Teacher Rating Scales

Parent and teacher reports offer additional and important perspectives; however, there are some potential limitations to using these instruments for assessing internalizing disorders in children. Parents and teachers may not know the nature or extent of the child's inner pressures and anguish. There is also often low concordance between child and parent reports of anxiety (Klein, 1991). Additionally, although not all data are consistent (see Krain & Kendall, in press), Frick, Silverthorn, and Evans (1994) reported that mothers tend to overreport anxiety symptoms in their children, and that this is related to the increased level of maternal anxiety. This finding would suggest that clinicians be aware of any distressing levels of parental anxiety (Bernstein, Borchardt, & Perwein, 1996). Among other potential limitations are the retrospective nature of the observations and the possibility of rater bias.

The most widely used rating scale is the Child Behavior Checklist (CBCL; Achenbach & Edelbrock, 1983), which has acceptable reliability, validity, and normative data. The 118-item CBCL assesses behavioral problems and social competencies. Items are scored 0, 1, or 2, depending on the degree to which the particular statement characterizes the child. The CBCL provides data on a child's level of disturbance on specific factors and offers discrimination between broadband, externalizing disorders and internalizing disorders: The CBCL does not identify/differentiate among the subtypes of anxiety described in DSM-IV. The CBCL also provides data on the child's participation in social activities and interactions with peers for evaluation of change. Using the items from the CBCL, a set of 16 items were found to have retest reliability and internal consistency, and to reliably differentiate anxiety-disordered and nondisordered youth (Kendall, Henin, MacDonald, & Treadwell, 1999). Following additional research, the CBCL-A may be a useful subscale to the CBCL for the identification youth with anxiety disorders.

There is also a version of the CBCL designed for teachers—the Teacher Report Form (TRF; Achenbach, 1991; Achenbach & Edelbrock, 1986). The primary teacher, using the TRF, rates the child's classroom functioning. Gathering and reviewing the TRF allows a comparison of the child's anxious behavior at home and in the school setting, and may be especially relevant for children whose fears involve social and evaluative situations. Keep in mind, however, that the classroom behavior of anxious children may not be seen as troubling to a teacher; thus, the TRF scores of some children with anxiety disorders are not necessarily extreme. The instrument provides useful information but is not linked to DSM diagnostic categories.

There is a parent version of the CQ-C, described earlier, called the Coping Questionnaire—Parent (CQ-P; Kendall, 1994). The parent rates the child's ability to cope with the three most anxiety-provoking situations identified from the diagnostic interview. The scale shows moderate interrater agreement and has been shown to be sensitive to treatment effects (Kendall & Marrs-Garcia, 1999).

Physiological Recordings

The physiological assessment of anxiety has received wide attention in the adult literature (see Himadi, Boice, & Barlow, 1985), yet little empirical data on these indicators exist in the child and adolescent population (Barrios & Hartmann, 1988; Beidel, 1988). Opponents of this method of assessing anxiety in children have cited the large imbalance between the extensive cost, in time and money, of gathering such information, and its relative yield (Barlow & Wolfe, 1981). Furthermore, the most commonly used physiological techniques, such as cardiovascular and electrodermal measures, lack adequate normative data for children. Children also appear to show idiosyncratic patterns of response during physiological assessment. Moreover, measures can be influenced by expectancy effects, emotions other than anxiety, and incidental motoric and perceptual activity (Wells & Virtulano, 1984; Werry, 1986).

Despite these somewhat daunting limitations, the physiological assessment of childhood anxiety should not be totally abandoned. Empirical investigations of autonomic responsivity in anxious children should be conducted, as the results of such work would increase our understanding of the psychophysiological expression of anxiety and help to develop normative data in this area. There is some evidence suggesting that the physiological activity of anxious children is somewhat similar to that of anxious adults (Beidel, 1988).

Family Variables

Family assessment is a relatively unexplored method of assessing factors associated with childhood anxiety. Since the cognitive-behavioral model acknowledges and is concerned with the influence of the family and other social contexts on childhood anxiety (Kendall, 1985, 1991), the paucity of established techniques to assess the family of the anxious child is a serious oversight. The Family Assessment Device (FAD; Epstein, Baldwin, & Bishop, 1983) is one potentially useful instrument that is currently available for assessing family functioning. The FAD is based on the McMaster model of family functioning. It measures six dimensions of family functioning (including communication, affective involvement, behavior control), has been found to possess adequate retest reliability, and differentiates between clinician-rated healthy and unhealthy families (Miller, Epstein, Bishop, & Keitner, 1985; Miller, Kabacoff, Keitner, Epstein, & Bishop, 1986). To date, this measurements of family functioning has not been applied specifically to families of anxious children. As mentioned earlier, one study of parents of children with anxiety disorders (Siqueland et al., 1996) found them to be somewhat controlling and reluctant to grant autonomy to the child. Other work (see Rapee, 1997) has described how anxious children—who are already avoidant—become increasingly avoidant after discussing with a parent problems to be solved. These findings were based on observational methods of assessing parent–child interactions, and it may be that advances in our knowledge will come through observational assessments.

Summary

The assessment of anxiety in children requires a multimethod approach, drawing information from structured clinical interviews, child self-report, parent and teacher ratings, behavioral observations, as well as family history and patterns of interaction. Each method has advantages and potential disadvantages that limit the merits of relying on a single assessment technique for diagnostic purposes. The multiple assessments should measure the nature of the child's anxiety and the role of family factors in the child's anxiety, and be sensitive to the evaluation of therapeutic change. Further work on these assessment strategies will improve the current resources, add to the normative data, and address the developmental changes occurring during childhood.

TREATMENT: PROCEDURES AND OUTCOMES

Over the last decade, interventions that target childhood anxiety disorders have received increased attention. The development of such treatments is consistent with the field's increasing understanding of the prevalence and impact of anxiety disorders in youth. Various forms of behavior therapy and cognitive-behavioral treatments have shown promise in treating childhood phobias and anxiety disorders. Through a developmentally sensitive synthesis of behavioral and cognitive treatment approaches, therapeutic gain can result for the anxious child (see Kendall, Howard, & Epps, 1988; Ollendick & King, 1998). The following discussion highlights features of cognitive-behavioral treatment, such as relaxation, building a cognitive coping template, problem solving, modeling, contingency maintenance, and imaginal and *in vivo* exposure. We also discuss an integrated treatment package for youth with anxiety disorders (see Kendall, Kane, Howard, & Siqueland, 1989), and the integrated program is illustrated with case examples. The treatment uses the *Coping Cat Workbook* (Kendall, 1992b). Last, a review of the research evaluations of these procedures is provided.

Integrated Cognitive-Behavioral Therapy for Anxious Children

The cognitive-behavioral treatment of anxiety disorders in children and young adolescents integrates the demonstrated efficiencies of the behavioral approach (e.g., exposure, relaxation training, role plays) with an added emphasis on the cognitive information-processing factors associated with each individual's anxieties (see treatment manuals; e.g., Kendall et al., 1989; Howard & Kendall, 1996b; Flannery-Schroeder & Kendall, 1996).[2] The overall goal is to teach children to recognize signs of overwhelming anxious arousal and to let these signs serve as cues for use of anxiety management strategies. Identifying the cognitive processes associated with excessive anxious arousal, training in cognitive strategies for anxiety management, and behavioral relaxation and performance-based practice opportunities are sequenced within the treatment program to build skill upon skill. The greatest emphasis is placed upon the following general strategies:

- Coping modeling
- Identification and modification of anxious self-talk
- Exposure to anxiety-provoking situations
- Role playing and contingent reward procedures

- Homework assignments ("Show That I Can" [STIC] tasks)
- Affective education
- Awareness of bodily reactions and cognitive activities when anxious
- Relaxation procedures
- Graduated sequence of training tasks and assignments
- Application and practice of newly acquired skills in increasingly anxiety-provoking situations

The structured treatment program is divided into two segments: Skills training occurs in the first eight sessions and skills practice in the second eight. The therapist guides the client through a gradual and progressive building of skills that the child later practices through a hierarchy of exposure tasks. Exposure tasks provide the child with opportunities to demonstrate his or her abilities in real-life situations and develop a sense of self-competence. Through rehearsal and multiple attempts, the child succeeds in situations that previously felt impossible and learns to rely on his or her own coping skills rather than depend on others for reassurance. The focus on cognitive processes and creating a coping template stems from an interest in helping the child internalize lessons and generalize skills across settings. The child is taught to attribute successes to his or her own burgeoning competence and that these skills can be used in a variety of situations, not just those practiced in session. To facilitate the learning process, the therapist assumes the posture of a collaborative coach who generates treatment goals with the child and tailors therapy interventions to the child's interests and abilities.

Throughout treatment, the therapist functions as a coping model, demonstrating the skill in each new situation. The child is then invited to participate with the therapist in role playing (e.g., tagalong; Ollendick, 1983). To make role plays less threatening, the therapist may role-play a situation first as the child follows along with him or her. Describing what he or she is feeling or thinking, the therapist asks the child if he or she is experiencing similar or different feelings. Ultimately, the child is encouraged to role-play scenes alone, practicing the newly acquired skills by him- or herself. Variations in role playing are used, depending on the child's skill level and understanding of concepts being introduced. With adolescents, the tag along procedure is often unnecessary. Similarly, role plays should represent situations relevant to the child. The therapist can derive role-play situations from the child's organized fear hierarchy or from external events that the child has reported to have occurred.

Therapist self-disclosure may also be appropriate to reinforce the therapist's role as a coping model. Therapist self-disclosure often takes the form of revealing past experiences that are relevant to the child's own experiences or describing out loud his or her thoughts and feelings about situations as they arise in therapy. For example, it may be appropriate for the therapist to disclose his or her own anxiety at meeting the child for the first session. This sort of disclosure normalizes anxiety and sets the tone for sessions to be a setting in which feelings can be discussed freely. The therapist works as an opportunist, seizing upon situations in which he or she can demonstrate to the child how to cope with a distressing situation. If the therapist trips, the best he can do is express his own anxiety ("Wow, I'm glad you didn't laugh at me. That would have been embarrassing") and then describe how he made himself feel better ("But I thought that even if you had laughed at me, that wouldn't mean that you didn't like me anymore"). By modeling a general process of coping with distress, the child begins to see how a competent adult copes with daily stresses.

The skills training sessions focus on four basic skill areas: awareness of bodily reactions to feelings and those physical symptoms specific to anxiety; recognition and evaluation of "self-talk," or what the child thinks and says to him- or herself when anxious; problem-solving skills, including modifying anxious self-talk and developing plans for coping; and self-evaluation and reward. In the sections that follow, a closer look at the various features of the treatment program is provided. To facilitate the child's involvement in the program and the transmission of useful information and ideas, the chapters of the *Coping Cat Workbook* parallel the treatment sessions. Thus, the child is working with session content and homework assignments that are coordinated within a workbook.

Relaxation

Relaxation training aims to teach children to develop awareness and control over their own physiological and muscular reactions to anxiety. In this procedure, major muscle groups of the body are progressively relaxed through systematic tension-releasing exercises (e.g., King et al., 1988). By tensing and relaxing various muscle groups, the individual learns to perceive sensations of bodily tension and to use these sensations as the stimuli to relax. During the initial instruction, the child is taught to identify the particular muscle groups and somatic sensations that uniquely characterize his or her own anxious states. This increased awareness of his or her own somatic reactions to anxiety allow the child to use an aroused physical state as an "early warning signal" to initiate relaxation procedures. Furthermore, greater awareness of individual responses to distress allows the child to target specific muscle groups that tense when anxious.

A therapist can also teach cue-controlled relaxation in which the child learns to associate a relaxed state with a self-produced cue word, such as "calm." While the child is totally relaxed, the cue word is subvocalized with each exhalation. The cue serves as a reminder of the relaxed state and can initiate muscle relaxation when used during a distressed state. Cue-controlled relaxation can be helpful when the child wishes to initiate muscle relaxation in a public setting but does not feel comfortable performing progressive relaxation techniques. When teaching both progressive and cue-controlled techniques, relaxation training scripts are often incorporated (e.g., Koeppen, 1974; Ollendick & Cerny, 1981). For example, a child is taught to tense and relax her stomach by imagining that she is squeezing through a fence or tensing and relaxing her hand muscles by pretending to squeeze the juice out of a lemon. Scripts differ depending on the age range of the targeted clients. Scripts for younger children are typically shorter in length and offer fewer distinctions among the muscle groups than scripts for adolescents or adults.

Weisman, Ollendick, and Horne (1978) demonstrated the efficacy of muscular relaxation procedures with normal 6- and 7-year-old children. They found that the procedures of both Ollendick and Cerny (1981) and Koeppen (1974) resulted in significantly reduced muscle-tension levels, as measured by electromyographic (EMG) recordings (both groups were superior to an attention-control group but did not differ from one another). This finding suggests that muscular relaxation procedures may be an effective counterconditioning agent for young children. Adding imaginal or *in vivo* exposure tasks to a relaxation training program (as in systematic desensitization) may enhance the therapeutic outcome of progressive relaxation. A recent review of controlled studies assessing the efficacy of treatments for childhood fears and phobias (see Ollendick & King, 1998) concluded that relaxation used in conjunction with gradual imaginal exposures is superior to relaxation training alone (Barabasz, 1973; Kondas, 1967; Mann & Rosenthal, 1969; Miller, Barrett, Hampe, & Noble, 1972), and the therapeutic benefit is greater still if *in vivo*, rather than imaginal, exposures are implemented (Kuroda, 1969; Ultee, Griffioen, & Schellekens, 1982). Thus, muscle relaxation may work best as a counterconditioning agent when the child first achieves an aroused emotional state, via exposure, similar to that produced by the anxiety-provoking stimulus.

Building a Cognitive Coping Template

Because cognition is theorized to be inextricably linked to emotion and behavior (Ingram, Kendall, & Chen, 1991), it is believed that dysfunction in either the behavioral or emotional realm can be ameliorated by identifying and challenging a child's distorted or unrealistic cognition. Cognitive-based therapies highlight the role of maladaptive thinking in dysfunctional behavior and operate by adjusting distorted cognitive processing to more constructive ways of thinking. Cognitive strategies typically consist of teaching the child to test out and reduce negative self-talk, generating positive self-statements, challenging unrealistic or dysfunctional negative self-statements, and creating a plan to cope with feared situations. Cognitive modeling, rehearsal, social reinforcement, and role play are all used to help the child build a coping template that helps to interpret future interactions with feared situations in a new light.

Building a cognitive coping template entails the identification and modification of maladaptive self-talk, along with building a new way to view situations—a new structure that is based on coping. The therapist works with the child to (1) remove characteristic misinterpretations of environmental events and (2) gradually and systematically build a frame of reference that includes strategies for coping. Accurate assessment and conceptualization of the dysfunctional thought structure are essential. For example, a child's fear of speaking in front of others may be based on legitimate grounds if the child has had difficulty with stuttering and has been teased in the past. However, it may be less realistic for the child to conclude that, because he stutters and is teased by some children, other children will refuse to be his friends. At this level, the therapist and child can create a coping template, including helpful self-talk, that challenges this inflexible belief structure. Guiding the child in asking questions such as, "Is it true that all of the other classmates will tease the child after a speech?" and "Will the child's current friends abandon him or her after being teased by others?" can help the child begin to understand that alternative perspectives exist.

The goal of building a new template for thinking is not so that the perceptions of stress will disappear forever, but so that the formerly distressing misperceptions and arousal, when seen through a cognitive coping structure, will serve as reminders for the use of coping strategies. It is also not the case that we strive to fill the anxious child with positive self-talk. Rather, it is recognized that the power lies not in positive self-talk but in the reduction of negative self-talk—a phenomenon termed "the power of non-negative thinking" (Kendall, 1984). At present, cognitive-based treatment of children with anxiety disorders has shown considerable promise (e.g., Eisen & Silverman, 1993; Kane & Kendall, 1989; Ollendick, 1995). Often cognitive strategies are used in combination with other forms of behavioral therapy (e.g., Friedman & Ollendick, 1989; Graziano & Mooney, 1980, 1982; Mansdorf & Lukens, 1987), and it has been suggested that self-talk and cognitive restructuring may require operant-based reinforcement strategies when used in treatments with children (e.g., Hagopian, Weist, & Ollendick, 1990). Further study is also required to determine if cognitive procedures actually alter those processes that are conceptualized as critical in the treatment model (i.e., whether distorted cognition changes as a result of treatment; Ollendick & King, 1998). Recent evidence suggests that changes in children's negative self-talk (but not positive self-talk) does indeed mediate change in anxiety associated with treatment (Treadwell & Kendall, 1996).

Problem Solving

Another component of the cognitive- behavioral approach to anxiety is problem solving. Early on, D'Zurilla and Goldfried (1971) outlined a 5-stage problem-solving sequence (see also Spivack & Shure, 1974; D'Zurilla & Nezu, 1999). The overall goal of teaching problem solving is training children to develop confidence in their own ability to help themselves meet daily challenges. In the first stage of problem solving (general orientation), the therapist focuses on helping the child understand that problems are a part of everyday life and encourages the child to inhibit his or her initial impulses (e.g., avoidance behavior). In the second stage, the child works to operationally define and formulate the problem into a workable problem with goals. The third stage in problem solving involves the generation of alternative solutions, the core of which lies in brainstorming. Here, ideas, both practical and outlandish, should be generated without judgment. Oftentimes, alternatives that appear implausible at first glance may be viable solutions once given more deliberate consideration. The therapist can model good brainstorming skills by generating both pragmatic and improbable alternatives, and encouraging the child to follow suit.

In decision making, the fourth stage, the child evaluates each alternative, choosing the most appropriate solution, and then puts the action into effect. The final stage consists of verifying the merit of the chosen solution. Training the child to ask him- or herself the following questions may help the child orient him- or herself in a problem-solving mind-set: (1) What is the problem? (2) What are all the things I could do about it? (3) What will probably happen if I do those things? (4) Which solution do I think will work best? and (5) After I have tried it, how did I do? In the end, problem solving helps the child become adept at generating alternatives in what may at first appear like hopeless situations.

Kleiner, Marshall, and Spevack (1987) reported that problem solving prevents posttreatment relapses of anxiety disorders. Twenty-six agoraphobic patients were randomly assigned to either an *in vivo* exposure treatment or *in vivo* exposure plus a problem-solving skills training program. All of the patients improved significantly after 12 treatment sessions. However, those in the *in vivo*–only procedure failed to show further gains at follow-up or relapsed, but those receiving training in problem solving continued to improve at follow-up. Thus, problem solving may enhance the therapeutic gains of treatment strategies, such as with *in vivo* exposure (e.g., Arnow, Taylor, Agras, & Telch, 1985; Jannoun, Munby, Catalan, & Gelder, 1980).

Contingent Reinforcement

In contrast to relaxation, systematic desensitization, and modeling, which all assume that fear must be reduced or eliminated before approach behavior will occur, contingency reinforcement procedures, based on operant conditioning principles, operate on a different assumption. Operant-based procedures focus on facilitating approach responses through appropriate reward and reinforcement, and focus less on the reduction of anxiety per se. Shaping, positive reinforcement, and extinction are the most frequently used contingency management procedures to reduce phobic or anxious behaviors.

Some children diagnosed with anxiety disorders will demonstrate a negative self-focus characterized by self-deprecating thoughts and doubts in self-confidence. Other anxious children may place exceedingly high standards for achievement on themselves and may be less forgiving than most if they fail to meet these standards. To help counter this unjustly critical belief structure, the therapist emphasizes the importance of rewarding oneself for effort and partial successes. The therapist might use the example of a dog learning a trick for the first time. When first learning to sit at its owner's command, a dog is not expected to achieve perfect success the first time, nor is it expected to perform consistently so. Likewise, the anxious child should be reminded that when he or she is initially attempting to accomplish a challenging task, perfect execution is not expected. Graduated practice and timely reinforcement will help the child develop confidence over time and lead to a growing sense of competence.

Reinforcement procedures contingent upon performance have been successful in modifying a wide variety of anxiety-related behavior, such as school phobic behavior (e.g., Ayllon, Smith, & Rogers, 1970) and avoidance of the dark (Leitenberg & Callahan, 1973). In comparison to other behavioral techniques, a contingency management program was shown to produce greater benefits for treating fear of the dark than a self-instruction group without reinforcement procedures (Sheslow, Bondy, & Nelson, 1983). Similarly, in a comparison between live modeling and reinforced practice in the treatment of children with water phobia (Menzies & Clarke, 1993), the reinforced practice condition produced statistically and clinically significant gains over live modeling procedures. Furthermore, there was no difference in efficacy between the reinforced practice condition when implemented alone or when combined with an added live modeling intervention.

Modeling

Modeling derives its conceptual roots from the social learning paradigm (Bandura, 1969, 1986) in which nonfearful behavior is demonstrated in the fear-producing situation so as to illustrate appropriate responses for the child. As a result, fear may be reduced and appropriate skills acquired. Variations of modeling include filmed (symbolic), live, and participant modeling. In filmed modeling, the anxious child watches a videotape of the model, while in live modeling, the model is in the presence of the anxious child. In participant modeling, the live model interacts with the anxious child and guides his or her approach to the feared stimulus. Regular corrective feedback and reinforcement for effort and partial success are required to help the child match the performance of the model (Ollendick & Francis, 1988).

Ross, Ross, and Evans (1971) demonstrated a successful use of modeling procedures in treating a 6-year-old boy who feared interaction with his peers. Generalized imitation, participant modeling, and social reinforcement were the main treatment procedures. Directly following treatment and upon follow-up, the child could interact positively with his peers and displayed few avoidance behaviors. Some studies indicate that interventions that include assisted participation (child participation with therapist modeling of approach behaviors) show greater change in avoidance behavior than treatments that make use of filmed or live modeling alone (Lewis, 1974; Ritter, 1968). Overall, modeling, in its various forms, has received support for its clinical utility in treating anxious and fearful children (e.g., Melamed & Siegel, 1975; Murphy & Bootzin, 1973) as well as helping children placed in stressful situations (e.g., medical procedures; Peterson, 1989).

Exposure-Based Procedures

Exposure entails placing the client in a fear-evoking experience, either imaginally or *in vivo*, to help the client acclimate to the distressing situation and to provide opportunities for the client to practice coping skills within simulated or real-life situations (Francis & Beidel, 1995; Marks, 1975). Exposures can be conducted in graduated measures or by flooding. In gradual exposure, the therapist and child generate a list of feared situations in a hierarchy from least to most anxiety provoking. The child then approaches each situation sequentially, moving up the hierarchy as his or her anxiety level permits. It is important that, at any level, the exposure is not so aversive that the experience actually reinforces the fear. Gradual exposures help the child build experience upon experience and develop a sense of mastery over time. It is important to note that the extent to which the child can discriminate between threatening and nonthreatening stimuli is linked to the exposure's effectiveness in producing fear reduction. The therapist will be careful to collaborate with the child when designing exposures so that the child has an understanding of the intended goals.

In flooding, a child participates in repeated and prolonged exposure to the feared stimulus and remains in the presence of the anxiety-provoking stimulus (either imaginal or *in vivo*) until his or her self-reported anxiety level diminishes. Typically, flooding is used in conjunction with response prevention, in which the child is prevented from engaging in avoidance behavior during exposure. Flooding and response prevention may create more distress than other exposure procedures (Francis & Beidel, 1995), and so the child's clear understanding of the treatment rationale is important. Accordingly, application with younger children should be considered thoughtfully.

In a single-case study of the utility of exposure in treating childhood anxiety, Francis and Ollendick (1990) followed a 16-year-old adolescent with generalized social phobia through a 3-month exposure intervention. The adolescent had a history of school refusal and avoidance of most social situations, and reported intense social-evaluative fears. A fear hierarchy of situations was developed that ranged from least (going to a shopping mall with someone) to most anxiety provoking (going to school alone and staying all day). Items from the hierarchy were used as homework assignments to be practiced between sessions. Tasks were completed in a gradual fashion, with repeated practice for each one. Although the adolescent was not able to return to her previous school, the exposure intervention did enable her to attend an alternative school program, obtain her GED, and enroll in a local community college. Although she still reported anxiety in some social situations, she no longer engaged in avoidance behaviors.

Examples from a Cognitive Behavioral Program

These cognitive-behavioral strategies form an integrated cogntive-behavioral program, such as the one used at the Child and Adolescent Anxiety Disorders Clinic of Temple University. The following case examples demonstrate how these procedures can be implemented when treating children with anxiety disorders. Special attention has been paid to the challenges that can arise during treatment and how therapists can manage difficulties within this treatment approach.

Affective Education

To introduce the concept of physical feelings and behavior, the therapist and child discuss how facial expressions and postures are related to different emotions. The child is taught that tense muscles and irregular breathing can be the first signs of distress. Concepts are first introduced in the abstract or by referring to others, rather than focusing on the child's own experience. The therapist uses pictures or drawings from magazines, books, or educational materials to outline and label different facial expressions and body postures for the child. Various emotions and their physical expression can be role-played by the therapist and child (e.g., feelings charades). Finally, the therapist helps the child become aware of his or her own physical reactions to anxiety.

Often, anxious youth appear to have difficulty distinguishing different feelings, particularly fear, sadness, and anger, and have difficulty seeing that emotions can be modified. The therapist aids the child in differentiating emotions by helping him or her identify the specific physical reactions that accompany each feeling. In the following example, a 10-year-old girl acts out an emotion from a feelings list. As the therapist attempts to name the feeling, she verbally describes the behavior she is using to make her guess. The therapist also uses multiple labels, which requires the child to consider each and decide whether to accept or reject the guess. In this way, she may develop a sense of the unique characteristics of each feeling and apply her own labels. At the end of the exchange, the girl associates her acted feeling to an experience she has had in the past. Children will often internalize experiences better when they have applied their own labels and to the extent that feeling is paired with a real-life experience.

THERAPIST: (*Child jumps around, looks jittery, and hits the table.*) You're drumming, you're jamming, you're breathing!

CHILD: That's not a feeling!

THERAPIST: You're right, that's not a feeling. You're breathing hard, you're intense.

CHILD: I don't know what that means.

THERAPIST: It may be that you're concentrating. You're holding your breath. You're working hard. Umm, you're stressed?

CHILD: What's that?

THERAPIST: It means like you're under a lot of pressure.

CHILD: Maybe. But it's on the list. It's a couple of things, all together.

THERAPIST: You look a little scared. Your eyes are really wide. You may be nervous.

CHILD: Nervous, scared, and worried. I'm like on stage and nervous.

THERAPIST: Oh, so you're taking deep breaths.

CHILD: Yeah, could you see my lips trembling?

THERAPIST: Yeah.

CHILD: It's like trying out for a play.

Once the children begin to identify their own physical symptoms of anxiety, they are taught to use these physical reactions as cues to begin cognitive coping and relaxation. The children are taught a modified, progressive muscle relaxation procedure, which first focuses on the three or four muscle groups most affected by their anxiety. The therapist can then model and discuss with the child times when using the relaxation may be useful.

For the younger child, a script that puts the exercise in a story-like scenario (e.g., Koeppen, 1974) encourages participation. A script by Ollendick and Cerny (1981) can be used for the older child. An audiotape of the therapist going through the relaxation procedure can be given to the child, enabling him or her to practice at home. In addition, the child can demonstrate the procedure to his or her own parents, who might like to practice with the child, or help find a time and a place to practice at home.

Focusing on either progressive or targeted relaxation exercises may be useful for children who do not yet feel comfortable disclosing their fears with the therapist. In a recent case, Eric, a 13-year-old boy, born with spina bifida and confined to a wheelchair, presented with a number of medically related fears. The child required numerous medical procedures, but his fears of intravenous needles, ramps, and elevators interfered on a regular basis. The parents reported that when confronted with needles, Eric would freeze up, have an "anxiety attack," and refuse to let the doctors near him. Similarly, Eric would resist being pushed up wheelchair access ramps for fear of slipping and falling. However, Eric acknowledged few of these fears in-session. When the therapist asked Eric about his feelings toward medical procedures or ramps, Eric would respond with a cavalier, "No problem." Rather than inducing a power struggle with the child, such situations might call for the therapist to emphasize relaxation skills. Rehearsing and practicing these skills in hypothetical situations (imaginal or *in vivo*) may provide the child with the opportunity to practice concrete strategies without necessarily having to self-disclose.

Self-Talk

The notion of self-talk, the things children say to themselves when they are anxious, is an important concept introduced in this training program. Self-talk includes the child's expectations and attributions about him- or herself, others, and situations. For the anxious child, these expectations seem to focus on negative self-evaluation, perfectionistic standards for performance, heightened self-focused attention or concern about what others are thinking, and concerns about failure or not coping. For example, when discussing an upcoming quiz in Bible study, a 12-year-old boy diagnosed with social phobia reported the following five fears: "I won't pass," "I'm going to do so bad that I'm going to be kicked out of school," "Everyone in my family is going to think I'm dumb," "I'll be really embarrassed," and "I won't have a confirmation party." Contained within this child's fears were doubts about self-competence, presupposed consequences for failure, and fears of public humiliation.

A variety of strategies may be employed to help children become aware of the thoughts they are thinking when they are anxious. The therapist points out that the way one thinks about things affects what he or she might feel or do in that situation. Cartoons with empty thought bubbles are often used to introduce the concept. At first, the cartoons can portray simple, nonthreatening scenes in which the character's thoughts are likely to be fairly obvious. As the child becomes comfortable with the task, more ambiguous or anxiety-provoking situations can be used. With the therapist's help, the child generates both anxiety-provoking and anxiety-reducing (coping) thoughts for the characters. To help the child generate coping self-statements, the therapist prompts the child with questions such as, "How likely is it that that will actually happen?", "How many times has it ever happened before?", "Could there be other ways to look at it?", or "How you know it will be as bad as you are expecting?" The therapist guides the child through an empirical, hypothesis-testing process in which both work to challenge the assumptions and beliefs that lead to anxiety and distress. Over the course of treatment, the child develops an alternative information-processing template that is based on coping.

In the following example, a child recounts the anxious thoughts he experienced prior to a science fair and the advice he received from a principal who noticed him worrying:

THERAPIST: Can you think of a situation where you were really nervous? Let's take the example you gave before—that science project. What kinds of things were you thinking?

CHILD: Oh no, will I get an "F"? What about the big kids? Will they make fun of me? I'm not going to do this. Well, I have to or I'll get an "F." . . . My principal was telling me not to worry about the big kids. And I was looking at their projects, and they weren't that great, so I don't know . . .

THERAPIST: What did you think of your principal's advice?

CHILD: I don't know. I guess it was okay, I guess . . .

The child appears comfortable disclosing his anxious self-talk and demonstrates some ability in producing coping thoughts. Early in treatment, such coping thoughts may not yield immediate anxiety reduction. Along the treatment process, anxious youth may become generally good at producing coping self-statements even when the child may not have fully internalized a coping belief structure. In the previous passage, the child admits that the other children should not worry him and acknowledges that an authority figure supports him for doing the best he can. However, as evidenced by his last reply, the child has difficulty believing the principal's advice. This phenomenon is not uncommon with anxious youth. Although the therapist can help the child build a coping template, homework assignments (STIC tasks), role plays, and exposure tasks are necessary to reinforce the message that the child has the ability to handle his own distressing situations. In the case described here, the therapist might ask the child to interview others at home to see what they would think of his science project, or how they would evaluate him if he did not win the contest. If his primary fear is being singled out by bullies, he could poll friends and ask how many of them had ever been teased, or how they had coped with their fear. Gaining confidence through practice and investigation helps the anxious child develop greater faith that his or her coping template will be of use in future challenges.

Problem solving is emphasized. The therapist helps the child begin to generate various alternative solutions to cope with a difficult situation and to select the most appropriate solution. Failing to believe there is anything they can do to make a situation less frightening, anxious children's only coping response is to withdraw from the anxiety-provoking situation. Discussion of nonthreatening situations can be used to introduce the problem-solving concept. For example, "you have lost your shoes in the house. What are some ways you could go about trying to find them?" The therapist provides other examples of situations and helps the child to generate alternatives, to evaluate these possibilities, and to choose the preferred solution.

At this point in the program, children have already been introduced to two different coping strategies: relaxation and changing anxiety-producing thoughts into coping thoughts. The child is reminded that in an anxious situation, he or she could take some deep breaths to calm down and begin to relax those parts of the body that might become tense. By asking what he or she is expecting to happen or what will happen, the therapist also helps the child to recognize his or her thoughts. As discussed previously, the therapist helps the child to challenge any distortions in thinking that may contribute to feelings of anxiety.

When possible, the child is encouraged to take concrete steps to improving his or her situation. These coping strategies are more specific to individual problems. Solutions may involve enlisting friends or family members for support or advice, thinking about or watching how others cope with situations, or rehearsing and practicing various skills in academic, performance, or social situations. For example, a child who was afraid of going into the snake house at the zoo (on a school trip) came up with the following possibilities to deal with the situation: "Take deep breaths," "Say everything is okay," "Listen to my tape player and think about the music," or "Be with a friend who is not scared and will not tease me." The child both generates and evaluates the different possibilities as much as he or she can and decides which solution feels best.

When practicing problem solving, younger children may want to choose a cartoon (television, movie) character or hero whom he or she admires or believes can cope with difficult situations. The therapist can encourage the child to think about how that character might handle anxiety-provoking situations. As a problem-solving strategy, the child can pretend to be that character or take that character along into scary situations for support. A 10-year-old boy who was afraid to walk home from school following a confrontation with an older child, who pushed him off his bike, used this method as one of his coping strategies. Next time he was nervous, he planned to take deep breaths and think, "Nothing will happen to me" or "I can handle this," or go into a store or to someone's doorstep. He also felt more confident if he brought "X-man" (a superhero figure) along with him on the walk and imagined that he would be right behind if he needed him.

Ratings and Reward

Teaching children self-evaluation and reward is an important fourth concept introduced in the program. Anxious children often have difficulty evaluating themselves accurately and/or set extremely high standards for success. The therapist can help children begin to think about possibly evaluating situations based on partial success. Children can learn to identify what things they liked about how they handled the situation, and what things they would like to do differently. The idea of rewarding themselves for accomplishments they are proud of is also introduced. Finally, children can learn to generate a list of possible self-rewards, ranging from spending more time in an activity they like (e.g., riding bikes or reading), giving themselves a pat on the back, telling themselves, "I've done a good job," to spending time with family and friends.

In the following example, the therapist helps the 12-year-old boy, described earlier preparing for a Bible study quiz, develop a plan to cope with the upcoming exam. Initially, the child demonstrates acumen at listing anxious thoughts and generating coping thoughts to challenge his fears. In addition to identifying anxiety-producing and anxiety-reducing thoughts, the child and therapist collaboratively draft a list of actions that the child can take in preparation for the quiz. However, typical of anxious children, the boy has difficulty separating effort from outcome and places too much emphasis on his test grade when evaluating his coping performance. The therapist attempts to help the child distinguishing between one's effort and performance in coping and one's letter grade on a test:

THERAPIST: Let's say you do all these actions: You study by reading it, writing it, and saying it out loud.

CHILD: . . . writing it, saying it out loud, yep.

THERAPIST: And let's say you ask your parents to quiz you on it.

CHILD: They will.

THERAPIST: You make a pretend quiz up and you've checked off everything you needed to know. How are you going to rate yourself from 1 to 10?

CHILD: If I pass?

THERAPIST: No, for now, that doesn't matter. It's how well you do these things, regardless of whether you pass or fail, that you're rating yourself on.

CHILD: Oh . . . if I do really, really good, I'll give myself about a . . . a 7.

THERAPIST: (*surprised*) A 7? If you try at these things really hard, you're going to give yourself a 7 out of 10?

CHILD: Yeah, if I do really, really good, and I pass the test, then I'd give myself a 10, but see I'm only going to—

THERAPIST: —but see, you give this rating for how hard you tried to prepare and to cope, not on—

CHILD: —Yeah, 7—

THERAPIST: (*beginning to sound exasperated*)—but if you try really, really hard, then don't you deserve a 10, regardless of how you do.

CHILD: Oh, I guess, I'd give myself—

THERAPIST: So we're going to give you a 10. If you do all those things—

CHILD: If I don't, I get a zero.

THERAPIST: If you do none, then . . . then I'd give you a zero.

In the last statement, it would have been equally appropriate if the therapist had disagreed with the child and suggested that he deserved a 3, even if he had put none of his plans into action. Undoubtedly, the boy would have been surprised at this suggestion. However, the therapist could have reminded him that proceeding through the first three steps of coping (i.e., listing anxious self-talk, generating coping self-talk, generating actions that can help) is part of the battle. Although implementing his plan of action is the ultimate goal, the child should be rewarded for initiating the coping process and reminded that these are skills that take time to master.

The FEAR Plan

The four skills taught in the program are represented by the acronym, FEAR, as a way of helping children remember what things to do when they get nervous. As described in the *Coping Cat Workbook*, FEAR stands for the following:

F—Feeling frightened? (recognizing physical symptoms of anxiety)
E—Expecting bad things to happen? (recognizing self-talk and what one is worried about)
A—Actions and attitudes that will help (different behaviors and coping

statements the child can use in the anxiety provoking situation based on problem-solving)

R—Results and rewards (self-evaluation and self-rewards)

The child can make a sign, a wallet-sized card, or a decorated wall poster—each using the FEAR plan (or a personalized version of it). Even after the children have been taught many of these skills, they do not always use them in anxiety-provoking situations. Through imaginal and *in vivo* exposure, the second half of the program provides opportunities for children to practice their newly acquired skills in anxiety-provoking situations. Imaginal exposure to stressful situations is used to help children begin thinking through the various coping strategies that they might use in these situations. However, imaginal exposure does not always produce much visible anxiety except in the most anxious children, so it is often used as an intermediate step, prior to *in vivo* exposure. When planning *in vivo* exposures, low-anxiety situations are arranged first, followed by a gradual progression to higher-anxiety-producing situations.

The therapist presents the situation to be encountered, remarks about aspects of the situation that are likely to be troubling, and models behavior, using the different approaches in coping with the situation. The therapist then helps the child think through the steps to use when approaching the situation. The therapist and child then rehearse what might occur during the *in vivo* exposure using these coping steps, until the child feels calmer and ready to try the situation. Following the exposure, the child is helped to evaluate his or her performance and to think of a reward. When possible, the therapist should elicit the child's help in designing exposure tasks. *In vivo* exposures that result from a collaborative effort between the therapist and child are often among the most memorable and meaningful to the child.

Various *in vivo* situations can be set up in the office, such as taking a math test, giving a speech, reading a poem in front of a small audience or video camera, or introducing oneself to office personnel. Other *in vivo* exposures involve taking the child outside the office, for example, to a graveyard, zoo, or shopping center. Many naturally occurring academic and social situations can be arranged in schools with the help of teachers and guidance personnel. Following the first successful *in vivo* situation, the child often experiences a new sense of competency and more willingly engages in other anxiety-provoking situations. Given the new set of skills that the child can call on if feeling anxious, much of the treatment encourages risk taking. In the process, the therapist is mindful to normalize anxiety, stressing that fear is a normal but manageable experience.

The following example demonstrates a representative exchange between a child and therapist as they prepare for an *in vivo* exposure (first described in Kendall et al., 1991). The child is afraid to visit new places for fear of getting lost. When taken to a shopping mall, he came up with the following plan:

THERAPIST: So are you feeling nervous now?

CHILD: I don't know. Not really.

THERAPIST: How would you know you were starting to get nervous?

CHILD: My heart would start beating faster.

THERAPIST: (*recalling a common somatic complaint for this child*) What about your breathing?

CHILD: I might start breathing faster.

THERAPIST: And what would you be thinking to yourself?

CHILD: I might get lost or I don't know where I am.

THERAPIST: And what are some things you could do if you start getting nervous?

CHILD: I could take deep breaths and say everything is going to be okay.

THERAPIST: That's good, but what if you were unsure where you were or got lost?

CHILD: I could ask somebody.

THERAPIST: Yes, you could ask somebody. Would it be a good idea to ask one of the guards or policemen? How are you feeling? Do you think you are ready to give it a try?

The therapist and child agree on a number of trips to make within the mall, varying in distance and degree of familiarity. During the trip, the child was to ask the guard for directions so that he could feel comfortable doing this in the future.

Although conducted within a supportive environment, exposure tasks are intended to be challenging and anxiety provoking. The therapist can improve chances for child participation by incorporating elements that are fun for the child when designing tasks and assignments. Situations that are typically threatening for a child can appear more manageable when livened up with creative twists. For example, a child afraid of giving a speech can pretend to give a speech after winning an Academy Award, or the therapist might arrange for a child with social phobia to visit an arcade to get change for a video game. The child overcomes a challenge of interacting with others, but the situation provides natural reinforcement. A particularly valuable exposure task is one that permits the child to engage in an activity that is ordinarily somewhat prohibited. For a child concerned about public opinion, strutting through the library singing his favorite tune is a frightening proposition. But what child would turn down the rare opportunity to create a ruckus in the library with a consenting adult nearby? The therapist adheres to the principle that the engaging and creative exposure task is the memorable and effective one (Kendall, Chu, Gifford, Hayes, & Nauta, 1998).

It is important that the therapist remain flexible in the timing and planning of *in vivo* exposures. Traditionally, the therapist plans exposures in a hierarchical fashion, progressing from easiest to hardest for the child. At times, events that occur outside the therapy call for the therapist to adjust his or her plans to take full advantage of opportunities as they present themselves. This kind of opportunity often presents itself when the child experiences a stressful situation that would have been addressed or simulated later in the exposure stage. As described in more detail in Kendall et al. (1998), the following case illustrates how a therapist can appropriately adapt his or her plans to a child's concern as it arises. In the following example, the clinician had planned to address separation issues with his 11-year-old female client, who feared her father might leave her after they argued. The clinician was aware of this issue and, because of the severity of the fear, had planned to simulate an argument between the child and father for an exposure task later in treatment. The clinician's plan was challenged when the child arrived for the 12th session panicked and visibly distraught because she had just had an argument with her father. The therapist was confronted with a choice: Should he initiate relaxation exercises and tell her to hold her concerns off until a later date, when they could systematically build up to a related exposure, or should he rearrange his plans and devise a task that would address the presenting crisis while matching the child's current level of coping skills? Appropriately, the therapist chose the latter approach.

THERAPIST: So, Belinda, you've told me a lot of ways that you think your dad is mean to you. Are there any other thoughts except "madness" that are running through your thought bubbles? Do you ever worry about what your dad might be thinking of you?

CHILD: Yeah, I guess. Yeah, sometimes I worry that he'll be more mad at me, that he won't like me. Like, I'll come home and tell him some bad things that happened to me today, and he'll say I complain too much. He says all I ever do is complain. He doesn't care what happens to me.

THERAPIST: Do you really think he doesn't care about you?

CHILD: Well, he says he doesn't want to spend time with me because I complain too much. Then he says, "Well, Belinda, if I stopped spending any time with you, then you'd learn to appreciate the time I do spend with you."

In this scenario, the child is worried that being open with her feelings will drive her father away. Previous meetings with the father confirmed that he often felt overwhelmed by his daughter's emphasis on negative events and wished they could spend more time engaging in mutually enjoyable activities. When the father felt frustrated by his daughter's complaining, he would distance himself from her. This behavior elicited fear from his daughter and led to further clinging behavior. Through a series of role plays, the therapist helps Belinda articulate her feelings while at the same time helping her to understand her father's perspective. The therapist and child alternate roles. First, Belinda acts the role of the distant father, while the therapist models appropriate ways for Belinda to express her hurt feelings. Then, the therapist and child switch roles so that Belinda is portraying herself and the therapist provides a realistic portrayal of a father who might become irritable but is unlikely to be condemning. After a number of these rehearsals, Belinda and the therapist devise a realistic plan that allows Belinda to communicate openly with her father, including discussions of both negative and positive events that occur during the day. By the end of the session, Belinda invites her father into the therapy room, proposes her plan to him, and sets up a required schedule that would reward successful interactions with him.

Because the situation arises earlier than was expected, and because separation was determined to be such a central issue for Belinda, the therapist takes special care to provide additional role-playing rehearsals and stresses relaxation exercises and reducing initial somatic arousal. Although the therapist begins to discuss alternate ways for Belinda to interpret her interactions with her father, he does not expect her to invest fully in this coping structure at this point. Rather, the therapist provides the groundwork for challenging the child's long-held beliefs and fears of rejection, and plans to revisit these issues later.

Going "Hollywood"

Our program closes with the child contributing to the creation and production of a "commercial" about his or her experiences in the program; that is, the client is asked to help put together a video, booklet, or cassette tape to help tell other children about the ways to manage anxiety. We have produced "rap" tapes and videocassettes that are both humorous and impressively informative. It is our goal to set the stage for clients to endorse the program, and make a tape, for example, gives clear evidence of our interest in their support, provides a demonstration of their success, offers a tangible reward at the end of the program, and we suspect, helps to buttress the maintenance of the treatment-produced gains.

Working with Families

We recognize the importance of parental involvement in helping the child to overcome disproportionate anxiety. Although the cognitive-behavioral nature of the program focuses on helping the individual learn to think and behave differently, we also encourage parents to participate in a supportive role. Though the child-focused treatment program described herein does not focus on "family" therapy, parents are actively involved from the outset of the child-focused protocol. For instance, unless the parental responses to inventories and structured interview lead to a diagnosis of an anxiety disorder, the child is not accepted into the program. Once treatment has begun, the therapist meets with the parents after the third session to collaborate with them on treatment plans and to solicit their cooperation. At this meeting, we provide additional information about the treatment via an outline of the program and details where the child is in the program. We give the parents an opportunity to discuss their concerns about the child and provide further information that might be helpful to the therapist. We share impressions about what specific situations provoke the child's anxiety, and how the child typically reacts. Last, we offer specific ways that the parents can become involved in the program. For example, the parents are invited to sit in on part of the child's next session so that they can help the child practice relaxation skills. Also, they are invited to call the therapist if they can think of any further information that might be helpful, or if they have any questions. Depending on the age of the child and the quality of parental support, the therapist may ask the parents to help in other specific tasks assigned to the child in upcoming weeks.

Given the important role that parents can play in their child's treatment, therapists should be aware of the particular problems that families of anxious children may be experiencing. These problems may range from increased rates of anxiety disorders, as well as other types of pathology (for a review of increased anxiety disorders among relatives of anxiety probands, see Carey & Gottesman, 1981) to particular problems in parenting, such as overprotectiveness and guilt about the problems that their children are experiencing (see also Chorpita & Barlow, 1998).

Several studies have examined rates of anxiety in the relatives of anxiety disorder probands. Strong evidence has emerged supporting a familial pattern in rates of panic disorder among relatives of individuals with this disorder (Cloninger, Martin, Clayton, & Guze, 1981; Crowe, Noyes, Pauls, & Slyman, 1983; Crowe, Pauls, Slyman, & Noyes, 1980; Harris, Noyes, Crowe, & Chaudery, 1983; Torgersen, 1983). Moreover, there is some indication that female relatives are more susceptible than males, while male relatives may have a somewhat increased rate of alcoholism (Crowe et al., 1980). Studies comparing relatives of individuals who have a broad range of anxiety disorders with those of normal controls (Noyes, Clancy, Crowe, Hoenk, & Slyman, 1978; Solyom, Beck, Solyom, & Hugel, 1974) show significantly higher rates of pathology (e.g., alcoholism, depression, and anxiety) among the relatives of the anxious probands. Children of parents with depression and panic disorder have shown higher rates of depression and anxiety, and poorer rates of adjustment than children of controls (Sylvester, Hyde, & Reichler, 1987). Furthermore, there is some evidence suggesting that different types of parental anxiety (e.g., agoraphobia vs. generalized anxiety disorder) have a varying impact on the rates of clinical diagnosis and/or receiving a CBCL score in the clinical range (Silverman, Cerny, & Nelles, 1988).

Research suggests that families with anxious children may have increased rates of pathology, yet these typically correlational studies provide little insight into what to expect when working with parents in a clinical setting. Given the dearth of research in this area, many of the following suggestions stem from our clinical work and observations. It is our experience that parental involvement with overanxious youth ranges from underinvolved, in which parents appear to be unaware of their children's problems, to extreme overprotectiveness. Underinvolvement can lead to problems with keeping appointments or helping the child to keep his or her therapy-related material organized. Parents benefit from being informed of the negative impact that this can have on therapy. Overprotectiveness can interfere with the child's performing important tasks that are designed to build his or her sense of confidence. For example, one mother of a 12-year-old girl who had suffered from cancer as a young child expressed concern when the therapist said that she and the girl were going to leave the building and go to a nearby bookstore. The parent wanted to go along! Rather than getting into a power struggle with the concerned parent, the therapist simply announced that she and the girl were going together, and kept walking out the door. When dealing with such an overprotective parent, the therapist needs to strike a delicate balance between helping the child to become more independent while at the same time not increasing the parent's own anxiety and hence risking alienation from the treatment. One tactic may be to get the parent initially involved in suggesting or participating in some of the in vivo experiences that the child will complete. This allows the parent to maintain initial involvement with the child while also encouraging the child's independent behavior, since the parent does not continue with the in vivo experiences.

The therapist may also want to point out how parents communicate their own anxiety and overprotectiveness to their child. Parents may not be aware of how their well-intentioned communications might be interpreted by their child as cues to respond with anxiety and fear. For example, in a therapy session conducted with a mother and her 12-year-old son diagnosed with social phobia, the therapist had to demonstrate how the mother's messages about embarrassment in social situations were contributing to the child's fear of social situations. The child's self-reported goals for treatment were to make new friends and become more comfortable speaking to unfamiliar people. The child's coexisting diagnosis of expressive–receptive learning disability meant that he had real concerns about understanding and being understood by other children, which compounded his fears of talking to others.

Observing that the child was not ready for a social exposure task, the therapist chose an intermediate approach. As a STIC task, she suggested that the child begin acclimating to social environments by riding his bicycle around the neighborhood to get used to the idea of seeing unfamiliar children. The therapist recommended that the child not engage in any interactions, but simply ride down the block. Before he could respond, the mother interjected, "But if you ride down the street without saying anything, won't the other kids see you and think you're rude?" Although the parent's question was intended to help the child consider the consequences of his actions, the therapist pointed out that there are better ways to communicate this. The therapist recommended that instead of interjecting her own fears about possible negative outcomes, she might ask the child what he thought might happen and discuss the situation within a problem-solving framework.

Parents of anxious children may also express guilt about the child's anxiety. Helping them to cope with these feelings may involve a pragmatic discussion, suggesting that how the problem developed is not the issue; rather, it is important to focus on how they can contribute to helping their child cope at the present time. If the parent's own anxiety or other problems appear to be genuinely contributing to the child's anxiety, it is discussed with the parent. Such a discussion may involve observations and suggestions about how to change the "parent–child" interaction, and even recommendations for the parent's own treatment. More specifically, it may be helpful to find out what kinds of expectations the parents hold for their children—both academically and behaviorally. For instance, are they over-concerned with academic performance and therefore placing a lot of pressure on their child to achieve? Parents may also have inaccurate expectations about what is appropriate behavior given their child's developmental level. Helping parents to clarify what is and is not within the normal range of behavior may prevent inappropriate and anxiety-provoking responses to their child's normal behavior. Finally, it is important to help parents learn new ways of responding to their child's anxious behavior. The stress of dealing with an anxious child may lead parents to become sensitized to any signs of anxiety in their children. They may be hypervigilant and strongly react to any indication of anxiety, for example, by becoming anxious themselves or depressed when they feel helpless about what to do.

One therapist videotaped her session with an 8-year-old boy and his mother to make a dramatic point about the parent's hypervigilance around her son's somatic complaints and school-refusal behavior. Minutes before the child was to depart for school or other extracurricular activities, he would begin reporting a variety of physical symptoms, including stomach cramps, headaches, and diarrhea, and would claim he had to use the bathroom. In response to the child's complaints, the mother would ask a series of questions to assess the extent of his physical distress: "What's the matter?" "Does your throat hurt?" "Do your ears hurt?" "Are you going to be sick?" Once the mother began showing concern, the child's report of somatic symptoms would escalate until he became nearly incapacitated with pain, sickness, or fear. The therapist used the videotaping to demonstrate how the mother's questions contributed to the escalation of her child's physical symptoms. Presented with this evidence, the mother was able to see how her demonstrations of concern could actually contribute to her son's reported symptoms of distress. The mother admitted that she had believed she was "making it worse" in some way but was unaware of how or where the cycle began. Such demonstrations, if provided in a nonaccusatory, nonjudgmental manner, can provide parents with concrete information that helps explain current interactional patterns and gives direction for behavioral change.

Given the important role that parents play in the success of child-focused treatment for childhood anxiety disorders, and given the hypothesized roles family members may play in the genesis and maintenance of anxiety disorders, it should not be surprising that, in addition to the child-focused intervention, we have also developed a family intervention. The same strategies are employed, but the sessions include parental participation. A manual describing this program is available (Howard, Chu, Krain, Marrs-Garcia, & Kendall, 2000). Initial research has been conducted with family-focused cognitive-behavioral format (Howard & Kendall, 1996a). As discussed in greater detail later, Barrett, Dadds, and Rapee (1996) have implemented a family management component (i.e., affective education, contingent reinforcement schedules, and management of parental anxiety) for the families of anxious children and have reported positive results. We encourage the continued development of family-focused intervention and support models that target the interactive influence of family members.

For example, treatment for a separation-anxious child might address the child's need for greater independence by working on age-appropriate problem-solving or assertiveness skills in situations in which he or she may have previously unnecessarily relied on a parent, and concurrently examine and correct (testing out *in vivo*) parents' misperceptions of their child's competencies or equating good parenting with being overinvolved. One can imagine that without coordinating efforts between parents and children, a child's gains toward greater independence and management of fears may be mislabeled as disobedience or contribute to sadness in parents because they misattribute this change to their no longer being needed. Such responses could threaten the maintenance of the child's gains. By coordinating efforts, the new behavior in the child is concomitant with new beliefs or expectancies in the parents. Inversely, a parent's acquisition of new coping skills and overt behaviors, such as going to work rather than sleeping all day, will be coupled with the child's new attributions of strength to the parent and less fear for his or her safety. Although cognitive-behavioral treatment strategies for families are incorporated into our clinical research and practice, there remains the great need for empirical evaluation of when it is best to include, or not include, parents in the treatment of anxiety disorders in children and adolescents.

Research Outcomes

The American Psychological Association (APA) Task Force on Promotion and Dissemination of Psychological Procedures (1995) has provided guidelines for what should be considered "well-established," "probably efficacious," and "experimental" treatments (see also Chambless & Hollon, 1998). For a treatment to be considered efficacious, it must be shown to be more effective than a control (i.e., no treatment) in randomized clinical trials conducted by independent researchers. A recent review of empirically supported treatments for children with anxiety disorders (Ollendick & King, 1998) concluded that behavioral and cognitive-behavioral procedures represent the modalities that have received the most empirical support. For treating phobias, behavioral techniques—including imaginal and *in vivo* desensitization; live, filmed and participant modeling; as well as contingency management strategies—were granted "probably efficacious" or "well-established" status. For treating other anxiety disorders, cognitive-behavioral procedures with and without family anxiety management were deemed "probably efficacious."

Building upon a base of promising results from single-case design studies (e.g., Eisen & Silverman, 1993; Kane & Kendall, 1989; Ollendick, 1995), three randomized clinical trials conducted by two different research groups using cognitive-behavioral techniques constitute the weight of the evidence upon which these labels were applied (Kendall, 1994; Kendall et al., 1997; Barrett et al., 1996). Kendall (1994) conducted the first randomized clinical trial aimed at investigating the efficacy of cognitive-behavioral treatment (CBT) for 9- to 13-year-old youth with anxiety disorder. In the trial comparing a manual-based CBT to a wait-list control, 64% of children treated did not receive their principal anxiety disorder diagnosis at posttreatment and maintained their treatment gains at 1-year follow-up (Kendall, 1994). Longer-term follow-up assessments documented that the gains were maintained over a 2- to 5-year period (mean of 3.35 years) (Kendall & Southam-Gerow, 1996). The efficacy of this procedure was replicated in a second randomized trial with ninety-four 9- to 13-year-olds diagnosed with a primary anxiety disorder and randomly assigned to CBT and wait-list control (Kendall et al., 1997). At posttreatment, there were positive outcomes on a variety of measures for children in the treatment group over those in the wait-list control. These treatment gains were maintained and evident at 1-year follow-up (Kendall et al., 1997).

Several researchers have noted the need for additional involvement of parents/family in the treatment of childhood anxiety disorders (e.g., Dadds, 1995; Siqueland & Diamond, 1998). Adding a family management component to individual child CBT has produced encouraging results in clinical trials. Barrett, Dadds, and Rapee (1996) compared a CBT intervention based on Kendall's (1992b) program to an intervention that included the CBT intervention plus a family intervention (FAM). Seventy-nine 7- to 14-year-old children who met a primary diagnosis of overanxious disorder, separation anxiety disorder, or social phobia were included and randomly assigned to a CBT group, a CBT + FAM, or wait list control. All conditions lasted 12 weeks. The CBT condition paralleled that of Kendall (1994), whereas the CBT + FAM included a Family Anxiety Management component wherein parents were trained in contingency management strategies and communication and problem-solving skills, and taught to recognize and address their own emotional and anxious responses to stimuli. Sixty percent of both treatment conditions achieved a nondiagnosis status, compared to less than 30% of the wait-list control children. At the 12-month follow-up, no-diagnosis rates were 70% for the CBT and 95% for the CBT + FAM intervention groups. Other supportive data, using related intervention strategies, have also been reported (e.g., Last, Hansen, & Franco, 1998; Nauta, 1999; Silverman et al., 1999).

Based on this evidence and on the criteria put forth by the APA Task Force (1995) and Chambless and Hollon (1998), CBT for children with anxiety can be considered a "probably efficacious" treatment (see also Ollendick & King, 1998; Kazdin & Weisz, 1998). In light of the considerably significant positive results of the CBT + FAM condition, family components of cognitive-behavioral therapy deserve further attention and research efforts.

An interesting direction being explored in the area of cognitive-behavioral treatment for anxiety disordered youth is in prevention and early intervention for "at-risk" children and adolescents. The work of one group (Dadds et al., 1997; Dadds, Spence, Holland, Barrett, & Laurens, 1999) has provided preliminary evidence for the effectiveness of cognitive-behavioral and family-based group treatment for the prevention of anxiety in children and adolescents at risk for anxiety disorders. The Queensland Early Intervention and Prevention of Anxiety Project used a school-based screening procedure to identify children at risk for later anxiety disorders and then offered cognitive-behavioral skills training to children and parents. Educational sessions focusing on family involvement and parents managing their own anxious symptomatology were included. Both intervention and monitored groups showed improvements immediately at postintervention; however, at 6-month follow-up, only the intervention group maintained improvements, showing a reduced rate of existing anxiety disorder and preventing the onset of new anxiety disorders. At 12 months, the groups converged, but the superiority of the intervention group was evident again at 2-year follow-up (Dadds et al., 1999). Although prevention efforts are in their preliminary stages, such findings merit further investigation.

ACKNOWLEDGMENTS

Portions of the work reported here were supported by a research grant from the National Institute of Mental Health. We wish to acknowledge and to thank the authors of the chapter on this topic that appeared in the first edition of this book. As before, the effort was collaborative and reflects the input of each author, as well as the groundwork provided by the authors of the chapter in the first edition.

NOTES

1. Other childhood disorders, such as posttraumatic stress disorder (PTSD) and obsessive–compulsive disorder (OCD) also have anxiety as part of the central presenting problem. However, there are important differences, suggesting that PTSD and OCD require their own focused interventions. Readers interested in OCD, for example, should see Henin and Kendall (1997), Piacentini, Gitrow, Jaffer, Graae, and Whitaker (1994), and March (1995).
2. Readers interested in foreign-language translations of the treatment manuals or the *Coping Cat Workbook* should contact the publisher, Workbook Publishing, Ardmore, Pennsylvania (phone: 610-896-9797; fax: 610-896-1955). Readers interested in adaptations and applications in other countries or languages should consult the following resources: Kendall and DePietro (1995; in Italian, Italy); Masayi Ichii, University of the Ryukyus, Okinawa, Japan; Barrett, Dadds, and Rapee (e.g., 1996; in English, Australia); John Weisz and Michael Southam-Gerow, University of California at Los Angeles, for a Spanish version used in Los Angeles; Claire Hayes, University of Dublin, Ireland; Maaki Nauta, University of Groningen, the Netherlands; Susan Bogels, University of Maastricht, the Netherlands; Dominiek Bracke and Caroline Braet, University of Ghent, Belgium; Sandra Mendlowitz et al. (1999), Hospital for Sick Children, Toronto, Canada. Readers interested in prevention should see the report of Dadds et al. (1997) or consider the ongoing work of Dena Hirshfeld, Harvard/Massachusetts General Hospital, Boston.

REFERENCES

Achenbach, T. M. (1991). *Integrative guide for the 1991 CBCL/4-18, YSR, and TRF.* Burlington: University of Vermont.

Achenbach, T. M. (1993). Implications of multiaxial empirically based assessment for behavior therapy with children. *Behavior Therapy, 24,* 91–116.

Achenbach, T., & Edelbrock, C. (1986). *Manual for the TRF and the Child Behavior Profile.* Burlington: University of Vermont

Achenbach, T. M., & Edelbrock, C. S. (1978). The classification of child psychology: A review and analysis if empirical efforts. *Psychological Bulletin, 85,* 1275–1301.

Achenbach, T. M., & Edelbrock, C. S. (1983). *Manual for the Child Behavior Checklist and Revised Child Behavior Profile.* Burlington: University of Vermont, Associates in Psychiatry.

Achenbach, T. M., & McConaughy, S. H. (1992). Taxonomy of internalizing disorders of childhood and adolescence. In W. M. Reynolds (Ed.), *Internalizing disorders in children and adolescents* (pp. 19–60). New York: Wiley.

Achenbach, T. M., McConaughy, S. H., & Howell, C. T. (1987). Child/adolescent behavioral and emotional problems: Implications of cross-informant correlations for situational specificity. *Psychological Bulletin, 101,* 213–232.

Albano, A. M., Chorpita, B. F., & Barlow, D. H. (1996). Childhood anxiety disorders. In E. J. Mash & R. A. Barkley (Eds.), *Child psychopathology* (pp. 196–241). New York: Guilford Press.

American Academy of Child and Adolescent Psychiatry. (1993). AACAP official action: Practice parameters for the assessment and treatment of anxiety disorders. *Journal of the American Academy of Child and Adolescent Psychiatry, 34,* 976–986.

American Psychiatric Association. (1987). *Diagnostic and statistical manual of mental disorders* (3rd ed., rev.). Washington, DC: Author.

American Psychiatric Association. (1994). *Diagnostic and statistical manual of mental disorders* (4th ed.). Washington, DC: Author.

American Psychological Association Task Force on Promotion and Dissemination of Psychological Procedures. (1995). Training in and dissemination of empirically-validated psychological treatments: Report and recommendations. *Clinical Psychologist, 48,* 3–24.

Anderson, J. C. (1994). Epidemiological issues. In T. H. Ollendick, N. J. King, & W. Yule (Eds.), *International handbook of phobic and anxiety disorders in children and adolescents* (pp. 43–65). New York: Plenum Press.

Arnow, B. A., Taylor, C. B., Agras, W. S., & Telch, M. H. (1985). Enhancing agoraphobia treatment outcome by changing couple communication patterns. *Behavior Therapy, 16,* 452–467.

Ayllon, T., Smith, D., & Rogers, M. (1970). Behavioral management of school phobia. *Journal of Behavior Therapy and Experimental Psychiatry, 1,* 125–138.

Bandura, A. (1969). *Principles of behavior modification.* New York: Holt, Rinehart & Winston.

Bandura, A. (1986). *Social learning theory.* Englewood Cliffs, NJ: Prentice-Hall.

Barabasz, A. F. (1973). Group desensitization of test anxiety in elementary school. *Journal of Psychology, 83,* 295–301.

Barlow, D. (1992). Diagnosis, DSM-IV, and dimensional approaches. In A. Ehlers, W. Fiegenbaum, I. Florin, & J. Margraf (Eds.), *Perspectives and promises of clinical psychology* (pp. 13–21). New York: Plenum Press.

Barlow, D., & Wolfe, B. E. (1981). Behavioral approaches to anxiety disorders: A report on the NIMH-SUNY, Albany, Research Conference. *Journal of Consulting and Clinical Psychology, 49,* 448–454.

Barrett, P. M., Dadds, M. R., & Rapee, R. M. (1996). Family treatment of childhood anxiety: A controlled trial. *Journal of Consulting and Clinical Psychology, 64,* 333–342.

Barrett, P. M., Rapee, R. M., Dadds, M. M., & Ryan, S. M. (1996). Family enhancement of cognitive style in anxious and aggressive children. *Journal of Abnormal Child Psychology, 24,* 187–203.

Barrios, B. A., & Hartmann, D. B. (1988). Fears and anxieties. In E. J. Mash & L. G. Terdal (Eds.), *Behavioral assessment of childhood disorders* (2nd ed., pp. 196–264). New York: Guilford Press.

Bauer, D. (1976). An exploratory study of developmental changes in children's fears. *Journal of Child Psychology and Psychiatry, 17,* 69–74.

Beidel, D. C. (1988). Psychophysiological assessment of anxious emotional states in children. *Journal of Abnormal Psychology, 97,* 80–82.

Beidel, D. C. (1989). Assessing anxious emotion: A review of psychophysiological assessment in children. *Clinical Psychology Review, 9,* 717–736.

Beidel, D. C., Fink, C., & Turner, S. (1996). Stability of anxious symptomatology in children. *Journal of Abnormal Child Psychology, 24,* 257–269.

Beidel, D. C., Turner, S. M., & Morris, T. (1995). A new inventory to assess childhood social anxiety and phobia: The Social Phobia and Anxiety Inventory for Children. *Psychological Assessment, 7,* 73–79.

Bernstein, G. A. (1991). Comorbidity and severity of anxiety and depressive disorders in a clinic sample. *Journal of the American Academy of Child and Adolescent Psychiatry, 30,* 43–50.

Bernstein, G. A., & Borchardt, C. M. (1991). Anxiety disorders of childhood and adolescence: A critical review. *Journal of the American Academy of Child and Adolescent Psychiatry, 30,* 519–532.

Bernstein, G. A., Borchardt, C. M., & Perwein, A. R. (1996). Anxiety disorders in children and adolescents: A review of the past 10 years. *Journal of the American Academy of Child and Adolescent Psychiatry, 35,* 1110–1119.

Bierman, K. L. (1984). Cognitive development and clinical interviews with children. In B. B. Lahey & A. E. Kazdin (Eds.), *Advances in clinical child psychology* (Vol. 6, pp. 217–250). New York: Plenum Press.

Brady, E., & Kendall, P. C. (1992). Comorbidity of anxiety and depression in children and adolescents. *Psychological Bulletin, 111,* 244–255.

Campbell, S. B. (1986). Developmental issues. In R. Gittelman (Ed.), *Anxiety disorders of childhood* (pp. 24–57). New York: Guilford Press.

Carey, G., & Gottesman, I. (1981). Twin and family studies of anxiety, phobic, and obsessive disorders. In D. F. Klein & J. Rabkin (Eds.), *Anxiety: New research and changing concepts* (pp. 117–133). New York: Raven Press.

Chambers, W. J., Puig-Antich, J., Hirsch, M., Paez, P., Ambrosini, P. J., Tabrizi, M. A., & Davies, M. (1985). The assessment of affective disorders in children and adolescents by semi-structured interview. *Archives of General Psychiatry, 42,* 696–702.

Chambless, D., & Hollon, S. (1998). Defining empirically supported treatments. *Journal of Consulting and Clinical Psychology, 66,* 5–17.

Chorpita, B., & Barlow, D. (1998). The development of anxiety: The role of control in the early environment. *Psychology Bulletin, 124,* 3–21.

Chorpita, B. F., Brown, T. A., & Barlow, D. H. (1998). Perceived control as a mediator of family environment in etiological models of childhood anxiety. *Behavior Therapy, 29,* 457–476.

Cloninger, C. R., Martin, R. L., Clayton, P., & Guze, S. B. (1981). A blind follow-up and family study of anxiety neurosis: Preliminary analysis of the St. Louis 500. In D. F. Klein & J. Rabkin (Eds.), *Anxiety: New research and changing concepts* (pp. 137–148). New York: Raven Press.

Crowe, R. R., Noyes, R., Pauls, D. L., & Slyman, D. (1983). A family study of panic disorder. *Archives of General Psychiatry, 40,* 1065–1069.

Crowe, R. R., Pauls, D. L., Slyman, D. J., & Noyes, R. (1980). A family study of anxiety neurosis. *Archives of General Psychiatry, 37,* 77–79.

Dadds, M. (1995). *Families, children and the development of dysfunction.* London: Sage.

Dadds, M., Heard, P., & Rapee, R. (1991). Anxiety disorders in children. *International Review of Psychiatry, 3,* 231–241.

Dadds, M. R., Holland, D. E., Laurens, K. R., Mullins, K. R., Barrett, P. M., & Spence, S. H. (1999). Early intervention and prevention of anxiety disorders in children: Results at 2-year follow-up. *Journal of Consulting and Clinical Psychology, 67,* 145–150.

Dadds, M. R., Spence, S. H., Holland, D., Barrett, P. M., & Laurens, K. (1997). Early intervention and prevention of anxiety disorders: A controlled trial. *Journal of Consulting and Clinical Psychology, 65,* 627–635.

Daleiden, E., & Vasey, M. W. (1997). An information-processing perspective on childhood anxiety. *Clinical Psychology Review, 17,* 407–429.

Dong, Q., Yang, B., & Ollendick, T. H. (1994). Fears in Chinese children and adolescents and their relations to anxiety and depression. *Journal of Child Psychology and Psychiatry, 35,* 351–363.

Draper, T. W., & James, R. S. (1985). Preschool fears: Longitudinal sequence and cohort changes. *Child Study Journal, 15,* 147–155.

Dweck, C., & Wortman, C. (1982). Learned helplessness, anxiety, and achievement. In H. Krone & L. Laux (Eds.), *Achievement, stress and anxiety* (pp. 93–125). New York: Hemisphere.

D'Zurilla, T. J., & Goldfried, M. R. (1971). Problem-solving and behavior modification. *Journal of Abnormal Psychology, 78,* 107–126.

D'Zurilla, T., & Nezu, A. M. (1999). *Problem-solving therapy: A social competence approach to clinical intervention* (2nd ed.). New York: Springer.

Edelbrock, C., Costello, A. J., Duncan, M. K., Conover, N. C., & Kalas, R. (1986). Parent–child agreement on child psychiatric symptoms assessed via structured interview. *Journal of Child Psychology and Psychiatry, 27,* 181–190.

Edelbrock, C., Costello, A. J., Duncan, M. K., Kalas, R., & Conover, N. C. (1985). Age differences in the reliability of the psychiatric interview of the child. *Child Development, 56,* 265–275.

Eisen, A. R., & Silverman, W. K. (1993). Should I relax or change my thoughts? A preliminary examination of cognitive therapy, relaxation training, and their combination with overanxious children. *Journal of Cognitive Psychotherapy: An International Quarterly, 7,* 265–279.

Epstein, N., Baldwin, L., & Bishop, D. (1983). The McMaster Family Assessment Device. *Journal of Marital and Family Therapy, 9,* 171–180.

Fauber, R. L., & Long, N. (1991). Children in context: The role of the family in child psychotherapy. *Journal of Consulting and Clinical Psychology, 59,* 813–820.

Flannery-Schroeder, E., & Kendall, P. C. (1996). *Cognitive-behavioral therapy for anxious children: Therapist manual for group treatment.* Ardmore, PA: Workbook Publishing.

Fonseca, A. C., Yule, W., & Erol, N. (1994). Cross-cultural issues. In T. H. Ollendick, N. J. King, & W. Yule (Eds.), *International handbook of phobic and anxiety disorders in children and adolescents* (pp. 67–84). New York: Plenum Press.

Francis, G., & Beidel, D. (1995). Cognitive-behavioral psychotherapy. In J. S. March (Ed.), *Anxiety disorders in children and adolescents* (pp. 321–340). New York: Guilford Press.

Francis, G., & Ollendick, T. (1990). Behavioral treatment of social anxiety. In E. L. Feindler, & G. R. Kalfus (Eds.), *Casebook in adolescent behavior therapy* (pp. 127–146). New York: Springer.

Frick, P. J., Silverthorn, P., & Evans, C. (1994). Assessment of childhood anxiety using structured interviews: Patterns of agreement among informants and association with maternal anxiety. *Psychological Assessment, 6,* 372–379.

Friedman, A. G., & Ollendick, T. H. (1989). Treatment programs for severe nighttime fears: A methodological note. *Journal of Behavior Therapy and Experimental Psychiatry, 20,* 171–178.

Ginsburg, G., & Silverman, W. (1996). Phobic and anxiety disorders in Hispanic and Caucasian youth. *Journal of Anxiety Disorders, 10,* 517–528.

Ginsburg, G. S., La Greca, A. M., & Silverman, W. K. (1998). Social anxiety in children with anxiety disorders: Relation with social and emotional functioning. *Journal of Abnormal Child Psychology, 26,* 175–185.

Ginsburg, G. S., Silverman, W. K., & Kurtines, W. K. (1995). Family involvement in treating children with phobic and anxiety disorders: A look ahead. *Clinical Psychology Review, 15,* 457–473.

Gittelman, R. (Ed.). (1986). *Anxiety disorders of childhood.* New York: Guilford Press.

Graziano, A. M., & Mooney, K. C. (1980). Family self-control instruction for children's nighttime fear reduction. *Journal of Consulting and Clinical Psychology, 48,* 206–213.

Graziano, A. M., & Mooney, K. C. (1982). Behavioral treatment of "Nightfears" in children: Maintenance of improvement at 2½- to 3-year follow-up. *Journal of Consulting and Clinical Psychology, 50,* 598–599.

Hagopian, L. P., Weist, M. D., & Ollendick, T. H. (1990). Cognitive-behavior therapy with an 11-year-old girl fearful of AIDS infection, other diseases, and poisoning: A case study. *Journal of Anxiety Disorders, 4,* 257–265.

Harris, E. L., Noyes, R., Crowe, R. R., & Chaudery, M. D. (1983). A family study of agoraphobia. *Archives of General Psychiatry, 40,* 1061–1064.

Henin, A., & Kendall, P. C. (1997). Obsessive–compulsive disorder in childhood and adolescence. In T. Ollendick & R. Prinz (Eds.), *Advances in clinical child psychology* (Vol. 19, pp. 75–118). New York: Plenum Press.

Herjanic, B., Herjanic, M., Brown, F., & Wheatt, T. (1975). Are children reliable reporters? *Journal of Abnormal Child Psychology, 1,* 41–48.

Herjanic, B., & Reich, W. (1982). Development of a structured psychiatric interview for children: Agreement between child and parent on individual symptoms. *Journal of Abnormal Child Psychology, 10,* 307–324.

Himadi, W. G., Boice, R., & Barlow, D. H. (1985). Assessment of agoraphobia: Triple response measurement. *Behaviour Research and Therapy, 23,* 311–323.

Hodges, K., McKnew, C., Burbach, D. J., & Roebuck, L. (1987). Diagnostic concordance between the Child Assessment Schedule and the Schedule for Affective Disorders and Schizophrenia for School-age Children in an outpatient sample using lay interviewers. *Journal of the American Academy of Child and Adolescent Psychiatry, 26,* 654–661.

Howard, B. L., Chu, B., Krain, A., Marrs-Garcia, A., & Kendall, P. C. (2000). *Cognitive-behavioral family therapy for anxious children: Therapist manual* (2nd ed.). Ardmore, PA: Workbook Publishing.

Howard, B. L., & Kendall, P. C. (1996a). Cognitive-behavioral family therapy for anxiety disordered children: A multiple baseline evaluation. *Cognitive Therapy and Research, 20,* 423–443.

Howard, B. L., & Kendall, P. C. (1996b). *Cognitive-behavioral therapy for anxious children: Therapist manual.* Ardmore, PA: Workbook Publishing.

Ingram, R. E., & Kendall, P. C. (1986). Cognitive clinical psychology: Implications of an information processing perspective. In R. E. Ingram (Ed.), *Information processing approaches to clinical psychology* (pp. 3–21). New York: Academic Press.

Ingram, R. E., & Kendall, P. C. (1987). The cognitive side of anxiety. *Cognitive Therapy and Research, 11,* 523–537.

Ingram, R. E., Kendall, P. C., & Chen, A. H. (1991). Cognitive-behavioral interventions. In C. R. Snyder & D. R. Forsyth (Eds.), *Handbook of social and clinical psychology: The health perspective* (pp. 509–522). New York: Pergamon Press.

Jannoun, L., Munby, M., Catalan, J., & Gelder, M. (1980). A home-based treatment program for agoraphobia: Replication and controlled evaluation. *Behavior Therapy, 11,* 294–305.

Kane, M., & Kendall, P. C. (1989). Anxiety disorders in children: A multiple baseline evaluation of a cognitive-behavioral treatment. *Behavior Therapy, 20,* 499–508.

Kashani, J. H., & Orvaschel, H. (1988). Anxiety disorders in mid-adolescence: A community sample. *American Journal of Psychiatry, 145,* 960–964.

Kazdin, A., & Weisz, J. (1998). Identifying and developing empirically supported child and adolescent treatments. *Journal of Consulting and Clinical Psychology, 66,* 100–110.

Kendall, P. C. (1984). Behavioral assessment and methodology. In G. T. Wilson, C. M. Franks, K. D. Brownell, & P. C. Kendall, *Annual review of behavior therapy: Theory and practice* (Vol. 9, pp. 39–94). New York: Guilford Press.

Kendall, P. C. (1985). Toward a cognitive-behavioral model of child psychopathology and a critique of related interventions. *Journal of Abnormal Child Psychology, 13,* 357–372.

Kendall, P. C. (1991). Guiding theory for treating children and adolescents. In P. C. Kendall (Ed.), *Child and adolescent therapy: Cognitive-behavioral procedures* (pp. 3–24). New York: Guilford Press.

Kendall, P. C. (1992a). Childhood coping: Avoiding a lifetime of anxiety. *Behavioral Change, 9,* 1–8.

Kendall, P. C. (1992b). *Coping cat workbook.* Ardmore, PA: Workbook Publishing.

Kendall, P. C. (1994). Treating anxiety disorders in children: Results of a randomized clinical trial. *Journal of Consulting and Clinical Psychology, 62,* 100–110.

Kendall, P. C. (2000). *Childhood disorders.* London: Psychology Press.

Kendall, P. C., & Brady, E. U. (1995). Comorbidity in the anxiety disorders of childhood. In K. D. Craig & K. S. Dobson (Eds.), *Anxiety and depression in adults and children* (pp. 3–34). Newbury Park, CA: Sage.

Kendall, P. C., Chu, B., Gifford, A., Hayes, C., & Nauta, M. (1998). Breathing life into a manual: Flexibility and creativity with manual-based treatments. *Cognitive and Behavioral Practice, 5,* 177–198.

Kendall, P. C., & DiPietro, M. (1995). *Terapia scolastica dell'ansia: Guida per psicologi e insegnanti.* Trento, Italy: Edizioni Erickson.

Kendall, P. C., & Flannery-Schroeder, E. C. (1998). Methodological issues in treatment research for anxiety disorders in youth. *Journal of Abnormal Child Psychology, 26*(1), 27–38.

Kendall, P. C., Flannery-Schroeder, E., Panichelli-Mindel, S., Southam-Gerow, M., Henin, A., & Warman, M. (1997). Therapy for youth with anxiety disorders: A second randomized clinical trial. *Journal of Consulting and Clinical Psychology, 65,* 366–380.

Kendall, P. C., Henin, A., MacDonald, J. P., & Treadwell, K. R. II. (1999). *Parent ratings of anxiety in children: Development and validation of the CBCL-A.* Manuscript submitted for publication.

Kendall, P. C., Howard, B. L., & Epps, J. (1988). The anxious child: Cognitive-behavioral treatment strategies. *Behavior Modification, 12,* 281–310.

Kendall, P. C., & Ingram, R. (1987). The future of cognitive assessment of anxiety: Let's get specific. In L. Michelson & M. Ascher (Eds.), *Anxiety and stress disorders: Cognitive-behavioral assessment and treatment* (pp. 89–104). New York: Guilford Press.

Kendall, P. C., & Ingram, R. (1989). Cognitive-behavioral perspectives: Theory and research on depression and anxiety. In P. C. Kendall & D. Watson (Eds.), *Anxiety and depression: Distinction and overlapping features* (pp. 27–54). New York: Academic Press.

Kendall, P. C., Kane, M., Howard, B., & Siqueland, L. (1989). *Cognitive behavioral therapy for anxious children: Treatment manual.* Available from Kendall, Department of Psychology, Temple University, Philadelphia, PA 19122.

Kendall, P. C., Kortlander, E., Chansky, T., & Brady, E. (1992). Comorbidity of anxiety and depression in youth: Treatment implications. *Journal of Consulting and Clinical Psychology, 60,* 869–880.

Kendall, P. C., & Marrs-Garcia, A. (1999). *Psychometric analyses of a therapy-sensitive measure: The Coping Questionnaire (CQ).* Manuscript submitted for publication.

Kendall, P. C., Marrs-Garcia, A., Nath, S., & Sheldrick, R. C. (1999). Normative comparisons for the evaluation of clinical significance. *Journal of Consulting and Clinical Psychology, 67,* 285–299.

Kendall, P. C., Pellegrini, D., & Urbain, E. (1981). Assessment strategies for cognitive-behavioral procedure with children. In P. C. Kendall & S. D. Hollon (Eds.), *Assessment strategies for cognitive-behavioral interventions* (pp. 227–286). New York: Academic Press.

Kendall, P. C., & Ronan, K. R. (1990). Assessment of childhood anxieties, fears, and phobias: Cognitive-behavioral models and methods. In C. R. Reynolds & R. W. Kamphaus (Eds.), *Handbook of psychological and educational assessment of children: Personality, behavior, and context* (pp. 223–244). New York: Guilford Press.

Kendall, P., & Southam-Gerow, M. (1996). Long-term follow-up of treatment for anxiety disordered youth. *Journal of Consulting and Clinical Psychology, 65,* 883–888.

Kendall, P. C., & Warman, M. (1996). Anxiety disorders in youth: Diagnostic consistency across DSM-III-R and DSM-IV. *Journal of Anxiety Disorders, 10,* 452–463.

Kendall, P., & Watson, D. (Eds.). (1989). *Anxiety and depression: Distinctive and overlapping features.* New York: Academic Press.

King, N. J., Hamilton, D. I., & Ollendick, T. H. (1988). *Children's phobias: A behavioral perspective.* London: Wiley.

Klein, R. G. (1991). Parent–child agreement in clinical assessment of anxiety and other psychopathology: A review. *Journal of Anxiety Disorders, 5,* 187–198.

Kleiner, L., Marshall, W. L., & Spevack, M. (1987). Training in problem-solving and exposure treatment for agoraphobics with panic attacks. *Journal of Anxiety Disorders, 1,* 219–238.

Koeppen, A. S. (1974). Relaxation training for children. *Elementary School Guidance and Counseling, 9,* 12–21.

Kondas, O. (1967). Reduction of examination anxiety and "stage fright" by group desensitization and relaxation. *Behaviour Research and Therapy, 5,* 275–281.

Kortlander, E., Kendall, P. C., & Panichelli-Mindel, S. M. (1997). Maternal expectations and attributions about coping in anxious children. *Journal of Anxiety Disorders, 11,* 297–315.

Krain, A. L., & Kendall, P. C. (in press). The role of parental emotional distress in parent report of child anxiety. *Journal of Clinical Child Psychology.*

Krohne, H. W., & Hock, M. (1991). Relationships between restrictive mother–child interaction and anxiety of the child. *Anxiety Research, 4,* 109–124.

Kuroda, J. (1969). Elimination of children's fears of animals by the method of experimental desensitization: An application of learning theory to child psychology. *Psychologia, 12,* 161–165.

Lang, P. J. (1968). Fear reduction and fear behavior: Problems in treating a construct. In J. M. Shlien (Ed.), *Research in psychotherapy.* Washington, DC: American Psychological Association.

Last, C., Hansen, C., & Franco, N. (1998). Cognitive-behavioral treatment of school-phobia. *Journal of the American Academy of Child and Adolescent Psychiatry, 37,* 404–411.

Last, C., Hersen, M., Kazdin, A., Francis, G., & Grubb, H. (1987). Disorders in mothers of anxious children. *American Journal of Psychiatry, 144,* 1580–1583.

Last, C., Phillips, J. E., & Statfield, A. (1987). Childhood anxiety disorders in mothers and their children. *Child Psychiatry and Human Development, 18,* 103–117.

Last, C. L., Strauss, C. C., & Francis, G. (1987). Comorbidity among childhood anxiety disorders. *Journal of Nervous and Mental Disease, 175,* 726–730.

Leitenberg, H., & Callahan, E. J. (1973). Reinforced practice and reduction of different kinds of fears in adults and children. *Behaviour Research and Therapy, 11,* 19–30.

Lewis, S. A. (1974). A comparison of behavior therapy techniques in the reduction of fearful avoidance behaviors. *Behavior Therapy, 5,* 648–655.

Mann, J., & Rosenthal, T. L. (1969). Vicarious and direct counter-conditioning of test anxiety through individual and group desensitization. *Behaviour Research and Therapy, 7,* 359–367.

Mansdorf, I. J., & Lukens, E. (1987). Cognitive-behavioral psychotherapy for separation anxious children exhibiting school phobia. *Journal of the American Academy of Child and Adolescent Psychiatry, 26,* 222–225.

March, J. S. (1995). Cognitive-behavioral psychotherapy for children and adolescents with obsessive–compulsive disorder: A review and recommendations for treatment. *Journal of the American Academy of Child and Adolescent Psychiatry, 43,* 7–18.

March, J. S., & Albano, A. M. (1998). New developments in assessing pediatric anxiety disorders. In T. Ollendick & P. Prinz (Eds.), *Advances in clinical child psychology* (Vol. 20, pp. 213–242). New York: Plenum Press.

March, J. S., Parker, J., Sullivan, K., Stallings, P., & Conners, C. (1997). The Multidimensional Anxiety Scale for Children (MASC): Factor structure, reliability and validity. *Journal of the American Academy of Child and Adolescent Psychiatry, 36,* 554–565.

Marks, I. M. (1975). Behavioral treatments of phobic and obsessive–compulsive disorders: A critical appraisal. In M. Hersen, R. M., Eisler, & P. M. Miller (Eds.), *Progress in behavior modification* (pp. 65–158). New York: Academic Press.

Melamed, B. G., & Siegel, L. J. (1975). Reduction of anxiety in children facing hospitalization and surgery by way of filmed modeling. *Journal of Consulting and Clinical Psychology, 43,* 511–521.

Mendlowitz, A., Manassis, K., Bradley, S., Scapillato, D., Mienzitis, S., & Shaw, B. (1999). Cognitive-behavioral group treatments in childhood anxiety disorders: The role of parental involvement. *Journal of the American Academy of Child and Adolescent Psychiatry, 38*, 1223–1229.

Menzies, R. G., & Clarke, J. C. (1993). A comparison of *in vivo* and vicarious exposure in the treatment of childhood water phobia. *Behaviour Research and Therapy, 31*, 9–15.

Miller, L. C., Barrett, C. L., Hampe, E., & Noble, H. (1972). Comparison of reciprocal inhibition, psychotherapy, and waiting list control for phobic children. *Journal of Abnormal Psychology, 79*, 269–279.

Miller, I., Epstein, N., Bishop, D., & Keitner, G. (1985). The McMaster Family Assessment Device: Reliability and validity. *Journal of Marital and Family Therapy, 11*, 345–356.

Miller, I., Kabacoff, R., Keitner, G., Epstein, N., & Bishop, D. (1986). Family functioning in the families of psychiatric patients. *Comprehensive Psychiatry, 27*, 302–312.

Morris, R. J., & Kratochwill, T. R. (1983). *Treating children's fears and phobias: A behavioral approach*. New York: Pergamon Press.

Murphy, C. M., & Bootzin, R. R. (1973). Active and passive participation in the contact desensitization of snake fear in children. *Behavior Therapy, 4*, 203–211.

Nauta, M. (1999, September). *Cognitive interventions for parents of children with anxiety disorders*. Paper presented at the 29th meeting of the European Association for Behavioural and Cognitive Therapies, Dresden, Germany.

Neal, A. M., & Turner, S. M. (1991). Anxiety disorders research with African Americans: Current status. *Psychological Bulletin, 109*, 400–410.

Noyes, R., Clancy, J., Crowe, R., Hoenk, P. R., & Slyman, D. J. (1978). The familial prevalence of anxiety neurosis. *Archives of General Psychiatry, 35*, 1057–1059.

Ollendick, T. H. (1983). Reliability and validity of the Revised Fear Survey Schedule for Children (FSSC-R). *Behaviour Research and Therapy, 21*, 685–692.

Ollendick, T. H. (1995). Cognitive behavioral treatment of panic disorder with agoraphobia in adolescents: A multiple baseline design analysis. *Behavior Therapy, 26*, 517–531.

Ollendick, T. H., & Cerny, J. A. (1981). *Clinical behavior therapy with children*. New York: Plenum Press.

Ollendick, T. H., & Francis, G. (1988). Behavioral assessment and treatment of childhood phobias. *Behavior Modification, 12*, 165–204.

Ollendick, T. H., & King, N. J. (1994). Diagnosis, assessment, and treatment of internalizing problems in children: The role of longitudinal data. *Journal of Consulting and Clinical Psychology, 62*, 918–927.

Ollendick, T. H., & King, N. J. (1998). Empirically supported treatments for children with phobic and anxiety disorders: Current status. *Journal of Clinical Child Psychology, 27*, 156–167.

Ollendick, T. H., King, N. J., & Frary, R. B. (1989). Fears in children and adolescents: Reliability and generalizability across gender, age, and nationality. *Behaviour Research and Therapy, 27*, 19–26.

Ollendick, T. H., Matson, J. L., & Helsel, W. J. (1985). Fears in children and adolescents: Normative data. *Behaviour Research and Therapy, 23*, 465–467.

Orvaschel, H., & Weissman, M. M. (1986). Epidemiology of anxiety disorders in children: A review. In R. Gittelman (Ed.), *Anxiety disorders of childhood* (pp. 58–72). New York: Guilford Press.

Parker, G. (1983). *Parental overprotection: A risk factor in psychosocial development*. New York: Grune & Stratton.

Peterson, L. (1989). Coping by children undergoing stressful medical procedures: Some conceptual, methodological, and therapeutic issues. *Journal of Consulting and Clinical Psychology, 57*, 380–387.

Piacentini, J., Gitrow, A., Jaffer, M., Graae, F., & Whitaker, A. (1994). Outpatient behavioral treatment of child and adolescent obsessive–compulsive disorder. *Journal of Anxiety Disorders, 8*, 277–289.

Pollack, M., Otto, M., Sabatino, S., Majcher, D., Worthington, J., McArdle, E., & Rosenbaum, J.

(1996). Relationship of childhood anxiety to adult panic disorder: Correlates and influence on course. *American Journal of Psychiatry, 153,* 376–381.

Prins, P. J. (1986). Children's self-speech and self- regulation during a fear-provoking behavioral test. *Behaviour Research and Therapy, 24,* 181–191.

Puig-Antich, J., & Chambers, W. (1978). *The Schedule for Affective Disorders and Schizophrenia for School-Age Children (Kiddie-SADS).* New York: New York State Psychiatric Institute.

Quay, H. C. (1977). Measuring dimensions of deviant behavior: The Behavior Problem Checklist. *Journal of Abnormal Child Psychology, 5,* 277–289.

Rapee, R. M. (1997). The potential role of childrearing practices in the development of anxiety and depression. *Clinical Psychology Review, 17,* 47–67.

Reynolds, C. R., & Paget, K. D. (1983). National normative and reliability data for the Revised Children's Manifest Anxiety Scale. *School Psychology Review, 12,* 324–336.

Reynolds, C. R., & Richmond, B. O. (1978). What I Think and Feel: A revised measure of children's manifest anxiety. *Journal of Abnormal Psychology, 6,* 271–280.

Reynolds, C. R., & Richmond, B. O. (1979). Factor structure and construct validity of "What I Think and Feel": The Revised Children's Manifest Anxiety Scale. *Journal of Personality Assessment, 43,* 281–283.

Ritter, B. (1968). The group desensitization of children's snake phobias using vicarious and contact desensitization procedures. *Behaviour Research and Therapy, 6,* 1–6.

Ronan, K. R., & Kendall, P. C. (1997). Self-talk in distressed youth: States-of-mind and content specificity. *Journal of Clinical Child Psychology, 26,* 330–337.

Ronan, K., Kendall, P., & Rowe, M. (1994). Negative affectivity in children: Development and validation of a self-statement questionnaire. *Cognitive Therapy and Research, 18,* 509–528.

Ross, C., Ross, S., & Evans, T. (1971). The modification of extreme social withdrawal with guided practice. *Journal of Behavior Therapy and Experimental Psychiatry, 2,* 273–279.

Sanders, M. (1996). New directions in behavioral family intervention with children. In T. Ollendick & R. Prinz (Eds.), *Advances in clinical child psychology* (Vol. 18, pp. 283–330). New York: Plenum Press.

Scherer, M. W., & Nakamura, C. Y. (1968). A Fear Survey Schedule for Children (FSS-FC): A factor analytic comparison with manifest anxiety (CMAS). *Behaviour Research and Therapy, 6,* 173–182.

Shaffer, D., Fisher, P., Dulcan, M. K., Davis, D., Piacentini, J., Schwab-Stone, M., Lahey, B., Bourdon, K., Jensen, P., Bird, H., Canino, G., & Regier, D. (1996). The NIMH Diagnostic Interview Schedule for Children, Version 2. 3. (DISC 2. 3): Description, acceptability, prevalence rates, and performance in the MECA study. *Journal of the American Academy of Child and Adolescent Psychiatry, 49,* 865–877.

Sheslow, D. V., Bondy, A. S., & Nelson, R. O. (1983). A comparison of graduated exposure, verbal coping skills, and their combination in the treatment of children's fear of the dark. *Child and Family Behavior Therapy, 4,* 33–45.

Silverman, W., Kurtines, W., Ginsburg, G., Weems, C., Lumpkin, P., & Carmichael, D. (1999). Treating anxiety disorders in children with group cognitive-behavioral therapy: A randomized clinical trial. *Journal of Consulting and Clinical Psychology, 67,* 995–1003.

Silverman, W. K. (1991). *Guide to the use of the Anxiety Disorders Interview Schedule for Children—Revised* (child and parent versions). Albany, NY: Graywind.

Silverman, W. K., & Albano, A. M. (1997). *The Anxiety Disorders Interview Schedule for Children (DSM-IV).* San Antonio, TX: Psychological Corporation.

Silverman, W. K., Cerny, J. A., & Nelles, W. B. (1988). Familial influence in anxiety disorders: Studies on the offspring of patients with anxiety disorders. In B. B. Lahey & A. E. Kazdin (Eds.), *Advances in child clinical psychology* (Vol. 16, pp. 223–248). New York: Plenum Press.

Silverman, W. K., & Kurtines, W. M. (1996). *Anxiety and phobic disorders: A pragmatic approach.* New York: Plenum Press.

Siqueland, L., & Diamond, G. (1998). Engaging parents in cognitive behavioral treatment for children with anxiety disorders. *Cognitive Behavioral Practice, 5,* 81–102.

Siqueland, L., Kendall, P. C., & Steinberg, L. (1996). Anxiety in children: Perceived family environments and observed family interaction style. *Journal of Child Clinical Psychology, 25,* 225–237.

Solyom, M. D., Beck, P., Solyom, C., & Hugel, R. (1974). Some etiological factors in phobic neurosis. *Canadian Psychiatric Association Journal, 19,* 69–78.

Southam-Gerow, M., & Kendall, P. C. (2000). Emotional understanding in youth with anxiety disorders. *Journal of Child Clinical Psychology, 29.*

Spielberger, C. (1973). *Preliminary manual for the State–Trait Anxiety Inventory for Children ("How I Feel Questionnaire").* Palo Alto, CA: Consulting Psychologists Press.

Spivack, G., & Shure, M. (1974). *A problem-solving approach to children's adjustment.* San Francisco: Jossey-Bass.

Stallings, P., & March, J. S. (1995). Assessment. In J. S. March (Ed.), *Anxiety disorders in children and adolescents* (pp. 125–147). New York: Guilford Press.

Stark, K. D., Humphrey, L. L., Crook, K., & Lewis, K. (1990). Perceived family environments of depressed and anxious children: Child's and maternal figure's perspectives. *Journal of Abnormal Child Psychology, 18,* 527–547.

Strauss, C. C., Last, C. G., Hersen, M., & Kazdin, A. E. (1988). Association between anxiety and depression in children and adolescents with anxiety disorders. *Journal of Abnormal Child Psychology, 16,* 57–68.

Strauss, C., Lease, C., Kazdin, A., Dulcan, M., & Last, C. (1989). Multimethod assessment of the social competence of anxiety disordered children. *Journal of Child Clinical Psychology, 18,* 184–190.

Strauss, C., Lease, C., Last, C., & Francis, G. (1988). Overanxious disorder: An examination of developmental differences. *Journal of Abnormal Child Psychology, 16,* 433–443.

Sylvester, C., Hyde, T. S., & Reichler, R. J. (1987). The Diagnostic Interview for Children and Personality Interview for Children in studies of children at risk for anxiety disorders and depression. *Journal of the American Academy of Child and Adolescent Psychiatry, 26,* 668–675.

Torgersen, S. (1983). Genetic factors in anxiety disorders. *Archives of General Psychiatry, 40,* 1085–1089.

Treadwell, K. H., Flannery-Schroeder, E. C., & Kendall, P. C. (1994). Ethnicity and gender in a sample of clinic-referred anxious children: Adaptive functioning, diagnostic status, and treatment outcome. *Journal of Anxiety Disorders, 9,* 373–384.

Treadwell, K. H., & Kendall, P. C. (1996). Self-talk in anxiety-disordered youth: States-of-mind, content specificity, and treatment outcome. *Journal of Consulting and Clinical Psychology, 64,* 941–950.

Ultee, C. A., Griffioen, D., & Schellekens, J. (1982). The reduction of anxiety in children: A comparison of the effects of "systematic desensitization *in vitro*" and "systematic desensitization *in vivo*." *Behaviour Research and Therapy, 20,* 61–67.

Verhulst, F. C., Althaus, M., & Berden, G. F. M. G. (1987). Psychopathology in the offspring of anxiety disordered patients. *Journal of Consulting and Clinical Psychology, 55,* 229–235.

Weisman, D., Ollendick, T. H., & Horne, A. M. (1978). *A comparison of muscle relaxation techniques with children.* Unpublished manuscript, Indiana State University, Terre Haute.

Weisz, J. R., & Weiss, B. (1991). Studying the "referability" of child clinical problems. *Journal of Consulting and Clinical Psychology, 59,* 266–273.

Wells, K. C., & Virtulano, L. A., (1984). Anxiety disorders in childhood. In S. E. Turner (Ed.), *Behavioral theories and treatment of anxiety* (pp. 413–439). New York: Plenum Press.

Werry, J. S. (1986). Diagnosis and assessment. In R. Gittelman (Ed.), *Anxiety disorders of childhood* (pp. 73–100). New York: Guilford Press.

PART IV

SPECIAL POPULATIONS AND TOPICS

CHAPTER 7

Cognitive-Behavioral Interventions for Children with Chronic Health Conditions

James W. Varni, Annette M. La Greca,
and Anthony Spirito

As biomedical science has successfully developed treatment approaches to nutritional disorders and infectious diseases of childhood, there has been an increased emphasis on those children coping with chronic health conditions (Varni, 1983). Epidemiological surveys in the 1970s and early 1980s found that between 10% and 20% of children in Western developed countries had a pediatric chronic health condition (Wallander & Varni, 1998). An estimated 31% of children under 18 years of age, or almost 20 million children nationwide, were reported to have one or more chronic health conditions in 1988 (Newacheck & Taylor, 1992). Although chronic health conditions were quite common among children, a comparatively smaller number of children were severely affected by them (Newacheck & Taylor, 1992). However, in 1994, 18% of children nationwide, or 12.6 million, had a chronic physical, developmental, behavioral, or emotional condition that required health and related services of a type or amount beyond that required by children generally (Newacheck et al., 1998).

Although biologically very diverse, pediatric chronic health conditions have in common the features of significant duration and potential long-term impact on the daily lives of the children and their families (Varni,

1983). As a group, children with chronic health conditions have been found to be at increased risk for psychological and social adjustment problems (Stein, Westbrock, & Silver, 1998; Wallander & Varni, 1998). This common impact of pediatric chronic health conditions on psychosocial development has resulted in the noncategorical approach (Stein, Bauman, Westbrook, Coupey, & Ireys, 1993; Varni, 1983), in which descriptions of chronic health conditions are not based on specific diagnoses, but on the degree of burden caused by the condition (Stein et al., 1993). Given the noncategorical commonalties indigenous to pediatric chronic health conditions, the need for a standardized, generic measurement instrument to assess the impact of pediatric chronic health conditions is quite evident. Health-related quality of life (HRQOL) is a construct that neatly fits the demands of such a generic measurement instrument for pediatric chronic health conditions (Varni, Seid, & Kurtin, 1999). Measurement of HRQOL should be conducted prior to any intervention for children with chronic health conditions to facilitate the tailoring of the intervention to the perceived problems as reported by the child and his or her parents. The measurement of HRQOL is described first. Then we present a discussion of coping, empirically supported treatment, adherence, and pain.

HEALTH-RELATED QUALITY-OF-LIFE ASSESSMENT

The accurate, comprehensive measurement of health outcomes in pediatric chronic health conditions requires a standardized approach (Varni, Pruitt, & Seid, 1998). "Quality of life," "functional status," or "health status" are terms frequently used interchangeably in the assessment of the impact of a physical disorder, although HRQOL is the more comprehensive concept (Guyatt, Feeny, & Patrick, 1993). Similar to laboratory tests for biological disease, screening for HRQOL morbidity in a patient population requires a standardized test with established reliability and validity (Varni & Setoguchi, 1992). HRQOL, as a broad measure of health, is a multidimensional construct that includes primary domains of physical and mental health functioning, social and role functioning, disease- and treatment-related symptoms, and general perceptions of well-being (Gotay, Korn, McCabe, Moore, & Cheson, 1992; Ware & Sherbourne, 1992).

Measurement of HRQOL in pediatric populations is challenging because of several factors, including the importance of developmental considerations and questions regarding who is likely to be the best respondent for HRQOL assessment. The circumstances under which proxies' ratings of patients' quality of life are accurate and acceptable have been a topic of growing empirical scrutiny. Cross-informant inconsistency has been repeatedly found in adult HRQOL research between adult patients' self-reports of their HRQOL and the ratings of both health care providers and significant others (e.g., spouses) (Sprangers & Aaronson, 1992). In pediatrics, a lack of ideal congruence has been documented among child/adolescent, parent, teacher, and health care professional reports in the assessment of physically healthy children's adjustment (Achenbach, McConaughy, & Howell, 1987). Agreement among observers has been found to be lower for internalizing problems (e.g., depression, anxiety, pain, nausea) than for externalizing problems (e.g., hyperactivity, aggression, physical functioning). This discordance, or lack of agreement, among reporters of child/adolescent adjustment has been termed "cross-informant variance," and has been demonstrated in the HRQOL assessment of children with asthma (Guyatt, Juniper, Griffith, Feeny, & Ferry, 1997), cancer (Varni, Katz, Quiggins, Friedman-Bender, & Castro, 1998), and other pediatric chronic health conditions. Given that HRQOL derives from a person's perceptions of the impact of disease and treatment (Schipper, Clinch, & Olweny, 1996), the presence of cross-informant variance indicates a critical need to develop pediatric patient HRQOL self-report instruments to ensure that the child's perceptions are accurately measured. However, a reliable and valid parent proxy-report of HRQOL, in addition to the pediatric patient self-report, is important in at least two ways. First, children are rarely in the position to refer themselves for treatment, even when they are experiencing symptoms and problems. It is the parents' perceptions of the child's HRQOL that influence the likelihood that care will be sought. Thus, the parent's perception of HRQOL, while not necessarily reflecting the patient's experience with complete accuracy, is important instrumentally in seeking treatment for the child. Second, the use of a proxy rater to estimate patient HRQOL may be necessary when the patient is either unable or unwilling to complete the HRQOL measure. Given these considerations, the evaluation of HRQOL with parallel pediatric patient self-report and parent proxy-report forms is considered essential (Varni, Seid, & Rode, 1999). A description of the PedsQL™ is provided to illustrate the measurement of pediatric HRQOL.

The PedsQL™Measurement Model

The PedsQL™ 4.0 (Pediatric Quality of Life Inventory™, Version 4.0) builds on and expands a programmatic measurement instrument development effort in pediatric chronic health conditions by Varni and his associates during the past 15 years. Specifically, standardized measurement of pain, coping, and functional status in pediatric arthritis (Varni, Thompson, & Hanson, 1987; Varni, Wilcox, Hanson, & Brik, 1988), and functional status and health care satisfaction in pediatric limb deficiency (Pruitt, Varni, Seid, & Setoguchi, 1998; Pruitt, Seid, Varni, & Setogushi, 1999; Pruitt, Varni, & Setoguchi, 1996) provided the empirical experience for the development of pediatric patient self-report and parent proxy-report

HRQOL measurement instruments across a wide age range. A disease-specific HRQOL instrument, the Pediatric Cancer Quality of Life Inventory (PCQL), was first developed and field tested with 291 pediatric cancer patients and their parents (Varni, Katz, Seid, Quiggins, & Friedman-Bender, 1998), followed by the development of the 32-item (PCQL-32) short form and health care satisfaction module (Varni, Katz, Seid, Quiggins, Friedman-Bender, & Castro, 1998b; Varni, Quiggins, & Ayala, in press).

The PedsQL™ 1.0, originally derived from the PCQL pediatric cancer database, is a generic pediatric quality-of-life inventory designed to be utilized noncategorically (i.e., across multiple pediatric chronic health conditions) with generic core scales and disease-specific modules (Varni, Katz, Seid, Quiggins, & Friedman-Bender, 1998; Varni, Katz, Seid, Quiggins, Friedman-Bender, & Castro, 1998). Given that instrument development is an iterative process, the PedsQL™ 2.0 and 3.0 were further advancements in the measurement model, including additional constructs and items, a more sensitive scaling range, and a broader age range for patient self-report and parent proxy-report.

The development and field testing of the 23-item PedsQL™ 4.0 Generic Core Scales further enhanced the measurement properties of the PedsQL™ within the planned continuous iteration methodology. The pediatric self-report (ages 5–18) and parent proxy-report (ages 2–18) multidimensional PedsQL™ 4.0 encompass essential core domains for pediatric HRQOL: (1) Physical Functioning (8 items), (2) Emotional Functioning (5 items), (3) Social Functioning (5 items), and (4) School Functioning (5 items). The PedsQL™ 4.0 has recently been field tested with over 1,600 children and adolescents in pediatricians' offices, hospital specialty clinics, community settings, and in schools for healthy population norms. The findings from this field test support the reliability, validity, responsiveness, and practicality of the PedsQL™ 4.0 for pediatric populations with acute and chronic health conditions. For example, the PedsQL™ was able to demonstrate a "return to health" for children who had an acute health condition 3 months after the condition had been treated by comparing their PedsQL™ scores to the PedsQL™ scores of physically healthy children. Thus, measuring the HRQOL of children with acute and chronic health conditions can provide a standardized approach to both targeting interventions and, subsequently, evaluating the clinical significance of the outcome in comparison to healthy population norms. However, to increase the sensitivity of the PedsQL™ to the needs of specific groups of children with chronic health conditions, disease-specific or condition-specific modules are additionally required.

The PedsQL™ Disease-Specific Modules

The concept of integrating into one assessment instrument both generic core HRQOL scales and disease-specific modules was influenced by the measurement research conducted by the European Organization for Research and Treatment of Cancer (EROTC) study group (Sprangers, Cull, Bjordal, Groenvold, & Aaronson, 1993). Generic HRQOL measures permit comparisons across different diseases, between acutely and chronically ill patient populations, and between ill and healthy individuals. Because generic measures can be administered to a broad array of patients and populations, they can be particularly instrumental in making health policy decisions, such as the allocation of resources related to health, education, or social services (Varni, Seid, & Kurtin, 1999). The supplemental modules are intended to assess disease and treatment effects and other relevant HRQOL issues not sufficiently covered in the generic core measure.

The PedsQL™ 4.0 Generic Core Scales are designed to enable comparisons across patient populations, including healthy populations. The goal of the chronic health condition-specific modules is to assess functioning specifically related to disease or treatment effects within a circumscribed clinical sample. Disease-specific measures are presumed to be more sensitive to changes in disease states and consequently may be more useful in comparing treatments within a disease. However, disease-specific measures are limited in their usefulness for comparison across different patient populations and with healthy population norms. Thus, the PedsQL™ Measurement Model combines both assessment strategies: the clinical utility and sensitivity of a disease-specific measure, and the applicability of generic core scales across healthy and patient populations required for standardized comparisons among different groups.

The clinical utilization of the PedsQL™ can be illustrated by an example. A boy with arthritis is referred because of "adjustment problems." On the PedsQL™ 4.0 Generic Core Scales, it is evident that he is having social interaction problems with classmates. Additionally, on the PedsQL™ Arthritis Module, he reports problems with recurrent pain in his joints. However, his parents do not report any difficulties on the parent-proxy-report version of the PedsQL™. This cross-informant variance provides an opportunity for an intervention. Both the parent (in this case, the child's mother) and the child meet with the therapist and discuss their PedsQL™ reports. The parent now has the opportunity to become aware of the child's social interaction problems with classmates, and both the child and parent agree to a social skills training intervention to address this need. Additionally, the parent was not aware of the child's recurrent joint pain, and they both agree to discuss this with the child's rheumatologist, and also to learn several cognitive-behavioral strategies to cope more effectively with the pain. Three months later, the child and parent complete the PedsQL™ again, and points of progress and areas in need of more change are identified and discussed.

Interventions for children with chronic health conditions are often presented to children and their parents as opportunities to learn more effective coping strategies for handling the challenges of the child's condition. Standardized coping assessment provides a means for identifying coping strengths and deficits in a systematic manner.

COPING ASSESSMENT

The decade of the 1990s began with great interest in the study of coping in chronic health conditions. This interest, for clinicians and researchers alike, stemmed from the belief that processes such as coping might mediate the potential negative effects of a chronic health condition. Despite this promise, relatively few studies have examined coping among children with a chronic health condition. The extant studies can be grouped as follows those that compare (1) coping strategy use between healthy children and children with a chronic illness and (2) among children with different disorders; (3) coping strategy differences with medical and everyday stressors; and (4) the relationship of coping strategy use to outcome. Examples of studies in each of these areas are next described.

Comparison of healthy children to chronically ill children has revealed some differences in coping strategy use. For example, Phipps, Fairclough, and Mulhern (1995) found that children with cancer used avoidant coping more often than healthy children. Other studies have examined differences in coping strategy use across children with different chronic illnesses. Olson, Johansen, Powers, Pope, and Klein (1993) examined the cognitive coping strategies of 175 children with juvenile rheumatoid arthritis, asthma, and diabetes to each other and a control group of 145 healthy school children. Children with different illnesses reported very similar types of coping to common painful (venipuncture) or stressful events. Adolescents with a chronic illness were twice as likely to offer more complex coping responses to a recent, personal stressful event than healthy children and adolescents.

Several studies examining frequency of coping strategy use in response to medical and nonmedical stressors have found that coping strategies differ by stressor. For example, in a sample of children with a variety of chronic illnesses, Spirito, Stark, Gil, and Tyc (1995) reported that some coping strategies (i.e., social withdrawal, social support, wishful thinking, and resignation) were used equally across stressors (medical and nonmedical), whereas other strategies (i.e., distraction, blaming others, and emotional regulation) varied by type of stressor. Bull and Drotar (1991) found that children with cancer use different coping strategies when confronted with everyday stressors than they do with disease-related stressors. Other studies have not found differences across stressors. For example, children with chronic illness reported using direct action (e.g., hit something) and cognitive techniques (e.g., problem solving, distraction) more than other types of coping in response to both disease- and non-disease-related stressors (Bull & Drotar, 1991).

Even fewer studies have examined the relationship between coping strategy use and outcome in children with chronic illness. In children with diabetes, primary control coping strategies (i.e., those that are more active and problem-focused) have been shown to be related to fewer behavioral difficulties and somewhat better control of symptoms in children (Band, 1990; Band & Weisz, 1990).

Progress in the field has also been hampered somewhat because the theoretical conceptualization of coping varies by study. However, there are some similarities across approaches; that is, coping is typically viewed as a process rather than a trait-oriented construct that varies by situation. In addition, despite the use of different terminology, most studies distinguish between two basic types of coping: efforts to change the situation (labeled approach, active, primary control, or problem-focused), and efforts to manage the emotions associated with a stressor (labeled avoidance, passive, secondary control, or emotion-focused). In addition, the methods/measures used to assess the construct of coping vary across studies. Examples of parent-, child-, and interviewer-rated measures include the Coping Health Inventory for Children (Austin, Patterson, & Huberty, 1991), a parent-completed 45 item non-illness-specific questionnaire covering five general coping patterns in children 8 to 12 years of age; a short version of the Coping Strategies Inventory (Tobin, Holroyd, Reynolds, & Wigal, 1989), a self-report-process oriented measure examining problem- and emotion-focused coping; and the Role-Play Inventory of Situations and Coping Strategies (Quittner et al., 1996), an interviewer-rated measure of 31 written and analyzed vignettes of problem situations for children with cystic fibrosis; and other measures developed specifically for the studies cited earlier in the literature review.

The lack of a consistently applied coping measure in the field is perhaps not surprising, because it is unlikely that any one process measure of coping is suitable for all situations. For example, unpublished factor analyses of the Kidcope (Spirito, Stark, & Williams, 1988), a scale with 10 common coping strategies designed to cut across situations, have revealed both two-factor and single-factor structures, depending on the type of situation selected by chronically ill children (Spirito, 1996). For example, a two-factor structure (i.e., approach–avoidance) emerged when the problem selected involved aversive medical procedures, but a single-factor structure resulted when the stressor was an extended period of hospitalization. The changing factor structure reflects the fact that the function or classification of a coping strategy (e.g., adaptive–nonadaptive) does not remain identical across situations. Coyne and Gottlieb (1996) argue against the search for a "gold standard" self-report measure of coping and encourage researchers to consider other means of thoroughly assessing coping, such as semistructured interviews, diaries, and checklists designed to test hypotheses of a specific project rather than rely on imperfect published measures. Interview methods may prove to be the most useful approach to gathering data on coping strategies, because they enhance understanding of the nature of the coping process. Interviews derived from a theoretical model (e.g., monitoring/blunting; Miller, Sherman, Combs, & Kruus, 1992; primary/secondary/relinquishing control strategies;

Band, 1990) allow for the computation of summary scores for specific constructs, also important for theory development.

Finally, change in any single coping strategy as the result of an intervention may not be as appropriate a marker of the success of an intervention as changes in the pattern of coping strategy use. For example, Donaldson, Prinstein, Danovsky, and Spirito (1997) compared the pattern of scores on the Kidcope of 170 hospitalized, mostly chronically ill children reporting an illness-related stressor to more than 700 healthy children reporting on interpersonal, family, or school stressors, and found differences in individual strategy use but notable consistencies in the patterns of children's frequency of coping strategies across the four stressor categories. Intraclass correlations, computed to consider how the relationship of the 10 coping strategies on the Kidcope was similar across each pair of stressors, ranged between .77 and .97 (median $r = .89$). This suggests that children's coping profiles were similar across all four types of stressors. An intraclass correlation that considered all four profiles simultaneously revealed a coefficient of .89. Children across all four stressors reported using Wishful Thinking more than any other strategy, followed by Emotional Regulation and Problem Solving. All children utilized Self-Criticism, Blaming Others, and Resignation the least. This suggests that the examination of coping patterns yields information unique from that obtained regarding individual coping strategies. Future studies of children's coping, particularly outcome studies, might incorporate information about both individual coping strategies and patterns of coping strategies in response to different types of stress. The sequencing of the use of these coping strategies is also important and may be a key indicator of positive change resulting from an intervention.

The majority of the coping interventions this decade have focused on teaching active coping strategies for use with medical procedure-related pain in both chronically and acutely ill children. This literature has been reviewed elsewhere and indicates that these approaches are successful in improving pain and emotional distress outcomes for these children (Powers, 1999). Examples of these cognitive-behavioral strategies are discussed subsequently in the pain management section of this chapter. The next section briefly provides an overview on empirically supported interventions in pediatric psychology, which is the specialization in psychology that has most concerned itself with pediatric chronic health conditions.

EMPIRICALLY SUPPORTED TREATMENTS IN PEDIATRIC PSYCHOLOGY

In 1999, the *Journal of Pediatric Psychology* launched a special series on empirically supported treatments in pediatric psychology. This special series stemmed from an initiative that began in 1995, when the Division of Clinical Psychology of the American Psychological Association instituted a task force on effective psychosocial interventions across the life span. This task force was established to extend the work of a prior task force, which had identified interventions for adults that had empirical support in the literature. The authors of the articles in the special series of the *Journal of Pediatric Psychology* were asked to review all interventions in their topic area and indicate which studies were sufficiently rigorous to be considered as evidence for treatment efficacy by applying the criteria developed by the original task force on effective treatments (Chambless et al., 1996). These criteria primarily involve the use of randomized controlled trials with manualized treatments.

The *Journal of Pediatric Psychology* has thus far published reviews on procedure-related pain, recurrent abdominal pain, headache, disease-related pain, sleep disorders, disease symptomatology, feeding problems, enuresis, and encopresis. The reviews most pertinent to chronic disease in childhood include disease-related pain and disease symptomatology. Walco, Sterling, Conte, and Engel (1999) found relatively few controlled intervention trials for disease-related pain; consequently, the evidence did not result in classification of these interventions as empirically supported. However, the literature does support cognitive-behavioral interventions as promising (i.e., supported by one well-controlled study with a randomized design and one less well-controlled study) adjuncts to pharmacotherapy for musculoskeletal pain disorders such as juvenile rheumatoid arthritis (Walco et al., 1999). McQuaid and Nassau (in press) found the use of electromyographic (EMG) biofeedback for children with emotionally triggered asthma, and imagery techniques with suggestion for children undergoing chemotherapy, to be empirically supported interventions (i.e., supported by at least two separate well-controlled studies with a randomized design) for reducing disease-related symptoms for these two diseases. Relaxation training for children with emotionally triggered asthma and distraction with relaxation for children undergoing chemotherapy were identified as probably efficacious treatments (i.e., supported by one well-controlled study with a randomized design or two studies demonstrating superiority to wait-list control).

There are, however, problems associated with the task force criteria for identifying empirically supported treatments (see the series of articles published in *Clinical Psychology: Science and Practice*, 1996, Vol. 3, No. 3 and the *Journal of Consulting and Clinical Psychology*, 1998, Vol. 6, No. 1). For example, it has been suggested that the criteria neglect the role of therapist variables in client outcome; require qualitative judgment, and do not specify magnitude of effect or proportion of positive responders by which to judge whether a given treatment is effective (Weisz & Hawley, 1998). In addition, without access to the treatment manuals and contents of the sessions, it is unclear if treatment approaches with the same name truly reflect equivalent treatments (Weisz & Hawley, 1998). A number of other problems specific to pediatric psychology were encountered, including the wide age range in many studies, small sample size, and heterogeneity of medical diagnostic categories. Outcome markers vary by study, with few studies examining areas such as quality of life, cost–benefit analysis, or medical offset analyses (Drotar, 1997; Weisz & Hawley, 1998). In addition, the majority of research on children with chronic health conditions has focused on psychosocial factors related to having an illness rather than interventions to promote adaptation.

Future intervention research on children with chronic health conditions may find their strongest effects when examining disease-related variables, such as pain, which require a biobehavioral perspective to achieve the best results. These disease-related variables affect all children to a greater or lesser extent, whereas other psychological and behavioral factors associated with disease state (e.g., social functioning deficits) are more subtle and/or affect only a relatively small portion of any group with a chronic health condition, which makes it very difficult to find group effects of interventions. Alternatively, preventing further impairment may be achievable goals of these studies. Group designs will need a larger number of subjects from multisite studies to detect statistical and clinical significance than has typically been the case to date for intervention research in pediatric chronic health conditions.

In the next three sections we describe interventions for adherence to medical treatment regimens, pain management, and social-cognitive problem solving. These topic areas have received the most empirical research to date in the development of cognitive-behavioral interventions for pediatric chronic health conditions.

INTERVENTIONS FOR MEDICAL ADHERENCE

Treatment adherence is a major area of concern for child and adolescent health. Many children and adolescents do not adhere to prescribed medical treatments for a variety of ailments, ranging from acute illnesses and infections (e.g., Colcher & Bass, 1972; Mattar, Markello, & Yaffe, 1975) to chronic conditions such as asthma (Celano, Geller, Phillips, & Ziman, 1998) and diabetes (Johnson, Silverstein, Rosenbloom, Carter, & Cunningham, 1986). Overall, pediatric adherence rates are estimated to be about 50% (Litt & Cuskey, 1980), although rates of noncompliance may be as high as 89% for some treatments (Eney & Goldstein, 1976).

In response to these alarming statistics, in recent years, we have witnessed a dramatic increase in research on factors contributing to treatment adherence and, to a lesser extent, methods for improving treatment adherence (La Greca & Schuman, 1995). The ultimate goal of such efforts is to improve the health status of children and adolescents affected by disease.

Also contributing to growing interest in pediatric treatment adherence are recent advances in medical science. Along with the advent of life-saving medical treatments (e.g., for cancer and HIV infection) comes a rise in the number of individuals with chronic conditions—individuals whose lives would have previously been lost to disease. Furthermore, new technologies have ushered in more complex regimens for chronic diseases. For example, new methods for home blood glucose monitoring have led to more intensified treatment regimens for diabetes; intensified regimens can improve blood-glucose control and reduce the likelihood of health complications (e.g., retinopathy, nephropathy) (DCCT Group, 1993). Yet intensified regimens are also substantially more demanding than conventional treatments, and often include multiple daily blood-glucose tests, reevaluating and readjusting insulin needs daily or weekly, and continually regulating food intake and exercise. Thus, medical advances bring new challenges for treatment adherence as regimens become more complex and sophisticated.

In the sections that follow, four primary approaches to improving treatment adherence are discussed: education, supervision and/or monitoring, use of incentives, and family involvement and problem solving. The last section covers multicomponent interventions that utilize several strategies.

Educational Approaches

Children and families' knowledge of disease symptoms and regimen requirements are critical for adherence (La Greca & Schuman, 1995). The importance of education has been emphasized for treatment regimes that involve complex skills (e.g., factor replacement therapy for hemophilia), require major lifestyle modifications (e.g., obesity), or demand a high degree of self-regulation on the part of the child and the parent (e.g., diabetes). However, for complex regimens, education will likely need to be combined with other treatment strategies to have an impact on adherence.

As a primary intervention approach, education *alone* appears to be most appropriate for short-term medication regimens that are prescribed for acute illnesses. For example, for parents of children with streptococcal pharyngitis, Colcher and Bass (1972) provided information on how to administer medication, plus written instructions; these parents were substantially more adherent with medication administration to their children (80%) than those in the "usual care" group (50%).

Educational interventions are also important for children and families at the time of initial disease diagnosis (Delamater et al., 1990), and for adolescents with a chronic disease who are beginning to assume increased responsibility for their treatment regimen (La Greca & Skyler, 1991). Surveys indicate that professionals tend to overestimate adolescents' competence in regimen tasks (Wysocki et al., 1992). In such cases, it is critical that youngsters and families have the knowledge and skills necessary to carry out the treatment regimen effectively. However, knowledge alone is not sufficient for adherence to complex, chronic, or aversive treatment regimens (La Greca & Schuman, 1995). In such cases, adherence may be enhanced by adding other strategies (e.g., support, supervision, incentives) to an educational approach.

Supervision, Monitoring, and/or Feedback on Adherence

Supervision by Health Care Providers

Supervision by health care personnel holds promise as a method for enhancing adherence to short-term regimens or to certain aspects of chronic treatment regimens (e.g., reminders to take medication or to keep medical appointments). Supervision can take the form of more frequent medical visits, phone calls, or monitoring medication intake through assays of drug levels. Such strategies are often easy and cost-efficient to administer, but alone, they are insufficient for making a substantial impact on adherence to complex treatments.

Existing studies suggest that medical supervision alone may be effective in enhancing adherence to short-term regimens. For example, Fink, Malloy, Cohen, Greycloud, and Martin (1969) studied 274 children with acute medical problems, randomly assigning their families to a usual-care group or a nurse follow-up condition that provided increased supervision of medication administration. The adherence rate in the nurse follow-up condition was 59% compared with an 18% adherence rate for the control patients.

Medical monitoring and supervision can also improve levels of adherence with chronic pediatric conditions to some extent. Eney and Goldstein (1976) provided increased medical supervision and monitoring of salivary theophylline levels of 47 youth with asthma compared with 43 children receiving "usual care." Of those receiving supervision plus monitoring, 42% achieved therapeutic levels of theophylline versus only 11% of the usual-care group.

Increased medical supervision has also been a part of multicomponent intervention programs (Delamater et al., 1990; Epstein et al., 1981). However, the relative contribution of medical supervision or monitoring to multicomponent packages has not been systematically evaluated.

Visual Cues and Reminders

Reminders or cues, such as signs in key places (e.g., refrigerator or bathroom mirror), calendars, postcards, and telephone calls, may prompt the performance of regimen tasks. This approach merits consideration for (1) acute, short-term regimens; (2) initial phases of more complex, chronic treatment protocols; and (3) situations in which parents are attempting to increase children's involvement in their own medical management. In such cases, new health behaviors must be acquired and integrated into the individual's daily routine; cues and reminders might facilitate this process.

Reminders, such as telephone calls or postcards, are often used to assist pediatric appointment keeping. Casey, Rosen, Glowasky, and Ludwig (1985) investigated the use of telephone reminders, with or without an educational session, to increase appointment adherence for 183 children with otitis media. The "telephone reminder" group had the highest percentage of children who were adherent with follow-up appointments (56%) compared to 39% for the "education" group and 25% for the control group. The effectiveness of the telephone reminders was not enhanced by combining it with an educational intervention. Thus, telephone reminders can increase adherence with medical appointments, although the best level of adherence demonstrated in this study (56%) still fell below the ideal. Others have similarly found that phone-call reminders improve appointment keeping among children, adolescents, and their parents for a variety of pediatric conditions (Cavanaugh, 1990; Dini, Linkins, & Chaney, 1995; Friman, Finney, Rapoff, & Christophersen, 1985; O'Brien & Lazebnik, 1998). However, in all these studies, reminders did not improve adherence to 100%, suggesting that reminders alone are insufficient for some children and families.

Visual cues and reminders are often used to prompt performance of daily regimen tasks, such as medication adherence. In one well-controlled investigation, Lima, Nazarian, Charney, and Lahti (1976) studied the impact of two visual cues on adherence to a 10-day antibiotic regimen. The cues consisted of a clock printed on the prescription label with the appropriate times for medication administration circled, and a bright, red, 5" × 7" sticker for posting at home. The low-income patient sample included 158 children and adults with a variety of acute problems (e.g., otitis media, bronchitis). Findings revealed that children and parents were helped considerably more by the visual reminders than were the adult patients. Moreover, children in the "reminder" groups demonstrated adherence levels that were more than twice as high as the controls.

Lowe and Lutzker (1979) employed visual cues as part of a multicomponent intervention for a 9-year-old girl with diabetes. In order to improve adherence to urine testing, a memo with written instructions for the urine testing procedure was posted in the girl's bathroom. Although adherence improved from 16% to 35% with the reminder memo, this level was less than optimal. With the *addition of a token reward system* for urine testing, however, the girl's adherence rate reached 97%. Improvements in targeted adherence behaviors were maintained at 10-week follow-up.

Overall, these studies suggest that reminders can facilitate adherence behaviors. For difficult regimens, however, additional procedures, such as incentive for adherence, are necessary.

Self-Monitoring

Self-monitoring of disease symptoms or regimen behaviors may be a useful strategy for acute illnesses with short-term medication regimens. For example, Mattar et al. (1975) provided 33 parents with calendars to monitor a 10-day regimen of oral medication for their children's otitis media. Fifty-one percent of the intervention group was adherent, as compared with an 8.5% rate in 200 concurrent control cases. Parents also were provided with written instructions on medication use and a calibrated measuring device to ensure that accurate doses of medication were administered. Thus, the effects of intervention were attributable to this combined approach.

For complex treatment regimens, self-monitoring interventions have been less promising. For instance, during the baseline phase of an intervention study (Epstein et al., 1981), youngsters with diabetes monitored the results of daily glucose tests, as well as daily insulin administration. No effects on glucose control were observed over the 3- to 6-week monitoring periods.

Wysocki, Green, and Hustable (1989) also found that self-monitoring alone is not an effective intervention strategy for chronic, complex regimens. Adolescents with diabetes ($n = 30$) were instructed to self-monitor blood-glucose levels using reflectance meters with memory chips that automatically recorded each blood-glucose test. They were randomly assigned to either a "meter-alone" (i.e., self-monitoring) or "meter-plus-contract" (i.e., self-monitoring plus monetary incentives) condition; 12 additional patients served as conventional-therapy controls. Self-monitoring alone had no positive effect on adherence, in that blood-glucose testing frequency declined sharply during the 16-week intervention for the meter-alone group, but remained at or above baseline levels for the meter-plus-contract group. Thus, the addition of a incentives for self-monitoring may be necessary to achieve adequate levels of blood-glucose testing.

As these studies suggest, self-monitoring alone is likely to be of limited utility for illnesses with complex regimens. In fact, daily record keeping (i.e., self-monitoring), an adherence behavior many children and parents find difficult, has served as a target behavior in some adherence studies (Lowe & Lutzker, 1979). Another reason why self-monitoring may be limited as a treatment strategy is that youngsters often have little use for the information provided by monitoring activities. Unless information can be used to improve disease management, the potential benefits of this procedure are likely to be limited.

Incentives for Adherence Behaviors

Reinforcement contingencies for adherence behaviors have proved useful with medication regimens (Rapoff, Purviance, & Lindsley, 1988), as well as with complex, chronic treatments (Epstein et al., 1981; Lowe & Lutzker, 1979; Wysocki et al., 1989). For example, Lowe and Lutzker (1979) combined written instructions, parental home monitoring, and a token reward system to increase adherence to foot care, urine glucose testing, and diet in a 9-year-old girl with diabetes. Similarly, Carney, Schechter, and Davis (1983) used a combination of parental praise and a point system for self-monitoring blood-glucose levels several times per day. Improvements in home blood-glucose monitoring were evident for 2 of the 3 child participants; and gains were maintained at 4-month follow-up. With a larger sample, Wysocki et al. (1989) obtained higher levels of glucose monitoring when adolescents with diabetes received monetary reinforcement for their adherence behaviors than when no such incentives were provided.

Complex, lifestyle behaviors, such as exercise and dietary management, have also been responsive to reinforcement techniques. Greenan-Fowler, Powell, and Varni (1987) focused on 10 children with hemophilia (ages 8–15 years) using a contingency contract and token exchange system for adherence to prescribed exercises, completing self-monitoring forms, and attending group exercise sessions. Six-month follow-up data disclosed that average adherence ranged from 81% to 90% for study participants. Similarly, Killam, Apodaca, Manella, and Varni (1983) report success in improving adherence to a weight control regimen for 5 children, ages 7–12 years, with spina bifida. Given activity restrictions, children with spina bifida are at risk for becoming overweight, and many develop obesity. In this study, parents were instructed as to diet and exercise, as well as the use of contingent reinforcement for their children's weight control. Four of the children evidenced a therapeutic reduction in percentage overweight at the 6-month follow-up assessment, although considerable variability in weight loss was observed.

Reinforcement may enhance patients' or parents' participation in treatment. For instance, Finney, Lemanek, Brophy, and Cataldo (1990) used reinforcement to improve appointment keeping in children (ages 4–17 years) who had poor attendance at allergy and asthma clinics. Youngsters earned a coupon for each kept appointment, and four coupons earned a prize. Appointment adherence increased for 3 of 5 subjects and was maintained throughout the intervention. However, improvements were not maintained after reinforcement was discontinued; in fact, 2 subjects dropped below their preintervention levels of adherence. This study illustrates a potential pitfall: improvements may only last as long as the reinforcers are applied.

The interventions previously discussed used positive reinforcement to increase *adherence behaviors*. Other investigations have provided positive contingencies for *symptom reduction* rather than for adherence. For example, Epstein et al. (1981) combined parental praise and reinforcement for their child's negative glucose results (an indication of good metabolic control) with an educational intervention for children with diabetes and their parents. Using a multiple-baseline across-groups design, significant increases in the percentage of negative glucose tests were observed, and these gains were maintained at 22-week follow-up.

Although promising, reinforcement procedures have limitations. With rare exceptions, studies have relied almost exclusively on single-subject designs. Also, variable subject responsiveness (Killam et al., 1983) and treatment failures (Carney et al., 1983; Finney et al., 1990) have been evident. Furthermore, adherence levels are not consistently maintained when reinforcement is discontinued. Future studies might explore methods for modifying reinforcement over time to maintain long-term adherence gains. Perhaps immediate and frequent reinforcement is needed for complex or demanding tasks, or for younger or less motivated youth (Friedman & Litt, 1987). Over time, reinforcement might be contingent on longer periods of adherence or greater self-management. Although reinforcement can be beneficial in many cases, additional procedures will be essential to the broad-based, long-term success of adherence interventions.

Family Support and/or Problem Solving

Social Support and Family Involvement

Given the substantial role that families play in children's disease management (Chaney & Peterson, 1989; La Greca, Follansbee, & Skyler, 1990), interventions that involve family members are extremely important. In fact, although many of the studies reviewed thus far have included parents in the treatment program, few studies have directly tried to improve family support and problem solving regarding daily regimen tasks.

In one exception, Satin, La Greca, Zigo, and Skyler (1989) evaluated the effects of a 6-week multifamily intervention for 36 adolescents with diabetes. Adolescents were randomly assigned to one of two multifamily conditions or to a wait-list control condition. Multifamily sessions stressed effective communication skills around diabetes-specific situations, problem-solving strategies for diabetes management, and family support for adolescents' self-care. In one of the multifamily conditions, parents also simulated diabetes for 1 week, completing all aspects of a diabetes regimen (daily injections, multiple daily glucose tests, dietary plan, exercise prescription), in order to heighten awareness of the difficulties of daily management. Adolescents participating in the multifamily groups demonstrated significant improvements in self-care and metabolic control 6 months posttreatment relative to control youngsters. This program emphasized the role of family support, communication, and problem solving in improving adherence to a complex regimen.

Aside from families, benefits might also accrue from the involvement or support of peers (La Greca, 1990; La Greca et al., 1995). Some research indicates that peers with the same medical condition can facilitate youngsters' disease management (Anderson, Wolf, Burkhart, Cornell, & Bacon, 1989). Moreover, support from healthy peers may also play a role in determining the extent to which a youngster will carry out tasks that set him or her apart from peers, such as following prescribed dietary guidelines or testing glucose following a meal at school. The role of friends and healthy peers in supporting and encouraging youngsters' treatment adherence is just beginning to be investigated (Greco, Pendley, & McDonnell, 1999; La Greca et al., 1995).

Reducing Barriers to Adherence/Increasing Problem Solving

Despite the many different types of obstacles to medical management reported by children and parents (La Greca & Varni, 1993; Leickly et al., 1998; Simoni et al., 1997), few investigators have matched their intervention strategies to the types of problems that interfere with youngsters' medical management. In one exception, Schafer, Glasgow, and McCaul (1982) helped 3 children with diabetes reduce their barriers to daily glucose testing, insulin administration, and exercise. Based on children's and parents' reports of barriers to management tasks, individualized programs were designed, and specific goals for adherence were established. For glucose testing and exercise adherence, the combination of barrier reduction and goal setting was effective for 2 of the 3 children. However, a combination of barrier reduction, goal setting, and contingent reinforcement was needed to achieve a satisfactory adherence for one child, who had difficulty administering injections on time.

In an effort to reduce social barriers to treatment adherence, Gross, Johnson, Wildman, and Mullett (1981) used a combination of modeling and role-playing procedures to teach children how to handle difficult situations related to their diabetes management. Posttreatment and follow-up assessments indicated that the children could respond to social situations in a more assertive manner, although the impact of the intervention on daily diabetes management and disease control was not assessed.

In general, problem-solving approaches to adherence are appealing, as they teach the individual strategies for dealing with the various types of barriers that can affect daily health care. Several investigators have included problem-solving strategies in the context of a multicomponent package (Anderson, Wolf, et al., 1989; Delamater et al., 1990; Satin et al., 1989). However, the added value of problem-solving training as part of an multicomponent adherence intervention package has not yet been determined. These studies are discussed next.

Treating Adherence Comprehensively: Multicomponent Interventions

It may be unrealistic to expect that any one intervention strategy will lead to successful adherence among a diverse group of pediatric patients, and for diseases with multiple aspects with respect to adherence (e.g., medication, monitoring, food, exercise, etc.). A meta-analysis of 153 published studies that evaluated the effectiveness of interventions for adherence among adults (Roter et al., 1998) concluded that comprehensive interventions that combined educational, behavioral, and affective components were more effective than single-focus interventions; the same is likely to be the case for pediatric patients. Given the complexities of treatments for chronic disease and the multiple factors contributing to treatment adherence, several multicomponent intervention programs have been developed and are described here.

Delamater and colleagues (1990) evaluated a program for teaching self-management skills to newly diagnosed youngsters with diabetes, and their parents, that involved patient and parent education/instruction, patient and parent problem solving, increased medical supervision, and (parental) reinforcement of youngsters' adherence behaviors. Youngsters (ages 3–16 years) were randomly assigned to conventional treatment (CT), supportive counseling (SC), or self-management training (SMT). All children and their parents were regularly seen on an outpatient basis. Those in the SC condition also met with a counselor for supportive treatment nine times over 6 months. Children and parents in the SMT condition met for nine sessions that stressed monitoring of blood glucose, parental reinforcement of children's monitoring behaviors, and the use of monitoring data for making adjustments in the daily regimen. Children in the SMT group had significantly better metabolic control 1 and 2 years postdiagnosis than those receiving only CT; those in the SC group had metabolic functioning intermediate to the other groups.

In another study, Baum and Creer (1986) used multiple treatment strategies, including SMT, to improve adherence among 20 children with asthma (ages 6–16 years). Children and their families were randomly assigned to either a self-monitoring condition (SM) or self-monitoring plus self-management (SM/SMT). Those receiving SMT participated in an education session for parents and children, and a reinforcement system was instituted for youngsters' adherence with the SM task. Youngsters receiving SMT did not evidence greater gains in medication adherence relative to those in the SM group. However, children in the SM/SMT group were more likely to try to get away from the cause of an asthma attack, were more likely to manage an asthma attack by themselves and not immediately seek adult attention, and were more likely to institute other measures before resorting to medication. In short, the multicomponent intervention led to better asthma management.

In contrast to these family-based interventions, Anderson, Wolf, et al. (1989) worked with adolescents in peer groups, in addition to intervening with parents. Adolescents with diabetes ($n = 35$) were randomly assigned to either intervention or standard care conditions, and were seen in clinic every 3 to 4 months over an 18-month period. Adolescents and parents who received the intervention met in concurrent but separate groups at each clinic visit. Adolescent sessions focused on the use of self-monitoring of blood glucose (SMBG) as a tool for solving diabetes management problems. The adolescents also ate, exercised, and monitored blood glucose together, creating an atmosphere of peer support. In addition, clinic nurses routinely contacted adolescents between clinic visits, providing increased medical contact and supervision. Parent sessions focused on strategies for negotiating appropriate levels of parental involvement and adolescent responsibility for diet, exercise, and monitoring. Postintervention, metabolic control deteriorated in 50% of the adolescents in the standard care condition but only in 23% of the intervention group. Significantly more adolescents in the intervention group reported changing their exercise patterns based on information from SMBG. This is an example of an intervention that effectively combined education, self-monitoring, medical supervision, and family and peer support to prevent deterioration in metabolic control, although little effect on adherence behavior was observed.

More recently, Mendez and Belendez (1997) evaluated the effects of a behavioral program to increase treatment adherence among adolescents with diabetes. The treatment components included education, blood-glucose discrimination training, role playing, relaxation exercises, self-instructions, problem-solving strategies, and homework. Among the findings, barriers to treatment adherence were reduced among adolescents receiving treatment ($n = 18$) relative to the "usual-care" controls ($n = 19$). Furthermore, this change was maintained at 13-month follow-up.

In summary, multicomponent intervention programs appear to be promising for complex chronic conditions. One drawback, however, is that the effective "ingredients" of the various strategies that comprise the treatment packages are not known. Nevertheless, given the multiple demands of many treatment regimens, the development and evaluation of intervention programs that include multiple strategies will continue to be important.

Summary

This section provided an overview of common intervention strategies for improving medical adherence among children, adolescents, and families.

Studies were organized according to their primary intervention strategy, although many interventions incorporated more than one strategy. In reviewing this literature, several limitations are apparent. First, most of the studies have relied on single-subject research designs or group designs with small subject samples; few large-group studies are available. Second, treatment duration and follow-up periods have been brief, with few exceeding 6 months. Third, many investigations used a combination of intervention strategies (e.g., monitoring and incentives), but did not evaluate the separate components. Because of this, little is known about the effective ingredients of various treatment approaches.

Finally, few studies have matched the intervention to the types of adherence problems children and families experience. This is a critical issue in that most studies have found adherence behaviors to be complex and multifaceted. Especially for chronic health conditions, such as asthma or diabetes, treatment regimens may have several components (e.g., taking medication, monitoring medication effects, eating certain foods, exercising, avoiding situations that compromise health), and research strongly suggests that these different components may be unrelated to one another, and may have unique and different barriers to adherence (Freund, Johnson, Silverstein, & Thomas, 1991; Leickly et al., 1998; Simoni et al., 1997). Because multiple factors contribute to problems with treatment adherence, it would be useful to tailor interventions to youngsters' and families' specific areas of difficulty. Perhaps for this reason, multicomponent interventions that address adherence in a comprehensive manner seem to fare the best in terms of treatment effectiveness.

For acute illnesses with short-term medication regimens, strategies such as providing verbal and written instructions, visual cues or reminders, and increased medical supervision appear to be effective. However, the management of chronic health conditions, with complex regimens and negative health consequences for poor self-care, remains a serious challenge. For chronic regimens, the most success has been associated with programs that combine intervention strategies, such as intensive education, parental involvement, self-monitoring, medical supervision, and reinforcement procedures (e.g., Baum & Creer, 1986; Delamater et al., 1990), or that reflect a high degree of family involvement (e.g., Anderson, Wolf, et al., 1989; Delamater et al., 1990; Satin et al., 1989).

Improving pediatric adherence will continue to be an important area in the future. Of particular interest will be efforts to tailor intervention programs to the type of problems youngsters and families experience, as well as efforts to examine child and family characteristics that may predict treatment responsiveness. Such characteristics might include the child's developmental level, the severity and duration of the pediatric condition, comorbidity with other problems, the child's and family's experience of distress, and the degree of parental involvement in treatment (cf. La Greca & Varni, 1993).

PEDIATRIC PAIN MANAGEMENT

The empirical investigation of pediatric pain and distress has been an area of tremendous research effort in the past decade. In contrast to the lack of systematic attention previously reported (Varni, 1983), the number of data-based studies, review articles, and textbooks devoted to pain in infants, children, and adolescents has grown exponentially (Bush & Harkins, 1991; McGrath, 1990; McGrath & Unruh, 1987; Ross & Ross, 1988; Schechter, Berde, & Yaster, 1993; Tyler & Crane, 1990; Varni, Blount, Waldron, & Smith, 1995; Varni, Walco, & Katz, 1989). Given that whole textbooks have been written on pediatric pain, it is our intent to provide an illustrative review of the current state of the field by focusing on chronic and recurrent pain in juvenile rheumatoid arthritis. This pediatric chronic disease exemplifies the application of cognitive-behavioral therapy techniques to the management of pain and distress in children, and provides the context for a more in-depth presentation than would be feasible with a more broadly conducted literature review. Before we proceed to the separate discussion of pain in this chronic pediatric physical disorder, we present a conceptual overview.

Biobehavioral Model of Pediatric Pain

Varni (1983) delineated four primary categories of pediatric pain: (1) pain associated with chronic diseases (e.g., arthritis, hemophilia, sickle-cell disease, cancer); (2) pain associated with observable physical injuries or traumas (e.g., burns, lacerations, fractures); (3) pain not associated with a well-defined or specific chronic disease or identifiable physical injury (e.g., migraine and tension headaches, recurrent abdominal pain syndrome); and (4) pain associated with medical and dental procedures (e.g., lumbar punctures, bone marrow aspirations, surgery, injections, extractions). In this chapter, we describe cognitive-behavioral treatment interventions for chronic/recurrent pain that are guided by explicit conceptual models. Pharmacological treatment interventions for pediatric pain are not presented here (see Schechter et al., 1993).

Cognitive Development

A greater amount of attention has been directed to the cognitive-developmental level of the child in approaches to the task of pediatric pain assessment. It has been hypothesized that children's conceptualizations of pain may mirror Piaget's stages of cognitive development (Thompson & Varni, 1986; Varni, 1983). Support for the theory of developmental stages of pain perception has been found in a large-scale study of school-age children's definitions of pain (Gaffney & Dunne, 1986). The pattern of responses given by the children followed a developmental sequence consonant with Piaget's theory of cognitive development. With increasing age, the children in the study showed a shift from concrete, perceptually dominated perspectives to more abstract, generalized, and psychologically oriented views. In a second study (Gaffney & Dunne, 1986), children's understanding of the causality of pain showed a developmental pattern similar to that found in children's definitions of pain: Objective and abstract explanations of pain increased significantly with children's age. These findings emphasize the importance of children's conceptualizations of pain when investigators are conducting clinical assessments of pain perception across age groups.

Theoretical Framework

Increasingly in pediatric psychology, a priori conceptual models have empirically guided the nonexperimental research field, particularly for pediatric chronic physical disorders (see Varni & Wallander, 1988; Wallander & Varni, 1992, 1995, 1998). This research has focused on a multivariate conceptual model of stress and coping that has been developed to explain the observed variance in psychological and social adaptation among children with chronic physical disorders (e.g., Varni, Setoguchi, Rappaport, & Talbot, 1992; Varni & Setoguchi, 1993). It is a major tenet of this theoretical framework that empirical identification of modifiable risk and resistance factors can provide heuristic guidance for new treatment interventions for these children (see Varni, Katz, Colegrove, & Dolgin, 1993). Varni (1989) has extended this conceptual model of risk and resistance to pediatric pain in an attempt to account for the observed variability in pediatric pain perception and pain behavior.

The biobehavioral model of pediatric pain, as delineated by Varni (1989), is schematically presented in Figure 7.1. This multidimensional conceptual model hypothesizes a number of variables that may influence pediatric pain perception and pain behavior. The path diagram represented in Figure 7.1 has been developed in an effort to identify potentially modifiable constellations of factors to be targeted for cognitive-behavioral treatment. In the model, the precipitants include disease (e.g., arthritis), physical injury, and psychological stress. Intervening factors are biological predispositions (e.g., behavioral genetics or temperament, age, gender, cognitive development), family environment (e.g., family functioning, family pain models, family reinforcement style), cognitive appraisal (e.g., meaning of pain), coping strategies (e.g., problem- or emotion-focused strategies), and perceived social support. Functional status variables are hypothesized to be affected by and to affect pain perception and pain behavior.

The theoretical framework can be further broken down into pain antecedents, which have a casual role in pain onset or exacerbate pain intensity; pain concomitants (e.g., depression, anxiety), which occur only during a

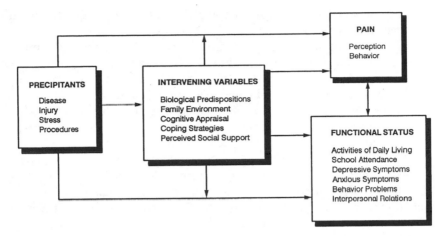

FIGURE 7.1. Biobehavioral model of pediatric pain. From Varni (1989). Reprinted by permission of the author.

painful episode, and which may be reciprocal; and pain consequences, which persist beyond pain relief and include long-term psychological, social, and physical disability (Varni, 1989; Varni et al., 1996a, 1996b).

On an individual-child basis, the conceptual model can inform the development of a tailored intervention. For example, if the child is experiencing a lack of family support or has coping skills deficits, then interventions can be targeted for these problem areas. For the child experiencing depressive symptoms associated with chronic pain, an approach that combines a direct intervention for pain, while also targeting the depressive symptoms, may most efficaciously ameliorate the child's distress. Thus, while the conceptual model has helped to guide empirical work, it has been our clinical experience that this framework can explicitly inform and organize conceptualization of the necessary clinical intervention for the individual child as well.

Pain Coping Construct

The construct of "coping with pain" refers to the process whereby the child engages in cognitive and/or behavioral strategies to manage painful episodes. By definition, coping efforts may be either adaptive or maladaptive, depending on their outcomes in terms of pain relief, emotional adjustment, or functional status. Thus, coping is conceptualized as a process mechanism and not as an outcome measure. The assessment of both adaptive and maladaptive pain coping strategies may provide heuristic guidance in explaining the variability in pain perception and pain behavior. Furthermore, the systematic study of pediatric pain coping strategies may contribute substantively to the conceptual understanding of the individual differences observed in patients' responses to pharmacological and cognitive-behavioral treatment modalities.

Although coping has been studied in pediatric pain populations to some degree, research has focused mostly on acute procedural pain (Siegel & Smith, 1989). In contrast, an extensive empirical literature has documented the effects of pain coping strategies on pain and adjustment in adult chronic pain patients (Jensen, Turner, Romano, & Karoly, 1991), resulting in significant advances in the conceptual understanding of the prediction of pain and adjustment by adult-oriented pain-coping strategies.

Within the biobehavioral conceptual model of pediatric pain, coping strategies are hypothesized to be a vital intervening factor (Varni, 1989). This theoretical framework served as the heuristic paradigm for the conceptual development of the Waldron–Varni Pediatric Pain Coping Inventory (PPCI). The PPCI was developed with the goal of facilitating a theory-driven programmatic research effort designed to further the understanding of the demonstrated individual differences in pediatric pain perception and pain behavior, and potentially to give empirical direction in the development and further refinement of cognitive-behavioral pain management treatment techniques for children.

The results of an initial investigation of the psychometric properties of the PPCI revealed a five-factor multidimensional structure for the cohort of 187 children and adolescents studied: (1) cognitive self-instructions, (2) seeks social support, (3) strives to rest and be alone, (4) cognitive refocusing, and (5) problem-solving self-efficacy (Varni et al., 1996b). It is anticipated that a taxonomy of pediatric pain coping strategies will emerge from this empirical effort, within the theoretical framework illustrated in Figure 7.1. Assessing pediatric pain coping strategies is consistent with an integrative cognitive-behavioral therapy framework that seeks to promote children's competency in confronting challenging biobehavioral problems.

Cognitive-Behavioral Treatment of Pediatric Pain

In the past several years, more and more investigators have generated a substantial database from which the clinical potential of cognitive-behavioral therapy techniques in managing pediatric pain has become evident (Bush & Harkins, 1991; McGrath, 1990). The primary cognitive-behavioral treatment techniques utilized in the management of pediatric pain and distress have been categorized by Varni (1983) as follows: (1) pain perception regulation modalities through such self-regulatory techniques as progressive muscle relaxation, meditation, and guided imagery; and (2) pain behavior modification, which identifies and modifies social and environmental factors that influence pain expression and rehabilitation. The following sections illustrate the applications of these cognitive-behavioral techniques to the management of chronic and recurrent pain in juvenile rheumatoid arthritis.

Chronic and Recurrent Pain in Juvenile Rheumatoid Arthritis

Juvenile rheumatoid arthritis (JRA) is one of the most common pediatric chronic diseases. In contrast to the rather extensive research literature on the assessment and management of pain in adult rheumatoid arthritis (RA), pain associated with JRA and the other pediatric rheumatic diseases remained a largely underdeveloped area of research and an undertreated clinical problem until recently (Varni & Bernstein, 1991). Numerous research studies have been published on RA pain, particularly as part of a quality-of-life assessment methodology including the three dimensions of physical disability, pain, and psychological functioning (Anderson, Firschein, & Meenan, 1989). Although pain has been well recognized as a significant problem to be managed in RA, similar recognition had not been forthcoming in JRA until very recently. This neglect has a number of potential causes, preeminent among them the previously inaccurate assessment methodologies for pediatric pain measurement (Varni & Bernstein, 1991).

The previous limitations of the available pediatric research literature on pain assessment and management in JRA have resulted in a relative lack of development of empirically derived guidelines within institutions and virtually no such development across institutions. As a result, both a general commitment to adequate management of pediatric pain and specific pain treatment protocols are left to the discretion of individual pediatric rheumatologists. However, given that there is not a one-to-one relationship between disease activity and pain intensity—psychological and social factors may modify the pain experience, focusing only on disease control may provide inadequate patient care. Measurement of pain should be considered as vital as measurement of disease activity parameters, and pain levels should be regularly assessed at all clinic visits as part of patient care quality assurance (Varni & Bernstein, 1991).

Pain Assessment

To facilitate the incorporation of accurate pain measures into pediatric rheumatology clinical trials, Varni and his associates developed the Pediatric Pain Questionnaire (PPQ), designed to be sensitive to children's particular cognitive developmental stages (Varni & Thompson, 1985). Although the PPQ is a comprehensive instrument, the three components that appear to be most germane for intervention studies are the PPQ's age-appropriate visual analogue scale (VAS), body outline, and pain descriptor list.

Visual Analogue Scale. Present pain and worst pain intensity for the previous week are assessed in the PPQ by a VAS. Each VAS is a 10-centimeter horizontal line with no numbers, marks, or descriptive vocabulary words along its length. The child VAS is anchored with developmentally appropriate pain descriptors (e.g., *Not hurting, Hurting a whole lot*) and happy and sad faces. The adolescent and parent VAS are anchored by the phrases *No pain* and *Severe pain,* in addition to the pain descriptors *Hurting* and *Discomfort.* The instructions for the VAS ask the child, adolescent, or parent to place a vertical line through the horizontal VAS line that represents the intensity of pain along the continuum from *No pain* to *Severe pain.*

The assessment of pediatric pain must fulfill the requirements for any measurement instrument, including reliability, validity, minimum inherent bias, and versatility (McGrath, 1986). As reviewed by McGrath, the VAS, although deceptively simple, has demonstrated the reliability, validity, minimum inherent bias, and versatility necessary for an objective pain measure in a variety of experimental and clinical pain studies. Historically, the VAS has been used extensively with adult pain patients because of its sensitivity and reproducibility (Huskinsson, 1983). As a continuous measurement scale, the VAS avoids the spurious clustering of pain reports that can occur with stepwise or categorical pain scaling methods (Levine, Gordon, Smith, & Fields, 1981). In both children and adults, the VAS has demonstrated excellent construct validity in postoperative medication studies, showing the expected reduction in pain subsequent to analgesia intake (Aradine, Beyer, & Tompkins, 1988; Levine et al., 1981; O'Hara, McGrath, D'Astous, & Vair, 1987; Taenzer, 1983) and in studies of chronic musculoskeletal pain, demonstrating the expected increase in perceived pain intensity with greater rheumatic disease activity (Thompson, Varni, & Hanson, 1987; Varni et al., 1987) and perceived stress and emotional distress (Varni et al., 1996a, 1996b). The child VAS has been shown to be a reliable and valid measure of pain perception in children as young as 5 years (McGrath & deVeber, 1986; Varni et al., 1987).

Body Outline. Body outline figures are very useful in helping children report the location of their pain (Savedra & Tesler, 1989). In the PPQ, age-appropriate body outlines are provided for children, adolescents, and parents. For children, a color-coded pain rating scale is used to measure both pain intensity and location. Four developmentally appropriate categories of pain descriptors are provided, along with eight standard crayons and the age-appropriate body outline. The child is instructed to color in the four boxes underneath each descriptive category representing pain intensity, and then to color in the body outline with the selected color-intensity match. In this way, the child can communicate to the health professional not only the exact location of multiple painful joint sites but also four levels of pain intensity. Body outlines can be effectively used with children as young as 5 years of age (Varni et al., 1987).

Pain Descriptors. Melzack (1975) made the case for sensory, affective, and evaluative pain descriptors in the original publication of the McGill

Pain Questionnaire (MPQ). Based on age-appropriate modifications of the MPQ, the PPQ contains a list of pain descriptors in order to assess the sensory, affective, and evaluative qualities of a child's pain experience. The child is instructed to circle the words from the list that best describe his or her pain.

In the PPQ, children are first given the opportunity to write down words that describe their pain before being presented with the word list. However, word recognition appears to be easier than generating their own words for younger children (Savedra & Tesler, 1989). Wilkie et al. (1990) have shown that pediatric pain descriptors from a supplied word list correlated significantly with pain intensity scores and the number of pain sites (concurrent validity), and also demonstrated significant test–retest reliability.

Comprehensive Assessment of Pediatric Pain

The degree of musculoskeletal pain experienced by a child with JRA (or an adult with RA) is the result of the interaction among disease activity, tissue damage, and a number of factors specific to the individual child (or adult). Consequently, there is no "right" amount pain for a given joint condition; the "right" amount is what the individual reports. Again, the veracity of a child's pain report should not be questioned. Rather, a search for the factors that influence pain perception and report is a more meaningful clinical approach.

Pain assessment encompasses the measurement not only of pain intensity, location, and quality, but also of what exacerbates or ameliorates pain perception. Consequently, a comprehensive assessment of pediatric pain requires a multifactorial approach (Thompson et al., 1987; Varni, Wilcox, & Hanson, 1988). A multidimensional assessment battery provides a comprehensive basis for developing pediatric chronic and recurrent pain management interventions.

Cognitive-Behavioral Management of Pain in Juvenile Arthritis

A comprehensive pain management approach in pediatric rheumatology should combine appropriate pharmacological agents with cognitive-behavioral therapy and physical modalities to optimize patients' quality of life (Varni & Bernstein, 1991). The primary cognitive-behavioral treatment techniques utilized in the management of pain in JRA are (1) pain perception regulation and (2) pain behavior modification.

Walco, Varni, and Ilowite (1992) have applied these cognitive-behavioral therapy techniques to the management of chronic and recurrent pain associated with JRA. The cognitive-behavioral intervention was based on the self-regulation treatment package originally developed by Varni and associates (Varni, 1981; Varni & Gilbert, 1982, Varni, Gilbert, & Dietrich, 1981) for the chronic musculoskeletal pain associated with hemophilic arthropathy.

Instruction in the cognitive-behavioral self-regulation of arthritic pain perception consisted of three sequential phases:

1. Each child was first taught a 25-step progressive muscle relaxation sequence involving the alternate tensing and relaxing of major muscle groups.

2. The child was then taught meditative breathing exercises, consisting of medium-deep breaths inhaled through the nose and slowly exhaled through the mouth. While exhaling, the child was instructed to say the word "relax" silently to him- or herself, and initially to describe aloud and subsequently visualize the word "relax" in warm colors, as if written in colored chalk on a blackboard.

3. Finally, the child was instructed in the use of guided imagery techniques consisting of pleasant, distracting scenes selected by the child, then to imagine him- or herself in a scene previously experienced as pain-free. Initially, the child was instructed to imagine actually being in the scene, not simply to observe him- or herself there. The scene was evoked by a detailed multisensory description by the therapist and subsequently described out loud by the child. Such scenes depended on the child's preference but could include detailed descriptions of the sound and sights of an ocean and beach. Once the scene was clearly visualized by the child, he or she was instructed to experiment with other, different scenes to maintain interest and variety. Additional guided imagery techniques involved invoking images that represented a metaphor for the sensory pain experience, and then altering the metaphor and thus the perception of pain. Specific images were based on sensory descriptors endorsed on the PPQ, with elaboration through subsequent discussion in an attempt to generate a concrete metaphor. For example, if a child described the pain as "hot," a metaphorical image might be that "Someone is in my knee with a blowtorch." An image was then generated of a blowtorch in the knee that was subsequently extinguished. Another alternative involved the use of colors. Children generated images in which painful sites appeared in a particular color that contrasted with pain-free tissue. They then imagined the colored area shrinking and then disappearing. Finally, for some of the older children, sessions began with a simple review of the nervous system, then images of "pain switches" were used to block the transmission of pain messages.

The children were instructed to practice these techniques on a regular basis in the home and were seen for a total of eight weekly individual sessions for maintenance and problem solving. Parents were seen on two occasions. In the first, a review of behavioral pain management techniques was provided. Specific suggestions for implementation with their children were made, including behavior modification techniques to encourage adaptive activities and to discourage maladaptive pain behaviors (Masek, Russo, & Varni, 1984). The second session, held 4–6 weeks after the first, served as a forum to discuss the implementation of behavioral pain management and to address questions that may have arisen.

Analysis of data on 13 children, ages 5–16 years, with JRA who completed the intervention indicated therapeutic effects with this cohort. In order to assess the immediate short-term effects of the intervention, the children were administered the PPQ's VAS for present pain just prior to engaging in the self-regulation techniques, and again immediately after completing the sequence (approximately 20 minutes are required to complete the self-regulation protocol). VAS data collected in the clinic setting demonstrated excellent immediate short-term benefits of the self-regulation techniques. At a 6-month follow-up assessment, the children's average home ratings of pain on the VAS were significantly lower. Although there was some increase of pain at the 12-month assessment relative to the 6-month follow-up assessment, the average pain intensity was still in the mild range. Parent VAS data essentially paralleled those of their children at the follow-up assessment periods. Functional status, as measured by the Child Activities of Daily Living Index (Varni, Wilcox, Hanson, & Brik, 1988) also showed improvement at the 6- and 12-month follow-up assessment periods relative to the pretreatment baseline.

The results of this study on the self-regulation of chronic musculoskeletal pain by children with JRA suggest the value of cognitive-behavioral techniques as components of comprehensive disease management. The findings support the potential of combining these cognitive-behavioral techniques with disease-modifying pharmacological treatments in order to minimize the recurrent "breakthrough" pain associated with JRA, and to maximize overall quality of life (Varni & Bernstein, 1991).

Although based on a relatively small sample size, these initial findings appear to have generalizability given that the identical cognitive-behavioral therapy treatment package was successfully utilized for chronic musculoskeletal pain associated with hemophilic arthropathy (Varni et al., 1981; Varni & Gilbert, 1982; Varni, Katz, & Dash, 1982). Other studies have also successfully employed cognitive-behavioral therapy for pain management in adult RA (Bradley et al., 1987; O'Leary, Shoor, Lorig, & Holman, 1988; Parker et al., 1988) and in JRA (Lavigne, Ross, Berry, Hayford, & Pachman, 1992). The consistency of the findings across various pediatric and adult musculoskeletal pain populations supports the potential generalizability of these initial findings. However, these results need to be replicated with a larger population of children with JRA in order for us to be truly confident of their actual generalizability.

PROBLEM-SOLVING SKILLS TRAINING
IN PEDIATRIC CANCER

The American Cancer Society estimated that 8,700 children would be newly diagnosed with cancer in 1998. Pediatric cancer has evolved from an inevitably fatal illness to a life-threatening chronic disease. Today, most children survive for 5 years or longer (Bleyer, 1990; Ross, Severson, Pollack, & Robison, 1996). Because of the declining death rate, it is predicted that by the year 2000, one in 1,000 young adults ages 20–29 years will be a survivor of childhood cancer given the current cure rate (Meadows & Hobbie, 1986).

Enhancing health-related quality of life (HRQOL) outcomes in pediatric cancer patients has been increasingly underscored (Mulhern, Hancock, Fairclough, & Kun, 1992; Varni, Katz, Seid, Quiggins, & Friedman-Bender, 1998). As the survival rate for pediatric cancer patients increases, psychological, social, and cognitive sequelae have and will continue to assume an increasingly prominent role in intervention and outcomes analyses.

Children and adolescents with cancer often experience disruptions in their social relations with peers, siblings, teachers, and parents due to illness-imposed limitations and extensive medical treatments (Katz, Rubenstein, Hubert, & Blew, 1988). Numerous authors have described the influences of social support and social competence on an individual's ability to tolerate stress such as that associated with a life-threatening illness (Johnson, 1986; Garmezy, 1983; Rutter, 1984; Varni & Katz, 1997) or physical handicap (Varni, Rubenfeld, Talbot, & Setoguchi, 1989). Social support refers to the perceived or actual positive regard expressed by significant others. Social competence refers to being accepted by peers and significant others (Harter & Pike, 1984).

Successful socializing experiences in childhood are associated with prosocial behavior, academic achievement, and the ability to withstand stress (Cole, Martin, Powers, & Truglio, 1996; Werner & Smith, 1982). Conversely, negative peer relationships during childhood are associated with academic failure, aggressive behavior, and psychopathology in childhood that often continue into adulthood. Because of their exposure to numerous negative, stressful experiences that can impair social relationships and social competencies, children with cancer are at risk for problems in these domains (Carpentieri, Mulhern, Douglas, Hanna, & Fairclough, 1993; Nassau & Drotar, 1997; Varni & Katz, 1997; Sawyer, Antoniou, Toogood, Rice, & Baghurst, 1993; Shelby, Nagle, Barnett-Queen, Quattlebaum, & Wuori, 1998). The literature supports the hypothesis that children with peer-relationship difficulties are at risk for feelings of loneliness, depression, poor self-esteem, and other long-term adjustment problems (Parker & Asher, 1987).

Previous research has demonstrated the importance of perceived social support from parents, teachers, and classmates as predictors of adjustment in children with chronic physical disorders (Varni, Babani, Wallander, Roe, & Frasier, 1989; Varni, Setoguchi, Rappaport, & Talbot, 1991; Varni & Setoguchi, 1993; Varni et al., 1992). These investigations demonstrate the potentially powerful effects of the social environment of the school setting, with perceived classmate social support the most significant predictor variable across depressive symptoms, trait anxiety, and general self-esteem. In particular, Varni, Katz, Colegrove, and Dolgin (1994) studied children newly diagnosed with cancer, finding that higher perceived classmate social support statistically predicted lower depressive symptoms, lower state and trait anxiety, lower social anxiety, and higher general self-esteem, as well as lower internalizing and externalizing behavior problems. Higher perceived teacher social support statistically predicted lower state anxiety and lower externalizing behavior problems. These findings underscore the importance of maximizing the social competence of children with cancer in order to facilitate positive social interactions with classmates and teachers.

Social Skills Training Interventions

Social skills training is one of the most promising and effective methods of enhancing children's social competence with peers (Elliott & Gresham, 1993). The basic premise of social skills intervention is that unaccepted or rejected children lack the requisite skills to develop and maintain peer relationships (Crick & Dodge, 1994). By teaching children these requisite social skills, one can improve peer relationships and ultimately enhance long-term development in such adjustment domains as school achievement, self-esteem, shyness/withdrawal, and depressive symptoms (Cole et al., 1996; Furman & Gavin, 1989). Since peer-relationship difficulties place children at increased risk for long-term adjustment problems, children for whom social skills training is successful would be expected to experience fewer subsequent adjustment problems than children who do not receive explicit social skills instruction (Parker & Asher, 1987).

Children prototypically exhibit deficits in interpersonal skills for three possible reasons: (1) a lack of specific behavioral abilities; (2) a lack of opportunity for peer interaction; and (3) emotional or cognitive factors that interfere with social skills performance. Social skills training is a means of transmitting new skills, strengthening existing skills, and eliminating psychological barriers to social skills performance.

Social skills training typically involves some form of modeling, behavioral rehearsal, corrective feedback, and reinforcement of prosocial behaviors such as demonstrating conversation skills, increasing cooperative play, positive peer interactions, peer acceptance, and making friends (Elliott &

Gresham, 1993). The most commonly used training methods are coaching and behavioral rehearsal with corrective feedback and reinforcement. Situations are based on the real-life experiences that children report encountering. Immediate feedback and suggestions for improvement are critical elements. "Homework" assignments encourage children to use the skills they are learning with their peers (La Greca & Santogrossi, 1980). Programs using these techniques have shown that in comparison to attention placebo and waiting-list control groups, the social skills training group has increased skill in a role-playing situation, greater verbal knowledge of how to interact with peers, and more initiation of peer interactions in the school setting (La Greca & Santogrossi, 1980).

A Social Skills Training Program for Children with Cancer

Ladd (1984) suggested that the development of a skills training curriculum must promote social skills that are ecologically valid (i.e., address social tasks that specific groups of children must perform competently to achieve designated outcomes). This ecologic approach is a crucial element in developing curricula that are relevant to the social challenges faced by children and adolescents with cancer and treatment side effects. Coping with peer teasing, minimizing isolation during periods of medical treatment, and feeling comfortable with interpersonal intimacy are of particular concern to children with cancer who have social skills deficits. Finally, parental involvement in the social skills training process is now recognized as vital in enhancing generalization and maintenance of training effects (Cousins & Weiss, 1993; Pfiffner & McBurnett, 1997).

We have developed a social skills intervention program that we tested in a randomized controlled clinical trial (Varni et al., 1993). Our social skills training program was designed to meet the generic needs of children with newly diagnosed cancer. The social situations and social skills included in the cognitive-behavioral therapy training approach were representative of actual social situations that have been clinically found to present difficulty for school-age children with newly diagnosed cancer (Katz, Dolgin, & Varni, 1990).

A comprehensive training manual was developed. Although a group format is possible, it was more convenient to schedule individual sessions. The program was conducted in three training sessions, with two follow-up sessions. Parents also received one session in the intervention condition to provide them with an overview of the approach, so that they could reinforce the child's use of strategies. Assessment of relevant psychosocial adjustment factors revealed that explicit social skills training benefits children with cancer when they return to their school environment. From this perspective, social skills training may be conceptualized as an effective secondary prevention intervention, the benefits of which may actually increase over time in pediatric cancer patients (Price, Cowen, Lorion, & Ramos-McKay, 1989).

Maternal Problem-Solving Therapy in Pediatric Cancer

Parents, particularly mothers of children and adolescents diagnosed with cancer, are at increased risk for emotional distress, including symptoms of posttraumatic stress. We have developed a Problem-Solving Skills Training Intervention (PSST) modeled after D'Zurilla's Problem-Solving Therapy approach (Varni, Sahler, et al., 1999). D'Zurilla and Goldfried (1971) first conceptualized problem-solving theory and research as a 5-stage process: (1) Problem Orientation, (2) Problem Definition and Formulation, (3) Generation of Alternative Solutions, (4) Decision Making, and (5) Solution Implementation and Solution Verification. A 1986 book and subsequent article by D'Zurilla described in detail the specific techniques in the problem-solving approach to stress management and prevention (D'Zurilla, 1986, 1990). Explicative, theoretically driven correlational and multiple regression analyses utilizing the Social Problem-Solving Inventory (SPSI) as a multidimensional self-report measure of social problem-solving ability have demonstrated the hypothesized relationships between problem-solving skills and psychological stress, depression, anxiety, coping, positive affectivity, negative affectivity optimism, pessimism, and knowledge acquisition (Chang & D'Zurilla, 1996; D'Zurilla & Chang, 1995; D'Zurilla & Nezu, 1990; D'Zurilla & Sheedy, 1991, 1992; Kant, D'Zurilla, & Maydeu-Olivares, 1997). Nezu and Nezu have further developed the social problem-solving therapy treatment studies (Arean et al., 1993; Nezu & Nezu, 1991; Nezu et al., 1994). Positive results have been demonstrated for the PSST interventions in decreasing emotional distress and enhancing HRQOL.

To make the overall philosophy and steps of the training intervention more easily understood and remembered, we previously developed the acronym "Bright IDEAS" and the logo of a lighted bulb. "Bright" signifies the sense of optimism about solving problems that is essential for successful implementation. The letters I (Identify the problem), D (Determine the options), E (Evaluate options and choose the best), A (Act), and S (See if it worked) signify the steps of problem solving as articulated by D'Zurilla and Nezu (1990) and reinterpreted by our group (Varni, Sahler, et al., 1999). The Bright IDEAS paradigm, as presented in our training manual (Varni et al., 1997), consists of six steps: (1) problem orientation philosophy (i.e., the overall Bright IDEAS approach), (2) problem definition and problem formulation (I), (3) generation of alternative solutions (D), (4) decision-making process (E), (5) solution implementation (A), and (6) solution verification (S). This randomized, currently ongoing clinical trial is further described in Varni, Sahler, et al. (1999).

SUMMARY

This chapter described the multiple levels at which cognitive-behavioral interventions may be used to mediate some of the recurrent stresses confronted by children with chronic health conditions. On an immediate basis, children may use such techniques in the context of self-regulation as a means of reducing levels of pain intensity, which may ultimately lead to enhanced health-related quality of life. On a much broader level, once one recognizes the power of peer relationships and social supports in mediating adjustment to chronic malfunctions, social-cognitive problem-solving techniques become central. As other factors mediating the stress–psychological adjustment relationship are identified, innovative cognitive-behavioral strategies for assessment and intervention can be devised and empirically tested.

REFERENCES

Achenbach, T. M., McConaughy, S. H., & Howell, C. T. (1987). Child/adolescent behavioral and emotional problems: Implications of cross-informant correlations for situational specificity. *Psychological Bulletin, 101,* 213–232.

American Cancer Society. (1998). *Cancer facts and figures—1998.* Paper presented at the meeting of the American Cancer Society, Atlanta, GA.

Anderson, B. J., Wolf, F. M., Burkhart, M. T., Cornell, R. G., & Bacon, G. E. (1989). Effects of peer-group intervention on metabolic control of adolescents with IDDM: Randomized outpatient study. *Diabetes Care, 3,* 179–183.

Anderson, J. J., Firschein, H. E., & Meenan, R. F. (1989). Sensitivity of a health status measure to short-term clinical changes in arthritis. *Arthritis and Rheumatism, 32,* 844–850.

Aradine, C. R., Beyer, J. E., & Tompkins, J. M. (1988). Children's pain perception before and after analgesia: A study of instrument construct validity and related issues. *Journal of Pediatric Nursing, 3,* 11–23.

Arean, P. A., Perri, M. G., Nezu, A. M., Schein, R. L., Christopher, F., & Joseph, T. X. (1993). Comparative effectiveness of social problem-solving therapy and reminiscence therapy as treatment for depression of older adults. *Journal of Consulting and Clinical Psychology, 61,* 1003–1010.

Austin, J. K., Patterson, J. M., & Huberty, T. J. (1991). Development of the coping health inventory for children. *Journal of Pediatric Nursing, 16,* 166–174.

Band, E. B. (1990). Children's coping with diabetes: Understanding the role of cognitive development. *Journal of Pediatric Psychology, 15,* 27–42.

Band, E. B., & Weisz, J. R. (1990). Developmental differences in primary and secondary coping and adjustment to juvenile diabetes. *Journal of Clinical Child Psychology, 19,* 150–158.

Baum, D., & Creer, T. (1986). Medication compliance in children with asthma. *Journal of Asthma, 23,* 49–59.

Bleyer, W. A. (1990). The impact of childhood cancer on the United States and the world. *Cancer Journal for Clinicians, 40,* 355–367.

Bradley, L. A., Young, L. D., Anderson, K. O., Turner, R. A., Agudelo, C. A., McDaniel, L. K., Pisko, E., Semble, E. L., & Morgan, T. M. (1987). Effects of psychological therapy on pain behavior of rheumatoid arthritis patients: Treatment outcome and six-month follow-up. *Arthritis and Rheumatism, 30,* 1105–1114.

Bull, B., & Drotar, D. (1991). Coping with cancer in remission: Stressors and strategies reported by children and adolescents. *Journal of Pediatric Psychology, 16*, 767–782.

Bush, J. P., & Harkins, S. W. (1991). *Children in pain: Clinical and research issues from a developmental perspective.* New York: Springer-Verlag.

Carney, R. M., Schechter, K., & Davis, T. (1983). Improving adherence to blood glucose testing in insulin dependent diabetic children. *Behavior Therapy, 14*, 247–254.

Carpentieri, S. C., Mulhern, R. K., Douglas, S., Hanna, S., & Fairclough, D. L. (1993). Behavioral resiliency among children surviving brain tumors: A longitudinal study. *Journal of Clinical Child Psychology, 22*, 236–246.

Casey, R., Rosen, B., Glowasky, A., & Ludwig, S. (1985). An intervention to improve follow-up patients with otitis media. *Clinical Pediatrics, 24*, 149–152.

Cavanaugh, R. M., Jr. (1990). Utilizing the phone appointment for adolescent follow-up. *Clinical Pediatrics, 29*, 302–304.

Celano, M., Geller, R. J., Phillips, K. M., & Ziman, R. (1998). Treatment adherence among low-income children with asthma. *Journal of Pediatric Psychology, 23*, 345–349.

Chambless, D., Sanderson, W. C., Shoham, V., Johnson, S. B., Pope, K. S., Crits-Christoph, P., Baker, M., Johnson, B., Woods, S. R., Sue, S., Beutler, L., Williams, D. A., & McCurry, S. (1996). An update on empirically validated therapies. *Clinical Psychologist, 49*, 5–18.

Chaney, J. M., & Peterson, L. (1989). Family variables and disease management in juvenile rheumatoid arthritis. *Journal of Pediatric Psychology, 14*, 389–403.

Chang, E. C., & D'Zurilla, T. J. (1996). Relations between problem orientation and optimism, pessimism, and trait affectivity: A construct validation study. *Behaviour Research and Therapy, 34*, 185–194.

Colcher, I. S., & Bass, I. S. (1972). Penicillin treatment of streptococcal pharyngitis: A comparison of schedules and the role of specific counseling. *Journal of the American Medical Association, 222*, 657–659.

Cole, D. A., Martin, J. M., Powers, B., & Truglio, R. (1996). Modeling causal relations between academic and social competence and depression: A multitrait multimethod longitudinal study of children. *Journal of Abnormal Psychology, 105*, 258–270.

Cousins, L. S., & Weiss, G. (1993). Parent training and social skills training for children with attention-deficit hyperactivity disorder: How can they be combined for greater effectiveness? *Canadian Journal of Psychiatry, 38*, 449–457.

Coyne, J. C., & Gottlieb, B. P. (1996). The mismeasure of coping by checklist. *Journal of Personality, 64*, 959–991.

Crick, N. R., & Dodge, K. A. (1994). A review and reformulation of social information-processing mechanisms in children's social adjustment. *Psychological Bulletin, 115*, 74–101.

Delamater, A. M., Bubb, J., Davis, S. G., Smith, J. A., Schmidt, L., White, N. H., & Santiago, J. V. (1990). Randomized prospective study of self-management training with newly diagnosed diabetic children. *Diabetes Care, 13*, 492–498.

Dini, E. F., Linkins, R. W., & Chaney, M. (1995). Effectiveness of computer-generated telephone messages in increasing clinic visits. *Archives of Pediatric and Adolescent Medicine, 149*, 902–905.

Donaldson, D., Prinstein, M., Danovsky, M., & Spirito, A. (1997). *Children's patterns of coping.* Paper presented at the 6th Florida Conference on Child Health Psychology, Gainesville, FL.

Drotar, D. (1997). Intervention research: Pushing back the frontiers of pediatric psychology. *Journal of Pediatric Psychology, 22*, 592–606.

D'Zurilla, T. J. (1986). *Problem-solving therapy: A social competence approach to clinical intervention.* New York: Springer.

D'Zurilla, T. J. (1990). Problem-solving training for effective stress management and prevention. *Journal of Cognitive Psychotherapy, 4*, 327–355.

D'Zurilla, T. J., & Chang, E. C. (1995). The relations between social problem solving and coping. *Cognitive Therapy and Research, 19*, 547–562.

D'Zurilla, T. J., & Goldfried, M. (1971). Problem-solving and behavior modification. *Journal of Abnormal Psychology, 78,* 107–126.

D'Zurilla, T. J., & Nezu, A. M. (1990). Development and preliminary evaluation of the Social Problem-Solving Inventory (SPSI). *Psychological Assessment, 2,* 156–163.

D'Zurilla, T. J., & Sheedy, C. F. (1991). The relation between social problem-solving ability and subsequent level of psychological stress in college students. *Journal of Personality and Social Psychology, 61,* 841–846.

D'Zurilla, T. J., & Sheedy, C. F. (1992). The relation between social problem-solving ability and subsequent level of academic competence in college students. *Cognitive Therapy and Research, 16,* 589–599.

Elliott, S. N., & Gresham, F. M. (1993). Social skills interventions for children. *Behavior Modification, 17,* 287–313.

Eney, R. D., & Goldstein, E. O. (1976). Compliance of chronic asthmatics with oral administration of theophylline as measured by serum and salivary levels. *Pediatrics, 57,* 513–517.

Epstein, L. H., Beck, S., Figueroa, I., Farkas, G., Kazdin, A. E., Daneman, D., & Becker, D. (1981). The effects of targeting improvements in urine glucose on metabolic control in children with insulin dependent diabetes. *Journal of Applied Behavior Analysis, 14,* 365–375.

Fink, D., Malloy, M. J., Cohen, M., Greycloud, M. A., & Martin, F. (1969). Effective patient care in the pediatric ambulatory setting: A study of the acute care clinic. *Pediatrics, 43,* 927–935.

Finney, J. W., Lemanek, K. L., Brophy, C. J., & Cataldo, M. F. (1990). Pediatric appointment keeping: Improving adherence in a primary care allergy clinic. *Journal of Pediatric Psychology, 15,* 571–579.

Freund, A., Johnson, S. B., Silverstein, J., & Thomas, J. (1991). Assessing daily management of childhood disease using 24-hour recall interviews: Reliability and stability. *Health Psychology, 10,* 200–208.

Friedman, I. M., & Litt, I. F. (1987). Adolescents' compliance with therapeutic regimens: Psychological and social aspects and intervention. *Journal of Adolescent Health Care, 8,* 52–65.

Friman, P. C., Finney, J. W., Rapoff, M. A., & Christophersen, E. R. (1985). Improving pediatric appointment keeping with reminders and reduced response requirement. *Journal of Applied Behavior Analysis, 18,* 315–321.

Furman, W., & Gavin, L. (1989). Peers' influence on adjustment and development: A view from the intervention literature. In T. J. Berndt & G. W. Ladd (Eds.), *Peer relationships in child development.* New York: Wiley.

Gaffney, A., & Dunne, E. A. (1986). Developmental aspects of children's definitions of pain. *Pain, 26,* 105–117.

Garmezy, N. (1983). Stressors of childhood. In N. Garmezy & M. Rutter (Eds.), *Stress, coping and development.* New York: McGraw-Hill.

Gotay, C. C., Korn, E. L., McCabe, M. S., Moore, T. D., & Cheson, B. D. (1992). Quality of life assessment in cancer treatment protocols: Research issues in protocol development. *Journal of the National Cancer Institute, 84,* 575–579.

Greco, P., Pendley, J. S., & McDonnell, K. (1999, April). *Obtaining reports of and measuring the effects of an intervention on peer support offered to adolescents with diabetes.* Paper presented at the Florida Conference on Child Health Psychology, Gainesville, FL.

Greenan-Fowler, E., Powell, C., & Varni, J. W. (1987). Behavioral treatment of adherence to therapeutic exercise by children with hemophilia. *Archives of Physical Medicine and Rehabilitation, 68,* 846–849.

Gross, A. M., Johnson, W. G., Wildman, H. E., & Mullett, M. (1981). Coping skills training with insulin dependent preadolescent diabetics. *Child Behavior Therapy, 3,* 141–153.

Diabetes Control and Complication Trial (DCCT) (1993). The effect of intensive treatment of diabetes on the development and progression of long-term complications in insulin-dependent diabetes mellitus. *New England Journal of Medicine, 329,* 977–986.

Guyatt, G. H., Feeny, D. H., & Patrick, D. L. (1993). Measuring health-related quality of life: Basic science review. *Annals of Internal Medicine, 70,* 225–230.

Guyatt, G. H., Juniper, E. F., Griffith, L. E., Feeny, D. H., & Ferry, P. J. (1997). Children and adult perceptions of childhood asthma. *Pediatrics, 99,* 165–168.

Harter, S., & Pike, R. (1984). The pictorial scale of perceived competence and social acceptance for young children. *Child Development, 55,* 1969–1982.

Huskinsson, E. C. (1983). Visual analogue scales. In R. Melzack (Ed.), *Pain measurement and assessment* (pp. 33–37). New York: Raven Press.

Jensen, M. P., Turner, J. A., Romano, J. M., & Karoly, P. (1991). Coping with chronic pain: A critical review of the literature. *Pain, 47,* 249–283.

Johnson, J. H. (1986). *Life events as stressors in childhood and adolescence.* Beverly Hills, CA: Sage.

Johnson, S. B., Silverstein, J., Rosenbloom, A., Carter, R., & Cunningham, W. (1986). Assessing daily management of childhood diabetes. *Health Psychology, 5,* 545–564.

Kant, G. L., D'Zurilla, T. J., & Maydeu-Olivares, A. (1997). Social problem solving as a mediator of stress-related depression and anxiety in middle aged and elderly community residents. *Cognitive Therapy and Research, 21,* 73 96.

Katz, E. R., Dolgin, M. J., & Varni, J. W. (1990). Cancer in children and adolescents. In A. M. Gross & R. S. Drabman (Eds.), *Handbook of clinical behavioral pediatrics* (pp. 129–146). New York: Plenum Press.

Katz, E. R., Rubenstein, C. L., Hubert, N. C., & Blew, A. (1988). School and social reintegration of children with cancer. *Journal of Psychosocial Oncology, 6,* 123–140.

Killam, P. E., Apodaca, L., Manella, K. J., & Varni, J. W. (1983). Behavioral pediatric weight rehabilitation for children with myelomeningocele. *American Journal of Maternal Child Nursing, 8,* 280–286.

Ladd, G. W. (1984). Social skills training with children: Issues in research and practice. *Clinical Psychology Review, 4,* 317–337.

La Greca, A. M. (1990). Issues and perspectives on the child assessment process. In A. M. La Greca (Ed.), *Through the eyes of the child: Obtaining self-reports from children and adolescents* (pp. 3–17). Boston: Allyn & Bacon.

La Greca, A. M., Auslander, W. F., Greco, P., Spetter, D., Fisher, E. B., Jr., & Santiago, J. V. (1995). I get by with a little help from my family and friends: Adolescents' support for diabetes care. *Journal of Pediatric Psychology, 20,* 449–476.

La Greca, A. M., Follansbee, D., & Skyler, J. S. (1990). Developmental and behavioral aspects of diabetes management in youngsters. *Children's Health Care, 19,* 132–137.

La Greca, A. M., & Santogrossi, D. A. (1980). Social skills training with elementary school students: A behavioral group approach. *Journal of Consulting and Clinical Psychology, 48,* 220–227.

La Greca, A. M., & Schuman, W. B. (1995). Adherence to prescribed medical regimens. In M. C. Roberts (Ed.), *Handbook of pediatric psychology* (2nd ed., pp. 55–83). New York: Guilford Press.

La Greca, A. M., & Skyler, J. S. (1991). Psychosocial issues in IDDM: A multivariate framework. In P. McCabe, N. Schneiderman, T. Field, & J. S. Skyler (Eds.), *Stress, coping and disease* (pp. 169–190). Hillsdale, NJ: Erlbaum.

La Greca, A. M., & Varni, J. W. (1993). Interventions in pediatric psychology: A look toward the future. *Journal of Pediatric Psychology, 18,* 667–679.

Lavigne, J. V., Ross, C. K., Berry, S. L., Hayford, J. R., & Pachman, L. M. (1992). Evaluation of a psychological treatment package for treating pain in juvenile rheumatoid arthritis. *Arthritis Care and Research, 5,* 101–110.

Leickly, F. E., Wade, S. L., Crain, E., Kruszon-Moran, D., Wright, E. C., & Evans, R. (1998). Self-reported adherence, management behavior, and barriers to care after an emergency department visit by inner city children with asthma. *Pediatrics, 101,* E8.

Levine, J. D., Gordon, N. C., Smith, R., & Fields, T. (1981). Analgesic responses to morphine and placebo in individuals with post-operative pain. *Pain, 10,* 379–389.

Lima, J., Nazarian, L., Charney, E., & Lahti, C. (1976). Compliance with short-term antimicrobial therapy: Some techniques that help. *Pediatrics, 57*, 383–386.

Litt, I. F., & Cuskey, W. R. (1980). Compliance with medical regimens during adolescence. *Pediatric Clinics of North America, 27*, 1–15.

Lowe, K., & Lutzker, J. R. (1979). Increasing compliance to a medical regimen with a juvenile diabetic. *Behavior Therapy, 10*, 57–64.

Masek, B. J., Russo, D. C., & Varni, J. W. (1984). Behavioral approaches to the management of chronic pain in children. *Pediatric Clinics of North America, 31*, 1113–1131.

Mattar, M. F., Markello, J., & Yaffe, S. J. (1975). Pharmaceutic factors affecting pediatric compliance. *Pediatrics, 55*, 101–108.

McGrath, P. A. (1986). The measurement of human pain. *Endodonics and Dental Traumatology, 2*, 124–129.

McGrath, P. A. (1990). *Pain in children: Nature, assessment, and treatment.* New York: Guilford Press.

McGrath, P. A., & deVeber, L. L. (1986). The management of acute pain evoked by medical procedures in children with cancer. *Journal of Pain and Symptom Management, 1*, 145–150.

McGrath, P. J., & Unruh, A. M. (1987). *Pain in children and adolescents.* Amsterdam: Elsevier.

McQuaid, E., & Nassau, J. (in press). Empirically supported treatments of disease related symptoms in pediatric psychology: Asthma, diabetes, and cancer. *Journal of Pediatric Psychology.*

Meadows, A. T., & Hobbie, W. L. (1986). The medical consequences of cure. *Cancer, 58*, 524–528.

Melzack, R. (1975). The McGill Pain Questionnaire: Major properties and scoring methods. *Pain, 1*, 277–299.

Mendez, F. J., & Belendez, M. (1997). Effects of a behavioral intervention on treatment adherence and stress management in adolescents with IDDM. *Diabetes Care, 20*, 1370–1375.

Miller, S. M., Sherman, H. D., Combs, C., & Kruus, L. (1992). Patterns of coping with short-term medical and dental stressors: Nature, complications, and future directions. In A. M. La Greca, L. J. Siegel, J. C. Wallender, & C. E. Walker (Eds.), *Stress and coping in child health* (pp. 157–190). New York: Guilford Press.

Mulhern, R. K., Hancock, J., Fairclough, D., & Kun, L. (1992). Neuropsychological status of children treated for brain tumors: A critical review and integrative analysis. *Medical and Pediatric Oncology, 20*, 181–191.

Nassau, J. H., & Drotar, D. (1997). Social competence among children with central nervous system related chronic health conditions: A review. *Journal of Pediatric Psychology, 22*, 771–793.

Newacheck, P. W., Strickland, B., Shonkoff, J. P., Perrin, J. M., McPherson, M., McManus, M., Lauver, C., Fox, H., & Arango, P. (1998). An epidemiologic profile of children with special health care needs. *Pediatrics, 102*, 117–123.

Newacheck, P. W., & Taylor, W. R. (1992). Childhood chronic illness: Prevalence, severity, and impact. *American Journal of Public Health, 82*, 364–371.

Nezu, A. M., Nezu, C. M., Faddis, S., Houts, P. S., DelliCarpini, L. A., Pfeiffer, E. J., & Rothenburg, J. L. (1994). *Problem solving and distress among recently diagnosed cancer patients.* San Diego:

Nezu, C. M., & Nezu, A. M. (1991). Assertiveness and problem-solving training for mildly mentally retarded persons with dual diagnoses. *Research in Developmental Disabilities, 12*, 371–386.

O'Brien, G., & Lazebnik, R. (1998). Telephone call reminders and attendance in an adolescent clinic. *Pediatrics, 101*, E6.

O'Hara, M., McGrath, P. J., D'Astous, J. D., & Vair, C. A. (1987). Oral morphine versus injected meperidine (Demerol) for pain relief in children after orthopedic surgery. *Journal of Pediatric Orthopaedics, 7*, 78–82.

O'Leary, A., Shoor, S., Lorig, K., & Holman, H. R. (1988). A cognitive-behavioral treatment for rehumatoid arthritis. *Health Psychology, 7*, 527–544.

Olson, A., Johansen, S., Powers, L., Pope, J., & Klein, R. (1993). Cognitive coping strategies of children with chronic illness. *Journal of Developmental and Behavioral Pediatrics, 14*, 217–223.

Parker, J. C., Frank, R. G., Beck, N. C., Smarr, K. L., Beuscher, K. L., Phillips, L. R., Smith, E. I., Anderson, S. K., & Walker, S. E. (1988). Pain management in rheumatoid arthritis patients: A cognitive-behavioral approach. *Arthritis and Rheumatism, 31*, 593–601.

Parker, J. G., & Asher, S. R. (1987). Peer relations and later personal adjustment: Are low-accepted children at risk. *Psychological Bulletin, 102*, 357–389.

Pfiffner, L. J., & McBurnett, K. (1997). Social skills training with parent generalization: Treatment effects for children with attention deficit disorder. *Journal of Consulting and Clinical Psychology, 65*, 749–757.

Phipps, S., Fairclough, D., & Mulhern, R. (1995). Avoidant coping in children with cancer. *Journal of Pediatric Psychology, 20*, 217–232.

Powers, S. (1999). Empirically supported treatments in pediatric psychology: Procedure-related pain. *Journal of Pediatric Psychology, 24*, 131–146.

Price, R. H., Cowen, E. L., Lorion, R. P., & Ramos-McKay, J. (1989). The search for effective prevention programs: What we learned along the way. *American Journal of Orthopsychiatry, 59*, 49–58.

Pruitt, S., Seid, M., Varni, J. W., & Setoguchi, Y. (1999). Toddlers with limb deficiency: Conceptual basis and initial application of a functional status outcome measure. *Archives of Physical Medicine and Rehabilitation, 80*, 819–824.

Pruitt, S. D., Varni, J. W., Seid, M., & Setoguchi, Y. (1998). Functional status in limb deficiency: Development of an outcome measure for preschool children. *Archives of Physical Medicine and Rehabilitation, 79*, 405–411.

Pruitt, S. D., Varni, J. W., & Setoguchi, Y. (1996). Functional status in children with limb deficiency: Development and initial validation of an outcome measure. *Archives of Physical Medicine and Rehabilitation, 77*, 1233–1238.

Quittner, A. L., Tolbert, V. E., Regoli, M. J., Orenstein, D., Hollingsworth, J. L., & Eigen, H. (1996). Development of the Role-Play Inventory of Situations and Coping Strategies (RISCS) for parents of children with cystic fibrosis. *Journal of Pediatric Psychology, 21*, 209–235.

Rapoff, M. A., Purviance, M. R., & Lindsley, C. B. (1988). Educational and behavioral strategies for improving medication compliance in juvenile rheumatoid arthritis. *Archives of Physical and Medical Rehabilitation, 69*, 439–441.

Ross, D. M., & Ross, S. A. (1988). *Childhood pain: Current issues, research, and management.* Baltimore: Urban & Schwarzenberg.

Ross, J. A., Severson, R. K., Pollack, B. H., & Robison, L. L. (1996). Childhood cancer in the United States: A geographical analysis of cases from the pediatric cooperative clinical trials groups. *Cancer, 77*, 201–207.

Roter, D. L., Hall, J. A., Merisca, R., Nordstrom, B., Cretin, D., & Svarstad, B. (1998). Effectiveness of interventions to improve patient compliance in juvenile rheumatoid arthritis. *Archives of Physical and Medical Rehabilitation, 69*, 439–441.

Rutter, M. (1984). Protective factors in children's responses to stress and disadvantage. In J. M. Jaffe, G. W. Albee, & L. D. Kelly (Eds.), *Readings in primary prevention of psychopathology.* Hanover, NH: University Press of New England.

Satin, W., La Greca, A. M., Zigo, M. A., & Skyler, J. S. (1989). Diabetes in adolescence: Effects of multi-family group intervention and parent simulation of diabetes. *Journal of Pediatric Psychology, 14*, 259–276.

Savedra, M. C., & Tesler, M. D. (1989). Assessing children's and adolescents' pain. *Pediatrician, 16*, 24–29.

Sawyer, M. G., Antoniou, G., Toogood, I., Rice, M., & Baghurst, P. A. (1993). A prospective study of the psychological adjustment of parents and families of children with cancer. *Journal of Paediatrics and Child Health, 29*, 352–356.

Schafer, L. C., Glasgow, R. E., & McCaul, K. D. (1982). Adherence to IDDM regimens: Relationship to psychosocial variables and metabolic control. *Diabetes Care, 6*, 493–498.

Schechter, N. L., Berde, C. B., & Yaster, M. (1993). *Pain in infants, children and adolescents.* Baltimore: Williams & Wilkins.

Schipper, H., Clinch, J. J., & Olweny, C. L. M. (1996). Quality of life studies: Definitions and conceptual issues. In B. Spilker (Ed.), *Quality of life and pharmacoeconomics in clinical trials* (2nd ed., pp. 11–23). Philadelphia: Lippincott–Raven.

Shelby, M. D., Nagle, R. J., Barnett-Queen, L. L., Quattlebaum, P. D., & Wuori, D. F. (1998). Parental reports of psychosocial competence in child survivors of acute lymphocytic leukemia. *Children's Health Care, 27*, 113–129.

Siegel, L. J., & Smith, K. E. (1989). Children's strategies for coping with pain. *Pediatrician, 16*, 110–118.

Simoni, J. M., Asarnow, J. R., Munford, P. R., Koprowski, C. M., Belin, T. R., & Salusky, I. B. (1997). Psychological distress and treatment adherence among children on dialysis. *Pediatric Nephrology, 11*, 604–606.

Spirito, A. (1996). Commentary: Pitfalls in the use of brief screening measures of coping. *Journal of Pediatric Psychology, 4*, 573–575.

Spirito, A., Stark, L., Gil, K., & Tyc, V. (1995). Coping with everyday and disease-related stressors by chronically ill children and adolescents. *Journal of the American Academy of Child and Adolescent Psychiatry, 34*, 283–290.

Spirito, A., Stark, L. J., & Williams, C. (1988). Development of a brief checklist to assess coping in pediatric patients. *Journal of Pediatric Psychology, 13*, 555–574.

Sprangers, M. A. G., & Aaronson, N. K. (1992). The role of health care providers and significant others in evaluating the quality of life of patients with chronic disease: A review. *Journal of Clinical Epidemiology, 45*, 743–760.

Sprangers, M. A. G., Cull, A., Bjordal, K., Groenvold, M., & Aaronson, N. K. (1993). The European Organization for Research and Treatment of Cancer approach to quality of life assessment: Guidelines for developing questionnaire modules. *Quality of Life Research, 2*, 287–295.

Stein, R. E. K., Bauman, L. J., Westbrook, L. E., Coupey, S. M., & Ireys, H. T. (1993). Framework for identifying children who have chronic conditions: The case for a new definition. *Journal of Pediatrics, 122*, 342–347.

Stein, R. E. K., Westbrook, L. E., & Silver, E. J. (1998). Comparison of adjustment of school-age children with and without chronic conditions: Results from community-based samples. *Journal of Development and Behavioral Pediatrics, 19*, 267–272.

Taenzer, P. (1983). Relationships among measures of pain, mood, and narcotic requirements. In R. Melzack (Ed.), *Pain measurement and assessment* (pp. 111–118). New York: Raven Press.

Thompson, K. L., & Varni, J. W. (1986). A developmental cognitive–biobehavioral approach to pediatric pain assessment. *Pain, 25*, 282–296.

Thompson, K. L., Varni, J. W., & Hanson, V. (1987). Comprehensive assessment of pain in juvenile rheumatoid arthritis: An empirical model. *Journal of Pediatric Psychology, 12*, 241–255.

Tobin, D. L., Holroyd, K. A., Reynolds, R. V., & Wigal, J. K. (1989). The hierarchical factor structure of the Coping Strategies Inventory. *Cognitive Therapy and Research, 13*, 343–361.

Tyler, D. C., & Crane, E. J. (Eds.). (1990). *Advances in pain research and therapy: Vol. 15. Pediatric pain.* New York: Raven.

Varni, J. W. (1981). Behavioral medicine in hemophilia arthritic pain management. *Archives of Physical Medicine and Rehabilitation, 62*, 183–187.

Varni, J. W. (1983). *Clinical behavioral pediatrics: An interdisciplinary biobehavioral approach.* New York: Pergamon Press.

Varni, J. W. (1989). *An empirical model for the biobehavioral investigation of pediatric pain.* Invited plenary address at the annual meeting of the American Pain Society, Phoenix, AZ.

Varni, J. W., Babani, L., Wallander, J. L., Roe, T. F., & Frasier, S. D. (1989). Social support and self-esteem effects on psychological adjustment in children and adolescents with insulin-dependent diabetes mellitus. *Child and Family Behavior Therapy, 11,* 1–17.

Varni, J. W., & Bernstein, B. H. (1991). Evaluation and management of pain in children with rheumatic diseases. *Rheumatic Disease Clinics of North America, 17,* 985–1000.

Varni, J. W., Blount, R. L., Waldron, S. A., & Smith, A. J. (1995). Management of pain and distress. In M. C. Roberts (Ed.), *Handbook of pediatric psychology* (2nd ed., pp. 105–123). New York: Guilford Press.

Varni, J. W., & Gilbert, A. (1982). Self-regulation of chronic arthritic pain and long-term analgesic dependence in a hemophiliac. *Rheumatology and Rehabilitation, 22,* 171–174.

Varni, J. W., Gilbert, A., & Dietrich, S. L. (1981). Behavioral medicine in pain and analgesia management for the hemophilic child with factor VIII inhibitor. *Pain, 11,* 121–126.

Varni, J. W., & Jay, S. M. (1984). Biobehavioral factors in juvenile rheumatoid arthritis: Implications for resarch and practice. *Clinical Psychology Review, 4,* 543–560.

Varni, J. W., & Katz, E. R. (1997). Stress, social support and negative affectivity in children with newly diagnosed cancer: A prospective transactional analysis. *Psycho-Oncology, 6,* 267–278.

Varni, J. W., Katz, E. R., Colegrove, R., & Dolgin, M. (1993). The impact of social skills training on the adjustment of children with newly diagnosed cancer. *Journal of Pediatric Psychology, 18,* 751–767.

Varni, J. W., Katz, E. R., Colegrove, R., & Dolgin, M. (1994). Perceived stress and adjustment of long-term survivors of childhood cancer. *Journal of Psychosocial Oncology, 12,* 1–16.

Varni, J. W., Katz, E. R., & Dash, J. (1982). Behavioral and neurochemical aspects of pediatric pain. In D. C. Russo & J. W. Varni (Eds.), *Behavioral pediatrics: Research and practice.* New York: Plenum Press.

Varni, J. W., Katz, E. R., Seid, M., Quiggins, D. J. L., & Friedman-Bender, A. (1998). The Pediatric Cancer Quality of Life Inventory-32 (PCQL-32): I. Reliability and validity. *Cancer, 82,* 1184–1196.

Varni, J. W., Katz, E. R., Seid, M., Quiggins, D. J. L., Friedman-Bender, A., & Castro, C. M. (1998). The Pediatric Cancer Quality of Life Inventory (PCQL): I. Instrument development, descriptive statistics, and cross-informant variance. *Journal of Behavioral Medicine, 21,* 179–204.

Varni, J. W., Pruitt, S. D., & Seid, M. (1998). Health-related quality of life in pediatric limb deficiency. In S. A. Herring & J. G. Birch (Eds.), *The child with a limb deficiency* (pp. 457–473). Rosemont, IL: American Academy of Orthopaedic Surgeons.

Varni, J. W., Quiggins, D. J. L., & Ayala, G. X. (in press). Development of the Pediatric Hematology/Oncology Parent Satisfaction survey. *Children's Health Care.*

Varni, J. W., Rapoff, M., Waldron, S. A., Gragg, R. A., Bernstein, B. H., & Lindsley, C. B. (1996a). Chronic pain and emotional distress in children and adolescents. *Journal of Developmental and Behavioral Pediatrics, 17,* 154–161.

Varni, J. W., Rapoff, M. A., Waldron, S. A., Gragg, R. A., Bernstein, B. H., & Lindsley, C. B. (1996b). Effects of perceived stress on pediatric chronic pain. *Journal of Behavioral Medicine, 19,* 515–528.

Varni, J. W., Rubenfeld, L. A., Talbot, D., & Setoguchi, Y. (1989). Family functioning, temperament, and psychological adaptation in children with congenital/acquired limb deficiencies. *Pediatrics, 84,* 823–830.

Varni, J. W., Sahler, O. J., Katz, E. R., Mulhern, R. K., Copeland, D. R., Noll, R. B., Phipps, S., Dolgin, M. J., & Roghmann, K. (1999). Maternal problem-solving therapy in pediatric cancer. *Journal of Psychosocial Oncology, 16,* 41–71.

Varni, J. W., Sahler, O. J., Mulhern, R. K., Katz, E. R., Copeland, D. R., Noll, R. B., Phipps, S., Dolgin, M. J., & Roghmann, K. (1997). *Maternal problem-solving training in childhood cancer.* Unpublished treatment manual.

Varni, J. W., Seid, M., & Kurtin, P. S. (1999). Pediatric health-related quality of life measurement technology: A guide for health care decision makers. *Journal of Clinical Outcomes Management, 6,* 33–40.

Varni, J. W., Seid, M., & Rode, C. A. (1999). The PedsQL™: Measurement model for the Pediatric Quality of Life Inventory. *Medical Care, 37,* 126–139.

Varni, J. W., & Setoguchi, Y. (1992). Screening for behavioral and emotional problems in children and adolescents with congenital or acquired limb deficiencies. *American Journal of Diseases of Children, 146,* 103–107.

Varni, J. W., & Setoguchi, Y. (1993). Effects of parental adjustment on the adaptation of children with congenital or acquired limb deficiencies. *Journal of Developmental and Behavioral Pediatrics, 14,* 13–20.

Varni, J. W., Setoguchi, Y., Rappaport, L. R., & Talbot, D. (1991). Effects of stress, social support, and self-esteem on depression in children with limb deficiencies. *Archives of Physical Medicine and Rehabilitation, 72,* 1053–1058.

Varni, J. W., Setoguchi, Y., Rappaport, L. R., & Talbot, D. (1992). Psychological adjustment and perceived social support in children with congenital/acquired limb deficiencies. *Journal of Behavioral Medicine, 15,* 31–44.

Varni, J. W., & Thompson, K. L. (1985). *The Varni/Thompson Pediatric Pain Questionnaire.* Unpublished manuscript.

Varni, J. W., Thompson, K. L., & Hanson, V. (1987). The Varni/Thompson Pediatric Pain Questionnaire: I. Chronic musculoskeletal pain in juvenile rheumatoid arthritis. *Pain, 28,* 27–38.

Varni, J. W., Walco, G. A., & Katz, E. R. (1989). Assessment and management of chronic and recurrent pain in children with chronic diseases. *Pediatrician, 16,* 56–63.

Varni, J. W., & Wallander, J. L. (1988). Pediatric chronic disabilities. In D. K. Routh (Ed.), *Handbook of pediatric psychology* (pp. 190–221). New York: Guilford Press.

Varni, J. W., Wilcox, K. T., & Hanson, V. (1988). Mediating effects of family social support on child psychological adjustment in juvenile rheumatoid arthritis. *Health Psychology, 7,* 421–431.

Varni, J. W., Wilcox, K. T., Hanson, V., & Brik, R. (1988). Chronic musculoskeletal pain and functional status in juvenile rheumatoid arthritis: An empirical model. *Pain, 32,* 1–7.

Walco, G., Sterling, C., Conte, P., & Engel, R. (1999). Empirically supported treatments in pediatric psychology: Disease-related pain. *Journal of Pediatric Psychology, 24,* 155–167.

Walco, G. A., Varni, J. W., & Ilowite, N. T. (1992). Cognitive-behavioral pain management in children with juvenile arthritis. *Pediatrics, 89,* 1075–1079.

Wallander, J. L., & Varni, J. W. (1992). Adjustment in children with chronic physical disorders: Programmatic research on a disability–stress–coping model. In A. M. La Greca, L. J. Siegel, J. L. Wallander, & C. E. Walker (Eds.), *Stress and coping in child health* (pp. 279–298). New York: Guilford Press.

Wallander, J. L., & Varni, J. W. (1995). Appraisal, coping, and adjustment in adolescents with physical disability. In J. L. Wallander & L. J. Siegel (Eds.), *Behavioral perspectives on adolescent health* (pp. 209–231). New York: Guilford Press.

Wallander, J. L., & Varni, J. W. (1998). Effects of pediatric chronic physical disorders on child and family adjustment. *Journal of Child Psychology and Psychiatry, 39,* 29–46.

Ware, J. E., & Sherbourne, C. D. (1992). The MOS 36-item short-form health survey (SF-36): I. Conceptual framework and item selection. *Medical Care,* 473–483.

Weisz, J., & Hawley, K. (1998). Finding, evaluating, refining and applying empirically supported treatments for children and adolescents. *Journal of Clinical Child Psychology, 27,* 206–216.

Werner, E. E., & Smith, R. S. (1982). *Vulnerable but invincible: A study of resilient children.* New York: McGraw-Hill.

Wilkie, D. J., Holzemer, W. L., Tesler, M. D., Ward, J. A., Paul, S. M., & Savedra, M. (1990). Measuring pain quality: Validity and reliability of children's and adolescents' pain. *Pain, 41*, 151–159.

Wysocki, T., Green, L., & Hustable, K. (1989). Blood glucose monitoring by diabetic adolescents: Compliance and metabolic control. *Health Psychology, 8*, 267–284.

Wysocki, T., Meinhold, P. A., Abrams, K. C., Barnar, M. U., Clarke, W. L., Bellando, B. J., & Bourgeois, M. J. (1992). Parental and professional estimates of self-care independence of children and adolescents with IDDM. *Diabetes Care, 15*, 43–52.

CHAPTER 8

Working with Adolescents
Guides from Developmental Psychology

Grayson N. Holmbeck, Craig Colder, Wendy Shapera,
Venette Westhoven, Laura Kenealy, and Anne Updegrove

The literature on child and adolescent therapy has matured to the point that there are numerous volumes devoted to the topic (e.g., Graham, 1998; Henggeler, Schoenwald, Borduin, Rowland, & Cunningham, 1998; Hibbs & Jensen, 1996; Kendall, 1991; Mash & Barkley, 1998; Reinecke, Dattilio, & Freeman, 1996; Rose, 1998; Stoiber & Kratochwill, 1998; Tolan & Cohler, 1993); this literature has also been the subject of several meta-analyses (e.g., Casey & Berman, 1985; Durlak, Fuhrman, & Lampman, 1991; Weisz, Weiss, Alicke, & Klotz, 1987; Weisz, Weiss, Han, Granger, & Morton, 1995). Despite such attention, it is also noteworthy that so little attention has been paid to the potential overlap between the field of developmental psychology and child and adolescent treatment (for relevant discussions, see Gordon, 1988; Holmbeck & Kendall, 1991; Holmbeck & Updegrove, 1995; Ivey, 1986; Kendall & Holmbeck, 1991; Kendall, Lerner, & Craighead, 1984; Shirk, 1988; Silverman & Ollendick, 1999; Weisz, 1997). It is virtually axiomatic that identical treatments cannot be applied with equal effectiveness across all individuals of all ages (Durlak et al., 1991; Shirk, 1999). On the other hand, even a cursory look at the child and adolescent therapy literature reveals that the "developmental level uniformity myth" (Kendall, 1984; Kiesler, 1966; Shirk, 1999) is alive and well in most published work.

Why has there been a lack of interface between these two fields? First, treatments for children and adolescents have been successful (Weisz, 1997).

Accordingly, one could argue that attending to a child's or adolescent's developmental level is not necessary to achieve satisfactory therapeutic gains. On the other hand, it is our contention that outcomes could be improved significantly by attending to "development"; indeed, children and adolescents prosper when there is a reasonable match between developmental level and environment (e.g., Eccles et al., 1993). With respect to cognitive-behavioral therapy (CBT), Kendall (1993) has argued that

> interventions with youth are perhaps best when they mesh effectively with the normal developmental trajectory. . . . A decided strength of the cognitive-behavioral strategy is that it works in a collaborative fashion with the youth and, correspondingly, fosters independent development. . . . (p. 243)

Second, although developmental psychologists have recently become concerned with adaptive and maladaptive variations in the course of development (e.g., the advent of developmental psychopathology as a field; Cicchetti, 1984), developmentalists and child clinicians have been less likely to collaborate on intervention research (Holmbeck & Kendall, 1991).

In this chapter, the focus is on the developmental changes and milestones of adolescence as they impact on the conduct of psychological therapy. First, we provide a rationale for why an exclusive focus on adolescents is justified. Second, we review findings of a literature search on CBT with adolescents, highlighting the general lack of attention paid to developmental factors in this literature. Third, we provide an overview of a developmental framework for understanding adolescent development and adjustment; in describing this framework, we also discuss clinical implications of each component of the model. Fourth, we discuss several developmental factors that clinicians will want to consider in their work with adolescent clients, namely, developmental myths, developmental psychopathology, developmental norms, developmental level, developmental transitions, and developmental predictors and protective factors. Fifth, we describe a clinical case (with examples from transcribed therapy sessions) that illustrates the importance of considering developmental factors when conducting therapy with adolescent clients.

WHY A SEPARATE CHAPTER ON ADOLESCENTS?

Adolescence is a transitional developmental period between childhood and adulthood that is characterized by more biological, psychological, and social role changes than any other stage of life except infancy (Feldman & Elliott, 1990; Hill, 1980b; Holmbeck, 1994; Lerner, Villarruel, & Castellino, 1999). "Change" is the defining feature of the adolescent period and there is considerable variability across individuals with respect to the onset, duration, and intensity of changes experienced in adolescence. Moreover, there are two transition points during this single developmental period—the transition to early adolescence from childhood, and the transition to adulthood from late adolescence (Steinberg, 1996).

Given the multitude of such changes, it is not surprising that there are also significant changes in the type and frequency of psychological disorders that are manifested during adolescence (as compared to childhood; Rutter, 1980). For some adolescents, it is a period of adaptation and improved mental health, but for others, it is a period of maladaptation and increasing levels of psychopathology. In short, it is a critical period in a child's development, when one's developmental trajectory can be dramatically altered in positive or negative directions.

In keeping with this developmental-psychopathology perspective, many scholars have attempted to identify risk and protective processes that are predictive of such individual differences in developmental pathways (Cicchetti & Toth, 1996; Rolf, Masten, Cicchetti, Nuechterlein, & Weintraub, 1990). Protective and vulnerability processes may have their greatest impact during life transitions or periods of dramatic developmental change (Rutter, 1990). In fact, some have argued that "the transitional nature and disequilibrium of adolescence represents an opportune period for intervention, as times of developmental change may result in a greater receptivity to intervention" (Cicchetti & Toth, 1996, p. xiii). We would argue further, however, that such opportunities are likely to be missed if one does not take developmental issues into account. Given that *change* is the defining feature of adolescence and given the opportunities for having a positive impact on a system that is in a state of flux, we believe that a focus on the adolescent period is a particularly effective way to demonstrate the importance and usefulness of a developmental perspective.

OVERVIEW OF RECENT RESEARCH ON COGNITIVE-BEHAVIORAL INTERVENTIONS WITH ADOLESCENTS

To determine the degree to which developmental factors have been considered in the design and evaluation of cognitive-behavioral interventions for adolescent clients, we conducted a computer search to identify empirical journal articles, book chapters, and journal reviews/meta-analyses of the literature published between 1990 and 1998, inclusively. We realize that a computer search is not likely to yield an exhaustive listing of all relevant papers, but we felt that this strategy would produce a representative collection of papers. We conducted our search by using various combinations of the following keywords: "cognitive," "behavioral," "adolescent," "therapy," and "treatment." We also did additional searches for authors who had multiple papers on the topic. These searches yielded a total of 756 overlapping entries. From this larger list, we selected the following: (1) empirical treatment-outcome studies employing CBT with adolescents (n = 34; studies that focused on a mixed sample of children and adolescents were not included); (2) book chapters on CBT with adolescents (n = 23); and (3) journal reviews/meta-analyses of empirical outcome studies of CBT with adolescents (n = 23). For the empirical journal articles, papers were coded for the following information (when relevant): (1) journal name, (2) title of publication, (3) authors, (4) year of publication, (5) age of participants (e.g., early, middle, late adolescence), (6) type of disorder targeted, (7) type of study (e.g., treatment outcome), (8) nature of treatment, (9) treatment specifics (e.g., number of sessions, length of treatment), (10) whether the treatment was manualized, (11) treatment setting, (12) statistical methods, and (m) whether developmental factors were discussed. This information was combined across studies and is provided in Table 8.1. Each book chapter and review/meta-analysis was reviewed to determine if developmental factors were taken into consideration.

The 34 empirical journal articles appeared in 18 different journals, with two or more papers coming from the following (number of papers in parentheses): (1) *Journal of the American Academy of Child and Adolescent Psychiatry* (n = 8); (2) *Journal of Consulting and Clinical Psychology* (n = 6); (3) *Behavior Therapy* (n = 3); (4) *Journal of Child and Adolescent Group Therapy* (n = 2); and (5) *Journal of Child and Youth Care* (n = 2). As can be seen in Table 8.1, major depression, anxiety disorders, conduct disorders, attention-deficit/hyperactivity disorder (ADHD), and obsessive–compulsive disorder were the most common targets of cognitive-behavioral interventions with adolescents. Participants in the interventions spanned the adolescent period, but were most likely to be in the early and middle adolescent age groups. Studies varied widely with respect to number of sessions, length of treatment, and whether a control group was included. Surprisingly, over 60% of the studies employed group therapy interventions. Over half (56%) were based on manualized treatments. The place of treatment was balanced between university/school-based and residential/hospital-based settings.

Most relevant to the current chapter was the finding that only 26% (9/34) of the empirical studies made mention of developmental issues when discussing the design/evaluation of the treatment. For those empirical journal articles that did mention developmental issues, what was the nature of these discussions? As can be seen in Table 8.2, only one of the empirical papers examined a developmental variable (i.e., age) as a moderator of treatment effects (Kendall et al., 1997). Some studies developed treatments by considering adolescent developmental issues (Belsher, Wilkes, & Rush, 1995; Etscheidt, 1991; Kastner, 1998; McGrath et al., 1992). One paper considered the utility of "parental involvement" when designing the treat-

TABLE 8.1. Review of Cognitive-Behavioral Treatment Outcome Studies Conducted with Adolescents (1990–1998; n = 34)

Dimensions and subcategories	No. of studies	% of total articles
Disorder targeted		
Major depression	11	32
Anxiety disorders	4	12
Conduct disorder	4	12
Attention-deficit/hyperactivity disorder	3	9
Obsessive–compulsive disorder	3	9
Oppositional defiant disorder	2	6
Disruptive behavior	2	6
Substance abuse	2	6
Mental retardation	1	3
Migraine headache	1	3
Panic disorder	1	3
Posttraumatic stress disorder	1	3
School refusal	1	3
Sexual offender	1	3
Social phobia	1	3
Stuttering	1	3
Age of participants		
"Adolescents"	4	12
Early adolescence	3	9
Early/middle adolescence	11	32
Middle adolescence	15	44
Early/middle/late	1	3
Control group?		
Yes	18	53
No	16	47
Number of sessions		
1–5	4	12
6–10	7	20
11–15	8	24
16–20	7	20
Over 20	2	6
Not given	6	18
Length of treatment		
1–5 weeks	5	15
6–10 weeks	4	12
11–15 weeks	4	12
16–20 weeks	6	18
Over 20 weeks	3	9
Not given	12	35
Individual or group?		
Individual	13	38
Group	21	62

TABLE 8.1. (*continued*)

Dimensions and subcategories	No. of studies	% of total articles
Manualized treatment?		
Yes	19	56
No	10	29
Not given	5	15
Treatment setting		
Secondary school	5	15
University clinic	11	32
Hospital		
Inpatient	1	3
Outpatient	5	15
Residential	7	20
Not given	5	15
Developmental issues discussed?		
Yes	9	26
No	25	74

Note. Early, middle, and late adolescence were defined with respect to the following age ranges: 11–14, 15–18, and 19–21 years, respectively (Steinberg, 1996). Percentages may not add up to 100% due to rounding.

ment (Ollendick, 1995), with another study examining the effect of parental involvement on treatment outcome (Lewinsohn, Clarke, Hops, & Andrews, 1990). Several empirical studies used outcome measures that were developed specifically for use with adolescents (Belsher et al., 1995; Lewinsohn et al., 1990; Ollendick, 1995; Vostanis, Feehan, & Grattan, 1998). Finally, some researchers interpreted their treatment-outcome findings in relation to developmental issues (Lewinsohn et al., 1990; Ollendick, 1995; Valliant, 1993).

Authors of book chapters (43%) and journal reviews/meta-analyses (43%) were more likely than authors of empirical papers to mention developmental issues when discussing the literature on CBT (10 of 23 articles in both cases). As can be seen in Table 8.2, reviews and chapters were most likely to discuss developmental issues in relation to the course of problem behavior and to advocate for adaptations of treatment manuals in line with developmental factors. Several authors included brief generic sections on developmental issues, with several discussing specific cognitive-developmental factors (see Table 8.2 for *n*s). Only three authors recommended that developmental variables be employed as possible treatment moderators.

What is perhaps equally interesting is what is *not* discussed in this literature. Although many authors advocate for adaptations of treatment manuals in ways that take development into account, few provide methods for doing so. Several authors also recommend that the therapist assess an

TABLE 8.2. Developmental Issues Discussed in Empirical Journal Articles ($n = 9$), Journal Reviews/Meta-Analyses ($n = 10$), and Book Chapters ($n = 10$) on Cognitive-Behavioral Therapy with Adolescents (1990–1998)

Developmental issue	n
Empirical journal articles ($n = 9$)	
Treatments developed by considering developmental issues.	5
Employed developmentally relevant outcome variables.	4
Interpreted findings in relation to developmental issues.	3
Considered issues relevant to parental involvement.	2
Employed a developmental variable as a moderator of treatment effects.	1
Journal reviews/meta-analyses/book chapters ($n = 20$)	
Advocates adaptations of treatment manuals for use with adolescents.	8
Discusses adolescent developmental issues in relation to etiology.	8
Section on "developmental issues" relevant to adolescents.	6
Discusses cognitive development or cognitive skills required for CBT.	5
Discusses importance of examining developmental status as a moderator of treatment effects.	3
Emphasizes developmental variability across adolescents.	2
Discusses issues relevant to parental involvement in treatment.	2
Proposes treatment model that varies as a function of stages of development.	2
Differentiates between normative development and psychopathology.	1
Suggests that treatments focus on contexts in which adolescents interact.	1
Emphasizes importance of maximizing match between developmental level and nature of CBT treatment.	1
Discusses developmentally based barriers to treatment of adolescents.	1

adolescent's cognitive-developmental level; again, little advice has been forthcoming for how to do so (although Bierman, 1988, is one exception in the area of cognitive-developmental understanding of social relationships).

Finally, almost half of the authors of reviews and chapters discuss developmental variability in relation to the course of psychopathology (e.g., child and adolescent depression); unfortunately, little is said about how this information can be taken into account when designing treatments. In summary, most authors who write about CBT for adolescents do not mention adolescent developmental issues. Of those that do, there is little in the way of specifics for how such information can be incorporated into the treatments that are conducted.

A FRAMEWORK FOR UNDERSTANDING ADOLESCENT DEVELOPMENT AND ADJUSTMENT

Given the lack of attention paid to developmental issues in studies of CBT with adolescents, we provide an overview of a developmental framework for understanding adolescent adaptation and adjustment (see Figure 8.1). We believe that an appreciation for the rapid developmental changes of adolescence and the contexts of such development will aid the clinician and treatment-outcome researcher in considering developmental issues in their clinical and research endeavors.

This framework summarizes the major constructs that have been studied by researchers in this field and is based on earlier models presented by Hill (1980b), Holmbeck (1994, 1996; Holmbeck & Kendall, 1991; Holmbeck & Updegrove, 1995), Steinberg (1996), and Grotevant (1997). See these references for more complete descriptions of the constructs reviewed (a thorough review of each construct is beyond the scope of this chapter). Each of the components of the model is reviewed in turn and relevant clinical issues are described.

The model presented here is biopsychosocial in nature, insofar as it emphasizes the biological, psychological, and social changes of the adolescent developmental period (see Figure 8.1). In addition to this focus on intraindividual development, we have also attempted to incorporate more recent discoveries from studies of contextual effects during adolescence. For example, recent research has gone beyond asking whether family vari-

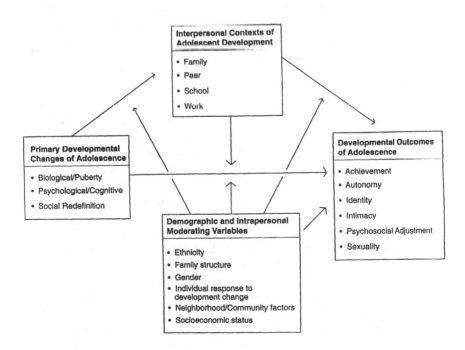

FIGURE 8.1. A framework for understanding adolescent development and adjustment. From Holmbeck and Shapera (1999). Copyright 1999 by John Wiley & Sons, Inc. Reprinted by permission.

ables are associated with adolescent adjustment outcomes and now attempts to isolate those contexts or circumstances in which such associations are most pronounced. In short, this model is both developmental and contextual (Steinberg, 1995).

At the most general level, the framework presented in Figure 8.1 indicates that the primary developmental changes of adolescence have an impact on the developmental outcomes of adolescence via the interpersonal contexts in which adolescents develop. In other words, the developmental changes of adolescence have an impact on the behaviors of significant others, which in turn influence the ways in which adolescents resolve the major issues of adolescence, namely, autonomy, sexuality, identity, and so forth.

For example, suppose that a young preadolescent girl begins to physically mature much earlier than her age-mates. Such early maturity will likely impact on her peer relationships, insofar as early maturing girls are more likely to date and initiate sexual behaviors at an earlier age than are girls who mature on time (Magnusson, Stattin, & Allen, 1985). Such impacts on male peers may influence her own self-perceptions in the areas of identity and sexuality. In this way, the behaviors of peers in response to the girl's early maturity could be said to *mediate* associations between pubertal change and sexual outcomes (and therefore account, at least in part, for these significant associations). We use the term "mediation" because of the proposed A → B → C relationship inherent in this example, whereby B is hypothesized to mediate associations between A and C (for a more thorough explanation of mediated effects, see Baron & Kenny, 1986; Holmbeck, 1997).

Such causal and mediational influences may vary depending on the demographic and intrapersonal context in which they occur (see Figure 8.1; "Demographic and Intrapersonal Moderating Variables"). Specifically, associations between the primary developmental changes and the developmental outcomes may be *moderated* by demographic variables such as ethnicity, gender, socioeconomic status and the like. We use the term "moderated" because it is expected that associations between the primary changes and developmental outcomes may *differ* depending on the demographic status of the individual (for a more thorough explanation of moderated effects, see Baron & Kenny, 1986; Holmbeck, 1997). For example, if associations between pubertal change and certain sexual outcomes *only* held for girls, we could infer that gender moderates such associations. In addition to serving a mediational role, as described earlier, the interpersonal contexts (i.e., family, peer, school, and work contexts) can also serve a moderational role in the association between the primary changes and the developmental outcomes. For example, early maturity may lead to poor adjustment outcomes *only* when families react to early pubertal development in certain ways (e.g., with increased restrictiveness and supervision); in this example, familial reactions to puberty moderate associations between pubertal development and adjustment.

Primary Developmental Changes of Adolescence

Upon further examination of the framework in Figure 8.1, we see that there are three types of primary developmental changes that occur during adolescence: biological/pubertal, psychological/cognitive, and social redefinition. They are viewed as "primary" because (1) they are universal across culture, and (2) they occur temporally prior to the developmental outcomes of adolescence (i.e., changes in autonomy, identity, sexuality, etc.). Despite the universality and intensity of these changes, there has unfortunately been a decided lack of attention to these developmental issues in the adolescent clinical literature (see Table 8.1; Holmbeck & Kendall, 1991; Holmbeck & Updegrove, 1995; Kazdin & Weisz, 1998; Kendall & Holmbeck, 1991; Kendall & Williams, 1986; Shirk, 1999; Tolan & Cohler, 1993; Weisz, 1997; Weisz & Weersing, 1999).

Biological/Pubertal Changes

More than any other stage of life except the fetal/neonatal period, adolescence is a time of substantial physical growth and change (Brooks-Gunn & Reiter, 1990). Tanner (1962) has charted most of the characteristics of these changes in males and females. Changes in body proportions, facial characteristics, voice, body hair, strength, and coordination are found in boys, and changes in body proportions, body hair, breast growth, and menarcheal status are found in girls.

Crucial to the understanding of this process is the knowledge that the peak of pubertal development occurs 2 years *earlier* in the modal female than in the modal male. *Intra*individual variation is also evident with respect to the onset of different pubertal changes (e.g., breast development typically occurs prior to menarche for girls). Moreover, there is substantial variation between individuals in the time of onset, duration, and termination of the pubertal cycle (Brooks-Gunn & Reiter, 1990), and these differences have social consequences. Thus, it is possible, for example, that two 14-year-old boys may be at very different stages of pubertal development, such that one boy has not yet begun pubertal changes and the other boy has experienced nearly all pubertal events.

Research also suggests that both *pubertal status* (an individual's placement in the sequence of predictable pubertal changes) and *pubertal timing* (timing of changes relative to one's age-peers) have an impact on the quality of family relationships and certain indicators of psychosocial adaptation (Alsaker, 1995; Buchanan, Eccles, & Becker, 1992; Holmbeck & Hill, 1991; Laursen, Coy, & Collins, 1998; Paikoff & Brooks-Gunn, 1991;

Petersen, 1988; Sagrestano, McCormick, Paikoff, & Holmbeck, 1999). With respect to pubertal timing, early maturing girls, for example, are at risk for a variety of adaptational difficulties (Holmbeck & Hill, 1991; Magnusson et al., 1985). Therapists working with such girls should be aware of their at-risk status. Early developing boys, on the other hand, are favored over later developing boys for involvement in athletic activities, dating, and social events (Richards, Abell, & Petersen, 1993).

Unlike the newborn, adolescents are aware of these physical changes, and this awareness may be pleasing or horrifying. A lack of information about puberty/sexuality can contribute to emotional upset (e.g., Ruble & Brooks- Gunn, 1982; Tobin-Richards, Boxer, & Petersen, 1982). Most of the psychological effects of pubertal changes are probably not direct but, rather, are moderated by responses of the individual or significant others to such changes (Holmbeck, 1996; Paikoff & Brooks-Gunn, 1991; Petersen, 1988; Petersen & Taylor, 1980; Richards & Petersen, 1987). In other words, the manner in which the family and peers respond to the adolescent's advancing development will impact on how such events are experienced.

Interestingly, there appear to be no links between physical development and cognitive development (e.g., an early maturing boy who appears more mature than the majority of his peers is not necessarily able to think more abstractly or complexly than others his age). Cognitive-behavioral therapists and significant others alike should not assume that physical changes are indicative of development in cognitive or psychological areas.

Psychological/Cognitive Changes

Perhaps most relevant to the interface between developmental psychology and CBT is the potential moderating effect of the adolescent's cognitive and psychological changes on the efficacy of treatment interventions. Although some efforts have been made to take cognitive development into account when designing treatments (e.g., Guerra, 1993; Kendall, 1984; Kendall et al., 1984; Shirk, 1988, 1999; Temple, 1997), few investigators have taken such development into account when conducting clinical intervention research (Durlak et al., 1991; Schleser, Cohen, Meyers, & Rodick, 1984). Thus, we have devoted extra space to this component of the model (both here and later in this chapter, when discussing the potential influence of "developmental level" on treatment outcome).

The Importance of "Cognition" in Theoretical Formulations: A Historical Perspective. CBT developed in response to the apparent inadequacy of conditioning paradigms to explain human behavior (Bandura, 1977; Rosenthal, 1982). The shortcomings of conditioning theories of behavior are evident when applying learning principles to therapy. For example, classical conditioning is the basis for systematic desensitization, which has been used to treat phobias. However, the success of classical conditioning depends on a variety of personal, social, and cognitive variables. In a therapeutic context, the client cannot be viewed as a passive recipient of stimuli. Instead, clients actively interpret a situation. Thus, an adequate account of classical conditioning must include cognitive processes.

Although theoreticians and practitioners developed a variety of ways to incorporate cognitive processes into models of abnormal behavior and therapies, all cognitive-behavioral approaches emphasize cognitive processes in the development, maintenance, and modification of behavior (Meichenbaum & Cameron, 1982). From a social-learning perspective (e.g., Bandura, 1977; Rotter, Chance, & Phares, 1972), for example, behavior is the product of cognitive processes that determine to what we attend, how we perceive events, whether we remember events, our degree of self-efficacy in performing a behavioral response, and the consequences we expect. Mahoney and Arnkoff (1978) suggested that the fundamental assumption of CBT is that cognitive or symbolic processes mediate behavior. From this assumption follow several treatment goals, including (1 identification of the cognitive processes that underlie the problem behavior, and (2) creation of learning experiences that will alter these processes and, in turn, behavioral patterns.

The Focus on "Cognition" in Treatment. Cognitive-behavioral therapies draw upon a number of techniques to change cognitive processes, which can be accomplished in an individual, group, or family format. Often, a therapist will try to identify maladaptive thoughts or assumptions (e.g., attributions, outcome expectancies) through questioning, imagery, and role playing. Once such a pattern is identified, the therapist and client work together to test its validity. New, more adaptive thoughts are encouraged and faulty assumptions are challenged. Occasionally, tasks are assigned outside of therapy to test the impact of maladaptive thought patterns or new ways of thinking. At this stage, an important goal of therapy is to review the outcomes of these assignments.

Another CBT technique is problem-solving training, which has been widely used to help adolescents develop adaptive responses during social conflicts. The training often includes skills development in self-monitoring, means–ends thinking, evaluation of probable consequences, selection of a solution, enactment, evaluation of the solution, and, if necessary, repeating the process to find an alternative solution (Temple, 1997). This approach grew out of research showing that normal and clinic populations differ in their problem-solving skills. For example, Spivack and colleagues (Spivack & Shure, 1974; Spivack, Platt, & Shure, 1976) found that children with emotional problems typically generate fewer solutions to hypothetical social problems, generate a higher proportion of antisocial solutions, and maintain inaccurate expectations about the probable consequences of their behavior. Systematic training in social problem-solving has been successful in treating adolescents with anger-control problems (Feindler & Ecton, 1986).

In general, the techniques of CBT emphasize self-reflection (thinking about how one thinks), consequential thinking (reflecting on the impact of a particular pattern of thinking or behaving), and consideration of future possibilities (thinking about how change in thinking or behaving might, in turn, impact on one's life in the future). Thus, the techniques of CBT rely on complex symbolic processes that typically require a high level of cognitive development. As suggested by Harrington, Wood, and Verduyn (1998) in their discussion of CBT as applied to clinically depressed adolescents,

> For a patient to have cognitive therapy . . . it is necessary to have not only the ability to experience negative cognitions, but also the capabilities to reflect on these cognitions and to engage in complex reasoning in which hypotheses are evaluated and alternative solutions to problems are generated. . . . A key feature of many cognitive therapies . . . is the ability to reflect on one's psychological interior and to consider private attributes of the self such as thoughts and feelings. Some of these are real and concrete but others are hypothetical. (p. 163)

Of course, some clients may not be capable of advanced symbolic processing, particularly in the domain of their problem. Although adolescence is often a time of dramatic cognitive development, there is also considerable interindividual variability in the degree to which such development has taken place. It follows, then, that an adolescent's level of cognitive development is likely to impinge on (or facilitate) the success of some CBT techniques (e.g., Bobbit & Keating, 1983; Kendall & Braswell, 1985; Schleser et al., 1984; Shirk, 1999). Indeed, a meta-analysis by Durlak et al. (1991) revealed that CBT is more likely to be effective with older (and more cognitively mature) adolescents.

Cognitive Development during Adolescence. Specifically, what are the cognitive changes of adolescence? Piaget (1970, 1972) has provided a comprehensive stage theory of cognitive development that has dominated this field of study. He identified adolescence as the period in which formal operational thinking emerges and adult-level reasoning can take place. Adolescents who have achieved such thinking abilities are able to think more complexly, abstractly, and hypothetically. They are able to think in terms of possibilities, and many are able to think realistically about the future.

Although, there is general agreement that a shift in thinking occurs during the transition from childhood to adolescence, critics of the Piagetian approach have suggested alternatives (Moshman, 1998). Proponents of the information-processing perspective, for example, have attempted to identify specific changes in cognitive activity that may account for advances in thinking. They maintain that there are significant advances in the following areas during adolescence: (1) processing capacity or efficiency (e.g., memory and organization of information); (2) knowledge base; and (3) cognitive self-regulation (Keating, 1990).

Sternberg's research on children's solutions to analogies illustrates how advances in information processing affect thinking (Sternberg, 1977; Sternberg & Nigro, 1980). In these studies, analogies were presented to 3rd-, 6th-, and 9th-graders, and to college students, and findings suggested age-related differences in the strategies employed. Older and younger participants seemed to employ similar strategies, but older participants were more complete and systematic in their approach to the problems. For example, in determining the relation between a pair of items, the 3rd- and 6th-graders tended to stop their search for a solution prematurely, before all possible relations were considered. These findings are consistent with an information-processing perspective. Adolescents have greater information-processing capacity than younger children, perhaps because they have automatized basic processes, have a broader knowledge base, and have increased short-term memory. These factors together make it easier for adolescents to simultaneously hold in mind multiple symbolic representations, rather than just one. Thus, they are better able to generate a complete list of solutions for the analogy problem and choose the best one. It is important to note that the information-processing and Piagetian perspectives are not necessarily mutually exclusive. Piaget's theory describes a qualitative shift in adolescent thinking that appears to begin around age 11 or 12, and the information-processing perspective complements this theory because it suggests possible cognitive features that underlie this shift.

In addition to the Piagetian and information-processing perspectives, a third approach to cognitive development during adolescence is the contextualist perspective. Vygotsky (1978) has suggested that psychological processes have a social basis. According to this approach, social interactions, particularly verbal communication, have an important influence on cognitive development. Lochman, White, and Wayland (1991) have applied a contextual approach to the development of problem solving. They note that caregivers structure their child's environment and resolve their child's problems, and through dialogue and observation, children internalize "idiographic" ways of perceiving the world and solving problems. This perspective on cognitive development is unique because it emphasizes the role of the cognitive "environment." Indeed, cognitive development does not occur in a vacuum but, rather, is fostered or hindered via interactions with the social world (Flavell & Ross, 1981; Higgins, Ruble, & Hartup, 1983; Overton, 1983; Shantz, 1975, 1983). Of interest here are the child's socially relevant cognitions, such as his or her understanding of significant others and their behaviors. The development of role-taking and empathy skills, the role of affect in understanding people, attributional processes in social situations, and prosocial behavior are a few of the social-cognitive developmental tasks that may influence progress in therapy (Guerra, 1993; Nelson & Crick, 1999).

Overall, it appears that during adolescence, a fairly sophisticated way of thinking develops, which is characterized by abstraction, consequential thinking, and hypothetical reasoning. Moreover, these cognitive processes are of central importance to CBT; that is, this approach to treatment emphasizes complex symbolic representation, which appears to become consolidated during adolescence. Although the processes that underlie the shift in adolescent thinking are not well understood, it appears that increases in efficiency, capacity, and attentional control are important factors. In addition, from a contextual point of view, environmental factors seem to be of importance.

Adolescents may benefit from treatment that initially focuses on changing/accelerating cognitive-developmental processes (Shirk, 1999), which in turn may influence the effectiveness of treatment (e.g., Temple, 1997, discusses strategies for helping adolescents to develop means–ends thinking and perspective taking); that is, the therapist may find it necessary to promote the developmental changes that are necessary for the child to benefit from subsequent therapeutic interactions (provided, of course, that the child is developmentally ready to experience such changes, and that there is adequate environmental support to maintain the changes). As with other forms of cognitive development, social-cognitive development can also be fostered by the therapeutic intervention (as well as by the therapeutic relationship itself; Guerra, 1993). Interestingly, therapists may find that adolescents' maladaptive cognitive beliefs are not as well developed as those of adults, thus making the former more amenable to treatment (Bowers, Evans, & Van Cleve, 1996). In short, basic knowledge of cognitive development and its application in therapy is likely to be very useful to CBT therapists.

Social Redefinition

A variety of changes in the social status of children occur during adolescence (Hill, 1980b; Steinberg, 1996). Although such social redefinition is universal, the specific changes vary greatly across different cultures. In some nonindustrial societies, public rituals (i.e., rites of passage) take place soon after the onset of pubertal change. In Western, industrialized societies, the transition is less clear, but analogous changes in social status do take place. Steinberg (1996) cites changes across four domains: *interpersonal* (e.g., changes in familial status), *political* (e.g., late adolescents are eligible to vote), *economic* (e.g., adolescents are allowed to work), and *legal* (e.g., late adolescents can be tried in adult court systems). In addition, adolescents are able to obtain a driver's permit and can get married. Leaving home in late adolescence (e.g., Moore, 1987) also serves to redefine one's social role. Finally, research suggests that stereotypical gender-role expectations are intensified during the adolescent period (Galambos, Almeida, & Petersen, 1990; Gilligan, Lyons, & Hanmer, 1990; Hill & Lynch, 1983).

Such changes in social role have clinical implications. Adolescents' abilities to adapt to changing societal expectations for acceptable behavior will vary. Expected roles are less clear in this culture than in less industrialized societies; there is little consensus about what constitutes "normal" behavior for adolescents in Western culture (e.g., conflicting messages concerning sexuality and substance abuse are frequently presented in the media). Given a lack of role clarity, psychopathology may be a frequent outcome of failure to sort through conflicting expectations.

Interpersonal Contexts of Adolescence

As indicated in Figure 8.1, there are four components included within the interpersonal context portion of the framework: (1) family, (2) peers, (3) school, and (4) work. As is clear from the work of Henggeler et al. (1998) on multisystemic treatment of antisocial behavior, the effectiveness of interventions can be enhanced by consideration of context. Adolescents are embedded within multiple systems; clearly, these systems are appropriate targets for interventions and are likely to be amenable to change (Kazdin & Weisz, 1998; Shirk, 1999; Weisz & Weersing, 1999).

Family Context

Adolescence is a time of transformation in family relationships (Collins, 1990; Hill, 1980a; Holmbeck, 1996; Paikoff & Brooks-Gunn, 1991; Steinberg, 1990; Walsh & Scheinkman, 1993). Scholars who have written about adolescence from a psychoanalytic perspective (Freud, 1958) have viewed this developmental period as a time of storm and stress, when extreme levels of conflict with parents result in a reorientation toward peers (for reviews, see Arnett, 1999; Holmbeck & Hill, 1988). Given that such views were based on clinicians' observations of adolescents with adjustment difficulties, it is not surprising that recent research involving large and more representative samples of adolescents has *not* supported these early storm-and-stress notions (Holmbeck & Hill, 1988; although, for an alternative perspective, see Arnett, 1999). Despite such disconfirming evidence, it appears that public policy and the public's beliefs are still in line with the out-of-date perspective (Buchanan et al., 1990; Holmbeck & Hill, 1988). For example, those who write for mass media publications will often invoke concepts such as rebelliousness and parent–adolescent conflict to make points about the negative nature of adolescence.

Despite the lack of serious relationship trauma during early adolescence, a period of increased emotional distance in the parent–adolescent relationship appears at the peak of pubertal change (Hill & Holmbeck, 1987; Holmbeck & Hill, 1991; Laursen et al., 1998; Paikoff & Brooks-Gunn, 1991; Papini & Sebby, 1987; Steinberg, 1990). Although there also may be an increase in conflict, most adolescents negotiate this period *without* severing ties with parents or developing serious disorders (Collins & Laursen, 1992; Holmbeck & Hill, 1988). Also, families with adolescents are more likely to conflict over mundane issues than basic values (Montemayor, 1983). Any discontinuities in the parent–child relationship during the transition to adolescence tend to occur against a backdrop of relational continuity (Cooper, Grotevant, & Condon, 1983; Holmbeck, 1996; Laursen & Collins, 1994).

The CBT therapist should be aware that transformations in attachments to parents are to be expected during adolescence and that some normative familial problems may arise because of difficulties in managing this transition. In fact, some have argued that the conflicts that arise during the transition to adolescence may serve an adaptive role (Cooper, 1988; Holmbeck, 1996). On the other hand, it is important for the therapist to evaluate whether an adolescent's adaptational difficulties are actually continuations of problems that began in early or middle childhood. Although difficulties that develop in childhood, as well as difficulties that develop anew in adolescence, may be in need of therapeutic attention, the latter are more likely to represent difficulties in negotiating the transition to adolescence (although pubertal and other biological factors also may play a role in the onset of some disorders).

One of the major tasks for parents during this developmental period is to be responsive to adolescents' needs for increasing responsibility and decision-making power in the family, while *at the same time* maintaining a high level of cohesiveness in the family environment. Parents who lack flexibility and adaptability during this developmental period, particularly in areas of strictness and decision making, tend to have offspring with less adaptive outcomes (Fuligni & Eccles, 1993; Holmbeck, Paikoff, & Brooks-Gunn, 1995; Kidwell, Fischer, Dunham, & Baranowski, 1983). Family therapy (Walsh & Scheinkman, 1993) can be used in combination with CBT to address this issue by facilitating such parental adaptability and developmental sensitivity.

It also appears that parent–adolescent relationships are altered by the cognitive changes discussed earlier. For example, adolescents are increasingly able and willing to discuss (and argue about) issues with their parents in more complex ways, to see the flaws in their parents' arguments, to imagine what it would be like to have different parents, and to think about their parent's marital relationship separate from their own relationships with them. Given these changes, mothers and fathers may benefit from viewing their child's adolescence as an opportunity to utilize increased questioning as a way to teach problem-solving skills. In short, the degree to which an adolescent has developed cognitively has clear implications for how a CBT intervention is implemented.

Peer Context

One of the most robust predictors of adult difficulties (e.g., dropping out of school, criminality) is poor peer relationships during childhood and adolescence (Parker & Asher, 1987). Most now agree that child–child relationships are necessities and not luxuries, and that these relationships have positive effects on cognitive, social-cognitive, linguistic, sex-role, and moral development (Berndt & Savin-Williams, 1993; Parker & Asher, 1987).

Peer relationships during childhood and adolescence appear to evolve through a series of developmental stages (e.g., Asher & Gottman, 1981; Berndt, 1981, 1983; Brown, 1990; La Greca & Prinstein, 1999; Selman, 1980; Youniss, 1980). Selman (1980, 1981), for example, presented a theory of the growth of interpersonal understanding, the stages of which correspond to developmental levels of social perspective taking. Many adolescents are increasingly able to employ advanced levels of role-taking skills that serve to enhance the maturity of their relationships. Sullivan (1953) also provided a stage theory for the development of peer relationships, in which he stressed the importance of interpersonal relationships and the differences between child–child and parent–child relationships (Youniss, 1980). With respect to adolescence, Sullivan described his notion of "chumship" and maintained that this (typically) same-sex friendship is a critical developmental accomplishment. It is with this relationship that the child presumably learns about intimacy, and this friendship serves as a basis for later close relationships. CBT therapists will want to facilitate the development of such "chumship" relationships in young adolescents who have few friends either by increasing the adolescents' involvement in extracurricular activities or by including them in group therapy.

Although families and peers each provide unique contributions to development and adjustment, it is also true that the family can provide a secure base for a child's exploration into the world of peers. Based on his review of the literature on peer relationships, Hartup (1983) suggested that healthy family relationships are a necessary basis for the development of healthy peer relationships, especially in light of the following findings: (1) Children and adolescents usually adhere to their parents' values even during increases in peer involvement; (2) parent and peer values are typically quite similar, especially with regard to important issues; and (3) differences between parent and peer values are more likely when adolescents have distant relationships with their parents, and when they associate with peers who endorse antisocial behaviors.

Thus, CBT therapists will need to assess the status and quality of their clients' peer relationships (Kendall & MacDonald, 1993), as well as the manner in which the family and peer environments are intertwined. With respect to the latter, therapists may want to involve older siblings in treatment in order to provide opportunities for adolescents to practice social skills that they will use in their interactions with peers (although the effectiveness of this strategy has not been tested). Moreover, parents should be encouraged to monitor their children's friendships (La Greca & Prinstein, 1999). Some have suggested that therapists should involve the adolescent's peers in the treatment (e.g., Bierman & Furman, 1984; La Greca & Prinstein, 1999; Lyman & Selman, 1985). Regardless of the specific strategy employed, friendship skills (e.g., conflict resolution) can be promoted via modeling and rehearsal (La Greca & Prinstein, 1999).

Cognitive-behavioral group therapy can often be a useful context when doing CBT with adolescents. As noted earlier, this is a commonly used intervention strategy with this age group. Because peers play an important role in shaping adolescent psychosocial development, group therapy with adolescents can be an effective means of challenging maladaptive patterns of thinking and behaving (Rose & Edleson, 1987).

School Context

Another context of adolescent development is the school environment. Scholars have maintained that we should be interested not only in the school's impact on cognition and achievement, but that we should also examine how the school is an important environment for the development of one's personality, values, and social relationships (Entwisle, 1990; Minuchin & Shapiro, 1983; Trickett & Schmid, 1993).

With increasing age, children are exposed to more complex school environments (Minuchin & Shapiro, 1983). Movement between schools (such as between an elementary school and a junior high school) can be viewed as a stressor, with multiple school transitions producing more deleterious effects (Petersen & Hamburg, 1986; Simmons & Blyth, 1987). Simmons and Blyth have found, for example, that children (and particularly girls) who switch from an elementary school into a junior high school (as opposed to staying in a K–8 school) show significant self-esteem decrements and that recovery in self-esteem is not likely for a sizable number of these young adolescents. Presumably, these decreases in self-esteem are due, at least in part, to movement from a protected environment (i.e., elementary school) to an impersonal environment (junior and senior high school).

As is the case with school transitions, the school environment also impacts on adolescent development. Physical setting, limitations in resources, philosophies of education, teacher expectations, curriculum characteristics, and interactions between teacher and student have been found to be related to a variety of child and adolescent outcomes (Minuchin & Shapiro, 1983; Rutter, Maughan, Mortimore, & Ouston, 1979). High school students, for example, appear to profit from nonauthoritarian teaching approaches (Rutter et al., 1979). Also, the high rate of dropouts in some school districts indicate that the school environment and the needs of the students have not been well matched (Eccles et al., 1993). On a positive note, larger schools provide larger numbers of peers as well as a larger variety of peers, with whom the adolescent can interact.

CBT therapists should be careful to assess the nature and quality of their adolescent clients' school environments (Trickett & Schmid, 1993); practitioners can work to enhance or to minimize various aspects of the school environment depending on their impact.

Work Context

The last context that we consider is the work environment (Greenberger & Steinberg, 1986; Lewko, 1987). Although more than 80% of all high school students in this country work before they graduate (Steinberg, 1996), and many government agencies have recommended that adolescents work, little research has been done on the effects of such work on adolescent development and the adolescents' relationships with significant others.

Based on the research that has been done (e.g., Greenberger & Steinberg, 1986), however, it seems clear that the work environment has both positive *and* negative effects on adolescent development. Although adolescents who work tend to develop an increased sense of self-reliance, they also tend to (1) develop cynical attitudes about work, (2) spend less time with their families and peers, (3) be less involved in school, (4) be more likely to abuse drugs or commit delinquent acts, and (5) have less time for self-exploration and identity development. The primary problem seems to be the monotonous and stressful nature of many adolescent jobs. CBT therapists need to attend to the balance between work and other aspects of an adolescent's life, the quality and impact of the work environment itself, and the adolescent's attitudes and beliefs about work.

Developmental Outcomes of Adolescence

As can be seen in Figure 8.1, the developmental changes of adolescence impact on the interpersonal contexts of adolescent development that, in turn, impact on the developmental outcomes of adolescence. In this section, the following developmental outcomes of adolescence are discussed: achievement, autonomy, identity, intimacy, psychosocial adjustment, and sexuality (see Figure 8.1).

Achievement

For the first time in one's life, decisions made during adolescence can have serious consequences for one's future education, career, and choice of extracurricular activities (Henderson & Dweck, 1990). Some adolescents decide to drop out of school, whereas others complete their education and graduate from high school. Some decide to continue on to college or graduate school. For those who remain in school, it is during high school that most adolescents are, for the first time, given the opportunity to decide which classes they want to take. Such decisions present new opportunities but also limit the range of possible employment and educational options available to the adolescent. After graduation from high school, adolescents typically decide whether they want to pursue more education or to seek full-time employment—a decision that is certainly affected by socioeconomic status. Finally, adolescence is a time of preparation for adult work roles, a time when vocational training begins. Given the increase in choices, one might expect to see an increase in anxiety around "life decisions."

The CBT therapist can aid the parent in serving as a guide or a model for the adolescent around these issues (rather than as an authority figure). Given the complexity of achievement decisions, adolescents also may benefit from naturally evolving or intervention-induced advances in cognitive abilities (i.e., the ability to employ future-oriented thinking, abstract reasoning, hypothetical thinking). Those who have developed these abilities are at an advantage when they begin to make education- and career-related decisions.

Autonomy

Autonomy is a multidimensional construct in the sense that there is more than one type of adolescent autonomy (Douvan & Adelson, 1966; Hill & Holmbeck, 1986; Steinberg, 1990). Emotional autonomy is the capacity to relinquish child-like dependencies on parents (Fuhrman & Holmbeck, 1995; Lamborn & Steinberg, 1993; Ryan & Lynch, 1989; Steinberg & Silverberg, 1986). Adolescents increasingly come to deidealize their parents, to see them as "people" rather than simply as parenting figures, and to be less dependent on them for immediate emotional support.

When adolescents are behaviorally autonomous, they have the capacity to make their own decisions and to be self-governing. CBT therapists who work with adolescents will likely confront developmental changes in their clients' level of behavioral autonomy. Being behaviorally autonomous does not mean that adolescents never rely on the help of others. Instead, they become increasingly able to recognize those situations where they have the ability to make their own decisions versus situations where they will need to consult with a peer or parent for advice.

The CBT therapist will want to be particularly attentive to the following autonomy-related issues as they arise during treatment: (1) the degree to which adolescents are responsible in managing the level of autonomy they have been granted, (2) whether parent and child have realistic expectations for the level of autonomy that should be granted in the future, (3) the degree to which there is a discrepancy between how much autonomy the parent is willing to grant and the amount of autonomy the adolescent is able to manage (Holmbeck & O'Donnell, 1991), (4) parents' responses to their child's attempts to be autonomous (i.e., do they have the ability to foster healthy levels of autonomy in their offspring?), (5) the degree of flexibility demonstrated by parents in changing their parenting around autonomy issues (Holmbeck et al., 1995), and (6) the degree to which the child is susceptible to peer pressure, which typically increases to a peak in early adolescence due in part to an increase in peer pressure prior to early adolescence and an accompanying decrease in susceptibility to parental pressure (Steinberg, 1996).

Autonomy development has implications for how parents and adolescents are involved in treatment (Forehand & Wierson, 1993; Shirk, 1999). For example, when conducting parent management training (PMT), such treatment "must be reconceptualized in terms of mutual rather than unilateral interventions" (Shirk, 1999, p. 64). Rather than parents being entirely in control of the intervention (as is the case with PMT as applied to *children*), parents *and* adolescents involved in PMT learn negotiation skills, and adolescents are instrumentally involved in the treatment (Shirk, 1999). Parents and therapists may want to utilize an approach where there is a balance between respecting and validating the input of the adolescent and maintaining some level of authority.

Identity

A major psychological task of adolescence is the development of an identity (Erikson, 1968; Harter, 1990). Adolescents develop an identity through role explorations and role commitments. One's identity is multidimensional and includes self-perceptions and commitments across a number of areas, including occupational, academic, religious, interpersonal, sexual, and political domains. Although the notion that all adolescents experience identity crises appears to be a myth, identity development is recognized as an important adolescent issue (Harter, 1990).

Research in the area of identity development has isolated at least four identity statuses that are defined with respect to two dimensions: commitment and exploration. These identity statuses are as follows: identity moratorium (exploration with no commitment), identity foreclosure (commitment with no exploration), identity diffusion (no commitment and no systematic exploration), and identity achievement (commitment after extensive exploration). A given adolescent's status can change over time, reflecting increased maturation and development or, alternatively, regression to some less adaptive identity status. Perhaps most importantly, an adolescent's identity status can also vary depending on the domain under consideration (e.g., academic vs. interpersonal).

It is important for the CBT therapist to recognize that the process of identity formation is different for males and females and that neither process should be pathologized. Identity development in males appears to involve struggles with autonomy and themes of separation, whereas identity development in females is more likely to be intertwined with the development and maintenance of intimate relationships (although both genders may experience either or both processes; Gilligan, 1982; Gilligan et al., 1990; Harter, 1990). With respect to self-esteem and perceived competence, CBT therapists may want to employ approval and positive-regard techniques with younger children but focus on self-efficacy beliefs in working with adolescents (Shirk, 1999).

Intimacy

It is not until adolescence that one's friendships have the potential to become intimate (Savin-Williams & Berndt, 1990). An intimate relationship is characterized by trust, mutual self-disclosure, a sense of loyalty, and helpfulness. Intimate sharing with friends increases during adolescence, as do adolescents' intimate knowledge of their friends. All relationships become more emotionally charged during the adolescent period, and adolescents are more likely to engage in friendships with opposite-sex peers than are children. Girls' same-sex relationships are described as more intimate than are those of boys. Having intimate friendships is adaptive; adolescents with such friendships are more likely to have high self-esteem. Some scholars have proposed that friendships change during the adolescent period because of accompanying social-cognitive changes. The capacity to exhibit empathy and take multiple perspectives in social encounters makes it more likely that friendships (and therapy relationships) will become similarly more mature, complex, and intimate. Again, adolescents may benefit from treatment that focuses on the development of perspective-taking skills given that such skills are precursors to the development of intimate relationships with others (Shirk, 1999).

In the same way that there are changes in the nature of adolescent peer relationships, therapeutic relationships with adolescents are more likely to become intimate and emotionally charged than is the case with younger children. Issues of trust, loyalty, and self-disclosure also become salient therapeutic concerns during this developmental period.

Psychosocial Adjustment

A host of psychosocial adjustment outcomes have been of interest to researchers who study the adolescent period. Handbooks on the topic typically have chapters on a variety of diagnostic categories (e.g., Tolan &

Cohler, 1993; Van Hasselt & Hersen, 1995; Weiner, 1992), namely, depression and anxiety disorders, suicidal behavior, conduct disorders and delinquency, substance-use disorders, eating disorders (anorexia and bulimia), schizophrenia, and academic underachievement. Studies that examine potential predictors of adjustment typically focus on a single outcome (e.g., delinquency) given that predictors for each type of outcome tend to vary across outcomes, and because the outcomes themselves tend to be multidimensional (Loeber, Farrington, Stouthamer-Loeber, & Van Kammen, 1998; Tolan & Cohler, 1993). Psychopathology can be assessed with self-, parent-, and/or teacher-report on questionnaires or with adolescent-report in diagnostic clinical interviews (e.g., Diagnostic Interview for Children and Adolescents; DICA; Reich, Shayka, & Taibleson, 1991).

It is important for the CBT therapist to be aware that there are dramatic changes in the rates of psychiatric disorders during the adolescent period (e.g., increases in rates of schizophrenia, decreases in rates of enuresis), with some disorders becoming major psychiatric problems for the first time during this developmental period (e.g., eating disorders; Rutter, 1980). The features of certain childhood disorders change as the child moves into the adolescent years (e.g., ADHD; Barkley, 1997), and there are also dramatic gender differences for some disorders during adolescence (e.g., depression; Nolen-Hoeksema, 1994). Many scholars have become interested in predictors of rates of change in disorders. For example, one might ask: Why do depression scores increase rapidly over time for some adolescents but not for others? To answer questions such as this, longitudinal studies with appropriate data-analytic techniques are needed.

The various problem behaviors of adolescence tend to be intercorrelated insofar as they tend to co-occur within the same individuals. One clustering scheme suggests that there are two broadband categories of psychopathology (Achenbach, 1982, 1985): *internalizing* problems (i.e., disorders that represent problems within the self, such as depression, anxiety, somatic complaints, and social withdrawal) and *externalizing* problems (i.e., disorders that represent conflicts with the external environment, such as delinquency, aggression, and other self-control difficulties). Alternatively, Jessor and colleagues (Jessor, Donovan, & Costa, 1991; Jessor & Jessor, 1977) have proposed that a "problem behavior syndrome" characterizes some adolescents, such that there tend to be high intercorrelations among several types of problem behavior (e.g., drug use, sexual intercourse, drinking, and aggression). According to problem behavior theory, such behaviors develop as a function of the same etiological factors and therefore tend to co-occur in the same individuals (findings that have been replicated in other laboratories; e.g., Farrell, Danish, & Howard, 1992; although, for an alternative perspective, see Loeber et al., 1998). Finally, some adolescents have multiple disorders (i.e., comorbidity; Biederman,

Newcorn, & Sprich, 1991; Loeber et al., 1998); treatment techniques often have to address multiple psychopathologies that may interact in various ways (e.g., ADHD is often comorbid with conduct disorder).

In summary, it is critical that the CBT therapist have knowledge of the various psychopathologies of adolescence. Most importantly, therapists will benefit from knowledge about developmental variations in the onset and course of these different pathologies and the degree to which there is overlap/comorbidity among the various disorders.

Sexuality

Most children have mixed reactions to becoming a sexually mature adolescent. Parents also have conflicting reactions to such increasing maturity. Despite the importance of this topic, we know very little about normal adolescent sexuality (whether heterosexual or homosexual), primarily due to the difficulty in conducting studies on this topic (Katchadourian, 1990).

There are a host of factors associated with the onset and maintenance of sexual behaviors. Pubertal changes of adolescence have both direct (hormonal) and indirect (social stimulus) effects on sexual behaviors. Ethnic and religious differences in the onset of sexuality also exist. Finally, personality characteristics (e.g., the development of a sexual identity) and social factors (e.g., parent and peer influences) also serve as antecedents to an early onset of adolescent sexual behaviors.

The increasing rates of sexually transmitted diseases among adolescents and the fact that many young adults with AIDS (acquired immune deficiency syndrome) probably became infected as adolescents would suggest that adolescent sexuality is deserving of considerable attention from mental health practitioners working with adolescents. Given the often conflictive nature of adolescent, peer, and parental responses to sexuality, CBT therapists may be called upon to serve as educators about sexual matters. Moreover, practitioners must be clear, direct, and thorough in their evaluation of adolescent sexual behaviors. This requires that therapists be aware of their own conflicts around issues of sexuality.

Use of the Framework for Understanding Adolescent Development

Having reviewed the different components of the framework, a few brief examples of how it can be used to understand the behavior of individuals may be helpful (a more extensive case example is presented later). Recall that the primary developmental changes of adolescence impact on interpersonal contexts that in turn impact on the developmental outcomes of adolescence (see Figure 8.1).

Example 1

Suppose that a young adolescent boy is recently able to take multiple perspectives in social interactions, think hypothetically, and conceive of numerous possibilities for his own behaviors. Such newly developed cognitive skills will impact on his familial relationships insofar as he is now able to imagine how his relationships with his parents could be different. He begins to challenge the reasoning of his parents and requests more decision-making power in his family. These changes may either be welcomed by the family and serve to facilitate growth and change within the family system or may be received more negatively and result in conflict. The accompanying changes in his relationships with his parents will in turn impact on his level of behavioral autonomy, the nature of his attachments to his parents, and his identity (see previous descriptions of each of these constructs).

Example 2

A 16-year-old girl has just obtained a driver's license and has decided that she will look for her first job to earn some spending money. Because she is now 16 years old, she recently gained a number of privileges that she did not have before (i.e., her social role has been redefined). She takes a job in a fast-food restaurant several miles from home and, because she now has a driver's license, she can get to work on her own. Her experiences at her job produce increases in feelings of autonomy and achievement as she begins to develop an occupational identity. Moreover, her peer group may become less school-based and more heterogeneous.

IMPLICATIONS OF DEVELOPMENTAL PSYCHOLOGY FOR THE USE OF COGNITIVE-BEHAVIORAL THERAPY WITH ADOLESCENTS

As suggested by Shirk (1988), "The psychological treatment of children can be informed, and advanced, by the introduction of developmental principles into clinical concepts and techniques" (p. 14). There are several developmental factors that are important to consider when working clinically with adolescent clients: (1) developmental myths, (2) developmental psychopathology, (3) developmental norms, (4) developmental level, (5) developmental transitions, and (6) developmental predictors and protective factors.

Developmental Myths

As mentioned earlier, it appears that therapists may inadvertently endorse the "developmental level uniformity myth" (Kendall, 1984; Kendall et al.,

1984), which is the tendency of clinicians to view children and adolescents of different ages as more alike than different. The consequence of a belief in this myth is that treatments are more likely to be applied without consideration of the developmental level (i.e., the social, emotional, and/or cognitive-developmental level) of the child or adolescent client.

More recently, Shirk (1999) has described a number of interrelated subtypes of the developmental-level uniformity myth. First, there is the "developmental continuity myth." This myth involves the assumption that therapies that are applied to adults can be applied with little modification to children with similar presenting problems. Unfortunately, adult treatments may be inappropriate for children and adolescents not only because of the complexities of language, but also because of the cognitive abilities required to participate in the treatment.

A second myth ("the developmental invariance myth") involves the assumption that a given disorder has a single etiological pathway (Shirk, 1999). Contrary to this assumption, it appears that *equifinality* and *multifinality* are more the rule than the exception (Cicchetti & Rogosch, 1996). Specifically, equifinality is the process by which a single disorder is produced via different developmental pathways ("Children may share the same diagnosis but not the same pathogenic process," Shirk, 1999, p. 65). Multifinality involves the notion that the same developmental events may lead to a variety of different adjustment outcomes (some adaptive, some maladaptive). Given past research support for the concepts of equifinality and multifinality (Cicchetti & Rogosch, 1996), it appears that CBT therapists are best served by gathering as much developmental and historical information as possible about a given child, in addition to what they already know about the etiology of the disorder in question.

The "developmental consistency myth" involves the assumption that the same developmental tasks are relevant across different ages. Contrary to this myth, (1) the clinical concerns that need to be addressed in treatment are likely to vary as a function of the developmental level of the child (e.g., the acquisition of certain conflict-resolution skills may be more relevant at certain ages than at others); (2) the therapeutic interventions that will successfully redirect a child from a maladaptive trajectory to an adaptive trajectory are likely to vary developmentally (Shirk, 1999); and (3) the presence of certain pathologies may make it more likely that a child will be off-time in the development of certain skills (e.g., an aggressive child with ADHD may not have developed appropriate social skills). An implication of the last issue is that the therapist may not only need to address the presenting symptoms (e.g., the ADHD and aggressiveness) but also the skills (e.g., social skills) that the child failed to develop as a consequence of having a severe behavior problem (Shirk, 1999).

Finally, "the myth of individual development" involves the assumption that treatment can proceed at the individual level without attention to contextual factors (Shirk, 1999). Contrary to this myth, Henggeler et al.

(1998) have documented the importance of attending to multiple systems (family, peer, school) in which the adolescent interacts. Similarly, if a family-oriented CBT approach is deemed optimal, the adjustment of the parents and the quality of parenting must be assessed prior to including the parents as part of the intervention (Kendall & MacDonald, 1993; Shirk, 1999).

Developmental Psychopathology

As already discussed, there is a decided lack of information concerning the effects of developmental level on treatment outcome (Kendall et al., 1984; Shirk, 1988; Tolan & Cohler, 1993). On the other hand, the related field of developmental psychopathology (e.g., Achenbach, 1982; Cicchetti, 1984; Cicchetti & Cohen, 1995; Cicchetti & Toth, 1996; Lewis & Miller, 1990) has seen much activity with the introduction of a new journal (*Development and Psychopathology*) and a rapid increase in research output.

Developmental psychopathology is an extension of developmental psychology insofar as the former is concerned with variations in the course of normal development (Rutter & Garmezy, 1983). Developmental psychopathology is also concerned with the continuity and discontinuity of certain psychological maladies (i.e., developmental transformations in the types and nature of psychopathology; e.g., Cicchetti, 1984; Cicchetti & Cohen, 1995; Masten, 1988; Rutter, 1980, 1985; Rutter & Garmezy, 1983; Sroufe & Rutter, 1984).

Research in the developmental psychopathology literature indicates that the frequency and nature of most disorders vary as a function of age. Regarding changes in frequencies, Loeber et al. (1998) have documented age shifts in the prevalence of certain disorders (e.g., delinquency, substance use, sexual behaviors, etc.). Loeber and his colleagues have also documented important differences between children and adolescents with early-onset problem behavior versus those with late-onset problem behaviors. Rutter (1980, 1985) summarized the changes that occur in behavior disorders from childhood to adolescence and concluded that roughly half of all adolescent disorders are continuations of those seen in childhood. Those that are new during adolescence (e.g., anorexia) tend to be quite different than those that began during childhood. There are increases in the rates of the following disturbances during adolescence, relative to rates during childhood: depression, bipolar affective disorders, attempted suicide, completed suicide, and schizophrenia. There are increases in the frequency of antisocial activities but not in the number of individuals involved. Animal phobias become less common during adolescence, and agoraphobia and social phobias become more common. Incidence of enuresis and encopresis is also less during adolescence. It is critical to note, however, that most adolescents do not develop mental disorders. The actual percentage of adolescents who do show symptoms, estimated as between 10% and 20% (Offer

& Offer, 1975; Rutter, 1980), is only slightly higher (perhaps less than 5% higher) than the rates for children or adults.

Regarding changes in the nature of disorders, Achenbach (1982, 1985, 1991; Achenbach & Edelbrock, 1981) has found, for example, that the nature of ADHD varies with age, with the various components of the disorder (i.e., impulsivity, inattention, and hyperactivity) being exhibited in varying degrees at different ages and in males versus females. The impulsivity and inattentiveness components of the disorder are much more likely to be evident during adolescence than is the hyperactivity component. Moreover, the manner in which impulsivity and inattentiveness are exhibited changes as children move into adolescence. Regarding depression, adolescent girls tend to exhibit symptoms of withdrawal, whereas younger depressed girls are less likely to exhibit this symptom. Similar age differences have been noted for other disorders falling within both the externalizing and internalizing categories (e.g., conduct disorders, anxiety).

The field of developmental psychopathology also addresses issues of continuity–discontinuity. Rutter (1985) suggests that antisocial behavior tends toward continuity insòfar as antisocial adults have "almost always" been antisocial children (although there also appear to be several subtypes of antisocial youth, each with its own developmental pathway; Tolan & Loeber, 1993). Depressed adults tend not to have been depressed children— with the onset of depression being less common in childhood. Finally, schizophrenia disorders are often not preceded by psychotic disorders during childhood. In a study of St. Louis youth, Robins (1966) found that multiple contacts with mental health professionals for antisocial acts were predictive of adult schizophrenia. In short, there is not a simple, continuous relationship between child, adolescent, and adult disorders.

The CBT clinician would want to have this knowledge of developmental psychopathology to enable him or her to develop hypotheses about the course of a given child's disturbance. Is it likely that the disturbance will change or abate, or stay the same over time? Is the disturbance typical of the problems that are usually seen for a child of that age? Without answers to these questions, the therapist may misdiagnose, be prone to apply inappropriate treatments, or be overly concerned about the presence of certain symptoms. If a therapist, for example, were asked to see an antisocial adolescent, it would certainly be important to understand the age changes (or, in this case, lack of changes) in the patterning of this disorder, as well as the healthy components of the disorder that should be maintained (e.g., high energy levels of antisocial adolescents).

Developmental Norms

The therapist who is knowledgeable about both normal and maladaptive adolescent development is at a great advantage when attempting to design a treatment, determine the conditions under which a treatment is efficacious, and/or apply a given treatment. Simply put, it is likely that the quality of adolescent treatment will "move up a notch or two" when the clinician is sensitive to adolescent developmental norms. Although we have thus far been critical of the existing clinical literature for not being attentive to the literature concerning normal development (Tolan & Cohler, 1993), this does not mean that efforts that take developmental factors into account do not exist.

Knowledge of developmental norms serves as a basis for making sound diagnostic judgments, assessing the need for treatment, and selecting the appropriate treatment. In terms of diagnosis, both overdiagnosis and underdiagnosis can result from a lack of, or erroneous knowledge of, developmental norms. A CBT clinician who lacks the knowledge that a given behavior is typical of the adolescent age period (e.g., increases in adolescent questioning of parental authority due to advances in cognitive development, increases in time spent with peers at the expense of time with family) is much more likely to *overdiagnosis* and to inappropriately refer such adolescents (and their families) for treatment.

With regards to *underdiagnosis*, it is a common belief that adolescents have extremely stormy and stressful relationships with their parents and that "detachment" from parents is the norm (Arnett, 1999; Holmbeck & Hill, 1988). On the other hand, research has not supported this notion—it appears that approximately 20% (rather than 100%) of adolescents have such relationships with their parents (for a review, see Holmbeck & Hill, 1988). It is interesting to speculate about the clinical implications of such erroneous "storm-and-stress" beliefs. Offer, Ostrov, and Howard (1981) have warned that "adolescents and their parents are not helped when experts tell them not to worry about their problems because the problems are a normal part of adolescence that will disappear with time. . . . Adolescents in the midst of severe identity crises or emotional turmoil are not just experiencing a part of normal growing up" (pp. 127–128). A problem results, then, when clinicians underdiagnose psychopathology during adolescence owing to storm-and-stress beliefs. Underdiagnosis is also possible when the same diagnostic criteria are applied to children and adolescents. For example, March and Mulle (1998) suggested that children tend to exhibit developmentally appropriate levels of obsessive–compulsive symptoms (e.g., normal children often insist that certain activities follow rigid routines). Such obsessive–compulsive behaviors are not typical of adolescents, however. Failure to recognize that such behaviors are developmentally inappropriate during the teenage years may lead to underdiagnosis.

Some changes during adolescence are normal, and these have implications for the selection of treatment. Given the adolescent's normal developmental trend toward greater autonomous functioning (Steinberg & Silverberg, 1986), certain treatments are more appropriate for this age group.

Self-control strategies (e.g., Feindler & Ecton, 1986; for a review of the developmental changes in self-control abilities, see Harter, 1983) are probably more useful with older adolescents than are behavioral programs in which parents are employed as behavior change agents (Guerra, 1993; Kendall & Williams, 1986; Shirk, 1999). Similarly, the work of Spivack and Shure (Shure & Spivack, 1978, 1980; Spivack et al., 1976) suggests that different cognitive–problem-solving strategies are relevant at different ages.

Even if a therapist's sense of what is normative is consistent with the research literature, a parent of an adolescent may need to be educated about typical adolescent behavior. Parents may use their own adolescence as "the norm," thus biasing their attributions about their child's behavior. Parents also have the additional task of integrating their own sense of what is normative with the norms and expectations of their child's peer group. Particularly for parents who are dealing with "adolescence" for the first time, the therapist can help to bring their expectations in line with what is known about normative behavior during the adolescent period.

Developmental Level

As suggested earlier, the importance of cognitive-developmental level as a moderator of treatment effectiveness has been stressed by many scholars in the field (e.g., Bobbitt & Keating, 1983; Furman, 1980; Guerra, 1993; Henggeler & Cohen, 1984; Holmbeck & Kendall, 1991; Holmbeck & Updegrove, 1995; Kendall, 1977; Kendall & Braswell, 1985; Kendall et al., 1984; Shirk, 1999). First, level of cognitive-development may be an important etiological factor in the onset and escalation of adolescent psychopathology. If so, the integration of cognitive developmental theory with etiological theories of psychopathology has important implications for intervention. Second, level of cognitive development may be an important factor in selecting optimal treatment strategies (Henggeler & Cohen, 1984).

Cognitive-Developmental Level and Etiology

Although there are many benefits to developing more sophisticated cognitive abilities, it is likely that the development of certain cognitive processes predisposes adolescents to psychopathology. In this section, we use adolescent depression as an example.

The initial onset of major depression often occurs in adolescence (Burke, Burke, Regier, & Rae, 1990; Durand & Barlow, 1997; Sorenson, Rutter, & Aneshensel, 1991). Could it be that advances in cognitive development are a precursor for the development of depression in at least a subset of adolescents? Interestingly, several theories of depression emphasize cognitive processes. The learned-helplessness theory posits that depression develops when a person responds to stressful events with internal, stable, and global attributions resulting in hopelessness about coping with negative life events (Seligman, 1975). Similarly, Beck (1976; Beck, Esptein, & Harrison, 1983; Clark & Beck, 1999) theorized that depression develops out of a negative schema or an enduring negative cognitive belief system characterized by a variety of cognitive errors about the self, the world, and the future. For example, an adolescent may make an overgeneralization error by assuming that he or she is rejected by all peers because two classmates refused to play basketball with him or her. According to cognitive theories of depression, people who make such errors much of the time are more likely to be depressed.

Adolescence marks the onset of hypothetical thinking and a new perspective on the world, which, in some cases, may be depressogenic given the occurrence of other factors (biological predisposition for mood disorders, stressful events, lack of social support, etc.). Hypothetical reasoning may be an important etiological factor, and it is often an important focus of cognitive treatments. From a cognitive-behavioral perspective, the goal of therapy is to help the client identify maladaptive thought patterns that result in depression and replace them with more adaptive thoughts and appraisals. This approach requires a client to think in terms of consequential thinking (e.g., If I keep thinking this way, I will remain depressed) and to think about possibilities (e.g., How will I feel if I think differently?). Since this level of abstract reasoning often emerges in adolescence, one would expect cognitive-behavioral treatment for depression to be effective with adolescents (Durlak et al., 1991). Indeed, a recent review suggests that cognitive-behavioral treatment for depression with adolescents successfully reduces depressive symptomatology (Marcotte, 1997).

Integrating cognitive development with the etiological theories may have important implications for intervention. As suggested earlier, formal operational thought may be an important etiological factor, and thus an important focus of treatment. Also, with regard to prevention, such an integration has implications for the timing of intervention. There may be optimal ages for implementing prevention programs, and it may be detrimental to intervene too early. A preventive intervention's effectiveness may be limited when the participant's experience forms no basis on which to relate personally to the curriculum (cf. Maggs, Schulenberg, & Hurrelmann, 1996). In the case of depression, at least from a cognitive-behavioral perspective, prevention efforts should target early adolescence when formal operations begin to emerge and when risk for depression increases.

Cognitive-Developmental Level and Optimal Treatment

Henggeler and Cohen (1984) discussed the role of child and adolescent cognitive development in family-oriented treatment for sexual abuse and divorce. They argued that behavioral approaches may be more appropriate for less cognitively mature children, whereas emotionally supportive approaches may be better suited for more advanced children, who are better able to reflect on the broader social and interpersonal consequences and effect of stressful events such as abuse or divorce. Specifically, in the case of sexual abuse, Henggeler and Cohen argued that treatment for the preoperational child will be quite different than treatment for the concrete operational child, or a formal operational child. Past research suggests that there are fewer negative effects for younger children than for older children (although the severity of the impact may also vary as a function of the nature and duration of the abuse; Tsai, Feldman-Summers, & Edgar, 1979). Preoperational children are less at risk because (1) they tend to not be aware of the negative social consequences of abuse; (2) they tend to feel less guilt, depression, and loss subsequent to the abusive act; and (c) they are less aware of the potential impact that the abuse may have on future heterosexual relationships. Behavioral approaches may be helpful for these less cognitively mature children because they may fear specific individuals or situations, and they may not be able to benefit from insight-oriented therapy. For the concrete operational child, on the other hand, the abuse is more likely to generate feelings of guilt and, as a result, emotional support may be more useful with such children. Similarly, the formal operational child will be more likely to understand the potential impact that abuse may play in disrupting *future* sexual relationships; such insights require discussion and support.

Regarding relations between cognitive development and child adjustment to divorce, preoperational children may be primarily concerned with the loss of parental attention and, as a consequence, behavior problems may emerge (Henggeler & Cohen, 1984). Again, behavioral techniques may be helpful in altering the consequences (i.e., rewards and punishments) of the child's behaviors. More cognitively mature children (and especially those adolescents who have role-taking skills) are able to understand that the lack of attention from parents may be a function of considerable marital stress as well as stress from other aspects of their parents' lives. On the other hand, adolescents are also more able to comprehend the seriousness of the "loss" of a parent. They are more able to verbalize their anger and concerns than are younger children; such verbal involvement on the part of the child may exacerbate the stress level of the parent. It is likely, then, that the adolescent will benefit from discussions with an objective outside person (i.e., a therapist).

In working with adolescents who have experienced a traumatic event, it is important that the therapist distinguish between new stressors *versus* stressors that occurred during childhood but are now being revisited anew during adolescence. Even if a sexually abused child, for example, received treatment at a young age, this child may need to receive treatment again as he or she confronts the developmental tasks of adolescence. Unlike young children, adolescents are able to understand the sexual aspects of the abuse. They may find it necessary to discuss these events with sexual partners. Moreover, their capacity for abstract reasoning allows them to comprehend the injustice of the events. Such a new perspective on an "old" event may necessitate additional therapeutic intervention. Indeed, treatment with children and adolescents may need to be administered *intermittently* at different critical periods rather than continuously at only one period of time.

Changes in a child's cognitive-developmental level also alter the nature of parent–child communication. As discussed earlier, adolescents are able to think more complexly and can think about possibilities; as a result, they may see flaws in their parents' arguments and also be more ready to question such flaws. This type of advanced thinking is to be encouraged, yet parents often feel threatened and challenged by this type of adolescent behavior. With such parents, the CBT therapist may want to use "reframing" techniques in the following manner. One could suggest to parents that their adolescent offspring are actually "asking" their parents (in their own inimitable way, of course) to help them learn to think. Telling adolescents, "Just do it because I said so!" does not prepare them for the myriad of choices and decisions they will face. However, a parent who is willing to engage in appropriate discussions with their adolescent concerning issues of rules, responsibilities, and decision-making is communicating to the child that there are multiple ways to view the same issue. Moreover, such discussions communicate to the child that all perspectives are important. Cognitive development is likely to be facilitated by such discussions insofar as this type of communication promotes more complex thinking abilities.

Weisz and Weersing (1999) have detailed several other cognitive developmental issues that are relevant to the treatment of adolescent clients. First, the degree to which a child or adolescent understands the purpose and process of therapy (as well as the concepts that are being taught) is critical. Second, the degree to which a child can perspective-take may place limits on the effectiveness of certain interventions where such skills are assumed. Third, a child's level of abstract reasoning is an important determinant of whether he or she will be able to participate in role-playing exercises and other hypothetical situations. Fourth, CBT, like all interventions, is dependent on language. The abilities to decode complex and abstract language, and engage in private speech may be important moderating factors for treatment effectiveness.

More generally, knowledge of developmental level can be used in a number of ways to modify treatment strategies. First, developmental level can provide a basis for designing alternate versions of the same treatment. Second, knowledge of developmental level may guide the stages of treatment. When teaching a child increasingly more complex levels of social interaction as part of social skills training, for example, the therapist could follow the developmental sequence of social play (Gelfand & Peterson, 1985). Finally, treatments can be used to advance the developmental level of the child or adolescent (see earlier discussion; La Greca & Prinstein, 1999); in other words, the developmental level of the adolescent can be the target of treatment.

Regarding the last point, social problem-solving training has been applied to a variety of adolescent clinical problems, such as anger and depression (Feindler & Ecton, 1986; Marcotte, 1997). Problem-solving training usually involves several sequential stages: the problem, generating potential solutions, evaluating solutions by predicting their potential consequences, and selecting the best solution. This requires sophisticated means–ends thinking and the capacity to simultaneously hold several mental representations (solutions) in mind. Deficiencies in problem solving may stem from a variety of sources, including low level of cognitive development or an impoverished fund of knowledge in the domain of social problem solving. Treatment can be viewed as an attempt to increase an adolescent's capacity to apply formal operational thinking to this psychosocial domain. For example, an adolescent with particularly limited cognitive skills may require intensive modeling and instruction in consequential thinking, later followed by practice and behavioral rehearsal. More cognitively sophisticated adolescents may be able to rely on discourse and talk about real-life problems, and how they might approach them differently. Leahy (1988) has similarly argued that "for children who are less able to take perspective on their thoughts than adults, socialization to treatment may involve building the cognitive skills that make treatment effective" (p. 202).

Developmental Transitions

A significant contribution in the area of developmental transitions is the work of Simmons and Blyth (1987). In their work with young adolescents, they have tested the hypothesis that a child who must confront multiple life changes that occur simultaneously is at risk for adjustment difficulties. They postulate that adolescents who experience multiple life changes are unable to "withdraw to a more comfortable, accustomed sphere or relationship when the latter is changing as well" (p. 304; e.g., a child who has just moved to a new school may be unable to seek support at home if his OR her parents are going through a divorce—two life changes that are frequently associated).

What implications do these findings have for treatment of adolescents? The results of Simmons and Blyth's (1987) work suggest that prevention efforts are needed for children who are about to experience multiple transitions. Such prevention efforts could occur at the level of a single therapist–client relationship or at a larger, school-based level. Kendall et al. (1984) argue that the focus of such prevention should be on the development of appropriate coping strategies to deal with upcoming transitions (also see

Compas, 1987). Here the focus would be on coping with future events rather than focusing on coping with current stressors; in this way, the CBT therapist is helping the adolescent to develop strengths, so that he or she is more able to manage adversity.

Developmental Predictors and Protective Factors

A clinician's knowledge of developmental predictors has a number of implications for the treatment of children and adolescents. If we know, based on longitudinal studies, that a specific set of behavioral deficits is related to more serious pathology later in the individual's life, we can then treat the less severe antecedent disturbance before having to deal with the more serious subsequent disturbance. This, of course, is the goal of all large-scale prevention efforts (see Dryfoos, 1990; Lerner et al., 1999), but it is relevant to individual psychotherapy as well. Earlier, we noted that prior knowledge of "developmental level" and "developmental transitions" can aid the CBT therapist in providing anticipatory interventions that circumvent the development of serious problems later on. We also believe that knowledge of developmental antecedents and consequences is critical in establishing coherent intervention efforts.

Loeber et al. (1998), in work on explanatory factors for the onset of problem behaviors in childhood and adolescence, identified a number of problem behaviors that can be detected early in childhood and are often associated with an escalation in problems later in development. For example, physical fighting, covert problem behaviors, and disobedience are risk factors for future delinquency and could be targets for intervention. Lack of guilt, poor school performance, and ADHD symptoms are additional explanatory risk factors for several problem behaviors that could be identified in younger children. By recognizing that the young child who presents with these behaviors is at risk for more severe problems later, the clinician is able to educate the family as to the importance of addressing these problems early in an effort to prevent the development of more severe pathology later.

As discussed earlier, the literature on peer relationships and later personal adjustment suggests that poor peer relationships early in childhood (e.g., lack of peer acceptance, aggressiveness, shyness, withdrawal) place the child at risk for developing later adjustment difficulties (for a review, see Parker & Asher, 1987). Although the causal links between early peer rejection and later psychopathology may be quite complex, such findings suggest that a peer-rejected child or adolescent may benefit greatly from an early intervention directed at social skills and peer acceptance. Knowledge of this research literature would make the CBT therapist more likely to gather information about an adolescent's peer status; if the child is rejected, a therapist with such knowledge would be more likely to address the child's peer relationships through treatment that promotes perspective taking (e.g., social skills training, group therapy). The informed CBT therapist will be well aware of the consequences of not addressing these problems and will also address these issues with the adolescent's family.

Thus far, we have discussed how certain behaviors in childhood and adolescence are predictive of future maladaptation. A number of writers have also stressed the notion that there are certain protective factors that make the child less likely to develop problem behaviors later in life. In part, protective factors are merely the reverse of vulnerability factors (e.g., secure attachment vs. insecure attachment; Rutter, 1987; Sroufe, 1988; Greenberg & Speltz, 1988), although this is not always the case (e.g., availability of an extrafamilial adult "mentor"). Garmezy (1985) discussed three categories of protective factors than seem to make the child most resilient: dispositional characteristics of the child, family cohesion, and the availability of external resources (including, but not limited to, the therapist). Clinicians would benefit from knowledge of this literature given that knowledge about protective factors can strengthen treatment endeavors; that is, therapists can identify opportunities for "protection" in the adolescent's life that can buffer the at-risk adolescent from developing later adaptational difficulties. In fact, the opportunity for engaging external resources for protection is more likely in the life of the adolescent (vs. the child) given the greater accessibility and frequency of external resources during this age period and the adolescent's greater ability to engage such resources on his or her own.

In summary, it appears that knowledge of developmental antecedents of later, more maladaptive, behaviors, is useful. Simply said, prevention efforts will enable the therapist ultimately to deal with a younger and less seriously disturbed clinical population. The alternative is that when faced with a lack of professional attention and a cumulation of negative consequences (e.g., Caspi, Elder, & Bem, 1987), disturbed children are more likely to "choose" those environments that exacerbate existing pathology.

CASE EXAMPLE: DEVELOPMENTAL FACTORS AND THE TREATMENT OF OBSESSIVE–COMPULSIVE DISORDER

To illustrate how an understanding of adolescent development can facilitate treatment, a case example is provided. A review of identifying information and presenting concerns is followed by a discussion of relevant developmental issues, with a particular focus on cognitive-developmental issues.

Identifying Information and Case History

Susan is a 14-year-old Caucasian ninth-grader. She was referred by a psychiatrist (Dr. J.) who had seen Susan for a medication evaluation. Dr. J. placed Susan on several medications (Prozac, Xanax, and Buspar) and recommended CBT to combat her severe obsessive–compulsive disorder (OCD). Susan lives with both natural parents and her sister (age 12). Susan's parents both attended college for 1 year and work full time.

Susan is petite and appears younger than her actual age. She presented as tense and high-strung. Susan receives straight A's in school and has a group of female friends with whom she socializes, including one "best friend" she has known since elementary school. Developmental milestones were reportedly reached on time or somewhat early. At intake, Susan reported frequent headaches and stomachaches; physical exams ruled out any medical cause for these symptoms.

There is a family history of anxiety problems on both the maternal and paternal sides. Susan's mother reports considerable anxiety and a past episode of depression that resulted in 2 years of outpatient therapy. Susan's maternal grandfather suffers from phobias and agoraphobia, as well as alcoholism, and a great aunt appears to have OCD. Susan's father reports that he is "moody" but has never sought treatment. Susan's paternal grandfather is an alcoholic and her paternal grandmother reportedly has anxiety problems for which she takes Xanax. Several paternal aunts reportedly have anxiety symptoms as well. Finally, a cousin on the paternal side has been diagnosed with bipolar disorder.

Presenting Concerns

At the time that Susan and her family presented for treatment, Susan was spending several hours per day doing compulsive behaviors or obsessive thinking. One of her most prominent symptoms was list making. Susan found it necessary to organize her entire day into a series of "systems" (e.g., a getting-ready-for-school system, a checking-homework system) and "lists" of things to do or to contemplate. Susan spent a good deal of time, both at home and at school, compulsively recording items on one of several lists. Often, these items were redundant with items on other lists, or were extremely trivial (e.g., Susan would write down every step of her bedtime routine, and would write down "go to the bathroom" and "stop at my locker" on her list of things to do during the day). Susan also had obsessive thoughts about the things she needed to do and things she felt she needed to consider or contemplate. For example, thinking about her family and the trouble she was causing them was an item that appeared on a list. Thus, her lists included actions to do (both compulsions and ordinary behaviors such as "brush teeth") as well as items relating to the content of her obsessions (such as "think about family"). She also had a symptom she called "nervous tics," which appeared to represent a voluntary motor compulsion consisting of a series of facial grimaces. Typically, Susan performed this compulsion a dozen or more times per day in response to feelings of anxiety triggered by any number of situations or thoughts.

At the start of treatment, Susan had recently spent an entire day writing and rewriting her lists. She became so distraught by her inability to stop this behavior that her parents eventually physically removed her from the table, carried her to the car, and drove around until Susan felt more under control. Susan had sporadic school absences, totaling 11 days in the first 2 months of school, and had been sleeping in her parents' bed due to distressing obsessive thoughts and some compulsive straightening of her pajamas and bedding at night.

Susan's symptoms began in early elementary school, and the family does not recall any precipitants or notable antecedent events. In first grade, she developed a routine involving using the bathroom. Her mother also recalls an episode that year in which Susan complained that she could not stop twisting her ankle back and forth. In third grade, she began her "tics." List making appeared while Susan was in the eighth grade. In September of ninth grade, as she began high school, Susan's symptoms worsened significantly.

Susan met DSM-IV criteria for OCD. At the start of treatment, Susan's symptoms were clearly and seriously interfering with her functioning both at home and at school. It appears that biological, cognitive, and social–environmental factors all played a role in the onset of her symptoms. CBT was begun based on the treatment manual provided by March and Mulle (1998).

General Developmental Issues Relevant to the Case

It appears that Susan has found several developmental tasks of early adolescence stressful and overwhelming. For example, her symptoms intensified just as she was making the transition to high school. As discussed earlier, a school transition is often a significant developmental stressor, particularly when it overlaps with other developmental changes or major life events. Having a more complicated schedule and more homework appears to have triggered Susan's thoughts about needing to be completely organized. Pubertal changes also appear to have been stressful for her. Interestingly, the week Susan began menstruating for the first time coincided with an increase in the intensity of her OCD symptoms. Moreover, Susan is somewhat immature in her social interests (e.g., she denies any interest in boys or dating; she was shocked that her younger sister has a "boyfriend," and she avoids socializing with older adolescents or mixed-sex groups). As noted earlier, she was also reported to be sleeping in her parents' bed, a behavior that is clearly developmentally atypical. All of these developmental concerns represent important components of Susan's problem that need to be integrated into a comprehensive treatment plan.

As her symptoms started to improve, Susan was able to behave in a more developmentally appropriate way. She began to sleep in her own bed and relied less on her mother for emotional support. These changes required some adjustment on the part of her mother, who was somewhat perplexed when Susan began to exhibit typical adolescent behaviors: "Sometimes I can tell she's upset, but she says, 'Mom, just leave me alone!' She's never been like this before. I don't know what to do. I want to help but everything I say seems to make it worse." Although Susan's mother worried about such incidents, Susan commented that they were "no big deal" and that her mother was overreacting.

Susan's parents also wondered about what role they should play in the treatment. In the March and Mulle (1998) treatment manual, parents may be included to varying degrees depending on the level of family pathology, the extent to which the compulsive rituals involve parents, and the developmental level of the child. In an early session, Susan's father commented, "She's doing great, but we're wondering if there's something we should be doing to help her more." Given the fact that Susan's family was basically functioning well and was not involved with her rituals, Susan's developmental level was "respected" by leaving it up to Susan how much she wanted her parents to be involved in the treatment. Susan appreciated having her parents in a supportive "cheerleader" role but chose not to utilize them as "cotherapists" (e.g., she did not want them to help her with her therapy homework). Despite some initial anxiety over whether they could be doing more, Susan's parents were able to allow her to take primary responsibility for her own treatment. Susan enjoyed having therapy time for herself, where she worked on skills and homework assignments independently.

Cognitive–Developmental Issues

There was evidence that Susan was beginning to develop formal operational cognitive abilities, as manifested by her ability to think hypothetically and abstractly. Susan was also able to consider different future possibilities. For example, fairly early in treatment, she remarked on what might happen in the future following treatment:

> "It might be hard when things change, like when I finish high school or start college and stuff. OCD might try to come back then. I think it'll be okay because I'll have the tools I learned, so I'll know how to deal. But if I didn't ever come to counseling, I guess it would be kind of overwhelming if the OCD got real bad and I didn't know what to do about it."

Here, Susan is considering both the *likely* future (i.e., as an adult, having completed therapy) and contrasts this to a different *unlikely* future (i.e., as an adult who never attended therapy).

As a formal operational thinker, Susan can also think about her own thinking. This was manifested in her OCD symptoms; she had obsessions about the content of her own thoughts (e.g., obsessively planning things she wanted to think about later). Susan frequently made lists of things she deemed important to think about (such as the difficulty she was causing her family). She was also concerned about the content and process of such thoughts (whether she had thought it through long enough or thoroughly enough). On the other hand, Susan's ability to think about her own thoughts was useful in CBT treatment. The therapist was able to help Susan step back from her thinking and challenge some of her thoughts, as in this exchange:

THERAPIST: How was that for you when you realized you had so much homework?

SUSAN: Well, for a minute I was like, "Oh my gosh, it's really a lot. I hope I don't get overwhelmed." But then I was like, "Wait. I know I won't. I can manage it."

Below is another example of Susan spontaneously challenging her thoughts when she had an obsessive worry about something bad happening if she forgot a chore:

"I just say, 'If I didn't let the dog out, what would be the worst thing that could happen—nothing.' "

One common feature of adolescent thinking is the belief in an "imaginary audience" (Elkind, 1967), which is the conviction that others are observing you closely and that they are as interested in what you are doing/thinking as you are about yourself. For example, like many adolescents, Susan was extremely distressed about a new haircut, despite the fact that it differed little from her usual style. Susan imagined that the change would be much more noticeable to others than was likely to be the case. Susan also sometimes believed that others were aware of her OCD symptoms. She commented that a friend "knows something is going on . . . with me making lists all the time and everything." When her symptoms began to improve, she felt this was obvious to school personnel as well: "I'm sure they [teachers] can tell it's much better for me now." Although it is reasonable to assume that others would notice obvious OCD symptoms, Susan was concerned that others would notice even the most subtle symptoms. The CBT therapist needs to be sensitive to this phenomenon as well as being reassuring and providing reality testing for the fears associated with being observed by an "imaginary audience."

In summary, this case demonstrates the utility of considering developmental factors when conceptualizing an adolescent therapy case. Susan was clearly dealing with a number of adolescent developmental issues, some of which exacerbated the nature of her OCD symptoms. Specifically, all of the following issues were relevant in this case: pubertal development, cognitive development, autonomy development with respect to her family relationships, school transitions, delayed peer/dating relationships, and parental involvement in treatment. Each of these factors was relevant not only to the conceptualization process but also to the treatment endeavor.

GENERAL CONCLUSIONS

Our informal review of the research literature revealed that there is an appreciable lack of interface between developmental psychology and clinical treatment with adolescents. This lack of attention has occurred despite numerous "calls" for research in this area (e.g., Holmbeck & Kendall, 1991; Santostefano, 1980; Shirk, 1988; Silverman & Ollendick, 1999; Tolan & Cohler, 1993). We also reviewed a framework for understanding adolescent development that illustrates the major developmental tasks of the adolescent period and discussed several developmental factors that are relevant to therapeutic interventions with adolescents.

Therapists who work with adolescents are encouraged to be involved with the developmental literature. A CBT therapist who neglects information on normative developmental processes during adolescence may be at risk for providing therapeutic interventions that do not "match" the developmental level of the adolescent. Moreover, uninformed therapists are more likely to overdiagnosis or underdiagnose maladaptive behavior. Knowledge of normal development can aid the therapist in formulating appropriate treatment goals, provide a basis for designing alternate versions of the same treatment, and guide the stages of treatment. We have stressed the importance of knowledge in the following areas for both researcher and therapist alike: developmental norms, developmental level, developmental transitions, developmental predictors, and developmental psychopathology.

Therapists may need to rethink how they do treatment. For example, it may be that intermittent, developmentally gauged treatments may be more effective than continuous treatment. Also, given the salience of peers during adolescence, "peer-oriented" approaches may be useful when working with clients who are withdrawn or isolated, or when attempting to facilitate social-cognitive development (e.g., perspective taking). Finally, efforts to integrate developmental psychology and clinical psychology should not stop with the therapist. Parents, teachers, and school administrators can be trained to think developmentally. Therapists can also work with parents to help them become more adaptable and sensitive to the changing developmental needs of their offspring during the adolescent transition.

ACKNOWLEDGMENTS

Completion of this chapter was supported in part by Research Grant Nos. 12-FY93-0621, 12-FY95-0496, 12-FY97-0270, and 12-FY99-0280 from the March of Dimes Birth Defects Foundation and a grant from the National Institute of Mental Health (No. R01-MH50423).

REFERENCES

Achenbach, T. M. (1982). *Developmental psychopathology* (2nd ed.). New York: Wiley.

Achenbach, T. M. (1985). *Assessment and taxonomy of child and adolescent psychopathology.* Beverly Hills, CA: Sage.

Achenbach, T. M. (1991). *Manual for the Child Behavior Checklist/4–18 and 1991 Profile.* Burlington: Department of Psychiatry, University of Vermont.

Achenbach, T. M., & Edelbrock, C. S. (1981). Behavioral problems and competencies reported by parents of normal and disturbed children aged 4 to 16. *Monographs of the Society for Research in Child Development, 46*(Serial No. 188).

Alsaker, F. D. (1995). Timing or puberty and reactions to pubertal changes. In M. Rutter (Ed.), *Psychosocial disturbances in young people: Challenges for prevention* (pp. 37–82). New York: Cambridge University Press.

Arnett, J. J. (1999). Adolescent storm and stress, reconsidered. *American Psychologist, 54,* 317–326.

Asher, S. R., & Gottman, J. M. (1981). *The development of children's friendships.* New York: Cambridge University Press.

Bandura, A. (1977). *Social learning theory.* Englewood Cliffs, NJ: Prentice-Hall.

Barkley, R. A. (1997). *ADHD and the nature of self-control.* New York: Guilford Press.

Baron, R. M., & Kenny, D. A. (1986). The moderator–mediator variable distinction in social psychological research: Conceptual, strategic, and statistical considerations. *Journal of Personality and Social Psychology, 51,* 1173–1182.

Beck, A. T. (1976). *Cognitive therapy and the emotional disorders.* New York: International University Press.

Beck, A. T., Epstein, N., & Harrison, R. (1983). Cognitions, attitudes, and personality dimensions in depression. *British Journal of Cognitive Psychotherapy, 1,* 1–16.

Belsher, G., Wilkes, T. C. R., & Rush, A. J. (1995). An open, multisite pilot study of cognitive therapy for depressed adolescents. *Journal of Psychotherapy Practice and Research, 4,* 52–66.

Berndt, T. J. (1981). Relations between social cognition, nonsocial cognition, and social behavior: The case of friendship. In J. H. Flavell & L. Ross (Eds.), *Social cognitive development: Frontiers and possible futures* (pp. 176–199). New York: Cambridge University Press.

Berndt, T. J. (1983). Social cognition, social behavior, and children's friendships. In E. T. Higgins, D. N. Ruble, & W. W. Hartup (Eds.), *Social cognition and social development: A sociocultural perspective* (pp. 158-189). New York: Cambridge University Press.

Berndt, T. J., & Savin-Williams, R. C. (1993). Peer relations and friendships. In P. H. Tolan & B. J. Cohler (Eds.), *Handbook of clinical research and practice with adolescents* (pp. 203–220). New York: Wiley.

Biederman, J., Newcorn, J., & Sprich, S. (1991). Comorbidity of attention-deficit hyperactivity disorder with conduct, depressive, anxiety, and other disorders. *American Journal of Psychiatry, 148,* 564–577.

Bierman, K. L. (1988). The clinical implications of children's conceptions of social relationships. In S. R. Shirk (Ed.), *Cognitive development and child psychotherapy* (pp. 247–272). New York: Plenum Press.

Bierman, K. L., & Furman, W. (1984). The effects of social skills training and peer involvement on the social adjustment of preadolescents. *Child Development, 55*, 151–162.

Bobbitt, B. L., & Keating, D. P. A. (1983). A cognitive-developmental perspective for clinical research and practice. In P. C. Kendall (Ed.), *Advances in cognitive behavioral research and therapy* (Vol. 2, pp. 198–241). New York: Academic Press.

Bowers, W. A., Evans, K., & Van Cleve, L. (1996). Treatment of adolescent eating disorders. In M. A. Reinecke, F. M. Dattilio, & A. Freeman (Eds.), *Cognitive therapy with children and adolescents: A casebook for practitioners.* New York: Guilford Press.

Brooks-Gunn, J., & Reiter, E. O. (1990). The role of pubertal processes. In S. S. Feldman & G. R. Elliott (Eds.), *At the threshold: The developing adolescent* (pp. 16–53). Cambridge, MA: Harvard University Press.

Brown, B. B. (1990). Peer groups and peer cultures. In S. S. Feldman & G. R. Elliott (Eds.), *At the threshold: The developing adolescent* (pp. 171–196). Cambridge, MA: Harvard University Press.

Buchanan, C. M., Eccles, J. S., & Becker, J. B. (1992). Are adolescents the victims of raging hormones? Evidence for activational effects of hormones on moods and behavior at adolescence. *Psychological Bulletin, 111*, 62–107.

Buchanan, C. L., Eccles, J. E., Flanagan, C., Midgley, C., Feldlaufer, H., & Harold, R. (1990). Parents' and teachers' beliefs about adolescence: Effects of sex and experience. *Journal of Youth and Adolescence, 19*, 363–394.

Burke, K. C., Burke, J. D., Regier, D. A., & Rae, D. S. (1990). Age of onset of selected mental disorders in five community populations. *Archives of General Psychiatry, 47*, 511–518.

Casey, R. J., & Berman, J. S. (1985). The outcome of psychotherapy with children. *Psychological Bulletin, 98*, 388–400.

Caspi, A., Elder, G. H., Jr., & Bem, D. J. (1987). Moving against the world: Life-course patterns of explosive children. *Developmental Psychology, 23*, 308–313.

Cicchetti, D. (1984). The emergence of developmental psychopathology. *Child Development, 55*, 1–7.

Cicchetti, D., & Cohen, D. J. (1995). *Developmental psychopathology.* New York: Wiley.

Cicchetti, D., & Rogosch, F. A. (1996). Equifinality and multifinality in developmental psychopathology. *Development and Psychopathology, 8*, 597–600.

Cicchetti, D., & Toth, S. L. (Eds.). (1996). *Rochester Symposium on Developmental Psychopathology: Vol. 7. Adolescence: Opportunities and challenges.* Rochester, NY: University of Rochester Press.

Clark, D. A., & Beck, A. T. (1999). *Scientific foundations of cognitive theory and therapy of depression.* New York: Wiley.

Collins, W. A. (1990). Parent–child relationships in the transition to adolescence: Continuity and change in interaction, affect, and cognition. In R. Montemayor, G. Adams, & T. Gullotta (Eds.), *Advances in adolescent development: Vol. 2. From childhood to adolescence: A transitional period?* (pp. 85–106). Beverly Hills, CA: Sage.

Collins, W. A., & Laursen, B. (1992). Conflict and relationships during adolescence. In C. U. Shantz & W. W. Hartup (Eds.), *Conflict in child and adolescent development* (pp. 216–241). New York: Cambridge University Press.

Compas, B. E. (1987). Coping with stress during childhood and adolescence. *Psychological Bulletin, 101*, 393–403.

Cooper, C. R. (1988). Commentary: The role of conflict in adolescent–parent relationships. In M. R. Gunnar & W. A. Collins (Eds.), *21st Minnesota symposium on child psychology* (pp. 181–187). Hillsdale, NJ: Erlbaum.

Cooper, C. R., Grotevant, H. D., & Condon, S. M. (1983). Individuality and connectedness in the family as a context for adolescent identity formation and role-taking skill. In H. D. Grotevant & C. R. Cooper (Eds.), *New directions for child development: No. 22. Adolescent development in the family* (pp. 43–59). San Francisco: Jossey-Bass.

Douvan, E., & Adelson, J. (1966). *The adolescent experience.* New York: Wiley.

Dryfoos, J. G. (1990). *Adolescents at risk: Prevalence and prevention.* New York: Oxford University Press.

Durand, V. M., & Barlow, D. H. (1997). *Abnormal psychology: An introduction.* New York: Brooks/Cole.

Durlak, J. A., Fuhrman, T., & Lampman, C. (1991). Effectiveness of cognitive-behavior therapy for maladapting children: A meta-analysis. *Psychological Bulletin, 110,* 204–214.

Eccles, J. S., Midgley, C., Wigfield, A., Buchanan, C. M., Reuman, D., Flanagan, C., & MacIver, D. (1993). Development during adolescence: The impact of stage-environment fit in young adolescents' experiences in schools and in families. *American Psychologist, 48,* 90–101.

Elkind, D. (1967). Egocentrism in adolescence. *Child Development, 38,* 1025–1034.

Entwisle, D. R. (1990). Schools and the adolescent. In S. S. Feldman & G. R. Elliott (Eds.), *At the threshold: The developing adolescent* (pp. 197–224). Cambridge, MA: Harvard University Press.

Erikson, E. (1968). *Identity: Youth and crisis.* New York: Norton.

Feindler, E. L., & Ecton, R. B. (1986). *Adolescent anger control: Cognitive-behavioral techniques.* New York: Pergamon Press.

Etscheidt, S. (1991). Reducing aggressive behavior and improving self-control: A cognitive-behavioral training program for behaviorally disordered adolescents. *Behavioral Disorders, 16,* 107–115.

Farrell, A. D., Danish, S. J., & Howard, C. W. (1992). Relationship between drug use and other problem behaviors in urban adolescents. *Journal of Consulting and Clinical Psychology, 60,* 705–712.

Feindler, E. L., & Ecton, R. B. (1986). *Adolescent anger control: Cognitive-behavioral techniques.* Elmsford, NY: Pergamon Press.

Feldman, S. S., & Elliott, G. R. (Eds.). (1990). *At the threshold: The developing adolescent.* Cambridge, MA: Harvard University Press.

Flavell, J. H., & Ross, L. (1981). *Social cognitive development: Frontiers and possible futures.* New York: Cambridge University Press.

Forehand, R., & Wierson, M. (1993). The role of developmental factors in planning behavioral interventions for children: Disruptive behavior as an example. *Behavior Therapy, 24,* 117–141.

Freud, A. (1958). Adolescence. *Psychoanalytic Study of the Child, 13,* 231–258.

Fuhrman, T., & Holmbeck, G. N. (1995). A contextual-moderator analysis of emotional autonomy and adjustment in adolescence. *Child Development, 66,* 793–811.

Fuligni, A. J., & Eccles, J. S. (1993). Perceived parent–child relationships and early adolescents' orientation toward peers. *Developmental Psychology, 29,* 622–632.

Furman, W. (1980). Promoting social development: Developmental implications for treatment. In B. B. Lahey & A. E. Kazdin (Eds.), *Advances in clinical child psychology* (Vol. 3, pp. 1–40). New York: Plenum Press.

Galambos, N. L., Almeida, D. M., & Petersen, A. C. (1990). Masculinity, femininity, and sex role attitudes in early adolescence: Exploring gender intensification. *Child Development, 61,* 1905–1914.

Garmezy, N. (1985). Stress-resistant children: The search for protective factors. In J. E. Stevenson (Ed.), *Aspects of current child psychiatry research* (Journal of Child Psychology and Psychiatry Book Suppl. No. 4, pp. 213–233). Oxford, UK: Pergamon Press.

Gelfand, D. M., & Peterson, L. (1985). *Child development and psychopathology.* Beverly Hills, CA: Sage.

Gilligan, C. (1982). *In a different voice: Psychological theory and women's development.* Cambridge, MA: Harvard University Press.

Gilligan, C., Lyons, N. P., Hanmer, T. J. (Eds.). (1990). *Making connections: The relational worlds of adolescent girls at Emma Willard School.* Cambridge, MA: Harvard University Press.

Gordon, D. E. (1988). Formal operations and interpersonal and affective disturbances in adolescents. In E. D. Nannis & P. A. Cowan (Eds.), *New directions for child development: No. 39. Developmental psychopathology and its treatment* (pp. 51–74). San Francisco: Jossey-Bass.

Graham, P. (1998). *Cognitive-behaviour therapy for children and families.* Cambridge, UK: Cambridge University Press.

Greenberg, M. T., & Speltz, M. L. (1988). Attachment and the ontogeny of conduct problems. In J. Belsky & T. Nezworski (Eds.), *Clinical implications of attachment* (pp. 178–218). Hillsdale, NJ: Erlbaum.

Greenberger, E., & Steinberg, L. (1986). *When teenagers work: The psychological and social costs of adolescent employment.* New York: Basic Books.

Grotevant, H. D. (1997). Adolescent development in family contexts. In W. Damon (Ed.), *Handbook of child psychology* (Vol. 3, pp. 1097–1149). New York: Wiley.

Guerra, N. G. (1993). Cognitive development. In P. H. Tolan & B. J. Cohler (Eds.), *Handbook of clinical research and practice with adolescents* (pp. 45–62). New York: Wiley.

Harrington, R., Wood, A., & Verduyn, C. (1998). Clinically depressed adolescents. In P. Graham (Ed.), *Cognitive-behaviour therapy for children and families* (pp. 156–193). Cambridge, UK: Cambridge University Press.

Harter, S. (1983). Developmental perspectives on the self-system. In P. H. Mussen (Ed.), E. M. Hetherington (Vol. Ed.), *Handbook of child psychology* (Vol. IV, pp. 275–386). New York: Wiley.

Harter, S. (1990). Self and identity development. In S. S. Feldman & G. R. Elliott (Eds.), *At the threshold: The developing adolescent* (pp. 352–387). Cambridge, MA: Harvard University Press.

Hartup, W. W. (1983). Peer relations. In P. H. Mussen (Ed.), E. M. Hetherington (Vol. Ed.), *Handbook of child psychology* (Vol. IV, pp. 103–196). New York: Wiley.

Henderson, V. L., & Dweck, C. S. (1990). Motivation and achievement. In S. S. Feldman & G. R. Elliott (Eds.), *At the threshold: The developing adolescent* (pp. 308–329). Cambridge, MA: Harvard University Press.

Henggeler, S. W., & Cohen, R. (1984). The role of cognitive development in the family-ecological systems approach to childhood psychopathology. In B. Gholson & T. L. Rosenthal (Eds.), *Applications of cognitive-developmental theory* (pp. 173–189). New York: Academic Press.

Henggeler, S. W., Schoenwald, S. K., Borduin, C. M., Rowland, M. D., & Cunningham, P. B. (1998). *Multisystemic treatment of antisocial behavior in children and adolescents.* New York: Guilford Press.

Hibbs, E. D., & Jensen, P. S. (1996). *Psychosocial treatments for child and adolescent disorders: Empirically based strategies for clinical practice.* Washington, DC: American Psychological Association Press.

Higgins, E. T., Ruble, D. N., & Hartup, W. W. (Eds.). (1983). *Social cognition and social development: A sociocultural perspective.* New York: Cambridge University Press.

Hill, J. P. (1980a). The family. In M. Johnson (Ed.), *Toward adolescence: The middle school* years (79th Yearbook of the National Society for the Study of Education, pp. 32–55). Chicago: University of Chicago Press.

Hill, J. P. (1980b). *Understanding early adolescence: A framework.* Carrboro, NC: Center for Early Adolescence.

Hill, J. P., & Holmbeck, G. N. (1986). Attachment and autonomy during adolescence. In G. J. Whitehurst (Ed.), *Annals of child development* (Vol. 3, pp. 145–189). Greenwich, CT: JAI Press.

Hill, J. P., & Holmbeck, G. N. (1987). Familial adaptation to biological change during adolescence. In R. M. Lerner & T. T. Foch (Eds.), *Biological–psychosocial interactions in early adolescence* (pp. 207–224). Hillsdale, NJ: Erlbaum.

Hill, J. P., & Lynch, M. E. (1983). The intensification of gender-related role expectations during early adolescence. In J. Brooks-Gunn & A. C. Petersen (Eds.), *Girls at puberty: Biological and psychosocial perspectives* (pp. 201–228). New York: Plenum Press.

Holmbeck, G. N. (1994). Adolescence. In V. S. Ramachandran (Ed.), *Encyclopedia of human behavior* (Vol. 1, pp. 17–28). Orlando, FL: Academic Press.

Holmbeck, G. N. (1996). A model of family relational transformations during the transition to adolescence: Parent–adolescent conflict and adaptation. In J. A. Graber, J. Brooks-Gunn, & A. C. Petersen (Eds.), *Transitions through adolescence: Interpersonal domains and context* (pp. 167–199). Mahwah, NJ: Erlbaum.

Holmbeck, G. N. (1997). Toward terminological, conceptual, and statistical clarity in the study of mediators and moderators: Examples from the child-clinical and pediatric psychology literatures. *Journal of Consulting and Clinical Psychology, 65,* 599–610.

Holmbeck, G. N., & Hill, J. P. (1988). Storm and stress beliefs about adolescence: Prevalence, self-reported antecedents, and effects of an undergraduate course. *Journal of Youth and Adolescence, 17,* 285–306.

Holmbeck, G. N., & Hill, J. P. (1991). Conflictive engagement, positive affect, and menarche in families with seventh-grade girls. *Child Development, 62,* 1030–1048.

Holmbeck, G. N., & Kendall, P. C. (1991). Clinical–childhood–developmental interface: Implications for treatment. In P. R. Martin (Ed.), *Handbook of behavior therapy and psychological science: An integrative approach* (pp. 73–99). New York: Pergamon Press.

Holmbeck, G. N., & O'Donnell, K. (1991). Discrepancies between perceptions of decision-making and behavioral autonomy. In R. L. Paikoff (Ed.), *New directions for child development: No. 51. Shared views in the family during adolescence* (pp. 51–69). San Francisco: Jossey-Bass.

Holmbeck, G. N., Paikoff, R. L., Brooks-Gunn, J. (1995). Parenting adolescents. In M. Bornstein (Ed.), *Handbook of parenting* (Vol. 1, pp. 91–118). Mahwah, NJ: Erlbaum.

Holmbeck, G. N., & Shapera, W. E. (1999). Research methods with adolescents. In P. C. Kendall, J. N. Butcher, & G. N. Holmbeck (Eds.), *Handbook of research methods in clinical psychology* (2nd ed., pp. 634–661). New York: Wiley.

Holmbeck, G. N., & Updegrove, A. L. (1995). Clinical–developmental interface: Implications of developmental research for adolescent psychotherapy. *Psychotherapy, 32,* 16–33.

Ivey, A. E. (1986). *Developmental therapy.* San Francisco, CA: Jossey-Bass.

Jessor, R., Donovan, J. E., & Costa, F. M. (1991). *Beyond adolescence: Problem behavior and young adult development.* New York: Cambridge University Press.

Jessor, R., & Jessor, S. L. (1977). *Problem behavior and psychosocial development: A longitudinal study of youth.* New York: Academic Press.

Kastner, J. W. (1998). Clinical change in adolescent aggressive behavior: A group therapy approach. *Journal of Child and Adolescent Group Therapy, 8,* 23–33.

Katchadourian, H. (1990). Sexuality. In S. S. Feldman, & G. R. Elliott (Eds.), *At the threshold: The developing adolescent* (pp. 330–351). Cambridge, MA: Harvard University Press.

Kazdin, A. E., & Weisz, J. R. (1998). Identifying and developing empirically supported child and adolescent treatments. *Journal of Consulting and Clinical Psychology, 66,* 19–36.

Keating, D. P. (1990). Adolescent thinking. In S. S. Feldman & G. R. Elliott (Eds.), *At the threshold: The developing adolescent* (pp. 54–89). Cambridge, MA: Harvard University Press.

Kendall, P. C. (1977). On the efficacious use of verbal self- instructional procedures with children. *Cognitive Therapy and Research, 1,* 331–341.

Kendall, P. C. (1984). Social cognition and problem solving: A developmental and child-clinical interface. In B. Gholson & T. L. Rosenthal (Eds.), *Applications of cognitive-developmental theory* (pp. 115–148). New York: Academic Press.

Kendall, P. C. (Ed.). (1991). *Child and adolescent therapy: Cognitive-behavioral procedures.* New York: Guilford Press.

Kendall, P. C. (1993). Cognitive-behavioral therapies with youth: Guiding theory, current status, and emerging developments. *Journal of Consulting and Clinical Psychology, 61,* 235–247.

Kendall, P. C., & Braswell, L. (1985). *Cognitive-behavioral therapy for impulsive children.* New York: Guilford Press.

Kendall, P. C., Flannery-Schroeder, E., Panichelli-Mindel, S. M., Southam-Gerow, M., Henin, A.,

& Warman, M. (1997). Therapy for youths with anxiety disorders: A second randomized clinical trial. *Journal of Consulting and Clinical Psychology, 65,* 366–380.

Kendall, P. C., & Holmbeck, G. N. (1991). Psychotherapeutic interventions for adolescents. In R. M. Lerner, A. C. Petersen, & J. Brooks-Gunn (Eds.), *Encyclopedia of adolescence* (pp. 866–874). New York: Pergamon Press.

Kendall, P. C., Lerner, R. M., & Craighead, W. E. (1984). Human development and intervention in childhood psychopathology. *Child Development, 55,* 71–82.

Kendall, P. C., & MacDonald, J. P. (1993). Cognition in the psychopathology of youth and implications for treatment. In K. S. Dobson & P. C. Kendall (Eds.), *Psychopathology and cognition* (pp. 387–432). San Diego: Academic Press.

Kendall, P. C., & Williams, C. L. (1986). Therapy with adolescents: Treating the "Marginal Man." *Behavior Therapy, 17,* 522–537.

Kidwell, J., Fischer, J. L., Dunham, R. M., & Baranowski, M. (1983). Parents and adolescents: Push and pull of change. In H. I. McCubbin & C. R. Figley (Eds.), *Stress and the family: Vol. I. Coping with normative transitions* (pp. 74–89). New York: Brunner/Mazel.

Kiesler, D. J. (1966). Some myths of psychotherapy research and the search for a paradigm. *Psychological Bulletin, 65,* 110–136.

La Greca, A. M., & Prinstein, M. J. (1999). Peer group. In W. K. Silverman & T. H. Ollendick (Eds.), *Developmental issues in the clinical treatment of children* (pp. 171–198). Boston: Allyn & Bacon.

Lamborn, S. D., & Steinberg, L. (1993). Emotional autonomy redux: Revisiting Ryan and Lynch. *Child Development, 64,* 483–499.

Laursen, B., & Collins, W. A. (1994). Interpersonal conflict during adolescence. *Psychological Bulletin, 115,* 197–209.

Laursen, B., Coy, K. C., & Collins, W. A. (1998). Reconsidering changes in parent–child conflict across adolescence: A meta-analysis. *Child Development, 69,* 817–832.

Leahy, R. L. (1988). Cognitive therapy of childhood depression: Developmental considerations. In S. R. Shirk (Ed.), *Cognitive development and child psychotherapy* (pp. 187–206). New York: Plenum Press.

Lerner, R. M., Villarruel, F. A., & Castellino, D. R. (1999). Adolescence. In W. K. Silverman & T. H. Ollendick (Eds.), *Developmental issues in the clinical treatment of children* (pp. 125–136). Boston: Allyn & Bacon.

Lewinsohn, P. M., Clarke, G. N., Hops, H., & Andrews, J. (1990). Cognitive-behavioral treatment for depressed adolescents. *Behavior Therapy, 21,* 385–401.

Lewis, M., & Miller, S. M. (1990). *Handbook of developmental psychopathology.* New York: Plenum Press.

Lewko, J. H. (Ed.). (1987). *New directions for child development: No. 35. How children and adolescents view the world of work.* San Francisco: Jossey-Bass.

Lochman, J. E., White, K. J., & Wayland, K. K. (1991). Cognitive-Behavioral assessment and treatment with aggressive children. In P. C. Kendall (Ed.), *Child and adolescent therapy: Cognitive-behavioral procedures* (pp. 25–65). New York: Guilford Press.

Loeber, R., Farrington, D. P., Stouthamer-Loeber, M., & Van Kammen, W. B. (1998). *Antisocial behavior and mental health problems: Explanatory factors in childhood and adolescence.* Mahwah, NJ: Erlbaum.

Lyman, D. R., & Selman, R. L. (1985). Peer conflict in pair therapy: Clinical and developmental analyses. In M. W. Berkowitz (Ed.), *New directions for child development: No. 29. Peer conflict and psychological growth* (pp. 85–102). San Francisco: Jossey-Bass.

Maggs, J. L., Schulenberg, J., & Hurrelmann, K. (1996). Developmental transitions during adolescence: Health promotion implications. In J. Schulenberg, J. Maggs, & K. Hurrelmann (Eds.), *Health risks and developmental transitions during adolescence* (pp. 522–543). New York: Cambridge University Press.

Magnusson, D., Stattin, H., & Allen, V. L. (1985). A longitudinal study of some adjustment processes from mid-adolescence to adulthood. *Journal of Youth and Adolescence, 14,* 267–283.

Mahoney, M. J., & Arnkoff, D. (1978). Cognitive and self-control therapies. In S. L. Garfield & A. E. Bergin (Eds.), *Handbook of psychotherapy and behavior change* (pp. 689–722). New York: Wiley.

Marcotte, D. (1997). Treating depression in adolescence: A review of effectiveness of cognitive-behavior treatments. *Journal of Youth and Adolescence, 26,* 273–283.

March, J. S., & Mulle, K. (1998). *OCD in children and adolescents: A cognitive-behavioral treatment manual.* New York: Guilford Press.

Mash, E. J., & Barkley, R. A. (1998). *Treatment of childhood disorders* (2nd ed.). New York: Guilford Press.

Masten, A. S. (1988). Toward a developmental psychopathology of early adolescence. In M. D. Levine & E. R. McAnarney (Eds.), *Early adolescent transitions* (pp. 261–278). Lexington, MA: Lexington Books.

McGrath, P. J., Humphreys, P., Keene, D., Goodman, J. T., Lascelles, M. A., Cunningham, S. J., & Firestone, P. (1992). The efficacy and efficiency of a self-administered treatment for adolescent migraine. *Pain, 49,* 321–324.

Meichenbaum, D., & Cameron, R. (1982). Cognitive behavior modification: Current issues. In G. T. Wilson & C. M. Franks (Eds.), *Contemporary behavior therapy: Conceptual and empirical foundations* (pp. 310–338). New York: Guilford Press.

Minuchin, P. P., & Shapiro, E. K. (1983). The school as a context for social development. In P. H. Mussen (Ed.), E. M. Hetherington (Vol. Ed.), *Handbook of child psychology* (Vol. IV, pp. 197–274). New York: Wiley.

Montemayor, R. (1983). Parents and adolescents in conflict: All families some of the time and some families most of the time. *Journal of Early Adolescence, 3,* 83–103.

Moore, D. (1987). Parent–adolescent separation: The construction of adulthood by late adolescents. *Developmental Psychology, 23,* 298–307.

Moshman, D. (1998). Cognitive development beyond childhood. In D. Kuhn & R. S. Siegler (Eds.), *Handbook of child psychology: Vol. 2. Cognition, perception, and language* (pp. 957–978). New York: Wiley.

Nelson, D. A., & Crick, N. R. (1999). Rose-colored glasses: Examining the social information-processing of prosocial young adolescents. *Journal of Early Adolescence, 19,* 17–38.

Nolen-Hoeksema, S. (1994). An interactive model for the emergence of gender differences in depression in adolescence. *Journal of Research on Adolescence, 4,* 519–534.

Offer, D., & Offer, J. B. (1975). *From teenager to young manhood: A psychological study.* New York: Basic Books.

Offer, D., Ostrov, E., & Howard, K. I. (1981). *The adolescent: A psychological self-portrait.* New York: Basic Books.

Ollendick, T. (1995). Cognitive behavioral treatment of panic disorder with agoraphobia in adolescents: A multiple baseline design analysis. *Behavior Therapy, 26,* 517–531.

Overton, W. F. (Ed.). (1983). *The relationship between social and cognitive development.* Hillsdale, NJ: Erlbaum.

Paikoff, R. L., & Brooks-Gunn, J. (1991). Do parent–child relationships change during puberty? *Psychological Bulletin, 110,* 47–66.

Papini, D. R., & Sebby, R. A. (1987). Adolescent pubertal status and affective family relationships: A multivariate assessment. *Journal of Youth and Adolescence, 16,* 1–15.

Parker, J. G., & Asher, S. R. (1987). Peer relations and later personal adjustment: Are low-accepted children at risk? *Psychological Bulletin, 102,* 357–389.

Petersen, A. C. (1988). Adolescent development. In M. R. Rosenzweig & L. W. Porter (Eds.), *Annual review of psychology* (Vol. 39, pp. 583–608). Palo Alto, CA: Annual Reviews.

Petersen, A. C., & Hamburg, B. A. (1986). Adolescence: A developmental approach to problems and psychopathology. *Behavior Therapy, 17,* 480–499.

Petersen, A. C., & Taylor, B. (1980). The biological approach to adolescence: Biological change and psychosocial adaptation. In J. Adelson (Ed.), *Handbook of adolescent psychology* (pp. 117–155). New York: Wiley.

Piaget, J. (1970). Piaget's theory. In P. H. Mussen (Ed.), *Manual of child psychology* (3rd ed., pp. 703–732). New York: Wiley.

Piaget, J. (1972). Intellectual evolution from adolescence to adulthood. *Human Development, 15,* 1–12.

Reich, W., Shayka, J. J., & Taibleson, C. (1991). *Diagnostic interview for children and adolescents (DICA-R-A; Adolescent version).* Unpublished interview, Washington University, St. Louis, MO.

Reinecke, M. A., Dattilio, F. M., & Freeman, A. (Eds.). (1996). *Cognitive therapy with children and adolescents: A casebook for practitioners.* New York: Guilford Press.

Richards, M., Abell, S. N., & Petersen, A. C. (1993). Biological development. In P. H. Tolan & B. J. Cohler (Eds.), *Handbook of clinical research and practice with adolescents* (pp. 21–44). New York: Wiley.

Richards, M., & Petersen, A. C. (1987). Biological theoretical models of adolescent development. In V. B. Van Hasselt & M. Hersen (Eds.), *Handbook of adolescent psychology* (pp. 34–52). New York: Pergamon Press.

Robins, L. (1966). *Deviant children grown up.* Baltimore: Williams & Wilkins.

Rolf, J., Masten, A. S., Cicchetti, D., Nuechterlein, K. H., & Weintraub, S. (1990). *Risk and protective factors in the development of psychopathology.* New York: Cambridge University Press.

Rose, S. D. (1998). *Group therapy with troubled youth: Cognitive-behavioral interactive approach.* Thousand Oaks, CA: Sage.

Rose, S. D., & Edleson, J. L. (1987). *Working with children and adolescent groups.* San Francisco: Jossey-Bass.

Rosenthal, T. L. (1982). Social learning theory and behavior therapy. In G. T. Wilson & C. M. Franks (Eds.), *Contemporary behavior therapy: Conceptual and empirical foundations* (pp. 339–366). New York: Guilford Press.

Rotter, J. B., Chance, J. E., & Phares, E. J. (1972). *Applications of social learning theory of personality.* New York: Holt, Rinehart & Winston.

Ruble, D. N., & Brooks-Gunn, J. (1982). The experience of menarche. *Child Development, 53,* 1557–1566.

Rutter, M. (1980). *Changing youth in a changing society: Patterns of adolescent development and disorder.* Cambridge, MA: Harvard University Press.

Rutter, M. (1985, July). *Some notes on psychopathology in adolescence.* Invited presentation at the workshop: Adolescence and Adolescent Development, sponsored by the Committee on Child Development Research and Public Policy, National Academy of Sciences, Woods Hole, MA.

Rutter, M. (1987). Psychosocial resilience and protective mechanisms. *American Journal of Orthopsychiatry, 57,* 316–331.

Rutter, M. (1990). Psychosocial resilience and protective mechanisms. In J. Rolf, A. S. Masten, D. Cicchetti, K. H. Nuechterlein, & S. Weintraub (Eds.), *Risk and protective factors in the development of psychopathology* (pp. 181–214). New York: Cambridge University Press.

Rutter, M., & Garmezy, N. (1983). Developmental psychopathology. In P. H. Mussen (Ed.), E. M. Hetherington (Vol. Ed.), *Handbook of child psychology* (Vol. IV, pp. 775–912). New York: Wiley.

Rutter, M., Maughan, B., Mortimore, P., & Ouston, J. (1979). *Fifteen thousand hours: Secondary schools and their effects on children.* Cambridge, MA: Harvard University Press.

Ryan, R., & Lynch, J. (1989). Emotional autonomy versus detachment: Revisiting the vicissitudes of adolescence and young adulthood. *Child Development, 60,* 340–356.

Sagrestano, L., McCormick, S. H., Paikoff, R. L., & Holmbeck, G. N. (1999). Pubertal development and parent–child conflict in low-income African-American adolescents. *Journal of Research on Adolescence, 9,* 85–107.

Santostefano, S. (1980). Clinical child psychology: The need for developmental principles. In R. L. Selman & R. Yando (Eds.), *New directions for child development: No. 7. Clinical-developmental psychology* (pp. 1–20). San Francisco: Jossey-Bass.

Savin-Williams, R. C., & Berndt, T. J. (1990). Friendship and peer relations. In S. S. Feldman & G. R. Elliott (Eds.), *At the threshold: The developing adolescent* (pp. 277–307). Cambridge, MA: Harvard University Press.

Schleser, R., Cohen, R., Meyers, A., & Rodick, J. D. (1984). The effects of cognitive level and training procedures on the generalization of self-instructions. *Cognitive Therapy and Research, 8*, 187–200.

Seligman, M. E. P. (1975). *Helplessness: On depression, development and death.* San Francisco: Freeman.

Selman, R. L. (1980). *The growth of interpersonal understanding: Developmental and clinical analyses.* New York: Academic Press.

Selman, R. L. (1981). The child as a friendship philosopher. In S. R. Asher & J. M. Gottman (Eds.), *The development of children's friendships* (pp. 242–272). New York: Cambridge University Press.

Shantz, C. U. (1975). The development of social cognition. In E. M. Hetherington (Ed.), *Review of child development research* (Vol. 5, pp. 257–324). Chicago: University of Chicago Press.

Shantz, C. U. (1983). Social cognition. In P. H. Mussen (Ed.), J. H. Flavell & E. M. Markman (Vol. Eds.), *Handbook of child psychology* (Vol. III, pp. 495–555). New York: Wiley.

Shirk, S. R. (Ed.). (1988). *Cognitive development and child psychotherapy.* New York: Plenum Press.

Shirk, S. R. (1999). Developmental therapy. In W. K. Silverman & T. H. Ollendick (Eds.), *Developmental issues in the clinical treatment of children* (pp. 60–73). Boston: Allyn & Bacon.

Shure, M. B., & Spivack, G. (1978). *Problem-solving techniques in childrearing.* San Francisco: Jossey-Bass.

Shure, M. B., & Spivack, G. (1980). Interpersonal problem-solving as a mediator of behavioral adjustment in preschool and kindergarten children. *Journal of Applied Developmental Psychology, 1*, 29–43.

Silverman, W. K., & Ollendick, T. H. (Eds.). (1999). *Developmental issues in the clinical treatment of children.* Boston: Allyn & Bacon.

Simmons, R. G., & Blyth, D. A. (1987). *Moving into adolescence: The impact of pubertal change and school context.* New York: Aldine De Gruyter.

Sorenson, S. B., Rutter, C. M., & Aneshensel, C. S. (1991). Depression in the community: An investigation into age of onset. *Journal of Consulting and Clinical Psychology, 59*, 541–546.

Spivack, G., Platt, J. J., & Shure, M. B. (1976). *The problem solving approach to adjustment.* San Francisco: Jossey-Bass.

Spivack, G., & Shure, M. B. (1974). *Social adjustment of young children: A cognitive approach to solving real-life problems.* San Francisco: Jossey-Bass.

Sroufe, L. A. (1988). The role of infant–caregiver attachment in development. In J. Belsky, & T. Nezworski (Eds.), *Clinical implications of attachment* (pp. 18–38). Hillsdale, NJ: Erlbaum.

Sroufe, L. A., & Rutter, M. (1984). The domain of developmental psychopathology. *Child Development, 55*, 17–29.

Steinberg, L. (1990). Interdependence in the family: Autonomy, conflict, and harmony in the parent–adolescent relationship. In S. S. Feldman, & G. L. Elliott (Eds.), *At the threshold: The developing adolescent* (pp. 255–276). Cambridge, MA: Harvard University Press.

Steinberg, L. (1995). Commentary: On developmental pathways and social contexts in adolescence. In L. J. Crockett & A. S. Crouter (Eds.), *Pathways through adolescence: Individual development in relation to social contexts* (pp. 245–253). Mahwah, NJ: Erlbaum.

Steinberg, L. (1996). *Adolescence* (5th ed.). Boston: McGraw-Hill.

Steinberg, L., & Silverberg, S. B. (1986). The vicissitudes of autonomy in early adolescence. *Child Development, 57*, 841–851.

Sternberg, R. (1977). *Intelligence, information, processing, and analogical reasoning: The componential analysis of human abilities.* Hillsdale, NJ: Erlbaum.

Sternberg, R., & Nigro, G. (1980). Developmental patterns in the solution of verbal analogies. *Child Development, 51,* 27–38.

Stoiber, K. C., & Kratochwill, T. R. (1998). *Handbook of group intervention for children and families.* Boston: Allyn & Bacon.

Sullivan, H. S. (1953). *The interpersonal theory of psychiatry.* New York: Norton.

Tanner, J. (1962). *Growth at adolescence* (2nd ed.). Springfield, IL: Thomas.

Temple, S. (1997). *Brief therapy for adolescent depression.* Sarasota, FL: Professional Resource Press.

Tobin-Richards, M. H., Boxer, A. M. N., & Petersen, A. C. (1982). The psychological significance of pubertal change: Sex differences in perceptions of self during early adolescence. In J. Brooks-Gunn, & A. C. Petersen (Eds.), *Girls at puberty: Biological and psychosocial perspectives* (pp. 127–154). New York: Plenum Press.

Tolan, P. H., & Cohler, B. J. (1993). *Handbook of clinical research and practice with adolescents.* New York: Wiley.

Trickett, E. J., & Schmid, J. D. (1993). The school as a social context. In P. H. Tolan & B. J. Cohler (Eds.), *Handbook of clinical research and practice with adolescents* (pp. 173–202). New York: Wiley.

Tsai, M., Feldman-Summers, S., & Edgar, M. (1979). Childhood molestation: Variables related to differential impacts on psychosexual functioning in adult women. *Journal of Abnormal Psychology, 88,* 404–417.

Valliant, P. (1993). Cognitive and behavioural therapy with adolescent males in a residential treatment centre. *Journal of Child and Youth Care, 8,* 41–49.

Van Hasselt, V. B., & Hersen, M. (Eds.). (1995) *Handbook of adolescent psychopathology.* New York: Lexington Books.

Vostanis, P., Feehan, C., & Grattan, E. (1998) Two-year outcome of children treated for depression. *European Child and Adolescent Psychiatry, 7,* 12–18.

Vygotsky, L. (1978). *Mind in society: The development of higher psychological processes.* Cambridge, MA: Harvard University Press.

Walsh, F., & Scheinkman, M. (1993). The family context of adolescence. In P. H. Tolan & B. J. Cohler (Eds.), *Handbook of clinical research and practice with adolescents* (pp. 149–172). New York: Wiley.

Weiner, I. B. (1992). *Psychological disturbance in adolescence.* New York: Wiley.

Weisz, J. R. (1997). Effects of interventions for child and adolescent psychological dysfunction: Relevance of context, developmental factors, and individual differences. In S. S. Luthar, J. A. Burack, D. Cicchetti, & J. R. Weisz (Eds.), *Developmental psychopathology: Perspectives on adjustment, risk, and disorder* (pp. 3–22). Cambridge, UK: Cambridge University Press.

Weisz, J. R., & Weersing, V. R. (1999). Developmental outcome research. In W. K. Silverman & T. H. Ollendick (Eds.), *Developmental issues in the clinical treatment of children* (pp. 457–469). Boston: Allyn & Bacon.

Weisz, J. R., Weiss, B., Alicke, M. D., & Klotz, M. L. (1987). Effectiveness of psychotherapy with children and adolescents: A meta-analysis for clinicians. *Journal of Clinical and Consulting Psychology, 55,* 542–549.

Weisz, J. R., Weiss, B., Han, S. S., Granger, D. A., & Morton, T. (1995). Effects of psychotherapy with children and adolescents revisited: A meta-analysis of treatment outcome studies. *Psychological Bulletin, 117,* 450–468.

Youniss, J. (1980). *Parents and peers in social development: A Sullivan–Piaget perspective.* Chicago: University of Chicago Press.

CHAPTER 9

Empirically Supported Treatments for Children and Adolescents

Thomas H. Ollendick and Neville J. King

The movement to identify, develop, disseminate, and use empirically supported treatments (initially referred to as empirically "validated" treatments; see Chambless, 1996; Chambless & Hollon, 1998; Chambless et al., 1996) has not been without significant controversy in the years since the publication in 1995 of a report by the Task Force on Promotion and Dissemination of Psychological Procedures. This report, commissioned by the Society of Clinical Psychology (a division of the American Psychological Association), recommended that treatments possessing empirical support should be promoted and disseminated for widespread use in clinical practice. On the surface, it hardly seemed possible that anyone could or would object to this report, or that the movement associated with it would become controversial. Surely, identifying, developing, and disseminating treatments that have empirical support should be encouraged, not discouraged, especially for a profession that is committed to the welfare of those served by its treatment interventions.

Sensible as this may seem, the task force report was controversial and served to divide the profession of clinical psychology and related mental health disciplines. In this chapter, we first define empirically supported treatments and then examine the current status of such treatments for children[1] who display a variety of behavior problems. In doing so, we illustrate the potential value of these treatments. Next, we illustrate and discuss some of the contentious issues associated with these treatments and their development and promulgation. We conclude our discourse by offering recommendations for future research and practice.

ON THE NATURE OF EMPIRICALLY SUPPORTED TREATMENTS

In 1995, the Society of Clinical Psychology Task Force on Promotion and Dissemination of Psychological Procedures, chaired by Diane Chambless, published its report on empirically validated psychological treatments. Task force members included representatives from a number of theoretical perspectives, including psychodynamic, interpersonal, and cognitive-behavioral points of view. This diversity in membership was an intentional step taken by the committee to emphasize a commitment to identifying and promulgating all psychotherapies of proven worth, not just those emanating from one particular school of thought. Defining empirically validated treatments proved to be a difficult task, however. Of course, from a research perspective, no treatment is ever fully validated. As noted in the task force report, there are always more questions to ask about any treatment, including questions about the essential components of treatments, client characteristics that predict treatment outcome, and the mechanisms or processes associated with behavior change. In recognition of this state of affairs, the term "empirically supported" was adopted to describe treatments of proven worth, a term that many agreed was more felicitous than "empirically validated."

Three categories of treatment efficacy were proposed in the 1995 report: (1) well-established treatments, (2) probably efficacious treatments, and (3) experimental treatments (see Table 9.1). The primary distinction between *well-established* and *probably efficacious* treatments was that a well-established treatment should have been shown to be superior to a psychological placebo, pill, or another treatment, whereas a probably efficacious treatment must be shown to be superior to a waiting-list or no-treatment control only.[2] In addition, effects supporting a well-established treatment must have been demonstrated by at least two different investigators or investigatory teams, whereas the effects of a probably efficacious treatment need not be (the effects might be demonstrated in two studies from the same investigator or investigatory team, for example). For both types of empirically supported treatments, characteristics of the clients must have been clearly specified (e.g., age, sex, ethnicity, diagnosis) and the clinical trials must have been conducted with treatment manuals. Furthermore, it was required that these outcomes be demonstrated in "good" group-design studies or a series of controlled single-case design studies. "Good" designs were those in which it was reasonable to con-

TABLE 9.1. Criteria for Empirically Validated Treatments

I. Well-established treatments
   A. At least two good between-group design experiments demonstrating efficacy in one or more of the following ways:
      1. Superior to pill or psychological placebo or to another treatment.
      2. Equivalent to an already established treatment in experiments with adequate statistical power (about 30 per group; cf. Kazdin & Bass, 1989)

or

   B. A large series of single case design experiments ($n > 9$) demonstrating efficacy. These experiments must have
      1. Used good experimental designs.
      2. Compared the intervention to another treatment in A.1.

Further criteria for both A and B:
   C. Experiments must be conducted with treatment manuals.
   D. Characteristics of the client samples must be clearly specified.
   E. Effects must have been demonstrated by at least two different investigators or investigatory teams.

II. Probably efficacious treatments
   A. Two experiments showing the treatment is more effective than a waiting-list control group.

or

   B. One or more experiments meeting the well-established treatment criteria A, C, D, but not E.

or

   C. A small series of single case design experiments ($n > 3$) otherwise meeting well-established treatment criteria B, C, and D.

clude that the benefits observed were due to the effects of treatment and not due to chance or confounding factors such as passage of time, the effects of psychological assessment, or the presence of different types of clients in the various treatment conditions (Chambless & Hollon, 1998; for a fuller discussion of research design issues, also see Kazdin, 1998; Kendall, Flannery-Schroeder, & Ford, 1999). Ideally, treatment efficacy would be demonstrated in randomized clinical trials—group designs in which patients would be assigned randomly to the treatment of interest, or one or more comparison conditions—or carefully controlled single-case experiments and their group analogues. Finally, *experimental* treatments were those treatments not yet shown to be at least probably efficacious. This category was intended to capture long-standing or traditional treatments that had not yet been fully evaluated, or newly developed ones not yet put to the test of scientific scrutiny. The development of new treatments was particularly encouraged. It was also intended that treatments could "move" from one category to another, depending on the empirical support available for that treatment *over time*; that is, an experimental procedure might enjoy probably efficacious or even well-established status as new findings became available. The categorical system was intended to be a dynamic—not static—one.

EMPIRICALLY SUPPORTED PSYCHOSOCIAL TREATMENTS FOR CHILD BEHAVIOR PROBLEMS

The 1995 Task Force Report on Promotion and Dissemination of Psychological Procedures identified 18 well-established treatments and seven probably efficacious treatments, using the criteria described previously and presented in Table 9.1. Of these 25 efficacious treatments, *three* well-established treatments for children (behavior modification for developmentally disabled individuals, behavior modification for enuresis and encopresis, and parent training programs for children with oppositional behavior) and *one* probably efficacious treatment for children (habit reversal and control techniques) were identified. As noted in that report, the list of empirically supported treatments was intended to be representative of efficacious treatments, not exhaustive. In recognition of the need to determine if additional psychosocial treatments were effective with children, concurrent task forces were set up by the Society of Clinical Psychology (Division 12, American Psychological Association) and the Section on Clinical Child Psychology (a section of the Society recently approved for division status and now Division 53 of the American Psychological Association). The two independent task forces joined efforts and in 1998 published their collective reviews in the *Journal of Clinical Child Psychology*, with Christopher Lonigan and Jean Elbert as coeditors of the special issue. Reviews of empirically supported treatments for children with autism, depression, anxiety disorders, attention-deficit/hyperactivity disorder (ADHD), and oppositional and conduct problem disorders were included in the special issue. As noted by Lonigan, Elbert, and Johnson (1998), the goal was not to generate an exhaustive list of treatments that met criteria for empirically supported treatments; rather, the goal was to focus on a number of high-frequency problems encountered in clinical and other settings serving children with mental health problems. As such, a number of problem areas were not reviewed, and the identification of empirically supported treatments for these other problem areas remains to be accomplished, even to this day. Overall, the goal was to identify effective psychosocial treatments for a limited number of frequently occurring disorders in childhood. A brief review of the findings with these various disorders follows.

Psychosocial Treatments for Autism

The efficacy of psychosocial interventions in the treatment of autism, a severe and chronic disorder that results in significant lifelong impairment, was examined by Rogers (1998). She reviewed the efficacy of 8 comprehensive treatment programs that were developed to reduce the level of impairment in these children, or stated differently, to change the nature of the outcome in autism and improve the overall functioning of children with autism. In general, the treatments sought to address multiple symptoms in children with varying levels of severity; not infrequently, they involved thousands of hours of treatment across several years. Although a variety of treatments based on different theories have been attempted and evaluated with autism, the treatment with the most support for its efficacy was found to be a behavioral one pioneered by Lovaas and his colleagues (Lovaas, 1987; McEachin, Smith, & Lovaas, 1993).

In the initial treatment study, 19 young children with autism (mean age = 32 months) were treated intensively with behavior modification procedures over a 2-year period of time. The children received more than 40 hours per week of 1:1 therapy based on operant teaching principles (i.e., reinforcement and punishment techniques) and delivered in home, school, and community settings. Parents were also taught to be therapists for their own children in order to continue the treatment in the absence of treatment personnel. These techniques were used to teach a wide range of social, language, cognitive, and self-care skills, as well as to reduce a variety of inappropriate behaviors such as tantrums and self-stimulatory behaviors. Treatment procedures were described in a manual (Lovaas et al., 1981), and videotapes of the treatment were developed. The efficacy of this intensive treatment program was compared to two control groups: (1) a group of 19 children who received a less intensive dose of the same treatment (i.e., about 10 hours per week over the 2 years), and (2) a group of 21 children who received treatment from a variety of community resources but did not have access to the behavioral programs. The treatment was evaluated after the children had completed first grade and again in early adolescence. At the time of the first follow-up, IQ scores and educational placements were contrasted. There was a mean IQ difference of 25 to 30 points between the children in the intensive behavioral group and those in the two control groups. In addition, significant differences were noted in educational functioning: Whereas 47% of the children in the intensive treatment had functioned well in typical first-grade classrooms, only 2% of the controls did so. Moreover, 53% of the combined control group children were in classes for children with severe disabilities, whereas only 10% of the children in the intensive treatment program were in such classrooms. In early adolescence, measures of school placement, IQ, and adaptive behavior were obtained on the children in the intensive and less intensive conditions (children receiving "treatment as usual" in the community were not followed further, since many of them received a variety of treatments in the interim, including behavioral treatments similar to those used in the intensive program). At early adolescence, 47% of experimental children continued to be educated in regular placements, without any evidence of educational handicaps. None of the less intensively treated children were in such placements. IQ differences noted after the first grade were stable, with differences of 30 points characterizing the two groups. Similar differences were noted on the adaptive behavioral measures.

As noted by Rogers (1998), although this study possessed many strengths, it also possessed a number of methodological weaknesses that preclude it from being an adequate test of the efficacy of the intensive behavioral treatment approach. The most serious weakness was that the children were not assigned randomly to treatment conditions, a specific criterion required by the task force to determine well-established and probably efficacious treatments. Other weaknesses included the failure of the investigators to document carefully the fidelity of treatment (i.e., adherence to the treatment protocol) and whether the children received "other" services from the community that might have enhanced treatment gains. Still, this study showed considerable treatment gains, and although methodological problems were evident, it remains one of the few studies with a reasonable and impressive experimental design in this literature. The significant gains should not be readily dismissed; autism, a difficult disorder to treat, is frequently refractory to behavior change.

Three other investigatory teams have examined the effectiveness of variants of the Lovaas intensive behavioral treatment program and have provided additional, albeit equivocal, support for its use (Anderson, Avery, DiPietro, Edwards, & Christian, 1987; Birnbrauer & Leach, 1993; Sheinkopf & Siegel, 1998). Unfortunately, Birnbrauer and Leach (1993) also failed to assign children randomly to treatment (9 children) or control (5 children) conditions (mean age of all children = 39 months); in addition, their behavioral treatment program was less intense than that of Lovaas (about 20 hours per week over a 2-year period). Moreover, fidelity of treatment was not ascertained and long-term follow-up data were not collected. As a result, although positive effects were obtained immediately following treatment, this study also failed to provide convincing evidence of the efficacy of the Lovaas treatment approach. Similarly, the study by Sheinkopf and Siegel, which entailed a retrospective analysis of 11 children (mean age = 33 months) whose charts indicated they had received intensive behavioral treatment (approximately 27 hours per week), similar to that recommended by Lovaas, failed to provide compelling support of its efficacy when compared to the outcomes of 11 children whose charts did not indicate the presence of such an intensive intervention. The study itself was compromised by a number of problems associated with retrospective reports. Finally, the study by Anderson et al. (1987) used a pre–post only group design to examine the effects of 1–2 years of home-based intensive behavioral interventions with 14 young children (mean age = 43 months). Therapy ranged from 15 to 25 hours per week. Although positive gains were made in language functioning, social functioning, and self-care skills, all of the children required special education services and none were mainstreamed full time into regular kindergarten or first-grade classrooms.

In summary, as noted by Rogers (1998), although the intensive behavioral program designed by Lovaas possesses empirical support, the studies themselves possess methodological weaknesses that compromise their scientific acceptability. Importantly, however, *no* other treatments for autism exist that approximate the level of support obtained for the Lovaas approach. Thus, we must conclude that although intensive behavioral programs demonstrate considerable promise, we have no well-established or even probably efficacious psychosocial treatments for autism at this time.

Psychosocial Treatments for Depression

The efficacy of a variety of psychosocial interventions in the treatment of depression was reviewed by Kaslow and Thompson (1998). Psychodynamic, interpersonal, cognitive-behavioral, and family systems interventions were examined separately for child and adolescent samples. Seven treatment outcome studies with children who had elevated levels of depressive symptoms (but not necessarily diagnosis of depression) were identified. All of the interventions were conducted in a group format and in school settings. Most treatments entailed less than 20 sessions and all were cognitive-behavioral or psychoeducational in nature. Commonly used interventions included social skills and social competency training, self-control therapy, cognitive restructuring, and problem-solving approaches. Collectively, these studies revealed that these similar, although not identical, approaches were efficacious in reducing depressive symptoms in children who were not formally diagnosed as depressed. In addition, gains for these children were maintained at follow-up intervals ranging from 4 weeks to 2 years. The majority of the studies adequately described the characteristics of the samples, used treatment manuals, and showed that the treatments were superior to waiting-list control conditions and, in at least one study conducted by Stark and colleagues, superior to an alternative treatment (traditional school counseling group). Although positive outcomes were noted in these 7 studies, only the self-control behavioral treatment program developed by Stark and colleagues (Stark, Reynolds, & Kaslow, 1987; Stark, Rouse, & Livingston, 1991; see therapist manual and client workbook developed by Stark & Kendall, 1996a, 1996b) approached the criteria for probably efficacious status, as defined by the 1995 task force. No treatments met criteria for well-established status.

Briefly, Stark and colleagues (1987) compared the relative efficacy of a 12-session group intervention involving self-control therapy (i.e., self-management skills focused upon self-monitoring, self-evaluating, and self-consequating skills) to a 12-session group intervention consisting of behavior problem-solving skills (i.e., education, self-monitoring of pleasant events, and group problem solving directed at improving social behavior), and to a wait-list control condition. Approximately 10 children in fourth to seventh grades were randomly assigned to each of the three groups. Findings suggested that the children in both active treatment groups showed reductions in depressive symptoms, whereas the wait-list control children evinced little change. Gains were maintained at an 8-week follow-up. In a second study, Stark et al. (1991) evaluated an expanded version of the self-control therapy used in the first study. The expanded version consisted of self-control and social skills training, assertiveness training, relaxation training, and cognitive restructuring, and was implemented in 24–26 sessions. This expanded treatment was compared to a traditional counseling condition designed to control for nonspecific elements of the intervention. Monthly family sessions were also held to bolster the gains made in the two groups and to help generalize them to the home setting. Twenty-six children in the fourth through seventh grades, randomly assigned to the two group conditions, participated. Postintervention and 7-month follow-up assessments showed decreases in self-reported depressive symptoms for children in both groups. However, at postintervention, children in the expanded self-control treatment group reported fewer depressive symptoms and endorsed fewer depressive cognitions than children in the attention control group, suggesting the superiority of the cognitive-behavioral intervention.

It should be evident that the self-control therapy evaluated in these studies differed both in duration and content, and that the second study provides only a partial replication of the first. Furthermore, as noted by Kaslow and Thompson (1998), none of the other 5 treatment-outcome studies used exactly the same treatment, although all were cognitive and behavioral in orientation. As a result, even though all 7 studies showed positive outcomes and the majority of them carefully defined characteristics of the children and used treatment manuals, none have been systematically replicated. Still, the 1987 and 1991 studies conducted by Stark and colleagues come closest to meeting the criteria for probably efficacious status. Both studies evaluated a variant of self-control therapy; however, the efficacy of self-control therapy has not been demonstrated by a second investigatory team, which precludes its achieving well-established status.

In their review, Kaslow and Thompson also examined the status of psychosocial treatments for adolescents with depression. As with children, only 7 treatment outcome studies were identified, 5 of which examined variants of cognitive-behavioral therapy (self-control therapy, problem solving, relaxation training, social skills, and cognitive restructuring); one examined interpersonal psychotherapy (which addresses the interpersonal, social, and developmental issues common to adolescents, with special attention to problems associated with depression); the other compared cognitive-behavioral approaches to systemic–behavioral family therapy (which combined techniques from functional family therapy and a problem-solving model, and included a focus on parenting and developmental concerns) and to a nondirective supportive control condition. Adolescents ranged in age from 13 to 18 years and were in the 9th to 12th grades. Six of the 7 treatments were delivered in a group format (1 used individual therapy) and 4 of the interventions were conducted in a school setting (3 were administered in outpatient clinic settings). As with the child studies, all 7 studies showed positive outcomes for the various treatments, reflecting superiority of the active treatments over wait-list control conditions. However, none of the active interventions proved to be superior to one another, reflecting both the absence of differences in the few studies that made such comparisons and the dearth of treatment-outcome studies conducted to date. Furthermore, only studies conducted by Lewinsohn, Clarke, and colleagues provided any indication of the replicability of findings associated with any one treatment and, then, only within the same group of investigators. No treatments met criteria for well-established status.

Briefly, the intervention studies conducted by Lewinsohn, Clarke, and colleagues are methodologically sophisticated; moreover, the findings support the probably efficacious nature of the cognitive-behavioral interventions studied (Lewinsohn, Clarke, Hops, & Andrews, 1990; Lewinsohn, Clarke, Rohde, Hops, & Seeley, 1996; for long-term follow-up of these treated youth, see Clarke, Rohde, Lewinsohn, Hops, & Seeley, 1999). Client characteristics were carefully specified, a treatment manual was used, two good group design studies were conducted, and follow-up data were obtained on the durability of treatment effects. In these studies, a cognitive-behavioral coping skills program was shown to be more effective that a wait-list control condition.

In the first study (Lewinsohn et al., 1990), 59 high school students who met diagnostic criteria for depressive disorders were assigned randomly to one of three conditions: a coping skills condition, a coping skills plus parental involvement condition, and a wait-list control condition. The coping skills intervention was conducted over fourteen 2-hour sessions and consisted of experiential learning and skills training, with attention to increasing pleasant activities, training in relaxation, controlling depressive thoughts, improving social interactions, and developing conflict resolution skills. The combined condition consisted of the coping skills intervention plus a seven-session complimentary parent intervention program designed to enhance the parents' ability to reinforce their adolescent's adaptive changes and to promote maintenance and generalization of the skills acquired by the adolescents. Participants in both active treatment conditions showed significant declines in depression compared to those in the wait-list condition; unexpectedly, the addition of the parental component to the coping skills interventions failed to produce additional effects. Similar findings were obtained in the second study (Lewinsohn et al., 1996), which also examined the potential effects of booster treatment sessions, serving to partially replicate the findings and to establish the coping skills program as a probably efficacious treatment.

Still, long-term follow-up of the youth treated in these studies revealed that about 25% experienced recurrence of depression within 24 months (Clarke et al., 1999). Somewhat higher recurrence rates were reported by Brent and colleagues in their 24-month follow-up of youth treated with cognitive-behavioral, systemic–behavioral family, and nondirective supportive therapies. Although cognitive-behavioral procedures were shown to be more effective than the other two treatments in the acute treatment phase, recurrence rates were equally high in all three treatment conditions (approximately 40%), suggesting the need for active maintenance programs in the follow-up phase (Brent, Kolko, Birmaher, Baugher, & Bridge, 1999).

Overall, for children and adolescents with depression, no treatments meet the criteria for well-established treatments and only the child studies conducted by Stark and colleagues (also see chapter by Stark et al., Chapter 5, this volume) and the adolescent studies undertaken by Lewinsohn, Clarke, and colleagues meet the criteria for probably efficacious interventions. Moreover, the long-term effectiveness of these interventions is questionable. As Kaslow and Thompson (1998) noted, this state of affairs should not be unexpected "given that the intervention literature on mood disorders in youth is in its infancy" (p. 153).

Psychosocial Treatments for Phobias and Anxiety Disorders

In 1998, we examined the status of empirically supported treatments for phobic and anxiety disorders in children (Ollendick & King, 1998). In undertaking this review, we examined phobic disorders first, followed by anxiety disorders. As in the Kaslow and Thompson review of depression in youth, we searched the literature for treatment-outcome studies in children based on psychodynamic, interpersonal, cognitive-behavioral, and family systems perspectives. No group outcome studies from an interpersonal perspective or from a family systems perspective were identified. Furthermore, no "good" outcome studies from a psychodynamic orientation were found. One uncontrolled outcome study conducted by Fonagy and Target (1994), using retrospective chart reviews of 196 children meeting diagnostic criteria for anxiety disorders at the Anna Freud Centre in London, suggested that child psychoanalysis might be effective (but then only for younger children who receive treatment four or five times a week for an average of 2 years).

However, no controlled group-outcome studies of psychodynamic psychotherapy were found.

For childhood phobias, we identified 2 treatments that attained well-established status (participant modeling, reinforced practice) and 5 treatments that could be described as being probably efficacious (imaginal and *in vivo* desensitization, live and filmed modeling, and cognitive-behavior therapy). These various interventions are based on principles of classical, vicarious, and operant conditioning, as well as information processing theories. A brief review of these findings follows.

Based on principles of counterconditioning and classical conditioning theory, imaginal and *in vivo* desensitization are variants of a procedure called systematic desensitization. In imaginal desensitization, the feared stimuli are presented imaginally, whereas in *in vivo* desensitization, the phobic stimuli are presented in real life. In both instances, the presence of other stimuli that elicit responses incompatible with fear (e.g., a positive relationship, relaxation, humor, food, imaginary character) are paired with the feared stimuli. Unexpectedly, and inconsistent with clinical lore, these procedures were not found to be well established; rather, they were found to be only probably efficacious; that is, in the majority of studies, these treatments were compared only to no-treatment or wait-list conditions, rarely to placebo or alternative treatments. Furthermore, when imaginal desensitization was compared to *in vivo* desensitization in a study with 24 water-phobic children between 5 and 10 years of age (Ultee, Griffioen, & Schellekens, 1982), *in vivo* desensitization was found to be the superior treatment. Thus, although imaginal desensitization has been found to be superior to no-treatment and to wait-list conditions, it has been found to be less efficacious than *in vivo* treatment, at least for younger children. However, inasmuch as *in vivo* desensitization has been shown to be superior to imaginal desensitization in only one study, it, too, can only be considered to be probably efficacious. Obviously, more research is needed to examine the efficacy of these frequently used procedures (Ollendick & King, 1998).

Drawing on vicarious conditioning principles, modeling capitalizes on the power of observational learning to overcome children's phobias. Theoretically, extinction of avoidance responses is thought to occur through observation of modeled approach behavior directed toward a feared stimulus without adverse consequences accruing to the model. Modeling can be symbolic (i.e., filmed), or live; furthermore, the phobic child can be assisted in approaching the feared stimulus (participant modeling) or prompted to display the modeled behavior without such assistance. In a number of studies, filmed and live modeling have been shown to be more effective than no-treatment or wait-list conditions but inferior to participant modeling in at least two studies (e.g., Lewis, 1974; Ritter, 1968). In the Lewis (1974) study, 40 water-phobic African-American boys between 5 and 12 years of age were randomly assigned to treatment conditions, and in the Ritter

(1968) study, 44 boys and girls, between 5 and 11 years of age, with snake phobias were randomly assigned to the treatment conditions. Thus, inasmuch as filmed and live modeling have been shown to be more effective than no-treatment or wait-list conditions, they can be said to be probably efficacious; however, participant modeling has been found not only to be more effective than no treatment but also more effective than either filmed or live modeling in two studies conducted by different investigatory teams. Participant modeling, therefore, can be said to enjoy well-established status based on the task force criteria.

In contrast to procedures based on classical or vicarious conditioning that assume that fear must be reduced or eliminated before approach behavior to the feared stimulus will occur, operant-based procedures such as contingency management make no such assumptions. Rather, these procedures attempt to alter phobic behaviors by manipulating their consequences. Shaping, positive reinforcement, and extinction are the most frequently used contingency-management procedures to reduce phobic behavior. As noted in our review, two studies have shown contingency management procedures to be more effective than no-treatment or wait-list control conditions (Leitenberg & Callahan, 1973; Obler & Terwilliger, 1970) in the treatment of fears and phobias related to dogs and the dark, and another two studies have shown these procedures to be more effective than verbal coping skills (Sheslow, Bondy, & Nelson, 1983) and live modeling (Menzies & Clarke, 1993) in the treatment of water phobias. In these studies, young children between 4 and 12 years of age were successfully treated.

Finally, two between-group outcome studies examined the use of cognitive-behavioral procedures (verbal self-instruction and cognitive restructuring) in the treatment of young children between 5 and 13 years of age, who were phobic of the dark (Graziano & Mooney, 1980; Kanfer, Karoly, & Newman, 1975). In both studies, these procedures were compared to no-treatment or wait-list control conditions. Given such outcomes, these cognitive-behavioral procedures can be viewed as possessing probably efficacious status.

In summary, a variety of behavioral and cognitive-behavioral procedures have been shown to be either well established or probably efficacious in the treatment of phobic disorders in children. Having stated this, however, it is clear that much more research is needed. Although children were randomly assigned to treatment conditions in these studies and the treatment procedures were reasonably well described, characteristics of the fearful or phobic children were only minimally specified (e.g., age, sex, diagnosis/extent of fear symptoms) and adequate statistical power was notably lacking (the sample sizes were relatively small in most studies). Moreover, most of the studies were undertaken with non-clinical-referred children. As such, the children and adolescents, and the treatments themselves may have differed substantially from clinic-referred children and adolescents and their families observed in clinic settings. Obviously, more research with clinic-referred children is necessary to establish the efficacy of these procedures in clinical settings.

Surprisingly, no controlled between-group design-outcome studies examining the efficacy of psychotherapy with children evincing anxiety disorders, other than simple or specific phobias, existed until recent years. However, several controlled single-case design studies provided preliminary support for the likely efficacy of behavioral and cognitive-behavioral procedures with overanxious and separation-anxious children (Eisen & Silverman, 1993; Kane & Kendall, 1989; Ollendick, 1995a; Ollendick, Hagopian, & Huntzinger, 1991). These early studies provided the foundation for the between-group design studies that followed. All evaluate the efficacy of cognitive-behavioral therapy. Cognitive-behavioral treatment for anxiety disorders in children, as pioneered by Kendall and his colleagues (e.g., 1992), is focused upon both cognitive and behavioral components. Cognitive strategies are used to assist the child to recognize anxious cognition, to use awareness of such cognition as a cue for managing anxiety, and to help the child cope more effectively in anxiety-provoking situations. In addition, behavioral strategies such as modeling, *in vivo* exposure to the anxiety cues, role play, relaxation training, and reinforced practice are used. Thus, these cognitive-behavioral procedures are broad in scope and incorporate many of the elements of treatments used with phobic children. In the first manualized between-group study, Kendall (1994) compared the outcome of this 16-session treatment to a wait-list control condition. Forty-seven 9- to 13-year-old children were assigned randomly to treatment or wait-list conditions. All the children met diagnostic criteria for one of the anxiety disorders, and over half of them were comorbid with at least one other psychiatric disorder. Treated children improved on a number of dimensions; perhaps the most dramatic difference was the percentage of children not meeting criteria for an anxiety disorder at the end of treatment— 64% of treated cases versus 5% of the wait-list children. At follow-up 1 and 3 years later, improvements were maintained (Kendall & Southam-Gerow, 1996). Kendall et al. (1997) reaffirmed the efficacy of this procedure with 94 children (ages 9–13) randomly assigned to cognitive-behavioral and wait-list control conditions. Seventy-one percent of the treated children did not meet diagnostic criteria at the end of treatment compared to 5% of those in the wait-list condition.

Subsequent to Kendall's first randomized clinical trial, his cognitive-behavioral therapy approach was evaluated independently by a different investigatory team in Australia (Barrett, Dadds, & Rapee, 1996). Children (7–14 years of age) were assigned randomly to one of three groups: cognitive-behavioral treatment, cognitive-behavioral treatment plus a family intervention, and a wait-list control. The cognitive-behavioral treatment was intended to be a replication of that used by Kendall (although it was shortened to 12 sessions). At the end of treatment, 57% of the anxious children in the cognitive-behavioral treatment were diagnosis free compared to 26% of the wait-list children; at 6-month follow-up, 71% of the treated children were diagnosis free (wait-list children were treated in the interim). Based on this study and the two studies conducted by Kendall and colleagues, we can conclude that cognitive-behavioral treatment is probably efficacious—it has been shown to be more effective than a wait-list control condition by two different investigatory teams. However, no studies have shown it to be superior to a psychological placebo or alternative treatment. In fact, this treatment has been shown to be less effective than another treatment, namely, the cognitive-behavioral plus family anxiety management treatment in the Barrett et al. (1996) study. In that study, parents were trained in how to reward courageous behavior and to extinguish reports of excessive anxiety in their children. More specifically, parents were trained in reinforcement strategies including verbal praise, privileges, and tangible rewards to be made contingent on facing up to feared situations. Planned ignoring was used as a method for dealing with excessive complaining and anxious behaviors; that is, the parents were trained to listen and respond empathetically to the children's complaints the first time they occurred but then to withdraw attention if the complaints persisted. In this treatment condition, 84% of the children were diagnosis-free immediately following treatment, a rate that persisted at 6-month follow-up. Thus, this treatment was superior to cognitive-behavioral treatment directed toward the child alone (57% diagnosis-free) and the wait-list control condition (26% diagnosis-free). In an earlier study, Dadds, Heard (Barrett), and Rapee (1992) demonstrated that the cognitive-behavioral treatment, supplemented with parental involvement, was superior to a wait-list control condition with 14 anxious children between 7 and 14 years of age. Thus, on the basis of these two studies conducted by these investigators, we can conclude that cognitive-behavioral treatment supplemented with family anxiety management procedures is also probably efficacious. Assuming it can be shown to be more effective than a cognitive-behavioral intervention alone by another investigatory team, it could rise to well-established status. It appears to be a very promising treatment package.

In summary, cognitive-behavioral and behavioral treatments have been shown to be effective with both phobic and anxiety disorders in children. It should be noted that these treatments have been used primarily with phobic children between 4 and 13 years of age and with anxious children between 7 and 14 years of age. As in other problem areas, additional research is required to determine whether these treatments will be effective with older adolescents.

Psychosocial Treatments
for Attention-Deficit/Hyperactivity Disorder

Pelham, Wheeler, and Chronis (1998) reviewed the current status of psychosocial treatments for attention-deficit/hyperactivity disorder (ADHD) in children and concluded that behavioral parent training programs and contingency management programs in the classroom met criteria for well-established treatments, as specified by the 1995 task force; cognitive interventions, however, failed to meet such criteria. A brief review of these findings and their implications follows.

Pelham et al. (1998) noted that although psychostimulant medications have relatively immediate and positive effects on many domains of functioning in children with ADHD, they do not produce long-term changes in academic achievement, classroom deportment, and peer relationships. Moreover, only about 70–80% of children with ADHD respond positively to a central nervous system stimulant regimen; the remainder shows either no response or an adverse response. Furthermore, of those children who do respond, the behavior of the majority is not normalized; that is, they continue to display relatively high rates of problematic behaviors. Given these findings, Pelham et al. (1998) argue for the inclusion of behavioral programs aimed at addressing these persistent and refractory behaviors. As noted earlier, behavioral parent training and behavioral interventions in the classroom have been recommended either to supplement the gains observed with stimulant medication or to be used on their own.

Behavioral parent training programs and behavioral interventions in the classroom are frequently combined in what Pelham et al. (1998) refer to as *clinical behavior therapy*. In typical behavioral treatment programs, parents are given a series of readings about the principles of behavior modification and are taught standard behavior management techniques such as time-out, response–cost, point systems, and contingent attention. Usually, these techniques are taught in a series of outpatient sessions lasting 10 to 20 weeks. At the same time, therapists work closely with the child's teachers to develop similar classroom management strategies that can be implemented in the school by the teachers; in addition, they assist the teachers in developing daily report cards that provide feedback to parents about their child's performance in the classroom. Typically, parents are asked to provide consequences for targeted classroom behavior at home (e.g., special rewards, time-out, response–cost). Such programs consistently show mild to moderate improvements in both classroom and home settings. Pelham et al. (1998) further note that these positive findings are enhanced when a consulting professional is available (in addition to the therapist) to work very closely with the teachers and parents. Under such conditions, greater control (and fidelity) is obtained over treatment implementation. Finally, these effects are enhanced even more when the peer relationships of children with

ADHD are specifically addressed. For a number of years, Pelham and his colleagues (e.g., Pelham & Hoza, 1996) have conducted an intensive Summer Treatment Program that has as a major purpose the improvement of social relationships in these children. The program is in effect 9 hours per day for 8 weeks and combines behavior management techniques with academic activities and sports skills training in a summer camp format.

At the present time, a combination of these various treatment components is being evaluated in the Collaborative Multimodal Treatment Study of children with ADHD (referred to as the MTA study; see Arnold et al., 1997; Richters et al., 1995). In this randomized clinical trial, the psychosocial package (behavioral parent training, school intervention, and a summer treatment program) is crossed with stimulant medication to produce the following four treatment groups each lasting 14 months, with 10- and 22-month follow-up periods: (1) psychosocial treatment alone, (2) pharmacological treatment alone, (3) combined psychosocial and pharmacological treatment, and (4) a community comparison control treatment. A large number of children are scheduled to be randomly assigned to each group (about 144 in each of the four cells). The children will be clinic-referred and most of them will be highly comorbid with other disorders, including the affective and conduct disorders. The treatments will be manualized, fidelity and adherence measures will be obtained, and a variety of outcome measures will be obtained (including measures of daily life functioning as well as specific ADHD symptomatology). Findings from this collaborative project are forthcoming and should be available within the next year or so.

A word of caution should be inserted about the limitations of the findings associated with these psychosocial treatments. First, the effects have been greater for younger than older children and adolescents with ADHD. For example, work by Pisterman and colleagues (1989, 1992) shows that behavioral parent training programs are highly effective with young children, whereas the work of Barkley, Guevremont, Anastopoulos, and Fletcher (1992) suggests caution when using such programs with adolescents. Similarly, positive effects associated with behavioral classroom interventions have been established with younger children but not adolescents. Quite obviously, systematic studies with children of varying ages (and developmental levels) are needed. Second, as with the stimulant medication studies, the effects of psychosocial programs are frequently short-lived. Studies examining the maintenance and generalization of the positive effects obtained in these studies are sorely needed. Third, controlled studies have *not* supported the use of cognitive-based procedures such as verbal self-instruction and cognitive modeling. Such procedures are frequently used in outpatient clinical settings to teach children a set of cognitive techniques that they can use to control their inattention and impulsive behaviors in extraclinic settings. As noted by Pelham et al. (1998), these findings are disappointing because these procedures were designed to provide the child internal mediators that would facilitate maintenance and generalization of the effects obtained from the behavioral programs. And, fourth, review of this literature provides no empirical support for the continued use of a variety of treatments that have been attempted with children with ADHD, including traditional one-to-one therapy, restrictive or supplemental diets, allergy treatments, biofeedback, pet therapy, and play therapy, among others. Pelham et al. (1998, p. 194) assert that "although some might argue that just because something has not been shown to be effective does not mean that it is not, we believe strongly that treatments should not be offered without reasonable evidence that they will ameliorate impairment and symptoms." We concur. Moreover, we would add that when certain treatments have been evaluated and have been shown *not* to produce beneficial effects, they should not continue to be in use—a practice that prevails in the treatment of children with ADHD. We shall return to this point later in a discussion of ethics and the use of empirically supported treatments.

In summary, in addition to stimulant medication regimens, behavioral parent training and behavioral classroom interventions have been shown to be well-established treatments for children with ADHD. Their effects are frequently short-lived, however, and additional research is called for to address this shortcoming.

Psychosocial Treatment for Oppositional and Conduct Problems

Oppositional and conduct problems are among the most commonly referred problems in child psychiatric clinics (see Greene & Doyle, 1999). Moreover, in the absence of effective treatment, a significant subset of these children become delinquent, and a significant minority become antisocial adults. Fortunately, in their review of the efficacy of psychosocial treatments for these youth, Brestan and Eyberg (1998) conclude that we now possess two well-established treatments and a host of probably efficacious treatments for these relatively refractory problems. A brief review of these treatments follows.

Unlike other child behavior problems reviewed in the Special Issue of the *Journal of Clinical Child Psychology,* several treatment studies have been conducted with these youth (Brestan and Eyberg located 82 outcome studies addressing these problems in 5,272 children and adolescents!). Two different "parenting" treatments were found to have the strong empirical support required for well-established status: Parent training programs based on the Patterson and Gullion (1968) book, *Living with Children,* and parent training programs based on Webster-Stratton's videotape modeling parent training program. Patterson and Gullion's program is based on operant principles of behavior change and is designed to teach parents to monitor targeted deviant behaviors, observe and reward incompatible be-haviors, and ignore or punish deviant behaviors. This program has been shown to be more effective than psychodynamic and client-centered ther-apy interventions, in addition to no-treatment control groups. Boys and girls, varying in age from early childhood to adolescence, have benefited from this approach. Overall, this approach has been shown to possess ro-bust effects in studies conducted with children and adolescents who have been referred by schools, family physicians, and juvenile courts; in addi-tion, these positive effects have been obtained by several different investiga-tory teams.

Webster-Stratton's (1984, 1990, 1994) parent training program is somewhat similar to that of Patterson and Gullion (1968); however, it is used primarily with very young, oppositional children who are at risk for development of more severe conduct problems. It includes a videotape se-ries of parent training "lessons" based in developmental and social learning theory. It is typically delivered to parents in small groups, with therapist-led group discussion of the videotape lessons. The treatment has been tested in several studies conducted by different investigatory teams in which it has been compared to wait-list control groups and to alternative parent train-ing formats. For the most part, these studies have typically included both boys and girls between 4 and 8 years of age, and it has been shown to be highly effective.

In addition to these two well-established treatments, Brestan and Eyberg (1998) identified 10 treatments that met criteria for probably effica-cious status. Some of these were variants of parent training, whereas others included child-centered and context-relevant treatments such as anger-con-trol training, anger-coping training, parent–child interaction therapy, prob-lem-solving skills training, rational–emotive therapy, and multisystemic therapy (for additional detail, see Lochman et al., Chapter 2, and Nelson & Finch, Chapter 4, this volume). Most of these treatments were evaluated in well-controlled, well-designed outcome studies and simply await systematic replication by a second research team before advancing to well-established status.

Although Brestan and Eyberg (1998, p. 183) noted that these various interventions "provide new and current standards of care" for children and adolescents with conduct disorder, it is evident that much research remains to be conducted before such a conclusion can be fully embraced. As with several other childhood problems and clinical disorders, considerably more research on a wide range of children with conduct disorder living in a vari-ety of familial and community contexts is required. The pioneering work conducted by Henggeler and colleagues on multisystemic therapy (e.g., Borduin et al., 1995; Henggeler, Melton, & Smith, 1992; Henggeler et al., 1986) represents the kind of work that will likely yield the best payoff.

Summary Comments

In summary, it is evident that very few well-established treatments have been identified for the treatment of child behavior disorders (see Table 9.2 for a summary). No well-established treatments have been identified for the treatment of autism, childhood depression, or childhood anxiety. Moreover, only two treatments have been shown to possess well-established status in the treatment of phobic disorders, ADHD, and conduct disorders, respectively. Although a stable of techniques appears promising and can be described as probably efficacious (see Table 9.2), it is evident that support for these interventions is meager at best. Rarely does any treatment have more than the two requisite studies that support its well-established or

TABLE 9.2. Well-Established and Probably Efficacious Psychosocial Treatments for Children

Problem/disorder	Treatments	
	Well-established	Probably efficacious
Autism	None	None
Depression	None	Behavioral self-control therapy Cognitive-behavioral coping skills

Anxiety	None	Cognitive-behavioral therapy
		Cognitive-behavioral therapy
		    plus family anxiety
		    management

Phobias	Participant modeling Reinforced practice	Imaginal desensitization *In vivo* desensitization Live modeling Filmed modeling Cognitive-behavioral therapy
ADHD	Behavioral parent training Operant classroom management	Cognitive-behavioral therapy

ODD/CD	Behavioral parent training
	
	Videotape modeling
	Parent training
		Anger control training with
		    stress inoculation
		Anger coping therapy
		Assertiveness training
		Delinquency prevention program
		Multisystemic therapy
		Parent–child interaction therapy
		Parent training program
		Problem-solving skills training
		Rational-emotive therapy
		Time out plus signal seat
		    treatment

Note. ADHD, attention-deficit/hyperactivity disorder; ODD, oppositional defiant disorder; CD, conduct disorder probably efficacious status (with the exception of parenting programs for children with oppositional and conduct problems and children with ADHD). It should also be evident that *all* of these probably efficacious and well-established treatments are based on behavioral and cognitive-behavioral principles. To some extent, however, we do not really know whether frequently practiced treatments from other orientations work or not (e.g., play therapy, interpersonal psychotherapy); in many instances, they simply have not been evaluated. Still, the value of identifying and promulgating treatments that do have support for their use is obvious. Demonstrating the efficacy of a treatment in well-controlled randomized trials may point the way to determining the effectiveness of the treatments in real-life clinical settings.

ON EMPIRICALLY SUPPORTED TREATMENTS: PROMISES AND PITFALLS

As noted in our opening comments, the movement to identify, develop, disseminate, and use empirically supported psychosocial treatments has been somewhat contentious. As noted by Ollendick (1999), three major concerns about this movement have been raised: (1) some treatments have been shown to be well-established and hence more effective than others and, as a result, the "Dodo Bird" effect (i.e., no treatment is superior to another) that has long characterized the state of psychosocial treatment interventions can no longer be asserted, (2) use of treatment manuals might lead to lockstep interventions and such "manually-driven" treatments might stifle creativity and flexibility in the therapy process; and (3) treatments shown to be effective in randomized clinical trials and based largely in university-based settings might not generalize to "real-life" clinical practice settings. What is the status of these concerns for empirically supported treatments for children and how might they be addressed? In the sections that follow, we examine these issues in more detail.

Differential Effectiveness of Psychosocial Treatments

Regarding the first issue, our review of the literature identifies a rather startling set of findings. It is obvious that interventions other than behavioral or cognitive-behavioral ones have not been examined adequately in controlled treatment-outcome studies and therefore cannot be said to be well-established or probably efficacious. Across frequently occurring problem areas of autism, depression, phobias, anxiety, ADHD, oppositonal behaviors, and conduct problems, for example, *no* randomized controlled trials using "good" experimental designs were found for psychodynamic psychotherapies or family systems therapies (with the exception of research in the area of oppositional behavior, wherein psychodynamic and family systems interventions were shown to be *less* efficacious than behavioral parenting programs; Brestan & Eyberg, 1998). In addition, only one study was found that examined the efficacy of interpersonal psychotherapy (Mufson et al., 1994), and that study was an uncontrolled one limited to the treatment of depression in adolescents. Inasmuch as these treatments have not been evaluated systematically, we simply do not know whether they are effective. They could be. Should we use such treatments, in the absence of evidentiary support? If so, how long should we continue to use them in the absence of support? If not, what forms of treatment will replace them? Clearly, our review documents that our clinical armamentarium is small and there are not many empirically supported treatments for most child behavior problems. Although behavioral and cognitive-behavioral treatment procedures fare better than other interventions (a conclusion identical to that of meta-analytic studies of treatment-outcome studies with children; for reviews that indicate the superiority of behavioral over "nonbehavioral" treatments, see Weisz, Weiss, Alicke, & Klotz, 1987; Weisz, Weiss, et al., 1995), we were able to identify only two well-established psychosocial treatments for specific phobias in children (participant modeling, reinforced practice), two well-established treatments for ADHD (behavioral parent training, operant classroom management), and two well-established treatments for oppositional and conduct problems using behavioral and cognitive-behavioral treatments (Webster-Stratton's videotape modeling parent training, Patterson's operant parent training program). Thus, even support for behavioral and cognitive-behavioral interventions is meager, at best. What should we do in our clinical practices in the absence of firmer support for our interventions? Unfortunately for the children and families we serve, we probably need to continue "treatment as usual" until such support is available; however, it seems to us that these alternative treatments, as well many behavioral and cognitive-behavioral ones, need to be submitted to systematic inquiry in randomized controlled trials before their routine use can be fully endorsed. Although we agree with Pelham et al. (1998, p. 194) that treatments should not be offered without "reasonable evidence that they will ameliorate impairment and symptoms," we simply do not have sufficient evidence at this time for the efficacy of psychosocial treatments for many child behavior problems (except perhaps, specific phobias, ADHD, and oppositional/conduct problems, where we also have a number of probably efficacious treatments). Although the utility of randomized controlled trials for obtaining "reasonable evidence" has been the focus of considerable debate (see Persons & Silberschatz, 1998), there is little doubt in our minds that such trials are well suited for establishing the *initial* efficacy of various treatments. Of course, the transportability of such treatments to practice settings, and their efficacy in such settings (effectiveness), must also be established (see later discussion).

Given the state of empirically supported psychosocial treatments and the need to rely on current clinical practices until support for additional treatments is garnered, one might rightfully ask, "What is the current status of 'treatment as usual' in clinical practice settings? And how effective is it?" Weisz, Huey, and Weersing (1998) examined this question in a reanalysis of their recent meta-analytic study (Weisz, Weiss, et al., 1995). They searched for studies involving treatment of clinic-referred children in service-oriented clinics, or clinical agencies, by practicing clinicians. Nine studies were identified (spanning a period of over 50 years!) that compared treatment "as usual" to a control group that received a no-treatment or placebo condition. Effect sizes associated with these nine studies were computed: they ranged from −.40 to +.29, with a mean effect size of .01, falling well below the average effect size obtained in their overall analyses (combining "research"- and "clinic"-based treatments). The effect size of .01 indicates that the treated children were no better off than the untreated children following treatment. Clearly, based on these analyses, outcomes associated with "treatment as usual" are unsatisfactory, if not alarming.

Similar outcomes were reported recently by Bickman and colleagues in their examination of a comprehensive mental health services program for children (Bickman, 1996; Bickman et al., 1995). Popularly known as the Fort Bragg Project, the United States Army spent $80 million to provide to children and their families an organized continuum of mental health care ("continuum of care" organized and coordinated by a case manager) and to test its cost-effectiveness relative to a more conventional and less comprehensive intervention (treatment as usual) in a matched comparison site. Although there is good evidence that the program produced better access to treatment and higher levels of client satisfaction, the program also cost significantly more and, most importantly, failed to show clinical and functional outcomes superior to those in the comparison site. In brief, the Fort Bragg children and their families received more interventions at a higher cost, but their outcomes were not improved by the increased intensity of treatment and cost.

In an even more recent study, Weiss, Catron, Harris, and Phung (1999) used a randomized controlled design to determine the effectiveness of child psychotherapy as typically delivered in an outpatient setting. A total of 160 children who presented with problems of anxiety, depression, aggression, and attention were randomly assigned to treatment and control conditions. Children were enrolled in normal elementary and middle schools (mean age was 10.3). Treatment was provided by mental health professionals hired through regular clinic practices (six were master's-level clinicians and one was a doctoral level clinical psychologist); therapists reported favoring cognitive and psychodynamic–humanistic approaches over behavioral ones. Treatment itself was open-ended, extensive in scope, and delivered over an extended 2-year period. Overall, results of the trial provided little support for the effectiveness of traditional child psychotherapy. Treatment produced an overall effect size of –.08! Despite the lack of a significant difference between treatment and control groups in regard to children's functioning, parents of children who received treatment reported higher levels of satisfaction with the services than control-group parents whose children received academic tutoring (a control for attention and the therapist–child relationship). These results, along with those of Bickman and colleagues, in addition to those reported by Weisz et al. (1998) in their meta-anlaytic review, argue persuasively for the importance of developing, validating, and transporting effective treatments to clinical settings. Apparently, "treatment as usual" is not treatment—such "treatments" have little support for their ongoing use.

One final comment should be offered about the ethics of continuing to provide treatments that have not been shown to be helpful to children and their families and, in fact, in some instances have been shown to be harmful (recall that the effect sizes for the nine clinic-based studies reviewed by Weisz et al. ranged from –.40 to +.29, and that the effect size reported by Weiss et al. was –.08). As psychologists, the identification, promulgation, and use of empirically supported treatments are certainly in accord with ethical standards asserting that psychologists "should rely on scientifically and professional derived knowledge when making scientific or professional judgments" (Canter, Bennett, Jones, & Nagy, 1994, p. 36). Yet, as noted in a lively debate on this issue (Eiffert, Schulte, Zvolensky, Lejuez, & Lau, 1998; Persons, 1998; Zvolensky & Eiffert, 1998, 1999), the identification and use of empirically supported treatments represent a two-edged sword. On the one hand, it might seem unethical to use a treatment that has not been empirically supported; on the other, inasmuch as few empirically supported treatments have been developed, it might be unethical to delimit or restrict practice to those problem areas and disorders for which treatment efficacy has been established. What, after all, should we do in instances when children and their families present with problems for which empirically supported treatments have not yet been developed? Quite obviously, there are no easy solutions here; nor can we address the issue in sufficient depth in this chapter. However, we are supportive of the conclusions reached by Kinscherff (1999) in an article entitled "Empirically Supported Treatments: What to Do until the Data Arrive (or Now That They Have)?" He suggests:

> Generally, clinicians should develop a formulation of the case and select the best approaches for helping a client from among the procedures in which the clinician is competent. Clinicians should remain informed about advances in treatment, including empirically supported treatments, and maintain their own clinical skills by learning new procedures and strengthening their skills in areas in which they are already accomplished. Because there

are limitations to how many treatments any one clinician can master, a key professional competence is knowing when to refer for a treatment approach that may be more effective for the client. This, in turn, requires at least a basic ongoing familiarity with the evolution of psychotherapeutic treatments and scientific basis for them in clinical populations. (p. 4)

We agree.

Manualization of Psychosocial Treatments

The recommendation that well-established and probably efficacious treatments *must* use a treatment manual was the second major source of controversy identified by Ollendick (1999). As noted by Chambless et al. (1996), there were two reasons for this requirement. First, inclusion of a treatment manual leads to an operational definition of the treatment; that is, a treatment manual provides a description of the treatment that makes it possible to determine whether the treatment was actually delivered as intended (i.e., treatment integrity). This allows for a better research design because it provides an indication of the integrity of the independent manipulation. Second, use of a manual allows other mental health professionals and researchers to know what the treatment actually consisted of and, therefore, exactly what procedures were supported in the efficacy trial. Manualization (as it has come to be called) is especially important in clarifying the many types or variants of therapy. For example, there are many types of cognitive-behavioral therapy or psychodynamic therapy. To say that cognitive-behavioral therapy or psychodynamic therapy is efficacious is largely meaningless. What type of psychodynamic therapy was used in this study? What form of cognitive-behavioral therapy was used in that study? There are many interventions and there are many variations of those interventions, that fall under any one psychotherapy rubric. As Chambless et al. (1996, p. 6) note, "The brand names are not the critical identifiers. The manuals are."

A flood of commentaries—some commendatory, others pejorative—filled several major journals, including the *American Psychologist, Journal of Consulting and Clinical Psychology, Clinical Psychology: Science and Practice, Clinical Psychology Review,* and *Psychotherapy.* Some authors viewed manuals as "promoting a cookbook mentality" (Smith, 1995, p. 40), "paint by numbers" (Silverman, 1996, p. 207), "more of a straightjacket than a set of guidelines" (Goldfried & Wolfe, 1996, p. 1007), "somewhat analogous to cookie cutters" (Strupp & Anderson, 1997, p. 78), and a "hangman of life" (Lambert, 1998, p. 391). Others viewed them in more positive terms (e.g., Chambless & Hollon, 1998; Craighead & Craighead, 1998; Heimberg, 1998; Kendall, 1998; King & Ollendick, 1998; Ollendick, 1995b, 1999; Strosahl, 1998; Wilson, 1996a, 1996b,

1998). Wilson (1998, p. 363), for example, asserted that "use of standardized, manual-based treatments in clinical practice represents a new and evolving development with far-reaching implications for the field of psychotherapy."

In its simplest form, a treatment manual can be defined as a set of guidelines that instruct or inform the user as to "how to do" a certain treatment (Ollendick, 1999). They specify and standardize treatment. Although many opponents of manual-based treatment support efforts for greater accountability with respect to the efficacy of psychotherapy, they are concerned that treatments evaluated in research settings will not be generalizable to "real-life" clinical settings and that manual-based treatments will need to be implemented in a lockstep fashion, with little opportunity for flexibility or clinical judgment in implementation of the treatment procedures. Seligman (1995, p. 967), for example, suggested that unlike the manual-based treatment of controlled, laboratory research, in which "a small number of techniques, all within one modality" are delivered in fixed order for a fixed duration, clinical practice "is self-correcting. If one technique is not working, another technique—or even modality—is usually tried." As noted by Wilson (1998), this characterization of manual-based treatment is inaccurate. A variety of treatments have been "manualized," including those based in psychodynamic (e.g., Strupp & Binder, 1984), interpersonal (e.g., Klerman, Weissman, Rounsaville, & Chevron, 1984), and behavioral (Patterson & Gullion, 1968) or cognitive-behavioral theory (e.g., Beck, Rush, Shaw, & Emery, 1979); moreover, these manuals allow for flexible use and, for the most part, are responsive to progress or regress in treatment.

One final comment about manuals should be offered. The movement to manualization existed long before the task force issued its report in 1995. Almost 30 years earlier, Patterson and Gullion (1968) published their now-classic book *Living with Children: New Methods for Parents and Teachers,* a "how to" parent manual that has served as the foundation for many behavioral treatments of children with oppositional, defiant, and conduct problems. Over a decade prior to the issue of the task force report (1995), Luborsky and DuRubeis (1984) commented upon the potential use of treatment manuals in a paper entitled "The Use of Psychotherapy Treatment Manuals: A Small Revolution in Psychotherapy Research Style." Similarly, Lambert and Ogles (1988) indicated that manuals were not new; rather, they noted, manuals have been used to train therapists and define treatments since the 1960s. On the one hand, the 1995 task force report simply affirmed a movement that had been present for some years and that had become the unofficial, if not official, policy of the National Institute of Mental Health for funding research studies exploring the efficacy of various psychotherapies. On the other hand, and this is where its actions became contentious, the task force report asserted that psychotherapies described and operationalized by manuals should be identified and disseminated to clinical training programs, practicing mental health professionals, the public, and to third-party payors (i.e., insurance companies, health maintenance organizations). Many authors were concerned that such actions were premature and that they would prohibit or, at least, constrain the practice of psychotherapies that had not been manualized, or not yet been shown to be efficacious. They also were concerned that the development of new psychotherapies would be stifled, if not temporarily curtailed. Although these are possible outcomes of the move to manualization and the evaluation of psychotherapies, they need not be the inevitable outcome. In fact, some have argued that these developments can serve to stimulate additional treatments by systematically examining the parameters of effective treatments as well as the therapeutic mechanisms of change (for examples, see Kendall, 1998; Wilson, 1998), a position with which we are in accord.

What is the current status of this movement toward manualization in the treatment of children? First, it should be clear that the studies summarized in our review of empirically supported treatments for children either used manuals or the procedures were described in sufficient detail so as not to require manuals (as originally suggested by the Task Force Report, 1995, and by Chambless et al., 1996). Addis and his colleagues (Addis, 1998; Addis, Hatgis, Soysa, & Zaslavsky, 1999), as well as Kendall and his colleagues (Kendall, 1998; Kendall & Chu, 2000; Kendall, Chu, Gifford, Hayes, & Nauta, 1998), have most eloquently addressed issues surrounding use of treatment manuals. As we noted earlier, manuals are simply guidelines that describe treatment procedures and therapeutic strategies, and in some instances, provide an underlying theory of change on which the procedures or techniques are based. In an interesting treatise on this topic, Addis et al. (1999) recommended viewing the tensions created by manualized treatment from a dialectical perspective. These authors offered a set of guidelines, or ways of thinking about manual-based treatment, that assist us in balancing effective adherence to treatment manuals with, at the same time, using these manuals flexibly for individual clients. In addition, Addis et al. provide guidelines that help us cut across different manualized treatments rather than being stuck on treatment specific interventions, a point especially useful in treating the majority of clients who present with comorbid disorders. As they note, one of the implications of viewing manualized treatments from a dialectical perspective is that apparent dichotomies related to manualized treatments can be viewed on two independent continua rather than on a single continuum, with one implicitly, if not explicitly, competing with the other. For example, although developing a therapeutic relationship may seem at odds with implementing specific therapeutic techniques, such need not be the case. The two are not mutually exclusive. Depending upon the stage of treatment or the timing within a treatment session, attention could be directed to one or the other, or both simultaneously. They are nonoverlapping dimensions. As noted by Addis et al. (p. 131), "The goal of working dialectically is not to remove tensions, but rather to tolerate, accept, and work creatively within them." The experience of tension itself may set the occasion for creative interventions that are consistent with manualized treatments. Similarly, although adhering to the treatment manual might seem at odds with adapting it for individual clients, it need not be; that is, in arriving at a possible synthesis of these two points, one might ask, "How does the manual provide a general framework for treating this individual?" and "What aspects of this particular client will facilitate my use of the treatment manual?" Such an approach allows the clinician to work with the tensions rather than fight them.

In a somewhat different vein, Kendall (1998) has recommended that we go beyond identification of the many perceptions about treatment manuals and undertake systematic research of the issues identified. He identified six (mis)perceptions that plague manual-based treatments: How flexible are they? Do they replace clinical judgment? Do manuals detract from the creative process of therapy? Does a treatment manual reify therapy in a fixed and stagnant fashion, and thereby stifle improvement and change? Are manual-based treatments effective with patients who present with multiple diagnoses or clinical problems? And are manuals primarily designed for use in research programs, with little or no use or application in service-providing clinics? Although answers to each of these penetrating questions are not yet available, he submits that careful research is needed to explore each of these perceptions. In addition, he provides some evidence from his own work with children who have anxiety disorders that at least some of these issues or questions may be pseudo ones, or at least not particularly esoteric ones. For example, flexibility of treatment implementation is an issue that many critics have raised; accordingly, it should be investigated empirically to determine if the degree to which a manual is implemented flexibly affects treatment outcome. Does it really make a difference? In a recent study by Kendall and Chu (2000) such an investigation was conducted.

Flexibility can be defined in a variety of ways; in this research, it was defined as a construct that measures the therapist's adaptiveness to the *specific* situation at hand, while adhering *generally* to the instructions and suggestions in the manual. Ratings on the degree to which the manual was implemented in a flexible manner were obtained from 18 different therapists who had implemented Kendall's cognitive-behavioral, manual-based treatment for anxious children (Kendall et al., 1992). Flexibility ratings were obtained retrospectively on a 13-item questionnaire, with each item rated on 1- to 7-point scale as to the extent of flexibility used in implementing treatment (e.g., "The manual suggests that clinicians spend 40–45 minutes of the session teaching the outlined skills to the child and 10–15 minutes of the session playing games. How flexible with this were you?" and "During therapy sessions, how flexible were you in discussing issues not related to anxiety or directly related to the child's primary diagnoses?"). First of all, results revealed that therapists reported being flexible in their implementation of the treatment plan (both in general and with specific strategies). Second, and perhaps unexpectedly, the indices of flexibility were *not* related to whether the children were comorbid with other disorders *or* treatment outcome. The important point here is that flexibility, however defined, is amenable to careful and systematic inquiry. Kendall (1998) asserts that other issues raised by the manualization of treatment are also amenable to empirical investigation and they need not remain in the area of "heated" speculation.

One additional example may help to illustrate how issues such as flexibility might be addressed empirically. In these studies, primarily conducted with adults, manual-based treatments have been "individualized" in a flexible manner by matching certain characteristics or profiles of the individuals being treated to specific elements or components of previously established effective treatments. These efforts have been labeled "prescriptive matching" by Acierno, Hersen, Van Hasselt, and Ammerman (1994). At the core of this approach is the belief that an idiographic approach to treatment is more effective in producing positive treatment outcomes than a nomothetic approach (e.g., not all patients who receive the same diagnosis or who present with similar behavior problems are *really* the same—the homogeneity myth put forth by Kiesler, 1966). For example, in one of these studies, Jacobson et al. (1989) designed individually tailored marital therapy treatment plans, in which the number of sessions and the specific modules selected in each case were determined by the couple's specific needs and presenting problems. Individualized treatments were compared to a standard cognitive-behavioral treatment program. Each was manualized. At posttreatment, unexpectedly, couples treated with individually tailored protocols could not be distinguished from those receiving standardized protocols. However, at 6-month follow-up, a greater proportion of couples receiving standardized treatment showed decrements in marital satisfaction, whereas a majority of those in the individually tailored program maintained their treatment gains, suggesting that individually tailored programs may help reduce relapses.

Similar, beneficial findings have been obtained in the treatment of adults with depression (Nelson-Gray, Herbert, Herbert, Sigmon, & Brannon, 1990). In this study, Nelson-Gray et al. assigned adult depressed patients to treatment protocols (e.g., cognitive treatment, social skills treatment) that were either matched or mismatched to their presenting problems (e.g., irrational cognitions, social skills problems). Those in the matched conditions fared better than those in the mismatched condition upon completion of treatment. Similarly, Ost, Jerremalm, and Johansson (1981) examined the efficacy of social skills training and applied relaxation in the treatment of adults with social phobia who were categorized as either "behavioral" or "physiological" responders. Physiological responders benefited most clearly from the applied relaxation training, whereas behavioral responders showed the most benefit from the social skills program. Not all studies with individualized treatments have produced such positive results, however. For example, Schulte, Kunzel, Pepping, and Schulte-Bahrenberg (1992) found that standardized treatment, contrary to expectations, proved more successful than either individualized or mismatched treatments in an investigation of adults with agoraphobia or specific phobias. Mersch, Emmelkamp, Bogels, and van der Sleen (1989) also failed to demonstrate the value of categorizing adults with social phobia into those with primarily cognitive or behavioral deficiencies and assigning them to matched or mismatched treatments. Matched treatments were not found to be superior to mismatched ones.

In the child arena, Eisen and Silverman (1993, 1998) have provided preliminary support for the value of prescriptive matching in the treatment of fearful and anxious children. In the first study, the effectiveness of cognitive therapy, relaxation training, and their combination was determined with 4 overanxious children, 6–15 years of age, using a multiple baseline design across subjects. The children received both relaxation training and cognitive therapy (counterbalanced), followed by a combined treatment that incorporated elements of both treatments. Results suggested that interventions were most effective when they matched the specific problems of the children; that is, children with primary symptoms of worry responded more favorably to cognitive therapy, whereas children with primary symptoms of somatic complaints responded best to relaxation treatment. Similar findings were obtained in the second study (Eisen & Silverman, 1998) with 4 children, between 8 and 12 years of age, who were diagnosed with overanxious disorder. The interventions that were prescribed on the basis of a match between the treatment and the response class (cognitive therapy for cognitive symptoms, relaxation therapy for somatic symptoms) produced the greatest changes and resulted in enhanced treatment effectiveness. These findings must be considered preliminary because of limitations associated with the single-case designs used to evaluate their efficacy; to our knowledge, no controlled group-design studies have been conducted examining these issues. Nonetheless, these studies, and those conducted with adult patients, show yet another possible way of individualizing treatment and exploring flexibility in the empirically supported treatment manuals.

In summary, issues with the manualization of treatment are many. However, as noted by Kendall (1998), most of these issues are open to experimental scrutiny. It seems to us that we could continue to debate the value of manualized treatments for a very long time, and such debate would likely be stimulating and fruitful; however, for the benefit of children and the families we serve, it seems to us that it would be more beneficial to get on with the business of developing manualized treatments for those problems and disorders for which we do not currently have empirically supported treatments and carefully refining those manuals that we do have to make them more clinician-friendly, determining how they can be used in a clinically sensitive and flexible manner.

Issues with Efficacy and Effectiveness: The Transportability of Treatments

Still, a third major concern about the empirically supported or evidence-based treatment movement is evident in differences between what have come to be called *efficacy* studies versus *effectiveness* studies (Hibbs, 1998; Hoagwood, Hibbs, Brent, & Jensen, 1995; Ollendick, 1999). Basically, efficacy studies demonstrate that the benefits obtained from a given treatment administered in a fairly standard way (with a treatment manual) are due to the treatment and not due to chance factors or to a variety of other factors that threaten the internal validity of the demonstration of efficacy. Typically, as noted by Seligman (1995), these studies are conducted in laboratory or university settings under tightly controlled conditions. Most consist of randomized clinical trials and clear specification of sample characteristics, features reflective of "good" experimental designs. Appropriate concern has been raised about the exportability of these "laboratory-based" treatments to the real world—the world of clinical practice. Arguments have been mustered that the "subjects" in randomized clinical trials do not represent real-life "clients," or that the "experimenter" therapists in these trials do not represent "clinical" therapists in applied practice settings. Moreover, it is argued, the settings themselves are significantly different—ranging from tightly controlled laboratory conditions to ill-defined and highly variable conditions in practice settings. Weisz, Donenberg, Han, and Weiss (1995) refer to practice settings as the "real test" or the "proving ground" of interventions. To many of us, this conundrum raises the ever-present concern about the need to build a strong bridge between science and practice, a bridge recommended over 50 years ago and embodied in the Boulder model of clinical training. Building this bridge is not easy, and a gap between efficacy and effectiveness studies remains.[3]

Nonetheless, it is evident that effectiveness studies demonstrating the external validity of psychotherapies are very important; moreover, they need to be conducted in a way that will allow us to conclude that the treatments are responsible for the changes observed in our clients, not chance or other extraneous factors. Demonstration of both internal and external validity is important. One should not be viewed as more important than the other. Of course, not all treatments shown to be efficacious in clinical trials research will necessarily be shown to be effective in clinical settings. Such failures may be associated with a host of difficulties, including problems in implementing the treatment procedures in less-controlled clinical settings and the "acceptability" of the efficacious treatments to clients and therapists alike. In the final analysis, whether the effects found in randomized clinical trials and conducted in research-based settings generalize to "real-world" clinical settings is an empirical question that awaits additional research (for further discussion of these issues, see Kendall & Southam-Gerow, 1995; Persons & Silberschatz, 1998).

The issues surrounding transportability and efficacy versus effectiveness studies are numerous and well beyond the scope of this chapter (e.g., training of therapists, supervision of therapists, homogeneous–heterogeneous samples, development of manuals, adherence to manuals, competence in executing manual-based treatment, and the acceptability of manual-based treatments to clinicians and clients, among others). Fortunately for us, Weisz et al. (1998) have examined this issue and identified a set of characteristics frequently associated with child psychotherapy outcome research that distinguishes efficacy from effectiveness research. They are reproduced in Table 9.3 under the headings of "Research Therapy" and "Clinic Therapy." As evident in Table 9.3, Weisz et al. characterize "research" therapy as serving relatively homogeneous groups of children that exhibit less severe forms of child psychopathology and present with single-

TABLE 9.3. Some Characteristics Frequently Associated with Child Psychotherapy in Outcome Research (Research Therapy) and in Clinics (Clinic Therapy)

Research therapy

Recruited cases (less severe, study volunteers)
Homogeneous groups
Narrow or single-problem focus
Treatment in lab, school settings
Researcher as therapist
Very small caseloads
Heavy pretherapy preparation
Preplanned, highly structured treatment (manualized)
Monitoring of therapist behavior
Behavioral methods

Clinic therapy

Clinic-referred cases (more severe, some coerced into treatment)
Heterogeneous groups
Broad, multiproblem focus
Treatment in clinic, hospital settings
Professional career therapists
Very large caseloads
Little/light pretherapy preparation
Flexible, adjustable treatment (no treatment manual)
Little monitoring of therapist behavior
Nonbehavioral methods

focus problems. Moreover, they suggest that such studies are conducted in research laboratories or school settings with clinicians who are "really" researchers, who are carefully trained and supervised, and who have "light" client loads. Finally, such studies typically use manualized treatments of a behavioral or cognitive-behavioral nature. In contrast, "clinic" therapy is characterized by heterogeneous groups of children that are frequently referred for treatment and have a large and diverse range of clinical problems. Treatment in such settings is, of course, delivered in a clinic or hospital by "real" therapists who have "heavy" caseloads, little pretherapy training, and who are not carefully supervised or monitored. Finally, treatment manuals are rarely used and the primary form of treatment is nonbehavioral. Clearly, a number of differences are highlighted. Although such distinctions are important to make, in our opinion they tend to be broad generalizations that may or may not be true for various studies conducted in laboratory *or* clinical settings. Moreover, they may serve to accentuate differences in types of studies rather than to define areas of rapprochement and, inadvertently, create a chasm, rather than a bridge, between laboratory and clinic research. We illustrate how these distinctions become blurred by describing three studies: (1) a "research" therapy study conducted by Kendall et al. (1997), (2) a "clinic" therapy study conducted by Weiss et al. (1999), and (3) a study examining the transportability of effective treatment into a practice setting (Tynan, Schuman, & Lampert, 1999).

In the Kendall et al. (1997) study, the efficacy of cognitive-behavioral treatment for anxious children was compared to a wait-list condition. Efficacy of treatment was determined at posttreatment and at 1-year follow-up. A randomized controlled trial was undertaken, detailed but flexible manuals were used, and the therapists were well-trained and supervised graduate clinicians who carried "light" clinical loads. Treatment was conducted in a university-based clinic. Ninety-four children (ages 9–13 years) and their parents participated. Children were referred from multiple community sources (not volunteers or normal children in school settings), all received primary anxiety disorder diagnoses (attesting to the relative severity of their problems), and the majority was comorbid with other disorders (affirming multiple problems in these children, including other anxiety disorders, affective disorders, and disruptive behavior disorders). In short, a relatively heterogeneous group of children was treated. Treatment was found to be highly effective both at posttreatment and 1-year follow-up. In reference to Table 9.3, it is evident that some of the characteristics associated with "research" therapy were evident in this study, and that in at least some respects, "clinic" therapy was enacted.

In the Weiss et al. (1999) study, traditional psychotherapy as routinely practiced in an outpatient setting (a school setting) was evaluated by comparing it to an attention-control placebo (academic tutoring). The seven therapists were hired through standard clinic practices (six were master's-level clinicians, and one was a doctoral-level clinical psychologist) and were allowed to select and use whatever intervention techniques they determined were necessary (most selected and used psychodynamic–humanistic or cognitive strategies). No manuals were used. They received no additional clinical training as part of the clinical trial and were provided with a minimal amount of supervision. One hundred and sixty children participated and were randomly assigned to one of the treatment conditions. The children, identified in the school setting through a mental health screening inventory conducted by the school system, presented with problems of anxiety, depression, aggression, and inattention. Diagnostic data were not obtained; however, the identified children were thought to represent a heterogeneous sample of children with multiple and serious problems. As noted earlier, traditional therapy, as implemented in this study, was determined to be largely ineffective. In reference to Table 9.3, it is evident that only some of the characteristics of "clinic" therapy were evident in this study, and that at least in some respects, "research" therapy was examined.

Finally, in the study undertaken by Tynan et al. (1999), the transportability of a well-established treatment for oppositional defiant disorder and ADHD in children between 5 and 11 years of age (behavioral parent management training and child social skills training) was examined in a "real-life" clinical setting (a child psychiatry outpatient clinic). Therapy was conducted in a group format and all children referred for ADHD or oppositional defiant disorder were assigned to the groups as the first line of treatment. Parents and children were treated in separate groups. Diagnostic interviews were conducted and the children all met diagnostic criteria for disruptive behavior disorders, and a majority was comorbid with other disorders. Problems were judged by the clinicians to be serious. Treatment was manualized and therapists were carefully trained and supervised by Tynan. No control group was used, and no follow-up data were reported. Nonetheless, the treatment was shown to be highly efficacious at posttreatment (effect size of .89 from pretreatment to posttreatment). Although several methodological problems are evident, this study illustrates the potential to extend findings from laboratory settings to clinical settings. This study also illustrates characteristics of "research" therapy and "clinic" therapy. To which is it more similar?

These three studies illustrate that demarcations between efficacy and effectiveness studies are not always easy or true to form. Perhaps more importantly, they illustrate the types of studies that are needed to be conducted that will bridge the gap between research and clinic settings.

Summary of Issues Attendant to Empirically Supported Treatments

Although other concerns about empirically supported treatments undoubtedly exist, these three major concerns (some treatments are more effective than others, use of treatment manuals and the independence of the therapist, and the transportability of treatments from the research setting to the clinical setting) seem central to most arguments in support or against this movement. For many of us, the movement toward determining the empirical status of our treatments holds considerable promise; for others, however, it signifies a major pitfall, full of lurking and unspecified dangers (Ollendick, 1999). Continued dialogue between clinicians and researchers on these issues is of utmost importance.

CONCLUSIONS

In this chapter, we have identified salient issues associated with empirically supported treatments and determined their significance for psychosocial treatments with children and adolescents. We have concluded that some treatments are more effective than others, that manualization need not be a stumbling block to providing effective psychotherapies in both research and clinic settings, and that the transportability of treatments from the laboratory setting to the practice setting is feasible. We have also noted that tensions remain about each of these issues, and we have illustrated avenues of rapprochement.

Somewhat unexpectedly, our overview of the status of empirically supported psychosocial treatments for children reveals that our armamentarium is relatively "light" and that much work remains to be done. We really do not have very many psychosocial treatments that have been shown to be well established in research settings, let alone clinical ones. Still, we assert that this is an exciting time and that we have the tools to close the oft-lamented gap between laboratory and clinic studies, and that rapprochement is possible. Children and their families presenting at our clinics deserve our concerted attention to further the true synthesis of these approaches and to transform our laboratory findings into rich and clinically sensitive practices.

NOTES

1. The term "children" is used throughout to refer to both children and adolescents, unless otherwise specified.
2. In a recent paper, Chambless and Hollon (1998) suggest that this criterion be dropped and that treatments found to be effective, whether in comparison to no treatment, another treatment, or a placebo, all be considered *efficacious*. Thus, if a treatment "works" for whatever reason, and if this effect can be replicated by two or more independent groups, then the treatment is likely to be of value clinically, and a case can be made for its clinical use. If there is one study supporting its efficacy, or if all of the research has been conducted by one investigatory

team, Chambless and Hollon consider the findings promising and label such a treatment as *possibly efficacious*, pending replication. We are not convinced of the wisdom of dropping the criterion related to distinction between treatments found to be superior to no treatment versus another treatment or a psychological placebo, and prefer the earlier distinction offered by the task force (1995). We have no reservations, however, about the label "probably efficacious" versus "possibly efficacious." Throughout this chapter, however, we use the terms "well-established" and "probably efficacious" as recommended by the initial task force in 1995.

3. The gap is being closed, however, as is illustrated later in this chapter.

REFERENCES

Acierno, R., Hersen, M., Van Hasselt, V. B., & Ammerman, R. T. (1994). Remedying the Achilles heel of behavior research and therapy: Prescriptive matching of intervention and psychopathology. *Journal of Behavior Therapy and Experimental Psychiatry, 25*, 179–188.

Addis, M. E. (1998). Evaluating the treatment manual as a means of disseminating empirically validated psychotherapies. *Clinical Psychology: Science and Practice, 4*, 1–11.

Addis, M. E., Hatgis, C., Soysa, C. K., & Zaslavsky, I. (1999). The dialectics of manual-based treatment. *the Behavior Therapist, 22*, 130–132.

Anderson, S. R., Avery, D. L., DiPietro, E. K., Edwards, G. L., & Christian, W. P. (1987). Intensive home-based early intervention with autistic children. *Education and Treatment of Children, 10*, 352–366.

Arnold, L. E., Abikoff, H. B., Cantwell, D. P., Conners, C. K., Elliott, G., Greenhill, L. L. Hechtman, L., Hinshaw, S. P., Hoza, B., Jensen, P. S., Kraemer, H., March, J., Newcorn, J., Pelham, W. E., Richters, J., Severe, J. B., Schiller, E., Swanson, J. M., Vereen, D., & Wells, K. (1997). National Institute of Mental Health collaborative multimodel treatment of study of children with ADHD (MTA): Design challenges and choices. *Archives of General Psychiatry, 54*, 865–870.

Barkley, R. A., Guevremont, D. C., Anastopoulos, A. D., & Fletcher, K. E. (1992). A comparison of three family therapy programs for treating family conflicts in adolescents with attention-deficit hyperactivity disorder. *Journal of Consulting and Clinical Psychology, 60*, 450–462.

Barrett, P. M., Dadds, M., & Rapee, R. M. (1996). Family treatment of childhood anxiety: A controlled trial. *Journal of Consulting and Clinical Psychology, 64*, 333–342.

Beck, A. T., Rush, A. T., Shaw, B. F., & Emery, G. (1979). *Cognitive therapy of depression.* New York: Guilford Press.

Bickman, L. (1996). A continuum of care: More is not always better. *American Psychologist, 51*, 689–701.

Bickman, L., Guthrie, P. R., Foster, E. M., Lambert, E. W., Summerfelt, W. T., Breda, C. S., & Heflinger, C. A. (1995). *Evaluating managed mental health services: The Fort Bragg experiment.* New York: Plenum Press.

Birnbrauer, J. S., & Leach, D. J. (1993). The Murdoch early intervention program after 2 years. *Behavior Change, 10*, 63–74.

Borduin, C. M., Mann, B. J., Cone, L. T., Henggeler, S. W., Fucci, B. R., Blaske, D. M., & Williams, R. A. (1995). Multisystemic treatment of serious juvenile offenders: Long-term prevention of criminality and violence. *Journal of Consulting and Clinical Psychology, 63*, 569–578.

Brent, D. A., Kolko, D. J., Birmaher, B., Baugher, M., & Bridge, J. (1999). A clinical trial for adolescent depression: Predictors of additional treatment in the acute and follow-up phases of the trial. *Journal of the American Academy of Child and Adolescent Psychiatry, 38*, 263–270.

Brestan, E. V., & Eyberg, S. M. (1998). Effective psychosocial treatments of conduct-disordered children and adolescents: 29 years, 82 studies, and 5,272 kids. *Journal of Clinical Child Psychology, 27*, 179–188.

Canter, M. B., Bennett, B. E., Jones, S. E., & Nagy, T. F. (1994). *Ethics for psychologists: A commentary on the APA ethics code*. Washington, DC: American Psychological Association.

Chambless, D. L. (1996). In defense of dissemination of empirically supported psychological interventions. *Clinical Psychology: Science and Practice, 3*, 230–235.

Chambless, D. L., & Hollon, S. D. (1998). Defining empirically supported therapies. *Journal of Consulting and Clinical Psychology, 66*, 7–18.

Chambless, D. L., Sanderson, W. C., Shoham, V., Bennett Johnson, S., Pope, K. S., Crits-Cristoph, P., Baker, M., Johnson, B., Woody, S. R., Sue, S., Beutler, L., Williams, D. A., & McCurry, S. (1996). An update on empirically validated therapies. *The Clinical Psychologist, 49*, 5–18.

Clarke, G. N., Rohde, P., Lewinsohn, P. M., Hops, H., & Seeley, J. R. (1999). Cognitive-behavioral treatment of adolescent depression: Efficacy of acute group treatment and booster sessions. *Journal of the American Academy of Child and Adolescent Psychiatry, 38*, 272–279.

Craighead, W. E., & Craighead, L. W. (1998). Manual-based treatments: Suggestions for improving their clinical utility and acceptability. *Clinical Psychology: Science and Practice, 5*, 403–407.

Dadds, M. R., Heard, P. M., & Rapee, R. M. (1992). The role of family intervention in the treatment of child anxiety disorders: Some preliminary findings. *Behaviour Change, 9*, 171–177.

Eifert, G. H., Schulte, D., Zvolensky, M. J., Lejuez, C. W., & Lau, A. W. (1998). Manualized behavior therapy: Merits and challenges. *Behavior Therapy, 28*, 499–509.

Eisen, A. R., & Silverman, W. K. (1993). Should I relax or change my thoughts? A preliminary examination of cognitive therapy, relaxation training, and their combination with overanxious children. *Journal of Cognitive Psychotherapy: An International Quarterly, 7*, 265–279.

Eisen, A. R., & Silverman, W. K. (1998). Prescriptive treatment for generalized anxiety disorder in children. *Behavior Therapy, 29*, 105–121.

Fonagy, P., & Target, M. (1994). The efficacy of psychoanalysis for children with disruptive disorders. *Journal of the American Academy of Child and Adolescent Psychiatry, 33*, 45–55.

Goldfried, M. R., & Wolfe, B. E. (1996). Psychotherapy practice and research: Repairing a strained alliance. *American Psychologist, 51*, 1007–1016.

Graziano, A. M., & Mooney, K. C. (1980). Family self-control instruction for children's nighttime fear reduction. *Journal of Consulting and Clinical Psychology, 48*, 206–213.

Greene, R. W., & Doyle, A. E. (1999). Affective modulation, self-regulation, and cognitive development: Implications of considering a reactive pathway to oppositional defiant disorder. *Clinical Child and Family Psychology Review, 2*, 129–148.

Heimberg, R. G. (1998). Manual-based treatment: An essential ingredient of clinical practice in the 21st century. *Clinical Psychology: Science and Practice, 5*, 387–390.

Henggeler, S. W., Melton, G. B., & Smith, L. A. (1992). Family preservation using multisystemic therapy: An effective alternative to incarcerating serious juvenile offenders. *Journal of Consulting and Clinical Psychology, 60*, 953–961.

Henggeler, S. W., Rodick, J. D., Bourdin, C. M., Hanson, C. L., Watson, S. M., & Utey, J. R. (1986). Multisystemic treatment of juvenile offenders: Effects on adolescent behavior and family interaction. *Developmental Psychology, 22*, 132–141.

Hibbs, E. D. (1998). Improving methodologies for the treatment of child and adolescent disorders: Introduction. *Journal of Abnormal Child Psychology, 26*, 1–6.

Hoagwood, K., Hibbs, E., Brent, D., & Jensen, P. (1995). Introduction to the special section: Efficacy and effectiveness in studies of child and adolescent psychotherapy. *Journal of Consulting and Clinical Psychology, 63*, 683–687.

Kane, M., & Kendall, P. C. (1989). Anxiety disorders in children: A multiple baseline evaluation of a cognitive-behavioral treatment. *Behavior Therapy, 20*, 499–508.

Kanfer, F. H., Karoly, P., & Newman, A. (1975). Reduction of children's fear of the dark by competence-related and situational threat-related verbal cues. *Journal of Consulting and Clinical Psychology, 43*, 251–258.

Kaslow, N. J., & Thompson, M. P. (1998). Applying the criteria for empirically supported treatments to studies of psychosocial interventions for child and adolescent depression. *Journal of Clinical Child Psychology, 27*, 146–155.

Kazdin, A. E. (1998). *Research design in clinical psychology* (3rd ed.). Boston: Allyn & Bacon.

Kazdin, A. E., & Bass, D. (1989). Power to detect differences between alternative treatments in comparative psychotherapy outcome research. *Journal of Consulting and Clinical Psychology, 57*, 138–147.

Kendall, P. C. (1994). Treating anxiety disorders in children: Results of a randomized clinical trial. *Journal of Consulting and Clinical Psychology, 62*, 100–110.

Kendall, P. C. (1998). Directing misperceptions: Researching the issues facing manual-based treatments. *Clinical Psychology: Science and Practice, 5*, 396–399.

Kendall, P. C., Chansky, T. E., Kane, M. T., Kim, R. S., Kortlander, E., Ronan, K. R., Sessa, F. M., & Siqueland, L. (1992). *Anxiety disorders in youth: Cognitive-behavioral interventions.* Needham Heights, MA: Allyn & Bacon.

Kendall, P. C., & Chu, B. C. (2000). Retrospective self-reports of therapist flexibility in a manual-based treatment for youths with anxiety disorders. *Journal of Clinical Child Psychology, 29*, 209–220.

Kendall, P. C., Chu, B., Gifford, A., Hayes, C., & Nauta, M. (1998). Breathing life into a manual: Flexibility and creativity with manual-based treatments. *Cognitive and Behavioral Practice, 5*, 177–198.

Kendall, P. C., Flannery-Schroeder, E., & Ford, J. D. (1999). Therapy outcome research methods. In P. C. Kendall, J. N. Butcher, & G. N. Holmbeck (Eds.), *Handbook of research methods in clinical psychology* (2nd ed., pp. 330–363). New York: Wiley.

Kendall, P. C., Flannery-Schroeder, E., Panichelli-Mindel, S., Southam-Gerow, M., Henin, A., & Warman, M. (1997). Therapy for youths with anxiety disorders: A second randomized clinical trial. *Journal of Consulting and Clinical Psychology, 65*, 366–380.

Kendall, P. C., & Southam-Gerow, M. A. (1995). Issues in the transportability of treatment: The case of anxiety disorders in youth. *Journal of Consulting and Clinical Psychology, 63*, 702–708.

Kendall, P. C., & Southam-Gerow, M. A. (1996). Long-term follow-up of a cognitive-behavior therapy for anxiety-disordered youth. *Journal of Consulting and Clinical Psychology, 64*, 724–730.

King, N. J., & Ollendick, T. H. (1998). Empirically validated treatments in clinical psychology. *Australian Psychologist, 33*, 89–95.

Kinscherff, R. (1999). Empirically supported treatments: What to do until the data arrive (or now that they have)? *Clinical Child Psychology Newsletter, 14*, 4–6.

Klerman, G. L., Weissman, M. M., Rounsaville, B. J., & Chevron, E. S. (1984). *Interpersonal psychotherapy for depression.* New York: Basic Books.

Lambert, M. J. (1998). Manual-based treatment and clinical practice: Hangman of life or promising development? *Clinical Psychology: Science and Practice, 5*, 391–395.

Lambert, M. J., & Ogles, B. M. (1988). Treatment manuals: Problems and promise. *Journal of Integrative and Eclectic Psychotherapy, 7*, 187–204.

Leitenberg, H., & Callahan, E. J. (1973). Reinforced practice and reduction of different kinds of fears in adults and children. *Behaviour Research and Therapy, 11*, 19–30.

Lewinsohn, P. M., Clarke, G. N., Hops, H., & Andrews, J. (1990). Cognitive-behavioral treatment for depressed adolescents. *Behavior Therapy, 21*, 385–401.

Lewinsohn, P. M., Clarke, G. N., Rohde, P., Hops, H., & Seeley, J. (1996). A course in coping: A cognitive-behavioral approach to the treatment of adolescent depression. In E. D. Hibbs & P. S. Jensen (Eds.), *Psychosocial treatments for child and adolescent disorders: Empirically based strategies for clinical practice* (pp. 109–135). Washington, DC: American Psychological Association.

Lewis, S. (1974). A comparison of behavior therapy techniques in the reduction of fearful avoidance behavior. *Behavior Therapy, 5*, 648–655.

Lonigan, C. J., Elbert, J. C., & Johnson, S. B. (1998). Empirically supported psychosocial interventions for children: An overview. *Journal of Clinical Child Psychology, 27*, 138–145.

Lovaas, O. I. (1987). Behavioral treatment and normal educational and intellectual functioning in young autistic children. *Journal of Consulting and Clinical Psychology, 55*, 3–9.

Lovaas, O. I., Ackerman, A. B., Alexander, D., Firestone, P., Perkins, J., & Young, D. (1981). *Teaching developmentally disabled children: The me book.* Baltimore: University Park Press.

Luborsky, L., & DeRubeis, R. (1984). The use of psychotherapy treatment manuals: A small revolution in psychotherapy research style. *Clinical Psychology Review, 4*, 5–14.

McEachin, J. J., Smith, T., & Lovaas, I. O. (1993). Long-term outcome for children with autism who received early intensive behavioral treatment. *American Journal on Mental Retardation, 97*, 381–384.

Menzies, R. G., & Clarke, J. C. (1993). A comparison of *in vivo* and vicarious exposure in the treatment of childhood water phobia. *Behaviour Research and Therapy, 31*, 9–15.

Mersch, P. P. A., Emmelkamp, P. M. G., Bogels, S. M., & van der Sleen, J. (1989). Social phobia: Individual response patterns and the effects of behavioral and cognitive interventions. *Behaviour Research and Therapy, 27*, 421–434.

Mufson, L., Moreau, D., Weissman, M. M., Wickramaratne, P., Martin, J., & Samoilov, A. (1994). Modificaiton of interpersonal psychotherapy with depressed adolescents (IPT-A): Phase I and II studies. *Journal of the American Academy of Child and Adolescent Psychiatry, 33*, 695–705.

Nelson-Gray, R. O., Herbert, J. D., Herbert, D. L., Sigmon, S. T., & Brannon, S. E. (1990). Effectiveness of matched, mismatched, and package treatments of depression. *Journal of Behavior Therapy and Experimental Psychiatry, 20*, 281–294.

Obler, M., & Terwilliger, R. F. (1970). Pilot study on the effectiveness of systematic desensitization with neurologically impaired children with phobic disorders. *Journal of Consulting and Clinical Psychology, 34*, 314–318.

Ollendick, T. H. (1995a). Cognitive-behavioral treatment of panic disorder with agoraphobia in adolescents: A multiple baseline design analysis. *Behavior Therapy, 26*, 517–531.

Ollendick, T. H. (1995b). AABT and empirically validated treatments. *the Behavior Therapist, 18*, 81–82.

Ollendick, T. H. (1999). Empirically supported treatments: Promises and pitfalls. *The Clinical Psychologist, 52*, 1–3.

Ollendick, T. H., Hagopian, L. P., & Huntzinger, R. M. (1991). Cognitive-behavior therapy with nighttime fearful children. *Journal of Behaviour Therapy and Experimental Psychiatry, 22*, 113–121.

Ollendick, T. H., & King, N. J. (1998). Empirically supported treatments for children with phobic and anxiety disorders: Current status. *Journal of Clinical Child Psychology, 27*, 156–167.

Ost, L. G., Jerremalm, A., & Johansson, J. (1981). Individual response patterns and the effects of different behavioral methods in the treatment of claustrophobia. *Behaviour Research and Therapy, 20*, 445–560.

Patterson, G. R., & Gullion, M. E. (1968). *Living with children: New methods for parents and teachers.* Champaign, IL: Research Press.

Pelham, W. E., & Hoza, B. (1996). Intensive treatment: A summer treatment program for children with ADHD. In E. Hibbs & P. Jensen (Eds.), *Psychosocial treatments for child and ad-

olescent disorders: Empirically based strategies for clinical practice (pp. 311–340). New York: American Psychological Association Press.

Pelham, W. E., Jr., Wheeler, T., & Chronis, A. (1998). Empirically supported psychosocial treatments for attention deficit hyperactivity disorder. *Journal of Clinical Child Psychology, 27,* 189–204.

Persons, J. B. (1998). Paean to data. *the Behavior Therapist, 21,* 123.

Persons, J. B., & Silberschatz, G. (1998). Are results of randomized controlled trials useful to psychotherapists? *Journal of Consulting and Clinical Psychology, 66,* 126–135.

Pisterman, S., Firestone, P., McGrath, P., Goodman, J. T., Webster, I., Mallory, R., & Goffin, B. (1992). The effects of parent training on parenting stress and sense of competence. *Canadian Journal of Behavioural Science, 24,* 41–58.

Pisterman, S., McGrath, P., Firestone, P., Goodman, J. T., Webster, I., & Mallory, R. (1989). Outcome of parent-mediated treatment of preschoolers with ADD with hyperactivity. *Journal of Consulting and Clinical Psychology, 57,* 628–635.

Richters, J. E., Arnold, L. E., Jensen, P. S., Abikoff, H., Conners, C. K., Greenhill, L. L., Hechtman, L., Hinshaw, S. P., Pelham, W. E., & Swanson, J. M. (1995). The National Institute of Mental Health collaborative multisite multimodal treatment study of children with attention-deficit/hyperactivity disorder (MTA): I. Background and rationale. *Journal of the American Academy of Child and Adolescent Psychiatry, 34,* 987–1000.

Ritter, B. (1968). The group desensitization of children's snake phobias using vicarious and contact desensitization procedures. *Behaviour Research and Therapy, 6,* 1–6.

Rogers, S. J. (1998). Empirically supported comprehensive treatments for young children with autism. *Journal of Clinical Child Psychology, 27,* 167–178.

Schulte, D., Kunzel, R., Pepping, G., & Schulte-Bahrenberg, T. (1992). Tailor-made versus standardized therapy of phobic patients. *Advances in Behaviour Research and Therapy, 14,* 67–92.

Seligman, M. E. P. (1995). The effectiveness of psychotherapy. *American Psychologist, 50,* 965–974.

Sheinkopf, S. J., & Siegel, B. (1998). Home-based behavioral treatment of young autistic children. *Journal of Autism and Developmental Disorders, 28,* 15–24.

Sheslow, D. V., Bondy, A. S., & Nelson, R. O. (1983). A comparison of graduated exposure, verbal coping skills, and their combination in the treatment of children's fear of the dark. *Child and Family Behavior Therapy, 4,* 33–45.

Silverman, W. H. (1996). Cookbooks, manuals, and paint-by-numbers: Psychotherapy in the 90s. *Psychotherapy, 33,* 207–215.

Smith, E. W. L. (1995). A passionate, rational response to the "manualization" of psychotherapy. *Psychotherapy Bulletin, 30*(2), 36–40.

Stark, K., & Kendall, P. C. (1996a). *Taking action: A workbook for overcoming depression.* Ardmore, PA: Workbook Publishing.

Stark, K., & Kendall, P. C. (1996b). Treating depressed children: Therapist manual for *Taking Action.* Ardmore, PA: Workbook Publishing.

Stark, K., Rouse, L., & Livingston, R. (1991). Treatment of depression during childhood and adolescence: Cognitive-behavioral procedures for the individual and family. In P. C. Kendall (Ed.), *Child and adolescent therapy: Cognitive-behavioral procedures* (pp. 165–206). New York: Guilford Press.

Stark, K. D., Reynolds, W. R., & Kaslow, N. J. (1987). A comparison of the relative efficacy of self-control therapy and a behavioral problem-solving therapy for depression in children. *Journal of Abnormal Child Psychology, 15,* 91–113.

Strosahl, K. (1998). The dissemination of manual-based psychotherapies in managed care: Promises, problems, and prospects. *Clinical Psychology: Science and Practice, 5,* 382–386.

Strupp, H. H., & Anderson, T. (1997). On the limitations of therapy manuals. *Clinical Psychology: Science and Practice, 4,* 76–82.

Strupp, H. H., & Binder, J. L. (1984). *Psychotherapy in a new key: A guide to time-limited dynamic psychotherapy*. New York: Basic Books.

Task Force on Promotion and Dissemination. (1995). Training in and disseminaiton of empirically validated treatments: Report and recommendations. *The Clinical Psychologist, 48*, 3–23.

Tynan, W. D., Schuman, W., & Lampert, N. (1999). Concurrent parent and child therapy groups for externalizing disorders: From the laboratory to the world of managed care. *Cognitive and Behavioral Practice, 6*, 3–9.

Ultee, C. A., Griffioen, D., & Schellekens, J. (1982). The reduction of anxiety in children: A comparison of the effects of "systematic desensitization *in vitro*" and "systematic desensitization *in vivo*." *Behaviour Research and Therapy, 20*, 61–67.

Webster-Stratton, C. (1984). Randomized trial of two parent training programs for families with conduct-disordered children. *Journal of Consulting and Clinical Psychology, 52*, 666–678.

Webster-Stratton, C. (1990). Enhancing the effectiveness of self administered videotape parent training for families with conduct-problem children. *Journal of Abnormal Child Psychology, 18*, 479–492.

Webster-Stratton, C. (1994). Advancing videotape parent training: A comparison study. *Journal of Consulting and Clinical Psychology, 62*, 583–593.

Weiss, B., Catron, T., Harris, V., & Phung, T. M. (1999). The effectiveness of traditional child psychotherapy. *Journal of Consulting and Clinical Psychology, 67*, 82–94.

Weisz, J. R., Donenberg, G. R., Han, S. S., & Weiss, B. (1995). Bridging the gap between laboratory and clinic in child and adolescent psychotherapy. *Journal of Consulting and Clinical Psychology, 63*, 688–701.

Weisz, J. R., Huey, S. J., & Weersing, V. R. (1998). Psychotherapy outcome research with children and adolescents: The state of the art. In T. H. Ollendick & R. J. Prinz (Eds.), *Advances in clinical child psychology* (Vol. 20, pp. 49–91). New York: Plenum Press.

Weisz, J. R., Weiss, B., Alicke, M. D., & Klotz, M. L. (1987). Effectiveness of psychotherapy with children and adolescents: A meta-analysis for clinicians. *Journal of Consulting and Clinical Psychology, 55*, 542–549.

Weisz, J. R., Weiss, B., Han, S. S., Granger, D. G., & Morton, T. (1995). Effects of psychotherapy with children and adolescents revisited: A meta-analysis of treatment outcome studies. *Psychological Bulletin, 117*, 450–468.

Wilson, G. T. (1998). The clinical utility of randomized controlled trials. *International Journal of Eating Disorders, 24*, 13–30.

Wilson, G. T. (1996a). Manual-based treatments: The clinical application of research findings. *Behaviour Research and Therapy, 34*, 295–314.

Wilson, G. T. (1996b). Empirically validated treatments: Reality and resistance. *Clinical Psychology: Science and Practice, 3*, 241–244.

Zvolensky, M. J., & Eiffert, G. H. (1998). Standardized treatments: Potential ethical issues for behavior therapists? *the Behavior Therapist, 21*, 1–3.

Zvolensky, M. J., & Eiffert, G. H. (1999). Potential ethical issues revisited: A reply to Persons. *the Behavior Therapist, 22*, 40.

Index